The Illustrated History of Freemasonry

1910

SCENE IN THE THIRD DEGREE OF THE MYSTERIES

Moses W. Redding

The Illustrated History of Freemasonry
By: Moses W. Redding

All rights reserved. No part of this book may be reproduced in any form without written permission from the publisher, except by a reviewer who may quote brief passages in a review to be printed in a newspaper or magazine

Printed: January, 2004

Published and Distributed by:
LUSHENA BOOKS, INC.
607 Country Club Drive, Unit E
Bensenville, IL 60106

ISBN: 1-1930097-71-9

Printed in the United States of America

The Illustrated History of Free Masonry.

THIS WORK CONTAINS

An Authentic History of the Institution from its Origin to the Present Time. Traced from the Secret Societies of Antiquity to King Solomon's Temple at Jerusalem, thence through the Roman Colleges of Builders, Travelling Bands of Masons, and the Guilds to Free Masonry.

Embellished with over 100 Fine Engravings, 73 of which are Full-Page Plates.

By MOSES W. REDDING,

AUTHOR OF RUINS AND RELICS OF THE HOLY CITY—MASONIC ANTIQUITIES OF THE ORIENT UNVEILED, SCARLET BOOK OF FREE MASONRY—STANDARD AHIMAN REZON, AND COMPENDIUM OF MASONIC LAW AND JURISPRUDENCE, ETC., ETC.

NEW YORK

REDDING & CO.

212 BROADWAY.

1910.

Entered according to Act of Congress in the year 1892, by
MOSES W. REDDING
In the Office of the Librarian of Congress at Washington.

Copyright, 1903, by
CHAS. L. COZZENS.

GEORGE S. FERGUSON CO.,
PRINTERS AND ELECTROTYPERS,
PHILADELPHIA.

MASONIC TEMPLE, CHICAGO.

PREFACE
AND INTRODUCTION.

ALL historians, the scope of whose works extends back of the age they live in, are dependent upon those who have gone before them for data; and as authorities, from prejudice, may pervert the information in their possession, it devolves on the faithful historian to critically examine the data he uses; or, in other words, he should constitute himself a tribunal, and summon every accessible witness, and from their testimony endeavor to find the facts. In this investigation he should exercise great discrimination in judging of both the competency and motives of witnesses.

In the preparation of this work, recourse has been had, not only to all the principal Masonic histories, old and new, but to much contemporaneous general history. And not the least among the difficulties to be overcome in the preparation of a work of this kind are the discrepancies between writers of different nationalities, caused by the strife to give their respective countries priority as to the origin of the Order.

The German writer conclusively shows (to himself) that the order originated in his country, and that the symbols are of Norse origin. While the Englishman, with a few strokes of his pen, demolishes the German's structure, and demonstrates that Guild Masonry originated in Britain. The greatest contention is found between English and German writers.

Where national pride is great, nothing is more certain than that the writers of each nation will claim priority and superiority as to the antiquity and value of its important institutions; therefore, we find on the question of the origin of Free Masonry, a great diversity of views on important points between such writers. As a sample of this, see the following from R. Freeke Gould, in The History of Free Masonry, vol i., p. 108:

Previous to the advent of literature, and a knowledge of the art of writing or transmitting history by engraved characters on monuments and tablets, it was necessarily done orally; consequently, if history was divested of all traditional authority, it would leave us but a meagre account of the earlier affairs of the human race.

It was the positive and earnest faith of the ancients in the spiritual—in Deity—that led them to blend religion with the affairs of life. Therefore the Mysteries were instituted for the instruction of man in all that could conduce to his physical and moral welfare.

While the Egyptians were advancing toward a higher civilization, they passed through several stages of culture in the arts and sciences, and their religious system kept pace with their intellectual advancement.

The results of their system are to be seen in the remains of Egyptian art among the ruins of structures throughout Egypt. The ruins of Memphis and Thebes alone exhibit astonishing attainments in architecture and sculpture.

The Egyptian system was the admiration of philosophers and scholars, and attracted the wisest and best men from all nations, who in turn disseminated the knowledge of the Egyptians throughout the world. Greece and Rome received ideas in art, science, philosophy, and religion from Egypt, and Hebrew Christianity owes to the Egyptians much of its knowledge of the attributes of Deity.

The Greek Philosophers, Magi of Persia, and Jewish Patriarchs all learned from the Egyptian priests their doctrines, mysteries, arts, and sciences. In short, many of the philosophers and rulers who made antiquity illustrious were pupils of initiation.

Therefore to Egypt, the land of speaking monoliths, the first great teacher of matters terrestrial and celestial, Masons have always looked with great interest as being the cradle of their initiation rites and ceremonies, and symbolism. On this point the best Masonic authorities agree.

The popular belief is, that the earlier ages of antiquity were buried in ignorance. But the history of the past, inscribed upon the monuments and tablets of the East, is confirmatory of the fact that art, if not science, existed in as great perfection during the continuance of the Egyptian, Assyrian, and Babylonian monarchies as at any period since.

For the sculptor may, in the exhumed figures of Thebes, Babylon, and Nineveh, behold the finest productions of the chisel, executed many centuries before Phidias or Canova were born. Deep under the mounds of ruins in the royal palace at Nineveh paintings have been found whose colors are bright after an interment of four thousand years; and though not rivalling the works of Raphael or Angelo, yet they exhibit great artistic skill.

The origin of language and the art of alphabetical writing may be studied in Assyrian and Egyptian inscriptions made long before Moses received the God-inscribed Tables of Law on the summit of Sinai. From the astronomical tables of Egypt and Babylon the astronomer may read important observations on the heavenly bodies, made five hundred years before Galileo gave to the world the system of planetary revolution.

The ancient tables of Nineveh and Babylon, inscribed a thousand years before the Old Testament was written, furnish the theologian with historical narratives illustrating and confirming the Bible history and prophecy. From the mythological inscriptions and hieroglyphic symbols he may also learn the doctrine of the Divine existence and of the soul's immortality.

ORIGIN.

To reach the origin of Free Masonry two lines of investigation are open to us, either of which leads to a satisfactory conclusion. First, the institution in its present form is mainly the outgrowth of the ancient Secret Societies, and of ancient Operative Masonry, both of which originated in Egypt. The important features of the initiation ceremonies and many of the symbols of Free Masonry are nearly identical with those of the ancient Societies, and plainly traceable back to Greece and Egypt. In showing the connection between ancient and modern practices it is immaterial which way we proceed, whether from the head of the stream toward its mouth, or trace it from its mouth to its source. But believing that it will render the subject more intelligible, I shall take the former course, and commence with the origin of the initiation ceremonies, as practiced in the secret societies of the earliest-known civilization, and follow by a sketch of the origin of architecture and its progress under the Roman Colleges, and their successors the Guilds—Guildic or Operative Masonry, to Free Masonry.

On the subject of the origin of the Order we have three classes of writers: The first, having the courage of its convictions, places the origin in Egypt and Greece; the second assigns it to the Roman Colleges and the Guilds; while the third, and last class—the Uriah Heap family, beg to name 1717 as the date, and London as the place of the origin of the Institution. Therefore the Masonic student who is travelling East in search of light, and finds himself in Egypt, can take the train there, at the commencement of the great Masonic Route. Others, according to where they find themselves, can step on the train at the way stations—the Temple of Eleusis, Greece; King Solomon's Temple, Jerusalem; the Colleges of Builders, Rome; at some of the stations of the Guilds, or meet the train on its arrival at its terminus in London.

As life is too short to complacently contemplate, much less read, masses of dry historical details, I have, so far as is compatible with an intelligent understanding of the subject, systematized and *condensed* this work, and have thus been able to present a large amount of information in a moderate compass.

THE AUTHOR.

CONTENTS.

CHAPTER I.
ANCIENT SECRET SOCIETIES AND MYSTERIES, ... 19

The Secret Societies of Egypt, Greece, Syria, and Rome.—Origin of Initiation.—Thrilling Scenes through which the Candidate passed in the Ancient Mysteries.—The Ritual, and Judgment of the Dead.—Description of a Temple Devoted to the Mysteries.—The Wonderful Labyrinth.

CHAPTER II.
IMAGES, FIGURES, SYMBOLS, ... 61

Origin of Masonic Symbols, Astronomical and Mechanical.—Their Original Signification.

CHAPTER III.
ARCHITECTURE, MASONRY, ... 89

Origin of the Builders' Art in Egypt.—Origin of the Pyramids, and Obelisk.—Their Original Purpose.—Remarkable Revelations from the Interior of the Pyramids.—The Magnificent Temple at Karnak.—Its Ruins.—Ancient Egyptian Houses.—Course of Architecture from Egypt.—Origin of the Different Styles.—Greek, Roman, Byzantine, Romanesque, Saracenic, etc.—Progress of Architecture under the Colleges of Builders and the Guilds.—Guildic Masonry.

CHAPTER IV.
KING SOLOMON'S TEMPLE, ... 150

The Building of this Remarkable Edifice.—Preparing the Timber in the Forests of Lebanon.—Cutting the Stone in the Great Subterranean Quarry.—Secret Meetings of the Master Workmen.—Completion and Dedication of the Temple.—Its Destruction and Commencement of the Captivity.—Ancient Tyre, Home of the Two Hirams.

CHAPTER V.
THE COLLEGES OF BUILDERS, ... 182

Their Lodges, Officers, and Practices closely Analogous to those of Free Masons.—They Carry on most of the Architecture, Engineering, and Masonry of their Time.—Build Splendid Public Edifices, Bridges, and Military Works.—From Rome, the Colleges Accompany the Roman Armies into Gaul, Germany, and Britain, where they Disseminate their Arts and Ethics.—Singular Remains of their Structures in those Countries.

CHAPTER VI.
GERMANY AND VICINITY, ... 199

The Romans Invade Germany, but Meet with a Stubborn Resistance, which Gave the Colleges of Builders Plenty of Occupation in Building Bridges, Forts, and Entrenched Camps. — B.C. 10 they cut a Canal through, between the Rhine and Issel, which Opened a Passage to the Zuider Zee. — Fighting Step by Step, the Romans so far Established Themselves in A.D. 100 that not only Markets, but Towns had Sprung Up in Various Places, and by 225, Manufactories, Temples, and Theatres were becoming Numerous. — Salzburg, Ratisbon, Augsburg, Strasburg, Basle, Baden, Cologne, and other Noted Cities were Founded. — All under the Supervision of the **Colleges of Builders,** whose Arts and Creed were so well Appreciated by the more Intelligent Natives, that they Eagerly Sought Initiation into this Roman Society, and thus its Arts and Creeds were Perpetuated Here under the Name of **Guilds.**

CHAPTER VII.
THE COLLEGES IN GAUL, FRANCE, ... 242

With the Roman Armies of Invasion they Enter Gaul. — Construct the Military Works and Bridges. — Build Vessels, Villages, Edifices, etc. — Ultimately Known as Compagnons. — **Guilds,** with Practices and Traditions very Similar to Ancient Masonry.

CHAPTER VIII.
ADVENT OF THE COLLEGES IN BRITAIN, ... 262

They enter the Country with Cæsar's Army of Invasion, 55 B.C. — The Natives Make a Determined Resistance. — Bloody Battles are Fought. — Fate of the Brave Caractacus, and of Queen Boadicea and her Beautiful Daughters. — Military Camps are Constructed at Different Places. — Under the Supervision of the **Colleges,** Towns grow up Around or Near these Camps. — Cities are Founded, notably London, Exeter, Dover, Chester. — After an Occupation of the Country for over Four Hundred Years the Romans leave it, but Everywhere leave the Strong Impress of Civilization, principally through the Operations of the *Colleges.* — Many Members of the Latter Remain and Continue their Organizations, which were Subsequently Known as **Guilds,** and Lastly as Free Masons. — Remarkable Remains of Roman Structures in Many Places. —1717, Free Masonry as it had Existed for Centuries, is now Freed from its Operative Domination, and its Doors are Thrown Open to Good and True Men, without Regard to Occupation or Religion. — Singular Ancient Masonic Documents.

CHAPTER IX.
ANCIENT YORK, ENGLAND, ... 375

This was the Chief Town of One of the Native Tribes when the Romans Landed in Britain. — It was Remodelled by the **Colleges of Builders.** — Several Roman Emperors Resided Here while Visiting the Island. — The First English Parliament was Held in this City. — King Edwin Resided near Here. — The City was also the Scene of the First General Assembly of Masons ever Held, and it has Held a Conspicuous Place in Masonic History since the Tenth Century.

CONTENTS. 11

CHAPTER X.
SCOTLAND.—EARLY HISTORY, ... 395

Free Masonry Makes its Appearance in this Country in the Fourteenth Century.—Quaint and Highly Interesting Documents of the Old Lodges at Perth, Scoon, and Aberdeen.—Old Documents, in which the Novel Ideas of the Ancient Scotch Craftsmen are expressed in the Rich Dialect of that Period.—A Singular Ancient Masonic Seal.—Robert Burns Master of a Lodge.—A Masonic Relic Left by Him.

CHAPTER XI.
RAPID SPREAD OF FREE MASONRY, ... 422

Its Introduction into the Countries of Europe, Asia, and Africa.—Free Masonry in Egypt, Greece, Turkey, Persia, Bombay, Calcutta, Australia, China, Japan, etc.

CHAPTER XII.
INTRODUCTION OF FREE MASONRY INTO NORTH AND SOUTH AMERICA AND ADJACENT ISLANDS, . 461

The First Lodges in the United States.—The First Lodges and Grand Lodges in all the Different States and Territories.—Primitive Proceedings in Early Lodges.—Remarkable Masonic and Social Career of a Prominent Mason.—He Builds a Castle and Marries a Beautiful Indian Girl.—Destruction of his Castle by the Indians.—Establishment of a Lodge at Crown Point in the Stirring Days of the Revolution.—A Mason Bound to the Stake by the Indians to be Burnt, but is Saved by Making the Sign of Distress.—Original and Highly Interesting Records of Various Old Lodges.—Washington's Headquarters at Morristown, N. J., in the Winters of 1777 and 1779.—A Lodge Opened there in which General Lafayette was Initiated.—Establishment of Lodges and Grand Lodges in the Countries of South America and the West India Islands.—Statistics of Free Masonry throughout the World.

CHAPTER XIII.
THE MARKS OF THE ANCIENT BUILDERS, ... 563

Marks Used at the Building of King Solomon's Temple.—Marks Found at Tyre and Sidon.—Marks Found in the Crypts of Old Churches and Cathedrals in Various Parts of Europe.

CHAPTER XIV.
ROYAL ARCH MASONRY.—ITS ORIGIN, ETC., ... 571

Origin of the Royal Arch Degrees.—The Captivity.—The Vaults Discovered Under the Site of King Solomon's Temple.—Remains of the Citadel and Tomb of Cyrus, King of Persia, at Ecbatana.—Establishment of the First Royal Arch Chapters in the United States.

CONTENTS.

CHAPTER XV.
THE A. AND A. SCOTTISH RITE, 33°, ... 592

Origin of this Rite.—Its Development and Rapid Spread in the East and West.—Its Advent in the West Indies and the United States.—Formation of the Different Bodies Representing the A. and A. Rite in this Country.—The Southern Jurisdiction.—Northern Jurisdiction.—Cerneau bodies.

CHAPTER XVI.
THE KNIGHTS TEMPLARS, ... 619

Origin of this Ancient Order.—The Knights of Chivalry.—Origin of the Crusades.—Peter the Hermit and His Hosts Set Out for Jerusalem, but are Nearly Annihilated by the Turks in Asia Minor.—Subsequent Crusades.—The Knights Templars and Knights Hospitalers, their Desperate Valor, and Wonderful Career of over Two Hundred Years.—They Defeat the Mohammedans in many Bloody Battles, but were Finally Overwhelmed by Numbers and afterward Robbed and Suppressed by the Pope and King of France.—De Molay and Two Hundred Knights Put to Death.—Suppressed, but Still Undaunted, They Maintain Their Organization in Different Countries.—Ultimately they Unite with the Free Masons and Hospitalers and thus Give Rise to Modern Knight Templary.—Establishment of the First Encampments in North America.—Grandeur of the Organization.

CHAPTER XVII.
THE MYSTIC SHRINE, ... 675

Reported Origin and History of the New Organization.—Institution of Mecca Temple in New York.—Establishment of Other Temples.—Growth of the Order in America.—List of Temples.

CHAPTER XVIII.
MISCELLANEOUS MATTERS CONNECTED WITH THE HISTORY OF FREE MASONRY, 679

Unique Old Documents.—The Grand Mystery of the Free Masons as Revealed by an Outsider in 1725.—Examination of Craftsmen in the Olden Time.—Dr. Plott's Account of the Free Masons.—The Four Crowned Martyrs.—Tomb of Adoniram at Saguntum.—Concerning King Canute, the Dane.—The Punishment of a Cowan in the Fifteenth Century.—Kitt's Cotti House, Its Symbolic Signification.—Bagdad, a Singular Old City Built by the Masonic Craftsmen.—Allahabad, Masonic Marks on Its Ancient Walls.—Satirical Lecture Given to a Young Craftsman in 1350.—Ancient Mexico, Its Mysteries.—Masonic Symbols Found on the Ruins of its Old Temples.—Ancient Peru, Its Hieroglyphics.—Masonry Among the Aborigines of North America.

ILLUSTRATIONS.

Masonic Temple, Chicago, ... *Frontispiece.*

CHAPTER I.

	PAGE
An Ancient Hall of Ceremonies,—Preparing for Initiation, ...	27
Graphic Initiation Scene, ...	31
The Third Degree,—Death and Resurrection, ...	35
Karnak, its Splendid Ruins, ...	43
The First Great Obelisk, ...	47
Judgment of the Dead, ...	53

CHAPTER II.

Apron Worn by Egyptian Kings, ...	63
The Ancient Ladder of Three Rounds, ...	66
The Lion's Paw, ...	75
Ancient Symbolism, Azoph, ...	78

CHAPTER III.

Monuments and Pyramids, showing how the Latter were Built, ...	91–93
The Temple at Karnak, Its Magnificent Hypostyle Hall, ...	97
Ancient Egyptian Houses, ...	99, 100
The Rameseum, ...	102
Columns of the Different Orders of Architecture, ...	107
A View in Pompeii, and the Mosque at Diarbeker, ...	111–113
Ruins of the Mashita Palace, ...	114
The Great Mosque at Constantinople, St. Sophia, ...	116
Interior of St. Sophia, ...	117
St. Mark's Cathedral, Venice, ...	122
The Sulemanie Mosque, ...	123
The Alhambra, ...	127
Beautiful Interiors of English Cathedrals, ...	130, 131
The Great Cathedrals, Cologne and Ratisbon, ...	134, 135
Dwellings of the Different Ancient Peoples, ...	139–143
Old Irish Architecture, ...	144

CHAPTER IV.

	PAGE
Getting out the Cedar Timber in the Forest of Lebanon,	152
The Great Subterranean Quarry.—Cutting Stone for the Temple,	153
Conveying the Timber in Floats to Joppa,	159
Ancient Joppa,	160
Building the Temple,	166
Destruction of the Temple.—Beginning of the Captivity,	167
The Clay Grounds,	172
The Mohammedan Mosque of Omar on the Site of the Temple,	173
Tomb of Hiram, King of Tyre,	177

CHAPTER V.

Remains of the Temple, Jupiter Stator, Rome,	186
The Appian Way,	187
Ancient Catacombs, Rome,	191
Roman Bridge across the Danube,	203

CHAPTER VI.

St. Goar,	202
Trent,	204
Oberwesel,	207
Hildesheim,	210
Cathedral at Worms,	213
Mayence,	217
Salzburg,	221
Rostock,	225
Nuremberg,	231
A Travelling Band of Masons in the Twelfth Century,	237

CHAPTER VII.

Mounted Gauls,	245
Ruins at Nismes,	248
Ancient Roman Gateway,	250

CHAPTER VIII.

Caractacus and His Wife before the Roman Emperor,	265
Roman Squadron on the Coast of Britain,	262
Roman Prisoner Before a British Chief,	269
Travel in England in the Fourth Century,	272
Remains of Ancient Chester,	273

	PAGE
Druid Altars,	277
Last of the Druids,	281
Canterbury Cathedral,	285
The Tower of London,	289
Chichester Cathedral,	293
An Old Street, London,	299
St. Paul's,	321

CHAPTER X.

Remains of Melrose Abbey,	398
A Relic Left by Robert Burns,	408
Holyrood Abbey,	414
Singular Symbolic Seal of the Ancient Abbey of Arbroath,	420

CHAPTER XI.

Amsterdam, The Montalbans Tower,	425
The Three Globes, Berlin,	431
Prison of the Inquisition, Barcelona,	445
A Relic of East Indian Fanaticism and Torture,	453

CHAPTER XII.

St. John's Hall, City of New York, 1760,	476
Tontine Tavern,	477
The Old Masonic Hall, Broadway and Duane Streets,	478
Masonic Temple, Philadelphia,	495
Masonic Temple, Boston,	503
Freeman's Tavern, Morristown, N. J.—A Relic of the Revolution and of Free Masonry,	513
Masonic Temple, Cincinnati, O.,	529
An Old Trading Post and Lodge Room,	536
Masonic Temple, Denver,	539
The Great Cathedral, Mexico,	547
Mexican Types,	548

CHAPTER XIII.

Marks of the Ancient Craftsmen,	565
An Abraxas Stone, now in the British Museum,	569

CHAPTER XIV.

Tomb of Cyrus, King of Persia,	577
Vaults Under the Temple,	581
Remains of Ecbatana, the Persian Capitol in the Time of Cyrus,	585
The Royal Arch of Heaven,	589

CHAPTER XVI.

	PAGE
Preaching the First Crusade,	617
The Four Leaders of the First Crusade,	621
Malta,	633

CHAPTER XVIII.

Bagdad, A.D. 762,	690
Fortress and City of Allahabad,	691
Egyptian Kings,	707
Chichen Itza, Yucatan,	714
House of Manco Capac, Peru,	715
Saguntum,	695

DIRECTIONS TO THE READER.

For greater convenience, and to present the testimony of authorities in a cumulative form, the notes, instead of being placed at the bottom of the pages, were carried to the end of each chapter, and are there indicated by numbers. Therefore, a star, or other mark in the text, is answered at the bottom of the page by the same mark, and by numbers corresponding to the numbers of notes as they will be found at the end of the chapter.

The following are among the authorities consulted :

History of Ancient Egypt	Rawlinson.
Egypt's Place in History	Bunsen.
Ancient Egyptians	Wilkinson.
Records of the Past	Birch.
Egypt from the Earliest Times	Birch.
Secret Societies of all Ages and Countries	Heckethorn.
The Essenes	Ginsburg.
The Gnostics	King.
The Mysteries of Free Masonry	Fellows.
Alphabets of the Seven Planets	Von Hammer
History of Architecture	Fergusson.
On Architecture	Hope.
History of Art	Lubke.
Archæologia	
Acta Latomorum	Thory.
Historie des anciennes Corporations	Ouin Lacroix.
The Romans in Britain	H. C Coote.
History and Development of the Guilds	Brentano.
English Guilds	Smith.
The History of Free Masonry, London Edition	R. Freeke Gould.
American Edition of the Same	Carson.
Masonic Sketches and Reprints	Hughan.

DIRECTIONS TO THE READER.

Early History and Antiquities of Free Masonry	Fort.
History of Free Masonry in Europe	Rebold.
History of Free Masonry	Laurie.
History of Free Masonry	Findel.
History of Free Masonry	Krause.
History of Free Masonry and Concordant Orders	Various Authors.
Masonic History and Digest	Mitchell.
Origin and Early History of Free Masonry	Steinbrenner.
Masonic History—The A. and A. Scottish Rite	Folger.
History of the Knights Templars	Addison.
History of the Knights Templars	De Vogue.
The Illustrations of Free Masonry	Preston.
The Traditions of Free Masonry	Pierson.
Land Marks of Free Masonry	Oliver.
Constitutions	Anderson.
Ahiman Rezon	Dermott.
Multa Paucis	
Encyclopædia of Free Masonry	Mackey.
Royal Cyclopædia of Free Masonry	
Encyclopædia Britannica	
Chambers's Encyclopædia.	
Dictionary of the Bible	Smith.
Cyclopædia of Biblical Literature	Kitto.
Clark's Commentaries	Adam Clark.
Decline and Fall of the Roman Empire	Gibbon.
History of Germany	Kolrausch.
History of England	Hume.
History of England	Macaulay.

☞ When referring to the principal authorities in this work, only the names of the authors will be given, as follows:

Rawlinson,	Heckethorne,	Chambers,	Mackey,	Addison,
Gould,	Folger,	Rebold,	Fergusson,	Findel, etc.

CHAPTER I.

ANCIENT SECRET SOCIETIES AND MYSTERIES.

The Secret Societies of Egypt, Greece, Syria, and Rome.—Origin of Initiation and Symbols.—Thrilling Scenes through which the Candidate passed in the Ancient Mysteries.—The Ritual and Judgment of the Dead.—Description of a Temple devoted to the Mysteries.—The Wonderful Labyrinth.

To establish the fact that the civilization of Egypt is the oldest known to history, and thereby reach the origin of the ancient societies of which Free Masonry is a descendant,* it will be necessary to compare the dates of the first appearance of the nations of antiquity in the great drama of life. While dealing with a subject that reaches back to the very twilight of time, reliable data is lacking to accurately fix dates so remote, yet from the results of modern research we gather the following: that the advent of Egypt in history was, at least, as early as 4500 B.C.; of Chaldea-Babylonia, not earlier than 3000 B.C.; India, 2500 B.C.; China, 2600 B.C.

Menes is by historians styled the first king of Egypt, yet who or what Menes was we have no certain information for determining. We know that the name "Menes" indicates the first Egyptian king, the beginning of the first dynasty of the old kingdom of pyramid-builders, whose capitol was Memphis. These, after a period of decadence, were superseded by kings of a different race from the south, 2571 B.C., and these in turn, after a brief rule, were conquered by an Asiatic race of Shepherd Kings, 1840 B.C.

The so-called Shepherd invasion was not completely successful, as Theban and Xoite dynasties coexisted with the Shepherds during the period of their stay.

* See notes 1, 2, 3, 4, 5, 7, 8, 14, pp. 53, 54, 56.

20   ANCIENT SECRET SOCIETIES AND MYSTERIES.

Finally the Shepherds were expelled, and the new kingdom was founded about 1640 B.C. From that time, to the present, the pathway of history is comparatively plain.

In the third century B.C. Manetho,* an Egyptian priest, by order of the king wrote a history of Egypt. He divided the history of the Egyptian kings into thirty dynasties, covering a period of 5000 years.

	B.C.
But Bockh places the accession of the first Egyptian king at	5702
Unger	5613
Mariette Bey	5004
Lenormant	5004
Brugsch Bey	4458
Lauth	4157
Ferguson	3906
Lepsius	3852
Bunsen	3623

As the above comprises some of the best and most recent authorities on this subject it would place the beginning of the first dynasty as early certainly as 4500 B.C.

The only country that has seriously competed with Egypt for the first mention in history is Chaldea-Babylonia. But the antiquity of Chaldean civilization compared with the Egyptian will be seen from the following carefully prepared table:

			Years.	Commencing B.C.
I.	1	Chaldean,	25	2438
II.	8	Medes,	224	2418
III.	11	Chaldeans,	258	2234
IV.	49	"	458	1976
V.	9	Arabians,	245	1518
VI.	45	Assyrians,	526	1273
VII.	8	"	122	747
VIII.	6	Chaldeans,	87	625
		Persian conquest.†		538

As inscriptions on tablets recently discovered among the ruins have confirmed the correctness of this table, it may be assumed to closely approximate the true chronology of that country from Nimrod to Cyrus.

* Rawlinson : Hist. An. Egypt, vol. ii., p. 6 ; Herodotus, xi., 100, 142 ; Ferguson, vol. i., p. 112.
† Ferguson, vol. i., pp. 144, 145.

ANCIENT SECRET SOCIETIES AND MYSTERIES. 21

Rawlinson says (vol. ii., p. 22): "The Old Empire of Manetho is a reality. It lives and moves before us in the countless tombs of Ghizeh, Saccarah, and Beni-Hassan, on the rocks of Assouan and the Wady-Magharah, on the obelisk of Heliopolis, and in numerous ancient papyri; its epochs are well marked; its personages capable in many cases of being exhibited distinctly; its life as clearly portrayed as that of the classical nations. And that life is worth studying. It is the oldest presentation to us of civilized man which the world contains, being certainly anterior, much of it, to the time of Abraham; it is given with a fulness and minuteness that are most rare, and it is, intrinsically most curious."

Intelligent man has, in all ages, realized the existence of two unseen but potent spirits—one, the spirit of good, from whom all blessings are derived, and the other the spirit of darkness, the evil spirit. Nowhere was the religious spirit so early and so fully manifested as in the Orient, the land of the Bible. This was especially true of Egypt, where the religious feeling was so strong that it entered into and mingled with all the affairs of life.*

The conditions under which the Egyptians lived also rendered them astronomers, as a knowledge of the movements of the principal planets was necessary to enable them to regulate their tillage, so strangely crossed by that disposition peculiar to their country.

From her wise men, astronomers, and leaders in religion came the priesthood of Egypt, and by the priesthood was developed the ancient system of science and religion designated the "Mysteries;" and prior to the Christian era all progress made in civilization was due to organizations known by the general name of Mysteries. The most noted of these societies were, first, the Egyptian,† commencing 2500 B.C., followed by the Eleusinian, Samothracian, Gnostics, Dionysian, and Mithraic.

The doctrine of the Egyptian Mysteries embraced Cosmogony, Astronomy, the Arts, Sciences, Religion, and the Immortality of the Soul.‡

By impressive rites and ceremonies they endeavored to lead the neophyte from darkness to light, from ignorance to knowledge, morality, and religion.

---

* See pp. 50 to 53; also notes 37, 38, 41, pp. 59, 60.
† Notes 6, 11, 15, 32, pp. 54, 55, 56, 59.
‡ Notes 9, 39, 42, pp. 55, 60; also Mysteries, p. 116.

At first only the better class, including candidates for the priesthood, were admitted into the Mysteries. Later, however, many from the ranks of the common people were initiated, but before proceeding further, they had to pass an examination so rigid, that comparatively but few could reach the greater Mysteries.

The priests, seeing that it was impossible for the neophyte to perceive the truths of science and religion except when illustrated by symbols, used symbols adapted to that purpose. Consequently *two* forms of ethics and religion began to prevail, one for the initiates in the *higher* Mysteries, and the other for the *mass*, who could perceive nothing beyond the symbol or image with which they were instructed. Therefore they naturally came to *worship* the *image*, hence became *Pagans*, with all that that term signifies, *including* the *orgies charged* to the Mysteries at large.

The knowledge of the symbolic language in which the priesthood concealed the real truths was carefully kept within the sacred circle of those who had been advanced to the highest grade of the Mysteries, but the public rites and ceremonies were open to all the people.

The great reverence shown the priests was due to their erudition, and the fact that the sacerdotal functions were hereditary. In fact, the Hierophants of Egypt constituted a sacred caste, which exercised such a controlling influence in the government that even the kings were to a great extent subject to its domination. The priests were divided into castes, and the castes were divided into different ranks. Their dress and mode of living were governed by strict rules, regulating and directing every act of the lives of kings and people.

Concerning the functions of the different ranks of the priesthood, we learn from Clemens of Alexandria that in their holy processions the Singer occupied the first place, carrying in his hands an instrument of music. He was obliged to learn two of the books of Hermes, one of which contained hymns addressed to the gods and the other the rules by which a prince ought to govern.

Next came the Horoscopus, holding a clock and a branch of a palm-tree, which were the symbols of astrology. He was required to be a complete master of the four books of Hermes, which treat of that science. One of these explained the order of the fixed stars, the second the motion and phases of the sun and moon, the other two determined the times of their periodical rising.

Then followed the Hierogrammatist, or Sacred Scribe, with a book and rule in his hand, to which were added the instruments of writing, ink and a reed. He had to know the hieroglyphics and those branches of science which belonged to cosmography—geography and astronomy, especially the laws of the sun, moon, and five planets; he should be thoroughly acquainted with the geography of Egypt, the course of the Nile, the furniture of the temples and of all consecrated places.

After these was an officer denominated Stolistes, who bore a square rule, as the emblem of justice, and the cup of libations. His charge included everything which belonged to the education of youth, as well as to sacrifices, first-fruits, hymns, prayers, religious pomp and festivals, and commemorations, the rules of which were contained in ten books. This functionary was succeeded by one called the Prophet, who displayed on his bosom a jar or vessel for carrying water, a symbol thought to represent the sacred character of the Nile. He was attended by persons bearing bread cut in slices. The duty of the Prophet, as President of the Mysteries, made it necessary for him to be perfectly acquainted with the ten books called sacerdotal, and which treated of the laws of the gods and of the whole discipline of the priesthood. He also presided over the distribution of the sacred revenue dedicated to the support of religious institutions.

Thoth was represented bearing in his hands a tablet and reed pen, sometimes a palm-branch and pen. It was his special office to be present in Amenti when souls were judged, to see their deeds weighed in the balance and record the result. It was he who composed the "Ritual of the Dead," at least its more important portions. He also wrote a book filled with wisdom and science.

There were altogether forty-two books of Hermes, the knowledge of which was necessary; of these thirty-six contained the philosophy of the Egyptians, and were carefully studied by the officers mentioned, and the remaining six comprised medicine and surgery.*

* See Mysteries, p. 95.

Egyptian mythology comprised a certain number of divinities, principal among which, were Osiris, Isis, Serapis, Hermes, Amun, Ptha, and Typhon.

Isis was the personification of universal nature, the parent of all things, the sovereign of the elements. On the front of the temple of Isis was cut this inscription: "I, Isis, am all that has been, is, or shall be, and no mortal hath ever unveiled me." This goddess was symbolized in different forms; first and principally, as the moon and as queen of the ocean. As queen of the ocean Isis is represented on ancient Egyptian coins as a girl holding a sistrum and unfurling a sail. Around her are the stars of heaven.

Osiris, the sun god, represented the abstract idea of the divine goodness or the attributes of Deity.

Serapis represented the principal attributes of the judge of the dead and the keeper of Hades.

Hermes was the god of science, art, and eloquence.

Amun was also a god of the sun; he was subsequently the Jupiter Ammon of the Romans and Zeus of the Greeks.

Ptha was the god of fire and life, and afterward the Prometheus of the Greeks.

Typhon represented the spirit of evil. His attributes were similar to those of Serapis.

In nearly all the earlier forms of religious worship God was worshipped under the symbol of the sun. We also find the sun alluded to in the Scriptures as the most perfect and appropriate symbol of the Creator.

The Mysteries, in their primitive form, taught the unity of God and the immortality of the soul of man as their cardinal doctrines, and that the sun was the symbol of Him whom the firmament obeys.*

The Ritual of the Mysteries was founded upon the legend of the death and resurrection of the sun-god, Osiris.

The Mysteries were in the form of a tragic drama, representing the singular death of Osiris, the search for his body by Isis, and its discovery and resurrection to life and power.

The attack of Typhon, the spirit of darkness, upon Osiris, who is slain,

---

* Note 10, p. 55; Mackey, pp. 514, 515; Macoy, p. 137; Stellar Theology, p. 20.

was enacted amid terrible scenes, during which the judgment of the dead and the punishments that the wicked suffered were represented as realities to the neophyte. Following this was the search for the body of Osiris, which was at last found concealed in the mysterious chest, after which the mutilated remains were interred amid exclamations of sorrow and despair. The ceremony closed with the return of Osiris to life and power, and amid effulgent beams of light, were seen the resplendent plains of Paradise.

Therefore the ceremonies represented a mystical death and descent into the infernal regions, where sin was purged away by the elements, and the initiated were said to be regenerated and restored to a life of light and purity. The ordeal was also a test of fortitude.

The Mysteries were celebrated once a year, when candidates were inducted into the degrees, viz.: of Isis, Serapis, and Osiris.*

The First Degree—Isis.

Of the ceremonies pertaining to these degrees we know but little, except that due inquiry was made as to the candidate's previous life, and at the time of initiation he was required to make confession. He was then taken charge of by a guide, who conducted him down through a low, dark passage to a subterranean apartment, where he met guards representing the tutelary deities of the temple, who demanded answers to certain questions, which, being given, he was conducted through another passage to the apartments for initiation, where he was subjected to severe trials, at the conclusion of which he was required to take a solemn and binding oath of secrecy and fidelity.

The Second Degree—Serapis.

This degree, like the first, was preparatory to the third, and the adept was required to take an additional obligation.

The Third Degree—Osiris.

After due time had passed, and the adept had given an exhibition of the requisite proficiency, he was raised to the third or highest degree, in which he

* See notes 19, 20, 21, 22, 23, p. 57; Mackey, pp. 242, 243.

represented Osiris, his death and resurrection. The conclusion of the obligation of this degree was as follows: "May my departed spirit wander in eternal misery, without a place of rest, should I ever violate the obligations conferred upon me by the Hierophants of the Sacred Mysteries."

Many of those who were initiated into the Mysteries entered the corporations of architects and builders, who erected the temples and other splendid edifices designed for the worship of Deity; in short, from this class came the rulers, priests, and architects of Egypt, its warriors and statesmen.

As the Eleusinian Mysteries were copied from the Egyptian, they constituted a complete reflex of them; and the Eleusinian having been practised down to A.D. 389 (see Hayden, p. 306), we have authentic data for a fuller description of their ceremonies—a description that will apply to the Egyptian Mysteries, as well as to the latter society.

The Eleusinian Mysteries.*

This institution was established in Greece, 1800 B.C., and when Eleusis was conquered by Athens, the inhabitants, while surrendering everything else, would not yield their mythologies and Mysteries.

The Mysteries were of two kinds—the Greater and the Less, the latter being preparatory to the Greater; and, like the Egyptian, they were celebrated once a year. For their purposes a magnificent temple of vast extent was erected at Eleusis. This edifice consisted of the sanctuary, or hall for the ceremonies of the Mysteries, the anactoron, or Holy of Holies, and a vast subterranean labyrinth for the ordeals pertaining to the induction of candidates into the degrees.† The ceremonies were grand and impressive throughout. The Hierophant (High Priest) sat in the east upon a magnificent throne and was arrayed in a splendid robe. Around him were seven brilliant lights representing the seven planets. The principal officers in attendance were the Priest, at the altar, the Dadochus, and the Herald. Over the head of the Hierophant a beautiful arch was represented, above which the moon and seven stars were seen. From his neck was suspended a golden globe. In addition to the officers, he had twenty-four attendants, clad in white

---
* Royal Masonic Cyclopædia, p. 193; also see note 16, p. 56.
† Note 33, p. 59; Mackey, p. 248.

HALL OF THE CEREMONIES IN THE TEMPLE OF THE ELEUSINIAN MYSTERIES.

ANCIENT SECRET SOCIETIES AND MYSTERIES.

robes, all wearing golden crowns, representing the twenty-four ancient constellations of the upper hemisphere.*

Rhea, who led the procession in search of the body of her lost companion, represented the moon.

The duty of the Dadochus—Torchbearer, was to impose silence on the assembly, and command the profane to withdraw.

The Priest officiated at the altar and wore a symbol of the moon. The Herald preserved order, compelled the uninitiated to retire at the command of the Dadochus, and punished all those who disturbed the sacred rites.

Bondmen and those with bodily defects were not admitted into the Mysteries.

The First Degree.

Previous to the initiation of a candidate due inquiry was made concerning his previous life; he was required to pass through a period of probation, make confession, and undergo lustration.† Finally, at the time appointed for the ceremonies, he was clothed in a dark robe and blindfolded. After being thus prepared he was conducted down through a dark and circuitous passage, into a cavern, where he heard the roar of wild beasts, the hissing of serpents, and was startled by terrible thunder and lightning. At length he was confronted by a massive door, on which was an inscription signifying that "he who would attain to the perfect state must be purified by the three great elements." Immediately after reading this the door slowly swung open and he was thrust into a place shrouded in darkness, where he was tossed about by a whirlwind. He was next compelled to cross a hall into which darted flames of fire, threatening his life. This ordeal passed, he was thrown into a dark and swift stream of water, across which he had to swim or drown. If the candidate had thus far exhibited manly courage and fortitude he was conducted to the great hall of the Mysteries, where, in the presence of the assembled priests and adepts, he took the oath of fidelity and secrecy. He then received the instructions and benediction.‡

---

* Stellar Theology, p. 12; Royal Masonic Cyclopædia, p. 194; Mackey, p. 247.
† See Mysteries of Free Masonry, pp. 137, 159; see notes 27–29, p. 58.
‡ See Gould, vol. i., p. 14; Stellar Theology, p. 10; also notes 13–24, 25, 26, pp. 55, 56, 57, 58.

The Second Degree.

After a twelvemonth's probation the candidate-adept was advanced to a higher degree. In the ceremonies of this degree sacrifice was made for the candidate and he took another oath or obligation. He was then invested with the sacred cloak, and mystic scarfs, a crown of palm-leaves was placed upon his head, and he was called Mystæ.

The Third Degree.

This degree represented the death of Bacchus (Osiris), the search for his body, and its resurrection. At the termination of another period of probation the adept was accorded a second advance—was raised to the third degree of the Mysteries. Therefore, after due preparation, he was conducted through a labyrinth amid horrible scenes into an apartment, the walls of which were draped in black and hung with emblems of death. Scenes of terror multiplied, and the horrors of Tartarus were seen in the distance. A tragic drama was enacted, in which a murder was committed by three ruffians, a bier rose before him on which lay a dead body. A funeral dirge was chanted, dusky phantoms (Rhea and attendants in search of the dead) passed before him, the corpse was missed from the bier, then suddenly a flood of dazzling light burst through the gloom, and standing in its centre the candidate in amazement saw the resurrected body. Exclamations of triumph and joy were now heard on every side, the fearful ordeal was over, and the brilliant spectacle of the Elysian fields and the bliss of the purified was presented.* In conclusion the candidate was conducted to the altar and took upon himself the obligation of this degree and was instructed in the Ritual. He was then called Epoptæ.

The horrors exhibited at the commencement of these ceremonies were intended to represent the condition of the wicked in another life, and the closing scene portrayed the abode of the blessed. The miseries of Tartarus and the happiness of Elysium were contrasted, being pronounced by the priests to be a true picture of what actually takes place in the future place of existence.

* See notes 28, 30, p. 58; also see Mackey, pp..247, 248, 249; Stellar Theology, pp. 13, 14; Royal Cyclopædia, p. 188; Macoy, pp. 124–129; Gould, vol. i., pp. 13, 14.

INITIATION SCENE IN THE MYSTERIES.

The Cabiri of Samothracia.

The three principal figures of the Egyptian ceremonial were carried to Berytus, in Phœnicia, and thence into several islands of the Ægean Sea. Their worship became very famous, especially in Lemnos, and in the island of Samothracia, which lies near it. They were called the Cabiri (cabirim, potentes), meaning the powerful gods.*

Many noted persons were initiated into these Mysteries, among whom we find such names as Orpheus, Hercules, and Ulysses.

Speaking of the Samothracian Mysteries, Voltaire asked ("Dict. Philo.") : "Who were the Hierophants—those sacred Free Masons who celebrated their ancient Mysteries—and whence came they?"

Gnostics.

The Gnostics were divided into many sects, and their Mysteries reach back to an early date. The best authorities agree that Gnosticism was an attempt to solve the problems of theology by combining the elements of the Egyptian Mysteries with the Jewish and Christian traditions.

The Dionysian Mysteries and Architects.

These Mysteries, like the others, comprised a tragedy—a murder, search for the body, its discovery and restoration to life. They were celebrated throughout Greece, Asia Minor, and Syria. Their Egyptian origin is shown by the fact that the Dionysian priests devoted themselves to the study and practice of architecture. About 1000 B.C. they established a society known as the Dionysian Architects, and were accorded the exclusive privilege of erecting the temples, and other public edifices. They were divided into companies, each one of which was governed by officers corresponding to the officers of a Masonic Lodge. They practised charity, had a system of secret words, and used several of the implements of Free Masonry.†

That a branch of this society was located at Tyre, at the time of the

---

* Note 31, p. 59; also Mysteries, p. 58.
† See Mackey, p. 222; Royal Masonic Cyclopædia, pp. 157, 158.

building of King Solomon's Temple, is well attested by history. In 300 B.C. they settled at Teos, where for centuries they practised their arts and Mysteries, making journeys to adjoining countries when their services were called for. In this way it is believed that at least a part of the travelling bands of Free Masons originated.

MITHRAISM.

The Mithraic Mysteries were essentially the same throughout as the Eleusinian, except that there were seven grades of the initiates. After passing through trying ordeals the neophyte was presented with an engraved amulet as a token of his admission into the brotherhood. He was also offered a crown, which, however, he was instructed to refuse, saying, "My only crown is Mithras." He was also marked in some indelible manner, the exact nature of which has not been ascertained.

The worship of Mithras was introduced into Rome at a very early date, and it soon became so popular in connection with the Serapis worship as to usurp the place of the ancient Roman deities, and during the second and third centuries of the empire Serapis and Mithras became the sole objects of worship, from the centre to the circumference of the Roman world.* From Rome the Mysteries soon found their way to Gaul, Germany, and Britain, and from inscriptions on tablets and tombs, and from other sources, we learn that they were practised in those countries as late as the tenth century.†

The Mithraism of the period to which the Roman Mithraic monuments belong have both a mythological and an astronomical character.

From the foregoing it appears that while the Mysteries embraced the arts and sciences, yet the great central idea of them all was, as previously stated, the unity of God and the immortality of the soul. Aspirations for purity and a higher life are everywhere manifest in their history.

In all the Mysteries regeneration was represented; an assassination took place, followed by a search for the body, its recovery and resurrection. In all such ceremonies grief and mourning are immediately followed by the most lively joy.

* See Gould, vol. i., p. 23.
† Stellar Theology, p. 106; note 17, p. 56; Gould, vol. i., p. 13; Mackey, p. 503.

SCENE IN THE THIRD DEGREE OF THE MYSTERIES.

ANCIENT SECRET SOCIETIES AND MYSTERIES.

As the Mysteries were practised in different parts of Europe to the time of the Guilds and bands of travelling Masons, a complete line of descent from the Egyptian Mysteries down to the Free Masonry of 1717 is shown. But the main line we shall see led through the Mysteries of Greece, the Roman Colleges of Builders, and the Guilds.*

THE ESSENES.

These peculiar people were a secret society of the Jews. They always rose before sunrise, assembled, and prayed with their faces turned toward the sun. Some were occupied in healing the sick, others in instructing the young, and all of them devoted certain hours to studying the mysteries of nature, revelation, and of the celestial hierarchy. The labor of the forenoon terminated at eleven, when they partook of their midday meal, each member taking his seat according to age.†

Every candidate passed through a novitiate which extended over three years. In the first stage, of twelve months, he had to turn all his property into the common treasury. He then received a copy of the ordinances, a spade, an apron (to be used at the lustrations), and a white robe. After the probation he was admitted into the second stage, which lasted two years. During this period he was admitted to a closer fellowship, and shared in the lustral rites, but could not hold an office or sit at the common table. After passing through the second stage of probation he was admitted to the third rank or degree. On his admission to this rank the candidate had to take a solemn oath to practise charity, and not to reveal the secrets of the order.

It is even claimed by ancient and modern authority that Christ was an Essene. This conclusion was arrived at from the following facts: As a sect they were distinguished for an aspiration after ideal purity, so as to ultimately attain an absolute standard of holiness.

They observed the sabbath with singular strictness, and they believed that to lead a pure and holy life, to mortify the flesh, and to be meek and lowly in spirit would bring them into closer communion with the Creator, therefore Christ would naturally associate himself with an order that was so congenial to his nature.

* Note 18, p. 56.   † See Gould, vol. i., pp. 26 to 34; also Laurie and Ginsburg.

Again Christ not being heard in public but once until he was thirty years old implies that he lived in seclusion with this fraternity.* And while he frequently denounced the Scribes and Pharisees, he never denounced, or in any way reflected, on the Essenes. Yet as their most important doctrines were taught in secret, and they having had grips and pass-words by which they recognized one another, Christ's association with them could only have been of a general nature.

Pliny states that, "Toward the west of the Dead Sea are the Essenes. They are a hermitical society, marvellous beyond all others throughout the whole earth. They live without women, without money, and in groves of palm-trees. Their ranks are daily made up by multitudes of new-comers who resort to them, and who, being weary of life, and driven by the surges of ill-fortune, adopt their manner of life. Thus it is that through thousands of ages (per sæculorum millia), incredible to relate, those people prolonged their existence without anyone being born among them, so fruitful to them are the weary lives of others."

Their existence under the name of Essenes is so fully attested by Josephus as to render it certain that they originated as early as 200 B.C.

In the earliest Masonic Ritual, or the one mentioned in the "York Constitutions," there is evidence of ceremonies that were obviously taken from the Roman colleges and that agree with the practices of the Essenes, and Soofes of Persia.

It has been claimed that there was a close similarity between the Essenes and the Pythagoreans; but the Pythagoreans were essentially polytheists, while the Essenes were monotheistic Jews. The Pythagoreans believed in the doctrine of metempsychosis, the Essenes did not believe in it.

Pythagoras taught that man could control his fortune; Essenism maintained that fate governs all things.

The Pythagoreans were aristocratic and exclusive, the Essenes were so meek and so friendly that all joined in bestowing great praise upon them.

* Mackey, p. 261.

PYTHAGORAS.

This renowned philosopher was a native of Samos, and a pupil of Pherecydes. He flourished, says Bayle, about five hundred years before Christ, in the time of Tarquin, last king of Rome.*

Pythagoras regarded music as something celestial and divine, and had such an opinion of its power over the human affections that he ordered his disciples to be wakened every morning and lulled to sleep every night by sweet sounds. He likewise considered it as greatly conducive to health, and made use of it in disorders of the body, as well as in those of the mind.

The first journey of Pythagoras from his native island was into Egypt, which was celebrated in his time for that kind of wisdom which best suited his genius and temper. On his way thither Jamblichus asserts that he visited Phœnicia and conversed with the prophets and philosophers who were the successors of Mochus, the Physiologist.

While in Egypt he was introduced to Amasia, the king, a distinguished patron of literary men, and thus obtained access to the colleges of the priests. He passed twenty-two years in Egypt, availing himself of all possible means of information with regard to the recondite doctrines of the priests, as well as of their astronomy, geometry, and other branches.

The brethren of the Pythagorean College at Crotona, called Coniobion, Cœnobium, about six hundred in number,† lived together as in one family with their wives and children, and the whole business of the society was conducted with perfect regularity. Every day commenced with a deliberation upon the manner in which it should be spent, and concluded with a retrospect of the events which had occurred and of the business transacted. Their dinner consisted chiefly of bread, honey, and water; for after they were fully initiated they denied themselves the use of wine. The remainder of the day was devoted to civil and domestic affairs, conversation, bathing, and religious ceremonies.

The Esoteric disciples of Pythagoras were taught after the Egyptian manner, by images and symbols, obscure and unintelligible to those who were

* Mysteries, p. 187.   † Ibid., p. 194.

not initiated into the mysteries of the school; and those who were admitted to this privilege were under the strictest obligation of secrecy with regard to the secret doctrines of their master.

He taught that the first step toward wisdom was the study of mathematics—a science which contemplates objects that lie midway between corporeal and incorporeal beings, and, as it were, on the confines of both, and which most advantageously inures the mind to contemplation.

The monad or unity is that quality which, being deprived of all numbers, remains fixed; whence called monad from to menein. It is the fountain of all numbers. The duad is imperfect and passive and the cause of increase and division. The triad, composed of the monad and duad, partakes of the nature of both. The tetrad is the most perfect. The decad, which is the sum of the four former, comprehends all arithmetical and musical proportions.

Next to mathematics, music had the chief place in the teachings of Pythagoras; he believing that music elevated the mind above the dominion of the passions, and inured it to contemplation. He considered music not only an art to be judged of by the ear, but as a science to be reduced to mathematical principles and proportions.

Besides arithmetic and music, Pythagoras cultivated geometry, which he had learned in Egypt, but he greatly improved it by investigating many new theorems, and by digesting its principles in an order more perfectly systematical than had before been done. Several Grecians about the time of Pythagoras applied themselves to mathematical learning, particularly Thales, in Ionia. But Pythagoras seems to have done more than any other philosopher of this period toward reducing geometry to a regular science.

He also taught that God is a soul, everywhere in nature; that the souls of men are derived from his supreme soul, which is immortal; that the principle of all things being unity, he believed that between God and man there is an infinite number of spiritual agents ministering from one to another, and to the great Supreme Soul.

He was killed in a riot, B C. 506, after having lived, according to the most probable statement of his birth, to the age of eighty years. After his death his followers paid a superstitious respect to his memory. They erected statues in his honor, and converted his house at Crotona into a temple of Ceres, and appealed to him as a divinity, swearing by his name.

After the death of the philosopher, the care and education of his children and the charge of his school devolved upon Aristæus of Crotona, who, having taught the doctrines of Pythagoras twenty-nine years, was succeeded by Mnesarchus, the son of Pythagoras. Pythagorean schools were afterward conducted in Heraclia by Clinias and Philolaus, at Metapontum by Theorides and Eurytus, and at Tarentum by Archytas, who is said to have been the eighth in succession from Pythagoras. The first person who divulged the Pythagorean doctrine was Phialorus.*

The First Temples of Egypt.

Although not of vital importance to this subject, yet it will be of interest to indicate, as near as possible, the commencement of the Egyptian Mysteries; therefore, as the weight of evidence gives *Memphis* † the greatest antiquity in Egyptian history, that city and its temples will be noticed first.

Memphis was the first capital of Egypt, was situated in the delta of the Nile, or Lower Egypt, and was founded in the first dynasty. According to Herodotus, the bed of the Nile was changed and an embankment made from one hundred stadia above Memphis to a short distance below the city, to protect it against inundations. The remains of this bank still exist. The city was composed of two portions, one being built of bricks and the other, in which was the citadel, of calcareous stone—" White Wall." In the citadel were some of the principal buildings.

The most remarkable features of the city were its temples and its necropolis, in which was the great pyramid, towering high in its centre.

Up to 1500 B.C. Memphis remained the religious capital of the old worship, and down to the death of Unas this city was the great seat of the Egyptian empire; but with the accession of the sixth dynasty there was a shift of power to the southward, to Abydos.

---

* Mysteries, p. 198.

† The principal seat of the Mysteries was at *Memphis*, in the neighborhood of the Great Pyramid. They were of two kinds, the Greater and the Less (Mackey, p. 242; also see Macoy, p. 124; Royal Cyclopædia, p. 188).

The temples of Memphis were numerous and magnificent, the first of which was near the centre of old Memphis. There was a temple of Isis, a temple dedicated to Proteus, a temple of the Apis having a peristyle and court, ornamented with figures, opposite the south propylæum of the temple of Ptha, and the temple of Ra. Some of the temples flourished in all their glory till the Persian conquest.

At Memphis were also the shrine of the Cabiri and the statues of Rameses II., one of which exists as the Fallen Colossus.

Thebes—Its First Temples.

It is believed by writers of note * that this city, as well as Memphis, was founded in the first Egyptian dynasty. But no remains of so early a date have yet been discovered. We find, however, that Sesonchosis, of the first dynasty of Theban kings, commenced to reign 2518 B.C., and its first temple was also erected soon after that time.

Thebes was situated on both sides of the Nile, and its remarkable ruins are divided into four principal groups—Karnak and Luxor on the east side of the river, and Medinet Habou, and Gournou on the west side. The distance between Karnak and Luxor is about two miles, which is also the distance between Medinet Habou and Gournou. In each of these quarters are the ruins of one or more splendid temples. This is especially the case at Karnak, where the remains show that over four thousand years ago there stood a temple at that place that was vast in its dimensions and magnificent in its architectural design and finish.

Half way between Medinet Habou and Gournou are the remains of still another temple belonging to Thebes—the Ramesseum, which in many of its details is equal to the great temple at Karnak. Next in importance among the temples of Egypt was the temple of Edfou, south of Thebes.

At Soan, near the mouth of the Nile, the ruins of a temple and of thirteen obelisks can still be traced. At Soleb, on the borders of Nubia, a temple now stands which is also scarcely inferior in magnificence to those of Thebes.

At Sedinga, not far below the third cataract, are the remains of a temple erected by Amenophis III., of the eighteenth dynasty.

* See Niebuhr, Dr. Thompson, Smith and Barnum's Dictionary of the Bible, p. 1103.

HYPOSTYLE HALL, KARNAK.

At Abydos the remains of two great temples of Osiris have been partially disinterred from the sand which overwhelmed them.

On the walls of one of these, the tablets of Abydos were discovered, which first gave connected lists of the kings. These lists nearly confirm those of Manetho, the second of which contains the names of seventy-six kings, ancestors of Manephthah, who reigned about 2000 B.C. But among the best preserved and most remarkable of the ruins of Egyptian edifices are those of the Temple of DENDERA (Tentyra). They present striking examples not only of practices in the ceremonies of the Mysteries, but of the advanced state that Egyptian architecture had attained to. The gateway in particular, which leads to the Temple of Isis, excites universal admiration.

Each front, as well as the interior, is covered with sculptured hieroglyphics, which were executed with a richness, elegance of form, and variety of ornament surpassing in many respects similar edifices found at Thebes and Philæ.

"Advancing along the ruins," says Dr. Richardson, "we came to an elegant gateway or propylon, which is of sandstone neatly hewn, and completely covered with sculpture and hieroglyphics remarkably well cut. Immediately over the centre of the doorway is the beautiful Egyptian ornament called the globe with wings,* emblematical of the glorious sun poised in the airy firmament of heaven, supported and directed in his course by the eternal wisdom of the Deity. The sublime phraseology of Scripture, 'The Sun of Righteousness shall rise with healing on his wings,' could not be more emphatically or more accurately represented to the human eye than by this elegant device."

The temple itself still retains much of its original magnificence. The centuries which have elapsed since the era of its foundation have scarcely affected it in any important part, and have impressed upon it no greater appearance of age than serves to render it more venerable and imposing. Another writer, who had seen innumerable monuments of the kind throughout the Thebaid, declared that these ruins exhibited the highest degree of architectural excellence that had ever been attained on the border of the Nile.

The portico consists of twenty-four columns, in three rows, each about twenty-two feet in circumference, thirty-two feet high, and covered with

* Mysteries, p. 97.

hieroglyphics. On the architrave are represented two processions of men and women bringing to Isis and to Osiris emblematical offerings. The interior of the pronaos is adorned with sculptures, most of them preserving part of the paint with which they had been covered. Those on the ceiling were peculiarly rich and varied, all illustrative of the union between the astronomical and religious creeds of the ancient Egyptians. The sekos, or interior of the temple, consists of several apartments, the walls and ceilings of which are likewise covered with religious and astronomical representations.

The rooms were lighted by perpendicular apertures in the ceilings, and, where it was possible to introduce them, by oblique ones in the sides. Therefore, the perpetual gloom in which the apartments on the ground floor of the sekos must have been buried was well calculated for the *mysterious practices* of the religion to which it was consecrated.

The ceiling of an adjoining room is divided into two compartments by a figure of Isis in very high relief. In one of them is the circular zodiac,* in the other a variety of boats, with four or five figures in each. Near this scene is a large lion, supported by four dog-headed figures, each carrying a knife. The walls of the third room are covered with several representations of a person : the first, at the point of death, lying on a couch, then *stretched out lifeless* upon a bier. †

The western wall of the great temple is particularly interesting for the extreme elegance of the sculpture.

In the centre of the ceiling of a chapel behind the temple is the face of Isis in high relief, illuminated by a body of rays issuing from the mouth of a long figure, which, in the other temples, appears to encircle the heavenly bodies.

About two hundred yards eastward from this chapel is a propylon of small dimensions, resembling in form that which conducts to the great temple, and, like it, built in a line with the wall which surrounds the sacred enclosure.

Still farther toward the east is another propylon, equally well preserved with the rest, about forty feet in height and twenty feet square at the base.

---

* Notes 34, 35, p. 59 ; Mysteries, p. 99.
† Traditions and Early History of Free Masonry, p. 220.

THE GREAT OBELISK, HELIOPOLIS.

ANCIENT SECRET SOCIETIES AND MYSTERIES. 49

Among the sacred figures on this building is an Isis pointing with a reed to a graduated staff held by another figure of the same deity.

Another remarkable structure was the LABYRINTH or Tower situated close to Lake Moeris, in which the priests were at one time lodged, and where the characters of the several works and the symbols of the public regulations were delineated.

"The remains of this building, recently discovered by Lepsius, shows that it was founded by Amenemha I., of the twelfth Egyptian dynasty, about 1800 B.C. This monarch was probably buried in it. This wonderful structure was built of Parian marble, Syenite granite, and porphyry—much of the work being beautifully polished. It contained three thousand chambers and passages said to be vaulted, half of the apartments were under ground and the others above. The upper chambers were decorated with reliefs, the lower were plain, and contained, according to tradition, the bodies of the founders of the building. When Herodotus and Strabo visited this edifice it was difficult to pass through it without the aid of a guide, and the opening of the doors echoed like the reverberation of thunder. For a long time great doubt prevailed whether any remains of the building existed, but it was discovered by Lepsius, who found part of the foundation or lower chambers close to the site of the Moeris lake, or modern Birket el-Keroun." *

THE OBELISK.

The first of these monuments to find place in history was that of Usurtasen I., erected at Heliopolis at least 2000 B.C. Referring to this obelisk, Rawlinson † says: "Originally it was beyond all doubt one of a pair placed in front of the great entrance to the Temple of the Sun—the Jachin and Boaz of the Egyptian sanctuary."

Thotmes I. erected two obelisks of large size before the sanctuary of the temple at Karnak. His daughter Hatasu erected two others before the second propylæon.

Thotmes III. erected several obelisks 1500 B.C., the first of which was set up to commemorate his conquest of Naharania, Mesopotamia. One of his

---
* See Chambers's Encyclopædia, vol. vii., p. 352; Rawlinson, vol. ii., p. 170.
† Ibid., vol. ii., p. 154.

Theban obelisks found its way to Rome, and stands in front of the church of St. John Lateran.

Of the other obelisks that Thotmes erected at Heliopolis, two at least were taken by Augustus to Alexandria, where they long remained, known as Cleopatra's Needles. Finally, in 1877, one of these ancient monuments was shipped to England, where, after severe vicissitudes it arrived, and was set up on the Thames Embankment. Another one was taken down by Commander Gorringe and brought to New York in 1880 and now adds its historic interest to Central Park.*

When lowering this obelisk at Alexandria, preparatory to shipping it, there was found under, or rather in, the pedestal the following Masonic emblems cut in the stone: The two Ashlars, an Apron, a Trowel, iron or steel, and a Trestle-board. What the original purpose of the obelisk was, is uncertain, but on this one, as on most of the others there were inscriptions—hieroglyphics setting forth the achievements of the reigning monarch.†

Religion.

Herodotus visited Egypt in the middle of the fifth century, and concerning their devotion, said: "The Egyptians are religious to excess, far beyond any other race of men."

"Writing was so full of sacred symbols, and of allusions to their mythology, that it was scarcely possible to employ it on any subject which lay outside of religion."

From their architectural remains it is seen that the temple dominates over the palace, both the temple and the tomb being the expression of religious ideas. The great temple of each city was the centre of its life.

That the Egyptians had correct conceptions of the attributes of God will be seen from the following quotations:

First, from a hymn inscribed on Egyptian papyri, now in the British Museum:

"He is not beheld;
His abode is not known.
No shrine is found with painted figures of him;

---

* Note 36, p. 59; Chambers's Encyclopædia, vol. viii., p. 714; Rawlinson, vol. ii, pp. 248, 260.
† Scarlet Book of Free Masonry, pp. 458-463.

> There is no building that can contain him.
> Unknown is his name in Heaven;
> He does not manifest his forms;
> Vain are all representations of him."

In another place God is thus described: "He hath made the world with his hand—its waters, its atmosphere, its vegetation, all its flocks, and birds and fish, and reptiles, and beasts of the field" (Translation by Chabas).

"He is their father, and they sons beloved of their father. He is the giver of life, toucher of the hearts, and Searcher of the Inward Parts is his name." "Let not thy face be turned away from us; the joy of our hearts is to contemplate thee."

> "Chase all anguish from our hearts.
> The spirits thou hast made exalt thee,
> Father of the father of all the Gods,
> Who raises the heavens, who fixes the earth,
> Maker of beings, author of existences,
> Sovereign of life, health, and strength, Chief of the Gods,
> We worship thy spirit, who alone hast made us;
> We whom thou hast made thank thee that thou hast given us birth.
> We give thee praise for thy mercy toward us."

Inscribed on the tombs is found this formula:

"I have given bread to the hungry, water to the thirsty, clothes to the naked, shelter to the stranger." This tenderness for suffering humanity is characteristic of the nation—Brotherly Love, Relief, and Truth.

An oracle of Apollo, quoted by Eusebius, says that the Egyptians were the first who disclosed by infinite actions the path that leads to the gods. The oracle is as follows:

> "The path by which to deity we climb
> Is arduous, rough, ineffable, sublime;
> And the strong massive gates, through which we pass
> In our first course, are bound with chains of brass.
> Those men the first, who of Egyptian birth,
> Drank the fair waters of Nilotic earth,

> Disclosed by actions infinite this road,
> And many paths to God Phœnicians showed.
> This road the Assyrians pointed out to view,
> And this the Lydians and Chaldeans knew."

Showing that the religion of the Egyptians originally comprised the essentials of Christianity, and that their moral code was both pure and exalted.

But the real *nature* and *attributes* of God could only be communicated to such as were initiated into the Mysteries, and gave unquestionable proofs of their fidelity and zeal. And to the initiate it was a startling and solemn revelation.

"It was difficult," says Plato, "to attain, and dangerous to publish the knowledge of the true God."

The Judgment of the Dead.

This singular ceremony was also embraced in the Mysteries, and was founded on the funeral rites of the Egyptians; and from its judgment in this world no Egyptian was exempt, be his position high or low; on this trial depended the right to an honorable burial.

The dead person was brought to the place of judgment, and to the foot of the tribunal, consisting of several judges, who inquired into his life and conversation. All whom the deceased had wronged, or who knew of his evil deeds, could testify to the same over his dead body. The decision was determined by the weight of evidence, without regard to the position of the deceased; therefore, at one time even a king who had led a wicked life might be excluded from burial in his own sepulchre and be buried among the rabble. The judgment at the funeral was believed to be the same as the deceased received in the invisible world at the same time.

When no accuser appeared, they ceased to lament the dead person, and his encomium was made. They commended his respect for religion, equity, moderation, chastity, and other virtues. His birth, which was supposed to be the same with all men, was never allowed as any virtue in him. All the assistants applauded these praises and congratulated the deceased on account of his being ready to enjoy an eternal repose with the virtuous.

ANCIENT SECRET SOCIETIES AND MYSTERIES. 53

The ceremony ended by thrice sprinkling sand over the openings of the vaults wherein they had put the corpse, bidding him thrice adieu.

These practices were almost everywhere copied, and were so many in-

JUDGMENT OF THE DEAD.

structions to the people, giving them to understand that death was followed by an account of which they were to give of their life before an inflexible tribunal; and that which was dreadful to the wicked was only a passage into a happier state for the good. Wherefore death was called the deliverance.*

NOTES FROM AUTHORITIES.

1. Documentary evidence, Craft symbolism, and oral relations alike take us back to Egypt and the East.

"One of the most learned of English Masons, the late Dr Leeson, in a lecture delivered at Portsmouth, on July 25, 1862, states: that Egypt was the cradle of Masonry. The Egyptians were the first to establish a civilized society and all the sciences must necessarily have been derived from this source." Gould, in History of Free Masonry, vol. iii., pp. 222-232.

2. "Egypt, remarkable for its historical interests, still retains in her wonderful monuments the earliest records of civilization. A land so ancient, that, even in the early days of Greece, it was considered to be of wondrous and remote antiquity.

* Note 40, p. 60.

54   ANCIENT SECRET SOCIETIES AND MYSTERIES.

Learning appears to have been pursued with great diligence and the education of an ancient philosopher was hardly considered complete until he had journeyed to Egypt, the cradle of the arts and sciences, and received from the lips of her priests some portion of their traditional lore. The mode of writing of the Egyptians was singular—they had three kinds of characters. The hieratic letters were used by the priests on sacred occasions; the demotic in all civil and secular matters; and the hieroglyphic to describe actions in a mysterious manner. The last-named consisted of pictures of every description of men, beasts, flowers, and instruments. The whole system of instruction was purely symbolic. Their philosophers concealed their particular tenets and principles of policy and philosophy under hieroglyphic figures, and expressed their ideas of government by signs and symbols." From an oration by J. Flavius Adams, M.D.

3. It has been forcibly observed, "that in all the legends of Free Masonry, the line of ascent leads with unerring accuracy through Grecian corporations back to the Orient." Fort, p. 183.

4. Says Adam Clark: "All knowledge, all religion, and all arts and sciences have travelled according to the course of the sun from east to west." Bazot tells us (in his Manuel du Franc-Maçon, p. 154) that "the veneration which Masons entertain for the East confirms an opinion previously announced, that the religious system of Masonry came from the East."

5. We are not to search for our antiquity in the mythology of Greece or Rome, we advance into remoter ages. We discover in the Ammonian and Egyptian rites the most perfect remains of these originals to whom our society refers. Traditions, p. 34; The Mysteries of Free Masonry, p. 220.

6. The irradiation of the Mysteries of Egypt shine and animate the secret doctrines of Phœnicia, Asia Minor, Greece and Italy. Heckethorn, Secret Societies of all Ages and Countries, vol. i., p. 78; Gould, iii., p. 223.

7. I see no reason why any pause should be made in our inquiry when we reach the Middle Ages. That era, no doubt, as well as the societies and associations coeval with it, is interesting to the archæologist, if it fixes a date, or channel, calculated to elucidate the transmission of Masonic science from the more remote past. Yet the greater number, not to go further, of the analogies or similarities which are so much dwelt upon have their examplers in the Mysteries to the extent that they are identical—we might with as much justice claim Egypt as the land of Masonic origin as limit our pretensions to a derivation from the Vehemic Tribunals of Westphalia. In the Mysteries we meet with dialogue, ritual, darkness, light, death, and reproduction. It admits of no doubt that the rites and theological expressions of the Egyptians were of universal acceptation. Gould, vol. iii., p. 236.

8. Ferguson, in History of Architecture, vol. i., p. 147, speaking of Assyrian architecture and the Egyptian pyramids, says: "It does not, it is true, rival that of Egypt in antiquity, as the pyramids still maintain a pre-eminence of 1,000 years beyond anything that has yet been discovered in the Valley of the Euphrates. There is nothing certain in India, that nearly approaches these monuments in antiquity, nor in China or the rest of Asia."

ANCIENT SECRET SOCIETIES AND MYSTERIES.

9. Pythagoras, Zoroaster, and Confucius drew their doctrines from the Mysteries. Clemens of Alexandria, speaking of the greater Mysteries, says: "Here ends all instruction. Nature and all things are seen and known." Had mortal truths alone been taught the initiate, the mysteries could never have deserved or received the magnificent eulogiums of the most enlightened men of antiquity ; of Pindar, Plutarch, Isocrates, Diodorus, Plato, Euripides, Socrates, Aristophanes, Cicero, Epictetus, Marcus Aurelius, and others. Traditions of Free Masonry, p. 225.

10. Our chief emblems originally from Egypt. . . . We have retained the Egyptian symbols of the sun and moon, as the emblems of God's power, eternity, omnipresence, and benevolence ; and thereby we signify that we are the children of light, and that the first foundation of our profession is the knowledge and adoration of almighty Mesouraneo, who seateth himself in the centre of the heavens ; and we have saved from oblivion many of their religious rites, in our initiation into the First Degree of Masonry, which otherwise would have slept in eternity. Mysteries of Free Masonry, p. 219.

11. The identity of the Masonic institutions with the ancient Mysteries is obvious from the striking coincidences found to exist between them. The latter were a secret religious worship, and the depository of religion, science, and art. Tradition dates the origin of the Mysteries back to the earliest period of time, and makes it coeval with the organization of society. Traditions, p. 13.

12. Albert Pike, in the Review, vol. ii., p. 33, says : "Such were the Mysteries and such the old thought, as in scattered fragments it has come down to us. The human mind still speculates on the great mysteries of nature, and still finds its ideas anticipated by the ancients, whose profoundest thoughts are to be looked for, not in their philosophies, but in their symbols, by which they endeavored to express the great ideas that vainly struggled for utterance in words, as they viewed the great circle of phenomena—birth, life, death or decomposition, and new life out of death—to them the great mysteries. Remember, while you study their symbols, that they have a profounder sense of those wonders than we have."

13. St. Cyril, of Alexandria, who was made bishop in A.D. 412, and died in 444, says in his seventh book against Julian : "These Mysteries are so profound and so exalted that they can be comprehended by those only who are enlightened. I shall not therefore attempt to speak of what is so admirable in them, lest by discovering them to the uninitiated I should offend against the injunctions not to give what is holy to the impure, nor cast pearls before such as cannot estimate their worth."

St. Chrysostom and St. Augustine frequently refer to the Mysteries of initiation. St. Augustine, 400 A.D., says : "I wish to speak openly of the Mysteries, but dare not on account of those who are uninitiated. I must therefore avail myself of disguised terms designating in a shadowy manner (where the whole Mysteries are celebrated) so as to exclude all uninitiated persons. Then guard the doors."

St. Augustine says to the initiated : "Having dismissed the Catechumenes, we have retained you only to be our hearers, because, besides those things which belong to all Christians in common, we are now to discuss to you of the sublime Mysteries which none are qualified to give except those who by the Master's sanction have the right to be present."

St. Gregory Narianzen, Bishop of Constantinople, A.D. 379, says: "You have heard as much of the Mystery as we are allowed to speak openly in the ears of all; the rest will be communicated to you in private and that you must retain yourself. . . . Our Mysteries are not to be made known to strangers."

St. Ambrose, Archbishop of Milan, who was born in 340 and died 393, says in his work De Mysteriis: "The Mysteries should be kept concealed, guarded by faithful silence, lest it should be inconsiderately divulged to the ears of the profane. . . . It is not given to all to contemplate the depths of our Mysteries; . . . that they may not be seen by those who ought not to behold them nor received by those who cannot preserve them."

14. The belief that Free Masonry derived its origin from the ancient Mysteries prevails in Europe and America. This theory was ably sustained by the learned antiquary Alexander Lenoir, in his celebrated work on the antiquity of Free Masonry, and his views were adopted by most of the Masonic writers of France.

15. Wheresoever the Mysteries were introduced they retained their primitive form, adapted to the customs and usages of the national religion. Hence, the same or similar ceremonies which were applied to Osiris and Isis in Egypt, the great source of secret and mysterious rites, were celebrated in Greece in honor of Bacchus and Rhea; at Eleusis they were applied to Ceres and Proserpine; in Tyre and Cyprus, to Adonis and Venus; in Persia, to Mithras and Mithra; in India, to Maha Deva and Sita; in Britain, to Hu and Ceridwin; in Scandinavia, to Odin and Frea; and in Mexico, to Tialoc and the Great Mother. These appear to be but different names for the deities. Oliver, in Signs and Symbols.

16. In discoursing, therefore, of the Mysteries in general, we shall be forced to take our ideas of them chiefly from what we find practised in the Eleusinian. Nor need we fear to be mistaken; the end of all being the same, and all having their common original from Egypt.

Herodotus, Diodorus, and Plutarch, who collect from ancient testimonies, expressly affirm, and in this all antiquity concurs, that the Eleusinian mysteries particularly retained the very Egyptian gods in whose honor they were celebrated. Mysteries of Free Masonry, pp. 106, 133.

17. Says Mr. King: "There is every reason to believe that, as in the East, the worship of Serapis was at first combined with Christianity, and gradually merged into it with an entire change of name, *not substance*, carrying with it many of its ancient notions and rites; so in the West a similar influence was exerted by the Mithraic religion." . And as there is no account of their decline, many have supposed that the worship of, and faith in, Mithras had survived down to comparatively modern times. Mysteries, p. 17.

18. Egypt has always been considered the birthplace of the Mysteries. It was there that the ceremonies of initiation were first established. It was there that truth was first veiled in allegory, and the dogmas of religion were first imparted under symbolic forms.

ANCIENT SECRET SOCIETIES AND MYSTERIES.

This system of symbols was disseminated through Greece and Rome and other countries of Europe and Asia, giving origin, through many intermediate steps, to that mysterious association which is now represented by the institution of Free Masonry. Mackey, p. 242.

19. The Isiac Mysteries would seem to be the First Degree among the Egyptians. The Second consisted of the Mysteries of Serapis. Of their nature we know scarcely anything. In the Mysteries of Osiris, which completed the series of Egyptian esoteric teaching, the lesson of death and resurrection were symbolically conveyed; the legend of the murder and restoration of Osiris was displayed to the affiliate in a scenic manner. Royal Masonic Cyclopædia, pp. 188, 189.

20. The First Degree, as we may term it, of Egyptian initiation was that into the Mysteries of Isis. The Mysteries of Serapis constituted the Second Degree of the Egyptian initiation. In the Mysteries of Osiris, which were the consummation of the Egyptian system, the lesson of death and resurrection was symbolically taught; and the legend of the murder of Osiris, the search for the body, its discovery and restoration to life is scenically represented. Mackey, pp. 242, 243.

21. Samuel L. Knapp, Esq., in a work entitled "The Genius of Masonry," says: "Behind this veil of Isis I have long thought was concealed our Masonic birth. I now fully believe it." Mysteries, p 121.

22. "The Mysteries of Osiris," says Heckethorn, "formed the Third Degree, or summit of Egyptian initiation."

23. In these, the legend of the murder of Osiris by his brother Typhon, was represented, and the god was personated by the candidate. Secret Societies of all Ages and Countries, vol. i., p. 75; Gould, iii., 249.

24. Apuleius (Met., book xi.), who had been initiated into all the Mysteries, speaks of those of Isis in the following way: "The priest, all the profane being removed to a distance, taking hold of me by the hand, brought me into the inner recesses of the sanctuary itself, clothed in a new linen garment. I approached the confines of death and having trod on the threshold of Proserpine, I returned therefrom, being borne through all the elements. At midnight I saw the sun shining with its brilliant light; and I approached the presence of the gods beneath, the gods above, and stood near and worshipped them. Behold I have related to you things of which, though heard by you, you must necessarily remain ignorant."

"This happy moment (de l' autopsia) was introduced," says Dupuis, "by frightful scenes, by alternate fear and joy, by light and darkness, by the glimmer of light, by the terrible noise of thunder, which was imitated, and by the apparitions of spectres, of magical illusions, which struck the eye and ears all at once." Royal Masonic Cyclopædia, p. 188; Mysteries, p. 144; also see Moore's Epicurean.

25. Dupuis says, in his "Recherches sur les Initiations:" "They exercised the candidates to cross by swimming a large extent of water; they threw them into it, and it was with great difficulty that they extricated themselves. They applied a sword and fire to their bodies; they made

58 ANCIENT SECRET SOCIETIES AND MYSTERIES.

them pass over flames. The aspirants were often in considerable danger, and Pythagoras, we are told, nearly lost his life in the trials. It was also at the same period that they celebrated the Pyrrhic or fire dance. And this illustrates the origin of the purification by fire and water, for having denominated the tropic of Cancer gate of heaven and of heat or celestial fire, and that of Capricorn gate of deluge or of water, it was imagined that the spirits of souls who passed through the gates on their way to and from heaven, were scorched or bathed; hence the baptism of Mithra and the passage through the flames, observed throughout the East long before." Mysteries, p. 147.

26. Volney says: "The truly grand tragedies, the imposing and terrible representations, were the sacred Mysteries, which were celebrated in the greatest temples in the world, in the presence of the initiated only. It was there that the habits, the decorations, the machinery were proper to the subjects; and the subject was, present and future life."

27. Confession was one necessary preparative for initiation. Those who were initiates also gave further security for their discretion; for they were obliged to make confession to their priests of all the most private actions of their lives; so that by this means they became the slaves to their priests, that their own secrets might be kept. It was upon this sort of confession that a Lacedemonian, who was going to be initiated into the Mysteries of Samothrace, spoke roundly thus to the priest: "If I have committed any crimes, surely the gods are not ignorant of them." Another answered almost after the same manner, "Is it to you or to God we ought to confess our crimes?" "It is to God," says the priest. "Well then, retire thou," answered the Lacedemonian, "and I will confess them to God." These Lacedemonians were not very full of the spirit of devotion—to man. Hist. of Oracles, p. 114, London, 1688, edit.; also Mysteries, p. 153.

28. The Scholiast on the Ranæ of Aristophanes says: "It was a universal opinion that he who had been initiated into the great Mysteries should obtain divine honors after death." Again, Isocrates affirms (Panegyr.): "The mysteries teach the initiated to entertain the most lively hopes touching death and immortality." Cicero also (De Leg., 1, ii., c. 14) praises these institutions for the same thing: "From them," says he, "we not only reap the advantage of greater happiness in this world, but we are instructed to hope for a better existence hereafter." Oliver, in Historical Landmarks of Free Masonry, vol. ii., p. 100.

29. They used as significant emblems the Theological Ladder; the triple support of the universal lodge, called by Masons Wisdom, Strength, and Beauty; the point within a circle, and many other legitimate emblems of Masonry; they used the same form of government, the same system of secrecy, allegory, and symbolic instructions, all tending to the same point, the practice of moral virtue. None were admitted without previous *probation* and initiation; the candidates were bound by solemn oaths, united by invisible ties, taught symbols, distinguished by signs and tokens, and compelled, by a conscientious adherence to the rules of the order they professed, to practise the most rigid morality, justice toward men, and piety to the gods. Oliver, in Signs and Symbols.

30. To disclose the Mysteries was a heinous offence, and the offender if caught was

ANCIENT SECRET SOCIETIES AND MYSTERIES.

doomed. The betrayers of the Mysteries were punished capitally and with merciless severity. Diagoras, the Melian, had revealed the Orphic, and Eleusinian Mysteries, on which account he passed with the people as an atheist, and the city of Athens proscribed him and set a price on his head. The poet Æschylus had like to have been torn in pieces by the people on the mere suspicion that in one of his scenes he had given a hint of something in the Mysteries.

31. The names of the Cabiri, with their significations, are thus given in Anthon's Class. Dictionary: Axieros is said to have signified in Egyptian the All-powerful One; Axiokersos is made to denote the Great Foundator; Axeokersa is consequently the Great Fecundatrix; and Casmilus, he who stands before the Deity, or he who beholds the face of the Deity. Mysteries, p. 59.

32. "Nor was it at Athens only that the worship and Mysteries of Isis, metamorphosed into Ceres, were established. The Bœotian worshipped the Great or Cabiric Ceres, and the ceremonies and traditions of their Mysteries were connected with those of the Cabiri in Samothrace. So in Argos, Phocis, Arcadia, Archia, Messenia, Corinth, and many other parts of Greece, the Mysteries were practised, revealing everywhere their Egyptian origin. Albert Pike, in Review; also see Rev. A. C. Arnold's History of Secret Societies; Bishop Warburton on the Mysteries; Oliver's History of Initiation; Apuleius Metamorphoses.

33. Ruins of ancient temples have been discovered in which the secret arrangement for carrying on the ceremonies of initiation were found complete. A temple of Isis which had these secret chambers has been uncovered at Pompeii, and now lies open to the day. Some English explorers who examined the ruins of the Temple of Eleusis discovered many evidences of the fact that the lower part had been arranged for secret ceremonies, there being deeply indented grooves to receive the pulleys which were probably used in the Mysteries to raise " a moving floor" with places for wedges, to fix it immovable at the desired height. There were also eight holes in blocks of marble raised above the floor; four on the right, and four on the left, adapted to receive pins of large dimensions. See Stellar Theology and Masonic Astronomy, p. 104.

34. In a room of the Temple of Tentyra the ceiling is divided into two compartments by a figure of Isis in very high relief. The wall of an adjoining room is covered with representations of an individual; first lying on a couch at the point of death, then stretched out lifeless upon a bier. Masonic readers will understand this without comment. Chambers's Encyclopædia, vol. iv., p. 295.

35. The signs of the zodiac portrayed in the centre of the roof of the Free Masons' Hall, London, are in accordance with the astronomical decorations of the ancient temples of Egypt. Celestial and terrestrial globes also compose a part of the Mason's emblems. Mysteries, pp. 97-99; Historical Landmarks, Oliver, p. 101.

36. As early as the twelfth dynasty the obelisk was invented and became an adjunct of the temple, its ordinary position being at either side of a doorway.

37. Religious laws and precepts were so numerous, so multiplied, that it was impossible to

exercise a profession, or even to obtain subsistence and provide for one's daily wants, without having constantly present to the memory the regulations established by the priests.

38. The gods of the popular mythology were understood in the esoteric religion to be either personified attributes of Deity, or parts of the nature which he had created, considered as informed and inspired by him.

39. No educated Egyptian priest certainly, no educated layman, conceived of the popular gods as really separate and distinct beings. All knew that there was but one God.

40. It was the universal belief that, immediately after death, the soul descended into the lower world and was conducted to the Hall of Truth (or "of the two Truths"), where it was judged in the presence of Osiris and the forty-two dæmones, the "Lords of Truth" and judges of the dead. Rawlinson, vol. i., pp. 321–329; Ritual of the Dead, ch. cxxv. (Bunsen, vol. v., p. 252); Herodotus, ii., 37, 60.

41. The most ancient of profane historians, and he who speaks in the most learned manner of the religion of the Egyptians, is Herodotus. According to him the Egyptians were the first people in the world who erected altars to the gods, made representations of them, raised temples to them, and had priests for their service. Never was any people, continues he, more religious. Mysteries, p. 218.

42. The sacred texts taught that there was a single Being, "the sole producer of all things both in heaven and earth. Himself not produced of any," "the only true living God, self-originated," "who exists from the beginning," "who has made all things, but has not himself been made." Rawlinson, vol. i., p. 324.

CHAPTER II.

IMAGES, FIGURES, SYMBOLS.

Origin of Masonic Symbols, Astronomical and Mechanical; Their Original Signification.

LANGUAGE was at first, extremely crude and equivocal, so that people would constantly be at a loss, on new conceptions or unusual occurrences, to render themselves intelligible to one another.

This necessarily set them to supplying the deficiencies of speech by significant signs; therefore, in the primitive ages of the world, conversation was carried on both by words and actions; from this came the phrase "voice of the sign." Improving upon what had arisen from necessity, they naturally came to expressing their ideas by objects, symbols, and pictures, and what was obscure in them was rendered clear by the simplicity and propriety of the name given each piece.

The necessity of personifying the objects the Egyptians wished to paint also suggested the use of allegorical pictures. Furthermore, they at that time had no knowledge of writing otherwise than by delineating the figures of objects intended.

Subsequently, when language had become sufficiently intelligible for the ordinary affairs of life, the material accessories were dispensed with by all except the priests, who, perceiving the advantages of symbols in illustrating religious ideas, retained them, making such changes as would adapt them to their purpose. From this was developed the symbolism of the Sacred Mysteries.*

A symbol is a sign or representation of something moral or intellectual by the image of material things. Another definition is that it is a visible

* See notes 1, 2, 3, p. 86.

sign by which a spiritual feeling or idea is communicated or expressed. The sun is a symbol of Deity; the acacia is a symbol of immortality, and the lamb is a symbol of innocence and meekness.

The ancient Mysteries comprised a series of symbols, and what was spoken consisted of accessory explanations of the image or act. Deity, in his revelations to man, used material images for the purpose of enforcing divine truths. Christ taught by symbols and parables. The cross is the vital and impressive symbol of Christianity.

CABLE-TOW.

The Masonic term "Cable-tow" was derived from the Hebrew word Kha Ble Tu, his pledge * (see Ezekiel xviii., 7). In the ancient Mysteries the initiate was invested with a sacred sash, which was said to possess the power of preserving the wearer from danger. It consisted of a cord of three times three strands, twisted together and fastened at the ends. It was a symbol of the Triune Deity.

CIRCUMAMBULATION.

This word is derived from the Latin circum, around, and ambulare, to walk; therefore to walk around the altar or some sacred shrine. The rite of circumambulation was a prominent feature of the ceremonies of the Mysteries.† This rite was in imitation of the apparent course of the sun from east to west by way of the south, and was accompanied by the chanting of a hymn to the sun-god.

In ancient Greece, when the priests were engaged in the rites of sacrifice, they walked three times around the altar, commencing at the east, then toward the south, the west, the north, and then to their starting-point, always following the course of the sun.

Among the ancient Hindoos circumambulation was always practised and always moving with the sun—to the right.

* See Traditions, p. 29 ; Mackey, p. 136.   † Notes 7, 8, pp. 86, 87.

IMAGES, FIGURES, SYMBOLS. 63

THE APRON—LAMB-SKIN.

The lamb-skin, or white leather apron, was an article of paraphernalia worn by the kings, priests, and scribes of Egypt. The apron of the king was of a prescribed and peculiar form, belonged exclusively to his rank, and was richly ornamented in front. The priests and the scribes, or hierogromats, likewise wore aprons appropriate to their sacerdotal functions.

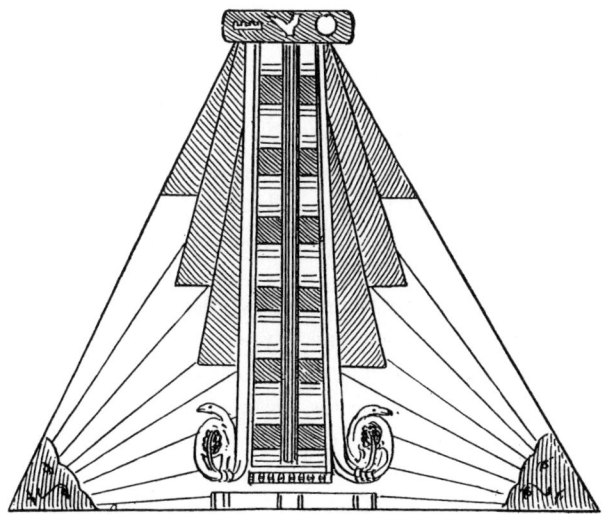

MYSTIC APRON WORN BY THE KINGS OF EGYPT.

When a candidate was initiated into the ancient Mysteries he was deemed regenerated and was invested with a white apron. The investment was very impressive and succeeded the communication of light. Since that time the lamb-skin apron has been used as an emblem of purity and distinction. With the ancient Essenes, the investiture of the apron formed an important part of the ceremony of initiation. It was the belief of the Essenes that purity and rectitude of conduct were most strikingly evinced by white raiment, particularly the white apron. When Aaron was consecrated he was invested with an apron. Samuel was girdled with an ephod or apron. St. John the Baptist went girdled with an apron of white leather. The apron is frequently found on Egyptian monuments.*

The Twenty-four Inch Gauge.

The twenty-four inch gauge was an Egyptian implement for measuring; it was also an emblem of a day divided into three parts, for labor, refreshment, and reflection and sleep.

The Northeast Corner, and the Corner-stone.

As it was the practice of the ancients to build their temples facing the east and lay the corner-stone at the northeast corner, it is believed that the corner-stone of King Solomon's Temple was laid at the northeast corner. Therefore the northeast corner has since been deemed the right place for the corner-stone of an edifice.†

The design, strength, and durability of the corner-stone are eminently symbolical. As the foundation and support of a massive building whose erection it precedes, it is, or should be, of material which will outlast all other parts of the edifice, so that when the ocean of time shall have overwhelmed all who were present at its laying, and the ruined edifice shall exhibit the ravages of centuries, the corner-stone will remain to tell, by its form, inscriptions, and deposit, that there once stood on that spot a building consecrated to a noble or sacred purpose by the zeal and liberality of men long since passed away. Likewise the durability of the corner-stone, in contrast with the decay of the building it helped to uphold, reminds the Mason that when his earthly tabernacle shall have passed away he has remaining a corner-stone of immortality—a spark from that Divine Spirit which pervades all nature, and which will survive the tomb and rise triumphant from the dust of death and the grave.

* Stellar Theology, p. 62; Mackey, p. 83; Royal Masonic Cyclopædia, p. 48.
† Stellar Theology, p. 78.

IMAGES, FIGURES, SYMBOLS.

The Lodge—Its Form, Lights, etc.

The name, lodge, comes from the German, Hutten-loge; Italian, loggia; and the Anglo-Saxon logian, and signified huts or cabins in which the ancient Masons lived when engaged upon a piece of work.* The form of the Masonic Lodge is, however, copied from the Tabernacle; and the Tabernacle was copied by Moses from the Egyptian temples.† It was a double cube, an emblem of the united powers of darkness and light in the creation. King Solomon's Temple and the altar of incense were double cubes, therefore Masonic Lodges are, or should be, of the same form.

Lodges should be situated due east and west, because "the sun, the emblem and glory of God, rises in the east and sets in the west." All ancient Temples faced the east.

Allegorically, the dimensions of the Lodge are without limit, and "its covering no less than the clouded canopy or starry-decked heavens." A Lodge has three lights, situated east, west, and south. They are so situated "in allusion to the sun, which rises in the east, reaches the meridian in the south, and disappears in the west."

The Square.

This implement and symbol originated in Egypt, its form being suggested by the division of a circle into four equal parts by lines drawn at right angles to each other. It was the Egyptian land measure, and it also became an emblem of justice, because by its aid the boundaries of land that were in dispute were adjusted and determined. There was an officer of justice who bore a square as an emblem of his office, and for use. The square was the first geometrical and artificial figure brought into use by operative masons.‡

The Compasses.

The angle of 60° alludes to the zodiac, being equal to two signs thereof. Sixty multiplied by the sacred number, three, becomes 180—the dimensions of the Royal Arch; hence the Craft when using the compasses as a symbol, set them at an angle of 60.°

* Mackey, p. 472, 473.   † Note 4, p. 86; Masonic World, vol. iv., No. 5.   ‡ Notes 5, 6, p. 86.

The Ladder of Seven Rounds.

One of the principal symbols of the ancient Mysteries was a ladder of seven rounds or steps. "The seven stages or steps were colored so as to represent the seven planetary spheres, according to the tints regarded by the

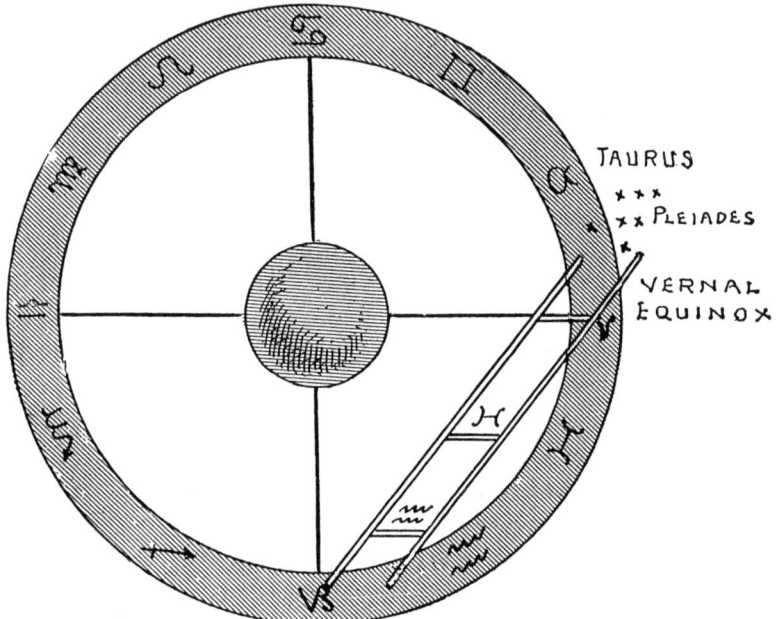

Ladder of Three Rounds.

ancients as appropriate to the seven luminaries, the basement being black, the color assigned to Saturn; the next orange, Jupiter; the third a bright red, Mars; the fourth the golden hue of the sun; the fifth pale yellow, the hue of Venus; the sixth dark blue, Mercury; the seventh silver, the moon."

The Ladder of Three Rounds.

This symbol is but a modification of the ladder of seven rounds, and is of the same general signification.

IMAGES, FIGURES, SYMBOLS. 67

This mystic ladder leads, first, to the "Seven Stars," or Pleiades, in the constellation Taurus, at the golden gates of spring; thence onward and upward to the Royal Arch of heaven, emblematically teaching that by the ladder of virtue the soul will at last pass the "cloudy canopy," even to the inmost circle of "the starry-decked heavens."

In the Masonic system the three principal rounds of the ladder are denominated Faith, Hope, and Charity. This symbol in the Mysteries is, however, universally furnished with seven rounds.

Masonic Pavement.

This pavement was originally used as flooring in Egyptian temples, and in other places where religious assemblies were held. It then represented the variegated face of the earth. The banqueting hall in the palace at Shushan was richly decorated with gold and silver, and was floored with a mosaic pavement of marble in four symbolical colors—red, white, blue, and black.

The Blazing Star,

says a learned writer, "refers to the sun, which lightens the earth with its refulgent rays, dispensing its blessings to mankind, and giving light and life to all things here below." This is the definition of the Blazing Star in the Grand Lodge of England.*

The Ashlars

represent the rough material and the finished work, both in a building and in a Mason.

St. John the Baptist.

From a well-authenticated tradition we learn concerning St. John the Baptist that his father and mother died when he was quite young, and that he was then adopted by the Essenes and finally became their Rabin. In that capacity he performed the duty of baptizing the initiates, and thus acquired the cognomen of John the Baptist. His stern integrity, continued preaching

*Notes 12, 13, p. 87.

against vice, and the unshaken firmness with which he met martyrdom rather than betray his duty to his master, made him a proper patron of the Masonic institution. The festival of St. John the Baptist occurs on the 24th of June.

St. John the Evangelist.

The mystical nature of his apocalyptic visions and his constant cultivation of brotherly love are the principal reasons that commend him to the veneration of the Fraternity. The festival in his honor is celebrated on the 27th of December.

St. John the Almoner

was the son of the King of Cyprus, and was born on that island in the sixth century. Early in life he gave up his prospects of succeeding his father on the throne, and went to Jerusalem, where he united with the Knights in works of charity; and to increase his facilities in this direction he erected a hospital for the accommodation of sick and indigent pilgrims. Rome canonized him under the name of St. John the Almoner, or St. John of Jerusalem. The days of his festival are January 23d and November 11th. St. John the Almoner was selected by the Knights Templars as their patron.

The Point Within a Circle

represents the earth as the centre around which the sun appears to annually revolve among the constellations of the zodiac. The parallel lines are the tropics of Cancer and Capricorn. The summer solstice is on the 21st of June, and the winter solstice on the 21st of December. These points are always marked by two parallel lines representing the tropics, as may be seen on any terrestrial map or globe.

Most of the ancient nations, when viewing the heavens, considered the east, the direction of the rising sun, as the starting-point. Consequently, the left hand would be north and the right hand south.

This ancient custom accounts for the fact that in this symbol the two lines representing the tropics are placed in a perpendicular instead of a horizontal position. In the Indian cave-temples the circle is found actually inscribed with the signs of the zodiac, in accordance with the practice of the ancients. Which is the most probable, that the Masons of the Middle Ages invented a symbol like this, suggested by their art, or that they inherited or adopted it from Eastern sources?

Another explanation is, that the point within the circle represents the Supreme Being; the circle indicates the annual circuit of the sun; and the parallel lines mark the solstices within which the circle is limited. The Mason who subjects himself to due bounds in imitation of that great luminary will not wander from the path of duty.

The Winding Stairs.

There are two versions of the origin of this legend. The first is principally derived from I. Kings vi., 5, 6. The second is the astronomical version.* The seven signs of the zodiac, from the vernal equinox to the first point of Scorpio, which wind in a glittering curve about the heavens, is emblematic of seven winding steps, leading to the place where corn, wine, and oil are brought forth to reward the husbandman. The sun reaches Aries on the 21st of March and Scorpio the 21st of October, passing successively through seven emblematic steps, corresponding with the ancient version of the Fellowcraft legend; also with the "seven semicircular steps" of the ancient "tracing-board" mentioned by Dr. Oliver.

In reference to the "winding stairs" conducting between the two pillars of the porch, Oliver further says: "The equinoctial points are called pillars because the great semicircle, or upper hemisphere, seems to rest upon them."

The Pillars and Globes.

Boaz is derived from Bo, and az, fire—the sun, the great morning fire. Jachin was derived from Jarac, the moon.†

The primitive signification of the words Jachin and Boaz will also be seen from Psalms lxxxix., 36, 37, speaking of David: "His seed shall endure for-

---

* See Mackey's Symbolism, chapter xxvi.; also, Stellar Theology, pp. 56–57.
† See Macoy's Cyclopædia, p. 246; Josephus, in Antiquities, Book viii., chapter iii., and note; Psalms xix.; and Gen. i., 14; Isaiah xi., 12; the Apocalypse xx., 9; also Mackey's Symbolism, chapter xiii.; Stellar Theology, pp. 75, 76; also Dr. Adam Clark.

ever, and his throne as the sun before me. It shall be established forever as the moon, and as a faithful witness in heaven. Selah."

It will be noticed in the text of I. Kings vii., 21, and in II. Chron. iii., 17, that only the names of those Pillars are given, and without any authentic explanation as to their significance; as " He shall establish," " In it is strength," are translators' notes, and at best can have only a collateral signification. That neither of the Globes would have been designed to represent the earth the following will show.

At the era of the building of King Solomon's Temple the world was supposed to be of an oblong form—a double cube. This was the belief of the Rabbins and the most enlightened of the Jewish nation, not only at that period but for centuries after.

The same description applied to representations of the face of the heavens, which, according to the belief of the ancients, was of the same form and size of the earth; the earth being the base, the sky or heavens the upper surface.

That the Globes represented the sun and moon will further be seen from a Masonic medal struck in 1798.*

From the foregoing it appears that the Pillars and the Globes must be considered collectively, and that they were symbols of Deity and his attributes. The Sun, as previously shown, was among all the ancient nations the emblem of God. The Moon was an emblem of wisdom, while the Pillars, with their crowning ornaments, were symbols of strength and beauty.

Further, from the definite description given in the Bible, in I. Kings vii., 15-24; II. Chron. iii., 15-17; Jer. iii., 21, 22, it is evident that they were made after Egyptian models. The " lily-work " on the capitals corresponded with the lotus-headed capitals of Egyptian architecture. The pomegranate was also a product of Egypt. The pomegranate-tree, with its beautiful fruit, is often seen on Egyptian sculptures.

The Liberal Arts and Sciences.

In an ancient Masonic manuscript the origin of the Seven Liberal Arts and Sciences was attributed to Euclid in the following: " He commensd yn the

---

* See Macoy's Cyclopædia—Medals.

IMAGES, FIGURES, SYMBOLS.

syens seven; gramatica ys the furste synes, y-wysse, dialectia the secunde so have y blysse, rethrica the thyrdde without nay,—musica ys the fourthe as yow say, astromia ys the v., by my snowte, arsmetica vi., without dowte, gemetria the seventhe maketh an ande." *

A record preserved in the Bodleian Library thus alludes to the arts invented by the Masons: "Whatte artes haueth the Maconnes techedde mankynde?"

"Ans. The artes, architectura, astronomia, geometri, numeres, musica, poesie, kymestrye, governmente, relygonne, and agricultura."

"How cometh the Maconnes more teachers than other menne?"

"Thehemselfe haueth alleine in arte of fyndynge new artes, whyche art the fyrste Maconnes receaud from Godde; by the whyche they fynde the whatte artes hem plesethe and the treu way of techynge the same."

The Legend of Euclid.

Euclid, being master of the liberal sciences, was consulted by the rulers of Egypt as to the best way of increasing the resources of the country so as to meet the demands of the rapidly increasing population for sustenance. His advice was that the intelligent sons of the nobility should be instructed in the liberal sciences, especially in geometry. This advice was immediately acted upon, and Euclid was empowered both to teach those young men the necessary arts and to superintend their labors after they became proficient. To render his plan more complete and acceptable to the rulers, he gave his skilled band charges that they should be loyal to the King and to the Lord for whom they worked, that they should call each other brother, and that the wisest and most skilled among them should be selected as Master.

The Equilateral Triangle, Letter G.

The Triangle is the true symbol of the Masonic science, geometry, for without a knowledge of its properties and use that science is impossible.

The Triangle is the same in form as the ancient Egyptian D, and the Greek delta, or letter D, and the equilateral triangle in the Greek tongue,

* Masonic Register, p. 30—Halliwell MS.; Mitchel, vol. i., p. 177.

as well as in other ancient languages, was the initial letter of the name of Deity. In the time of Pythagoras, oaths of importance were administered on the equilateral triangle, by which the name of God was directly invoked.

In the Middle Chamber of King Solomon's Temple, in plain view of all who entered, was a triangle, in which was inscribed י, signifying the ineffable name. The triangle with a Yod in the centre was also one of the original symbols of Free Masonry; but finally the explanation of this symbol was lost, and the initial of the English word " God," took its place, and a new explanation given.

As architecture could not be carried on without a knowledge of geometry, and G being the initial letter of that word, it also came to be a part of the Masonic signification of that letter.*

Sibola.—Shibboleth.

The Eleusinian Mysteries, being derived from the Mysteries of Isis, were known to the Greeks by the name of Ceres, also Cybele. Ceres was the Goddess of Harvest, and, like the beautiful virgin of the zodiac, was represented bearing spears of ripe corn. Isis, in the Egyptian zodiac, occupied the place of Virgo, and was represented with three spears of wheat in her hand.

The Syrian name for an ear of corn was sibola, identical with shibboleth, which the Ephraimites pronounced sibboleth—nearly correct. This word also signified "a stream of water." A sheaf of wheat near a river was one of the emblems of the Eleusinian and Dionysian Mysteries. The river originally referred to was the Nile, whose overflow enriched the soil and brought forth the harvest of Egyptian grain, which was at that time symbolically represented by the ears of corn (wheat) hanging by a river. This version of the emblem is much more rational than the tradition describing the brutal slaughter of forty-two thousand men by a barbarian, who offered up his own innocent daughter as a burnt offering. Would the Guild Masons of the Middle Ages have been likely to invent such an emblem?

The CORNUCOPIA, or Horn of Plenty, alludes to the constellation Capri-

---

* See Mackey, p. 379; Stellar Theology, p. 71.

cornus—to the arrival of the sun among the stars of that constellation. At that time the fruits of the earth—Corn, Wine, and Oil, have been gathered in and stored, so that although the frosts of winter come to destroy vegetation, the husbandman is still blessed with plenty.*

Another explanation is, that Bacchus, with other mythological deities, being attacked by Typhon, they at once assumed different shapes and plunged into a river, Pan, or Bacchus, leading the way, the part of his body which was under water taking the form of a fish, and the other part that of a goat. This god presided over the flocks and herds; he was also the god of plenty. Subsequently, the Horn of Capricornus, the Goat, became a symbol of plenty.

The Broken Column.

Rhea was represented as Cœlus and Terra, daughter of Sky and Earth. She was also represented as the mother of Jupiter, and the wife of Saturn, with his Scythe, or Time. In the Dyonysian Mysteries, Dyonysius, identical with Osiris, is represented as being slain. Rhea, identical with Isis and Virgo, goes in search of his body, which she at last finds, and causes it to be buried with great honors.

In the left hand Virgo holds a spear of ripe wheat, for which Masons have substituted the sprig of acacia, as an emblem of immortality. Her right rests on the broken column, because the ancients figured Virgo, under the name of Rhea, with her right hand resting on a column.†

The Trowel.

This was one of the first implements used by the ancient craftsmen in Egypt. A Trowel and Square were found under the pedestal of the ancient Egyptian Obelisk when it was taken down at Alexandria a few years since, to be brought to this country.

The Three Ruffians

in the tragedy of the Third Degree are the three autumnal months—the end of the year. The mystical Hiram, the Sun, was said to be slain by these

---

* Note 14, p. 88.   † Stellar Theology, pp. 68, 69.

74 IMAGES, FIGURES, SYMBOLS.

three months, which he successively meets on his way to the winter solstice, or southern quarter of the zodiac; and on the 23d of December, the shortest day in the year, the Sun was said to lie dead, buried beneath the rubbish of the dead vegetation of summer, in the midst of which, however, still blooms the evergreen, emblematic of spring—renewed life.

In Egypt the search for the slain Master, Osiris, the Sun, was said to be carried on by Isis, and in Syria by twelve Fellowcrafts, representing the twelve signs of the zodiac, and it was found by Aries, the first of the three western signs. Proceeding west, the next sign after Capricorn is Aquarius, the Waterman, anciently known as the Sea-faring Man, and this is also the next to the three western signs, the three Fellowcrafts, who are searching for the three Ruffians, the autumn months.

The month of April is represented by the Junior Warden, who fails to raise the body as April fails to raise the sun. May represents the Senior Warden, who also fails to raise it. June is represented by the Master, who raises it—as June raises the sun to its highest elevation of the year.*

The Lion's Paw.

"This emblem was found in the sarcophagus of one of the great kings of Egypt, entombed in the pyramid erected to his memory. It brings to mind the representation of the king's initiation into those greater mysteries of Osiris held to be the highest aim of the wise and devout Egyptian."

The emblem may be thus explained: The form that lies dead before the altar is that of Osiris, the personified Sun God, whom the candidate represents in the drama of raising, lying dead at the winter solstice, slain by the grim Archer—November, the fatal month of the year, for the Sun. The figure of the Lion grasping the dead Sun God alludes to the constellation Leo, which prevailed 4,000 years ago, raised the Sun God to his place of power and glory on the summit of the grand royal arch of heaven at the summer solstice, and denoted then, as it does now, that the Sun and the candidate are raised from a symbolical death to life and power by the strong grip of the Lion's Paw, or, as it has later been termed, "the Lion of the tribe of Judah."

* Notes 9–10, p. 87.

IMAGES, FIGURES, SYMBOLS. 75

The cross which the Lion holds in his other paw is the ancient Egyptian symbol of eternal life. The figure erect at the altar is doubtless that of the Grand Hierophant, with his hand raised in an attitude of command, forming a right angle, with eyes fixed upon the emblematic lion as he gives the sign of command that Osiris, or the candidate, be raised from death and darkness to light and life.*

From all of which it appears that the Lodge, its position, form, dimensions,

LION'S PAW.

lights, and furniture, also its principal officers, their stations and duties—the movements of the candidate, in fact, much of the important symbolism of Free Masonry have an astronomical significance and are of Egyptian derivation.

Masons are also instructed to travel toward the east in search of light, because the sun rises in the east and is the great source of light.

WISDOM, STRENGTH, AND BEAUTY.

In the ancient mysteries these three pillars represented the great emblematical triad of Deity. In the Hindu mysteries, Brahma, Vishnu, and Siva were considered a triune god and designated "Tri Muti." Brahma was said to be the Creator, Vishnu the Preserver, and Siva the Judge or Destroyer. Hence in their ceremonies the representative of Brahma was seated in the East, that of Vishnu in the West, and that of Siva in the South.

* See Stellar Theology, p. 48; note 15, p. 88.

The All-seeing Eye.

The ancient Egyptians emblematically and hieroglyphically represented the Sun God, Osiris, by the figure of an open eye, emblematic of the sun, which from the midst of the heavens beholds all things, and by whose heat and light we are enabled to live and see. This emblem was found engraved over the entrance to temples and tombs, and was peculiar to Omniscience.

The Anchor

was stamped on ancient Syrian coins and signified Hope—hope for security at the termination of a voyage, and hope for the happy life to come.

The Forty-seventh Problem of Euclid.

The invention of this problem was attributed to the noted philosopher, Pythagoras.

The Hour-Glass

was one of the first-known implements for measuring time. Its lesson is time past and future, the present being the point of union between the upper and lower cells. The Greeks held it as symbolic of Zeus—god of the present instant of time, as Kronos was of the past.

Clemens of Alexandria, describing one of the religious processions of the Egyptians, informs us that the Singer went forth bearing the symbol of music, and that he was followed by the Horoscopus bearing an hour-glass as the measure of time, showing that the hour-glass was one of the sacred astronomical emblems of the Egyptians.

The Scythe.

The scythe is an emblem of the great leveller—Time.

The Coffin

is an Egyptian emblem of the womb of the universe. The Egyptian coffin was usually inscribed with the history, creed, and character of the dead; a judgment on the life of the departed.

The Acacia

is an emblem of a continuation of life while the rest of the vegetable world is dead or dying. It is also an emblem of innocence. The species referred to is the sensitive acacia which shrinks from the touch, and therefore is a symbol of that innocence which shrinks from the rude touch of the world.

The acacia is a native of Egypt and Syria; it is also the acanthus of Herodotus and Strabo.*

The thickets of acanthus, alluded to by Strabo, still grow above Memphis, at the base of the low Lybian hills. In going from the Nile to Abydos the traveller rides through a grove of acacia, once sacred to Apollo, and sees the canal traversing it the same as when the geographer visited that city. (Wilkinson's Ancient Egyptians, chapter vi.).

Sign and Word of Master Mason.

The first sign of a Master Mason alludes to the sun, when raised to the third sign of the zodiac from the vernal equinox, the point of its brightest light. The Mason who has taken the third degree has attained an equal Masonic elevation.

Masonic Colors.

1. Blue, azure blue, the color of the vast vault of Heaven, is symbolic of universal friendship. With the Egyptians, Chaldeans, Chinese, and the Druids, blue was a sacred color. It was the color of one of the Vails of the Tabernacle, also of one of the great Vails of the Temple.

2. Purple (red and blue combined). This was also the color of one of the Vails of the Tabernacle, and of the great curtain over the entrance to the Holy of Holies in the Temple. In the American Rite, purple is symbolical of union, from the mixture of red and blue—Mark Master, Past Master, and Most Excellent Master.

3. Red—scarlet. As the image of fire it was used by the Egyptians to designate life, love, and zeal. Scarlet was the color of the third Vail of the Tabernacle, and one of the colors of the curtain of the Sanctuary of the Temple.

* Stellar Theology, p. 70.

IMAGES, FIGURES, SYMBOLS.

4. White. This is one of the most ancient and most generally diffused of all the colors. In the Mysteries it constituted, as it does in Masonry, the investiture of the candidate. It has always had the signification of innocence and purity. In Egypt, the spirits of the dead were supposed to be clothed in white because that color was the symbol of the regeneration of the soul. The Essenes wore white robes.*

Black has always been a symbol of mourning. Still the colors for mourning differ in different countries.

Yellow. This color was anciently symbolical of light—Divine light.

Green. With the Egyptians this color symbolized the Creator, Preserver, and Instructor of man.

ANCIENT SYMBOLISM.

ANCIENT SYMBOLISM.

An evidence of the transmission of Egyptian symbols through the Gnostics is afforded by a singular engraving in the Azoth Philosophorum of Basil Valentine, a philosopher who flourished in the seventh century. This piece is mostly occupied by Masonic Symbolism. It shows a winged globe inscribed with a triangle within a square and compasses on which reposes a dragon. On the dragon stands a human figure with two heads, surrounded by the sun, moon, and stars. One hand of the figure holds a square, the other holds a compass. In the globe is seen a point within a circle.†

* Light, pp. 6, 10; Note 11, p. 32; Mackey's Cyclopædia, p. 174, etc.
† See Mackey, p. 789.

ASTRONOMY.

To enable the reader to understand the relation of Masonic Symbolism to Astronomy, a sketch of the leading facts of that science will be given.

As the attributes of God and the immortality of the soul are the most exalted and sublime of all truths, they could only be symbolized by the most glorious and sublime objects in nature—the sun, moon, and stars. "The heavens declare the glory of God, and the firmament showeth his handiwork."

First, the Ecliptic.

This is an imaginary circle in the heavens surrounding the earth, and represents the apparent path of the sun each year among the stars.

The Zodiac

is a belt of stars, extending 8° on each side of the ecliptic, and is therefore 16° wide. This glittering belt is a complete circle of 360° in circumference, divided into twelve equal parts of 30°, each marking the place which the sun occupies during each of the twelve months of the year. Each division of the zodiac is marked by a separate group of stars, called a constellation. Each constellation was named after a certain "living creature," originally emblematic of the month in which the sun enters that constellation.

The word zodiac was derived from the Greek *zodiakos*, from *zo-on*, an animal, compounded directly from the primitive Egyptian *zo*, life, and *on*, a being.

The Twelve Constellations

are:

Aries, the Ram;	Leo, the Lion;	Sagittarius, the Archer;
Taurus, the Bull;	Virgo, the Virgin;	Capricornus, the Goat;
Gemini, the Twins;	Libra, the Scales;	Aquarius, the Waterbearer;
Cancer, the Crab;	Scorpio, the Scorpion;	Pisces, the Fishes.

These constellations are designated by certain characters, known as the "signs of the zodiac," and are as follows:

♈ ♉ ♊ ♋ ♌ ♍ ♎ ♏ ♐ ♑ ♒ ♓

The sign Aries is a remaining representation of the head and horns of a ram. Taurus of the face and horns of a bull. Gemini denotes the twins seated side by side; the ancient statues of Castor and Pollux consisted of two upright pieces of wood united by two cross-pieces. Cancer still resembles the claws of a crab. Leo resembles a crouching lion. In Virgo the resemblance is lost. Libra is a picture of a scale-beam. The sign Scorpio displays the sting of that creature. Sagittarius, the Archer, is well represented by his sign. Again in Capricornus the resemblance is lost. The sign Aquarius resembles the waves of the sea. In Pisces the resemblance of two fishes joined is seen.

In process of time, from convenience in writing, the original pictorial representations denoting the constellations were changed to the present arbitrary signs.

ARIES.

Twenty-two hundred years ago this was the first constellation of the zodiac; but by reason of the precession of the equinoxes it is now the second. It is known by two bright stars, about 4° apart, which are in the horns of the ram.

TAURUS

is next to Aries in the zodiac, and is one of the most celebrated and splendid of all the constellations. The Pleiades are in Taurus. The face of the bull is known by five bright stars forming the letter V, called the Hyades: the most brilliant of these is Aldebaran, which is much used by navigators. The tips of the horns of the bull are indicated by two bright stars. The Pleiades shine brightly near his shoulder. Orion faces the bull, and is known by four bright stars which form a large parallelogram; in the centre of this is a diagonal row of stars, known as the belt of Orion. Two stars of the parallelogram indicate his shoulders, and two his feet. A line of smaller stars and a beautiful nebula form his sword. A short distance below Orion is the sun-star Sirius, the Sothis of the Egyptians. These two stars with Betelgeux, in the shoulder of Orion, form a nearly perfect and beautiful triangle whose sides are each 26°. They are frequently alluded to by Virgil in the "Georgics," and these constellations render this quarter of the heavens sublime and brilliant.

Gemini

is the next constellation in the zodiac, and its principal stars are Castor and Pollux. They are of the first and second magnitude, and about $4\frac{1}{2}°$ apart.

Cancer

is composed of a group of small stars of the third and fourth magnitudes.

Leo.

This is a beautiful and celebrated constellation. It is known by six bright stars situated in the neck and head of the lion, in the form of a sickle. One of its most brilliant stars is Regulus, and being situated almost exactly in the ecliptic, it is of great importance to navigators in determining their longitude. The remarkable meteoric showers of November proceed from the constellation Leo.

Virgo.

This is known as the beautiful virgin of the zodiac. She is represented as holding a spear of wheat in her left hand, marked by a brilliant star, called Spica. In the Egyptian zodiac Isis occupied the place of Virgo.

Libra

is represented by the figure of a person holding a pair of scales. This constellation contains four stars in the form of a quadrilateral.

Scorpio

somewhat resembles the object after which it is named, and is very conspicuous in the evening sky of July.

Sagittarius

the Archer, follows Scorpio, and is represented as half horse and half man, in the act of shooting an arrow from a bow. This constellation is composed of several bright stars in the form of an inverted dipper.

CAPRICORNUS,

the Goat, is composed of fifty-one small stars.

AQUARIUS.

This constellation is represented by the figure of a man pouring water from a jar. The stars are small and unimportant.

PISCES.

This is also an unimportant constellation, and is represented by two fishes.

The ancients also designated the sun, moon, and planets by hieroglyphic astronomical signs, as follows:

    Sun, ☉.   Mercury, ☿.   Venus, ♀.   Saturn, ♄.
    Moon, ☽.   Mars, ♂.   Jupiter, ♃.

All these signs have come down to us from remote antiquity.

The zodiac has four principal points, +, the two solstitial and two equinoctial points, which divide the circle of the zodiac into four equal parts, anciently marked by the stars Fomalhaut, Aldebaran, Regulus, and Antares.

THE SOLSTITIAL POINTS

mark the extreme northern and southern limits of the movement of the sun. When the sun reaches his extreme northern limit, the summer solstice, it is in Cancer; and the winter solstice, or his southern limit, is in Capricornus. The distance of the sun north or south of the equator is called his northern or southern declination. When the sun reaches either solstitial point he begins to turn back toward the other, at first so slowly as to seem to stand still. For this reason these points are called "solstitial," from the Latin *sol*, the sun, and *sistere-stiti*, to cause to stand. For convenience of explanation the sun is said to move north and south; but it is really the motion of the earth, first inclining toward the north pole and then toward the south pole. In June the sun enters Cancer, and on the 21st reaches his greatest northern

IMAGES, FIGURES, SYMBOLS.   83

declination. As the sun advances north his rays fall more vertically, and thus cause the change from winter and spring to summer in all countries north of the equator. This apparent movement of the sun from one solstitial point to another is the cause of the change of the seasons.

THE EQUINOCTIAL POINTS

are where the sun crosses the celestial equator, twice yearly in his circuit of the zodiac, at two opposite points, distant from each other 180°, and in time, six months. The point where the sun crosses in March, coming north, is called the vernal equinox; and the other, where he crosses in September, going south, is called the autumnal equinox. At these periods the days and nights are of equal length, and hence are called equinoctial points, from the Latin *æquus*, equal, and *nox*, night. These two points are in the signs Aries (♈) and Libra (♎).

THE PRECESSION OF THE EQUINOXES.

In the movements of the planets a gradual change of place is constantly going on as to the point where the sun crosses the celestial equator. Therefore the sun does not cross the equator at the same place each year, but crosses a short distance back of the point of his crossing the previous year. As a consequence, the equinoctial point is annually falling back at a uniform rate.

Twenty-two hundred years ago the sun crossed the equator in the constellation Aries, but in the progress of centuries the place of the sun's crossing has fallen back 30°, so that it now crosses in the constellation Pisces.

The four cardinal points of the zodiac will, however, continue to be marked by the signs (♋, ♑, ♈, and ♎), without regard to the constellations which the sun actually enters at those periods; otherwise astronomers would not be able to register upon the face of the heavens the apparent movement of the stars. Although the equinoctial point is constantly falling back, yet, as it causes the stars apparently to advance, it is called the precession of the equinoxes.

The rate of this motion is but little more than fifty and a quarter seconds of a degree each year; it therefore takes the equinoctial point about 2,140 years to fall back a sign, or 30°, and a period of 25,791 years to make a complete revolution of the whole circle of the zodiac. As Plato taught that at the expiration of that period the world woul begin anew, it would be interesting to know when it first took its place in the planetary system.

The ancients began the year at the vernal equinox. Starting with the sun at that point and following his progress toward the north, on the 21st of June the summer solstice is reached—the longest day in the year—and the sun has then attained its greatest brilliancy. Through the summer months his heat and power are at the greatest, but as he approaches the sign Libra, the autumnal equinox, the days begin to shorten, and in October and November they grow short and dark with great rapidity; and finally the cold and stormy winds herald the approach of winter. The sun's rays rapidly grow weaker, until Capricorn is reached at the winter solstice, December 21st—the shortest day in the year—death of the sun.* For the next two months the sun seems to lie dead in the cold embrace of winter—the origin of the death and resurrection scenes portrayed in the Egyptian and later Mysteries.

Ancient Astronomy.

The Egyptians had made great progress in astronomy, geometry, and other sciences, even before the time of Menes. They " were also the first to discover the solar year, and to portion out its course into twelve parts." They " obtained this knowledge from the stars." Cæsar had recourse to the Egyptian astronomer Sosigenes for the correction of the calendar. Plato ascribes the invention of geometry to the Egyptians. Herodotus also says : " Geometry first came to be known in Egypt, whence it passed into Greece " (book ii., chap. cix.). The Egyptians knew the true system of the universe. (Wilkinson's " Ancient Egyptians ; " " Herodotus," book ii., chap. iv.)

Their knowledge of astronomy embraced the following facts: That the sun is the centre of the solar system, and that the earth and other planets revolve about it in fixed orbits. That the earth is round and revolves on its own axis, thus producing day and night. That the moon revolves about the earth, and that it shines by the reflected light of the sun. The calcula-

* See Stellar Theology, pp. 24–31.

IMAGES, FIGURES, SYMBOLS.   85

tion of eclipses; the obliquity of the ecliptic, and that the Milky Way is a collection of stars. The power of gravitation, and that the heavenly bodies are attracted to a centre. Pythagoras, who introduced the true system of the universe into Greece, received it from Œnuphis, a priest of On, in Egypt.*

Ideler says: "The Chaldeans knew the mean motions of the moon with an exactness which induced the Greek astronomers to use their calculations for the foundation of a lunar theory."

Rawlinson also says: "We are informed by Simplicius that Calisthenes, who accompanied Alexander to Babylon, sent to Aristotle from that capital a series of astronomical observations, which he had found preserved there, extending back to a period 2234 B.C."

The Romans used Chaldean observations which extended back to 721 B.C. Diodorus Siculus says the Chaldeans attributed comets to natural causes, and could foretell their reappearance. He stated that their recorded observations of the planets were very ancient and very exact.

From their great proficiency in astronomy it follows that the ancients possessed the telescope, as the discovery of many of the astronomical facts known to the Egyptians and Chaldeans would be impossible without it.†

Layard, speaking of the discovery of a lens among the ruins of Babylon, says: "This lens was found in a chamber of the ruins called Nimroud. It is plano-convex, an inch and a half in diameter and nine-tenths of an inch thick. It gives a focus of four and a half inches from the plane side." Pliny says that in his time "artificers used emeralds to assist the eye," and that "they were concave, the better to collect the visual rays." ‡

---
* Rawlinson's Herodotus, Appendix to chapter vii., book ii., and authorities there quoted.
† Stellar Theology, pp. 31–33.
‡ Layard's Nineveh and Babylon, chapter viii., pp. 16, 17.

NOTES FROM AUTHORITIES.

1. Heckethorn, in his valuable work on the Secret Societies of all Ages and Countries, says: "From the first appearance of man on the earth, there was a highly favored and civilized race, possessing a full knowledge of the laws and properties of nature, and which knowledge was embodied in mystical figures and schemes, such as were deemed appropriate emblems for its preservation and propagation. These figures and schemes are preserved in Free Masonry, though their full meaning is no longer understood by the fraternity. The aim of all secret societies was to preserve such knowledge as still survived, or to recover what had been lost. Free Masonry is the *résumé* of the teachings of *all* these societies."

2. "The first learning of the world," says Dr. Stukeley, "consisted chiefly of symbols." Gould, i., p. 21.

3. According to Dr. Armstrong, the symbols and emblems of Free Masonry are divided into three different species: first, such as are derived from the various forms of the ancient Mysteries; secondly, such as are derived from the Mason's craft, as the Square and Compasses; and, thirdly, those which are derived from the Temple of Solomon, the East, the Ladder of Jacob, etc. Gould, iii., p. 229.

4. From an oration delivered by Frederick Dalcho, M.D., before the Grand Lodge of South Carolina, 1801: "It must be evident to every Free Mason, that the situation of the Lodge and its several parts are copied after the Tabernacle and Temple, and represents the universe as the Temple in which the Deity is everywhere present."

5. In the works of the oldest of the Chinese classics we find distinct allusions to the symbolism of the Mason's art. In the writings of Mencius (B.C. 280) it is taught that men should apply the Square, Compasses, and the Level, figuratively to their own lives, and if they would walk in the straight paths of wisdom, they must keep themselves within the bounds of honor and virtue. In Book VI. of his Philosophy, he says: "A Master Mason, in teaching his apprentices, makes use of the Compasses and the Square. Ye who are engaged in the pursuit of wisdom must also make use of the Compasses and Square." Gould, vol. i., pp. 22, 23.

6. The Masonic Square, the Level, and the Mallet, all carefully displayed upon the memorial of the Roman architect, shows how important a feature the mechanical practice of the art was considered, in estimating the calling to which the Master belonged. Gould, vol. i., p. 44.

7. "The Masonic Rite of circumambulation strictly agrees with the ancient one," and that as "the circumambulation is made around the Lodge just as the sun was supposed to move round the earth, we are brought back to the original symbolism" of the sun's apparent course about the earth. Mackey, Symbolism of Freemasonry, chap. xxi.

IMAGES, FIGURES, SYMBOLS.

8. In the Indian Mysteries, the Candidate made three circuits around the hall to the right, crossing each time when he reached the south, saying: "I copy the example of the sun, and follow his beneficent course." Masonry has retained the circuits but lost the explanation, which is: "That in the Mysteries the Candidate represents the sun, both in his course from east to west, and in his declination southward toward the reign of Typhon (darkness and winter) there to be slain figuratively, and after a brief period to rise again from the dead and commence his ascent northward," typical of a new life, a new year. Stellar Theology, p. 59.

9. "In the Mysteries all was astronomical, but a deeper meaning lay hid under the astronomical symbols. While the bewailing the loss of the sun, the Epopts were in reality mourning the loss of that light whose influence is life. The passing of the sun through the zodiac gave rise to the myths of the incantations of Vishnu, the Labors of Hercules, etc.; his apparent loss of power during the winter season, and the restoration thereof at the winter solstice, to the story of the death, descent into hell, and resurrection of Osiris and of Mithras." Heckethorn, Secret Societies of all Ages and Countries, vol. i., pp. 19, 20; Gould, vol. iii., p. 225.

10. "The ancient Egyptians, says Julius Firmicus (Astron., lib. 2, c. 4.), divide each sign of the zodiac into three different sections; and each section was under the direction of an imaginary being, whom they called Decan, or chief of ten. Among the Greeks, also, the youths who served the tables were called diaconi, deacons; that is, ministers, attendants." Mysteries, p. 300.

11. Speaking of the ancient Priesthood, Dupuis says: "The priests clothe themselves in white, a color assigned to Aromaze, the god of light."

That white as an emblem of purity and innocence descended to the aborigines of America is shown by the fact that the Prophet who accompanied Black Hawk and other chiefs to Washington, as hostages for the faithful performance of the treaty made with their nation (1833), thus addressed the President: "Father, I have come this day clothed in white (pointing to his leather doublet), in order to prove that my intentions are of the most pacific nature, and (raising his hands to heaven) I call upon the Great Spirit of myself and forefathers to witness the purity of my heart on this occasion." Mysteries, pp. 218, 219.

12. "The Blazing Star" must not be considered merely as the creature which heralded the appearance of T. G. A. O. T. U., but the expressive symbol of that Great Being himself, who was described by the magnificent appellations of the Day Spring, or Rising Sun, the Morning Star, and the Bright and Blazing Star." Oliver, Symbol of Glory, p. 292.

13. In the lectures revised by Dr. Hemming and adopted by the Grand Lodge of England, at the union in 1813, and now constituting the authorized lectures of that jurisdiction, we find the following definition: "The Blazing Star, or glory in the centre, refers us to the sun, which enlightens the earth with its refulgent rays, dispensing its blessings to mankind at large, and giving life and light to all things here below." Mackey, p. 117.

IMAGES, FIGURES, SYMBOLS.

14. Corn was employed in the elucidation of the Mysteries of Eleusis, dedicated to Ceres, hence popularly regarded as the Goddess of Agriculture, furnishing mortals with the "staff of life." Wine, "the blood of the Sun," venerated by the ancients as a universal medicinal remedy for bodily ills, was a significant feature in the Mysteries of Bacchus, or the Deity of Prolific Fecundity. Oil was a substitute for water in the work of purification and consecration in all religious rites, memory of which is conserved in the title of Messiah, "The Christ, or the Anointed of the Lord." Masonic Chronicle, 1888, p. 266.

15. The twelve Fellowcrafts who were deputed for this service (search for Grand Master Hiram) represented the twelve signs of the zodiac; one of whom would be sure to find their Grand Master Hiram—the personification of Osiris, the Sun.

It may be remarked that the lamentations uttered for the death of the Grand Master Hiram is in exact accordance with the customs of the Egyptians, in their celebrations of the fabled death of Osiris, the Sun; of the Phœnicians, for the loss of Adonis, and of the Greeks, in their mystic rites of the Eleusinian Ceres.

The strong paw of the Lion wrests Osiris from the clutches of Typhon and places him in his wonted course, the archetype of the rising of Grand Master Hiram by the Strong Grip of Lion's Paw. Mysteries of Freemasonry, pp. 267, 281, 283, 284.

CHAPTER III.

ARCHITECTURE.—MASONRY.

Origin of the Builders' Art in Egypt.—Origin of the Pyramids and Obelisk.—Their Original Purpose.—Remarkable Revelations from the Interior of the Pyramids.—The Magnificent Temple at Karnak.—Its Ruins.—Ancient Egyptian Houses.—Course of Architecture from Egypt.—Origin of the Different Styles.—Greek, Roman, Byzantine, Romanesque, Saracenic, etc.—Progress of Architecture Under the Colleges of Builders.

As the Egyptian Mysteries comprised religion, art, and science, architecture was associated with religion from the first. Subsequently, upon the increased demand for the services of architects, minor organizations of the Mysteries were established, and at points more and more remote from the old centre of Egyptian worship. Into those societies not only Egyptians but foreigners were initiated; and in this way a knowledge of the Mysteries soon reached other countries, notably Greece and Rome. Thus religion and art came early to walk hand in hand: and among the first and grandest works of art were the temples of religion—expressions of the adoration of man for Deity.

Finally, when the Mysteries were generally discontinued, after Christianity had become the State religion of the Roman Empire, the architects who were initiates in the Mysteries, in order to retain a monopoly of the higher secrets of their art, decided to keep up—perpetuate the old society, and from that date until the eighteenth century, architecture-masonry was the principal repository of the religious elements of the Mysteries. Therefore we will now consider architecture, and trace its course from the banks of the Nile to Rome, where its connection with religion was fully disclosed in the colleges of builders, who transmitted this union of science and religion to their successors, the Guilds.

ARCHITECTURE.—MASONRY.

In all inquiries as to the origin of Masonic institutions by writers who assign to it an ancient, or a comparatively modern, origin, architecture is necessarily the subject in and through which their investigations are principally carried on. And it is through this channel that the essentials of the institution have reached us.

The civilization of Egypt, being the oldest, the first advance in the builders' art was necessarily made by her people.*

The architecture of Egypt originated principally in the construction of the monumental tombs of its kings; the first being those of Meydoun and Saccarah, in the first dynasty, in the second century of Egyptian history.

The Egyptians believing that the preservation of the body after death contributed to the duration of spiritual existence in the future life, conceived the idea of enbalming the dead and placing the bodies in repositories constructed for permanence.† The general form of their tombs was that of a truncated pyramid.

External embellishments were confined to the doorways or entrances, which were curiously carved and the lintels rounded. Door-posts were represented in stone on the sides of the doorway; an imitation of lattice work appears above; and at the sides are alternate pilasters and depressions adorned with panelling.

The interior is often found to be elaborately decorated with colored bas-reliefs, representing either mystic ceremonies, or scenes of daily life.

It was but a small advance on the pyramidal tombs to conceive the idea of adding to their height, solidity, and durability, by the superimposition of further stories constructed on a similar plan. An example of this stage of construction is seen in the singular monument at *Meydoun*. This structure stands upon a rocky knoll, has a square base about 200 feet each way, and rises in three stages at an angle of 74° 10″, to an elevation of nearly 125 feet.

The gratifying effect of elevation, gained by means of stages, and the increased durability by greater extent, soon suggested a larger structure. An example of this is seen at *Saccarah*, where stands an edifice similar in general character to that of Meydoun, but built in six instead of three stages; the stone decreasing in size from the first stage to the top of the pyramid. It is

---

* See notes 1, 2, 3, 4, pp. 146, 147.   † See note 5, p. 147.

ARCHITECTURE.—MASONRY. 91

also considerably larger on the ground, and its altitude 75 feet higher than the Meydoun monument.

Beneath this pyramid, and almost under its apex, is a chamber paved with granite blocks, which, when discovered, contained a sarcophagus, and was connected with the external world by concealed passages.

Leading into a small chamber, is a doorway ornamented at the sides by green cubes of baked clay with enamelled surfaces, alternating with blocks of limestone. On the lintels which covered the doorway, at the top, were hieroglyphics.

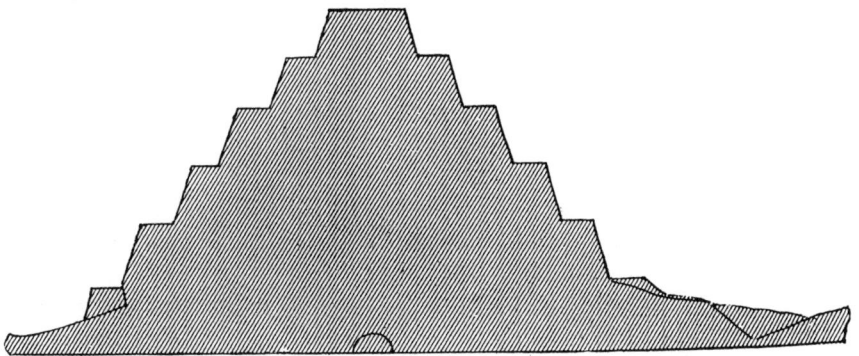

A Pyramid Before its Sides were Finished.

The next thing that would naturally suggest itself to an artistic mind would be the external finish, by smoothing the exterior, either by cutting down the angles of the stages to a uniform level, or by filling up the spaces between the top of each step and the side of the succeeding one; both of which plans the Egyptians subsequently followed.

The next advance in the size of these structures is found in one of the pyramids of Ghizeh. It exceeds the Saccarah structure in its height by eighteen feet. It was built in steps or stages,* like the Saccarah monument. The lower half of the pyramid was covered with several layers of a beautiful red granite, bevelled at the joints.

* Note 7, p. 147. See Bunsen, Egypt's Place in Universal History, vol. ii., p. 166; Rawlinson, vol. i., pp. 190 to 217; Fergusson, vol. i., p. 100.

ARCHITECTURE.—MASONRY.

Under the apex, sunk down in the native rock on which the pyramid stands, is a series of chambers, in one of which was found the sarcophagus of the monarch whom tradition pointed out as the builder of the monument.*

The roof of this chamber was composed of huge blocks, set obliquely and extending from the side walls, on which they rested, to the centre, where they met at an obtuse angle. (The incipient arch.) The granite slabs covering the sides were fastened to the rock and to each other by iron clamps, two of which were found *in situ*.

This sarcophagus was remarkable. With the exception of the lid, it was formed of a block of blue-black basalt, and still exhibited marks of the saw which was used in quarrying it. At the ends were reproduced doorways, which were imitations of woodwork, while the sides represented the façade of a palace. The dimensions of the sarcophagus were 8 feet long, 3 feet high, and 3 feet wide. It was carved and polished with great care, and was a beautiful object.

Passing over the many intermediate pyramids, we come to the great pyramid of Ghizeh, the largest edifice which the world contains. It is 200 yards northeast of the second pyramid.

Its original height is estimated at 485 feet, or higher than St. Paul's, London. The length of its side was 764 feet, and its area a little over thirteen acres.†

The stones in the lowest course were 30 feet in length, by 5 feet in thickness, but as in the other pyramids, they decreased in size in the different courses, until at the top they were only 18 inches thick.

In the middle of its northern front is an entrance from the thirteenth stage up from the base, which conducts by an incline to a subterranean chamber, deep in the rocks, and nearly under the apex of the pyramid. This chamber measures 46 feet by 27, and is 11 feet high. The passage is so low and narrow that it is necessary to creep through it in a stooping position. Over the entrance are two stones, placed at an angle which meet at the top, so that they support each other and act as an *arch* by supporting the superincumbent masonry. This construction continues along the passage until it enters the

---

* Rawlinson, vol. i., note 3, p. 197.
† See note 6. p. 147; also Rawlinson, vol. i., p. 204.

MEYDOUN MONUMENT.

PYRAMID OF SACCARAH.

ARCHITECTURE.—MASONRY.

rock at a distance of about 40 yards from the outside. It continues on through the rock in the same line 70 yards, then horizontally 9 yards to a subterranean chamber.

Again, at the distance of 21 yards from the entrance, an ascending passage leads from the descending one 124 feet toward the heart of the pyramid, then divides, and a low horizontal gallery, 110 feet long, leads to a room called the "Queen's Chamber," which is 19 feet by 17 in size, and is roofed in with sloping blocks at a height of 20 feet in the centre. Proceeding again, in the line of the ascending passage, a longer and much loftier gallery is reached, which is joined by a short passage to the great central chamber, where was found the sarcophagus of Cheops, or Khufu. The dimensions of this chamber are 34 feet by 14 feet in height. It is wholly composed of granite, and is beautifully polished.

In the construction of the chambers and passages of these pyramids, the Egyptian architects exhibited great skill and technic powers.*

Near the base of the great pyramid are found numerous tombs, whose walls bear the cartouche of the same king—Suphis. His name was also found in one of the chambers of the great pyramid. These are adorned with paintings so artistic as to enable us to fully realize the state of ancient Egyptian society.

Still more striking than the paintings are the portrait statues which have recently been discovered; nothing more realistic has been achieved since the invention of photography.†

The Great Temple at Karnak—Its Wonderful Ruins.

This immense edifice was commenced by Sesostris—Osortasen, of the Twelfth Dynasty, 2435 B.C., who erected a sanctuary here. Then came the Shepherd domination, which lasted over five centuries, after which the work was resumed, and prosecuted by successive monarchs—Amenophis, Thotmes I., Thotmes III., Maneptha, Rhamesis the First, and the Bubasite Kings, until completed—occupying many centuries of time; each century contributing its advance in art; so that when completed, it fully exemplified the culmination of Egyptian architecture.

* Notes 8 and 9, pp. 147, 148.   † Note 13, p. 148.

The grand entrance was through a long avenue of Crio sphinxes facing each other. This led to a portal between two lofty pylons, one of which remains nearly complete, and is 135 feet high. The portal led into a great court, which was supported by round pillars and a double line of columns down the centre. This court and the corridors are 275 feet long by 329 feet wide—comprising an area of over 90,000 feet.

Adjoining, and forming a part of the Great Temple, was a shrine or sanctuary, 160 by 80 feet. This was ornamented throughout with sculptures and inscriptions which exhibit great skill and care in their execution.*

On the side of the court facing the great entrance were two more pylons even higher than the first, and from them projected two masses like the antæ of a portico, between which a flight of seven steps led up to a vestibule 50 by 20 feet. From this, a broad and lofty passage conducted to the hypostyle hall, the climax of this vast edifice. Its length was 340 feet by 170 feet in width.

This superb hall was supported by massive and beautiful columns (see illustration), which were divided into three groups. Twelve columns, each 66 feet high and 11 feet in diameter, formed the main or central avenue, while each of the great wings was supported by 61 smaller columns.

These were arranged in seven rows of seven columns in a row, and two rows of six each; making the internal area of this hall 56,000 feet, and the area externally of the main edifice over 90,000 feet.

The main avenue was illumined by light from the Clerestory—light as bright as from the noonday sun, but without its heat. The arrangement of the columns in the wings was such, that they appeared to be gradually fading into obscurity, and finally lost in space. This, with the massiveness and beauty of the forms, and the brilliancy of their colored decorations, demonstrated the astonishing possibilities of the science of architecture.

Projecting into the great hall was a vestibule enclosed by thick walls, flanked at the angles by square piers. Beyond this was a long corridor, open to the sky, and on each side stood a lofty obelisk of rose-colored granite, covered with hieroglyphics.

* See note 12, p. 148; also Rawlinson, vol. i., pp. 230 to 241; and Fergusson, vol. i., pp. 118 to 121.

ARCHITECTURE.—MASONRY. 97

Still further on was another vestibule, beyond which was a cloistered court, 240 by 62 feet. Its roof was supported by square piers with colossi in

HALL OF THE GREAT TEMPLE, KARNAK.

front. Just inside of this court, on each side of the entrance, stood two more obelisks, 100 feet in height and 8 feet square at the base.

Proceeding again, another short flight of stairs led up to a portal opposite to that at the main entrance of the cloistered court. This portal opened into a vestibule 40 by 20 feet, with a doorway in the middle of each side which conducted to the adytum.

This apartment was about 120 feet square and comprised a central hall of finely polished granite, 52 by 64 feet, which was flanked on either side by a set of small apartments.

Both the large and small rooms were everywhere adorned with painted sculptures and hieroglyphical legends.

Passing from this, a porch or ante-room was reached, and from this room a doorway 8 feet wide led into the Holy Place, 20 by 14 feet, from which another passage of the same width as the last conducted into the Holy of Holies—the great objective point toward which all the arrangements of this immense temple tended.

This sacred place was 27 feet by 14, and its walls and ceiling were decorated in a manner appropriate to its purpose.

This sanctum sanctorum, with its inner and outer apartments, its porch and larger approaches, will suggest to both the Masonic student, and the student of Architecture, that this superb Egyptian Temple was the prototype of the Temple of Solomon at Jerusalem. The old temple at Edfou, Upper Egypt, also affords important points of similarity to the Jewish Temple, so that there is no doubt but that the latter was copied from one or both of these edifices.

This immense structure, considered as a whole, presents the following remarkable particulars:

Its length, outside of all, was 1,200 feet, and its width about 340—nearly an oblong, and giving an area of 396,000 feet. It comprised two great courts, one of which was colonnaded; an oblong cloister, supported by piers, ornamented with colossi—two great pillared halls—one of them with its pylons covering more ground than the Cathedral at Cologne—the largest of all the northern cathedrals; and compared with this edifice, the mass comprising St. Peter's and the Vatican is insignificant.

Altogether, this vast and magnificent edifice at Karnak was the crowning glory of Egyptian architecture, and in many respects surpassed the grandest achievements of the Mediæval Craftsmen.

ARCHITECTURE.—MASONRY.

ANCIENT EGYPTIAN HOUSES.

Among the pictorial representations which ornament Egyptian structures are illustrations of private residences. In one, there is a representation of the façade of a house, the centre, and two wings. The centre, which is higher than the rest, is crowned by a roof shaped like a truncated pyramid; at the base of this is a projecting cornice, and below the cornice a plain wall, through which is a door at the right hand corner. At the right of the door is a wing,

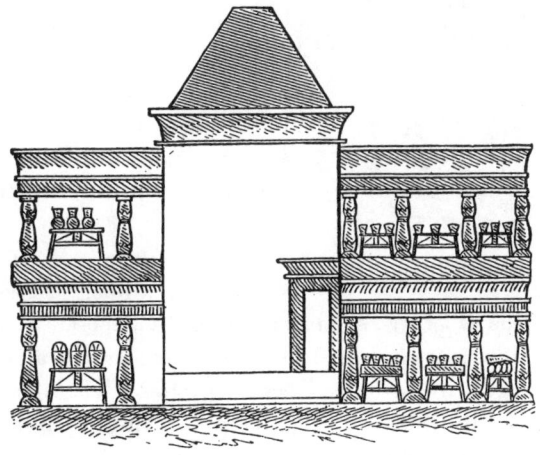

ANCIENT EGYPTIAN HOUSE.

SECTION OF AN EGYPTIAN HOUSE.

which consists of two stories, each ornamented with four pillars, forming in the one case a colonnade, in the other a gallery. The left wing is similar to the other, but shorter, and is ornamented with two pillars to each story. The wings have an architrave above the pillars, and are then crowned with a double cornice.*

Another picture exhibits the courtyard of a three-story mansion of much elegance, and apparently decorated for a festival. The central doorway is supported on either side by slender pillars representing a lotus-plant. Inside the doorway is seen a staircase, which conducts to the upper apartments. The

* Fergusson, vol. i., p. 131; Rawlinson, vol. i., pp. 258, 259.

staircase is represented as being carpeted, and having a mat at the foot of the first step. To the left is seen a doorway and three small windows protected by perpendicular bars. Over this rises a story built of wood or bricks, and broken by two windows, with the blinds drawn nearly to the bottom.

At the top is an open gallery with painted cornice, supported by four pillars. On the right of the main entrance the wall is plain, with the exception of a low doorway. Above it a drapery or awning is seen.

EGYPTIAN HOUSE, WITH COURT.

The next floor exhibits pillars at either end, and between them appears to be another awning. Above this is a range of short pillars supporting an upper gallery or half-story, but too low to have been inhabited. The front is crowned by a cornice painted in stripes of red, blue, and white, and resting at either end of the house on a lotus pillar.

GLASS.

Among the arts known to the Egyptians was that of making glass. From remains of glass articles, and from hieroglyphics, it appears that they were proficient in this manufacture at a very early period of their national existence. The process is represented in the paintings of Beni Hassan, executed in the reign of that monarch. Ornaments of glass have been found having the same specific gravity as that of English glass. Many glass bottles and vases have been found in the tombs, some of them of very remote antiquity. Such was their skill in this art that they successfully counterfeited the amethyst and other precious stones.

Winckelmann believes that glass was more generally used in ancient than in modern times, being used by the Egyptians even for coffins.

BABYLONIA.—ASSYRIA.

As early as 2000 B.C.,* the builders' art was sufficiently advanced in the Euphrates Valley to entitle it to a place in the history of architecture; this is demonstrated by the remarkable ruins recently discovered and uncovered at Wurka Mughear, Abu Shuhrein, Kaleh Shergat, at Khorsabad, Koyunjik, and Nimroud. In the mounds of these places the remains of structures have been found that are in many respects wonderful. This is especially true of the great observatory and palace at Khorsabad, the Temple, Birs Nimroud, and the palace of Ashurbanipal at Nimroud. The materials used were mostly sun-dried brick and alabaster slabs.

But of vastly greater importance than the architecture of this country, are the records—history engraved on tablets—that were found near where they had once been systematically arranged around the halls of noted structures. These tablets supply a long stretch of ancient history that otherwise would have been lost.

Assyrian architecture may be said to have reached down to the destruction of Babylon by Cyrus, 538 B.C.; yet the only impression it made on subsequent civilization was to the east and south of the Euphrates, as but little, if any, connection between it and western, or European, architecture has yet been proved.

Having now reached the domain of classical architecture, a definition of the term, and an explanation of its primary elements, are in order.

Architecture, according to Webster, is the art or science of building. Another definition is: ornamental construction. Its primary elements are the Column, the Arch, and the Dome.

* Fergusson, vol. i., p. 150.

COLUMNS.

The first dwellings of mankind were caves, and tents made of bark, and the skins of animals. The first improvement on this where timber was plenty, was wooden structures: either of logs laid horizontally one upon the other—log-houses—or buildings supported by posts; with posts for doorways, etc. Where timber was scarce, recourse was had to stone and brick. Therefore, the first pillars made of the durable materials might, or might not, have been suggested by the posts or pillars used in wooden buildings.

From the oldest of the rock-cut tombs in Egypt, the pillar can be traced from a plain pier to a *Doric Column.* At first it was a mere pier, square or rectangular; then the projecting angles were cut away, and the shape became octagonal; finally the octagon was rounded off into a circle. For greater strength and elegance, the base and entablature were added. Next, ornamentation was attempted, and that sort of fluting appears which subsequently characterized the Doric order of the Greeks.*

In the tombs of Beni Hassan, in Middle Egypt, there are pillars having sixteen shallow curved indentations, which are carried in straight lines from the top to the bottom of the columns, streaking them with delicate varieties of shade and light—adding greatly to their richness and effect.

RHAMESSION COLUMN, THEBES.

There is another still more elegant column which is found occasionally in the early tombs, which deserves notice. This column imitates four reed or lotus stalks, bound with a ligature over the top, above which they swell out and form a capital. It was sometimes delicately colored with streaks and bars of blue, and other colors, which rendered its appearance very effective.

* See Rawlinson, vol i., pp. 219, 220; Fergusson, vol. i., p. 248.

ARCHITECTURE.—MASONRY.

THE ARCH; ITS ORIGIN.

The first appearance of the arch was in Egypt, in the arched roofs of tombs, and small chambers, in the vicinity of the pyramids. The arch is also found in the chambers and passages in the pyramids, notably the third. As this pyramid was erected in the fourth dynasty, or nearly 3,000 years B.C., it places the arch among the first inventions of the ancient builders.*

In the rear of the Rhamession, at Thebes, there are a series of arches built of brick, and evidently of the same age as the building itself. In Ethiopia, the porches of some of the pyramids, built as early as the tenth century B.C., have arched roofs built of stone, in both the round and pointed forms.† Other early examples of the pointed arch have been found in the ruins of Khorsabad, in the arched gateways of that city. The façade of one, in particular, was beautiful, and all of these arches were constructed in accordance with the true principle of the arch. Just when or by whom the pointed arch was introduced in Europe, is uncertain, but all churches in Provence (France), from the time of Charlemagne to that of St. Louis, were vaulted, and the pointed arch was introduced by Abbot Suger, at St. Denis, in 1144. ‡

THE DOME

Was invented by the Romans about 400 B.C. The Romans being familiar with the arch, its form suggested to them the Dome. It was first used in Italy as a roof for churches, but later it took its proper place as the crowning glory of temples and other edifices. This is illustrated by the Dome of the Pantheon, one of the grandest expressions of architecture in existence. Other noted domes are St. Peter's, Rome; St. Paul's, London; St. Sophia, Constantinople; St. Vitale, Ravenna; San Marco, Venice; and the Capitol, at Washington.§

GRECIAN ARCHITECTURE.

Tradition alleges that a colony of Egyptians under Cecrops were among the first settlers of Attica; but the predecessors, if not the ancestors, of the

---

* Notes 10 and 11, p. 148 ; Rawlinson, vol. i., pp. 198–206.
† Hope, pp 122–146.   ‡ Fergusson, vol. i., p. 448.
§ See Fergusson, vol. ii., pp. 436–438 ; Chambers, vol. iv., p. 504.

Helenes were the Pelasgians (1184 B.C.),* and they were the first people to develop art in Greece. In consequence, however, of the length of time that has elapsed since the Pelasgic races ruled in that country, the architectural remains of their structures are few. The most remarkable of these yet discovered are the tombs of the kings of Mycenæ, which, in Homeric times, was one of the most important of their cities. The largest and most perfect of these tombs is that of Aretus. The largest chamber is 48 feet 6 inches in diameter, and was of the shape of a regular equilateral-pointed arch. The dome was lined internally with plates of brass or bronze, nails of which metals are now found there; and the holes from which other nails have been drawn, or have dropped out, are still to be seen all over the place.

Larrissa, Argos, and Ephyra, were three of their fortified cities. They constructed dams, water-works, and canals that exhibited great skill. They were also familiar with navigation. Of their sculpture, the principal relics are the head of Medusa and the image of Orpheus.

Grecian architecture, however, as we know it, first appeared at Corinth nearly under the Cypselidæ (650 B.C.), having undergone a great transformation in the meantime. On its reappearance it was no longer characterized by the ornate art of Mycenæ, but had assumed the characteristics of Egyptian art, and with more than Egyptian massiveness.

Grecian architecture was originally divided into three styles: the Doric, Ionic, and the Corinthian. As the Doric art progressed the early massive forms gave place to more elegant and slender proportions.

The Doric was the order that the Greeks specially cultivated, so as to make it exclusively their own. When first introduced from Egypt, it partook of Egyptian solidity; but it gradually became attenuated to the lean form of the Roman order of the same name. The columns of this order were at first 4.47 diameters high, then 6.025, and at last 7.015.† It has no ornaments on its capital except triglyphs. Notwithstanding this, the Doric order will doubtless always be admitted to belong to a higher class of art, because all its forms and details are better adapted to their purpose than those of either of the other styles.

---

* Fergusson, vol. i., pp. 241, 242; Chambers, vol. i., p. 845; vol. vi., p. 169; vol. xi., p. 1026.
† Fergusson, vol. i., pp. 243, 244, 248, 249.

The oldest example of the Doric style is a temple at Corinth, of the age of Cypselus (about 650 B.C.). The remains of this temple show that the various members of the style were fully developed, all being of a massive and heavy description, strongly resembling its prototype at Beni Hassan, in Egypt.*

The temple of Theseus (438 B.C.) and that of Jupiter at Olympia (440 B.C.), Apollo Epicurius at Bassæ, and Minerva at Sunium, are examples of the Doric style.

But of all the great temples of Greece, the most celebrated was the Parthenon; the only octastyle Doric temple in that country, and of its class the most beautiful building in the world. This edifice was built entirely of white marble; and the masonry in this, as in other Doric works of importance, is put together with the most perfect workmanship.

Ionic.

This style took its rise about 500 B.C., and to a certain extent depends upon ornamental carving for its effects. Its columns are nine diameters high, and its entablature is adorned with volutes, and its cornices have modillions. These exhibit the most perfect execution and workmanship, all being drawn and cut with the greatest possible exactness.

Those details and ornaments which were only painted in the Doric, were carved in the Ionic order, and therefore remain visible to the present day.†

The oldest example of the Ionic style was the temple on the Ilissus, dating from about 484 B.C. Following this is the beautiful little temple dedicated to Nike Apteros, the Wingless Victory, which stood in front of the Propylæ at Athens. The last and most perfect example of this order is the Erechtheum, on the Acropolis, its date being about 420 B.C., the great epoch of Athenian art.

In the Ionian and other colonies of Asia Minor many fine examples of this style were erected, among which was the celebrated temple of Diana, at Ephesus.

* Chambers, vol. vi., pp. 169, 170; also notes, 14, 15, and 16, p. 149.
† Fergusson, vol. i., p. 254; Chambers, vol. vi., pp. 170, 171.

Corinthian.

This was the next style introduced in Greece, and combines to some extent the characteristics of both the preceding. The capitals of this order were copied from the bell-shaped capitals of Egypt, as the Doric was from their oldest pillars.

But like everything in art that the Grecians touched, they soon rendered it Greek by the freedom and elegance with which they treated it. This column is ten diameters high, and its capital is adorned with two rows of leaves and eight volutes or scrolls, which sustain the abacus. The cornice has modillions, and the frieze is beautifully ornamented.

The Corinthian is the most florid of the styles invented by the Greeks, and from its richness and splendor, it afterward became a great favorite with the Romans, in whose hands Greek art spread over the Empire. One of the oldest and most beautiful example of the Corinthian order is the Choragic monument of Lysicrates, built 335 B.C. It is one of the most striking works of art of the merely ornamental class to be found in any part of the world.

The largest example of this order is the temple of Jupiter Olympius at Athens. This, however, may be called a Roman building on Grecian soil, having been commenced in its present form under Antiochus Epiphanes, by the Roman architect Cossutius, and finished by Hadrian.

Greek columns were at first supposed to be bounded by straight lines, but it has been ascertained that they have an entasis or convex profile in the Parthenon to the extent of $\frac{1}{550}$ of the height. While this cannot be perceived in ordinary positions, yet the lack of it gives that rigidity and poverty to columns so observable in modern edifices.*

The *technical* classification and designation of Greek temples is determined by the mode in which the columns of the porticos are arranged. The cella, or temple proper, is a square chamber contained within four walls; the simplest form of portico is called distyle in antis, the two side walls being continued past the end wall, and terminated with antæ, with two columns between.

* Fergusson, vol. i., pp. 250–259; Chambers, vol. vi., p. 170.

ORDERS AND STYLES OF ARCHITECTURE.

fillet ; 2, cyma recta ; 3, corona ; 4, ovolo ; 5, ca-
; 6, upper fascia ; 7, lower fascia ; 8, abacus ; 9,
; 10, colareno ; 11, astragal ; 12, fillet. or reglet ;
   ; 14, plinth ; 15, surbase ; 16, base.

ARCHITECTURE.—MASONRY.

Where the portico has four columns between the antæ, it is called tetrastyle. These temples generally had the same arrangement at both ends. In front of both ends of the plan distyle in antis, there was frequently placed a range of six columns, and from the flank column a row was continued along both sides. This arrangement is called peripteral, and the temple is designated hexastyle and peripteral.

The Parthenon is an exception to the above, as it had a hexastyle portico at each end of the cella, in front of which is placed an octastyle portico, and seventeen columns on each side.

A range of columns around a temple, or square, is called peristyle.*

CARYATIDES.

The name, as well as their being used only in conjunction with the Ionic order and its details, all point to an Asiatic origin for this questionable form of art.

ROMAN ARCHITECTURE.

We next come to the culminating period of ancient civilization. We first saw art originate and become thoroughly established in Egypt. Early Pelasgic art has been indicated in Asia, Greece, and Etruria. Next in Greece, under the Cypselidæ, we see all these elements gathered together, the best qualities taken from each, so that the whole formed the most perfect and beautiful combination of intellectual power and architectural science that the world had yet witnessed. After a brilliant but brief domination over the arts by Greece, all the different styles of architecture were collected in Rome, and thence spread their influence over the world. †

The earliest inhabitants of Rome were also Pelasgians; these were followed by Aryans. Their principal neighbor on one side was Etruria, also a Pelasgian nation; on the other side was Magna Græcia, originally colonized by Hellenic settlers of kindred origin. Therefore, Rome derived her architecture directly and indirectly from Greece. Indirectly, at first, through the Pelasgians and Etruscans, and later directly from Greece.

---

* Chambers, vol. vi., p. 171; Fergusson, vol. i., pp. 259-261.
† Fergusson, vol. i., pp. 294-303.

The advance made at first in architecture by the Etruscans is exhibited by the remains and representations of their bridges, gates, and aqueducts; and many examples of Etruscan art are found in their tumuli, which still exist in great numbers.

Time has reduced most of them to nearly the level of the ground, while a few of the larger ones still retain an imposing appearance. Although nearly all have been rifled at some early period, yet treasure and curiosities are still discovered in them.

One of the most remarkable of these structures, opened in modern times, is at Cervetere, known as the Regulini Galeassi Tomb.

Bedsteads, shields, arrows, and vessels were hung in a curious recess in the roof, doubtless representing a place for hanging such vessels in the house of the living. The treasures found in this tomb are in the oldest style of Etruscan art.*

Roman architecture may be said to have been the transition form between the Greek and Gothic. The Romans adopted the Greek form of decoration; they decorated their exteriors with columns crowned by straight architraves and cornices, and inside these they formed the real construction with arches and vaults.

The use of the latter gradually extended, especially in the construction of the interiors. By means of arches the Romans were able to roof in large areas without encumbering the floor with pillars. This was carried out in many important structures, such as the baths of Caracalla, Diocletian, and the Basilica of Constantine. In their works of public utility—aqueducts, bridges, etc., the Romans always used the arch as the fittest mode of construction.

The arcuated form came more and more into use, until it was universal. The Romans also conformed the Greek decoration to the circular arches by bending the entablature around the curves, as in the palace of Diocletian, at Spalatro.

To the Romans, therefore, is due a great improvement, if not the perfection, of the arcuate construction, together with a well-developed internal decoration. The early Christians adopted the Roman forms of construction and

* Fergusson, vol. i., pp. 286-290.

ARCHITECTURE.—MASONRY.

decoration, and this was particularly conspicuous in their sacred edifices built during the Middle Ages.

In Egypt, architecture was applied to palaces, temples, and tombs; in Greece, almost wholly to temples and theatres; and in Etruria, to tombs. But in Roman cities we find temples basilicas theatres, amphitheatres, baths,

An Interior View, Pompeii.

tombs, arches of triumph, bridges, and aqueducts, all equally objects of architectural skill.

One of the first strides in advance made by the Romans was by developing the arch and using it as a vault. The most perfect example of this was the rotunda of the Pantheon.

But with the primitive orders of the Greeks, they not only added nothing to the Doric or Ionic, but the latter suffered at their hands. With the Corinthian they were more successful, as they added fulness and strength to its capital, and thereby contributed to the perfection of an order which, for richness, proportion, and architectural fitness, has hardly been surpassed.

Among the Roman examples of this style are the temple of Jupiter Stator, the Pantheon, and the Maison Carrée at Nimes.*

Composite Order.

But, not satisfied with the Corinthian, the Romans attempted to improve it, and in doing this they hit upon what is known as the Composite Order. Its columns were ten diameters high, and its capital has two rows of leaves of the Corinthian and the volutes of the Ionic. Its cornices have modillions.

A decidedly Roman order is the Composite Arcade. This was a combination of Grecian and Etruscan architecture, Etruscan with a Grecian front.

Sassanian Architecture.

For the sake of maintaining the sequence of this history, the architecture of Persia, and its vicinity, will be noticed here.

The Sassanidæ dynasty derived its name from Sassan, grandfather of Ardisher, the king who ascended the throne of Persia A.D. 226.

As their religion required no temples, their public buildings were mostly palaces. These structures were built principally of sun-dried brick and wood, and were profusely ornamented with gold, silver, and rich hangings, beautiful in color and embroidery. An example of this style is the great Mosque at Diarbekr. This building was originally a palace, and was erected in the latter part of the third century. Another beautiful example, was the palace at Mashita, built early in the seventh century.

Not only in the early, but in the middle, ages, artists from Constantinople were eagerly sought after by both the monarchs of the Orient and the sovereigns of the Occident.

During the reign of the Sassanide dynasty, Greek artisans were in demand at the Persian court. A prince of this royal race, Nashervan by name, made the singular request of some Grecian philosopher to come and instruct young men of distinction in Greek theology.

* See Chambers, vol. x., p. 360 ; Fergusson, vol. i., pp. 300, 301.

ARCHITECTURE.—MASONRY.

Romanesque—Christian.

This style was introduced between the reigns of Constantine and Justinian, and was a modification of the classical Roman form. To the eastward it merged into the Byzantine style during the reign of Justinian, A.D. 527 to 564. In Italy and the south of France, the Romanesque continued to be prac-

Ruins of the Great Mosque at Diarbekr.

tised till the seventh century, and finally was merged into what came to be known as the Gothic.*

Among the noted examples of this style in Rome are St. Peter's, A.D. 330; St. Paul's, 386; Quattro Coronati, 625; and St. Clement's, 1118.

There were also octagon and circular churches; the latter were the prototypes of the Christian Baptisteries.

The earliest churches of the Christians at Constantinople and elsewhere, were closely imitated after the Basilica—Hall of Justice—such changes only having been made as the exigencies of the rites and ceremonies of the Christians required.

* Fergusson, vol. i., pp. 396–399.

They not only adopted the plans and mode of construction of the Romans, but used the actual materials of Roman buildings which had been destroyed by the barbarians.

In remote districts, where the builders had to prepare new material, they followed as closely as they could the Roman plans of construction. In process of time, when decorations were again desired, the new styles retained some of the original forms; each style depending for its peculiar character on the particular Roman form it retained and developed.

Ancient Palace at Mashita—Restored.

BYZANTINE ARCHITECTURE.

The style of architecture known as Byzantine, arose in the East, soon after Constantine transferred the government of the Roman Empire to Byzantium, and, until the seventh century, is said to be the Byzantine. The second, or Neo-Byzantine, included those forms which were practised in the East from the eighth century, till it was superseded by the Renaissance.

The Byzantine style was principally established by the church of St. Sophia—the great mosque of Constantinople.

The Mosque St. Sophia.

INTERIOR VIEW, ST. SOPHIA.

ARCHITECTURE.—MASONRY.

The fundamental principles of this style, as applied to churches, was a varied application of the Roman arch; its exhibition in the form of the dome being its most characteristic feature.* In the St. Sophia, the dome covered the principal central portion of the church, and was supported by strong and lofty pillars, held together by bold arches. To this central space was joined others of smaller size, which were covered by half cupolas or arches of more ordinary construction.

Frequently churches were erected in the form of a Greek cross, with the cupola rising in the centre, and smaller or semi-cupolas surmounting the four arms.

Many other details, such as the square capitals tapering downward, and the bold projecting mouldings ornamented with foliage seemed to have owed their strength and origin entirely to the ingenuity of Byzantine architects. The constant use of the apse is, after the cupola, their most marked feature.

St. Sophia.

The original church of St. Sophia was erected by Constantine, and was burned to the ground in the fifth year of Justinian (A.D. 532). It was rebuilt by the colleges of builders and Greek craftsmen, by order of Justinian; the architects being Anthemius of Thralles, and Isodorus the elder. It was completed 537 A.D.

In the same year a part of the dome fell, in consequence of an earthquake; but this damage was soon repaired, leaving the structure very nearly as it now stands.

While viewing his completed work, Justinian exclaimed, "I have surpassed thee, O Solomon!" He did not realize the extent to which his edifice excelled King Solomon's Temple, nor that in some respects he had surpassed the Pantheon at Rome. It is even now an open question whether a Christian church exists whose interior is equal to this marvellous creation of Byzantine art.†

Of the other beautiful mosques erected in Constantinople, that of Suleimanie,

---
* Note 17, p. 149.
† Fergusson, vol. ii , p. 443; Rebold, pp. 283-287.

completed in 1555, remains unsurpassed, and compares favorably with the church of St. Sophia.*

For several centuries Byzantium continued to be the centre of art and literature; the relation of Constantinople to the rest of the world being the same as Athens was to remote antiquity.

Byzantine architecture found its way into foreign lands, and one of the first edifices erected in this style was built at Ravenna. It was constructed in the form of a Greek cross, and was erected about the middle of the fifth century.

The cathedrals of Angoulême, Worms, Speyer, Mayence, and the church of St. Castor, at Coblenz, Santa Maria, of Cologne, all betray the singular characteristics of Byzantine architecture.

A large and prominent example of the Byzantine style, is the Doge's Palace, Venice. Its erection was commenced in 813, and through all its additions and alterations it retained its Byzantine character until 1301, but from that time until 1423, the alterations were principally executed in Gothic.

Cathedral of St. Mark's.

The present edifice was commenced in 997, the original building having been burnt down in a riot the previous year. It was completed, including the mosaics and internal decorations, in 1094. The first part erected, was the interior, covered by the five great domes which are arranged in the form of a Latin cross. The central one, and that in front, are 42 feet in diameter internally; the other three, 33 feet each. This cathedral is Byzantine with Gothic and Renaissance additions. Its interior is said to be the most impressive in Western Europe.† Subsequently Byzantine edifices profited by the example of St. Mark's.

* Fergusson, vol. ii., p. 540.

† Recently a crypt has been discovered and cleared out, which extends under the whole of the eastern part of the church, 86 feet by 74. Its vaults are supported by fifty-six monolithic columns, 5 feet 6 inches high; the whole height from the floor to the arch crown being 9 feet. In the centre, immediately under the altar of the upper church, on a raised platform between four stone piers, originally rested the relics of St. Mark; this part being more highly decorated than the rest of the crypt. There seems no doubt that this crypt, in all its details, forms part of the church as re-erected in the eleventh century, and is interesting as remaining almost unaltered to the present day. Fergusson, vol. ii., pp. 362–392.

St. Mark's, Venice.

SULEIMANIE MOSQUE.

The fascinating power of Byzantine art not only extended from the Orient to the Occident, but its influence reached the land of the Cossack; and in the year 955 the Russian Princess Olga, on her return from Constantinople, built at Kieff, a church in the form of a Greek cross. Near the close of the tenth century the Grand Duke Valdimar embraced the Christian religion and adopted the Greek ritual. Immediately after this he erected at Kieff, under the supervision of a Byzantine architect, a cathedral, which was dedicated to the name, " Divine Wisdom."

Santa Croce, at Florence, is remarkable for the great men who lie buried beneath it, and Santa Maria Novella possesses something exceptional in that city, a façade; but neither of these has anything to redeem its defects in the eye of an architect.

Saracenic.

This style was developed by the Mohammedans in the latter part of the seventh century, and it prevailed in the East, in Northern Africa, and in Spain.*

Wherever the Saracens successfully established themselves, they immediately turned their attention to beautifying the towns and villages by erecting sumptuous edifices; and for this purpose Abd-er Rahman, the Mussulman, ruler of Spain, procured for Cordova a Byzantine architect. In the year 820, a son of Haroun-al-Raschid, a friend of Charlemagne, applied to the Greek Empire for the best works extant, in order to have them translated into Arabic and used in the colleges of Borna, Corfu, Cairo, Tripoli, and Tunis.

Noted structures of this style were the great Mosque at Damascus, the Madrissa at Ispahan, the Khan's Palace at Khiva, the Suleimanie Mosque in Constantinople, the Kaitbey Mosque at Cairo, a Minaret at Tunis, and the Alcazar and Alhambra in Spain.

In 936 the Caliph Abd-er Rahman determined to erect at Zara, near Seville, the royal castle known as the Alcazar, and secured the services of the most skilful architects from Bagdad and Constantinople, to design the work and superintend the craftsmen employed on it. This castle, when completed, was noted for its peculiar style of architecture and its strength.

* See Fergusson, vol. ii., pp 497, 516, 520, 540; Fort, p. 347.

THE ALHAMBRA.

This singular edifice was erected at Granada by the craftsmen of several nations, under Mohammed ben Alhamer, and completed by Yousouf in 1354.

As a whole, this was in many respects a wonderful structure. The palace, when completed, constituted an expression of the combined styles of the architectural art of that period. In fact, in many of its details and general effect, it has not been surpassed in modern times.

The style of architecture pertaining to the tombs, which forms a prominent feature of Saracenic architecture, is missing in Spain. The Moors seem to have been of a purely Semitic race, either from Arabia, or descendants of the old Phœnician settlers on the southern coast.

BAGDAD.

In the ninth century Haroun-al-Raschid got a large number of the craft together at Bagdad, and repaired, improved, and enlarged that singular old city, principally in the Saracenic style. (See p. 695.)

GOTHIC ARCHITECTURE.

Under this title are comprised the principal styles of architecture which prevailed in Western Europe from the middle of the twelfth century to the sixteenth.

But, as previously stated, the pointed arch constructed with wedge-shaped voussoirs was used by the Ethiopians as early as the tenth century B.C., and by the Assyrians in the eighth century. The Saracens also used it at Cairo in the seventh century A.D.[*] All the churches in Provence (France), from the time of Charlemagne to the reign of St. Louis, were vaulted on the principle of the pointed arch.

The term Gothic was at first bestowed by Renaissance architects on the mediæval styles as a term of reproach. The name, however, outlived the reproach at first implied, and a feeling of admiration has succeeded; as the

---
[*] Fergusson, vol. i., p. 448.

PART OF THE ALHAMBRA.

Gothic now ranks as one of the noblest and most complete styles of architecture ever developed.

The first vaults constructed were simple, semi-circular tunnel vaults; but it was found that these, besides being gloomy, required massive walls to resist their thrust. An attempt was then made to obviate this difficulty by transverse arches thrown across at intervals under the tunnel-vault, to act as strengthening arches. Buttresses with a slight projection were supplied outside to support these, and a beam of wood was sometimes introduced at the wall-head, from buttress to buttress, to assist in resisting the thrust of the vault.

This, with a few other improvements, was the origin of the groin rib, the development of which played so important a part in Gothic vaulting.*

Improvements in vaulting went on to the last of the twelfth century, when the principles of the Gothic style were fully developed.

Therefore it will be seen that this style was not the invention of a nation or an individual, but a growth from an early period—a gradual development mostly necessitated by structural requirements.

The transition from the round Gothic to the true pointed Gothic style in France took place with the revival of the National power.

One of the earliest, if not the earliest, examples we have of the fully developed Gothic style is the Cathedral of St. Denis, in which are deposited the remains of the kings of France. This cathedral was founded by the Abbé Suger, in 1144. The Cathedral of Notre Dame, the magnificent Cathedrals of Chartres, Rheims, Amiens, Beauvais, Bourges, and many others of this style soon followed.†

Following the Norman conquest, in 1066, the architecture of England made a marked stride in advance; and nearly all the great cathedrals of that country were either rebuilt or remodelled in the twelfth and thirteenth centuries.

The first appearance of the pointed arch in England is believed to be at the rebuilding of the Cathedral of Canterbury, after the fire of 1174. The architect who superintended that work for the first five years was William of Sens (France). The details and arrangements are so different from anything

---

* See Chambers, vol. vi., pp 83–86.
† Fergusson, vol. i., p. 532; vol. ii., pp. 53, 246, 321, 407.

130　　　　ARCHITECTURE.—MASONRY.

NAVE, LINCOLN CATHEDRAL.

else of the same age in England, that his influence on the style of the building can hardly be doubted.

Yet, down to the year 1200, the round arch was currently employed in con-

ARCHITECTURE.—MASONRY. 131

junction with the pointed. At that time, however, it gave way to the latter, which dominated for three centuries; and it is in the cathedrals of the

VIEW IN PETERBOROUGH CATHEDRAL.

twelfth and thirteenth centuries that are found the noblest developments of the Gothic style.

In Germany the Gothic style early found a congenial home, and among its grandest achievements were the Cathedrals of Cologne and Strasburg.

The great typical cathedral of Germany is that of Cologne.

Its dimensions are 466 feet in length, by 275 in width, being the largest cathedral of Northern Europe; and also one of the noblest expressions of the adoration of man for Deity ever erected in any country.

Among the edifices—monuments of the craftsmen's skill, erected during the thirteenth century, are Westminster Abbey, the Cathedral at Lichfield, the Cathedrals of Paris, Rheims, Chartres, Rouen, Bruges, Amiens, Beauvais, Strasburg, and Cologne.

In the fourteenth century the Cathedrals of York and Exeter, and King's College at Cambridge; the cathedrals of Metz, Perpignan, Meaux, Auxerre, Tours, Como, Milan, Seville, Barcelona, and the Ducal Palace at Venice, were erected.

Renaissance.

This style followed the Gothic, and was derived from the Venetian style of Italian architecture, which made its appearance in the fifteenth century. From Italy this style soon found its way into France, and thence into England and other countries.*

In Brief.

1. **Egyptian Architecture** was established as early as 2500 B.C.—First Temple at Memphis erected.
    The great Temple at Karnak commenced, 2435 B.C.
    Scope, or field of operations of Egyptian Architecture, Egypt, Syria, and Greece.
2. **Greek Architecture,** established 1250 B.C.—Mycenæ founded at that time.
    Pelasgian art, from 1200 B.C. to 655.
    Greek architecture proper, commenced 650 B.C.
    Cypselidæ, building of Temple at Corinth at the above date.†
    Selinus founded, and a Temple commenced 626.
    Doric order invented 650 B.C.
    Ionic invented 500 B.C.

---

* Chambers, vol. vii., p. 54, and vol. x., p. 188.
† Fergusson, vol. i., p. 231.

ANCIENT ROMAN TOWER—CATHEDRAL AT RATISBON.

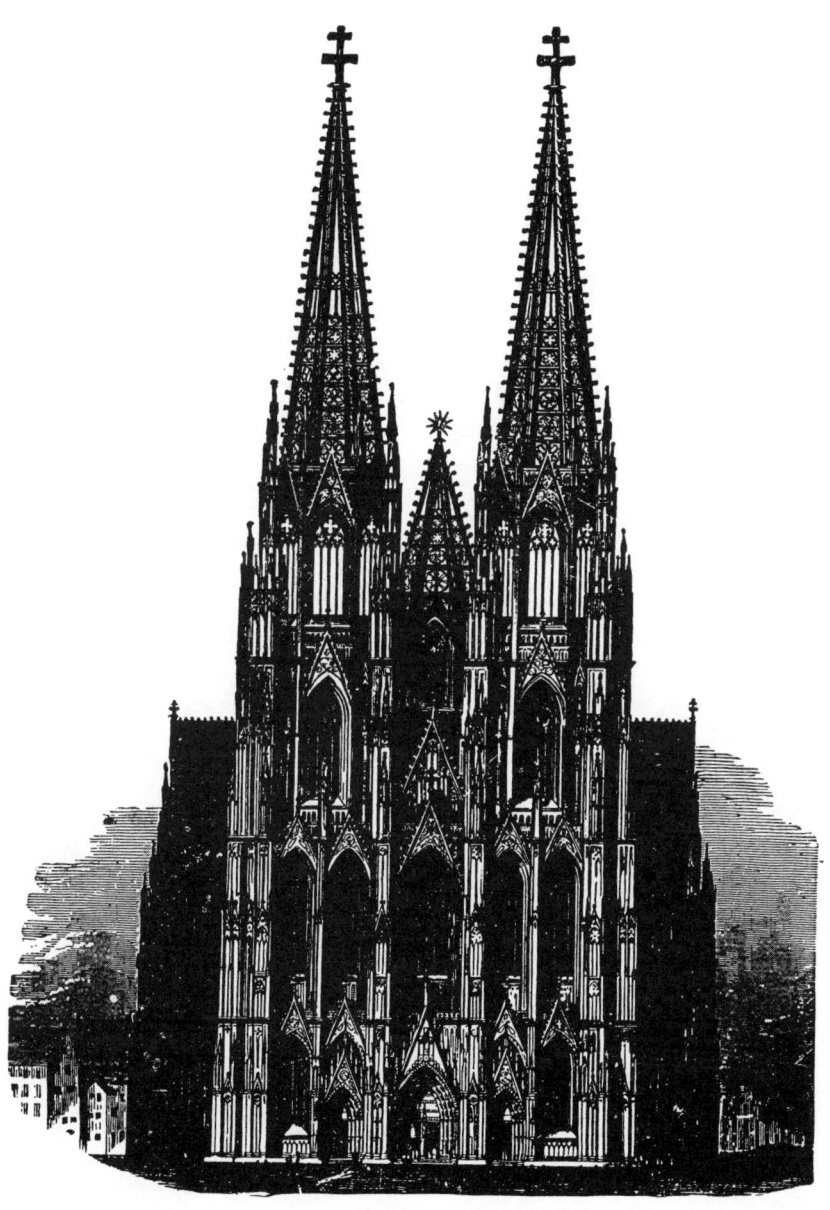

CATHEDRAL OF COLOGNE.

Corinthian invented 336 B.C.
Theron, at Agrigentum, commenced great Temple 480.
Climon, at Athens, Temple of Thesus, built 469.
Pericles, at Athens, Parthenon finished 438.
Temple of Jupiter, at Olympia, finished 436.
Erectheium, at Athens, finished 335.
Monument of Lysicrates, at Athens, 335.
Scope of Greek architecture, Greece and Italy.
3. **Roman Architecture,** established 616 B.C.
The Temple of Jupiter Capitolinus commenced at that time.
Pantheon erected A.D. 13.
Colosseum A.D. 70.
Destruction of Pompeii, 79.
Trajan's Column erected, 98.
Diocletian's Palace at Spalatro, 284.
Maxentius Basilica at Rome, 306.
Constantine, transfer of Empire to Constantinople, 328.
Scope of Roman Architecture, Southern Europe.
4. **Sassanian Architecture,** established 250 A.D.
Scope, Persia and vicinity.
5. **Romanesque,** established 450 A.D., Italy and Greece.
6. **Byzantine**—Roman and Greek combined. Established A.D. 330.
The old Byzantine practised until the eighth century, then the Neo-Byzantine till the twelfth century.
St. Sophia erected, and dedicated A.D. 537.
Scope, Greece, Asia Minor, and Italy.
7. **Saracenic Architecture.** Mohammedan—dates from the Hegira, A.D. 622.
Scope, Asia Minor, Northern Africa, and Spain.
8. **Gothic Architecture.** Developed between the seventh and twelfth centuries. Scope, Europe.
Cologne Cathedral, erected 1248. One of the grandest expressions of art in the world.
Strasburg Cathedral, first erected in 800. Destroyed by lightning 1007. Rebuilt in the fourteenth century.

138 ARCHITECTURE.—MASONRY.

9. **Renaissance** style, established in the middle of the fifteenth century. Scope, Italy, France, and England.

Noted Structures.

The great Pyramid of Ghizeh erected 3000 B.C.
The vast Temple at Karnak, 2435 B.C.
King Solomon's Temple, 1004 B.C.
Temple of Jupiter Stator, Rome, 685 B.C.
Temple of Diana at Ephesus, 552 B.C.
Parthenon, Athens, dedicated to Minerva, 442 B.C.
Pantheon, Rome, a circular temple, 27 B.C.
Colosseum, Rome, circular, 75 A.D.
CANTERBURY CATHEDRAL, founded A.D. 602. Destroyed by the Danes, 1011. Rebuilt 1130. Again burnt, and rebuilt 1184. The great tower completed 1495.
THE TOWER, London, first built 1078.
CHICHESTER CATHEDRAL, built in the thirteenth century.
LINCOLN CATHEDRAL, founded 1127.
LICHFIELD CATHEDRAL, founded 1148.
Notre Dame, Paris, 1163.
The Alhambra, Spain, founded 1250.
ST. PETER'S, Rome, begun 1506. Finished 1626.
ST. PAUL'S, London, begun 1675. Finished 1710.

Dwellings of Different Races—from the Iron Age to the Renaissance, in the Fifteenth Century.

No. 1. This illustration is from a dwelling of baked clay, recovered from a lake in Italy. Its immersion under water is accounted for from the fact that the lake occupies the crater of an extinct volcano.

2. An Egyptian house, 1400 B.C.
3. Hebrew, 1000 B.C.

Roman. 9.	Russian. 13.
Gaul. 10.	Byzantine. 14.
Gallic, Roman. 11.	Arabian. 15.
German. 12.	Chinese. 16.

ARCHITECTURE.—MASONRY.

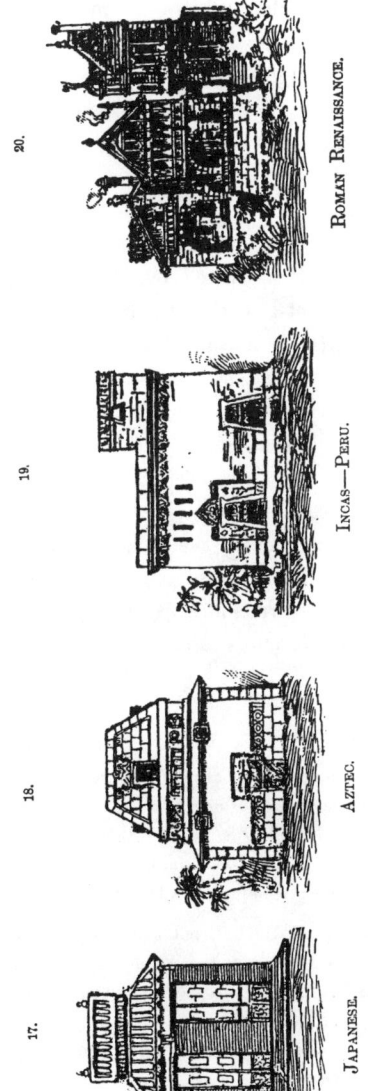

4. Etruscan, 800 B.C.
5. Assyrian, 500 B.C. The ruins of this house were found in a good state of preservation.
6. Phœnician, 400 B.C.
7. Greek, 420 B.C. This house was divided into two parts: one for the women and children, and the other for the father and grown-up sons. The houses of the well-to-do were handsomely furnished with pottery, couches, etc.
8. Persian, 100 B.C. Persian houses of the present day differ but little from the one here shown.
9. A Roman house of A.D. 20.
10. Gaul—France, 75 B.C. Circular structures with round roofs.
11. Roman—Gallic.
12. German; time of the Roman occupation.
13. Russian; suburbs of Moscow.
14. Byzantine, A.D. 400.
15. Arabian. Ancient and modern.
16. Chinese.
17. Japanese.
18. Mexico—Aztecs.
19. Peru—Incas.
20. Roman Renaissance.

From the foregoing we find that from Egypt the builders' art proceeded north to Syria, and after manifesting itself in King Solomon's Temple, it proceeded westward to Greece, where it was greatly developed and perfected. Proceeding westward again, it came to the Tiber; for on the absorption of Greece by the Roman Empire, B.C. 146, the arts and sciences of the Greeks found a ready market in Rome. From Rome and Greece, architecture proceeded into Gaul, Germany, and the British Isles.

Although the Romans gave their names to certain styles of architecture, yet they were nearly all originally copied from, or suggested by, Greek models. This will be readily understood from the fact that the Italian craftsmen were, from the first, constantly reinforced by Greek artisans. Finally, after Italy had become replete with both public and private structures, and Christianity had created a demand for church edifices beyond that country, the Corporations of Builders began to extend their operations into the northern and western portions of Europe.

The independent corporations had been preceded, however, by the Colleges of Builders, that had accompanied the Roman armies in their campaigns of conquests.* To summarize, architecture as we know it, originated on the banks of the Nile; took its course along the eastern shore of the Mediterranean, then westward to Greece, Italy, France, Germany, and Britain.

NOTES FROM AUTHORITIES.

1. In any consecutive narrative of the architectural undertakings of mankind, the description of what was done in Egypt necessarily commences the series, not only because the records of authentic history are found in the valley of the Nile long before the traditions of other nations had assumed anything like tangible consistency, but because, from the earliest dawn the inhabitants of that mysterious land were essentially and pre-eminently a building race.

2. Fortunately there is hardly a building in that country which is not adorned with the name of the king in whose reign it was erected. In royal buildings they are found on every wall and pillar. The older cartouches are simple and easily remembered, and when we find the buildings thus dated by the builders themselves, and their succession recorded by subsequent kings on the walls of their temples, we feel perfectly certain of our sequence, and nearly so of the actual dates of the buildings; they are, moreover, such a series as no other country

* Notes 14 and 15, p. 197.

TOWER OF KILREE, KILKENNY.

ST. KEVEN'S KITCHEN.

OLD IRISH ARCHITECTURE.

in the world can match either for historic interest or architectural magnificence. Fergusson, History of Architecture, vol. i., pp. 89, 124.

3. The history of Egypt will always be, to a very large extent, a history of art. Art had, so far as we know, its birth and earliest development in the valley of the Nile. Rawlinson, xi., p. 33.

4. The palaces, tombs, and temples of Upper Egypt, present to us the earliest known instances of architecture, sculpture, and painting. Kitto, vol. i., p. 604.

5. The Egyptians had a profound belief in the reality of the life beyond the grave, and a conviction that that life was, somehow or other, connected with the continuance of the body. They embalmed the bodies of the dead in a most scientific way; and having thus, so far as possible, secured them against the results of natural decay, they desired to secure them against the malice of enemies. Rawlinson, vol. i., p. 210.

6. The Egyptians, as stupendous in their excavations as the Hindoos, are far more so in those edifices, like the temples of Thebes and the pyramids of Memphis, raised on the surface of the ground, in which blocks of stone of immense weight, conveyed to a great distance from the quarry, elevated to a surprising height, and cut and interwoven with others in the most ingenious and solid manner, imply mechanical powers and skill of the highest description, of which the Hindoo buildings give no example.

To talk of Egyptian architecture, at least in its public monuments, is to discuss what, in respect of size, of integral component parts, and solidity of the whole, is most astonishing. Hope on Architecture, pp. 10, 14.

See also Birch, Egypt from the Earliest Times, pp. 32, 41; Lenormant, Manuel d'Histoire Ancienne, vol. i., pp. 537, 538; Fergusson, History of Architecture, vol. i., p. 98; Brugsch, Egypte, pp. 51-59, etc.

7. Herodotus (11, 125) expressly notices that the stones were raised in this way, a step at a time, by machines placed on the step below. Mr. Perring found marks of the use of such machines wherever the upper surface of the original steps was exposed to view. He conjectured that the machine used was the polyspaston of Vitruvius. Vyse, Pyramids of Ghizeh, vol. i., p. 197.

8. No one can possibly examine the interior of the great Pyramid without being struck with astonishment at the wonderful mechanical skill displayed in its construction. The immense blocks of granite, polished like glass, and so fitted that the joints can scarcely be detected.

Nothing can be more wonderful than the extraordinary amount of knowledge displayed in the construction of the discharging chambers over the roof of the principal apartment, in the alignment of the sloping galleries, in the provision of ventilating shafts, and in all the wonderful contrivances of the structure. All these, too, are carried out with such precision, that notwithstanding the immense superincumbent weight, no settlement in any part can be detected to the extent of an appreciable fraction of an inch. Rawlinson, vol. i., p. 214, quoting Fergusson.

9. These builders were able, first of all, to emplace their construction with astronomical exactness; secondly, to employ in them, wherever it was needed, masonry of the most massive and enduring kind; thirdly, to secure the chambers and passages, which were essential features of such structures, by contrivances of great ingenuity, perfectly adapted to their purpose; and fourthly, by their choice of lines and proportions, to produce works which, through their symmetry and the imposing majesty of their forms, impress the spectator, even at the present day, with the feelings of awe and admiration, such as are scarcely excited by any other architectural constructions in the whole world. Rawlinson, vol. ii., p. 82. Vyse, Pyramids of Ghizeh, vol. i., p. 176.

10. Circumstances have come to light, one after another, tending to throw the date more and more backward, until at length it seems to be admitted that in Egypt the arch existed in the time of Joseph. The observations of Rosillini and of Sir J. G. Wilkinson led them irresistibly to this conclusion. In the valley of Dayr el Medeeneh, at Thebes, are several tombs of the early date of Amenophis. Among the most remarkable of these is one whose brick roof and niche, bearing the name of the same Pharaoh, proves the existence of the arch at the remote period of B.C. 1540. Wilkinson's Topography of Thebes, p. 8.

To the same period belong the vaulted chambers and arched doorway which yet remain in the brick pyramid of Thebes (Wilkinson, Ancient Egyptians, iii., p. 317). The most ancient, actually existing, arches of stone occur at Memphis, near the modern village of Saqqara. Kitto, vol. i., p. 203.

11. It is generally supposed that the Egyptians were ignorant of the true principles of the arch, and only employed two stones meeting one another at a certain angle in the centre, when they wished to cover a larger space than could be conveniently done by a single block. This, however, seems to be a mistake, as many of the tombs and chambers around the pyramids and temples at Thebes are covered by stones and brick arches of a semicircular form, and perfect in every respect as far as the principles of the arch are concerned. Fergusson, vol. i., p. 204.

12. Of all the great structures of Egypt, the Temple of Karnak is the grandest expression of Egyptian art, and compares favorably with the greatest of mediæval cathedrals. See Rawlinson, vol. i., pp. 230–241.

13. They (the Egyptians) understand also, better than any other nation, how to use sculpture in combination with architecture, and to make their colossi and avenues of sphinxes group themselves into parts of one great design, and at the same time to use historical paintings, fading by insensible degrees into hieroglyphics on the one hand, and into sculpture on

the other, linking the whole together with the highest class of phonetic utterance. With the most brilliant coloring they thus harmonized all these arts into one great whole, unsurpassed by anything the world has seen during the thirty centuries of struggle and aspiration that have elapsed since the brilliant days of the great kingdom of the Pharaohs. Fergusson, vol. i., p. 139.

14. It is known, from the testimony of Diodorus Siculus, and from the conformity of the Athenian laws with those of the Egyptians, that the first inhabitants of Attica were an Egyptian colony. We have several proofs that it originally came from the city of Sais.

15. There is no doubt that the Doric style took its origin from the rock-cut tombs of Beni Hassan, in Egypt. Modern discoveries have shown that Greece owed much to the earlier civilization of the countries which preceded it in history. To the architecture of Egypt almost every feature of Greek architecture can be traced. See Fergusson, vol. i., pp. 110–242.

16. There exists in Egypt a class of temples called mameisi. They are of a simple peristylar form, with columns in front and rear, the latter being built into a wall and seven square piers on each flank. What renders them more than usually interesting to us is the fact that they were undoubtedly the originals of the Greek peristyle forms, that people having borrowed nearly every peculiarity of their architecture from the banks of the Nile. We possess tangible evidence of peristyle temples and protodoric pillars erected in Egypt, centuries before the oldest known specimen in Greece. Fergusson, vol. i., pp. 126, 127.

17. When the Romans transferred their capital to the shores of the Bosphorus, the semi-oriental nation seized on their own circular form, and, modifying and moulding it to its purpose, wrought out the Byzantine style ; in which the dome is the great feature. Fergusson, vol. i., p. 297.

CHAPTER IV.

KING SOLOMON'S TEMPLE.

The Building of this Remarkable Edifice.—Preparing the Timber in the Forests of Lebanon.—Cutting the Stone in the Great Subterranean Quarry. — Striking Scenes, the Ancient Craftsmen at Work. — Secret Meetings of the Master Workmen.—Completion and Dedication of the Temple.—Its Destruction and Commencement of the Captivity.

THE next Masonic landmark on the grand highway of time is Mount Moriah, and the next notable expression of the builder's art after leaving Egypt was the Temple of Solomon. There also at the building of the Temple we get the first notice of a society or lodge of artisans.

The preparation of the site and the building of the Temple involved a vast amount of labor and required a multitude of workmen, therefore the Masters and Supervisors found it expedient to hold secret meetings for instruction on the work and for mutual assistance.

As Moses and other Jews of the better class who had resided in Egypt had been initiated into the Sacred Mysteries, and had transmitted the same to the Jewish people, they had entered largely into the religious rites of the Jews previous to the reign of King Solomon. The Egyptian system being both secular and religious,* its essentials soon found their way into the Masters' meetings; and tradition says that the first meetings were held in a valley near Jerusalem, the better to guard against intrusion; but subsequently, for greater convenience, they built a cabin-lodge, on Moriah, near the work of the Temple.

This lodge was presided over by a Master of the Craft, and the meetings were held at stated periods, taking care that none entered except those who had been initiated and could make themselves known.†

* Notes 1 to 7, pp. 180, 181. † Note 9, p. 181.

KING SOLOMON'S TEMPLE.   151

The topography of the site of Jerusalem when in a state of nature would have shown a very rough locality. The Tyropean Valley ran through it from north to south, with what was subsequently known as Mount Zion on the west and Mount Moriah on the east. Moriah is a rocky spur, extending from the mountains on the north of Jerusalem about 2,000 feet in a southeasterly direction and terminating in a sharp and nearly perpendicular point.

The height of Mount Moriah at its highest point was 140 feet above the Valley of Jehoshaphat on the east, 70 feet above the Tyropean Valley on the west, and 2,360 feet above the Mediterranean.

Rugged as was this rocky hillock, it was the scene of three remarkable events. First, Abraham here prepared to offer his son a sacrifice; second, David erected an altar here on which to offer up sacrifices to appease the destroying angel; third, it was the site of the Temple of Solomon — Real and Mythical.

The erection of this edifice was managed by three men, noted in sacred and profane history. First, by Solomon, King of Israel, who furnished the money and precious metals and had the general supervision of the undertaking; second, Hiram, King of Tyre, who furnished men and material, mostly cedar timber; third, Hiram Abif,* also a Tyrian, a talented and skilful artificer, who superintended the manufacture of the vessels and ornamentation of the Temple.

The friendly relations that existed between Solomon and Hiram, King of Tyre, was the natural outcome of the long period of peace that had existed between the Jews and Phœnicians. According to Phœnician historians, King Solomon also married a daughter of the King of Tyre.

Hiram Abif was of a mixed race, his father being a skilful Tyrian mechanic and his mother a Jewess. His genius and acquirements were such as to place him early in life at the head of his profession in his own country. Therefore King Hiram could see no more practical way of assisting his friend Solomon than by giving him the service of such a skilful artificer.

The first thing to be done was to prepare the top of Mount Moriah for the Temple, its porch and courts. This alone was a herculean task, as Moriah extended from the hills like a promontory, sharp at the top, with its sides

* Note 7, p. 181.

and the south end falling away nearly perpendicular. Therefore to make a level area of the required size, nearly as much labor was necessary as was involved in the largest of the pyramids. As it would require a vast amount of stone and earth to level up the south end, it was decided to do it by a series of columns resting on the bed-rock and supporting a massive platform above.

Temple Area.

A better idea of the magnitude of the undertaking will be had when the extent of the rough hill that was to be made level is given. The Temple inclosure, or area, was 1,500 feet long, by an average of 950 feet wide, being widest at the north end. The surrounding walls were from eight to ten feet thick at the base by four feet at the top, and from fifty to seventy-five feet high above the surface on the Kedron Valley side. The platform over this work being so massive as to render it proof against fire and falling ruins during the destruction of the several temples above, some of the original work at the south end is still to be seen, and is minutely described by recent explorers. The entrance to it from the south end and from above was small, and known to but few, even in Solomon's time.

The corner-stone of King Solomon's Temple was laid in the month of May, 1012 B.C., and in the fourth year of the reign of King Solomon; and the Temple was completed in seven years, five months, and twenty-seven days.

Following the preparation of the site, the material that entered into the erection of the Temple and the sources from whence they were derived will next be considered.

Stone.

First in order, is the large amount of stone used in such a structure. Geology discloses the fact that Mount Moriah consists of tertiary limestone, the upper strata of which is hard and compact, while the underlying stratum is soft and white, but hardens rapidly on exposure to the air. It was of this latter stone that the mason-work of the Temple was built. But it is only a short time since, and then by accident, that this discovery was made. Dr. Barclay,* coming into the city one evening by way of

---

* An American missionary.

Getting Out the Cedar Timber in the Forest of Lebanon.

The Great Subterranean Quarry.

the Damascus gate, noticed that his dog acted strangely, close to the base of the ancient city wall, and on investigation discovered a small aperture extending down under the wall, through which it was evident that some animal was in the habit of passing. As Mohammedan law is very strict concerning the Temple area, forbidding any displacement of stone or soil in or about the sacred precincts, the discoverer waited until the following night, when with a small party of assistants, with implements for digging, he repaired to the hole under the wall, and as a precaution against wild animals and reptiles the dog was sent forward, and when it was evident that he had not met with anything serious, digging was commenced in earnest. Following the aperture, it led them down into the ground for a distance of ten feet, then horizontally a short distance to the southward, when they were astonished to find themselves in a large cavern, the cimmerian darkness of which was only intensified by their small lamp. Subsequent investigation, however, disclosed the fact that this was nothing less than the great quarry from which the stone for the Temple had been taken. This cavern is a short distance northwest of the Temple area, and under that part of Jerusalem now called Bezetha, the Mohammedan quarter. The largest apartment in the cavern is 750 feet by 100 feet wide and an average of 30 feet high. At intervals, pillars of rock were left to support the top of the cavern. From this apartment a labyrinth of smaller rooms opened in every direction, and in all of them chippings and other evidences of the work done here were found.

When this quarry was operated, it was lighted by many small lamps set in niches in the wall. This is shown both by the niches, and by streaks of soot left by the smoke of the lamps, some of the soot-lines being as black and bright as when they were made nearly three thousand years ago.

The floor of the quarry is uneven and is everywhere littered with chippings, and stones split from the sides of the quarry are lying around in various states of finish, showing that for some reason the masons had suddenly quit their work, never to return.

As the bed of this quarry was higher than the Temple area, the blocks of stone were doubtless rolled out of the southern end, and thence to that part of the site where they were to be used, but by what process of engineering these great blocks were elevated into position we have no means of knowing.

The illustration of this quarry at page 154 is from a sketch made by an artist on the spot, and the costumes of the workmen are in accordance with the descriptions given in the Scriptures and by contemporaneous writers.

Cedar.

Next in importance to the stone was the cedar used in the Temple. This was cut in the renowned forests of Mount Lebanon, near two mountain streams called the Nar el Kelb and Kadisha, their head waters being about fifteen miles from the sea. Here this timber was cut, hewn, finished, and marked or numbered, and then conveyed down the course of these streams to the sea, where it was made into rafts or floats. The rafts were manned, and taken down the coast of the Mediterranean to Joppa—a very hazardous undertaking at best.

There are small harbors at the mouth of both streams, which rendered them convenient places for making up the rafts and preparing them for the sea. The harbor at the mouth of the Nar el Kelb is a short distance north of Beyrout. One side of the harbor is formed by a rocky promontory, and on the sides of the higher rocks inscriptions have been cut by invaders and conquerors from Assyria, Macedonia, Egypt, and France.

Thirty-five miles north of this harbor is the inlet of the Kadisha. This is an ancient port, and here are ruins of very ancient buildings. What a busy and graphic scene these two harbors presented three thousand years ago! For here the many craftsmen of Hiram and King Solomon were engaged in making up the fragrant and beautiful cedar timber into rafts preparatory to its voyage to Joppa. In the forest, fifteen miles above, was another busy scene. Clad in their peculiar costume and using their unique tools, were many thousands of men at work. Some felling the giants of the forest; groups of craftsmen, under the superintendence of skilled workmen, or Masters, were squaring and finishing the timber for the Temple; while others were conveying it down the watercourses to the harbors below.

And when it is considered that they had then to traverse the boisterous Mediterranean for a distance of one hundred and thirty miles, it will be seen that it not only required care in putting the rafts together, but also skill in

Conveying the Timber in Floats to Joppa.

JOPPA.

handling them on the route. Tradition says that for greater safety they secured three rafts together, one after the other, and that they were propelled by sails and oars.

On the arrival of the rafts at Joppa, another difficulty had to be overcome, as the rocky shore was so steep that each piece of timber had to be lifted twenty feet to the landing above. From the landing, the timber was carried thirty-five miles to Jerusalem on the backs of asses and mules — a difficult and tedious operation; for their lack of facilities had to be made up by a large force of men and animals, and by severe and often dangerous labor.

Over three years were occupied in cutting and preparing the timber and dressing the stone in the quarries. At length, after the material was all on, or near, the site of the Temple, the two bodies of men from the forest and quarries united for the purpose of placing it convenient for use. Finally, when everything was ready and the process of erection commenced, every piece exactly fitted the place it was designed for.

This splendid edifice consisted of three courts: the Porch, the Sanctuary, and the Holy of Holies.* Passing through the eastern entrance of the wall, the first court, or Court of the Gentiles, was reached. This court was so named because the Gentiles were permitted to go no farther. Proceeding across this court, a passage through a low wall was reached, from which fifteen steps led up into the Court of the Women, and beyond this court was that of the Men. To these two courts the Jews came daily for the purpose of offering up prayers to Deity. Beyond the last-named court was the Court of the Priests, and in the centre of this, was the Altar of Burnt Offerings. From the Court of the Priests twelve steps led to the Temple proper, which consisted, first, of the Porch; second, the Sanctuary; third, the Holy of Holies. At the entrance to the Porch was a splendid gate of Corinthian brass. On one side of this gate was a pillar named Jachin, and on the other side one called Boaz. Passing from the Porch, the Sanctuary was reached through a portal across which hung a beautiful veil of many colors, which mystically represented the universe.

In the Sanctuary were arranged the various utensils for worship in the

* Note 8, p. 181.

Temple, among which were the Altar of Incense, the Ten Golden Candlesticks, and the Ten Tables of Stone on which offerings were laid previous to sacrifice.

Crossing the broad Sanctuary, the Holy of Holies, or innermost chamber, was reached. At the entrance to this sacred place there were two doors of olive-wood, beautifully sculptured, inlaid with precious metals, and further adorned with veils of blue, purple, scarlet, and fine linen. The Holy of Holies contained the Ark of the Covenant, overshadowed by the Cherubim. As this place was said to have been rendered most sacred by the very presence of God, it was deemed a sacrilege worthy of death for anyone except the High Priest to enter it, and even he could only enter it once a year, on the Day of Atonement.

East Gate—Gate Facing the Sun.

The ancient East Gate of the Temple enclosure was of a size and style worthy of its purpose. Its length was 70 feet, its width 55 feet, and it projected 6 feet outside of the wall. Two beautiful columns divided it into a double arcade, lighted at the west end by two domes. Its interior was ornamented with rich carvings, producing a grand and imposing effect. A massive stairway led up 25 feet to the platform above.

Dedication of the Temple.

From the time the corner-stone was laid, the work on the Temple was steadily prosecuted, until it was completed, which was in a little more than seven years, so that it was dedicated in 1004 B.C., or in the year 3000 according to Hebrew chronology. At its dedication there were assembled the priests, the elders, the heads of the tribes and all the men of Israel—a great multitude, to take part in the dedication of the most beautiful temple hitherto erected in Syria. The Ark of the Covenant having been brought from the City of David, it was deposited with great solemnity in its place in the Holy of Holies. "And it came to pass, when the priests came out of the Holy Place, that the Cloud filled the house of the Lord, so that the priests could not stand to minister because of the Cloud: for the glory of the Lord had

BUILDING THE TEMPLE

DESTRUCTION OF THE TEMPLE—THE CAPTIVITY.

filled the house of the Lord. And it came to pass, when Solomon had finished the house of the Lord, and the King's house, and all Solomon's desire which he was pleased to do, that the Lord appeared unto Solomon a second time, as he had appeared unto him at Gibeon. And the Lord said unto him, I have hallowed this house which thou hast built, to put my name there forever."

The Mosque, Dome of the Rock.

This renowned and beautiful edifice was erected by Constantine on the site of King Solomon's Temple, over the spot then believed to be the Holy Sepulchre. It is octagonal, 160 feet in diameter; its columns are of marble of the most precious kinds, and either belonged to the Temple of Herod or to that erected by Hadrian on the same spot. Its Mosaics are beautiful, though much altered in design by Mohammedans, who have added painted glass of beautiful patterns and exquisite color to the windows.*

Hiram Abif—The Real and the Mystical.

There are two accounts of the building of King Solomon's Temple. One account gives the actual history of that event and describes the three noted men who figured in it. The other account is traditional and allegorical.

In one account Hiram Abif appears as a real person, just as he was; in the other he appears as a mystical personage. He was really the cunning craftsman employed by King Solomon to beautify and adorn the actual Temple; he was an emblematic being, representing the sun, who by his magnetic power raises the Royal Arch of heaven and beautifies and adorns the terrestrial and celestial spheres. Therefore his name has a twofold meaning, significant of his real and of his mystical character.

In the Masonic tradition the mystical Hiram is represented as being an architect, superintending the building and drawing out the plans for the Temple.

But according to the Bible and Josephus, Hiram was no architect at all—drew out none of the designs for the Temple.

* Fergusson, vol. ii., p. 432.

The mystical Hiram of Masonic tradition is represented as having lost his life in a singular manner just before the completion of the Temple, and with some of his designs unfinished; while according to the sacred Scriptures, the real Hiram lived to finish all his labors in and about the Temple, and for King Solomon. That the Hiram of history mentioned in the Bible and by Josephus is a different personage from the traditional Hiram, will be seen by the following:

The designs, form, and dimensions of the Temple were all given by divine inspiration and command (II. Chron. iii.). To have altered or modified them in the smallest particular would therefore have been a sin, which would have called down the instant and terrible punishment of Jehovah. Hiram is nowhere mentioned or described in the Bible as being an architect or builder, but in I. Kings vii. he is described as being "filled with wisdom, and understanding, and cunning to work all works in *brass*."

Josephus thus mentions Hiram: "This man was skilful in all sorts of work, but his chief skill lay in working in gold, silver, and brass, by whom were made all the mechanical works about the Temple, according to the will of Solomon" ("Antiquities," Book VIII., Chapter iii., p. 4).

Nowhere is there a word said about his having anything to do with the management of the building of the Temple; but, for evidence on this point, see I. Kings vii.; II. Chron. iv., 11–19; also Josephus. From which we learn what part of the work of the Temple Hiram really did do—that he made for King Solomon the two pillars of brass called Jachin and Boaz, and their ornaments; the molten sea of brass with twelve oxen under it; the ten brazen lavers with their bases, and many pots, shovels, and flesh-hooks, together with all the other altar furniture to be used in the Temple.

All of these articles were made of bright brass, and were cast in the clay grounds between Succoth and Zeredatha (II. Chron. iv.; I. Kings vii., 45–46). Therefore the scene of Hiram's labors must have been over fifty miles from Jerusalem, or two days' journey. This distance, with the making of the moulds and the patterns for the great number of large and small pieces, many of them difficult of construction, renders it evident that Hiram must have been occupied most of his time at the place where he made the Temple furniture, rendering it impossible, under the circumstances, that he could

THE CLAY GROUNDS.

Mosque of Omar—Dome of the Rock.

KING SOLOMON'S TEMPLE.

have supervised the work in Jerusalem, or even visited it daily during the building of the Temple.

Besides these works in brass, we are told that Hiram made for the Temple, of pure gold, ten candlesticks for the altar, with flowers, lamps, and tongs, bowls, snuffers, basins, censers, and hinges of gold for the Holy Place and for the doors of the Temple. All being the work of a " cunning worker in metals," not of an architect or builder.

The historical Hiram lived to finish all his work. " So Hiram made an end of doing all the work that he had made King Solomon for the house of the Lord " (II. Chron. iv.).

Therefore, as the historical Hiram was no architect, and did not suffer death before the completion of the Temple, it follows that it was the mystical Hiram—Osiris, representing the sun—who meets with that fate near the completion of the emblematic Temple, the year. (See p. 88.)

Summary of the Temples of Jerusalem—the Jews.

King Solomon's Temple commenced, 1012 B.C.; dedicated, 1004 B.C.; plundered by Shishak, 971 B.C.; restored by Joash, 856 B.C.; robbed and polluted by Ahaz, 740 B.C.; restored by Hezekiah, 726 B.C., but he gave the treasures of the Temple as a ransom, 711 B.C.; desecrated by Manasseh, 698 B.C.; repaired by Josiah, 624 B.C.

Nebuchadnezzar carried a part of the sacred vessels to Babylon, 606 B.C.

He plundered and burnt the Temple, and carried the principal inhabitants captive to Babylon, 588 B.C.

Cyrus gave the decree to Zerubbabel and other Jews to return and rebuild the Temple, 536 B.C.

It was completed in the second year of Darius, 515 B.C.

Pillaged by Ptolemy Lagos,* 320 B.C.

Plundered by Antiochus, 170 B.C.

Plundered by Crassus, 54 B.C.

Rebuilt by Herod, 18 B.C.

* Chambers's Encyclopædia, vol. ix., p. 912.

Finally it was destroyed by Titus, 70 A.D.

The Mohammedan mosque of Omar now stands on its site.

The destruction of the Israelitish nationality by the Roman legions caused the Jews to disperse into Persia and other provinces of the Roman empire, and wherever they settled, they immediately became famous as astronomers, mathematicians, and geometricians. The Moors of Spain were also greatly indebted to their Jewish subjects for an institution of learning controlled by rabbis from Jerusalem. The fame of this institution was such that many scholars were attracted to it from the cities of Spain and from abroad. Several Israelites gained distinction by writing learned treatises on geometry.

Later, Charlemagne commissioned a Jew of great Oriental learning to visit the East, for a special purpose; and another Jew brought him many costly foreign fabrics, which the emperor highly prized.

In Alexandria the rabbis enumerated over twenty thousand scholars to whom Judaistic theology was taught. Learned rabbis declared that all the lore of their fathers was not transmitted in writing, but that much of it had been perpetuated by Moses, in an oral form. Such traditions were recorded in books with interpretations by erudite Jews.

The Israelites were numerous in Rome during the age of Julius Cæsar, and their customs and creed very largely influenced the residents of the great metropolis.

Ancient Tyre—The Home of the Two Hirams.

Tyre was founded in 1250 B.C., two hundred and thirty-eight years before the corner-stone of King Solomon's Temple was laid. Even in the days of David it was a stronghold for its commerce.

This ancient port is one hundred and fourteen miles north of Jerusalem and eighty-seven miles up the coast from Joppa. The old city stood on the mainland in the rear of the present town, and at first bore the name of Palæ-tyrus, or old Tyre. The site of the present town was an island until the invasion by Alexander the Great, 350 B.C., when, in order to attack the city to greater advantage, he built a causeway out to it from the mainland. Subse-

TOMB OF HIRAM, KING OF TYRE.

quently the action of the sea caused the sand to accumulate around and over the causeway, until it became solid land, forming a peninsula of the whole.

The articles of export were the famous Tyrian dye, sugar, glass, and other manufactured goods. Sugar-cane was cultivated near Tyre, and sugar was made similar to that now made in the Southern States and in the West Indies.

The Tyrians worshipped Hercules as a god, and built and dedicated a temple to him. Tyre also possessed many other splendid edifices, but, like individuals and nations, it had its birth, a period of activity, and then its death, so that the few ruins of it now to be seen may be likened to its grave-stone bearing an inscription commemorating its former greatness.

Many columns and floors of marble lie buried under the rubbish all over the site of the old city. Hundreds of beautiful columns and capitals, many of them whole, have been carried away to Joppa and other places, and built into modern structures. The large amount of such ruins attests the grandeur and wealth of this ancient commercial city. At the time of Christ, Tyre contained a population of 150,000, but it is now a miserable Arab village of 3,000 inhabitants.

Anything relating to Hiram Abif being of interest to Masons, one of the traditions which have been transmitted to us will be noticed.

A few years before the building of the Temple, Hiram Abif, as the agent of the King of Tyre, purchased some curious and valuable stones of an Arabian merchant, who told him that they had been found by accident on an island in the Red Sea. The King directed his agent to go and investigate the truth of the report, which he did; and he had the good fortune to discover many precious stones called topaz, with which the King of Tyre richly adorned his palaces and temples. Subsequently these stones were brought in the ships of Tyre for the service of King Solomon.

King Hiram's Tomb.

On the crest of a hill about six miles from Tyre, is a massive sarcophagus resting on a lofty pedestal of dark-gray stone. The dimensions of this sarcophagus are twelve feet eleven inches, by five feet eight inches wide, and three feet six inches deep. The lid is roof-shaped and three feet six inches high in the centre. A small hole has been broken through one end of the tomb, but whether it was done by curiosity-seekers or by robbers in search of valuables is not known. The great antiquity of this tomb, its massive proportions, and the commanding position it occupies, strongly corroborate the tradition that it is King Hiram's tomb. The country surrounding it is now dotted with Arab villages embowered in groves of olives, pomegranates, and oranges.

Carthage, so renowned in ancient history, was founded by a colony from Tyre, 869 B.C.

The skill of the Carthaginians in masonry was such as shows them to have been a highly intelligent people. Their marble temples, gold statues, splendid palaces, ships, and forts, point them out as occupying a prominent position among the nations of the earth; and when it is considered that their ships sailed on every known sea, carrying on a trade with all the known world, it is not surprising that they so long disputed with the Romans the right of universal empire.

NOTES FROM AUTHORITIES.

1. In "A brief examination of the Rev. Mr. Warburton's Divine Legation of Moses," London, 1742, are the following remarks:

"We have no profane records that can reach by many hundred years so high as the ancient state and constitution of the religion and priesthood of Egypt, in and before the days of Moses. But as the Mosaic constitution itself was accommodated to the natural temper and bias of people perfectly Egyptianized, and who knew nothing but the language, religion, laws, and customs of Egypt; and as this people could never be brought off from the religion and customs to which they had been naturalized, the history of Moses and the prophets gives one almost as just and adequate a notion of the religion, priesthood, and worship of Egypt, as if their own history had been handed down to us. Mysteries, p. 118.

2. In a German work by C. L. Reinhold, entitled "The Hebrew Mysteries," or the oldest religious Freemasonry, it is affirmed that the Mosaic religion was an initiation into mysteries, the principal forms and regulations of which were borrowed by Moses from the secrets of the old Egyptians.

3. Josephus says that: "The high and sublime knowledge which the Gentiles with difficulty attained in the celebration of their mysteries, was habitually taught to the Jews at all times."

Moses could not have been left in ignorance of this mysterious knowledge, because, as he himself informs us, he was acquainted with "all the learning of Egypt." Traditions, pp. 18, 19.

4. A steady and uninterrupted intercourse of the Hebrews of Egypt with those of Palestine, propagated the secret mysteries of the former among the Israelites, and ultimately gained a well-defined status in the creeds of the Jews.

5. Clemens of Alexandria affirms that Moses studied in the colleges of the priests of Egypt, and there learned arithmetic, geometry, symbols, and hieroglyphics; which Justin Martyr called the emblematical part of the Egyptian Scriptures.

6. The method of instruction by symbols, which had been in use in Egypt from the earliest times, was subsequently adopted by the Jews, who thenceforth interpreted their sacred writings allegorically. In this way Egyptian philosophy gradually found its way into the Jewish schools. And the Egyptian Platonic, Pythagorean, and Oriental afterward became blended with their doctrines and ancient faith, and appears in their scriptures. See Gould, vol. iii., p. 63. Brucker's Historia Critica Philosophiæ; also Ginsburg.

7. To the name of Hiram, in the original Hebrew, from which Abif is taken, the affix is Abbi, the possessive case of Abba; which signifies father, figuratively, a superior. His proper address then is my father, in court style my lord. In this sense it is equivalent to Adonis, Baal, or Osiris, all names of the sun.

8. In reference to the pattern given to David for the Temple, Pireson, in "Traditions of Freemasonry," says: "There is another belief that the temple was built upon a plan corresponding with one of the temples at Edfou, in Upper Egypt. This latter had its porch, the entrance to which was between two pyramidal moles; the entrance conducted to a court surrounded with pillars, and winding stairs furnished access to a middle chamber." Traditions and Early History of Freemasonry, pp. 18, 19, 20, 176.

9. Such Fraternities had become so numerous in Rome at the commencement of the reign of Numa Pompilius, that he deemed it advisable, both for their encouragement and regulation, to make them a ward of the state. From this period they flourished under the name of Colleges of Builders till the eighth century, when they, with slight modifications, began to be known as Guilds, by which name they were principally known down to 1717, to the transformation from operative to speculative masonry.

CHAPTER V.

COLLEGES AND GUILDS.

The Colleges of Builders.—Their Lodges, Officers, and Practices Closely Analogous to Those of Free Masons.—They Carry on Most of the Architecture, Engineering, and Masonry of Their Time.—Build Splendid Public Edifices, Bridges, and Military Works.—From Rome, the Colleges Accompany the Roman Armies into Gaul, Germany, and Britain.

FOLLOWING the course of architecture westward, the next grand landmark in the history of the ancient craft is Rome; for here the idea of combining for the promotion of a common purpose, as manifested at the building of King Solomon's Temple, next appeared; and here the different interests of society were first represented by regular organizations, known as Colleges or Guilds.

Whenever, in the history of the world, civilization has reached that point where art and trade began to be practised, men engaged in a common pursuit have combined together for the promotion of their common and joint interests. Hence, in the early history of Rome we find such organizations, notably, the Colleges of Builders.*

The term "collegium" originally signified a number of persons voluntarily associated together for a particular purpose.

Among the most noted of these organizations were the Roman Colleges of Builders, established about 715 B.C. The object of these societies was instruction in architecture and kindred arts, in religion,† mutual advancement and assistance.

The first regulation established was, that no meeting was competent to act with less than three members present. ‡

* Notes 1, 2, p. 195. † Notes 6–11, pp. 195, 196.
‡ Notes 4, 5, 9, pp. 195, 196; also, Rebold, pp. 35, 259.

Each College was presided over by a Magister, which is exactly translated by the English word "master." The next two officers were the Decuriones, whose duties were nearly identical with those of Masonic Wardens, the Master's orders being given through them. Next in order was the Scriba, or Secretary, Athesaurensis, or Treasurer, and lastly, a Sacerdos, or Chaplain, who conducted the religious services.

Monthly dues were imposed for the general and special purposes of each College, for the assistance of needy brethren, and for the burial of their dead, etc.

In their corporate capacity, the Colleges could hold property. They had a common chest, a common cult, and permanent places of meeting.

On the death of a member, he was publicly interred in a common sepulchre, or columbarium, all the survivors being present.

Members were not liable for the debts of their College, but the property of the College itself could be seized. They could sue or be sued by their syndicus or actor.

Each College celebrated three days, viz., its natal day, caræ cognationis, dies violarum and dies rosæ.

The members called themselves Fraters. "For among them," says Mr. Coote, "existed the dear bond of relationship which, though artificial, was that close alliance which only a common sentiment can make."

The College held secret meetings at stated periods, in which candidates were initiated, and craftsmen advanced to a higher grade and received esoteric instructions.*

The candidates for admission were elected by the voice of the members.†

When a man was admitted into the fraternity of a College, he was said to be a co-optatus in collegium. The verb "co-optare," employed to signify an election into a College, comes from the Greek *optomai*, "to see, to behold." This same word gives origin, in Greek, to *epoptes*, "a spectator or beholder," one who has attained to the first degree in the Eleusinian Mysteries.

Furthermore, those Colleges that were sanctioned by the government were called "Collegia licita," or lawful Colleges, while those not authorized

* Note 8, p. 196. † Note 10, p. 196.

were called "Collegia illicita," equivalent to lawfully constituted, and clandestine Colleges.*

In the Colleges there were three grades of initiates—apprentices, fellow-workmen, and masters. Their meetings were opened by a religious ceremony—not sectarian, but recognizing Deity as the Grand Architect of the Universe.

The ritual comprised and taught certain religious ceremonies, a knowledge of the obligations and duties imposed upon the initiate, a knowledge of certain symbolisms, and secret modes of recognition, and the oath and its inviolability. The Fellowcraft was also instructed in the use of the implements of masonry, especially the square plumb, level, chisel, and mallet.

To render a member eligible for the position of Master, he had to make due proficiency in the arts and trades for the execution of civil, naval, and hydraulic architecture.

The Colleges comprised the civil and engineering science of the period in which they flourished; therefore, accompanying each legion of the Roman armies, in their campaigns of conquest, was attached a brigade of the Fraternities, whose duties were to design and construct the military roads, intrenched camps, and fortifications, and direct the labors of the soldiers and workmen in the execution of these works.† They were subject to the commanders of the legions only in matters pertaining to the movements of the army and military works, but otherwise they maintained all their privileges. On the return of an army, after a career of conquest, many of the Fraternities would remain in the conquered countries and engage in the erection of houses, bridges, and public edifices, disseminate their arts and doctrines, and found towns and cities. In this way several of the most noted ancient cities, both in Britain and on the Continent, were founded—notably, the cities now known as London, York, St. Albans, in England, and Strasburg, Cologne, and Paris, on the Continent.

Subsequently, the Colleges were known as Guilds; and as the centuries advanced they improved their system, and not only kept abreast of the civilization of the day, but often led it.‡

---

* Note 3, p. 195. † Also see Rebold, pp. 71–73, 263.
‡ Note 7, p. 195. Also notes 14–20, pp. 197, 198.

REMAINS OF THE TEMPLE OF JUPITER STATOR.

THE APPIAN WAY.

COLLEGES AND GUILDS.

One of the earliest works the Colleges were engaged on was a temple to Jupiter Stator.

From 610 to 500 B.C. they prosecuted the erection of several renowned temples, a great sewer, the Cloaca maxima, through Rome, a strong wall around the Viminal, Quirinal, and Esquiline Hills, which were then included in the city limits. They also completed two extensive circuses; and between 500 and 480 B.C. they erected the temples to Saturn, Mercury, and Castor-Pollux.

The year 451 B.C. was noted for the creation of the laws of the Twelve Tables, the eighth of which was for the regulation of the Colleges of Builders.

Sixty-one years later Rome was sacked by the Gauls, and a part of its monuments destroyed, but they were re-erected by the Colleges.

Between 312 and 285 B.C. the celebrated Appian Way was constructed by the Colleges, or Fraternities, as they were now often called. They also constructed the first great aqueduct. The temple to Romulus, on which was placed the first sun-dial, was also erected about this time.

During the fifty years following (275 B.C.) the Romans conquered most of Gaul, and with the army came a large number of Fraternities, who proceeded to fortify strategic points, and construct great highways. They also founded the city of Cordova, in Spain, and Empordorum, in Gaul.

After the defeat of Hannibal by the Romans, the Fraternities erected a temple to commemorate the event.

The first city hall and court of justice in Rome was erected by the Fraternities, 125 B.C.

Prior to 75 B.C. military colonies were established by the Romans throughout Gaul, one colony in the vicinity of Massillia (Marseilles) and another near Arles. Arles afterward became the capital of the Kingdom of Arles. Here the Fraternities erected an amphitheatre, obelisk, and other noted works, the ruins of which are still to be seen.

Subsequently, Julius Cæsar completed the conquest of Gaul, comprising what is known as France, and ordered the Fraternities to reconstruct and enlarge the cities now known as Treves, Rheims, Rouen, Bordeaux, Besançon, Lyons, Toulouse, and Paris.

They also erected in Paris two new temples, one to Isis, and one to Mithra.

Jewish architects in Rome were admitted into the Colleges of Builders A.D. 10. At this time particular attention was paid to teaching the Egyptian Mysteries in the Colleges; and in the writings of Vitruvius Pollio he describes and extols the doctrines of the Fraternity, which, clothed in allegory and illustrated by symbols, then formed the basis of the teachings of those colleges.*

F. Vespasian caused the Colleges to erect the famous Colosseum, A.D. 70. This vast structure was capable of containing 100,000 people; and under the supervision of the Fraternities 12,000 captive Jews were compelled to assist in its construction.

Marcus Aurelius caused the Colleges to construct the road from Civita to Arles, A.D. 168.

The break between the Government and the Fraternities, that had for some time existed on account of the new religion, was widened during the latter part of the reign of Aurelius, and later by Diocletian, by renewed and cruel persecutions of the proselytes, comprising a large portion of the Fraternities; and as a consequence, many of those who could not leave Rome found secure, if dismal, retreat in the vast Catacombs of the city against the bloody edicts issued against them. By sallying forth secretly by night, they managed to secure provisions, and thus existed in this noisome abode for years. Finally many of the more venturesome, including members of the Colleges—Masons—made their escape to France and England.†

In the great procession ordered by Gallienus, in Rome (A.D. 263), the Colleges marched with shields and banners, having their place after the sacerdotal hierarchy. Later, in the triumphant march of Aurelian, celebrating his victory over Zenobia, the Colleges attached to his army appeared in the procession, bearing their banners.

Under the orders of the Emperor Aurelian, the Fraternity erected two temples to the Sun at Palmyra (A.D. 275). These edifices surpassed in grandeur the temples at Heliopolis.

In A.D. 313, Constantine the Great not only stopped the persecutions of the Christians, but caused a decree to be issued which established Christianity as the religion of the state.

* Note 13, p. 196. † Rebold, pp. 277-281.

Ancient Catacombs, Rome.

COLLEGES AND GUILDS.

The seat of government of the Roman Empire was transferred to Byzantium, A.D 328. And as the frequent irruptions of the northern savages rendered the occupation of the better class of artisans precarious in Rome, they soon after followed the imperial family to the new metropolis. They the more readily sought the new capital, as many of them were Greeks by nativity, and preferred to consecrate their talents to the land of their birth. Therefore, Constantinople became the headquarters of master architects and other skilled artificers; and from the Byzantine Empire art again proceeded westward—light from the east again flashed forth to remote countries.

Immediately after removing to Byzantium, Constantine, by edict, placed the Colleges under the patronage of the Empire, and gave them immunity from all civil exactions, including taxation. Thus the Colleges were established by imperial recognition, and when the code was promulgated in 438, all the privileges and immunities previously granted were confirmed to them.

A.D. 330, Constantine changed the name of Byzantium to Constantinople, and commenced immense improvements, which necessitated the assistance of many architects and workmen. Consequently, the Masonic Fraternities came here in great numbers. The foundations of the Church of Saint Sophia having already been laid, the work on this unique and splendid edifice was pushed to completion. Subsequently, this church was destroyed by fire, but was re-erected, A.D. 550. Finally the Turks converted it into a mosque, and thus it remains at this time.

As the colleges of artificers travelled extensively in the East and Europe, they were brought into contact with all forms of national life, and were subjected to the adventitious circumstances attendant upon a sojourn in distant countries; therefore, they travelled and worked in regularly organized bodies and always maintained the Colleges—Guilds.*

RACES.

As the terms Celtic, Gaul, Picts, and Scots will frequently occur hereafter in this work, a brief explanation of them will not be amiss here.

The Celtic nations were a group of the Aryan family that came from Asia, claimed by some to be Scythians, who invaded Europe, and finally set-

* Notes 12 to 20, pp. 196–198.

tled in Spain, France, Northern Italy, Belgium, and the British Isles. All the above countries, except Britain, were designated by the Romans as Gallia—Gaul.*

The Picts, or Pictish, were a Celtic race, and were first known to history in the northeast of Scotland. Their descendants are now found in Ireland, the Highlands of Scotland, a part of Wales, and the north of France.

The Scoti, or Scots, were also a Celtic people from Ireland.

The Turanian races were the first to people the world beyond the limits of the original cradle of mankind.

In the ancient world the typical Turanians were the Egyptians; in the modern, the Chinese and Japanese, and perhaps the Mexicans.

The Turanians existed in the valley of the Euphrates before the Semitic or Aryan races came there. The Tunguses in the north, the Mongols, Turks, and all the tribes generally described as Tartars, are Turanians.

The oldest people in Europe of this family are the Pelasgi and the Etruscans. The race also appears in the Magyars, Finns, and Lapps, but ultimately they were everywhere overpowered by the Aryans who drove them into remote corners.

The Semitic Races

developed themselves in the track of country between the Mediterranean, Tigris, and Red Sea; also in Abyssinia, and colonized the northern coast of Africa.

The Turanians were builders; the Semitic races never erected a building worthy of the name. When King Solomon decided to build the Temple at Jerusalem, he had recourse to Turanians to take the lead in the work.

In Assyria the remains of splendid palaces have been found that were more or less Semitic, but having been built of wood and sun-dried bricks, their history was only preserved from the accident of their having been so clumsily built as to bury themselves with their tablets in their own ruins. †

---

* Aryan designates the ethnological division of the human race called Indo-European. It consists of an Eastern and Western branch. The Eastern branch comprises the people of Persia, Armenia, Afghanistan, and of Northern Hindoostan. The Western branch comprises the people of Europe, with the exception of the Turks, Magyars of Hungary, and the Finns of Lapland.

† See Fergusson, vol. i., p. 70; Haydn's Dates, p. 399.

·The Aryans first appear prominently in the Western world in Greece, where by a union with the Pelasgi, a people apparently of Turanian race, they produced a civilization more brilliant than anything the world had before seen.

The Aryans next appear in Rome, mixed with the Turanians, Etruscans, and Celtic tribes of Italy; and lastly in Northern Europe.*

NOTES FROM AUTHORITIES.

1. Plutarch and other historians ascribed the first organization of the Roman Colleges to Numa Pompilius, second king of Rome; although, as Newman conjectures, similar organizations previously existed among the Alban population. See Mackey, p. 653.

2. In proceeding with the inquiry into the early history of the Collegia, it will suffice, I think, as regards their extreme antiquity, to state that while their institutions have been commonly ascribed to Numa, this figure of speech is most probably only another way of expressing that their existence was coeval with that of Rome itself.

3. A lawfully constituted College was legitimum, and an unlawful one, illicitum. The distinction is not clearly laid down.

4. No College could consist of less than three members. So indispensable was this rule that the expression, tres faciunt collegium, "Three make a College," became a maxim of the civil law.

5. In its constitution the College was divided into decuriæ and centuriæ, bodies of ten and one hundred men; and it was presided over by a magister and by decuriones—a master and wardens. Among other officers there was a treasurer, sub-treasurer, secretary, and archivist.

To each candidate on his admission was administered an oath. Dues and subscriptions were imposed to meet the expenses of the College. The History of Free Masonry, by Gould, pp. 40-42.

6. Peculiar religious rites were also practised, perhaps with a veil of secresy; and those forms of worship constituted an additional bond of union. Palgrave, Rise and Progress of the English Commonwealth, vol. i., p. 332.

7. Although no rules are extant of any of the trade Colleges of the Romans, some of those in use among the Colleges, Cultorum Dei, have descended to us. Of one of these last-mentioned corporations, the rules or by-laws are given by Mr. Coote, who next cites corresponding regulations of three Guilds (or, as he prefers to style them, Colleges), established in

* See Fergusson, vol. i., pp. 55-75; Chambers, vol. v., pp. 9-16.

London, Cambridge, and Exeter, respectively, composed of gentlemen or persons unconnected with trade ; and having carefully compared the rules of the British Guild with those of the College Cultores Dei already quoted, their resemblances are placed in formal juxtaposition, and he adds : " These coincidences, which cannot be attributed to imitations or mere copying, demonstrate the *absolute identity* of the *Guild* of England with the *Collegium* of Rome and of Roman Britain." Gould, vol. i., p. 43 ; Coote, The Romans in Britain, pp. 390–413.

8. These Colleges held secret meetings, in which the business transacted consisted of the initiation of neophytes into their fraternity, and of mystical and esoteric instructions to their apprentices and journeymen. They were, in this respect, secret societies like Masonic Lodges. The first regulation, which was an indispensable one, was that no College could consist of less than three members.

Each College was presided over by a chief or president, whose title of Magister is exactly translated by the English word "Master." The next officers were the Decuriones. They were analogous to the Masonic "Wardens."

9. There was also in the Colleges a Scriba, or "Secretary," who recorded its proceedings ; a Thesaurensis, or "Treasurer," who had charge of the common chest ; a Tabularius, or keeper of the archives, equivalent to the modern "Archivist ; " and lastly, as these Colleges combined a peculiar religious worship with their operative labors, there was in each of them a Sacerdos, or priest, who conducted the religious ceremonies, and was thus exactly equivalent to the "Chaplain" of a Masonic Lodge.

10. In the Colleges, applicants for admission were elected, as in the Masonic Lodges, by the voice of the members. Mackey, p. 654.

11. The partly religious character of the Roman Colleges of Artificers constitutes a very peculiar analogy between them and Masonic Lodges. The history of these Colleges shows that an ecclesiastical character was bestowed upon them at the very time of their organization by Numa.

12. It cannot be doubted that Krause is correct in this theory : that the incunabula, the cradle or birthplace of the modern Masonic Lodges, is to be found in Roman Colleges of architects.

13. But when we view Free Masonry in a higher aspect, when we look at it as a science of symbolism, the whole of which symbolism is directed to but one point, namely, the elucidation of the great doctrine of immortality of the soul, and the teachings of the two lives, the present and the future, we must go beyond the Colleges of Rome, which were only operative associations, to that older type to be found in the *Ancient Mysteries,* where precisely the same doctrine was taught in precisely the same manner. Mackey, 657, 658.

COLLEGES AND GUILDS.

14. On page iv of preface to Fort's Early History and Antiquities of Free Masonry, he says: "The immediate argument and scope of this treatise may be briefly stated as follows. To commence with a narrative of the state of fine arts at the decline and fall of the Roman Empire, and also of the propagation of architecture and its kindred sciences by bodies of builders, who developed into Middle-Age Free Masons.

15. Again, at page 40, in speaking of the presentation of the Greek artists in the eighth century, he says: "Upon their arrival in Italy and in Southern Europe, they were quickly associated with the corporations of builders."

15½. After the sixth century, translators and commentators designate the Roman corporations as Guilds as often as they do Colleges. See Gould, vi., p. 39.

GUILDS.

16. We cannot wonder that, at a period when artificers and artists of every class, from those of the most mechanical, to those of the most intellectual, nature, formed themselves into exclusive corporations of architects, which in conformity to the general style of such corporations, assumed that of Free and Accepted Masons, and was composed of those members who, after a regular passage through the different stages of apprenticeship, were received as masters and entitled to exercise their profession on their own account.

17. Those Italian corporations of builders, therefore, whose services ceased to be necessary in the countries where they had arisen, now began to look abroad toward those northern climes, for that employment which they no longer found at home; and a certain number united and formed themselves into a single greater association or fraternity, which proposed to seek occupation beyond its native land; and in any ruder foreign region, however remote, where new religious edifices and skilful artists to erect them, were wanted, to offer their services.

18. Whenever they came in the suite of missionaries, or were called by the natives, or arrived of their own accord to seek employment, they appeared headed by a chief surveyor, who governed the whole troop, and named one man out of every ten, under the name of warden, to overlook the nine others.

Even in England, as late as the reign of Henry VI., in an indenture of covenants made between the church wardens of a parish in Suffolk, and a company of Free Masons, the latter stipulated that every man shall be provided with a pair of white leather gloves and an apron; and that a Lodge, properly tiled, should be erected at the expense of the parish, in which to hold their meetings. See Hope on Architecture, pp. 229 to 238.

19. Hughan, one of England's noted historians, says: "Believing as we do that the present associations of Free Masonry are an outgrowth of the Building corporations and Guilds of

the Middle Ages, as also the lineal descendants and sole representatives of the early secret Masonic Sodalities, it appears to us that their ancient laws and charges are specially worthy of preservation, study, and reproduction."

20. In Germany, and in Germany alone, we have, among the archives of chapters, found actual working drawings of edifices erected, or to be erected, on such a scale, and so complete and minute, as to prove that on the spot, and among the local Lodges of Free Masons, existed as well the head that invented, as the hand that executed, those monuments.   Hope, p. 423.

CHAPTER VI.

GERMANY AND VICINITY.

The Romans Invade Germany but Meet with a Stubborn Resistance, which Gave the Colleges of Builders Plenty of Occupation in Constructing Bridges, Forts, and Entrenched Camps.—B.C. 10, they Cut a Canal through between the Rhine and Issel, and Opened a Passage to the Zuider Zee.—Fighting Step by Step, the Romans so far Establish Themselves in A.D. 100, that not only Markets but Towns had Sprung up in Various Places, and by A.D. 225 Manufactures, Temples, and Theatres were Becoming Numerous.—Salzburg, Ratisbon, Augsburg, Strasburg, Basle, Baden, Cologne, and other Noted Cities were Founded.—All under the Supervision of the Colleges, whose Achievements were so well Appreciated by the more Intelligent Natives that they Eagerly Sought Initiation into this Roman Society, and thus its Arts and Ethics were Perpetuated here under the name of Guilds.

HAVING sketched the operations of the Colleges of Constructors in Rome, and in the Roman armies, their advent into Germany, and the noted events pertaining to their stay in that country will now be given.

In the year 113 B.C. the Romans, who were guarding the passes into Italy, were confronted by a wild and unknown tribe from across the Danube.

Soon after this, they defeated the Romans near Norega, in the mountains. Carbo, who commanded the Romans here, had proved treacherous to them, for upon their request to remain on friendly terms with him, he had provided them with false guides, who misled them among the mountains, while he advanced by a shorter route and fell unexpectedly upon them. For this breach of faith they fought the Romans furiously, and would have utterly destroyed them had not a heavy storm intervened and assisted the latter in their flight.

Whence these hordes originally came no one knew. They called themselves Cimbri and Teutoni. It appears, however, that the Cimbri had for a considerable length of time been wandering about, and had already fought with many nations, and now, quitting the Danube, appeared upon the Roman frontiers. Whether they are to be considered as collective tribes intent upon migrating, or only as troops of warriors seeking adventures, or people who had formed themselves by degrees into one entire mass or nation by the junction of different tribes, and required a country wherein to settle, cannot be positively decided.

The Romans, who were contemplating the conquest of the whole earth, were astonished to now find themselves defeated by a horde whose name they scarcely knew; therefore, they quickly collected together another large army under the Consul Marcus Manlius, and sent it to the assistance of Scipio, whose legate, Scaurus, had been vanquished. But the envy and dissension that existed between the generals now paralyzed their action, which the Germans took advantage of, and gave them such a battle that eighty thousand Romans and their allies were left dead upon the field.

The Consul Marius, however, soon collected another large army and conducted it over the Alps to the river Rhodanus (the Rhone), and there formed a defensive camp, where he rested and drilled his troops for a short time. He then moved on to Aquæ Sextæ, the present Aix, in the south of France, where a multitude of the Germans were ready to dispute his further progress. Here a terrible battle ensued, which resulted in such a route of the Germans that the Romans killed and took prisoners more than one hundred thousand. Shortly after this battle, the Prince of the Teutoni, Teutobod, was taken prisoner in his flight across the mountains, and was subsequently forced to form in Rome the chief ornament in the triumphant train of Marius; and according to the account of the Romans, he was so tall that his figure rose above all the trophies. The arms and booty were burnt as a great sacrifice to the gods, excepting only what was preserved of the most costly and rare. This battle took place in the year 102 B.C., eleven years after the battle of Noreja.

Subsequently, Julius Cæsar appeared upon the scene and confronted Ariovistus, a vain German chief, who had invaded Gaul and gained some advantages. To Cæsar's request for an interview, Ariovistus returned an insolent reply, which soon resulted in a fierce and bloody battle, in which the Germans were defeated with great slaughter.

When the Germans were driven to flight, they hastened toward the Rhine. But the Roman cavalry overtook the greater part, and but few, among whom was Ariovistus, saved themselves by swimming or by traversing the river in small boats. His two wives were killed in the flight, and of his two daughters, one was slain and the other taken prisoner. Ariovistus himself was not again heard of.

Cæsar next began the subjection of the Gallic tribes, which he conquered one after the other, and kept constantly advancing to the lower Rhine. Intelligence then came to him that two German tribes had passed over that river to seek a new settlement in Gaul. He therefore determined to build a bridge across the Rhine and make the Germans feel in their own country the power of Rome. In ten days he constructed, with much ingenuity, below the place where the Moselle falls into the Rhine, a large wooden bridge, and crossed it with his army.

Cæsar's design was to attack the confederation of the Suevi; they, however, retreated with their wives and children far back into the interior of the forest, and there awaited the enemy. But Cæsar, finding that they had selected their ground with great prudence, did not consider it advisable to follow them thus far. He therefore halted only eighteen days on the right bank of the Rhine, devastated with fire and sword the vicinity of the siege, where the Siganbri then dwelt, and then returned across the river.

Later Cæsar again crossed the Rhine, and again the Germans retired to their forest strongholds, upon which he re-crossed the river as before; and after this he did not again pass into Germany, but endeavored to raise troops from among them to serve in his legions. This was easy to do among such a brave people, where there were always bold men ready to go forth for pay, booty, and the love of war. Cæsar was likewise a hero, who well understood how to win the hearts of his warriors; he always led them to victory. German subsidies helped him thenceforth to win his battles, and at Pharsalus, where he fought the last battle against Pompey, and where it was decided which of the two should rule the world, they afforded him important aid. Cæsar was assassinated 44 B.C.

The Romans also attacked those tribes which dwelt upon the sides of the Alps toward Germany—Tyrol—tribes partly of Gallic and partly of un-

St. Goar.
(For the subjects of illustrations see pages 240 and 241.)

known origin, who, being unable to defend themselves against their skilled enemies, were not only conquered, but many of them were sold as slaves.

This contest was concluded in the year 15 B.C. Henceforward the river Danube was, on the east side, the boundary between the Romans and the Germans. From the other side, however, the river Rhine was no longer to

ANCIENT ROMAN BRIDGE ACROSS THE DANUBE.

remain so, for Augustus sent his stepson, Claudius Drusus, a hero competent to accomplish great works, to attack the Germans in their own country.

In the years from 12 to 9 B.C. he warred with the Suevi, Usipeti, and other tribes, and passed on from the lower Rhine to the rivers Lippe and Ems, as far as the Elbe. But his invasion did not result in conquests. He, however, prepared the way for further operations, as he caused his *Colleges of Constructors* to build strong forts at the mouths of the rivers which emptied into the Rhine and the North Sea, thus enabling him to convey into the country a portion of his army with greater security upon a fleet of small vessels, and to transport their provisions conveniently after.

For this purpose he also commenced a canal and united the Rhine, between Doesberg and Isselort, with the Issel. By means of this canal the Rhine was brought into connection with the Zuider Zee, the Flevum Ostium * of the ancients; and the Romans, henceforth, by means of this outlet, were enabled to have communication with the North Sea from all their strongholds on the Rhine. Drusus also took this mode of uniting himself with the Friesi and of reaching the mouth of the Ems by sea, where he likewise built a fort, opposite to the present Emden. On the Rhine he built forts, and strongly fortified Bonn and Mentz, the last upon the border against the Suevi, and provided them with bridges and flotillas for their defence. Also upon the Taunus Mountains, near the present Hamburg, he built a fort as a defence against the Chatti.

In his last campaign, Drusus advanced from his fort on the Taunus Mountains into the land of the Chatti, beat them, as well as the Marcomanni, under Marbodius, and forced the latter to retreat further eastward; but although he was victorious, he lost his life; for on his return he fell from his horse, and died a few weeks afterward from his injuries.

Tiberius, his brother, succeeded him in the command. He was of an artful and deceptive disposition; and besides arms, he employed finesse against his enemies; and by the aid of the strong forts placed on the Rhine and its affluents, and of the frontier walls which inclosed the occupied country, the northwestern portions of Germany, nearly as far as the Weser, appeared to be already subdued—a Roman province.

* History of Germany by Kohlrausch, p. 51.

Since the invasion of the German country a multitude of its youths had arrived at Rome; some as hostages, some as prisoners, and many were in the Roman service. These became acquainted with Roman military affairs, their art of government, and their craft, civil and military.

This, and the campaigns and forts of Drusus, and the cunningly devised

TRIENT—TRENT.

arts of Tiberius, had not only rendered the intercourse between the Romans and Germans extensive, but so intimate as to effect a great change in the National manners and customs of the latter. Under the supervision of the Colleges of builders, bridges and dikes were built across the morasses; towns with markets sprang up around the Roman camps, which enticed the Germans to purchase and barter. The Roman Governor, Sentius Saturninus, who was in Germany in the year 6 A.D., contributed much to these changes, as he was a man who united honesty with affability; and as many of the Germans worked under the Colleges in their military and civil works, it came to pass that many of the more intelligent were received into their ranks.

Yet, notwithstanding the submission and conformity of the Germans to Roman laws and customs, the love of liberty was as strong as ever with them, and only needed a competent leader to precipitate a revolt.

Among the German youths who had resided in Rome was Arminius (by some called Hermann), the son of Segimer, Prince of the Cherusci, who, by distinguished military service, had acquired the right and dignity of a Roman citizen and knight, and had returned to his country well instructed and practised in all the arts of war. With these advantages and a determination to free his country from the Roman domination, he soon managed to gain the confidence of his countrymen, and become their leader. He first, from the disaffected tribes, got together a large army, which he concentrated in the depths of the Teutoburger forest, in the present principality of Lippe-Detmold.

Around his position on all sides were mountains and narrow valleys, with nowhere a beaten path visible—nothing but a thickly-grown and impenetrable wood.

Into this trap the Romans under Varus, who was now in command, were tempted to advance. It was in the stormy autumn season—heavy rains had made the ground slippery and every step unsafe, while the tempest above roared. Warriors, beasts of burden, loaded with baggage and ammunition, all pressed heedlessly on as in perfect security. But suddenly, from out of the thickets on all sides, the German hordes charged upon them, and by dint of numbers and desperate fighting, succeeded after a two days battle, in nearly annihilating the Roman army.

Upon receipt of this terrible news, Tiberius was hastily despatched to the Rhine with a rapidly collected army. But to his astonishment, he found everything quiet; and not being disposed to penetrate the country far in quest of an enemy, nothing was accomplished. In a short time afterward he succeeded Augustus in the Empire, and transferred to his nephew, Germanicus, the son of Drusus, the management of the war against the Germans.

Germanicus, having in mind the great example of his father, resolved to revenge the defeat of Varus; therefore, he made such preparations as insured his success. He collected a large fleet of vessels, with deep and broad holds, and smaller ones with flat bottoms for landing. Everything being ready, he embarked his army of not less than ninety thousand men, and passing through the Fossa Drusiana into the North Sea, landed at the mouth of the Ems. Here the Chauci were obliged to supply an auxiliary army, and the Angrivari were forced into subjection on the lower Weser. The Romans then advanced and took a position between the present Minden and Vlotho. Here they were attacked by Arminius, at the head of the Germans, and a battle ensued; but after a long and fierce contest the Germans were defeated.

Of the subsequent fate of Arminius, Tacitus relates that he was murdered in the year 21, in the thirty-seventh year of his age.

Although the Romans were successful in the last campaign, they thought no more of subduing Germany, but applied themselves solely to securing their frontiers against the incursions of the German tribes and Eastern hordes. As a stroke of policy, the Emperor Claudius granted to the chief seat of the Ubi, the distinction of a colony of his retired veterans; and later, in honor of his consort, Agrippina, born on that spot, it was called Colonia Agrippina (*Cologne*).

The allied tribes were now frequently overrunning the Roman territory, but were temporarily checked by Marcus Aurelius, who however, died from his exertions during the campaign at Windobona (the present Vienna), in the year 180.

A.D. 225.—At this time the Germans had become acquainted with money and many luxuries. The Romans had planted the vine on the Rhine, and constructed roads, cities, manufactories, theatres, fortresses, temples, and altars. Roman merchants brought their wares to Germany, and carried back amber, feathers, furs, slaves, and the very hair of the Germans; for it was now the fashion in Rome to wear light flaxen wigs instead of the natural hair.

From the foregoing sketch of history, it will be seen that the long intercourse between the Germans and Romans had, as a consequence, resulted in thoroughly familiarizing the former with the essentials of Roman civilization—especially the arts and ethics of the Colleges, as many of the more intelligent natives had joined the latter after having assisted them in their works. The operations of the Colleges included the founding of the following cities—viz., Salzburg, Ratisbon, Augsburg, Basle, Strasburg, Baden, Spires, Worms,

OBERWESEL.—OCHSENTHRUM.

Mentz, Treves, Cologne, and Bonn. Remains of their military works are also still to be seen.

The time was, however, near at hand when the Roman sway would terminate in Germany, for the Germans from the west, and the Goths from the banks of the Vistula and the Black Sea, were pressing the Romans east and west. The Emperor Valens, in an attempt to stay the progress of the Goths under Fridigern, was defeated, and taking refuge in a hut was discovered, and the hut burnt over his head. This occurred in 378.

The Emperor Theodosius contrived to weaken the Goths by divisions, and made Fridigern's successor, Athanaric, conclude a peace.

Theodosius died in the year 395, and his two sons, Honorius and Arcadius, divided the Empire between them. Arcadius took his seat at Constantinople, and Honorius in Italy. The first division was called the Eastern, and the second the Western, Empire. Soon after this, Alaric the Goth advanced against Italy, against Rome itself; and in this once proud metropolis the terror of the people amounted to a panic. For since six hundred years they had seen no enemy before their city, nor during eight hundred years had they beheld an enemy within their walls; hence the title, the "Eternal City." When the Romans fully realized their great peril, they promised to comply with the demands of Alaric, which were five thousand pounds of gold and thirty thousand of silver, besides a multiplicity of rare and costly articles. To meet this demand they were obliged to have recourse to the ornaments and decorations of the ancient temples; and it is said that, among the statues of their divinities, that of Valor was also melted down.

Notwithstanding this great sacrifice and humiliation, Alaric marched on Rome the second time and took it by storm. This took place on the 23d of August, in the year 410. The Goths plundered the palace, and houses of the nobles; but they so far moderated their ire, that they did not burn the city.

Following this were the ravages of Attila the Hun; but singularly enough, the crowning catastrophe was to come from Africa—Carthage—as Genseric the Vandal king came over, overthrew and devastated Rome in 455.

Passing over the intervening general history, we arrive at a period when Christianity began to exercise a decided influence on the affairs of nations, and give a different turn to civilization, the arts, and sciences.

Winifred, who afterward received the title of Bonifacius (the Beneficent), was one of the first who rendered the new status conspicuous in Germany. He labored from the year 718 to 755, with inexhaustible courage, for Christianity in Franconia, Thuringia, on the Rhine, and among the Saxons and Friesi. He also possessed a knowledge of architecture, which enabled him to collect the communities into villages, and thus lay the foundations of new towns.

As many of the Germans had received their first knowledge of the Masonic art from their intercourse with the Romans and their Colleges of Builders, they were prepared to co-operate with him in his laudable designs. To facilitate his operations he divided his force into two classes, "Magistri Operum," or Masters, and Operui, or Craftsmen. In addition to these, laymen were employed, under the supervision of the Magistri, and as there were many men of intelligence among them they gradually became possessed of the skill and esoteric principles of their masters, so that ultimately they became strong enough to separate themselves from the ecclesiastical fraternities, and not only form organizations of their own, but monopolize the construction of important edifices throughout the country.

OLD GATE HOUSE, HILDESHEIM.
(For subjects of illustrations see pages 240 and 241.)

Charlemagne (768–814) also paid great attention to architecture and

GERMANY AND VICINITY.

agriculture in his dominions, which was soon imitated by the Ecclesiastics, who, with axe and fire vigorously attacked the gloomy forests, and opened up to cultivation vast areas of forest lands; and in connection with companies of *Craftsmen*, commenced to erect church edifices and other buildings upon the cleared ground. Previous to the time of Charlemagne, houses were mostly constructed of wood—stone was seldom used, and tile was rare. The wooden cabins contained but one room, from the middle of which arose a single post, which furnished a support for the roof. But under Charlemagne stone dwellings as well as public edifices of stone were introduced. The celebrated palaces of the Emperor at Aachen, Ingelheim, and the residences of the nobility, were built of stone. As an illustration of the style of the day, one of the Emperor's dwellings contained eleven work-rooms, three sleeping apartments, and two for storage.

950. From this time forth wooden structures were torn down, and in every direction arose new buildings, larger and more elegant than those that preceded them. A.D. 1001 the Church of St. Benigne and the rotunda at Dijon were constructed. From 1005 to 1020 there were erected at Rheims, Tours, Cambrai, Orléans, Limoges, and in other towns in France, numerous cathedrals and other edifices, affording employment to a large array of craftsmen. Clugny Abbey still possesses a curious structure which dates back to the year 1088.

The Cathedral at Amiens was completed in 1288. Sainte Chapelle was built in 1248, and Notre Dame, of Paris, was finished in 1275. The Cathedral at Worms was also completed in the thirteenth century.*

LOMBARDY.

Although the building fraternities were found located in that part of Cisalpine Gaul afterward known as Venice and Lombardy, as early as 288 B.C., yet it was not until several centuries later that their history here became conspicuous.

In the spring of 568 King Alboni broke up from Hungary with all his Longobardian men, their women and children, accompanied by twenty thousand

---

* Fort, pp. 38–71.

Saxons, and leaving the country to their allies, the Avari, they set out to locate themselves in a land more fruitful, and under skies more genial. It was a beautiful morning, when from the heights of one of the mountains of the Alps, afterward called the King's Mountain, the astonished strangers cast their eyes down upon what was for the future to be their country.

The conquest of Pavia, at the confluence of the Ticino and the Po, soon followed, and Alboni's dominion in Upper Italy was established. Subsequently he made Pavia the chief city of those districts. In Lower Italy, also, this people conquered beautiful tracts of land and founded the principality of Benevento, which comprises the greater portion of the present kingdom of Naples; and it was only by the intervention of the Franks that the Longobardi were prevented from taking possession of the whole of Italy.*

The Longobardi being ignorant of the builder's art, had recourse to the *Roman Colleges*, and *Byzantine workmen*. Numerous structures were erected in Northern Italy by them, including a church dedicated to St. John the Baptist, near Milan, in which the celebrated iron crown was preserved.

After the fall of the Roman Empire, Lombardy became a centre of trade, art, and architectural science, and from thence went forth Colleges or Guilds of Masons into the northern and western parts of Europe. This also contributed to the origin of the German Guilds of the Mediæval Ages.†

King Rotharis of Lombardy promulgated an edict, which expressly mentions the Colleges of Builders, and their Masters as Magistri.

In A.D. 1054 a large number of the craft united in Lombardy for the purpose of reviving the operations of the Colleges, and their design was seconded by the Church, the Abbots, and Prelates, many of whom esteemed it an honor to become members of the Fraternity and participate in their secrets.

Lombardy long maintained its pre-eminence as an active centre of the arts, wherever fragments of the Colleges of Builders were located, they having survived the ordeal of many wars, and fully maintained their old organization; but they now passed under the name of Free Corporations—*Guilds*.

* History of Germany, by Kohlrausch, p. 81.
† Mackey's Cyclopædia, p. 823; Rebold, pp. 50, 73, 297.

CATHEDRAL AT WORMS.

STRASBURG.

The original Cathedral of Strasburg was founded in 504, but in 1007 it was struck by lightning and nearly destroyed. The present edifice was commenced in 1015. Its spire is four hundred and sixty-six feet high, being one of the highest in the world. The nave and the western front is the glory and boast of this edifice, and possesses, in a remarkable degree, all the beauties of the German style. The details are pure and beautiful, and the design is of peculiar boldness. Altogether, this is one of the finest Gothic edifices in Europe.

The Cathedral at Ratisbon, although much smaller, is another beautiful specimen of German art. It was commenced in the year 1275.

It was at the Masonic Congress at Strasburg, in 1275, under Erwin of Steinbach, that the German fraternity, in imitation of their English brethren, assumed the name of *Freemasons* and established a system of regulations for the government of the craft.

OLD DOCUMENTS.

As the internal workings of the Masonic Institution during the Mediæval Ages will be best seen from the old manuscripts and documents that have been preserved and brought to light, the most important of those belonging to Germany, France, and England will be presented in connection with the Masonic history of those countries.

THE STRASBURG CONSTITUTIONS.*

Item: No craftsman or master shall be received in the Fraternity who goes not yearly to the Holy Communion, or who keeps not Christian discipline, or who squanders his substance at play; but should anyone be inadvertently accepted into the Fraternity who does these things as aforesaid, then shall no master nor fellow keep fellowship with him until he desists therefrom, and has been punished therefor by those of the Fraternity.

* Unimportant portions are omitted.

No craftsman nor master shall live in adultery while engaged in masonry; but if such a one will not desist therefrom, then shall no travelling fellow nor Mason work in company with him, nor keep fellowship with him.

If a master have a complaint against another master for having violated the regulations of the craft, or a master against a fellow, or a fellow against another fellow, any master or fellow who is concerned therein shall give notice thereof to the master who presides over the Fraternity, and the master who is informed thereof shall hear both parties, and set a day when he will try the cause; and meanwhile, before the fixed or appointed day, no fellow shall avoid the master, nor master drive away the fellow, but render services mutually until the hour when the matter is to be heard and settled. This shall all be done according to the judgment of the craftsmen, which shall be observed accordingly. Moreover, the case shall be tried on the spot where it arose, before the nearest master who keeps the Book of Statutes, and in whose district it occurred.

Item: Every Parlirer * shall honor his master, be true and faithful to him according to the rule of Masonry, and obey him with undivided fidelity, as is meet and of ancient usage. So also shall a fellow.

And when a travelling fellow-craft desires to travel further, he shall part from his master and from the Lodge in such wise as to be indebted to no one, and that no man have any grievance against him, as is meet and proper.

A travelling fellow, in whatever Lodge he may be employed, shall be obedient to his master and to the parlirer, according to the rule and ancient usage of Masonry, and shall also keep all the regulations and privileges which are of ancient usage in the said Lodge.

If a complaint be made involving a greater punishment, as, for instance, expulsion from Masonry, the same shall not be tried or judged by one master in his district, but the two nearest masters who are intrusted with the copies of the Statutes, and who have authority over the Fraternity, shall be summoned by him, so that there may be three. The fellows also who were at work at the place where the grievance arose shall be summoned also, and whatsoever shall be with one accord agreed upon by those three, together with all the fellows, or by a majority thereof, in accordance with their oath

---

* Parlirer (orator, speaker) held an intermediate position between the fellow and the master.

Mayence—Mentz.

and best judgment, shall be observed by the whole Fraternity of craftsmen.

Item: If two or more masters who are of the Fraternity be at variance or discord about matters which do not concern Masonry, they shall not settle these matters anywhere but before Masonry, which shall judge and reconcile them as far as possible.

If a mason or fellow fall sick, or a fellow who is of the Fraternity, and has lived uprightly in Masonry, be afflicted with protracted illness and want for food and necessary money, then shall the master who has charge of the box lend him relief and assistance.

The Statutes of the Parlirers and Fellows.

No craftsman or master shall set at work a fellow who commits adultery, or who openly lives in illicit intercourse with women, or who does not yearly make confession, and goes not to the Holy Communion, according to Christian discipline, nor one who is so foolish as to lose his clothing at play.

Item: If any fellow should wantonly take leave of a Grand Lodge or from another Lodge, he shall not ask for employment in the said Lodge for a year to come.

The Apprentices.

No craftsman nor master shall knowingly accept as an apprentice one who is not of lawful birth, and shall earnestly inquire thereof before he accepts him, and shall question such apprentice on his word, whether his father and mother were duly united in lawful wedlock.

Although by Christian discipline every Christian is bound to provide for his own salvation, yet it must be duly remembered by the masters and craftsmen.*

THE BROTHER BOOK.†

The Ordinances and Articles of the Fraternity of Masons, renewed at the Chief Lodge at Strasburg on St. Michael's Day MDLXIII.

* Steinbrenner, pp. 84 to 95. † Gould, vol. i., p. 119.

The First Article.

That if any article in this book be too hard or heavy, or any be too light, then may those who are of our Guild, being in a majority, alter, lessen, or increase such articles, according to the times, the necessities of the land, and the course of affairs.

And when there is a general summons they shall meet together in chapter form, according to the contents of this book, and their resolutions shall be kept on the oath which each one has taken. . . .

Whoso comes into this Guild of his own good will, as hereafter stands written in this book, he shall promise to keep every point and article if he be of our craft of Masonry. . . And be it masters or fellows, they shall and must conduct themselves honorably, and none shall be wronged by them; therefore have we taken power in these Ordinances to punish them on the occasion of every such act.

Whoever it be, either master or fellow, who shall oust from his work another master who is of this Guild of craftsmen, or shall apply for the work that he possesses, be it large or small, the same shall be brought to task, and no master or fellow shall have any communion with him. And no fellow who is of this Guild shall enter into his employ so long as he possesses the work which he has dishonorably obtained; nor until he shall have made restitution and given satisfaction to him who was thus dispossessed of the work; and also until he shall have been punished by the masters, who are enjoined to do so by the Guild.

And no craftsman or master shall take money from a fellow for showing or teaching him anything touching Masonry.

No craftsman or master shall be received into the Guild who goes not yearly to the Holy Sacrament, or keeps not Christian discipline, and squanders his substance in play. But should anyone be inadvertently accepted into the Guild who does these things as aforesaid, no master shall keep company with him; nor shall any fellow stand by him until he shall have ceased to do so, and been punished by those of this Guild.

If a fellow takes work of a master who has not been advanced in this

THE OLD CASTLE AT SALZBURG.

Guild of craftsmen, he shall not be punished therefor; but nevertheless, the fellow shall keep the Ordinances as hereinbefore and hereafter written. And what it behooves him to give to the Guild, that shall be done by him. . . .

But if a fellow would take unto himself a lawful wife, and not being employed in a Lodge, would establish himself in a city, he shall on every Ember week pay four pennies, as long as he shall not be employed in one of the Lodges.

It is also further decided, as regards the driving away : If it happen that anything be reported of a master or fellow, a matter of hearsay, repeated from one to the other, so long as it is not certain ; and if the aforesaid is not righteously convicted thereof, he shall be avoided or driven away by no one, but pursue his work until such time as it shall be really brought home to him, and he be righteously convicted.

It is also decided, that where a matter begins and takes its rise, there it shall be settled, or in the nearest Lodge where a book lies. And neither party shall appeal until plaint and answer take place and are heard, nor carry the matter further than aforesaid, unless it be rejected there.

All those, be they masters or fellows, who are of this Guild, shall hold in obedience all points and articles as stand both before and hereafter written. But if anyone should perchance break one of the points and become punishable, and if afterward he be obedient to the regulations by sufficing to that which has been ordered as amends, he shall have done sufficient, and be released from his vow as regards the article wherefore he has been punished.

CONCERNING THE PUNISHMENTS THAT MAY ENTAIL EXPULSION FROM THE CRAFT.

If a complaint be laid before a master, such as would entail the greater punishment ; for instance, if anyone is to be forbidden the craft, that shall the master of a district not hear or judge of alone, but call to his aid the two nearest masters, who also possess a book and power according to these ordinances ; that there may be three of them, and also the fellows that are in the employ where the complaint arose ; and that which these three, together with the fellows, unanimously or by a majority, shall then decide on their oath and to the best of their judgment, that shall hereafter be maintained by the whole body of craftsmen.

When Quarrels Arise, not Concerning Masonry.

Should it be that two or more masters who are of this Guild be at variance or discord about matters which do not concern Masonry, they shall not, on account of this difference, summon one another anywhere but before the craft and brotherhood; and they shall judge and reconcile them to the best of their ability.

All masters and craftsmen who are of this Guild, and have Lodge employment, shall each possess a box, and every fellow shall pay thereto every week one penny, and every master shall faithfully collect such money and whatever else may be due, and annually account for it to the Guild where the nearest book lies, that the poor may be relieved, and the necessities of our Guild provided for.

Should it be that a master or fellow be put to expense, or defray anything on account of the Guild, and notice be given how the same occurred, such expense, be it large or small, shall be returned to such master or fellow out of the Guild box. And also, if anyone come to grief with justice or other things touching this Guild, then shall everyone, be he the master or fellow, be helpful to the other, and lend him assistance on his oath to the Guild. Nevertheless, no one shall, of his own accord, without advice of other masters and fellows, put the Brotherhood to any expense.

A travelling fellow, in whatever Lodge he may be employed, shall be obedient to his master and warden, according to the rule and ancient usages of Masonry, and shall also keep all the regulations and privileges which are of ancient usage in the said Lodge.

And a fellow shall not revile his master's work, either secretly or openly. . . .

No master or craftsman shall employ any fellow who consorts with a woman in adultery, or who openly lives a dishonorable life with women, or who goes not to the Holy Communion according to Christian discipline, or one who is so foolish as to game away his clothing. Should it be that a craftsman or work-master have a travelling fellow in his employment, and wish to discharge him, he shall not discharge him except of a Saturday or pay evening, that he may know how to travel on the morrow, unless he have

Rostock.

given cause of offence. The same shall also be done by a fellow, if he demand his discharge.

Likewise the fellow shall, in the future, make no more mutinies or conspiracies to leave any employ collectively. But should a master behave otherwise than right in any case, he shall be summoned before the craft, and submit to its judgment. . . .

No fellow shall go out from the Lodge without leave; or if he go to his broth or any other meal, not remain out without leave; nor shall any make Holy Monday. If anyone do so, he shall stand to punishment by the master and fellows, and the master shall have power to discharge him in the week when he will.

In the first place, every apprentice, when he has served his time and is declared free, shall promise the craft, on his truth and honor, in lieu of oath, that he will disclose or communicate the mason's greeting and *grip* to no one, except to him to whom he may justly communicate it, and also that he will write nothing thereof.

And no one shall alter, of his own will and power, his mark which has been granted and lent him by a craft; but if he will ever desire to alter it, he shall only do it with the knowledge, will, and approval of a whole craft.

THE TORGAU ORDINANCES, 1462.*

Concerning the worshipful Masters of Stone-masons of the Craft, the Wardens, and the Fellows.

All Articles and Statutes, as they are written in the Book; how each and every one in his conduct and station in the craft shall demean himself, both here in Zwickau and elsewhere, in all lands as in the Book, so stands hereafter written, each article separately. . . . And all these articles have been drawn up from the letter of the ancient Lodge rites, that were instituted by the holy crowned martyrs, to the honor and praise of the Holy Trinity and Mary Queen of Heaven.†

* Gould, vol. i., p. 134.
† Valuable facts are disclosed in these statutes, concerning the general government and practices which then prevailed within the Lodge, that we do not get from the Strasburg constitutions or Brother Book.

1. Therefore have we made divers rules and statutes with the help of God.

. . . .

And for God's service shall every master of a work, be it great or small, give on each fast of our lady one old goat.

And every fellow shall give every week to the box one penny for God's service.

And every one shall keep his time according to the ancient traditionary usages of the land; if he do that he is free, and even if he do it not with council, according to the usages of the land and the craft.

And every master shall be upright in all things. He shall incite neither warden, nor fellow, nor apprentice to evil, nor to ought whence harm may arise.

And every master shall keep his Lodge free from all strife, yea, his Lodge shall he keep pure as the seat of justice.

Therefore shall no master allow a harlot to enter his Lodge; but if any one have ought to commune with her, he shall depart from the place of labor so far as any one may cast a gavel.

If other masters learn thereof, they shall fine him for each offence in five pounds of wax.

A master shall appoint his warden, master and warden being both present; and he shall appoint no warden unless he be able thereto, so that the craftsmen and he be supplied. . . .

When a master has set a warden, the fellows shall swear to be obedient unto him as a master, and the warden shall pledge master and fellows.

And the master has power, if he so will, to rest in the Lodge at vesper tide.

And if any fellow shall make a journey for the Guild in that concerns the craft his expenses also shall be paid him out of the box.

And if a master or fellow come free of the craft or trade, and demand a mark of a work-master, to him shall he grant his wishes, and he shall give for the service of God that which shall be adjudged of masters and fellows. And to masters and fellows shall he pledge the mark doubly.

No master shall withhold his mark from his apprentice for a further space than xiiij days, unless it be that the apprentice has wasted his master's time; he shall then first do his behest before that and the feast.

And no master shall show any reluctance to pledge his apprentice's mark, and the several clericals whom he may bid thereto, with a penny wheaten bread of xv. gr., a loaf of xv. gr., meat, and two stoups of wine; and the apprentice shall not bid more than x. fellows; and if he bid more, then shall he buy more, that the master suffers not thereby.

The master shall knock with three blows, the warden with two consecutively, and one for announcements at morning, noon, and eve, as is the old usage of the land.

The master may appoint an apprentice who serves for knowledge to the office of warden, if he be able to maintain it.

The master may lend his apprentice a mark to travel with during his apprenticeship, if the master have no employment, and must let him travel.

No master shall allow his apprentice to pledge his mark, unless he have served his time.

No master shall lay snares for another and entice away his apprentice, so reads the letter.

No master shall employ any one who has brought himself to shame or dishonor, either by word or deed; he is worse than a hound; him shall the master set down as void of honor, likewise also the fellows.

And a master may hold a General Court in his Lodge over his own fellows, and he shall judge righteously by his oath, and not of hatred, or of friendship, or of enmity.

And furthermore, no master shall judge alone of that which touches honor or good repute; but there shall be together three masters who shall then judge such matters.

And he shall every quarter-day hold a hearing of lords and craftsmen, whether any offence were, whether they have wasted time, lived riotously, gamed, or otherwise acted disorderly, whence harm might come to wardens or master; that they shall make known to the master, that he may punish therefor as is meet.

Every warden shall preserve his Lodge, and all that he has shown to, and all that is entrusted to him.

And if any fellow be in need on account of sickness, and have not wherewithal to live because he lieth sick, he shall be assisted from the box, and if he recover he shall pay it.

And if any fellow shall make a journey for the Guild, in that, that concerns the craft, his expenses shall also be paid him out of the box.

THE CHARTER OF COLOGNE.*

It is claimed that in 1535, a general assembly of representatives of the progressive Lodges was convened at Cologne, under the direction of Herman, Bishop of that city, and there prepared and adopted the Charter of Cologne.

From the Charter.

" We, the Elect Masters of the venerable Society sacred to John, or of the Social Order of Freemasons, rulers of the Lodges or tabernacles constituted at London, Edinburgh, Vienna, Amsterdam, Paris, Lyons, Frankfort, Hamburg, Antwerp, Rotterdam, Madrid, Venice, Ghent, Konigsberg, Brussels, Dantzic, Middleburg, Bremen, and in the City of Cologne, in the year, month, and day after mentioned.

" Our President being the Master of the Lodge established in this city—a venerable brother and most learned, prudent, and judicious man, called to preside over these deliberations, by our unanimous vote—do, by these letters, addressed to all the above-mentioned Lodges—to our brethren present and future—declare, that forasmuch as we have been considering the designs which, in these calamitous times, embroiled by civil dissensions and discord, have been imputed to our aforesaid Society, and to all the brethren belonging to this Order of Freemasons, or of John, opinions, machinations, secret as well as openly detected; all of which are utterly foreign to us, and to the spirit, design, and precepts of the Association.

. . . .

" Therefore, having all these considerations in view, it hath seemed to us expedient, and even absolutely necessary, to expound the true state and origin of our Order, and to what it tends, as an institution of charity itself, and

* See Gould, vol. ii., p. 496.

NUREMBERG.

to give forth to the Lodges or conclaves of our Society the principles thus expounded.

. . . .

"For these causes, by these universal letters, compiled according to the context of the most ancient monuments which are extant, concerning the objects of the institution, the rights, and customs of our most ancient and our most secret Order, we, Elect Masters, influenced by the most solemn sanctions, adjure all fellow-laborers, to whom these presents now or in time hereafter may come, that they withdraw not themselves from the truth contained in this document. Moreover, to the enlightened as well as to the darker world, whose common safety concerns and strongly interests us, we announce and proclaim:

"**A.** That the Society of Freemasons, or order of brethren attached to the solemnities of St. John, , . . . are *more ancient* than any Order of Knights, . . . and existed in Palestine and Greece, as well as in every part of the Roman Empire, long before the Holy Wars and the times of the expeditions of the above-mentioned Knights into Palestine.

. . . .

"**B.** That our Association now, as formerly, consists of the three degrees of Disciple, Fellow, and Master—the last, or Master, admitting of Elect Masters and Superior Elect Masters.

. . . .

"**C.** That among the Doctors, Masters of this Order, cultivating the sciences of mathematics, astronomy, and other studies, a mutual interchange of doctrine and light was maintained, which led to the practice of electing, out of those who were already Elect Masters, one in particular, who, as excelling the rest, should be venerated as Supreme Elect Master or Patriarch.

. . . .

"**D.** The government of our Society, the mode and rule according to which the rays of the flaming light be imparted and diffused among the illuminated brethren, as well as the profane world, rest entirely with the highest Elect Masters.

. . . .

"**E.** To us it is by no means clear that this association of brethren, prior to the year 1440 were known by any other denomination than that of Brethren of John. But at that time, we are informed, the Fraternity, especially in Valence and in Flanders, began to be called by the name of Freemasons.

"F. Although, in works of benevolence, we pay no regard to religion or country, we, however, consider it safe and necessary, hitherto, to receive none into our Order but those who, in the society of the profane and unenlightened are professedly Christians.

. . . . . .

"G. To those duties which are commanded and undertaken by a solemn oath, are added those of fidelity and obedience to the secular rulers lawfully placed over us.

"H. The principles on which we act, and all these, our efforts, to whatever purpose and direction they may tend, are expressed in these two precepts: 'Love and regard to all men as brethren and relations; render to God what is God's, and to Cæsar what is Cæsar's.'

"I. The secrets and mysteries which veil our undertakings conduce to this end; that without ostentation we may do good, and without disunion of action, prosecute our designs to the uttermost.

"K. We celebrate, annually, the memory of St. John, the forerunner of Christ and patron of our community.

"L. These, and the rest of the corresponding ceremonies of the Institution, though represented in the meetings of the brethren by signs, or speech, or otherwise, do, nevertheless, differ totally from the rites of the churches.

"M. He is considered a brother of the Johannite Society, or Freemason, who, in a lawful manner, by the help and under the direction of some Elect Master, with the assistance of at least seven brethren, is initiated into our Mysteries, and who is ready to prove his adoption by the signs and tokens which are used by other brethren, but in which signs and words are included those which are in use in the Edinburgh Lodge, or Tabernacle, and its affiliated Lodges, as also in the Hamburg, Rotterdam, and Middleburg Tabernacles, and in that which is found erected at Venice.

. . . .

"N. Nothing is more necessary than a certain conformity among all those who are dispersed throughout the world, as members of one aggregate body;

wherefore these present letters, testifying the nature and spirit of our Society, shall be sent to all and sundry Colleges of the order existing.

. . . .

   Signed, " Hermanus, A. Nobel,
        Carlton,   Ignatius de la Torre,
        Jo. Bruce,   Doria,
        Fr. Von Upna, Jacob Uttinhove,
        Cornelius Banning, Falk,
        Colligni,   Nicholas Van Noot,
        Virieux,   Phillipus-Melancthon,
        Johannis Schroeder, Huyssen,
        Hofmann,   Wormer Abel,
          Jacobus Prepostius."

Concerning the authenticity of the Charter of Cologne we have the following:

There was between 1519 and 1601, in the city of Amsterdam, Holland, a Lodge whose name was Het Vredendall, or the Valley of Peace.

In the latter year Romanish fanaticism caused this Lodge to be closed; but in 1637 it was revived under the name of Frederick's Valley of Peace. In this lodge-room, at the time of its restoration, there was found a *chest, bound with brass, secured with three locks and three seals*, which, according to a protocol, published on the 29th of January, 1637, contained the following documents:

1. The original warrant of constitution of the Lodge, Het Vredendall.
2. A roll of all the members of the Lodge, from 1519 to 1601.
3. The original charter, given to the Brotherhood at the City of Cologne, of which the document here presented is a translation.

In 1821, Dr. Krause published it in his celebrated work, " The Three Oldest Masonic Documents."

A Dutch writer, P. J. Schouten, who had seen the original document, describes it as being written on parchment, in Masonic cypher, in the Latin language, the characters uninjured by time, and the names signed, not in cypher, but in the ordinary character. The Latin is that of the Middle Ages.

The learned antiquaries of the University of Leyden testified that the paper on which the register of this Lodge was written is of the same kind that was used in Holland at the beginning of the sixteenth century, the time of its date, and that the characters of which it is composed are of the same period. This register refers to the Charter of Cologne, as existing at that time; so that, if the learned men of Leyden were correct, the Charter must be nearly three centuries old.

Hermann V., Bishop of Cologne, whose name as Hermanus heads the list of the subscribers to the Charter, was afterward censured by the Church for having presided over this assembly.

The Charter asserts that there were many irregular Masons and false systems in 1535, and that true Masonry was only to be found in nineteen Lodges represented at Cologne, showing that that society had detached itself from the general body of Masons.

The Official Register of the Grand Lodge of Scotland, published at the end of its "Laws and Constitution" (edition 1852, p. 60), states that the "Lodge of Edinburgh, No. 1," was instituted in 1518, seventeen years before the promulgation of the Charter of Cologne.

There has also recently been discovered a transcript in French of the *minutes* of a Lodge at La Haye, from the date of its Constitution, January 29, 1637, during its entire first year. This Lodge, moreover, is declared to be a *continuation* of a *still older* Lodge at *Amsterdam*, a list of whose members existed, extending from 1519 down to 1601, when the Lodge lapsed into slumber by reason of popular troubles and prosecution of a war.

More singular still, the Lodge at La Haye worked four degrees: Apprentice, Companion, Master, and Master Elect, into which degree it appears that His Highness Frederick Henry, Stadtholder of the Netherlands, had been initiated previous to 1637.

Also see Mackey in *American Masonic Review* for 1859, pp. 51 to 61, and authorities there quoted. Also, *Masonic Chronicle*, February, 1890, pp. 70 to 74.

TRAVELLING CRAFTSMEN.—THEIR DRESS, ETC.

In the Mediæval Ages the Craft often travelled in search of employment; and during these journeys they were usually under the lead of an experienced architect. As they were always well armed and travelled in companies, they had little to fear from the marauding bands who infested the highways. In the centre of the companies was a pack-horse who carried their tools and provisions, which was under the care of the Oblati.*

Craftsmen of that period were clad in a singular costume, consisting of a short tunic of woollen material, black or gray, open at the side, a gorget with a cowl or hood attached, and a leather girdle from which was suspended a short, heavy sword, and a small leather sack or satchel.

Over the tunic they wore a black scapulary, which, while at labor, they tucked beneath their girdles; but when employed in religious exercises or on festival days it was allowed to hang loosely over their garments. The Oblati wore clothes in like manner, with the exception of the Moxetta and Scapulary. In summer they wore tunics of linen, and in winter of woollen. They wore a broad felt or straw hat, tight-fitting leather breeches, and long boots. These costumes were retained unchanged in form for several centuries.†

The Fraternity, from the nature of their art, were continually brought into contact with all classes and conditions of people, and were therefore far ahead of their contemporaries in general knowledge and education.

Indications of their opposition to the prevailing corruption of the Church exists to this day in many of the ancient edifices erected by their hands. In the Church of St. Sebaldus, at Nuremberg, is a carving in stone representing a nun in the embrace of a monk. In one of the upper corridors of the Strasburg Cathedral there is a sculptured representation of a religious procession. First comes a bear, carrying a cross; next follows a hog and a goat, bearing a case with religious reliques, in which is a sleeping fox.

In the Church of Doberan, Mecklenburg, is an altar-piece still in a good

---

* They were youths who waited on the Masons, fetched wood, water, stone, and tended the sick in the hospital.
† Steinbrenner, p. 69.

state of preservation, which exhibits in the foreground several priests turning a mill, in which the dogmas of the Church are being ground out.*

NOTED CITIES IN GERMANY.

Work of the Old Craftsmen.

ST. GOAR.

1. This is one of the oldest towns in Germany. It claims to be older than Rome, but it was doubtless first built by the Romans.

WORMS.

2. This city was founded by the Romans, and was by them called Borbetomagus. It was plundered by the Alemanni in 354 A.D., and by Attila in 451. It was rebuilt by Clovis in 475, and in 806 Charlemagne resided here.

The most striking feature of this old city is its cathedral. It was founded in the eighth century, but was not completed until the twelfth. It is a massive edifice, partly in the Byzantine style, with four towers.

MAYENCE—MENTZ.

3. This city was also founded by the Romans. It has several remarkable towers, one of them being over four hundred feet high. It has numerous old churches and chapels. This city is very strongly fortified.

TRENT.

4. This is the ancient Tridentum, founded by an Alpine tribe, the Tridentini. Among its examples of mediæval architecture are ruined castles, embattled walls, spires, towers, and a cathedral. The cathedral was begun in 1212, and is a beautiful specimen of the Romanesque style of Lombardy.

HEIDELBERG

5. is one of the ancient cities of Germany, in the grand duchy of Baden. Among its noted buildings is the Church of the Holy Ghost, which

* See Steinbrenner, in Traditions, pp. 75, 76, 80.

A Travelling Band of Masons.

GERMANY AND VICINITY.

is divided through the centre by a partition-wall. On one side Catholic service is carried on, and on the other side the Protestants worship at the same time.

HILDESHEIM

6. is an old town of Hanover, founded in the eighth century. It is noted for its very old houses and gateways.

In 1868, while some soldiers were digging in the vicinity of the old gate, illustrated on page 210, they discovered, at the depth of nine feet, sixty silver vessels, of the best period of Roman art.

SALZBURG.

7. This is an old city founded in, or before, the tenth century. One of its most noted and conspicuous features is the old feudal castle.

ROSTOCK.

8. This city was founded in the eleventh century. Among the noted works of the old Craftsmen are St. Peter's and St. Catherine's churches. The former has a tower four hundred feet high.

NUREMBERG

9. is another city dating from the eleventh century. It was a free city in 1219, and in 1532 a Diet was held here which secured religious liberty to the Protestants.

CHAPTER VII.

THE COLLEGES IN GAUL—FRANCE.

With the Roman Armies of Invasion they enter Gaul. — Construct the Military Works and Bridges.—Build Vessels, Villages, Edifices, etc.— Ultimately Known as Compagnons.—With Practices and Traditions very Similar to Ancient Masonry.

FOLLOWING the career of the Colleges in Germany, their advent and operations in France will now be sketched.

In following the rise and progress of the Guilds of France, it is necessary to consider that, until comparatively recent times, France was not a homogeneous State. On the arrival of Cæsar—58 B.C.—he found it divided into three very distinct nationalities, which he named Gallia Belgica, Gallia Aquitania, and Gallia Propria, or Celtica.* The Aquitani came from Spain, and were of African origin. The Belgæ were Teutons, their language and customs Gothic, and the Celts were the original inhabitants, whose descendants are now found in Gallicia and Brittany.

During the Roman conquest of Gaul (70 to 55 B.C.) the building fraternities, besides constructing the many extensive military works needed, also made other great improvements throughout the country—founding and building towns, edifices, bridges, and highways. Gaul had, at this time, a population of three millions.

Subsequently, Augustus continued the improvements commenced by Cæsar, employing all the different bands of constructors—not only the Masonic corporations, but wood-workers. Thus, temples, monuments, roads, private buildings, and ships were being built, presenting a scene of the greatest activity even as early as 27 B.C.†

* Chambers, vol. iii., pp. 16, 17. Hayden, p. 768.
† Rebold, pp 65–67. Chambers, vol. v., p. 518.

THE COLLEGES IN GAUL—FRANCE.

The great Roman highways were marked from their starting-point with mile-stones from five to eight feet high, and the distance given in miles and leagues.

As a means of Romanizing the people, Augustus founded a large number of military colonies. This policy succeeded so well that those colonies originated nearly all the old cities of France; among which are Bordeaux, Besançon, Bourges, Rheims, Rouen, Toulouse, Paris, and Trèves. Each of these cities had its forum, theatre, temples, aqueducts, and schools.

Between 306 and 336 France was divided into seventeen provinces. Many districts are now celebrated for the very products which then constituted their staple industries; and splendid ruins still testify to the opulence of the ancient citizens.

Roman sway and prosperity in Gallia, however, at last reached a period in which it was destined to be interrupted, and later terminated, as the country was constantly invaded by the German tribes, the most persistent of which was the Franks, who, advancing step by step, finally secured permanent possession of the country.

History first distinctly mentions this people about the middle of the third century as a union of North German tribes.* Flavius Vopiscus first names them in the life of the Emperor Aurelian, about 242. They were a very strong and bold people. Their opinion of themselves is expressed in the introduction to the Salic Law, where it states that "The high-famed nation of the Franks, who have God for their judge, are brave in war, profound in council, firm in union, noble, manly in form, bold, and prompt." Such was the nation which, though small in numbers, by strength and courage burst the yoke of the Romans.

They traversed Roman territory, particularly Gaul, from one end to the other, and even crossed the Pyrenees into Spain and took the city of Tarragona. The Romans, in the third century, had so frail a tenure of these countries that the Franks and other warlike hordes, among whom were the Burgundians and Vandals, had possession of seventy considerable cities in Gaul.

About the year 482 Clovis, the son of Gilderich, became Prince of the Salian Franks, and eventually king of all the Franks. He first attacked the

---
* History of Germany, Kohlrausch, p. 65.

Roman Governor Syragrius and defeated him at Soissons (Suessiones), and occupied the country as far as the Loire. This took place in the year 486, and practically terminated the Roman rule in Gaul.

The kingdom of the Franks was subsequently divided into two great portions, Neustria and Austrasia, or the Western and Eastern Kingdoms. In the Western Kingdom the Roman manners and language maintained their superiority; but in the East those of the Germans predominated.

During the occupation of the country by the Romans, the Masonic Corporations had made a practice of receiving into their membership Gauls of the better class; and on the departure of the Romans they reorganized and elected their own officers, and devoted themselves principally to erecting church edifices; in fact, they became attached to the Church, and might be termed Masonic Ecclesiastics. Among the noted architects of this kind, between 659 and 740, were St. Ferol, St. Elor, Bishop of Noyon, Dalmac, Bishop of Rhodes, and Agricola, Bishop of Chalons.

About the year 700 the Grand Steward over the Kingdom of the Franks was Pepin, a careful and prudent man, who restored order and justice, held the old March Assemblies regularly, and so won the love and confidence of the people by restoring their rights, that he was enabled to make the office hereditary in his family.

His son, Charles Martel, who was Grand Steward after him, saved the whole of Christianity at this time from a great impending danger—Mohammedanism.

Savage hordes had suddenly appeared from the southeast, and had in a short time traversed extensive tracts with fire and sword, subjecting all to their dominion. No nation could withstand them; their arms were irresistible, and struck their opponents like lightning. These strangers were the Arabs, and they derived their impetus from the new faith. For he whom they called their prophet, Mohammed, had announced to them much from the doctrines of Moses and of the Saviour; besides which, he promised to this people, who were addicted to sensual pleasures beyond everything, great rewards and eternal bliss in Paradise if they fought zealously for their new religion, and extended it over all countries.

After the Mohammedans had overrun Spain, they crossed the Pyrenees

MOUNTED GAULS.

THE COLLEGES IN GAUL—FRANCE.

and fell upon France. At the same time they showed themselves below Constantinople with a large army and a fleet; so that they embraced in their operations the whole of Europe from east to west, determined upon conquering and proselyting it. Constantinople, however, with its strong walls and Greek fire, which the inhabitants used against the ships of their enemy, checked them. And in France they were opposed by the powerful hero, Charles Martel, who, with his Franks, crossed the river Loire to meet the enemy, and came upon them on the wide plain between the cities of Tours and Poitiers.

Here, on a Saturday in October, 732, a terrible battle was fought, and the Arabs were repulsed with great slaughter, as nearly three hundred thousand fell, together with their general, Abderrahman.* Those who remained fled toward Southern France, whence Charles soon drove them forth, and placed forever a boundary against them on that side. For this wonderful deed he was highly honored throughout all countries. He died in the year 741.

In 753 Pope Stephen crossed the Alps to secure the assistance of Pepin (successor of Martel) against the Longobardian King Aistulph, who had conquered Ravenna and demanded tribute and submission from the Pope. Pepin promised aid, and retained him through the winter at his court. Here the Pope repeated the anointment of the King as already performed by the Holy Boniface, anointing also his two sons, Carloman and Charles (after he had himself lifted the latter, then twelve years old, from the font), and then presented to the Franks those members of the newly-created dynasty as alone legitimate. In the spring of the year 755 the king advanced against Italy, defeated Aistulph at Susa, conquered Ravenna, with the surrounding country, which had previously belonged to the Greek Emperors, and presented it to the Pope. This formed the beginning of the Papal States.

The termination of the Roman domination in France did not terminate Roman civilization; for at the time of Charlemagne, Craft Guilds, successors to the Roman Colleges, were established in the principal cities of that country. Roman industries and traditions were perpetuated till a late date; for

* History of Germany, p. 88.

even in the fourteenth century industries still flourished which had created the opulence of Roman Gaul.*

Many Roman edifices also exist in a complete state of preservation; showing that, despite the ravages of the Gothic hordes, some cities were never destroyed or even deserted. At Rheims a triple arch of Roman construction is still used as one of the city gates—the Porte-de-Mars.

REMAINS OF A ROMAN TEMPLE AT NISMES.

Arles, once the metropolis of Gaul, possesses the ruins of an amphitheatre, two temples, also a Roman triumphal arch in excellent preservation.

At Nismes is the famous Maison Carrée. It is 76 feet in length, 39 feet in height and breadth, with 26 columns, each standing 27 feet from the ground. It is in nearly as good a condition as when erected in honor of the grandsons of Augustus. This ancient city has also an amphitheatre nearly as large as that of Rome, and in a better state of preservation.†

* Note 1, p. 260. † Gould, vol. i., p. 183.

THE COLLEGES IN GAUL—FRANCE.

FRENCH GUILDS.

The Colleges of Builders flourished in France during the Roman occupation; but soon after the departure of the Romans the name, "College" was dropped, and Compagnonnage and Guilds substituted, under which names they were known until the reorganization of the Masonic bodies, in 1717.

The first French Guild that was authorized by law was that of the Marchands *de l'eau de Paris*. The document in which this company was legally recognized bears date A.D. 1121, wherein Louis VI. grants certain privileges which had been previously vested in him, and in which it is treated as an already *ancient* institution.

This Guild all French writers claim to be a direct successor of the Nautæ Parisiaci, one of the Roman Colleges.* The grounds for this belief being its great antiquity, and the fact that a College—Nautæ—did exist here under the Romans. In the reign of Tiberius Cæsar the Nautæ erected an altar to Jupiter, and in digging in the eighteenth century, on the spot where the Hôtel de Ville now stands, this ancient altar was unearthed. It bears the following inscription:

"TIB. CÆSARE.
AVG. IOVI. OPTVM
MAXSVMO . . . . M
NAVTÆ PARISIACI
PVBLICE POSIERV
IN."

The oldest Code of the French Guilds, which has been preserved, is that of Boileau—date about 1260. In it there is evidence of a much earlier existence. This Code unites, under the banner of St. Blaize, the masons, stone masons, and plasterers.

CODE OF THE MASONS.—BOILEAU.†

He may be a mason in Paris who wishes, provided, always, that he knows the handcraft, and that he works after the usages and customs of the craft, and they are these:

None may have in his employ but j apprentice; and if he have an ap-

---
* Gould, vol. i., p. 185; also note 4, p. 260.
† Ibid., vol. i., p. 197.

prentice, he may not accept him for less than vj years service; but for longer service may he well accept him, and also for pay, if he be able to obtain it. And if he accept him for less than vj years, then is he cast in a fine of xx sols, to be paid to the Chapel of St. Blaise, unless they be his own sons born only in honorable wedlock.

And the king who is at this time, and to whom God grant long life, has granted the mastership of the masons to Master William, of Saint Patu, for so long as it shall please him. Which Master William took oath in Paris, within the precincts of the palace aforesaid, that he would the aforesaid craft well and loyally keep to the best of his power, as well for poor as rich, for weak as strong, for so long as it shall please the king that he shall keep the said craft; and afterward the said Master William did take the form of oath aforesaid, before the Provost of Paris, at the *Chastelet.*

And every mason, and every mortarer, and every plasterer, shall swear by the saints that he will keep the craft aforesaid well and truly, each one in his place; and if they know that anyone do ill in anything, and not act according to the usages and customs of the craft aforesaid, that they will lay the same before the master whensoever they shall know thereof, and on their oath.

The master whose apprentice shall have served and completed his time, shall appear before the master of the craft, and bear witness that his apprentice had served his time well and truly; and then the master who keeps the craft shall cause the apprentice to swear by the saints that he will conform to the usages and customs of the craft well and truly.

And no one shall work at this craft after the strike of 3 P.M., at Notre Dame, during flesh time, and of a Saturday in Lent, after vespers shall have been chanted at Notre Dame, unless it be to close an arch or stairway, or to close a door-frame placed on the street. And if anyone work beyond the hours aforesaid, unless it be of necessity in the works aforesaid, he shall pay iiij pence as a fine to the master who keeps the craft, and the master may seize the tools of him who shall be recast in the fine.

The master of the craft has cognizance of the petty justice and fines of the masons, and of their workmen and apprentices, as long as it shall please the king, as also of deprivation of their craft, and of bloodless beatings, and of *clameur de proprete.*

Ancient Roman Gateway.

And if any of the aforesaid craftsmen be summoned before the master who keeps the craft, and he absent himself, he shall pay a fine of iiij pence to the master; and if he appear at the time and acknowledge his fault, he shall forfeit; and if he pay not before the night, he shall be fined iiij pence to the master; and if he deny and be found to have done wrong, he shall pay iiij pence to the master.

The master who rules the craft cannot levy but one fine for each offence; and if he who has been fined is so stiff-necked and so false that he will not obey the master or pay his fine, the master may forbid him the craft.

If any one of the afore-mentioned crafts, whose craft shall have been forbidden him by the master, shall nevertheless use his craft, the master may seize his tools and keep them until he have paid the fine; and if he forcibly resist, the master shall make it known to the Provost, and the Provost shall compel him.

The masons and the plasterers owe the watch duty, and the tax and the other dues which the other citizens of Paris owe the king.

The mortarers are free of watch duty, and all stone-masons, since the time of Charles Martel, as the wardens (preudomes) have heard tell from father to son.

The master who keeps the craft in the name of the King is free of the watch duty for the service he renders in keeping the craft.

He who is over sixty years of age, and he whose wife is in child-bed, so long as she lies abed, are free of watch, by order of the king.

Statutes and Ordinances Made by the Masters.—Mason Architects of the City of Montpellier.

According to their ancient privileges, which have been lost and destroyed during the troubles and wars which have been in this country, and now re-enacted under the good pleasure of our Sire the King, and of the Court of Monsieur, the Governor of the said city.

Item. The fellow (compagnon) who shall desire to present himself for the said mastership shall have served previously, and accomplished, his three years of apprenticeship which he shall cause to be sufficiently made apparent, and also that after his said apprenticeship he has served the masters of the said city or elsewhere for three or four years.

Item. Every Saturday or Sunday each master shall be required to place in the box each week, to be employed for the benefit of poor masters and fellows, widows and orphans of the said masters, ten pence of Tours, and the fellows working for hire, three pence of Tours.

Item. Every apprentice shall be required to place in the box, immediately on his entering upon his apprenticeship, fifteen sols of Tours, to be employed as already said; which fifteen sols the master who has received the said apprentice shall himself place in the said box, whether or no he be reimbursed by the said apprentice; and the said master shall be required to inform thereof the said apprentice, or he who undertakes for him the payment of the said fifteen sols.

" *Vised* at the council of the office of the Royal Domain, in the Court of the Government of the City of Montpellier, the regulations containing statutes made and agreed by the Master Masons working at the art of masonry and architecture in the said city, conformably to what they used to do of old times."

In 1493 Peyre Borgonhon, Master Mason, reports to the Consuls of Montpellier that he could no longer find masons to work at the fortifications under four sous per diem; and these, " after taking information respecting the prices elsewhere, and considering also that the days in the month of April were among those of the longest of the year, resigned themselves to pay the price asked." This is one of the earliest strikes in the building trade.

THE COMPANIONAGE, OR LES COMPAGNONS DU TOUR DE FRANCE.

The "Companionage" signified the associations formed by the journeymen of France for mutual instruction, support, and assistance.* They practised a real initiation—a mystic reception—and cherished venerable legends.

In 1814 Agricol Perdiguier published his " Livre de Compagnonnage," giving as accurate an account of their history and traditions as the nature of his oath would permit. In the same year a talented authoress published a work,

* Gould, vol. i., pp. 212–228.

"Le Compagnon du Tour de France." Attention being thus called to the Companionage, the subject was investigated by other writers, several of whom were themselves companions.

The Companionage was composed of three great divisions. The principal division was denominated Sons of Solomon, and the others were called respectively, Sons of Maître Jaques, and the sons of Maître Soubise. They all concurred in ascribing their origin to the Stone Masons of Solomon.*

In whatever town a charge was deposited, there the craftsman found a house of call devoted to his purpose, and a branch of the society. These towns were called Villes du devoir, or du tour de France.†

The villes *du tour de France* were Marseilles, Lyons, Avignon, Nismes, Montpellier, Clermont Ferrand, Bordeaux, Nantes, and Paris. Tours, Chalons-sur-Saône, Beziers, La Rochelle, Angoulême, Saumur, Orléans, and later Alger—all included in the Roman occupation.

Introduction or Initiation.

In Perdiguier's own handicraft we find the following customs and arrangements prevailing: A young workman presents himself, and requests to be made a member of the Society. His sentiments are inquired into, and if his replies are satisfactory, he is embauché.

At the next General Assembly he is brought into an upper room, where, in presence of all the companions and affiliés, a series of questions are asked him, to ascertain that he has made no mistake—that it is into this society, and not in some other, that he wishes to enter. The ordinances are then read to him, and he is asked whether he can, and will, conform thereto. If he replies, "Yes," he is affiliated and conducted to his proper place in the room. If he is of the right material he receives the Degree of the Companionage, and is eligible to its various offices.

In this Society there were three further degrees: compagnon reçu, compagnon fini, and initiated compagnon—compagnon initié. All these degrees

---
* Notes 2, 3, 5, pp. 260, 261.
† The word devoir is equivalent to "charge," suggestive of ancient Masonic charges. The British charges are a written Code of Rules of Conduct prefaced by a traditional history of the craft, which exactly corresponds with that of the French devoir. Gould, vol. i., p. 216.

were attended with a ceremony of which Thory, writing a generation earlier than Perdiguier, says: "Their *initiations* are accompanied by secret forms, and their unions existed from time immemorial."

Perdiguier, mourning the obliteration of the ancient landmarks and customs, says of *another* society: "They have no mystery, no initiation, no distinctions."

The assemblies of the craft were usually held on the first Sunday of every month, and at the banquets each member paid an equal sum.

The privileges and advantages to which a member was entitled were various. Upon his arrival in a town or city he was directed where to find employment.

In case of sickness, the members took turns in visiting him, and providing for his wants. In some of these societies he was granted a sum of ten sous per diem during the time he remained in the hospital, the amount of which was presented to him on his leaving. If he should be cast into prison for any ordinary offence he was assisted in every possible way.

Each Society had an officer called Rouleur, whose duties were onerous. He welcomed new arrivals, found them work, and on their desiring to leave, saw that all their old scores were cleaned off, and then accompanied them to the gates of the town. It was also his duty to convoke the assemblies.

The Sons of Solomon provided their members with work as follows: The Rouleur introduced the applicant to his new master, who advanced five francs toward his future wages. This sum the Rouleur retained, advising the journeyman to be careful to earn it.

When a companion brought disgrace upon his Society, a special meeting was called, and in presence of the assembly he was forced on his knees, the companions standing round and drinking to his damnation; during which time he was compelled to drink water until nature rebelled and he was unable to imbibe any more, when it was poured over him. The glass which he used was broken, and his colors were torn from him and burned; the Rouleur then led him round the room, each companion bestowing a buffet, not to hurt him, but as an expression of contempt. He was then led to the door, and made his exit in manner set forth in the "Lay of St. Nicholas."

> "And out of the doorway he flew like a shot,
> For a foot flew up with a terrible thwack,
> And caught the foul demon about the spot
> Where his tail joins on to the small of his back."

In reference to King Solomon, Perdiguier says: "The Sons of Solomon claimed that this king gave them a charge, and incorporated them fraternally within the precincts of the Temple." He also says: "The stone-masons (of this Fraternity, S. of S.) are counted the most ancient of the Companions." Concerning the tradition of Maitre Jacques, Perdiguier adds: "There is one which enjoys an extended acquaintance with the very many Compagnons du Devoir. It is from this that I extract, without changing a single word, the following details.

The Tradition of Maitre Jacques.

"Maitre Jacques, one of the Masters of Solomon, and a colleague of Hiram, was born in a small town called Carte, now St. Romili, in the south of Gaul. He was a son of Jacquin, a celebrated architect, and devoted himself to stone-cutting. At the age of fifteen he left his family and travelled into Greece, then the centre of the fine arts, where he entered into close alliance with a philosopher of the highest genius, who taught him sculpture and architecture. He soon became celebrated in both these arts.

"Hearing that Solomon had summoned to himself all the famous men, he passed into Egypt, and thence to Jerusalem. He did not at first gain much distinction among the workmen; but at last, having received an order from the chief master to construct two columns, he sculptured them with such art and taste that he was accepted as a master.

"Maitre Jacques arrived in Jerusalem at the age of twenty-six. He remained there only a short time after the construction of the Temple; when many masters wishing to return to their country, they took leave of Solomon loaded with benefits.

"Maitre Jacques and Maitre Soubise made their way back to Gaul. They had sworn never to part; but before long M. Soubise, a man of violent character, becoming jealous of the ascendency which M. Jacques had acquired over their disciples, and of the love which they bore him, separated from his friend and chose other disciples.

M. Jacques landed at Marseilles, and M. Soubise at Bordeaux. Before commencing his travels M. Jacques chose thirteen Compagnons and forty disciples, and being deserted by one of them, he chose another. He travelled three years, leaving everywhere the memory of his talents and virtues. One day, being at some distance from his disciples, he was assailed by ten of the followers of M. Soubise, who attempted to assassinate him. In order to save himself he plunged into a swamp, the canes (or reeds, in French " joncs ") of which not only supported him, but afforded a refuge from the blows of his assailants. While these cowards were seeking some means of reaching him, his disciples arrived and effected his rescue.

He then withdrew to St. Beanne. One of his disciples called Jeron betrayed him to the disciples of M. Soubise. One day after sunrise, M. Jacques being alone, engaged in prayer in his accustomed spot, the traitor arrived, accompanied by the executioners, and gave as usual, the kiss of peace, which was the preconcerted death-signal. Five villains at once fell upon, and killed him with five dagger wounds.

His disciples arrived too late, but yet in time to receive his last farewell. "I die," he said, "for God has so willed it. I forgive my assassins, and forbid you to follow them." He pronounced a few more words which they were unable to understand, and crossing his arms over his breast, expired in his forty-seventh year—four years after leaving Jerusalem, and 989 B.C.

The funeral ceremonies lasted three days. The procession crossed forests and mountains, and encountered a terrible storm, but at length arrived at the final resting-place, where the body was lowered into the grave. The Elder descended beside it, the Companions covering both with a pall; and after the former had given the Guilbrette they covered the grave with large stones and sealed it with heavy bars of iron, after which they made a great fire, and threw into it their torches and all that had been used during the obsequies of their master. His raiment was preserved in a chest. Subsequently the sons of M. Jacques separated, and divided among themselves his clothing, which was thus distributed :

" His hat to the hatters ; his tunic to the stone-masons ; his sandals to the locksmiths; his cloak to the joiners; his belt to the carpenters; his staff to the wagon-makers."

"After the division of the articles belonging to M. Jacques, the act of faith was found which was pronounced by him on the day of his reception (as master probably) before Solomon, Hiram, the High Priest, and all the Masters."

Their funeral ceremonies were peculiar. If a companion died his Society undertook all the expenses of his interment. The deceased was carried by four or six of his fellows, who changed from time to time. On the coffin were placed two canes crossed, a square and compass interlaced, and the colors of the Society. Each companion wore black crape on his left arm and on his cane, and wore his colors. They marched to the church, and thence to the cemetery, in two lines, placed the coffin on the edge of the grave, and then formed around it the "living circle." The Master next addressed the mourners, then all knelt on one knee and offered up prayer to Deity. The coffin was then lowered, after which two canes were placed on the ground beside the grave so as to form a cross.

Two Companions then took their places, each within one of the quarters of the cross, turned half around on the left foot, moved the right foot forward so as to face each other, and thus occupied with their feet the four quarters of the cross. They then took each other by the right hand, whispered in each other's ear, and embraced. All went through this ceremony in turn, knelt again on the edge of the grave, offered up a prayer, threw three lumps of earth on the coffin, and retired.

In some cases the ceremony concluded as follows: After the coffin was lowered a Companion descended and placed himself beside it; a cloth was stretched over the mouth of the grave, and lamentations arose from below, to which the Companions above replied. The concealed Companion then gave a portion of the guilbrette to the deceased.

The first public Masonic edifice built in France was in Marseilles, and entitled "The Lodge of St. John." It was 58 feet long, 30 broad, and 42 feet high. It was decorated with paintings of the best artists. At the bottom of the hall, under a gilded canopy with blue hangings and trimmed with gold, was a painting representing the "Genius of Masonry," supporting the portrait of the then King of France, with an inscription in Latin, the translation of which is, "The Masons of Marseilles have erected this monument of their affection to their most beloved king."

A genius seated below the pedestal presents with one hand this inscription, and with the other the arms of the Lodge, with their motto, " Deo, Regi, et Patriæ, Fidelitas "—fidelity to God, our king, and country. Above, is a genius which crowns the king.

To the right of this is another splendid painting, representing the wisdom of Solomon, with this inscription above it, " Prudencia "—prudence.

To the left is another, representing the courage of St. John the Baptist in remonstrating with Herod upon his debaucheries, with the inscription, " Fortitudo." *

NOTES FROM AUTHORITIES.

1. Much of the account of the Compagnonnage has been drawn from Gould's History of Free Masonry, vol. i., pages 212, 241, 249 ; and the following are among his conclusions : " We may add to the preceding the great probability that the French Guilds were direct descendants of the Roman Colleges without serious break of continuity, and that the trade guilds, at their earliest stage, preserved a modification of the ancient mysteries, which may also have been previously celebrated by the Colleges. Their ceremonies continued to be practised in secret, the masterpiece and the banquet only being allowed to become known to the outside world."

2. 1. " Sons of Solomon " certainly remind us in general terms of our fraternity. 2. Companions de liberté, free company of Free Masons. 3. Devoir is a literal translation of our English charge, and the documents appear to be of very similar form. 4. " General Assembly " is a term common to both societies. 5. Accepted companion and initiated companion sound strangely familiar. 6. Passed companion presents a remarkable coincidence with our own expression.

3. Perdiguier, who was a " Compagnon," writes of the organization as a Free Mason would of Free Masonry, *i.e*, without disclosing aught of an esoteric character ; but the legend and customs are carefully described. Gould, vol. i., pp. 240, 241, 249.

4. In France, especially in the south, the continuation of the Colleges was unbroken ; for there the Roman Law predominated throughout all the vicissitudes of government, and at the Revolution, it superseded the Federal Law of the Pays Coutumier. Coote, Romans of Britain, ii., pp. 390-413.

* Register, p. 509.

5. According to Dr. Luio Brentano, who published, in 1870, an essay on the history and development of Guilds, England is the birth-place of the Mediæval Guilds, from whom he says that the modern Free Masons emerged. They existed, however, in every country of Europe, and we identify them with the Compagnons du Tour de France, and the Baucorporationen of Germany.

Besides being brotherhoods for the care of the temporal welfare of their members, the Craft Guilds were, like the rest of the Guilds, at the same time religious fraternities.

In this respect the Craft Guilds of all countries are alike; and in reading their Statutes, one might fancy sometimes that the old Craftsmen cared only for the well-being of their souls.

We find innumerable ordinances also as to the support of the sick and poor; and to afford a separate asylum for distress, the London Companies early built dwellings near their halls. Mackey, pp. 310 and 311.

CHAPTER VIII.

ADVENT OF THE COLLEGES IN BRITAIN.

They Enter the Country with Cæsar's Army of Invasion, 55 B.C.—The Natives Make a Stubborn Resistance.—Bloody Battles take Place.—Fate of the Brave Caractacus, and of Queen Boadicea and her Beautiful Daughters.—Military Camps are Constructed at Different Places.—Under the Supervision of the Colleges, Towns grow up Around or Near these Camps.—Cities are Founded, Notably London, Exeter, Dover, Chester.—After an Occupation of the Country for over Four Hundred Years the Romans Leave it, but Everywhere Leave the Strong Impress of Civilization—Principally Through the Operations of the **Colleges,** *which were Subsequently Known as Guilds, and Lastly as Free Masons.—Remarkable Remains of Roman Structures in Many Places. —1717, Free Masonry, as it Had Existed for Centuries, is now Freed from its Operative Domination, and its Doors Thrown Open to Good and True Men, without Regard to Occupation or Religion.—Singular Ancient Masonic Documents.*

B.C. 55. Cæsar determined upon the conquest of Britain, and after making due preparations he embarked the infantry of two legions in eighty vessels, at or near where Calais now stands. His cavalry were embarked at another place fifteen miles distant.

Having a fair wind, Cæsar arrived on the coast of Britain the morning following, but not finding a suitable place to land, he sailed along the shore until three o'clock, when he disembarked at Deal, where he found a large body of the British ready to dispute his progress; but although his cavalry had not arrived and the natives fought with desperate valor, yet they were forced to retreat with heavy loss.

Following this, the Romans advanced into the country in various directions,

Roman Squadron off the Coast of Britain

but always meeting with such stubborn resistance that their operations finally came to a stand; and for nearly one hundred years after the invasion, the only result to Rome was a small annual tribute paid by a few chiefs.

In 43 A.D., however, Claudius despatched four legions under Aulus Plautius against Britain, and he succeeded, after several desperate engagements, in reducing the southern portion of the country to the condition of a Roman province.

A.D. 50, Plautius was succeeded by Ostorus Scapula, who pressed the war vigorously, and, to secure the Roman conquest in that part of the country, he caused his Colleges to erect fortifications on the banks of the Severn and Avon. He next settled a strong colony of his veterans with some Colleges at Camalodunum, both to hold in check the neighboring warlike tribes and to spread a knowledge of the useful arts among the people. Scapula then advanced against Caractacus, one of the bravest of the brave British chiefs, whom he found strongly fortified,* and his works were so well defended that the first attack of the Romans was repulsed, with considerable loss. Persistence and discipline, however, prevailed; their works were carried by assault, and the brave chief, his wife, and daughter, were taken prisoners. Later on, Caractacus was sent a prisoner to Rome, and on coming in sight of the city, he remarked to his guard that he was astonished that the possessors of such magnificence should envy him a poor hovel in Britain.

The next events of importance in the Roman conquest of the island were the capture of the Island of Mona—Anglesey—by Suetonius, and the desperate battle fought with Boadicea, widow of Prastagus, king of the Iceni.† Prastagus had for many years been a faithful ally of Rome, and on his death, the better to secure a portion of his inheritance to his family, he named his daughters and the Roman Emperor as his joint heirs; but instead of compliance with this modest arrangement, the Roman Procurator took possession of the whole in the name of the Emperor. This aroused the indignation of Boadicea, and she remonstrated against the robbery, but instead of redress she was severely beaten with rods, and her two beautiful daughters were dishonored before her eyes. The intelligence of these outrages spread like wild-fire, and the Iceni and Trinobants first attacked and captured the

---

* Note 1, p. 369. † Hume, vol. i., pp. 6, 7.

Colony of Camalodunum; defeated the ninth legion, that was marching to its relief; took Londinium and Verulamium, and the blow was so overwhelming that only a fragment of the army and a small portion of the inhabitants escaped alive. The rage of the insurgents against the inhabitants was caused by their quiet submission to the Romans.

In 62, however, Suetonius got together a force large enough to act on the offensive and marched against the enemy, whose success had drawn a multitude from all quarters into their ranks, which the Romans found occupying a good position and under the command of Boadicea. Just before the commencement of the struggle Boadicea was seen slowly advancing along the lines of her army, standing in a singular-looking chariot. She was enveloped in a mantle, encircled by a heavy gold chain, her long hair reaching to her feet, and she thus addressed her army: " Britons are accustomed to fight under a woman. Avenge me as a woman of your own class; avenge my liberty outraged, my body torn by the scourge; and avenge my innocent daughters dishonored." Exasperated by her words, the Britons rushed to the attack, and a fierce and bloody battle was fought; yet notwithstanding the great inferiority of the Romans in numbers, their firmness, splendid discipline, and the knowledge that no quarter would be given if defeated, carried them through the terrible onslaught of the enemy and to victory, which not only ended in a rout, but in the slaughter of over eighty thousand Britons. As soon as Boadicea saw that she was defeated, she ended her life with poison.

Passing over some minor events, we next come to the administration of Agricola, who was appointed governor of Britain A.D. 78. He first repressed a revolt of the Ordovices; then pushed his conquest to the river Tay and fortified several strategic points. Still advancing north, he crossed the Forth to the frontier of Caledonia, where he caused his Colleges to construct a military wall with towers, from the Forth across the country to the Clyde.

Afterward, when Agricola had by force and wise management brought the country into a state of peace, he improved the opportunity to disseminate the useful arts and a taste for Roman amusements among the people. He promoted the erection of temples, forums, and other public works by grants from the treasury, and caused the sons of the chiefs to receive special instructions from his *Colleges of Builders*.

CARACTACUS AND HIS WIFE BEFORE THE ROMAN EMPEROR.

As the Caledonians * were still giving the Romans trouble in the north, Agricola (A.D. 85) advanced into their country, met them on the Grampian hills, 30,000 strong, under Galgacus, and after a sanguinary battle put them to flight, leaving 10,000 dead on the field. Undaunted by defeat, however, the Caledonians continued to harass the Romans; so that on the arrival of Hadrian in Britain (A.D. 123) he found that he could not maintain the Roman power up to the wall of Agricola, and therefore built a second wall across the country nearly 100 miles south of the first, and soon after this the broad belt between the two walls was practically abandoned to the tireless Caledonians.

During the stay of the Emperor Hadrian he resided at York, where by the aid of the Colleges he made some important improvements as well as in other parts of the province.

The next event of note in the Roman occupation was the arrival of the Emperor Septimus Severus, A.D. 208. He found the Caledonians overrunning the northern portions of the country, even menacing the Roman domination on the Island, but with his legions of veterans he defeated them with great slaughter, and again brought them to terms.

Notwithstanding this, knowing the bitter enmity of the northern tribes both against the Romans and the Britons, Severus caused his *Colleges* to construct a formidable line of fortifications across the country, immediately north of the wall of Hadrian. This new line of works consisted of a massive stone wall, with towers at regular distances apart. The towers, however, were placed on hills or projecting rocks, even though the wall made a *détour* to reach such a position. Hence the towers served both as points of observation and defence. During Severus's stay he also resided at York, and died there A.D. 211.

The next matter worthy of consideration in this connection was the arrival of Carrausius, in 287.

During the persecutions of the Christians in Rome, large numbers of the people, including many members of the Colleges of Builders, took refuge in Britain, and these, uniting with those already there, comprised among their number many men of great intelligence and skill throughout the country; so that when Carrausius, in command of the Roman navy, took possession of

* Note 10, p. 370.

Britain and proclaimed himself Emperor, he found it necessary to conciliate them in order to strengthen his precarious position; therefore he restored and confirmed all their ancient privileges. This was done at his residence, Verulam (Saint Albans), A.D. 290. Among the immunities and privileges granted them at this time were *freedom* from taxation and the supervision of all public works, from which circumstance they were sometimes called Free Masons.

When Carrausius negotiated with the Colleges on his landing, they were represented by Albanus, who had the general oversight of the Fraternity in that country. Albanus was also a convert to Christianity, and in his zeal for the new faith he undertook to convert Carrausius; but his Pagan Majesty was pleased to consider this so presumptuous that nothing less than death could atone for the affront. Therefore he decreed that Albanus should be beheaded, which was done in 293.* But, as if in retribution, Carrausius was himself assassinated three years later.

During the sway of Carrausius in Britain (287–295), he employed the *Colleges* in the erection of public edifices, some of which rivalled those of Rome.

Following Carrausius came Constantinus, who, like his predecessors, made York his home. His rule was so judicious and conciliatory that he was held in great esteem by the people. He died in 306, and soon after his death his wife Helena inclosed London with a stone wall. Constantinus was succeeded by his son, the celebrated Constantine. On his accession to the throne religious toleration was restored throughout the Empire, and Christianity made great progress in Britain.

At this time a hierarchy was established, and at the council of Arles, in 314, the Bishops of York, London, and Camalodunum assisted.

The last event of any importance in the Roman occupation was the arrival, in 343, of Theodosius, who marched against the Scots and succeeded in driving them back into their mountains.

But Rome, torn by internal dissensions and hard pressed by Northern and Eastern hordes, was compelled to abandon Britain in 416.

Notwithstanding that much of the Roman rule had been tyrannical, yet their intercourse with the people of the island had greatly improved the condition of the latter.

* Notes 8 and 9, p. 376.

A ROMAN PRISONER BEFORE A BRITISH CHIEF.

ADVENT OF THE COLLEGES IN BRITAIN.

The Colleges of Builders had constructed for the legions, intrenchments and fortified camps, and, as time advanced, temples, dwellings, bridges, and other extensive improvements followed; thus laying the foundations of towns and cities. So that, even in the second century, over eighty of the former, and not a few of the latter, had arisen south of the Tyne, including York, London, Chester, Lincoln, Dover, and Colchester. And as the more intelligent of the natives were admitted into the bodies of constructors, the builder's art had spread so rapidly that architecture, as early as the third century, had attained a degree of perfection in Britain not to be found in any other Roman province. As the public and private works had been carried on by both Romans and the natives, under the supervision of the *Colleges*, the great influence exercised by this organization in the formation of society, the development of *Guildic* Masonry, and the useful arts will readily be seen.*

Britain was also indebted to Rome for her first code of laws, municipal government, and civil tribunal.†

Evidences of Roman civilization are still to be seen, in structures and the ruins of them, at Dover Castle, Lincoln, Richborough Castle, Chester, St. Albans, York, Porchester, Leicester, and Colchester. The most remarkable and most interesting remains of Roman works are those of the wall and towers extending across the country from Wallsend on the Tyne to Bowness in Cumberland. This wall runs so closely to a wall of earth and stone that some believe the two were constructed at the same time, but according to the most authentic accounts the earth wall is much the oldest.‡ One of the most noticeable features of the ruins of the stone wall and towers is, as previously stated, the uniform straightness of its course except where the towers are located. The outer face of the wall was built of blocks of ashlar, and the interior was filled with rubble and mortar. Near the wall, at nearly regular intervals, were stations or camps sometimes comprising a large tower, while at a distance of about a Roman mile there were placed small towers. Considerable architectural finish was given to these towers by the Roman craftsman. Says an English writer: "For nineteen miles out of Newcastle the road to Carlisle runs on the foundations of the wall, and during the summer months its white, dusty surface contrasts well with the surrounding verdure.

---

* Notes 2 and 3, pp. 369, 370. † Note 4, p. 370. ‡ Probably the wall of Hadrian.

Often will the traveller, after attaining some of the steep acclivities of his path, observe the road stretching for miles to the east and west of him, resembling a white ribbon on a green ground."

TRAVEL IN BRITAIN IN THE LAST PART OF THE ROMAN OCCUPATION.

The next important remains of Roman military works is Richborough Castle, in Kent. It is a parallelogram, embracing in its area nearly five acres. The walls are 23 feet high and 11 feet thick at the bottom and 10 feet at the top. First, there are several courses of flint, then two courses of bonded tile,

Ancient Chester.

and from this to the top of the wall there are alternate sections of ashlar and tile.

Another interesting relic is Newport Gate. It was the north gate of the Roman city, Lindum, and from it a military road leading toward the Humber may still be seen. This gate forms the principal entrance into the city from that side.

Another reminder of the Roman occupation is the ancient city of Chester. The two main streets cross each other at right angles and were cut through the solid rock. The houses were built on the ungraded ground from six to ten feet above the level of the streets, and had passages and stairs cut up to them from the streets below. These old streets and several of the Roman houses are still to be seen; also many other evidences of the presence of the Romans, such as "Arthur's Oven," mosaic pavements, metallic implements of war, of architecture, art, bronze, inscriptions, etc.

But one of the most unique of all the Roman remains is Pharos Tower, in Dover Castle. Its form is octagonal, and it was built of alternate courses of tufa, flint, and Roman brick—the latter nearly two feet long. An arched doorway leads into the south side of the tower. On the east side of it is a lofty arch, faced with stone, the soffit of which was turned with brick. This arch doubtless once communicated with some building adjoining.

The Druids of Britain.—Their Mysterious Rites, etc.

When the Romans first invaded Britain, the inhabitants were famous, even among foreign nations, for their superior knowledge of the principles, and zeal for the rites, of their religion. The esoteric doctrines of the Druids were so similar to those of the ancient Egyptians and subsequent societies, that several writers claim to see a close analogy between them.

That the mysteries of the Druids originated in the East, is shown by the great annual festival they held on May 1st, in honor of Belinus, or the sun. On this day prodigious fires were kindled in all their sacred places, and on the tops of all their cairns, and many sacrifices were offered to that glorious luminary, which at that time began to shine upon them with great warmth. Of this festival there are still some vestiges remaining, both in Ireland and in the Highlands of Scotland, where May 1st is called Beltian, that is, the fire of Bel, or Belinus.

In some of their largest temples, particularly that of Stonehenge, they had laid stones of prodigious weight on the tops of standing pillars, which formed a kind of circle aloft in the air, and added much to the grandeur of the whole.

The temple at Classerness (Island of Lewis), was constructed on geometrical and astronomical principles, in the form of a cross and a circle. The circle consisted of twelve upright stones, in allusion to the solar year, or the twelve signs of the zodiac; the east, west, and south are marked by three stones each, placed without the circle in direct lines, pointing to each of those quarters; and toward the north is a double row of twice nineteen stones, forming two perpendicular parallel lines, with a single elevated stone at the entrance. In the centre of the circle stands, high exalted above the rest, the gigantic representative of the Deity, to which the adoration of his worshippers was peculiarly directed.*

Among the ancient Britons, and some other ancient nations, the laws were not considered as the decrees of their princes, but as the commands of their gods. Therefore violations of the laws were not regarded as crimes against prince or state, but as sins against Heaven, for which the Priests, as ministers of Heaven, had alone the right of taking vengeance. The Druids exercised the prerogatives of explaining and executing the laws, in their full extent. "All controversies," says Cæsar, "both public and private, are determined by the Druids. If any crime is committed, or any murder perpetrated, if any disputes arise about the division of inheritances, or the boundaries of estates, they alone have the right to pronounce sentence; and they are the only dispensers both of rewards and punishments." This oligarchy had one engine which contributed much to procure submission to their decisions. That was the sentence of excommunication, which they pronounced against persons, or tribes, when they refused to submit to their decrees. The interdicts of the Druids were no less dreadful than those of the Popes, when their power was at its greatest height.

* See Mysteries, pp. 201, 206, 238; Toland Druids, vol. i., p. 90; also History of Great Britain by Robert Henry, D.D.

Druid Altar.

"The garments of the Druids were remarkably long; and when employed in religious ceremonies, they always wore a white surplice. They usually carried a wand in their hands, and wore a kind of ornament encased in gold, about their necks, called the Druid's egg. Their necks were likewise decorated with gold chains, and their hands and arms with bracelets; they wore their hair short, and their beards remarkably long.*

"The Druids had one chief, or Arch-Druid, in every nation, who acted as high-priest, or pontifex maximus. They had absolute authority over the rest, and commanded, decreed, and punished."

Suetonius Paulinus, who was governor of Britain under Nero, A.D. 61, observing that the isle of Anglesea was the great seat of disaffection to the Roman government, and the asylum of all who were forming plots against it, determined to subdue it. Therefore he conducted his army to the island, and defeated the Britons who attempted to defend it, though they were animated by the presence, prayers, and exhortations of a great multitude of Druids; and not content with cutting down their sacred groves, demolishing their temples, overturning their altars, he burned many of the Druids in the fires which they had kindled for sacrificing the Roman prisoners, if the Britons had gained the victory. So many of the Druids perished on this occasion, that they were never able to make any considerable figure after this period.

Anglo-Saxons.

We now come to an event that was destined to change not only the history of Britain, but the history of the Masonic Fraternities—the advent of the Jutes, Saxons,† and Anglii in that country.

The Britons being deserted by the Romans, and consequently subjected to incursions of their tireless enemies, the Scots, Picts, and Northern pirates, they invited the first-named people to come to their assistance. The

---

* See Edinburgh Encyclopædia.

† The Saxons' confederation was named in the year 288, by Eutropius; it was formed of the remaining Lower German tribes, who had not joined the Franks, or had again separated themselves from them. Amm. Marcellinus next mentions the Saxons as the neighbors of the Franks, about the middle of the fourth century. The greatest territorial extension which they gained up to the time of Charlemagne was from the Danes; and in addition they occupied Lower Saxony and the greater portion of Westphalia, the banks of the Elbe, Weser, Aller, Ems, Lippe, and Ruhr. History of Germany, p. 65.

remedy, however, proved to be worse than the disease, for after their new allies had repulsed the Scots, they settled in the land, and true to the instincts of their natures, they committed cruel and brutal barbarities on the people, not hesitating to ransack and destroy whole villages where any defence was made against them. Then the term "Anglo-Saxon" was equivalent to savagery; now it is the general title of two great nations.

These tribes of people came to Britain in the following order:

First, the Jutes; second, the Saxons; and lastly, between 527 and 547, came the Anglii. The latter, like the Jutes, came from Schleswig, and there is still a corner of Schleswig called *Anglen*. Therefore it was doubtless from the Anglii and their country that the national name "England" originated. A part of the descendants of the Colleges of Builders also took the name Anglo-Saxon Guilds; and from 750 to 975 these Guilds had become so numerous and influential that their ordinances were not only sanctioned, but frequently imitated, in legislation. In fact, legislation as early as the latter part of the seventh century was merely a reproduction of the older laws of the Colleges or *Guilds*. In the year 715, by the decree of King Ina, the Guildic brethren, who had slain a thief, were rendered liable to a prescribed penalty.*

In the time of Alfred the Great, the amercements to which these bodies were subjected for the murder of a Guildic member were defined with precision. The Judicia Civitatis Londoniæ, A.D. 924–940, contains ordinances for the maintenance of social duties in the Guildships.

The statute of one of the Guilds at Cambridge throws much light upon the internal structure of these sodalities at that time. It was called thegnagilde.† The following are the vital elements in the creed of this oath-bound society:

"Members shall swear on the reliques [holy-dome] that they will help, aid, and assist each other, in spiritual and secular matters, and that the corporation itself shall sustain the personal difficulties of brethren who have justice with them."

Conspicuous among the exemplars of the esoteric teachings of the Colleges, was Austin, a Christian and architect, who came to England in A.D. 557 for the purpose of converting the Anglo-Saxons to Christianity. He placed

---

* Note 7, p. 370; Fort, p. 392. † Fort, p. 404.

THE LAST OF THE DRUIDS.

himself at the head of the Masonic Colleges, augmented their membership from the more intelligent of the new-comers, and assisted them out of the difficulties that the recent wars had involved them in. Austin subsequently became Archbishop of Canterbury, thus enabling him to still further assist the Fraternity by giving them work on churches, etc. It was in this manner that a part of the building fraternities became attached to the monasteries, and operated with them for nearly four centuries.

Among the grand old edifices of England is the Cathedral of Canterbury. Its nucleus, or commencement, was a church built and used by the Roman Christians, in the fourth century. To this additions were made until the latter part of the eleventh century. In 1174 the choir was destroyed by fire, and was rebuilt under William of Sens.

Notwithstanding the temporary affiliation of the Colleges with the Church, he who aspired to the rank of master had to prove to the Craft that he had travelled in Italy and the East, and possessed a knowledge of the architecture of those countries. In this way the Masonic bodies, in connection with the Church, became the conservators of the science and art of that period; and the esteem in which these corporations were held was such as to create a circle of activity and influence that embraced a large portion of Western Europe. This prosperous state of affairs was soon, however, to meet with a temporary but severe reverse. For, as the cohesion of the different tribes, and peoples who were to constitute the British nation was not yet strong enough to enable them to defend the country against the Danes, that people repeatedly overran the richest portion of the island; and between 845 and 870 they plundered and then burned nearly all the church edifices and other public buildings, together with the records and ancient documents of the churches and Lodges that had been preserved in the monasteries. These wars paralyzed the operations of the Craft until peace was fully restored. Then, however, in consequence of the general destruction of public buildings, the services of the Fraternities were in great demand; and the travelling bands were everywhere seen proceeding to localities where building operations were going on; consequently the Masonic institution soon felt the impetus of the renewed activity, and from this time forth it constantly increased both in numbers and influence.

Transition State.

Prior to the eighth century, the building fraternities had nearly all passed under the title of Colleges of Builders, but, in consequence of the national peculiarities of the people within the scope of their operations, and of improvements in their system, they began to change their title, and were in the eighth Century known as Brother Masons and Compagnons in France; Guilds and sometimes Free Masons in England; Colleges and Guilds in Germany; and Colleges and Masonic Fraternities in Italy. This, therefore, may be termed the transition period, for in a few years we find that the name, "Colleges of Builders" had nearly disappeared, and in its place the terms Guild and Free Mason were used.

When we consider the wonderful change that has been wrought in North America in less than four centuries, and then consider that the Roman occupation of France, Germany, and Britain extended over a period of four centuries, it will be evident that, as a consequence, Roman civilization made a strong impression upon the people of those countries.

The most durable and still visible impression was made by that feature of civilization expressed by the arts and sciences, as these had everywhere been disseminated directly by the *Colleges of Constructors,** and later, indirectly, by the Church, after it had allied itself with architecture and the Colleges. Hence, the process by which the external and internal workings of the Roman Collegia reached the Guilds of the Mediæval Ages will be clearly discernible, or in other words, it will be seen that the *Guilds* were simply a continuation of the *Colleges*.

Separation of Church and Art.

Luxury and dissipation having found its way into the Church, religious services had become but little better than mockery. This, and the domineering spirit shown by the Church toward lay Craftsmen, caused such dissatisfaction as resulted, in the eleventh century, in the withdrawal of the laity from the domination of the priests and the formation of independent Guilds, thus

* Notes 5 and 6, p. 370.

CANTERBURY CATHEDRAL.

resuming the plan of the old Colleges of Builders. And at the commencement of the twelfth century, not only architecture, but the other arts, had passed from the monasteries to the lay architects—the Guilds.* The formation of independent lay Guilds was also hastened by the attitude of the nobility toward artisans. Disregard of personal rights and numberless acts of violence drove the people to combine for their defence, and prominent among the defensive associations were the Masonic Guilds, who frequently defied not only the nobles, but royal authority. Therefore, at this time the Masonic Guilds assumed not only a definite, but a controlling, position in mediæval society.

In " Historical Account of Master and Free Mason," p. 420, we find that the Master Masons of England, in addition to the work they did for the government, were employed in the invention of military stratagems. The construction of all the public works, exclusive of church buildings, was also under the supervision of the Guilds.

THE ADMISSION OF NEW MEMBERS INTO GUILDS IN THE TWELFTH CENTURY.

Before opening a lodge a guard was stationed at the entrance of the cabin in which the meetings were held, to prevent the uninitiated from entering or seeing the transactions within. A candidate for admission had to meet the following requirements : He must be *free-born*, of a certain age, *physically sound*, and exhibit satisfactory evidence of his capacity to acquire a knowledge of Masonry and kindred arts. As in the Colleges of Builders, so in the Guilds, an initiation fee was required of the candidate.

All instruction necessary to enable the apprentice to become a Fellow was imparted to him, together with such grips and pass-words as prevented imposition from the uninitiated, attesting that the requirements then in vogue were substantially the same as now prevail in Free Masonry.

The time of an apprenticeship varied. In Germany it was fixed at five years; in France, six ; in England, seven years. Upon the expiration of the term the Craftsman was entitled to ask and receive advancement to the degree of Fellow or Companion, which grade in the line of promotion was exclusively recognized by the mediæval Masons.

* Note 12, p. 371.

In the thirteenth century apprentices, upon their advancement to the degree of Fellow, took the prescribed oath upon the Scriptures or Holy-Dome, which were held by a Senior Warden. The exact length of time that the obligated candidate remained a Fellow is not known, but it is inferable that when initiated into the secrets of this degree, he received the essentials of the mystic rites of the brotherhood, and when the prescribed time and proficiency entitled him to the final grade of Master, or third degree, it was conferred upon him. He was then instructed in the powers and duties pertaining to that degree, together with the secret symbolism which constitutes the groundwork of the institution, as the mystical and geometrical secrets of the Order were given in this degree.

The Masters held regular quarterly meetings, at which the affairs of the Fraternity were discussed and arranged; those who had violated any of the rules and regulations were tried and punished, and the meetings concluded with a feast. Early in the fourteenth century the Guilds were endowed with power to select by ballot any reputable citizen and accept him as a member. One Guild in England, whose origin was traceable beyond the Norman conquest, elected the clergy to membership.

In 1272, Edward I. reigned, and his son, Edward, was the first Prince of Wales—the Welsh having submitted to his father. In 1285 the laying of the cap-stone of Westminster Abbey was celebrated by a great concourse of Masons, with great pomp.

In 1331 King Edward III. became a member of a Guild in London, and his example was frequently followed by his successors, and the nobility of the kingdom.

Tracing the progress of the Craft in Britain, England, Germany, and France down to A.D. 1300, we find that they had so increased in numbers and importance that all the architecture of Europe was in their hands. Large bands of them, under the name of travelling Free Masons, passed from place to place, constructing cathedrals where such edifices were to be built.*

But that this order occupied a position in history of vastly more importance

---

* In a work entitled Parentalia, the author thus speaks of the Guilds: "Their government was regular, and where they fixed near a building in hand, they made a camp of huts. A surveyor governed in chief; every tenth man was called a Warden and overlooked each nine."

THE TOWER, LONDON.

GUILDS AND MASONS.

than a purely mechanical association, will be seen from the fact that since the sixth century it has numbered among its Grand Masters, or presiding officers, fourteen kings and princes and twelve dukes, who esteemed it an honor to belong to the Ancient Order.

In 1351 the craft, under William of Wykeham, were engaged in the erection of Windsor Castle; and here occurred a strike, as the men refused to proceed with the work unless their wages were raised. Their demands being refused, they abandoned the work in a body, but as the government did not then depend upon their votes an act was passed, compelling the recalcitrants to resume labor or be branded. They resumed labor.

The ancient records show that in 1422 there was a Lodge in successful operation at Canterbury, and the name of Thomas Staplyton is recorded as Master, John Morris Custos as Warden; there were also fifteen Fellow Crafts, and three Entered Apprentices named in the same record.

In the year 1438 the Grand Masters of Scotland are accorded jurisdiction by James II., King of Scotland, who also authorized them to establish special tribunals in the principal cities for the trial of Craftsmen for Masonic offences. For this privilege each Master Mason was to pay annually into the State Treasury a tax of four pounds. Each Grand Master was likewise authorized to have a reception fee collected for each new member. Immediately after this the King nominated William St. Clair to the position of Grand Master adjunct for the lodges of Scotland.

In 1442 Henry VI., King of England, was initiated into the Masonic fraternity, and his example was followed by nearly all the gentlemen of his court. As the King and these gentlemen were admitted as accepted Masons, it is supposed that all the details of initiation were not observed.

In 1607, James I. proclaimed himself protector of Free Masonry in his kingdom.

In 1666, a great conflagration took place in London, by which over 40,000 houses and ninety churches were destroyed. As such a wide-spread disaster left a large portion of the inhabitants without shelter, an army of builders was required at once. Therefore, a call was extended to the Masonic fraternity throughout Europe to repair to London and co-operate with the craft there in rebuilding the burnt city.

Soon after the commencement of these building operations the craft organized themselves into lodges, and this action was followed by placing the lodges under the Lodge of St. Paul.

In the reign of Henry VII., the Grand Master of the Order of St. John, at Rhodes, assembled all the knights in grand convocation, and chose Henry their protector. Subsequently, by virtue of his office of Protector, Henry appointed John Islip, the Abbot of Westminster, and Sir Richard Bray, Wardens, through whom his summons was issued for convening an assembly of Master Masons at his palace. And, on the assembling of the Craft, a grand procession was formed, under charge of the King, who walked to the East of Westminster Abbey and there laid the corner-stone of the King's Chapel, according to the ancient usages of the Order.*

During the reign of Edward VI. and the bloody Catholic Mary, but little of Masonic interest transpired. Elizabeth ascended the throne in 1558.

At this time the Fraternity had become so numerous in the south of England that it was deemed proper to district the kingdom, and appoint a Master in Chief of each district. Accordingly, Sir Francis Russel, Earl of Bedford, was chosen to take charge of the Masons in the Northern division, and Sir Thomas Gresham of the Southern; but the General Assembly continued to meet at York, where the records were at this time kept.

Sir Thomas Gresham superintended the building of the first Royal Exchange. The corner-stone of this English Bourse was laid on June 7, 1566, and it was finished in November, 1567. In 1570, the Queen, having dined with Sir Thomas, and been shown by him through the building, with which she was particularly pleased, she caused the name of the edifice to be proclaimed, by herald and trumpet, the *Royal Exchange*.

Charles Howard, Earl of Effingham, was next chosen Master, and presided in the south of England until 1588, when George Hastings, Earl of Huntingdon, was chosen Master, and served in that office until the death of Queen Elizabeth, in 1603.

On December 27, 1561, a general assembly of Masons met at York, and had organized for business, when, by order of Queen Elizabeth, a detachment of soldiers proceeded to their hall for the purpose of dissolving the

* Mitchel, vol. i., p. 184.

Chichester Cathedral.

assembly; but the officer commanding the troop, finding that the meeting had no political significance, so reported to the Queen, who revoked her order.

1590. King James of Scotland conferred upon Patrick Copland the right of filling the office of Senior Warden of Free Masons in Banff, Kincardine, and Aberdeen. Eight years later, at a general meeting in Edinburgh, new statutes from all the Lodges in Scotland were accepted and adopted.

Free Mason—Origin of the Term.

Several causes contributed to establish the prefix *Free*, to Mason. First, and principally, as the secrets could be extorted from *slaves*, none but *free* men were admitted into the hermetic societies.* Second, in many localities, the fraternity were exempt from taxes, made *free* of them, and were therefore called *Free* Masons. The French Masons made a practice of calling each other Frère (Brother), hence *Free* Mason. Lastly, the *free* stone-workers were often called Free Masons. Although this term had been in use for centuries,† yet it did not begin to appear on records much before the fourteenth.‡

The following examples are from old records, and from epitaphs in churchyards.

In 1535 the Dean and Chapter of Wells granted to William Atwodde, Free Mason, the office previously held in the church by William Smythe, with a yearly salary. The letter of appointment makes known that the salary in question has been granted to Atwodde for his good and faithful service in his art of Free Masonry.

" Rec. of the gudman Stefford, Fremason for the holle stepyll wt Tymbr, Iron and glas xxxviijl."

1550. The free mason heuyth the harde stone's and Hewyth of hre one pece and there another, tyll the stones be fytte and apte for the place where he wyll laye them. Euen so God the heavenly free mason builde thys christen churche, and he frameth and polysheth us, whiche are the costlye and precyous Stones wyth the crosse and afflicyon, that all abomynacyone and wickedness which do not agree unto thys gloryous buyldynge, myghte be removed and taken out of the waye I. Petr. II.

* Notes 13 and 14, p. 371. † Note 18, p. 372. ‡ Notes 15, 16, 17, pp. 371, 372.

1590. March 19th. John Kidd, of Leeds, Free Mason, gives bond to produce the original will of William Taylor, junr., of Leeds.

On a tomb in the Church of St. Helen, Bishopsgate, is the following:

"Here lyeth the bodie of William Kerwin of this city of London, Freemason, who departed this lyfe the 26th day of December ano 1594."

Among the epitaphs in Holy Trinity Churchyard, Hull, is the following: 1708, Dec. 27; under the above date Sarah Roebuck, late wife of John Roebuck, Freemason.

Entick, describing the two armories in the Tower of London, says: "It was begun by King James II., but finished by King William, who erected the small armory, in which he with Queen Mary his consort dined in great form, having all the Warrant Workmen . . . to attend them, dressed in white gloves and aprons, the usual badges of the Order of Free Masonry." *

Elias Ashmole.

This eminent mason and antiquary was the only child of Simon Ashmole, of Litchfield, in which city he was born May 23, 1617. At the age of sixteen he went to reside with his cousin, Thomas Paget, Esq., in London, where he remained for several years. In 1638 he married Eleanor, daughter of Peter Mainwaring, and during the same year became a solicitor in chancery. In 1641 he was sworn an attorney to the common pleas. He then practised law and prosecuted his studies till March, 1646, when he was made a Captain in Lord Ashley's regiment at Worcester, and on June 12 he was made Comptroller of the Ordnance. After the surrender of Worcester he withdrew to Cheshire, and on October 16th of the same year he was made a Free Mason.† Subsequently he returned to London, and having lost his wife several years previous, he married Lady Mainwaring in 1649. He at this time had for friends and associates men of note; and in 1661 he was admitted a Fellow of the Royal Society.

---

* Gould, vol. iii., pp. 154-167.

† There is, therefore, nothing to induce the supposition that the secrets of Free Masonry, as disclosed to Elias Ashmole in 1646—in aught but the manner of imparting them—differed materially, if at all, from those which passed into the guardianship of the Grand Lodge of England in 1717. Gould, vol. iv., p. 364.

He was the author of several important works, including hermetic works and a Masonic Ritual. He died May 18, 1692, aged seventy-five.

From Ashmole's Diary.

"Oct. 16, 4.30 p.m.—I was made a Free Mason at Warrington, in Lancashire, with Col. Henry Mainwaring, of Karincham, in Cheshire. The names of those that were then of the Lodge were Mr. Rich. Penket, Warden; Mr. James Collier, Mr. Rich. Sankey, Henry Littler, John Elam Rich, and Hugh Brewer."

Nothing of a Masonic character transpired in his intercourse with the fraternity that Ashmole thought worth recording again, until 1682, but at that date we find the following:

"March 16, 1682. 10.—About 5 p.m. I rec'd a summons to appear at a lodge to be held the next day at Mason's Hall, London. 11.—Accordingly I went, and about noone were admitted into the Fellowship of Masons Sir William Knight, Capt. Rich. Borthwick, Mr. Will. Woodman, Mr. Wm. Grey, Mr. Samuel Taylour, and Mr. William Wise.

"I was the Senior Fellow among them (it being thirty-five years since I was admitted). There were present beside myself the fellows after named: Mr. Thomas Wise, Mr: of the Masons Company this year. Mr. Thomas Shorthose, Mr. Thomas Shadbot. Wainsdford Esq., Mr. Nick: Young, Mr. John Shorthose, Mr. William Hamon, Mr. John Thompson, and Mr. Will: Stanton. We all dyned at the Halfe Moone Tavern in Cheapeside, at a noble dinner prepared at the charge of the New — accepted Masons."

The Rules or Orders of the Alnwicke Lodge.

"Orders to be observed by the Company and Fellowship of Freemasons att a Lodge held at Alnwicke, Septr. 29, 1701, being the Genl Head Meeting Day.

"First, it is ordered by the said Fellowship thatt there shall be yearly Two Wardens chosen upon the said Twenty-ninth of Septr., being the Feast of St. Michaell, the Archangell, which Wardens shall be elected and appoynted by the most consent of the Fellowship.*

* Gould, vol. iv., p. 262.

"Item. Thatt noe Mason shall take any work thatt any of his Fellows is in hand with all—to pay for every such offense the sum of.......£2. 6s. 8d.

"Item. Thatt noe Mason shall take any Apprentice (but he must) enter him and give him his charge within one whole year after. Nott soe doing, the master shall pay for every such offense .... 3s. 4d.

"Item. Thatt every master for entering his apprentice shall pay .....6d.

"Item. Thatt every Mason when he is warned by the Wardens or other of the Company, and shall nott come to the place appointed, except he have a reasonable cause to show the Master and Wardens to the contrary; nott soe doing shall pay .... 6s. 8d.

"8th Item. Thatt noe Mason shall show (shun) his Fellow or give him the lye, or any ways contend with him or give him any other name in the place of meeting, than Brother or Fellow, or hold any disobedient argument, against any of the Company reproachfully, for every such offense shall pay, 6d.

"Item. If any Mason, either in the place of meeting or att work among his Fellows, swear or take God's name in vain, thatt he or they soe offending shall pay for every time .... 5s. 4d.

"Item. Thatt if any Fellow or Fellows shall att any time or times discover his Master's secretts, or his owne, be it nott onely spoken in the Lodge or without, or the secretts or councell of his Fellows, thatt may extend to the damage of any of his Fellows, or to any of their good names, whereby the science may be ill spoken of, for every such offense, he shall pay ...£1 6s. 8d.

"Item. Thatt noe Fellow or Fellows within this Lodge shall att any time or times call or hold assemblys to make any Mason or Masons free: Nott acquainting the Master or Wardens therewith, for every time so offending shall pay .... £3 6s. 8d.

"Item. Thatt all Fellows being younger shall give his elder Fellows the honor due to their degree and standing. Alsoe thatt the Master Wardens, and all the Fellows of this Lodge doe promise severally and respectively to performe all and every the orders above named, and to stand bye each other (but most particularly to the Wardens and their successors) in sueing for all and every the forfeitures of our said Brethren, contrary to any of the said orders, demand therefor being just made." *

* Gould, vol. iv., p. 267.

AN ANCIENT STREET—LONDON.

"At a true and perfect Lodge kept at Alnwicke, at the house of Mr. Thomas Davidson, one of the Wardens of the same Lodge, it was ordered that for the future noe member of the said Lodge, Master, Wardens, or Fellows should appear at any Lodge to be kept on St. John's day without his *apron* and common *square* fixed in the belt thereof; upon pain of forfeiting two shillings and six pence, each person offending, and that care be taken by the Master and Wardens for the time being, that a sermon be provided and preached that day at the parish church of Alnwicke by some clergyman at their appointment; when the Lodge shall all appear with their aprons on, and common squares as aforesaid, and that the Master and Wardens neglecting their duty in providing a clergyman to preach as aforesaid shall forfeit the sum of ten shillings."

From the Records of Smallwell Lodge—Entered Apprentices.

"For as much as you are contracted and bound to me of our Brethren: We are here assembled together with one accord to dictate unto you the Laudable Dutys appertaining unto those yt are Apprentices to those who are of the Lodge of Masonry, which if you take good heed unto and keep, will find the same worthy your regard for a worthy Science: for at the building of the Tower of Babylon, and Citys of the East, King Nimrod the son of Cush, the Son of Ham &c., gave charges and orders to Masons, as also did Abraham in Egypt. King David and his son King Solomon, at the building of the temple at Jerusalem, and many more Kings and Princes of worthy memory from time to time and did not only promote the ffame of the 7 Liberal Sciences, but formed Lodges and gave and granted their commissions and Charters to those of, or belonging to the Science of Masonry, to keep and hold their assemblys for correcting of faults, or making of Masons, when, and where, they pleased."

After the restoration of Charles II., who had suffered much in exile and knew the value of Masonry, he embraced the earliest opportunity to restore the ancient Order to its wonted prosperity. Therefore on the 27th of December, 1663, a General Assembly of Masons was held under the authority of the King.

At this Assembly, Henry Jermyn, Earl of St. Albans, was chosen Grand

Master, and after the transaction of preliminary business the following resolutions were adopted:

"1. That no person of what degree soever be made or accepted a Freemason, unless in a regular lodge, whereof one to be a Master or Warden in that limit or division where such lodge is kept, and another to be a Craftsman in the trade of Freemasonry.

"2. That no person hereafter shall be accepted a Freemason but such as are of able body, honest parentage, good reputation, and an observer of the laws of the land.

"3. That no person hereafter who shall be accepted a Freemason shall be admitted into a Lodge or assembly until he has brought a certificate of the time and place of his acceptation from the Lodge that accepted him unto the Master of that limit or division where such Lodge is kept, and the said Master shall enroll the same in a roll of parchment, to be kept for that purpose, and shall give an account of all such acceptations at every General Assembly.

"4. That every person who is now a Freemason shall bring to the Master a note of the time of his acceptation, to the end that the same may be enrolled in such priority of place as the brother deserves; and that the whole company and Fellows may the better know each other.

"5. For the future the said Fraternity of Freemasons shall be regulated and governed by one Grand Master, and as many Wardens as the said Society shall think fit to appoint at every annual General Assembly.

"6. That no person shall be accepted unless he be twenty-one years old, or more."

SPECULATIVE MASONRY.

1717. We have now arrived at the second, and grand epoch in the history of the ancient craft. This begins with the reorganization of Free Masonry, the disappearance of the operative domination in the Society, and its assumption of a speculative or philosophic character. Notwithstanding the fact that members of the Masonic Guilds, both in England and in other countries, had for many centuries been known as Free Masons, and that their esoteric teachings had gradually become more and more of a speculative character,* yet until this time their membership had principally been composed

* Notes 20, 21, 22, pp. 372, 373.

of operative Masons. Now, however, a change is to be made by which the temples of the Fraternity are to be thrown open to good and true men without reference to their calling, religion, or nationality.

In 1703 the Lodge of St. Paul, after due deliberation, passed the following important resolution : " RESOLVED, THAT THE PRIVILEGES of Masonry shall no longer be confined to OPERATIVE MASONS, but be free to men of all professions, provided that they are regularly approved and initiated into the Fraternity." The object of this act was to augment the membership of the Society by the admission of men in the different ranks of life, and thereby perpetuate its philosophical and religious principles as taught by allegories and symbols.

But on account of the opposition of some influential members, this change was not adopted by the fraternity at large until 1717. At that time a general assembly was convened in London, the resolution of 1703 adopted, and the first real Grand Lodge constituted.

Soon after the establishment of the Grand Lodge of England it commenced to organize lodges, and this suggested the necessity of better regulations. Therefore, in 1718, George Payne, then Grand Master, requested the brethren to unite with him in collecting all the old documents and records pertaining to the subject.* The result was the collection of considerable important data, including the Gothic constitutions, from which he compiled and arranged a series of charges and regulations. These were submitted to the Grand Lodge under Montagu, in September, 1721, and after its consideration by that body, they empowered Dr. James Anderson to revise and prepare the same as a Code of Law and Doctrine for the use of the Lodges in England. This, by the assistance of Payne and Desaguliers, he did, and at the meeting of the Grand Lodge held at the Queen's Arms, St. Paul's Churchyard, on December 27, 1721 (being the Festival of St. John the Evangelist), the same was presented for approbation. Upon which a committee of fourteen learned brothers was appointed to examine the manuscript and report.

On March 25, 1722, at a Grand Lodge held at the Fountain Tavern, in the Strand, the committee reported that they had examined the manuscript containing the history, charges, regulations, etc., of Masonry, and after some

---
* See Gould, vol. iv., pp. 280-348.

amendments had *approved* of the same. The G. L. approved of the conclusions of the committee, and directed that the book be published, * which was done, and submitted to that body in print, January 17, 1723, under the title: "The Book of Constitutions of the Freemasons; containing the History, Charges, Regulations, etc., of the most Ancient and Right Worshipful Fraternity. For the use of the Lodges."

Thus originated the famous "History, Charges, and Regulations of the Most Ancient and Right Worshipful Fraternity."

Returning to the year 1717, the establishment of the historic Grand Lodge of that date, together with a sketch of succeeding Grand Lodges, will now be given, and in the peculiar language of Dr. Anderson:

"King George I. entered London most magnificently on September 20, 1714. And after the rebellion was over, 1716 A.D., the few Lodges at London, finding themselves neglected by Sir Christopher Wren, thought fit to cement under a Grand Master as the Center of Union and Harmony, viz., the Lodges that met."

"No. 1.   . . .   Ale-house, in St. Paul's Churchyard.

"2.   At the Crown Ale-house, in Parker's Lane, near Drury Lane.

"3.   At the Apple-Tree Tavern, in Charles Street, Covent Garden.

"4.   At the Rummer and Grapes Tavern, in Channcel Row, Westminster.†

"They and some old Brothers met at the said Apple-Tree, and having put into the chair the oldest Master Mason (now the Master of a Lodge), they constituted themselves a Grand Lodge pro Tempore in Due Form, and forthwith revived the *Quarterly* communication of the Officers of Lodges (call'd the Grand Lodge), resolved to hold the Annual Assembly and Feast, and then to chuse a Grand Master from among themselves till they should have the Honour of a Noble Brother at their Head. ‡

"Accordingly, on St. John Baptist's Day, in the third year of King George I., 1717 A.D., the Assembly and feast of the Free and accepted Masons was held at the foresaid Goose and Gridiron Ale-house. §

"Before Dinner, the oldest Master Mason (now the Master of a Lodge), in

---

* See Mitchell, pp. 241, 242. Also Notes 23, 24, and 26, p. 373.
† Gould, vol. iv., p. 279.   ‡ Note 25, p. 373.
§ The first four Grand Masters were elected under the banner of the old Lodge of St. Paul. See Gould, vol. iv., note 4, p. 282.

the Chair, proposed a list of proper Candidates; and the Brethren by the majority of Hands elected Mr. Anthony Sayer, Gentleman, Grand Master of Masons, who being forthwith invested with the Badges of Office and Power by the said oldest Master, and install'd, was duly congratulated by the Assembly, who pay'd him the Homage; Mr. Jacob Lamball, Carpenter, and Captain Joseph Elliot, Grand Wardens.

"Sayer, Grand Master, commanded the Masters and Wardens of Lodges to meet the Grand Officers every *Quarter* in Communication, at the Place that he should appoint in his Summons sent by the Tyler.

"Assembly and Feast at the said Place, 24 June, 1718. Brother Sayer having gathered the Votes, after Dinner proclaim'd aloud our Brother George Payne, Esq., Grand Master of Masons, who being duly invested, install'd, congratulated, and homaged, recommended the strict Observance of the Quarterly Communication; Mr. John Cordwell, City Carpenter, and Mr. Thomas Morrice, Stone-cutter, Grand Wardens. And desired any Brethren to bring to the Grand Lodge any old Writings and Records concerning Masons and Masonry, in order to show the Usages of antient Times; and this year several old Copies of the Gothic Constitutions were produced and collated.

"Assembly and Feast at the said Place, 24 June, 1719. Brother Payne having gather'd the Votes, after Dinner proclaim'd aloud our Reverend Brother John Theophilus Desaguliers, LL.D. and F.R.S., Grand Master of Masons, and being duly invested, install'd, congratulated, and homaged, forthwith reviv'd the old regular and peculiar Toasts or Healths of the Free Masons. Now several old Brothers, that had neglected the Craft, visited the Lodges; some Noblemen were also made Brothers, and more new Lodges were constituted. Mr. Anthony Sayer foresaid and Tho. Morrice, Grand Wardens.

"Assembly and Feast at the foresaid Place, 24 June, 1720. Brother Desaguliers having gather'd the Votes, after Dinner proclaim'd aloud George Payne, Esq., again Grand Master of Masons, who being duly invested, install'd, congratulated, and homag'd, began the usual Demonstration of Joy, Love, and Harmony. Mr. Thos. Hobby, Stone-cutter, and Mr. Rich. Ware, Mathematician, Grand Wardens.

"This Year, at some private Lodges, several very valuable manuscripts (for they had nothing yet to print) concerning the fraternity, their Lodges, Regulations, Charges, Secrets, and Usages (particularly one writ by Mr. Nicholas Stone, the Warden of Inigo Jones) were too hastily burnt by some scrupulous Brothers; that those papers might not fall into strange Hands.

"At the Quarterly Communication or Grand Lodge, in ample Form, on St. John Evangelist's Day, 1720, at the said Place.

"It was agreed, in order to avoid disputes on the Annual Feast-day, that the new Grand Master for the future shall be named and proposed to the Grand Lodge some time before the Feast, by the present or old Grand Master; and if approv'd that the Brother proposed, if present, shall be kindly saluted; or even if absent, his Health shall be toasted as Grand Master Elect.

"Also agreed, that for the future the New Grand Master, as soon as he is install'd, shall have the sole Power of appointing both his Grand Wardens and a Deputy Grand Master (now found as necessary as formerly) according to antient Custom, when Noble Brothers were Grand Masters.

"Accordingly

"At the Grand Lodge in ample Form on Lady-Day, 1721, at the said place, Grand Master Payne proposed for his Successor our most Noble Brother John, Duke of Montagu, Master of a Lodge; who, being present, was forthwith saluted Grand Master Elect, and his Health drank in due Form; when they all express'd great Joy at the happy Prospect of being again patronized by noble Grand Masters. . . .

"Payne, Grand Master, observing the number of Lodges to increase, and that the General Assembly requir'd more Room, proposed the next Assembly and Feast to be held at Stationers' hall, Ludgate Street; which was agreed to.

"Then the Grand Wardens were order'd, as usual, to prepare the feast, and to take some Stewards to their Assistance, Brothers of Ability and Capacity, and to appoint some Brethren to attend the Tables; for that no strangers must be there. But the Grand Officers not finding a proper Number of Stewards, our Brother Mr. Josiah Villeneau, Upholder in the Burrough Southwark, generously undertook the whole himself, attended by some Waiters, Thomas Morrice, Francis Bailey, &c.

"Assembly and Feast at Stationers' Hall, 24 June, 1721, in the 7th Year of King George I.

SPECULATIVE MASONRY. 307

"Payne, Grand Master, with his Wardens, the former Grand Officers, and the Masters and Wardens of 12 Lodges, met the Grand Master Elect in a Grand Lodge at the King's Arms Tavern, St. Paul's Churchyard, in the Morning; and having forthwith recognized their Choice of Brother Montagu, they made some new Brothers, particularly the Noble Philip, Lord Stanhope, now Earl of Chesterfield; And from thence they marched on Foot to the Hall in proper Clothing and due Form; where they were joyfully receiv'd by about 150 true and faithful, all clothed.

"After Grace said, they sat down in the antient manner of Masons to a very elegant Feast, and dined with Joy and Gladness. After Dinner and Grace said, Brother Payne, the old Grand Master, made the First Procession round the Hall, and when return'd he proclaim'd aloud the most noble Prince and our brother,* John Montagu, Duke of Montagu, Grand Master of Masons. . . . Montagu, Grand Master immediately called forth . . . John Beal, M.D., as his Deputy Grand Master. . . .

"In like Manner his Worship call'd forth and appointed Mr. Josiah Villeneau and Mr. Thomas Morrice, Grand Wardens, who were invested and installed by the last Grand Wardens.

"Upon which the Deputy and Wardens were saluted and congratulated as usual.

"Then Montagu, G. Master, with his Officers and the old officers, having made the 2d procession round the Hall, Brother Desaguliers made an eloquent Oration about Masons and Masonry; And after great Harmony, the Effect of brotherly Love, the Grand Master thank'd Brother Villeneau for his Care of the Feast, and ordered him as Warden, to close the Lodge in good time.

"The Grand Lodge in ample Form on September 29, 1721, at King's Arms foresaid, with the former Grand Officers and those of 16 Lodges.

"His Grace's Worship and the Lodge finding fault with all the Copies of the old Gothic Constitutions, order'd Bro. James Anderson, A. M., to digest the same in a new and better Method.

"The Grand Lodge in ample Form on St. John's Day, 27 Dec., 1721, at the said King's-Arms, with former Grand Officers and those of 20 Lodges.

"Montagu, Grand Master, at the Desire of the Lodge, appointed 14

* Gould, vol. iv., pp. 282, 283.

learned Brothers to examine Brother Anderson's Manuscript, and to make report. This Communication was made very entertaining by the Lectures of some old Masons.

"Grand Lodge at the Fountain, Strand, in ample Form, 25 March, 1722, with former Grand officers and those of 24 Lodges.

"The said Committee of 14 reported that they had perused Brother Anderson's Manuscript, viz., the History, Charges, Regulations, and Master's Song, and after some Amendments had approv'd of it: Upon which the Lodge desir'd the Grand Master to order it to be printed. Meanwhile ingenious Men of all Faculties and Stations being convinced that the Cement of the Lodge was Love and Friendship, earnestly requested to be made Masons, Affecting this amicable Fraternity more than other Societies, then often disturbed by warm disputes.

"Grand Master Montagu's good Government inclin'd the better Sort to continue him in the Chair another Year; and therefore they delay'd to prepare the Feast.

"May 25th, 1722 —Met the Duke of Queensboro', Lord Dunbarton, Hinchinbroke, &c., at Fountain Tavern Lodge, to consider of (the) feast of St. John's."

"Nov. 3rd,[*] 1722.—The Duke of Wharton and Lord Dalkeith visited our lodge at the Fountain.

"But Philip, Duke of Wharton, lately made a Brother, tho' not the Master of a Lodge, being ambitious of the Chair, got a Number of Others to meet him at Stationers' Hall, 24 June, 1722. And having no Grand Officers, they put in the Chair the oldest Master Mason (who was not the present Master of a Lodge, also irregular), and without the usual decent Ceremonials, the said old Mason proclaimed aloud: Philip Wharton, Duke of Wharton, Grand Master of Masons, and Mr. Joshua Timson, Blacksmith, and Mr. William Hawkins, Mason, Grand Wardens; but his Grace appointed no Deputy, nor was the Lodge opened and closed in due form.

"Therefore the noble Brothers and all those that would not countenance Irregularities, disown'd Wharton's Authority, till worthy Brother Montagu heal'd the Breach of Harmony by summoning the Grand Lodge to meet

---

[*] The entries of May 25 and November 3, 1722, are from Dr Stukely's Diary and introduced to fill a break that occurs here in Anderson's account. See Gould, vol. iv., p. 288.

SPECULATIVE MASONRY.

17 January, 1723, at the King's-Arms foresaid, where the Duke of Wharton, promising to be true and Faithful, Deputy Grand Master Beal proclaim'd aloud the most noble Prince and our Brother, Philip Wharton, Duke of Wharton, Grand Master of Masons, who appointed Dr. Desaguliers the Deputy Grand Master, Joshua Timson foresaid, and James Anderson, A. M., Grand Wardens, for Hawkins, demitted as always out of Town, when former Grand Officers, with those of 25 Lodges, paid their Homage.

" G. Warden Anderson produced the new book of Constitutions, now in print, which was again approv'd, with the Addition of the Antient Manner of Constituting a Lodge.

" Now *Masonry* flourished in Harmony, Reputation, and Numbers; many Noblemen and Gentlemen of the first Rank desir'd to be admitted into the *Fraternity*, besides other Learned Men, Merchants, Clergymen, and Tradesmen, who found a Lodge to be a safe and pleasant Relaxation from Intense Study or the Hurry of Business, without Politicks or Party. Therefore the Grand Master was obliged to constitute more new Lodges and was very assiduous in visiting the Lodges every Week with his Deputy and Wardens; and his Worship was as well pleas'd with their kind and respectful Manner of receiving him, as they were with his affable and clever conversation.

" Grand Lodge in ample Form, 25 April, 1723, at the White Lion, Cornhill, with former Grand Officers and those of 30 Lodges, call'd over by G. Warden Anderson, for no Secretary was yet appointed; when Wharton, Grand Master, proposed for his Successor the Earl of Dalkeith (now Duke of Buckleugh), Master of a Lodge, who was unanimously approv'd and duly saluted as Grand Master Elect." *

At a meeting held April 28, 1724, Grand Master Dalkeith proposed the Duke of Richmond as his successor, and he was saluted as Grand Master elect.

"At the assembly and feast, June 24, 1724, Grand Master Dalkeith, his Deputy and Wardens, visited the Duke of Richmond, in the morning, at his house in Whitehall, who, with many brothers duly clothed, proceeded in coaches from the West to the East, and were handsomely received at the hall by a large assembly.†

* Note 27, p. 373; Gould, vol. iv, p. 290. † Mitchel, p. 244.

"The Grand Lodge met, and having confirmed their choice of . . . Grand Master, adjourned to dinner. Dinner being ended, Grand Master Dalkeith made the first procession around the tables, viz., Bro. Clinch to clear the way;

"The Stewards, two and two abreast with white rods;

"Secretary Cowper, with the bag, and on his left the master of a Lodge, with one great light;

"Two other great lights borne by two masters of Lodges;

"Former Grand Wardens proceeding one by one, according to juniority;

"Former Grand Masters proceeding according to juniority;

"Sorrel and Senex, the two Grand Wardens;

"Desaguliers, Deputy Grand Master, alone;

"The Sword carried by the Master of the Lodge to which the sword belonged;

"The Book of Constitutions on a cushion carried by the Master of the Senior Lodge present;

"Richmond, Grand Master elect, and Grand Master Dalkeith.

"During the procession around the table three times, the brethren stood up and faced about with regular salutations; and when returned, Bro. Dalkeith stood up and, bowing to the assembly, thanked them for the honor he had of being Grand Master, and then proclaimed aloud to the most noble prince and our Bro. Charles Lenox, Duke of Richmond and Lenox, Grand Master of Masons. The Duke having bowed to the assembly Bro. Dalkeith invested him with the ensigns and badges of his office and authority, installed him in Solomon's Chair, and wishing him all prosperity sat down at his right hand. Upon which the assembly joined in due homage, affectionate congratulations, and other signs of joy." . . .

This concludes the first *seven* years—the eventful period in the history of the Grand Lodge of England.

December 15, 1730.—" Brother Sayer attended the Grand Lodge to answer the complaint made against him, and after hearing both parties, and some of the Brethren being of the opinion that what he had done was clandestine, others that it was irregular, the question was put whether what was done was clandestine, or irregular only, and the Lodge was of the opinion that it was irregular only; whereupon the Deputy Grand Master told Brother Sayer that he was acquitted of the charge against him, and recommended it to him to do nothing so irregular for the future." . . .

"In April, 1735, Lord Weymouth was installed Grand Master, and to give our readers some idea of the estimation in which the fraternity was then held by the nobility and gentry, we mention the following individuals as being present on that occasion, viz.: The Dukes of Richmond and Athol; the Earls of Crawford, Winchelsea, Balcarras, Weyms, and London; the Marquis of Beaymont; Lords Cathcart and Vene Bertre; Sir Cecil Wray and Sir Edward Mansell."*

ORDER OBSERVED IN MASONIC PROCESSIONS IN 1742.

Tyler to clear the way.
The Music.
The First light, carried by the Master of the fourth Lodge.
The Wardens of the Steward's Lodge.
The Master of the Steward's Lodge.
The Grand Secretary with the bag.
The Grand Treasurer with the staff.
The Provincial Grand Masters, juniors to walk first.
All Past Junior Grand Wardens, juniors to walk first.
All Past Senior Grand Wardens, juniors to walk first.
The Second Light, carried by the Master of the third Lodge.
All former Deputy Grand Masters, juniors to walk first.
The Third Light carried by the Master of the second Lodge.
The Junior Grand Warden.   The Senior Grand Warden.
The Deputy Grand Master.
The Master of the Senior Lodge, with the Constitution on a cushion.
The Grand Master elect.
The Sword Bearer, carrying the Sword of State.
The Grand Master.

On April 3, 1747, a resolution was passed discontinuing for the future the usual procession on the feast day. "The occasion of this prudent regulation was that some unfaithful brethren, disappointed in their expectations of the

* Mitchell, p. 255.

high offices and honors of the society, had joined a number of the buffoons of the day in a scheme to exhibit a mockery of the public procession to the grand feast."

Other Notable Events.

Lord Byron was elected Grand Master on April 30, 1747, and presided over the fraternity until March 20, 1752, when he proposed Lord Carysfort as his successor.

In 1787, the Prince of Wales, Sir Samuel Hulse, Col. Stanhope, Lord Lake, and others petitioned the Duke of Cumberland, then Grand Master, for a warrant to constitute a new Lodge, to be called Prince of Wales Lodge. This petition was granted in 1787. Sir Samuel Hulse was named the first Master, Col. Stanhope and Lord Lake, Wardens. Soon after this, however, the Prince of Wales was made Master of the Lodge, and in 1792 the Dukes of York and Clarence were elected Wardens, which offices they filled until the Prince of Wales ascended the throne.*

In 1827, Humber Lodge laid the corner-stone of a new Masonic Hall, the ceremony of which commenced as follows:

Dep. G. M.—I hereby, in the presence of all these Worshipful Masters, Wardens, and Deacons, and in the presence of all these Master Masons, worthy and diligent workmen of our secret Craft, do ask of you and your company if you know yourself at this time to have done anything contrary to the law of Masonry, which has not been told to the provincial authorities, and whereby you should be suspended from your work?

W. M.—We are good Masons at this very time.

D. P. G. M.—Have you among your company any brother guilty of brawlings, strife, and disobedience in open Lodge?

W. M.—We have none, Right Worshipful Master.

D. P. G. M.—Have you among your company any brother who, in open lodge, is guilty of drunkenness, common swearing, or profane words?

W. M.—We have none, Right Worshipful Master.

D. P. G. M.—Have you authority to do this day's work?

*Mitchell, p. 388.

W. M.—We have, Right Worshipful Master, and, with your permission, will here read it.

The authority was then read, the procession formed, and the corner-stone laid in ample form.*

SCHISMS.

As every publication of the schisms and contentions that have from time to time taken place in the different bodies of Free Masonry, furnishes material with which cranks and fanatics can assail the institution, their publication is neither profitable nor dignified. Consequently all such matters will receive but little further notice in this work than is necessary to maintain the sequence of current Masonic history.

In consequence of the erasure of lodges for not attending the quarterly meetings and non-payment of dues to the Grand Lodge as instituted in London in 1717, both members and lodges commenced in 1739 to dissent and rebel against the Grand Lodge.† The seceders did not at first set up a Grand Lodge, but simply held themselves independent of all authority—denied the right of a general governing head. They professed to be governed by the ancient law which authorized any number of Masons to assemble when and where they please, and there to make Masons. But dissatisfaction and discontent increased until 1752, when the schism culminated in an open rebellion and the establishment of an independent body, which at first they termed "Grand Committee."

On February 5, 1752, the seceders met at the Griffin Tavern, in Holborn, London, where were present the representatives of Lodges from No. two to ten inclusive, when upon the representation of John Morgan, the Grand Secretary, that he wished to retire from office, Lawrence Dermott was examined as to his qualifications for the position, and unanimously chosen Grand Secretary. Later on he became Deputy Grand Master; and being both aggressive and energetic, he did not hesitate to take any advantage of the other body, within his power. Therefore he designated his Grand Lodge the "Ancient York Masons," and the Grand Lodge of England "The Moderns." But upon ascertaining that the "Grand Lodge of All England" at

* Mitchell, p. 390. † Note 28, p. 373.

York was still in operation, he dropped the name "York" and took the title of "Ancients." This significant distinction helped his society immensely.* The new body was furnished with a constitution by Dermott, which he termed the "Ahiman Rezon," the first edition of which was published in 1756, under the title "Ahiman Rezon: or a Help to a Brother."

In 1771 John, the third Duke of Athol, was installed Grand Master, and in 1775 he was succeeded by the fourth Duke of Athol. From this fact the "Ancients" were also called Athol Masons; and during the Grand Mastership of the Athols they granted dispensations for lodges in North America which ultimately resulted in capturing the Grand Lodges of several States.

The trouble between the Grand Lodge of England, established in 1717 at London, and the Lodge of All England, at *York*, was caused by the establishment of lodges by the first-named Grand Lodge at different places in Yorkshire. The culminating point appears to have been the establishment of a lodge in the city of York itself in 1761. This spurred the York Grand Lodge into renewed activity, which was manifested by the establishment of lodges in territory especially claimed by the Grand Lodge at London. But this, as well as the Dermott schism, was healed at the general reconciliation in 1813.

On St. John's Day, December 27th of that year, the brethren of the several lodges who had been previously reobligated and certified by the Lodge of Reconciliation were arranged on the two sides of Free Mason's Hall, in such order that the two Fraternities were completely intermixed. The two Grand Masters seated themselves, into equal chairs, on each side of the throne. The Act of Union was then read and accepted, ratified, and confirmed by the Assembly.

"One Grand Lodge was then constituted. The Duke of Kent then stated that the great view with which he had taken upon himself the important office of Grand Master of the Ancient Fraternity, as declared at the time, was to facilitate the important object of the Union, which had been that day so happily consummated. He therefore proposed His Royal Highness the Duke of Sussex to be Grand Master of the United Grand Lodge of Ancient Freemasons of England for the year ensuing. This being put to vote, was carried unanimously, and the Duke of Sussex received the homage of the Fraternity." †

* Notes 29 and 30, p. 374. † Gould, vol. iv., pp. 414, 447, 502.

GRAND MASTERS "GRAND LODGE OF ENGLAND," FROM A.D. 1717.

"MODERNS."

1. 1717. Anthony Sayer.
2. 1718. George Payne.
3. 1719. J. T. Desaguliers, LL.D., F.R.S.
4. 1720. George Payne (re-elected).
5. 1721. John, Duke of Montague.
6. 1722. Philip, Duke of Wharton.
7. 1723. Francis Scott, Earl of Dalkeith.
8. 1724. Charles Lennox, Duke of Richmond.
9. 1725. James Hamilton, Lord Paisley.
10. 1726. William O'Brien, Earl of Inchiquin.
11. 1727. Henry Hare, Lord Coleraine.
12. 1728. James King, Lord Kingston.
13. 1729–1730. Thomas Howard, Duke of Norfolk.
14. 1731. Lord Lovel (Earl of Leicester).
15. 1732. Anthony Brown, Lord (Viscount) Montague.
16. 1733. James Lyon, Earl of Strathmore.
17. 1734. John Lindsay, Earl of Crawford.
18. 1735. Thomas Thynne, Lord (Viscount) Weymouth.
19. 1736. John Campbell, Earl of Loudoun.
20. 1737. Eduard Bligh, Earl of Darnley.
21. 1738. Henry Brydges, Marquis of Carnarvon.
22. 1739. Robert, Lord Raymond.
23. 1740. John Keith, Earl of Kintore.
24. 1741. James Douglas, Earl of Morton.
25. 1742–1743. John, Lord (Viscount) Dudley and Ware.
26. 1744. Thomas Lyon, Earl of Strathmore.
27. 1745–1746. James, Lord Cranstoun.
28. 1747–1751. William, Lord Byron.
29. 1752–1753. John Proby, Lord Carysfort.

30.	1754–1756.	James Brydges, Marquis of Carnarvon (Duke of Chandos).
31.	1757–1761.	Sholto Douglas, Lord Aberdour.
32.	1762–1763.	Washington Shirley, Earl Ferrers.
33.	1764–1767.	Cadwallader, Lord Blaney.
34.	1768–1771.	Henry Somerset, Duke of Beaufort.
35.	1772–1776.	Robert Edmund, Lord Petre.
36.	1777–1781.	George Montague, Duke of Manchester.
37.	1782–1790.	H. R. H. Duke of Cumberland.
38.	1791–1812.	H. R. H. the Prince of Wales (His Majesty George IV.).
39.	1813.	H. R. H. Augustus Frederick, Duke of Sussex.*

GRAND-MASTERS "GRAND LODGE OF ALL ENGLAND, HELD AT YORK."

"YORK MASONS."

1.	1705.	Sir George Tempest, Baronet.
2.	1707.	The Rt. Hon. Robert Benson, Lord Mayor of York.
3.	1708.	Sir William Robinson, Baronet.
4.	1711.	Sir William Hawkesworth, Baronet.
5.	1713.	Sir George Tempest, Baronet.
6.	1714.	Charles Fairfax, Esq.
7.	1720.	Sir Walter Hawkesworth, Baronet.
8.	1725.	Edward Bell.
9.	1726.	Charles Bathurst.
10.	1729.	Edward Thompson.
11.	1733.	John Johnson, M.D.
12.	1734.	John Marsden.

(Hiatus.)

13.	1761–1762.	Francis Drake, F.R.S.
14.	1763–1764.	John Sawry Morritt.
15.	1765–1766.	John Palmer.
16.	1767.	Seth Agar.

* McClenachan, vol. i., pp. 52, 53.

SPECULATIVE MASONRY. 317

17. 1768-1770. George Palmer.
18. 1771-1772. Sir Thomas Gascoigne, Baronet.
19. 1773. Charles Chaloner.
20. 1774-1775. Henry Stapleton.
21. 1776-1779. William Siddall.
22. 1780. Francis Smyth, Jr.
23. 1782. Robert Sinclair.
24. 1783-1784. William Siddall.
25. 1790. Thomas Kilby.
26. 1792. Eduard Wolley.

GRAND MASTERS " GRAND LODGE OF ENGLAND."

"ANCIENTS."

1. 1753. Robert Turner.
2. 1754-1755. Edward Vaughan.
3. 1756-1759. Earl of Blessington.
4. 1760-1765. Earl of Kelly.
5. 1766-1770. The Hon. Thomas Matthew.
6. 1771-1774. John, third Duke of Athol.
7. 1775-1781. John, fourth Duke of Athol.
8. 1782-1790. Earl of Antrim (Marquis of Antrim).
9. 1791-1813. John, fourth Duke of Athol.
10. 1813. H. R. H. Duke of Kent.

GRAND MASTERS OF THE " UNITED GRAND LODGE OF ENGLAND."

1. 1813-1842. H. R. H. Duke of Sussex, K.G.
2. 1843-1869. Earl of Zetland, K.G.
3. 1870-1874. Marquis of Ripon, K.G.
4. 1874-1901. H. R. H. Albert Edward, Prince of Wales.
5. 1901- Duke of Connaught.

SPECULATIVE MASONRY.

Sir Christopher Wren.

As frequent mention is made of this distinguished architect in connection with the History of Free Masonry in England, he by some writers having been made to pose as G. M., a brief sketch of his life will be of interest to the Fraternity.*

Sir Christopher was the son of Dr. Wren, and was born in Wiltshire, October 20, 1632. In his fourteenth year he was entered as a gentleman commoner in Wadham College, Oxford. Even at this early age he was noted for his mathematical knowledge, and was an inventor of several mathematical and astronomical instruments. At the age of twenty-one he was elected a Fellow of All Souls' College and had achieved distinction as an inventor of scientific instruments, etc.

In 1660 he was appointed by King Charles II. one of a commission to superintend the restoration of St. Paul's Cathedral. Before, however, the designs could be carried into execution, the great conflagration occurred which laid a great part of London, including St. Paul's, in ashes.

Soon after the great fire, he was appointed assistant to Sir John Denham, the Surveyor-General, in the great work of rebuilding the city. Meeting with opposition to his plans for the future restoration of the burnt districts, he abandoned his position with Denham, but subsequently he superseded him. Having then full scope for his genius, he erected a large number of churches and other public edifices. But the crowning work of his life was the erection of St. Paul's Cathedral, which was begun in 1675 and completed in 1710. Notwithstanding that the authorities seriously altered his plans, yet this Cathedral is held to be one of the finest edifices in Europe to-day.†

When surveying the ground to begin this mighty edifice, there was an occurrence that was regarded by many as an omen of good. Having determined the outward lines for the foundation of the building, he found the centre, and sent a laborer for a stone to mark the spot, who seizing upon the first he came to among the rubbish, brought up part of an old grave-stone, having on it but a single word of the original engraving, viz., Resurgam.

In the progress of the work on the foundations, Wren met with an

---

* See Gould, vol. iii., pp. 3–55. † Note 19, p. 372.

unexpected difficulty. He began to lay the foundation from the west end, and had progressed successfully to the east end, where the bottom was very good; but as he went on to the northeast corner, which was the last, and where nothing was expected to interrupt, he came upon a pit, where all the pot-earth had been robbed by the potters of old times.

Here were discovered quantities of urns, broken vessels, and pottery ware of divers sorts and shapes. How far this pit extended northward there was no occasion to examine. "It was no little perplexity to fall into this pit at last." He wanted but six or seven feet to complete the design, and this fell into the very angle northeast. He knew very well that under the layer of pot-earth there was no other good ground to be found till he came to the low-water mark of the Thames, at least forty feet lower. His artificers proposed to him to pile, which he refused, for the piles may last forever when always in water, otherwise they would rot. His endeavors were to build for eternity. He therefore sunk a pit about eighteen feet square, to the depth of forty feet, where he found a firm sea-beach, which confirmed the opinion of many that the sea had been, in ages past, where St. Paul's Church stands.

The following is from a paper prepared by Sir Christopher Wren in his old age, designed as a letter of instruction to those who might succeed him:

"Since Providence, in great mercy, has protracted my age to the finishing the Cathedral church of St. Paul's and the parochial churches of London, in lieu of those demolished by the fire, and being now constituted one of the commissioners for building, pursuant to the late act, fifty more churches in London and Westminster, I shall presume to communicate, briefly, my sentiments, after long experience; and without further ceremony. . . .

"I conceive the churches should be built, not where vacant grounds may be cheapest, purchased in the extremities of the suburbs, but among the thicker inhabitants, for convenience of the better sort, although the site of them should cost more—the better inhabitants contributing most to the future repairs, and the ministers and officers of the church, and charges of the parish.

"I could wish that all burials in churches might be disallowed, which is not only unwholesome, but the pavement can never be kept even, nor the pews upright; and if the churchyard be close about the church, this is also inconvenient, because the ground being continually raised by the graves occasions in time a descent by steps into the church, which renders it damp and the walls green, as appears evidently in all old churches.

"It will be inquired, Where, then, shall be the burials? I answer, in cemeteries seated in the outskirts of the town. And since it has become the fashion of the day to solemnize funerals by a train of coaches (even where the deceased are of moderate condition), though the cemeteries should be half a mile or more distant from the church. . . . This being enclosed with a strong, brick wall, and having a walk round and two cross-walks decently planted with yew-trees, the four quarters may serve four parishes, where the dead need not be disturbed at the pleasure of the sexton. . . .

"In these places beautiful monuments may be erected; but yet the dimensions should be regulated by an architect, and not left to the fancy of every mason; for thus the rich, with large marble tombs, would shoulder out the poor, when a pyramid, a good bust on a pedestal, will take up little room in the quarters, and be more proper than figures lying on marble beds. The walls will contain escutcheons and memorials for the dead, and the area good air and walks for the living. . .

"The capacity and dimensions of the new churches may be determined by a calculation. It is, as I take it, pretty certain that the number of inhabitants for whom these churches are provided are five times as many as those in the city who were burnt out. . . .

"The churches, therefore, must be large; but still, in our reformed religion, it should seem vain to make a parish church larger than that all present can both hear and see distinctly. The Romanists, indeed, may build larger churches. It is enough if they hear the murmur of the mass and see the elevation of the host; but ours are to be fitted for auditories. I can hardly think it practicable to make a single room so capacious, with pews and galleries, as to hold above two thousand persons, and all to hear the service and both to hear distinctly and see the preacher. I endeavored to effect this in building the parish church of St. James, Westminster, which I presume is the most capacious, with these qualifications, that hath yet been built; and yet, at a solemn time when the church was much crowded, I could not discern, from a gallery, that two thousand were present. . . .

St. Paul's.

OLD ENGLISH DOCUMENTS AND MSS.

"Concerning the placing of the pulpit, I shall observe: A moderate voice may be heard fifty feet distant before the preacher. . . . A Frenchman is heard further than an English preacher, because he raises his voice and never sinks his *last* words. I mention this as an insufferable fault in the pronunciation of some of our otherwise excellent preachers, which schoolmasters might correct in the young as a vicious pronunciation. . . ."

OLD DOCUMENTS AND MSS.

These invaluable additions to Masonic history were preserved by the old Lodges and by descendants of officers and members of old Lodges, and subsequently were gathered into the British Museum, Bodleian Library, and other repositories, where they are now to be seen.

From this source selections will be made that will indicate the internal operations of the Order—show what the institution was in England from the fourteenth to the seventeenth century.

FROM THE HALLIWELL MSS.

Date, 1390.*

The clerk Euclyde on thys wyse hyt fonde,
Thys craft of gemetry yn Egypte londe.
Yn Egypte he taw3 hte hyt ful wyde,
Yn dyvers londe on every syde;
Mony erys afterwarde, y understonde,
3er that the craft come ynto thys londe.
Thys craft come ynto Englond, as yzow say,
Yn tyme of good kynge Adelstonus day;
He made tho bothe halle and eke bowre,
And hye templus of great honowre,
To sportyn hym yn bothe day and ny3th,
And to worschepe hys God with all hys my3th.
Thys good lorde loved thys craft ful wel,
And purposud to strengthyn hyt every del,
For dyvers defawtys that yn the craft he fonde;
He sende aboute ynto the londe

* Masonic Register, p. 17.

After all the masonus of the crafte,
To come to hym ful evene stȝst 3 fte,
For to amende these defautys alle
By good consel, 3 ef hyt myt 3 th falle.
A semble thenne he cowthe let make
Of dyvers lordis, yn here state,
Dukys, erlys, and barnes also,
Kny 3 thys, sqwyers, and mony mo,
And the gret burges of that syte,
They were ther alle yn here degre;
These were ther uchon algate,
To ordeyne for these masonus astate.
Ther they sow 3 ton by here wytte,
How they my 3 thyn governe hette;

The furste artycul of thys gemetry :—
The mayster mason moste be ful securly
Bothe stedefast, trusty, trwe,
Hyt shal hymever thenne arewe :
. . . . .

The secunde artycul of good masonry,
As 3 e mowe hyt here hyr specyaly,
That every mayster, that ys a mason,
Most ben at the generale congregacyon,
So that he hyt resonable y-tolde
Where that the semble schal be holde;
And to that semble he most nede gon,

The thrydde artycul for sothe hyt ysse,
That the mayster take to no prentyss,
But he have good seuerans to dwell
Seven 3 er with hym, as y 3 ow telle.
. . . . .

The fowrthe artycul thys moste be,
That the mayster hym wel be-se,
That he no bondemon prentys make,
Ny for no covetyse do hym take.
. . . . .

The fyfthe artycul ys swvthe good,
So that the prentes be of lawful blod;

> The mayster schal not, for no vantage,
> Make no prentes that ys outrage;
> Hyt ys to mene, as ȝe mowe here,
> That he have hys lymes hole alle y-fere;
> To the craft hyt were great schame,
> To make an halt mon and a lame,
> For an unperfyt mon of suche blod
> Schulde do the craft but lyttul good.
> Thus ȝe mowe knowe everychon,
> The craft wolde have a my ȝ thy mon;
> A maymed mon he hath no my ȝ ht,
> ȝe mowe hyt knowe long zer ny ȝ ht.

LANSDOWNE MS.

(In the British Museum, and known as the Burghley Papers.—Sixteenth Century.)

" Here Begineth the True Order of Masonrie.

" The might of the Father of the Heavens the Wisdome of the Glorious Son, And the goodness of the Holy Ghost three persons and one God be with us now and ever Amen.

" Good brethren and Fellows our purpose is to show you how and in what manner this Noble and Worthy Craft of Masonry was first founded and begun, And afterwards how it was confirmed by worthy Kings Princes and by many other Worshipfull men, And also to all those that be heere, We minde to shew you the Charge that belongs to every trew Mason to keep, for in good ffaith if you take good heed it is well worthy to be kept for A worthy Craft and curious Science. Srs there be Seaven Liberall Sciencies of the which the Noble Craft of Masonry is one, And the Seaven be these, The first is Gramer and that teacheth a man to Spell and Write trewly, The second is Rethorick and that teacheth A man to speake faire and Subtill, The third is Lodgick and that teacheth A man to deserne the trew from false, The ffowrth is Arethmatick and that teacheth A man to Reckon and Account all manner of Accompts, the fifth is Geometry and that teacheth A man* and Measure of Earth and of all things, of the which this Science is called Geometry, The sixth is called Musick : and that teacheth A man to sing with Voyce and

---

* Blank spaces in the original. Hughan, p. 207.

Tongue and Organ Harp and Trump, The Seaventh is called Astronemy and that teacheth A man to know the Course of the Sunn and the Moone and the Stars, these be the *Seaven Liberall Sciences* of the which all be founded by one which is *Geometry*, and thus a man, may prove that all the Seaven Sciences be founde by Geometrie for it Teacheth a Man and Measure ponderation that worketh any Craft but he worketh by some Mott or Measure And every man that buyeth or selleth they buy or sell some weight or Measure, And all this is Geometry, And the Merchant and all other Craftmen of the Seaven Sciences, and the Plowmen and Tillers of the Earth and Sowers of all manner of Graines Seeds and Vine plants, and Setters of all manner of ffruits : ffor Gramer or Arethmatick nor Astronomy nor none of all the Seaven Sciences can no man find Mott or Measure in without *Geometry* wherefore methinks that the said Science of Geometry is most worthy, And all the others be founded by it. But how this worthy Science and Craft was first founded and begun I shall tell you before *Noyes* fflood there was A man which was called *Lameth* as it is written in the Bible in the 4th Chapter of Genesis, and this Lameth had 2 Wifes the one called Ada the other Sella, by the first wife Ada he begat a Sonne and a daughter And these 4 Children found the beginning of all these Crafts and Sciencies in the World, ffor the Eldest Sonne *Gabell* found the Craft of Geometry and he fed flocks of sheep and Lambs in the ffields : And first wrought houses of Stone and he and his Brother *Tuball* found the Crafts of Musick song of mouth harp and Organs and other Instruments. The third Brother Tubalican found the Smith Craft of Gold and Silver Iron and Copper and Steel, And the daughter found the Craft of Webbing and these children knew well that God would take vengeance for Sinn either by ffire or Water, wherefore they wrought the Scyences they had founded in 2 *Pillers* of Stone, that they might be found afterwards, and the one Stone was called Marble for that would not burne in the ffire, And the other Stone was called Latherne that would not be drowned with water ; Our Intent is to tell you how and in what manner these stones were found that these Sciences was written on. . . . Armes the father of the Wiseman he found one of the 2 Pillers of Stone and found the Science written therein and he taught it to others.

. . . And the worthy *Mr. Ewclides* gave it the name of Geometry, and how it is called through out all the World *Masonrie* Long after when the Children of Israell were come into the Land of Berhest which is now called the Countrey of Jerusalem where King David begun the Temple that is now called Templum Dei, and is named with us the *Temple* of *Jerusalem* and the same King David Loued Masons then right well and gave them good pay, and he gave the Charges and Manners that he learned in *Egipt* which were given by that worthy Doctor Ewclid and other more charges that you shall hear afterwards; And after the decease of King David, then reigned *Solloman* that was King Davids Sonne and he performed out the Temple that his father had begun and he sent after Masons into Diverse Countreys and into Diverse Lands and he gathered them together so that he had 24000 Workers of Stone and were all named Masons and he chosed out of them 3000 and were all ordained to be Masters, Rulers and Governors of his worke, and was there a King of another Region which men called *Iram* and he loved well King Solloman and gave him Timber to his worke and he had a Sonne that was called a man that was a Master of Geometry, and was chiefe Master of all his Masonrie & of all his Graving, Carving and all other Masonry that belonged to the Temple, this is witnessed in the Holy Bible (in Libro Regium quarto et Tertio) and this same Solloman confirmed both the charges and the Manners which his ffather had given, and thus was the worthy Craft of *Masonrie* confirmed in that Countrey of Jerusalem. And many other Regions and Kingdoms men walked into Diverse some because of Learning to learn more cunning, and some to teach them that had but little cunning, . . . and thus came this Noble Craft into ffrance and England, in that season stood void as fforagine Charge of Masons until St. Albanes and St. Albanes was a worthy Knight and Steward to the King of his household and had Government of his Realme and also of the makeing of the Walls of the said Towne, and he loved well Masons and cherished them much and made their pay right good for he gave iijis vjd a week and iijd before that time all the Land a Mason took but one penny a day and his meat till St. Albones mended it and he gott them a *Charter* of the King and his Councell for to hold a Generall Councell and gave it to name Assembly. Thereat was he himselfe and did help to make *Masons* and gave them Charges as you shall heare afterwards, soone after the Decease of St. Albones there came Diverse Warrs into

England out of Diverse Nations so that the good rule of Masons was distirbed and put downe vntill the tyme of *King Adelston* in his tyme there was a worthy King in England that brought this Land into good rest and he builded many great workes and buildings, therefore he loved well Masons for he had a Sonne called Edwin the which Loved Masons much more than his ffather did and he was soe practized in Geometry that he delighted much to come and talke with Masons and to Learne of them the Craft, And after for the love he had to Masons and to the Craft, he was made Mason at Windsor and he got of the King his ffather a *Charter* and commission once every yeare to have *Assembley* within the Realme where they would within England and to correct within themselves ffaults & Tresspasses that were done as touching the Crafts, and he held them an Assembley at *Yorke* and there he made *Masons* and gave them Charges and taught them the Manners, and Commands the same to be kept ever afterwards And tooke them the Charter and Commission to keep their Assembley, and Ordained that it should be *renewed* from King to King, and When the Assembley were gathered together he made a Cry that all old Masons or young that had any *Writings* or Understanding of the *Charges* and manners that were made before their Lands wheresoever they were made *Masons* that they should shew them forth. There were found some in ffrench, some in Greek some in Hebrew and some in English, and some in other Languages, and when they were read over and overseen well, the intent of them was understood to be all one, and then he caused a Book to be made there of how this worthy Craft of *Masonrie* was first founded and he himselfe Commanded and also then caused that it should be read at any tyme when it should happen any Mason or Masons to be made to give him or them their *Charges*, and from that time untill this Day Manners of Masons have been kept in this Manner and forme as well as Men might Governe it and ffarther more at diverse Assembleys have been put and Ordained diverse Charges by the best advice of *Masters* and *ffellows* (Tunc vnus ex Senioribus contat Librum et ille poneret manam Suam Super Librum) Every man that is a Mason take good heede to these Charges, If any man finde himselfe guilty in any of these Charges wee pray that he may amende himselfe or principally for dread of God you that be charged take good heede that you Keep all these Charges well for it is a great perill to a man to forsware himself upon the Booke.

Charges.

"*The First Charge* is that you shall be true to God and holy Church and to use noe Error or Heresie you vnderstanding and by wise mens teaching, also that you shall be Leige men to the King of England without Treason or any ffalsehood and that you know noe Treason or treachery but that ye amend and give knowledge thereof to the King or his Councell also that ye shall be true to one another (that is to say) every Mason of the Craft that is Mason allowed you shall doe to him as you would be done to yo selfe.

"*Secondly* and ye shall keep truely all the Councell of the Lodge or of the Chamber, and all the Councell of the Lodge that ought to be kept by the way of Masonhood also that you be noe theefe nor theeves to yor Knowledge free that you shall be true to the King Lord or Master call all Masons yo ffellows or yor Brethren and noe other names.

"*Fowerthly* also you shall not take your ffellows wife in Villoney nor deflowre his Daughter or Servant nor put him to disworship also you shall truely pay for yo meat or drinke wheresoever you goe to Table or Board whereby the Craft or Science may be slandered, These be the Charges Generall that belonge to every true Mason both Masters and Fellows.

"*Now I will rehearse other Charges single for Masons Allowed.*

"*First* that noe Mason take on him noe Lords worke nor other mans but if he know himselfe well able to performe the worke soe that the Craft have noe Slander.

"*Secondly* also that noe Master nor ffellow shall take noe Prentice for lesse than Seaven yeares and that the prentice be able of Birth that is *ffree borne* and of *Limbs whole* as a Man ought to be and that noe Mason or ffellow take no Allowance to be maid Mason without the Assent of his ffellows at the least Six or Seaven, that he that be maide be able in all degrees that is free borne and of a goode Kindred true and no bondsman and that he have his right Limbes as a man ought to have.

"*Sixthly* also that none slander another behind his back to make him loose his good name.

"*Seventhly* that noe ffellow in the house or abroad answere another vngodly or reprovable without cause.

"*Eighthly* also that every Master Mason be noe coman player at the Dice Cards or hazard nor at any other vnlawful playes through the which the Science or Craft may be dishonored.

"*Ninethly* also that noe Mason use no Lechery nor have been abroad whereby the Craft may be dishonored or Slandered.

"*Tenthly* also that no ffellow goe into the Towne by night except he have a ffellow with him who may beare record that he was in an honest place.

"*Eleventhly* also that every Master and ffellow shall come to the Assembly if it be within 50 Miles of him if he have any warning and if he have tresspassed against the Craft to abide the award of the Master and ffellows.

. . . .

"*These* be all the Charges and Covenants that ought to be read at the makeing of a Mason or Masons.

"The Almighty God who have you & me in his Keeping Amen.

HARLEIAN MSS.,* No. 1942. Date 1600.

26. "Noe person (of what degree soever) bee accepted a free mason, unless hee shall have a lodge of five *free masons;* at least, whereof one to be a *master*, or *warden*, of a limit, or division wherein such lodge shall be kept, and another of the trade of Free Masonry."

27. "That no p'son shal bee accepted a free mason, but such as are of able body, honest parentage, good reputacon and observes the laws of the land."

28. "That noe p'son hereafter bee accepted free mason, norshall bee admitted into any Lodge or assembly untill hee hath brought a *certificate* of the time of adoption from the Lodge yt accepted him, untill the Master of that limit, and devision, where such Lodge was kept, which sayd Master shall enrole the same in parchm't in a role to bee kept for that purpose, to give an acct of all such acceptions at every *General Assembly.*"

29. "That every p'son who now is a free mason, shall bring to the Master a note of the time of his acception to the end the same may bee enroll'd in such priority of place of the p'son shall deserve, and to ye end of the whole company and fellows may the better know each other."

*Gould, vol. i., p. 88.

30. "That for the future the sayd Society, Company and fraternity of free masons shall be regulated and governed by one Master, and assembly and Wardens, as ye said Company shall so fit to chose at every *yearly* assembly."

31. "That no p'son shal bee accepted a free mason or know the secrets of the said Society until he hath taken the oath of secrecy hereafter following: I, A. B. Doe, in the presence of Almighty God and the Fellows and brethren here present, promise and declare that I will not at any time hereafter by any act or circumstance whatever, reveal or make known any of the secrets, privileges, or counsels of the Fraternity of free masonry, which at this time, or any time hereafter shallbee made known unto mee soe help me God and the Holy contents of this book.

The Apprentice Charge.

1. "That he shall be true to God and the Holy Church, the prince, his M^r. and Dame whome he shall serve."

2. "And that he shall not steale nor peke away his M^r. or dames goods, nor absent himselfe from their service, nor goe from them about his oun pleasure by day or by night without their licence."

3. "And that he do not committ adultery or fornication in his Master's house with his wife, daughter, or servant, or any other."

4. "And that he shall keepe counsil in all things spoken in Lodg or Chamber by any Masons, fellows, or freemasons."

5. "And that he shall not hold any disobedient argument against any freemason, nor disclose any secret whereby any difference may arise amongst any Masons, or fellows, or apprentices, but Reverently to behave himselfe to, all freemasons being sworne brethren to his M^r."

6. "And not use any carding, diceing, or any other unlawful games."

7. "Nor haunt Taverns or alehouses there to waste any man's goods, without Licence of his M^r. or some other freemason."

8. "And that he shall not commit adultery in any man's house where he shall worke or be tabled."

9. "And that he shall not purloyn nor steal the goods of any p'son, nor willingly suffer harme or shame or consent thereto, during his said

apprenticeship either to his Mr. or dame, or any other *freemason*. But to withstand the same to the utmost of his power, and thereof to informe his said M^r. or some other freemason, with all convenient speed that may be."

General Charges Following the Buchanan MSS.

"(1.) The charges are that you shall bee true men to god and his holy church: that you use noe heresie nor errors in your understanding to distract mens teacheings.

"(2.) And alsoe that you bee true men to the Kinge without any treason or falsehood and that you shall know noe treason or falsehood but you shall amend it or else give notice thereof to the Kinge and Councell or other officers thereof.

"(3.) And alsoe that you shall be true each one to other that is to say to every Master and Fellow of the Craft of Masonrie that be *free* masons allowed and doe you to them as you would that they should doe to you.

"(4.) And alsoe that every free Mason Keepe councill truly of the secret and of the Craft and other Councill that ought to bee Kept by way of Masonrie.

"(5.) And alsoe that noe Mason shall be a Thiefe or accesary to a thiefe as farr forth as you shall know.

"(6.) And alsoe you shall be true men to the Lord and Master you serve and truly see to his profitt and advantage.

"(7.) And alsoe, you shall call Masons your fellows or Brethren and noe other foule name nor take your fellows wife violently nor desire his daughter ungodly nor his servant in villanie.

"(8.) And alsoe that you truly pay for your table and for your meate and drinke where you goe to table.

"(9.) And alsoe you shall doe noe villanie in the house in which you table whereby you may be ashamed.

"These are the Charges in general that belong to all free masons to keepe both Masters and Fellows.*

"These bee the Charges *singular* for every Master and Fellowe as followeth:

* Gould, vol. i., p. 98.

Special Charges.

"(1.) First that noe Mason take upon him noe Lord's worke nor other mens worke unless hee know himselfe able and skillfull to perform it soe as the Craft have noe slander nor disworshipp but that the Lord and owner of the worke may bee well and truly serve.

"(9.) And alsoe that noe fellow within the Lodge or without the Lodge missweare one another ungodly without any just cause.

"(10.) And alsoe that everyone reverence his fellow elder and put him to worshipp.

"(11.) And alsoe that noe Mason play att Cards or Dice or any other game whereby they should slander.

"(12.) And alsoe noe Mason shall bee a Common Ribald in Lech'ary to make the Craft slandered.

"(13.) And alsoe that noe fellow shall goe into the towns in the night thereas is a Lodge of Fellowes without some Fellowes that may beare him witnesse that hee was in a honest place.

"(14.) And alsoe that every Master and Fellow shall come to the Assembly if it be within seven miles about him if hee have warning or else to stand to the award of Master and Fellowes.

. . . .

"These charges that you have received you shall well ana truly keepe not disclosing the secresy of our Lodge to man woman nor child : Sticke nor stone : thing movable nor immovable soe God you helpe and his holy Doome.

"Amen . . . Finis."

An Epitome of Articles and Points, in Operation in the Fourteenth Century.

fifteen articles for the "mayster mason"

1. He must be "stedefast, trusty, and trewe," and upright as a judge.
2. "Most ben at the generale congregacyon," to know it where it "schal be holde."
3. Take apprentices for seven years "Hys craft to lurne, that ys profytable."

4. " No bondemon prentys make . . . Chef yn the logge he were y-take."
5. " The prentes be of lawful blod," and " have hys lymes hole."
6. " To take of the Lord for hyse prentyse, also muche as hys felows."
7. " Schal no thef" accept, " lest hyt wolde turne the craft to schame."
8. " Any mon of crafte, be not also perfyct, he may hym change."
9. " No werke he undurtake, but he come bothe hyt ende and make."
10. " Ther schal no mayster supplante other, but be as systur and brother."
11. He ought to be " bothe fayr and fre," and " techyt by hys mychth."
12. " Schal not hys felows werk deprave," but " hyt amende."
13. His apprentice " he hym teche," in all the requisite particulars.
14. So " that he, withynne hys terme, of hym dyvers poyntes may lurne."
15. Finally, do nothing that " volde turne the craft to schame." *

FIFTEEN POINTS FOR THE CRAFTSMEN.

1. Most love wel God, and holy churche and mayster and felows."
2. Work truly for " huyres apon werke and holydays."
3. Apprentices to keep " their mayster conwsel " in chamber " yn logge."
4. " No mon to hys craft be false," and apprentices to " have the same lawe."
5. Masons to accept their pay meekly from the master, and not to strive.
6. But to seek in all ways " that they stonde wel yn Goddes lawe."
7. Respect the chastity of his master's wife, and " his felows concubyne."
8. Be a true mediator " To his mayster and felows fre," and act fairly to all.
9. As steward to pay well, and truly " To mon or to wommon, whether he be."

* See Gould, vol. i., pp. 82, 83.

10. Disobedient masons dealt with by the Assembly, the law, and forswear the craft.

11. Masons to help one another by instructing those deficient in knowledge and skill.

12. The decisions of the Assembly to be respected, or imprisonment may follow.

13. " He schal swere never to be no thef," and never to succour any of " fals craft."

14. Be true " to hys lygh Lord the Kinge," and be sworn to keep all these points.

15. And obey the Assembly on pain of having to forsake the craft and be imprisoned.

FROM THE SLOAN MS., 3329. DATE, 1659.

" *The Mason word and everything therein contained* you shall keep secret; you shall never put it in writing directly or indirectly ; you shall keep all that we or you attend ; shall bid you keep secret *from man, woman or child, stock or stone,* and never reveal it but to a *brother* or in a *Lodge* of *Freemasons* and truly observe the charges in any Constitucion all this you promise and swear faithfully to keep and observe without any manner of *equivocation* or *mental reservation* directly or indirectly so help you God and by the contents of this book. " So he kisses the book, etc." *

From the catechism, Sloan MS. :

(Q.) " What is a just and perfect or just and lawful Lodge ? "

(A.) " A just and perfect Lodge is two *Interprintices*, two Fellow Crafts, and two Masters, more or fewer, the more the merrier, the fewer the better cheer, but if need require five will serve ; that is two Interprintices, two Fellow Crafts, and one Master, on the *highest hill* or *lowest valley* of the world without the crow of a cock or the bark of a dog."

(Q.) " What were you sworn by ? "

(A.) " By God and the square."

* Gould, vol. iv., p. 317.

THE MANUSCRIPT OF HENRY VI.*

Certayne Questyons wyth Answers to the same, concernyng the Mystery of Maconrye: Wrytenne by the Hande of Kinge Henrye, the Sixthe of the Name, and faythfullye copyed by me, John Leylands, Antiquarius, by the commande of his Highnesse.

They be as followthe:

Q. What mote ytt be?

A. Ytt beeth the skylle of nature, the understondynge of the myghte that ys hereynne and its sondrye werekynges; sonderlyche, the skylle of rectenyngs, of waightes, and metynges, and the treu manere of faconnyge all thynges for manne's use, headlye, dwellynges, and buyldunges of alle kinds, and alle odher thynges that make gudde to manne.

Q. Where dyd ytt begynne?

A. Ytt dyd begynne with the ffyrste menne yn the este, which were before the ffyrste menne of the weste, and comynge westlye, ytt hathe broght herwythe alle comfortes to the wyld and comfortlesse.

Q. Who did brynge ytt westlye?

A. The Venetians whoo, beynge grate merchaundes, comed ffyrste ffrome the este ynn Venetia, ffor the commedytye of marchaundysynge bey the redde and myddllonde sees.

Q. Howe comde ytt yn Engelonde?

A. Peter Gower, a Grecian, journeyedde ffer kunnynge yn Egypte, and yn Syria, and yn everyche land whereas the Venetians hadde plaintedde Maconrye, and wynnage entrance yn al lodges of Maconnes, he lerned muche, and retournedde and woned yn Grecia Magna wachsynge, and becommynge a myghtye wyseacre, and gratelyghe renowned, and here he framed a grate lodge at Groton and maked manye Maconnes, whereffrome, yn processe of tyme, the arte passed yn Engelonde.

Q. Do the Maccones descouer here artes unto odhers?

A. Peter Gower, whenne he journeyedde to lernne, was ffyrste made, and anonne techedde; evenne so shulde all odhers beyn recht. Natheless Maconnes hauthe alweys yn everyche tyme from tyme to tyme communicatedde

---

* See Fort, pp. 417, 418; Mitchell, p. 174.

to mankynde soche of her secretted as generally che myghte be usefulle; they hauthe keped bache soche allein as shulde be harmfulle yff they commed yn euylle hannded, oder soche as ne myghte be helpynge wythouten the techynges to be joynedde herwythe in the lodge, oder soche as do bynde the frered more stronglyche together, bey the proffyte, and commodyte commynge to the confrerie herfromme.

Q. Whatte arts haythe the Maconnes techedde mankynde?

A. The arts agricultura, *architectura*, astromomia, *geometria*, *numeres*, musica, poesis, kymistrye, governmente, and relygyonne.

Q. Howe comme the Maconnes more teachers than odher menne?

A. The hemselfe hauthe allein in arts of fyndynge neue artes, whyche artes the ffyrste Macconnes receued from Godde; by the whyche they fynde the wharre artes hem plesethe, and the treu way of techynge the same. Whatte odher menne doethe ffynde out, ys onllche bey channce, and herefore byt lytel I tro.

Q. Whatte dothe the Maconnes concele and hyde?

A. They concellethe the art of ffyndynge neue artes and thatt ys for here own proffyte, and preise; they concelethe the art of kepynge secrettes, thatt soe the worlde mayeth nothinge concele from them. They concelethe the art of wunderwerckynge, and of fore sayinge thynges to comme, that so they same artes may not be usedde of the wyckedde to an euylle end; they also concele the arts of chaunges, the wey of wynnynge the facultye of Abrac, the skylle of becommynge gude and parfyghte wythouten the holpynges of fere and hope; and the universalle longage of Maconnes.

Q. Wylle teche me thay same artes?

A. Ye shalle be techedde yff ye be worthye, and be able to lerne.

Q. Dothe alle Maconnes *kunne* more than odher menne?

A. Not so. Thay onlyche hauthe recht, and occaysonnee more then odher menne to kunne, butt many doeth fale yn capacity, and manye more doeth want industrye, thatt ys perneccessarye for the gaynynge all kunnynge.

Q. Are Maconnes gudder menne then odhers?

A. Some Maconnes are not vertuous as some odher menne; but yn the moste, they be more gudde than they would be yf they war not Maconnes.

Q. Doth Maconnes love eidher odher myghtylye as beeth sayde?

A. Yea veryche, and yt may not odherwise be ; for gude menne, and true, kennynge eidher odher to be socher, doeth alweys love the more as thay be more gudde.

Here endthe the questyonnes and awnsweres.

A letter from Mr. John Locke to the Right Honorable Thomas, Earl of Pembroke, concerning the foregoing old manuscript :

May 6th, 1696.

MY LORD : *I have at length, by the help of Mr. Collins, procured a copy of that MS. in the Bodleian Library, which you were so curious to see ; and in obedience to your Lordship's commands, I herewith send it to you.*

The MS., of which this is a copy, appears to be about one hundred and sixty years old; yet (as your Lordship will observe by the title) it is itself a copy of one yet more ancient by about one hundred; for the original is said to be the handwriting of King Henry VI.

I am, My Lord, your Lordship's most ob't and most humble servant,

JOHN LOCKE.

LIST OF THE PRINCIPAL OLD CHARGES, ETC.

1. Halliwell, *book form*, late fourteenth century.
2. Cooke, *book*, early fifteenth century.
3. Lansdowne, *ordinary* MS., sixteenth century.
3a. Melrose, No. 1, form and material not known, date, 1581.
4. Grand Lodge, *roll*, 1583.
5. York, No. 1, *roll*, seventeenth century.
6 and 7. Wilson, *ordinary* MS., seventeenth century.
8. Ignio Jones, *book* (*folio* MS.), 1607.
9. Wood, *book*, 1610.
10. York, No. 3, *roll*, 1630.
11. Harleian, 1,942, *ordinary* MS., seventeenth century.
12. Harleian, 2,054, *ordinary* MS., seventeenth century.
13. Sloane, 3,848, *ordinary* MS., 1646.
14. Sloane, 3,329, *ordinary* MS., 1659.
14a. Lechmere, *roll*, late seventeenth century.

15. Buchanan, *roll*, seventeenth century.
16. Kilwinning, *lodge record*, 1675.
17. Atcheson Haven, *lodge record*, 1666.
18. Aberdeen, *lodge record*, 1670.
19. Melrose, No. 2, *lodge record*, 1674.
20. Hope, *roll*, seventeenth century.
21. York, No. 5, *roll*, seventeenth century.
22. York, No. 6, *roll*, seventeenth century.
22a. Colne, No. 1, *roll*, late seventeenth century.
23. Antiquity, *roll and lodge record*, 1686.
24. Supreme Council, *roll*, 1686.
25. York, No. 4, *roll*, 1693.
25a. Colne, No. 2, *roll*, early eighteenth century.
26. Alnwick, *lodge record*, 1701.
27. York, No. 2, *roll*, 1704.
28. Scarborough, *roll* (?), 1705.
29. Papworth, *roll*, 1714.
30. Gateshead, *lodge record*, 1730.
31. Rawlinson, *ordinary* MS., 1730.
31a. Harris, *roll*, eighteenth century.

Nos. 1, 2, and 6, of these MSS. are vellum, ordinary MS.; Nos. 4, 5, 9, 10, 14, 15, 20, 22, 23, 24, 27, and 31, are parchment; the rest are paper.

THE PRINCIPLES OF FREE MASONRY
AS SET FORTH IN THE
CHARGES AND REGULATIONS
OF THAT MOST ANCIENT AND RIGHT WORSHIPFUL FRATERNITY, PROMULGATED IN GRAND LODGE AT LONDON, JAN. 17, 1723.[*]

THE CHARGES OF A FREE MASON,

Extracted from the ancient Records of Lodges beyond Sea, and of those in England, Scotland, and Ireland, for the use of the Lodges in London, to be read at the making of New Brethren, or when the Master shall order it.

[*] Gould, vol. iv., pp. 288, 289.

THE CHARGES AND REGULATIONS OF 1723.

The General Heads, *viz.*:

I. Of God and Religion.
II. Of the Civil Magistrate Supreme and Subordinate.
III. Of Lodges.
IV. Of Masters, Wardens, Fellows, and Apprentices.
V. Of the Management of the Craft in Working.
VI. Of Behaviour, viz. :
1. In the Lodge while Constituted.
2. After the Lodge is over and the Brethren not gone.
3. When Brethren meet without Strangers, but not in a Lodge.
4. In Presence of Strangers not Masons.
5. At Home and in the Neighbourhood.
6. Towards a Strange Brother.

I. *Concerning God and Religion.*

A Mason is oblig'd, by his Tenure, to obey the moral Law; and if he rightly understands the art, he will never be a stupid Atheist, nor an irreligious Libertine. But though in ancient Times Masons were charg'd in every Country to be of the Religion of that Country or Nation, whatever it was, yet 'tis now thought more expedient only to oblige them to that Religion in which all Men agree, leaving their particular Opinions to themselves; that is, to be good Men and true, or Men of Honour and Honesty, by whatever Denominations or Persuasions they may be distinguish'd; whereby Masonry becomes the Centre of Union, and the Means of conciliating true Friendship among Persons that must have remain'd at a perpetual Distance.

II. *Of the Civil Magistrate Supreme and Subordinate.*

A Mason is a peaceable Subject to the Civil Powers, wherever he resides or works, and is never to be concern'd in Plots and Conspiracies against the Peace and Welfare of the Nation, nor to behave himself undutifully to inferior Magistrates; for as Masonry hath been always injured by War, Bloodshed, and Confusion, so ancient Kings and Princes have been much dispos'd to encourage the Craftsmen, because of their Peaceableness and Loyalty, whereby they practically answer'd the Cavils of their Adversaries, and promoted the Honour of the Fraternity, who ever flourish'd in Times of Peace. So that if a Brother should be a Rebel against the State, he is not to be countenanc'd in his Rebellion, however he may be pitied as an unhappy Man; and, if convicted of no other Crime, though the loyal Brotherhood must and ought to disown his Rebellion, and give no Umbrage or Ground of political Jealousy to the Government for the time being; they cannot expel him from the Lodge, and his Relation to it remains indefeasible.

III. *Of Lodges.*

A Lodge is a place where Masons assemble and work: Hence that Assembly, or duly organiz'd Society of Masons, is call'd a Lodge, and every Brother ought to belong to one, and to be subject to its By-Laws and the General Regulations. It is either particular or general, and will be best understood by attending it, and by the Regulations of the General or Grand Lodge hitherto annex'd. In ancient Times, no Master or Fellow could be absent from it especially when warn'd to appear at it, without incurring a severe Censure, until it appeared to the Master and Wardens that pure necessity hinder'd him.

The Persons admitted Members of a Lodge must be good and true Men, free-born, and of mature and discreet Age, no Bondmen, no Women, no immoral or scandalous Men, but of good Report.

IV. *Of Masters, Wardens, Fellows, and Apprentices.*

All Preferment among Masons is grounded upon real Worth and personal Merit only: . . . . Therefore, no Master or Warden is chosen by Seniority, but for his Merit. . . . .

Only *Candidates* may know, that no *Master* should take an *Apprentice*, unless he be a perfect Youth, having no Maim or Defect in his Body, that may render him uncapable of learning the Art, and of being made a Brother, and then a Fellow-Craft in due Time, even after he has served such a term of years as the Custom of the Country directs; and that he should be descended of honest Parents; that so, when otherwise qualify'd, he may arrive to the Honour of being the Warden, and then the Master of the Lodge, the Grand Warden, and at length the Grand Master of all the Lodges, according to his Merit.

No Brother can be a Warden until he has pass'd the part of a Fellow-Craft; nor a Master until he has acted as a Warden, nor Grand Warden until he has been Master of a Lodge, nor *Grand Master* unless he has been a Fellow-Craft before his Election, who is also to be nobly born, or a Gentleman of the best Fashion, or some eminent *Scholar*, or some curious *Architect*, or other *Artist*, descended of honest Parents, and who is of singular great Merit in the Opinion of the *Lodges.*

And for the better, and easier, and more honourable Discharge of his Office, the Grand Master has a Power to chuse his own Deputy Grand Master, who must be then, or must have been formerly, the Master of a particular Lodge, and has the Privilege of acting whatever the Grand Master, his Principal, should act, unless the said Principal be present, or interpose his Authority by a Letter.

These Rulers and Governors, supreme and subordinate, of the ancient Lodge, are to be obey'd in their respective Stations by all the Brethren, according to the old Charges and Regulations, with all Humility, Reverence, Love, and Alacrity.

V. *Of the Management of the Craft in Working.*

All Masons shall work honestly on working Days, that they may live creditably on *holy* Days; and the time appointed by the Law of the Land, or confirm'd by Custom, shall be observ'd.

The most expert of the Fellow-Craftsmen shall be chosen or appointed the *Master*, or Overseer of the Lord's Work; who is to be call'd Master by those that work under him. The Craftsmen are to avoid all ill Language and to call each other by no disobliging Name, but Brother or Fellow; and to behave themselves courteously within and without the Lodge.

None shall discover Envy at the Prosperity of a Brother, nor supplant him, or put him out of his Work, if he be capable to finish the same; for no

THE CHARGES AND REGULATIONS OF 1723.

Man can finish another's Work so much to the Lord's Profit, unless he be thoroughly acquainted with the Designs and Draughts of him that began it.

When a Fellow-Craftsman is chosen Warden of the Work under the Master, he shall be true both to Master and Fellows, shall carefully oversee the Work in the Master's absence to the Lord's Profit; and his Brethren shall obey him.

All Masons employ'd, shall meekly receive their Wages without Murmuring or Mutiny, and not desert the Master till the Work is finish'd.

A younger Brother shall be instructed in working, to prevent spoiling the Materials for want of Judgment, and for encreasing and continuing of brotherly love.

All the Tools used in working shall be approved by the Grand Lodge.

No Labourer shall be employ'd in the proper Work of Masonry; nor shall *Free Masons* work with those that are not free, without an urgent Necessity; nor shall they teach Labourers and unaccepted Masons, as they should teach a *Brother* or *Fellow*.

VI. *Of Behaviour.*

1. IN THE LODGE WHILE CONSTITUTED.

You are not to hold private Committees, or separate Conversation, without Leave from the Master, nor to talk of any thing impertinent or unseemly, nor interrupt the Master or Wardens, or any Brother speaking to the Master: Nor behave yourself ludicrously or jestingly while the Lodge is engaged in what is serious and solemn; nor use any unbecoming Language upon any Pretence whatsoever; but to pay due Reverence to your Master, Wardens, and Fellows, and put them to worship.

If any Complaint be brought, the Brother found guilty shall stand to the Award and Determination of the Lodge, who are the proper and competent Judges of all such Controversies (unless you carry it by Appeal to the Grand Lodge), and to whom they ought to be referr'd, unless a Lord's Work be hinder'd the mean while, in which Case a particular Reference may be made; but you must *never go to Law* about what concerneth *Masonry*, without an absolute Necessity apparent to the *Lodge*.

2. BEHAVIOUR AFTER THE LODGE IS OVER AND THE BRETHREN NOT GONE.

You may enjoy yourselves with innocent Mirth, treating one another according to Ability, but avoiding all Excess, or forcing any Brother to eat or drink beyond his Inclination, or hindering him from going when his Occasions call him, or doing or saying anything offensive, or that may forbid an easy and free Conversation; for that would blast our Harmony, and defeat our laudable Purposes. Therefore no private Piques or Quarrels must be brought within the Door of the Lodge, far less any Quarrels about Religion, or Nations, or State Policy, we being only, as Masons, of the Religion above-mention'd; we are also of all Nations, Tongues, Kindreds, and Languages, and are resolv'd against all Politicks, as what never yet conduc'd to the Welfare of the Lodge, nor ever will. This Charge has been always strictly enjoin'd and observ'd; but especially ever since the Reformation in Britain, or the Dissent and Secession of these Nations from the Communion of Rome.

3. BEHAVIOUR WHEN BRETHREN MEET WITHOUT STRANGERS, BUT NOT IN A LODGE FORM'D.

You are to salute one another in a courteous manner, as you will be instructed, calling each other Brother, freely giving mutual Instruction as shall be thought expedient, without being overseen or overheard, and without encroaching upon each other, or derogating from that Respect which is due to any Brother, were he not a Mason: For though all Masons are as Brethren upon the same Level, yet Masonry takes no Honour from a Man that he had before; nay rather it adds to his Honour, especially if he has deserv'd well of the Brotherhood, who must give Honour to whom it is due, and avoid ill Manners.

4. BEHAVIOUR IN PRESENCE OF STRANGERS NOT MASONS.

You shall be cautious in your Words and Carriage, that the most penetrating Stranger shall not be able to discover or find out what is not proper to be intimated; and sometimes you shall divert a Discourse, and manage it prudently for the Honour of the worshipful Fraternity.

THE CHARGES AND REGULATIONS OF 1723.

5. BEHAVIOUR AT HOME AND IN YOUR NEIGHBOURHOOD.

You are to act as becomes a moral and wise Man; particularly, not to let your Family, Friends, and Neighbours know the Concerns of the Lodge, &c. but wisely to consult your own Honour, and that of the ancient Brotherhood, for Reasons not to be mention'd here. You must also consult your Health, by not continuing together too late, or too long from home, after Lodge Hours are past; and by avoiding of Gluttony or Drunkenness, that your Families be not neglected or injured, nor you disabled from working.

6. BEHAVIOUR TOWARDS A STRANGE BROTHER.

You are cautiously to examine him, in such a Method as Prudence shall direct you, that you may not be impos'd upon by an ignorant false Pretender, whom you are to reject with Contempt and Derision, and beware of giving him any Hints of Knowledge.

But if you discover him to be a true and genuine Brother, you are to respect him accordingly; and if he is in want, you must relieve him if you can, or else direct him how he may be reliev'd; You must employ him some Days, or else recommend him to be employ'd. But you are not charged to do beyond your Ability, only to prefer a poor Brother, that is a good Man and true, before any other poor People in the same Circumstance.

Finally, All these Charges you are to observe, and also those that shall be communicated to you in another way; cultivating Brotherly Love, the Foundation and Capestone, the Cement and Glory of this ancient Fraternity, avoiding all Wrangling and Quarrelling, all Slander and Backbiting, nor permitting others to slander any honest Brother, but defending his Character, and doing him all good Offices, as far as is consistent with your Honour and Safety, and no farther. And if any of them do you Injury, you must apply to your own or his Lodge; and from thence you may appeal to the Grand Lodge at the Quarterly Communication, and from thence to the annual Grand Lodge, as has been the ancient laudable Conduct of our *Fore-fathers in every Nation;* never taking a legal Course but when the Case cannot be otherwise decided, and patiently listning to the honest and friendly Advice of Master and Fellows, when they would prevent your going to Law with Strangers, or would excite you to put a speedy Period to all Law Suits, that so you may mind the Affair of Masonry with the more Alacrity and Success; but with respect to Brothers or Fellows at Law, the Master and Brethren should kindly offer their Mediation, which ought to be thankfully submitted to by the contending Brethren; and if that Submission is impracticable, they must however carry on their Process, or Law-Suit, without Wrath and Rancor (not in the common way), saying or doing nothing which may hinder Brotherly Love and good Offices to be renew'd and continu'd; that all may see the benign Influence of Masonry, as all true Masons have done from the Beginning of the World, and will do to the End of Time.

General Regulations,

Compiled first by Mr. George Payne, Anno 1720, when he was Grand Master, and approved by the Grand Lodge on St. John Baptist's Day, Anno 1721, at Stationer's Hall, London; when the most noble Prince John Duke of Montagu was unanimously chosen our Grand Master for the year ensuing; who chose John Beal, M. D., his Deputy Grand Master; and Mr. Josiah Villeneau and Mr. Thomas Morris, Jun., were chosen by the Lodge Grand Wardens. And now, by the Command of our said Right Worshipful Grand Master Montagu, the author of this book has compar'd them with, and reduc'd them to, the ancient Records and immemorial Usages of the Fraternity, and digested them into this new Method, with several proper Explications, for the Use of the Lodges in and about London and Westminster.

I. The *Grand Master*, or his Deputy, hath Authority and Right, not only to be present in any true Lodge, but also to preside wherever he is, with the Master of the Lodge on his Left hand, and to order his Grand Wardens to attend him, who are not to act in particular Lodges as Wardens, but in his Presence, and at his Command; because there the Grand Master may command the Wardens of that Lodge, or any other Brethren he pleaseth, to attend and act as his Wardens pro tempore.

II. The Master of a particular Lodge has the Right and Authority of congregating the Members of his Lodge at pleasure, upon any Emergency or Occurrence, as well as to appoint the time and place of their usual forming:

And in case of Sickness, Death, or necessary Absence of the Master, the senior Warden shall act as Master pro tempore, if no Brother is present who has been Master of that Lodge before; for in that Case the absent Master's Authority reverts to the last Master then present; though he cannot act until the said senior Warden has once congregated the Lodge, or in his Absence the junior Warden.

III. The Master of each particular Lodge, or one of the Wardens, or some other Brother by his Order, shall keep a Book containing their By-Laws, the Names of their Members, with a List of all the Lodges in Town, and the usual Times and Places of their forming, and all their Transactions that are proper to be written.

IV. No Lodge shall make more than Five new Brethren at one Time, nor any Man under the Age of Twenty-five, who must be also his own Master; unless by a Dispensation from the Grand Master or his Deputy.

V. No man can be made or admitted a member of a particular Lodge, *without previous notice one Month* before given to the said Lodge, in order to make due Enquiry into the Reputation and Capacity of the Candidate; *unless* by the *Dispensation aforesaid.*

VI. But no Man can be enter'd a Brother in any particular Lodge, or admitted to be a Member thereof, without the unanimous Consent of all the Members of that Lodge then present when the Candidate is propos'd, and their Consent is formally ask'd by the Master; and they are to signify their Consent or Dissent in their own prudent way, either virtually or in form, but with Unanimity: Nor is this *inherent Privilege subject* to a *Dispensation;* because the Members of a particular Lodge are the best Judges of it; and if a fractious Member should be imposed on them, it might spoil their Harmony, or hinder their Freedom; or even break and disperse the Lodge; which ought to be avoided by all good and true Brethren.

VII. Every new Brother at his making is decently to cloath the Lodge, that is, all the Brethren present, and to deposite something for the Relief of indigent and decay'd Brethren, as the Candidate shall think fit to bestow, over and above the small Allowance stated by the By-Laws of that particular Lodge; which Charity shall be lodg'd with the Master or Wardens, or the Cashier, if the Members think fit to chuse one.

And the Candidate shall also solemnly promise to submit to the Constitutions, the Charges, and Regulations, and to such other good Usages as shall be intimated to them in Time and Place convenient.

VIII. No Set or Number of Brethren shall withdraw or separate themselves from the Lodge in which they were made Brethren, or were afterwards admitted Members, unless the Lodge becomes too numerous; nor even then, without a Dispensation from the Grand Master or his Deputy : and when they are thus separated, they must either immediately join themselves to such other Lodge as they shall like best, with the unanimous Consent of that other Lodge to which they go (as above regulated), or else they must obtain the Grand Master's Warrant to join in forming a new Lodge.

If any Set or Number of Masons shall take upon themselves to form a Lodge without the Grand Master's Warrant, the regular Lodges are not to countenance them, nor own them as fair Brethren and duly form'd, nor approve of their Acts and Deeds; but must treat them as Rebels, until they humble themselves, as the Grand Master shall in his Prudence direct, and until he approve of them by his Warrant, which must be signify'd to the other Lodges, as the Custom is when a new Lodge is to be register'd in the List of Lodges.

IX. But if any Brother so far misbehave himself as to render his Lodge uneasy, he shall be twice duly admonish'd by the Master or Wardens in a form'd Lodge; and if he will not refrain his Imprudence, and obediently submit to the Advice of the Brethren, and reform what gives them Offence, he shall be dealt with according to the By-Laws of that particular Lodge, or else in such a Manner as the Quarterly Communication shall in their great Prudence think fit; for which a new Regulation may be afterwards made.

X. The Majority of every particular Lodge, when congregated, shall have the Privilege of giving Instructions to their Master and Wardens, before the assembling of the grand Chapter, or Lodge, at the three Quarterly Communications hereafter mention'd, and of the Annual Grand Lodge too; because their Master and Wardens are their Representatives, and are supposed to speak their Mind.

XI. All particular Lodges are to observe the same Usages as much as possible; in order to which, and for cultivating a good Understanding among

Free Masons, some Members out of every Lodge shall be deputed to visit the other Lodges as often as shall be thought convenient.

XII. The Grand Lodge consists of, and is form'd by, the Masters and Wardens of all the regular particular Lodges upon Record, with the Grand Master at their Head, and his Deputy on his Left-hand, and the Grand Wardens in their proper Places; and must have a Quarterly Communication about Michaelmas, Christmas, and Lady-Day, in some convenient Place, as the Grand Master shall appoint, where no Brother shall be present, who is not at that time a member thereof, without a Dispensation; and while he stays, he shall not be allowed to vote, nor even give his Opinion, without Leave of the Grand Lodge ask'd and given, or unless it be duly ask'd and given, or unless it be duly ask'd by the said Lodge.

All Matters are to be determin'd in the Grand Lodge by a Majority of Votes, each Member having one Vote, and the Grand Master having two Votes, unless the said Lodge leave any particular thing to the Determination of the Grand Master for the sake of Expedition.

XIII. At the said Quarterly Communication, all Matters that concern the Fraternity in general, or particular Lodges, or single Brethren, are quietly, sedately, and maturely to be discours'd of and transacted: Apprentices must be admitted Masters and Fellow-Craft only here, unless by a Dispensation. Here also all Differences, that cannot be made up and accommodated privately, nor by a particular Lodge, are to be seriously considered and decided: And if any Brother thinks himself aggrieved by the Decision of this Board, he may appeal to the annual Grand Lodge next ensuing, and leave his Appeal in Writing with the Grand Master, or his Deputy, or the Grand Wardens.

Here also the Master or the Wardens of each particular Lodge shall bring and produce a List of such Members as have been made, or even admitted in their particular Lodges since the last Communication of the Grand Lodge: And there shall be a Book kept by the Grand Master, or his Deputy, or rather by some Brother whom the Grand Lodge shall appoint for Secretary, wherein shall be recorded all the Lodges, with their usual Times and Places of forming, and the Names of all the Members of each Lodge; and all the Affairs of the Grand Lodge that are proper to be written.

They shall also consider of the most prudent and effectual Methods of collecting and disposing of what Money shall be given to, or lodged with them in Charity, towards the Relief only of any true Brother fallen into Poverty or Decay, but of none else; But every particular Lodge shall dispose of their own Charity for poor Brethren, according to their own By-Laws, until it be agreed by all the Lodges (in a new Regulation) to carry in the Charity collected by them to the Grand Lodge, at the Quarterly or Annual Communication, in order to make a common Stock of it, for the more handsome Relief of poor Brethren.

They shall also appoint a Treasurer, a Brother of good worldly Substance, who shall be a Member of the Grand Lodge by virtue of his office, and shall be always present, and have Power to move to the Grand Lodge any thing, especially what concerns his Office. To him shall be committed all Money rais'd for Charity, or for any other Use of the Grand Lodge, which he shall write down in a Book, with the respective Ends and Uses for which the several Sums are intended; and shall expend or disburse the same by such a certain Order sign'd, as the Grand Lodge shall afterwards agree to in a new Regulation: But he shall not vote in chusing a Grand Master or Wardens though in every other Transaction. As in like manner the Secretary shall be a Member of the Grand Lodge by virtue of his Office, and vote in everything except in chusing a Grand Master or Wardens.

The Treasurer and Secretary shall have each a Clerk, who must be a Brother and Fellow-Craft, but never must be a Member of the Grand Lodge, nor speak without being allow'd or desir'd.

The Grand Master, or his Deputy, shall always command the Treasurer and Secretary, with their Clerks and Books, in order to see how matters go on, and to know what is expedient to be done upon any emergent Occasion.

Another Brother (who must be a Fellow-Craft) should be appointed to look after the Door of the Grand Lodge; but shall be no member of it.

But these Offices may be farther explain'd by a new Regulation, when the Necessity and Expediency of them may more appear than at present to the Fraternity.

XIV. If at any Grand Lodge, stated or occasional, quarterly or annual, the Grand Master and his Deputy should be both absent, then the present Master of a Lodge, that has been the longest a Free Mason, shall take the

Chair, and preside as Grand Master pro tempore; and shall be vested with all his Power and Honour for the time; provided there is no Brother present that has been Grand Master formerly, or Deputy Grand Master; for the last Grand Master present, or else the last Deputy present, should always of right take place in the Absence of the present Grand Master and his Deputy.

XV. In the Grand Lodge none can act as Wardens but the Grand Wardens themselves, if present; and if absent, the Grand Master, or the Person who presides in his Place, shall order Private Wardens to act as Grand Wardens pro tempore, whose Places are to be supply'd by two Fellow-Craft of the same Lodge, call'd forth to act, or sent thither by the particular Master thereof; or if by him omitted, then they shall be call'd by the Grand Master, that so the Grand Lodge may be always compleat.

XVI. The Grand Wardens, or any others, are first to advise with the Deputy about the Affairs of the Lodge or of the Brethren, and not to apply to the Grand Master without the Knowledge of the Deputy, unless he refuse his Concurrence in any certain necessary Affair; in which Case, or in case of any Difference between the Deputy and the Grand Wardens, or other Brethren, both Parties are to go by Concert to the Grand Master, who can easily decide the Controversy and make up the Difference by virtue of his great Authority.

The Grand Master should receive no Intimation of Business concerning Masonry, but from his Deputy first, except in such certain Cases as his Worship can well judge of; for if the Application to the Grand Master be irregular, he can easily order the Grand Wardens, or any other Brethren thus applying, to wait upon his Deputy, who is to prepare the Business speedily, and to lay it orderly before his Worship.

XVII. No Grand Master, Deputy Grand Master, Grand Wardens, Treasurer, Secretary, or whoever acts for them, or in their stead pro tempore, can at the same time be the Master or Warden of a particular Lodge; but as soon as any of them has honourably discharg'd his Grand Office, he returns to that Post or Station in his particular Lodge, from which he was call'd to officiate above.

XVIII. If the Deputy Grand Master be sick, or necessarily absent, the Grand Master may chuse any Fellow-Craft he pleases to be his Deputy pro tempore: But he that is chosen Deputy at the Grand Lodge, and the Grand Wardens too, cannot be discharg'd without the Cause fairly appear to the Majority of the Grand Lodge; and the Grand Master, if he is uneasy, may call a Grand Lodge on purpose to lay the Cause before them, and to have their Advice and Concurrence: In which case, the Majority of the Grand Lodge, if they cannot reconcile the Master and his Deputy or his Wardens, are to concur in allowing the Master to discharge his said Deputy or his said Wardens, and to chuse another Deputy immediately; and the said Grand Lodge shall chuse other Wardens in that Case, that Harmony and Peace may be preserv'd.

XIX. If the Grand Master should abuse his Power, and render himself unworthy of the Obedience and Subjection of the Lodges, he shall be treated in a way and manner to be agreed upon in a new Regulation; because hitherto the ancient Fraternity have had no occasion for it, their former Grand Masters having all behaved themselves worthy of that honourable Office.

XX. The Grand-Master with his Deputy and Wardens, shall (at least once) go round and visit all the Lodges about Town during his Mastership.

XXI. If the Grand Master die during his Mastership, or by Sickness, or by being beyond Sea, or any other way should be render'd uncapable of discharging his Office, the Deputy, or in his Absence, the Senior Grand Warden, or in his Absence the Junior, or in his Absence any three present Masters of Lodges, shall join to congregate the Grand Lodge immediately, to advise together upon that Emergency, and to send two of their Number to invite the last Grand Master to resume his office, which now in course reverts to him; or if he refuse, then the next last, and so backward: But if no former Grand Master can be found, then the Deputy shall act as Principal, until another is chosen; or if there be no Deputy, then the oldest Master.

XXII. The Brethren of all the Lodges in and about London and Westminster, shall meet at an Annual Communication and Feast, in some convenient Place, on St. John Baptist's Day, or else on St. John Evangelist's Day, as the Grand Lodge shall think fit by a new Regulation, having of late Years met on St. John Baptist's Day: Provided,

The Majority of the Masters and Wardens, with the Grand Master, his Deputy and Wardens, agree at their Quarterly Communication, three Months

THE CHARGES AND REGULATIONS OF 1723.

before, that there shall be a Feast, and a General Communication of all the Brethren: For if either the Grand Master, or the Majority of the particular Masters, are against it, it must be dropt for that Time.

But whether there shall be a Feast for all the Brethren, or not, yet the Grand Lodge must meet in some convenient Place annually on St. John's Day; or if it be Sunday, then on the next Day, in order to chuse every Year a new Grand Master, Deputy, and Warden.

XXIII. If it be thought expedient, and the Grand Master, with the Majority of the Masters and Wardens, agree to hold a Grand Feast, according to the ancient laudable Custom of Masons, then the Grand Wardens shall have the care of preparing the Tickets, seal'd with the Grand Master's Seal, of disposing of the Tickets, of receiving the Money for the Tickets, of buying the Materials of the Feast, of finding out a proper and convenient Place to feast in; and of every other thing that concerns the Entertainment.

But that the Work may not be too burthensome to the two Grand Wardens, and that all Matters may be expeditiously and safely managed, the Grand Master, or his Deputy, shall have power to nominate and appoint a certain Number of Stewards, as his Worship shall think fit, to act in concert with the two Grand Wardens; all things relating to the Feast being decided amongst them by a Majority of Voices; except the Grand Master or his Deputy interpose by a particular Direction or Appointment.

XXIV. The Wardens and Stewards shall, in due time, wait upon the Grand Master, or his Deputy, for Directions and Orders about the Premises; but if his Worship and his Deputy are sick, or necessarily absent, they shall call together the Masters and Wardens of Lodges to meet on purpose for their Advice and Orders; or else they may take the Matter wholly upon themselves, and do the best they can.

The Grand Wardens and the Stewards are to account for all the money they receive, or expend, to the Grand Lodge, after Dinner, or when the Grand Lodge shall think fit to receive their Accounts.

If the Grand Master pleases, he may in due time summon all the Masters and Wardens of the Lodges to consult with them about ordering the Grand Feast, and about any Emergency or accidental thing relating thereunto, that may require Advice; or else to take it upon himself altogether.

XXV. The Masters of Lodges shall each appoint one experienc'd and discreet Fellow-Craft of his Lodge, to compose a Committee, consisting of one from every Lodge, who shall meet to receive, in a convenient Apartment, every Person that brings a Ticket, and shall have Power to discourse him, if they think fit, in order to admit him, or debar him, as they shall see cause; Provided they send no Man away before they have acquainted all the Brethren within Doors with the Reasons thereof, to avoid mistakes; that so no true Brother may be debarr'd, nor a false Brother, or mere Pretender, admitted. This Committee must meet very early on St. John's Day at the Place, even before any Persons come with Tickets.

XXVI. The Grand Master shall appoint two or more trusty Brethren to be Porters, or Door-keepers, who are also to be early at the Place, for some good Reasons; and who are to be at the Command of the Committee.

XXVII. The Grand Wardens, or the Stewards, shall appoint beforehand such a Number of Brethren to serve at Table as they think fit and proper for that Work; and they may advise with the Masters and Wardens of Lodges about the most proper Persons, if they please, or may take in such by their Recommendation; for none are to serve that Day, but free and accepted Masons, that the Communication may be free and harmonious.

XXVIII. All the Members of the Grand Lodge must be at the Place long before Dinner, with the Grand Master or his Deputy at their Head, who shall retire, and form themselves. And this is done in order,

1. To receive any Appeals duly lodg'd, as above regulated, that the Appellant may be heard, and the Affair may be amicably decided before Dinner, if possible; but if it cannot, it must be delay'd till after the new Grand Master is elected; and if it cannot be decided after Dinner, it may be delay'd, and referr'd to a particular Committee, that shall quietly adjust it, and make Report to the next Quarterly Communication, that Brotherly love may be preserv'd.

2. To prevent any Difference or Disgust which may be feared to arise that Day; that no Interruption may be given to the Harmony and Pleasure of the Grand Feast.

3. To consult about whatever concerns the Decency and Decorum of the

Grand Assembly, and to prevent all Indecency and ill Manners, the Assembly being promiscuous.

4. To receive and consider of any good Motion, or any momentous and important Affair that shall be brought from the particular Lodges, by their Representatives, the several Masters and Wardens.

XXIX. After these things are discuss'd, the Grand Master and his Deputy, the Grand Wardens, or the Stewards, the Secretary, the Treasurer, the Clerks, and every other Person, shall withdraw, and leave the Masters and Wardens of the particular Lodges alone, in order to consult amicably about electing a new Grand Master, or continuing the present, if they have not done it the Day before; and if they are unanimous for continuing the present Grand Master, his Worship shall be call'd in, and humbly desir'd to do the Fraternity the Honour of ruling them for the Year ensuing: And after dinner it will be known whether he accepts of it or not: For it should not be discovered but by the Election itself.

XXX. Then the Masters and Wardens, and all the Brethren, may converse promiscuously, or as they please to sort together, until the Dinner is coming in, when every Brother takes his Seat at Table.

XXXI. Some time after Dinner the Grand Lodge is form'd, not in Retirement, but in the Presence of all the Brethren, who yet are not Members of it, and must not therefore speak until they are desir'd and allow'd.

XXXII. If the Grand Master of last Year has consented with the Master and Wardens in private, before Dinner, to continue for the Year ensuing; then one of the Grand Lodge, deputed for that purpose, shall represent to all the Brethren his Worship's good Government, &c. And turning to him, shall in the Name of the Grand Lodge, humbly request him to do the Fraternity the great Honour (if nobly born, if not) the great Kindness of continuing to be their Grand Master for the Year ensuing. And his Worship declaring his Consent by a Bow or a Speech, as he pleases, the said deputed Member of the Grand Lodge shall proclaim him Grand Master, and all the Members of the Lodge shall salute him in due Form. And all the Brethren shall for a few Minutes have leave to declare their Satisfaction, Pleasure, and Congratulation.

XXXIII. But if either the Master and Wardens have not in private, this Day before Dinner, nor the Day before, desir'd the last Grand Master to continue in the Mastership another Year; or if he, when desir'd, has not consented: Then,

The last Grand Master shall nominate his Successor for the Year ensuing, who, if unanimously approv'd by the Grand Lodge, and if there present, shall be proclaim'd, saluted, and congratulated the new Grand Master as above hinted, and immediately install'd by the last Grand Master, according to Usage.

XXXIV. But if that Nomination is not unanimously approv'd, the new Grand Master shall be chosen immediately by Ballot, every Master and Warden writing his Man's Name, and the last Grand Master writing his Man's Name too; and the Man, whose name the last Grand Master shall first take out, casually or by chance, shall be Grand Master for the Year ensuing; and if present, he shall be proclaim'd, saluted, and congratulated, as above hinted, and forthwith install'd by the last Grand Master, according to Usage.

XXXV. The last Grand Master thus continued, or the New Grand Master thus installed, shall next nominate and appoint his Deputy Grand Master, either the last or a new one, who shall be also declar'd, saluted, and congratulated as above hinted.

The Grand Master shall also nominate the new Grand Wardens, and if unanimously approv'd by the Grand Lodge, shall be declar'd, saluted, and congratulated, as above hinted; but if not, they shall be chosen by Ballot, in the same way as the Grand Master: As the Wardens of private Lodges are also to be chosen by Ballot in each Lodge, if the Members thereof do not agree to their Master's Nomination.

XXXVI. But if the Brother, whom the present Grand Master shall nominate for his Successor, or whom the majority of the Grand Lodge shall happen to chuse by Ballot, is, by Sickness or other necessary Occasion, absent from the Grand Feast, he cannot be proclaim'd the New Grand Master, unless the old Grand Master, or some of the Masters and Wardens of the Grand Lodge can vouch, upon the Honour of a Brother, that the said Person, so nominated or chosen, will readily accept of the said Office; in which case the old Grand Master shall act as Proxy, and shall nominate the Deputy and

Wardens in his Name, and in his Name also receive the usual Honours, Homage, and Congratulation.

XXXVII. Then the Grand Master shall allow any Brother, Fellow-Craft, or Apprentice to speak, directing his Discourse to his Worship; or to make any Motion for the good of the Fraternity, which shall be either immediately consider'd and finish'd, or else referr'd to the Consideration of the Grand Lodge at their next Communication, stated or occasional. When that is over,

XXXVIII. The Grand Master or his Deputy, or some Brother appointed by him, shall harangue all the Brethren, and give them good Advice: And lastly, after some other Transactions, that cannot be written in any Language, the Brethren may go away or stay longer, as they please.

XXXIX. Every Annual Grand Lodge has an inherent Power and Authority to make new Regulations, or to alter these, for the real Benefit of this ancient Fraternity: Provided always that the old Land-Marks be carefully preserv'd, and that such Alterations and new Regulations be proposed and agreed to at the third Quarterly Communication preceding the Annual Grand Feast; and that they be offered also to the Perusal of all the Brethren before Dinner, in writing, even of the youngest Apprentice; the Approbation and Consent of the Majority of all the Brethren present being absolutely necessary to make the same binding and obligatory; which must, after Dinner, and after the new Grand Master is install'd, be solemnly desir'd; as it was desir'd and obtain'd for these Regulations, when propos'd by the Grand Lodge, to about 150 Brethren, on St. John Baptist's Day, 1721.

Postscript.

Here follows the Manner of constituting a New Lodge, as practis'd by his Grace the Duke of Wharton, the present Right Worshipful Grand Master, according to the ancient Usages of Masons.

A new Lodge, for avoiding many Irregularities, should be solemnly constituted by the Grand Master, with his Deputy and Wardens; or in the Grand Master's Absence, the Deputy shall act for his Worship, and shall chuse some Master of a Lodge to assist him; or in case the Deputy is absent, the Grand Master shall call forth some Master of a Lodge to act as Deputy pro tempore.

The Candidates, or the new Master and Wardens, being yet among the Fellow-Craft, the Grand Master shall ask his Deputy if he has examin'd them, and finds the Candidate Master well skill'd in the noble Science and the royal Art, and duly instructed in our Mysteries, &c.

And the Deputy answering in the affirmative, he shall (by the Grand Master's Order) take the Candidate from among his Fellows, and present him to the Grand Master; saying, Right worshipful Grand Master, the Brethren here desire to be form'd into a new Lodge; and I present this my worthy Brother to be their Master, whom I know to be of good Morals and great Skill, true and trusty, and a Lover of the whole Fraternity, wheresoever dispersed, over the Face of the Earth.

Then the Grand Master, placing the Candidate on his left Hand, having ask'd and obtain'd the unanimous Consent of all the Brethren, shall say: I constitute and form these good Brethren into a new Lodge, and appoint you the Master of it, not doubting of your Capacity and Care to preserve the Cement of the Lodge, &c., with some other Expressions that are proper and useful on that Occasion, but not proper to be written.

Upon this the Deputy shall rehearse the Charges of a Master, and the Grand Master shall ask the Candidate, saying, Do you submit to these Charges, as Masters have done in all ages? And the Candidate signifying his cordial Submission thereunto, the Grand Master shall, by certain significant Ceremonies and ancient Usages, install him, and present him with the Constitutions, the Lodge-Book, and the Instruments of his Office, not all together, but one after another; and after each of them, the Grand Master, or his Deputy, shall rehearse the short and pithy Charge that is suitable to the thing presented.

After this, the Members of this new Lodge, bowing all together to the Grand Master, shall return his Worship Thanks, and immediately do their Homage to their new Master, and signify their Promise of Subjection and Obedience to him by the usual Congratulation.

The Deputy and the Grand Wardens, and any other Brethren present, that are not Members of this new Lodge, shall next congratulate the new

THE CHARGES AND REGULATIONS OF 1723.

Master; and he shall return his becoming Acknowledgments to the Grand Master first, and to the rest in their Order.

Then the Grand Master desires the new Master to enter immediately upon the Exercise of his Office, in chusing his Wardens: And the new Master calling forth two Fellow-Craft, presents them to the Grand Master for his Approbation, and to the new Lodge for their Consent. And that being granted,

The senior or junior Grand Warden, or some Brother for him, shall rehearse the Charges of Wardens; and the Candidates being solemnly ask'd by the new Master, shall signify their Submission thereunto.

Upon which the new Master, presenting them with the Instruments of their Office, shall, in due Form, install them in their proper Places; and the Brethren of that new Lodge shall signify their Obedience to the new Wardens by the usual Congratulation.

And this Lodge being thus compleatly constituted, shall be register'd in the Grand Master's Book, and by his Order notify'd to the other Lodges.

APPROBATION.

Whereas by the Confusions occasion'd in the Saxon, Danish, and Norman Wars, the Records of Masons have been much vitiated, the Free Masons of England *twice* thought it necessary to *correct their Constitutions, Charges, and Regulations; first in the Reign of King Athelstan* the Saxon, *and long after in the Reign of King Edward IV.* the Norman: And Whereas the old Constitutions in England have been much interpolated, mangled, and miserably corrupted, not only with false Spelling, but even with many false Facts and gross Errors in History and Chronology, through Length of Time, and the Ignorance of Transcribers, in the dark illiterate Ages, before the Revival of *Geometry* and *ancient Architecture*, to the great Offence of all the learned and judicious Brethren, whereby also the Ignorant have been deceiv'd.

And our late Worthy Grand Master, his Grace the Duke of Montagu, having order'd the Author to peruse, correct, and digest, into a new and better Method, the History, Charges, and Regulations of the ancient Fraternity; He has accordingly examin'd several Copies from Italy and Scotland, and sundry Parts of England, and from thence (tho' in many Things erroneous), and from several other ancient Records of Masons, he has drawn forth the above written new Constitutions, with the Charges and General Regulations. And the Author, having submitted the whole to the Perusal and Corrections of the late and present Deputy Grand Masters, and of other learned Brethren, and also of the Masters and Wardens of particular Lodges at their Quarterly Communication: He did regularly deliver them to the late Grand Master himself, the said Duke of Montagu, for his Examination, Correction, and Approbation; and His Grace, by the Advice of several Brethren, order'd the same to be handsomely printed for the use of the Lodges, though they were not quite ready for the Press during his Mastership.

Therefore, We, the present Grand Master of the Right Worshipful and most ancient Fraternity of Free and accepted Masons, the Deputy Grand Master, the Grand Wardens, the Masters and Wardens of particular Lodges (with the Consent of the Brethren and Fellows in and about the Cities of London and Westminster) having also perused this performance, Do join our laudable Predecessors in our solemn Approbation thereof, as what We believe will fully answer the End proposed; all the valuable Things of the old Records being retain'd, the Errors in History and Chronology corrected, the false Statements and the improper Words omitted, and the whole digested in a new and better Method.

And we ordain That these be receiv'd in every particular Lodge under our Cognizance, as the only Constitutions of Free and Accepted Masons amongst us, to be read at the making of new Brethren, or when the Master shall think fit; and which the new Brethren shall peruse before they are made.

PHILIP, DUKE OF WHARTON, *Grand Master.*

J. T. DESAGULIERS, LL.D. and F.R.S., *Deputy Grand Master.*

JOSHUA TIMSON,
WILLIAM HAWKINS, } *Grand Wardens.*

And the Masters and Wardens of particular Lodges, viz.:

I. Thomas Morris, sen., *Master;* John Bristow, Abraham Abbot, *Wardens.*

II. Richard Hail, *Master;* Philip Wolverston, John Doyer, *Wardens.*

III. John Turner, *Master ;* Anthony Sayer, Edward Cale, *Wardens.*
IV. Mr. George Payne, *Master ;* Stephen Hall, M.D., Francis Sorrell, Esq., *Wardens.*
V. Mr. Math. Birkhead, *Master ;* Francis Baily, Nicholas Abraham, *Wardens.*
VI. William Read, *Master ;* John Glover, Robert Cordell, *Wardens.*
VII. Henry Branson, *Master ;* Henry Lug, John Townshend, *Wardens.*
VIII. , *Master ;* Jonathan Sisson, John Shipton, *Wardens.*
IX. George Owen, M.D., *Master ;* Eman Bowen, John Heath, *Wardens.*
X. , *Master ;* John Lubton, Richard Smith, *Wardens.*
XI. Francis, Earl of Dalkeith, *Master ;* Captain Andrew Robinson, Colonel Thomas Inwood, *Wardens.*
XII. John Beal, M.D. and F.R.S., *Master ;* Edward Pawlet, Esq., Charles More, Esq., *Wardens.*
XIII. Thomas Morris, jun., *Master ;* Joseph Ridler, John Clark, *Wardens.*
XIV. Thomas Robbe, Esq., *Master ;* Thomas Grave, Bray Lane, *Wardens.*
XV. Mr. John Shepherd, *Master ;* John Senex, John Bucler, *Wardens.*
XVI. John Georges, Esq., *Master ;* Robert Gray, Esq., Charles Grymes, Esq., *Wardens.*
XVII. James Anderson, A.M., the Author of this Book, *Master ;* Gwinn Vaughan, Esq., Walter Greenwood, Esq., *Wardens.*
XVIII. Thomas Harbin, *Master ;* William Attley, John Saxon, *Wardens.*
XIX. Robert Capell, *Master ;* Isaac Mansfield, William Bly, *Wardens.*
XX. John Gorman, *Master ;* Charles Garey, Edward Morphey, *Wardens.*

ANCIENT LANDMARKS.

The Ancient Landmarks of Free Masonry are:
I. Belief in the existence of God.
II. Secrecy.
III. The modes of recognition—signs, grips, and words.

IV. Must congregate in regular Lodges.
V. Lodges must be tiled.
VI. Lodges must have a Book of the Law.
VII. Qualifications of Candidates; must be Sound, mentally and physically; Free Born, of lawful Age and well recommended.
VIII. Secret ballot.
IX. Division into three degrees: E. A., F. C., and M. M.
X. Legend of the third degree.
XI. Gen'l gov't by a Grand Master.
XII. Gov't of Lodges by a Master and two Wardens.
XIII. Right of appeal to the Grand Lodge.
XIV. Right of representation in Grand Lodge.
XV. Visitors must be vouched for, or examined.
XVI. Prerogatives of Grand Master to preside over any Assembly of the Craft, and to grant dispensations.
XVII. That Masonic instruction is a right and a duty of Masons.

FREE MASONRY IN IRELAND.

ALTHOUGH Free Masonry was introduced into this country in, or before, 1720, yet the earliest minutes of the Irish Craft are found in the "Munster Records," comprising the proceedings of a "*Grand* Lodge" and Lodge, dating from the year 1726.*

MINUTES OF THE GRAND LODGE OF MUNSTER, 1726–33.

"At an assembly and meeting of the Grand Lodge for the Province of Munster, at the house of M[r]. Herbert Phaire, in Cork, on S[t]. John's Day, being the 27th day of December Ano Dm. 1726. The Hon[ble]. James O'Brien, Esqr[e], by unanimous Consent elected Grand Master for the ensueing yeare; Springett Penn, Esqr[e], appointed by the Grand Master as his Deputy.

"WALTER GOOLD, Gent[e].,
THOMAS RIGGS, Gent[e]., } appointed Grand Wardens."

* Gould, vol. v., pp. 28–35.

FREE MASONRY IN IRELAND.

"S: Jons Day, Decembr 27th, 1727.

"At a meeting of the Rt. Worshipful the Grand Lodge of Free Masons for the Province of Munster, at the house of Herbert Phair, in the City of Corke, on the above day, the Grand Master and the Deputy Grand Master not being present, Willm Lane, Master of the Lodge of Corke, being the oldest Master present, acted as Grand Master pro tempore.

"It appearing to the Grand Lodge that severall Lodges within this Province have neglected to pay their attendance wch is highly resented, in order to prevent the like for the future, and punish such as shall not conform themselves to their duty: It is agreed unanimously that for the future no excuse shall be taken from the Masters and Wardens of any Lodge for their non-attendance unless a suffict. number appear, or that they send, at the time of such excuse, the sum of twenty-three shill. stg., to be disposed of as the Grand Lodge shall direct; the number deem'd suffict. to be not less than three. It is further resolv'd that the Master and Wardens who have absented themselves on this day doe and are hereby obliged to pay the like sum of 23s., to be dispos'd of as aforsd, except such as have justly excus'd y^{m}selves: And it is recommended to the Grand Master for the time being, that when he shall appoint any Master of a Lodge, that such Master shall oblige and promise for himself and Wardens that they comply with the aforemention'd rule, and moreover, that every Master and his Wardens shall require as many of his Lodge as he possible can assure himself can have no just reason for absenting themselves to attend at ye Grand Lodge. And further, it is resolved that this Rule be read or recited to all Mastr^s and Wardens at their election or nomination.

"Ordered that these regulations be recommended to the several Lodges within our precincts.

"Ordered that the Deputy Grand Warden of this R^t. Worshipfull Lodge, in their names, doe return thanks to Thos. Rigs, Esq., for his exelent speech in ye opening this Grand Lodge, and for all other his former service.

"Ordered that M^r. Thos. Wallis, sec^d. deputy Grand Warden, doe attend and open our next Grand Lodge.

"Ordered that this Grand Lodge be adjourned to ye next St. John's day, at this House of Brother Herbert Phair.

"W^м. Lane, p. tempe, G. M.
Thos. Riggs, } G. W.
Thos. Wallis, }
Ja. Crooke, *Treasurer and Secretary*."
(And six others without Titles.)

"St. John's Day, June 24, 1728.

"At a meeting of the Rt. Worshipfull ye Grand Lodge of Free Masons for the Province of Munster, at ye House of Bro: Herbert Phair, in ye City of Corke, on ye above day, The Honble. James O'Bryan was unanimously elected Grand Mastr. Robt. Longfield, Esq., appointed by the Grand Mast'. as his Deputy. Samuel Knowles, Esq., and Mr. Thos. Wallis appointed Grand Wardens.

"Ord^d. that Mr. John Wallis and Mr. St. George Van Lain be suspended from this Lodge for their Contempt offer'd this Rt. Worshipfull Grand Lodge this day in refusing attendance though regularly summond, and appearing afterward before ye windows at ye time of their sitting ; and that they, before they be recd. again, doe make a proper publick acknowledgmt of their behaviour, and to pay, each of them, two British Crowns to ye Treasurer of G^d. Lodge for ye benefit of ye poore Brethren.

"Thos. Wallis, } G. W. Ja. O'Bryen, G. M.
Saml. Nolers, }   Robt. Longfield, D. G. M."

"St. John's Day, June 24, 1730.

"At ye Grand Lodge held at Bro^r. Phaire's this day, Col. W^m. Maynard was by a unanimous Consent of ye Brethren then present Elected Grand Master for ye ensuing year, & M^r. Thos. Riggs elected Deputy Grand Master, W^m. Gallaway and Jo^n. Gamble, Esq^rs., Grand Wardens ; Mr. Sam^{ll}. Atkins, Secretary to s^d. Lodge.

"Thỏ'. Wallis, G. M. pro temp.
Adam Newman, G. W.
James Crooke, pro temp., G. W."

"Ordered that this Grand Lodge be adjourned to Bro^r. Phaire's on St. John ye Baptist's Day, wh. will be in ye year 1731.

"Thos. Riggs, D. G. M.
W^m. Galwey, G. W.
John Gamble, G. W."

"St. John's Day, June 24th, 1730.

"Humble supplication being made from some Brethern at Waterford to have Warrant from our Grand Lodge for assembling & holding Regular Lodges there, according to ancient Costome of Masonry ; it is agreed ye Petition shall be received from s^d. Brethern to be approved and granted as they shall shew themselves Qualified at our next Grand Lodge."

"The like application from some Brethern at Clonmell, ye like order for their approbation."

1731.—"At a Grand Lodge held the 24th Day of June at Mr. Herbert Phaire's, S^d. Grand Lodge was adjourned to Monday, the 9th Day of Augt. 1731.

"W^m. Galwey, Mastr."

"At a Grand Lodge held at Mr. Herbert Phaire's, Monday the 9th Day of August 1731, by unanimous Consent the Rt. Honble. James Lord Baron of Kingston was elected Grand Master.

"W^m. Galwey, Mast^r."

"August the 9th, 1731.—Mr. Adam Newman appointed Depty. Grand Mr., Jonas Morris and Wm. Newenham, Esqrs., Grand Wardens, by the Rt. Worshipful the Grand Master, the Rt. Honble. James Lord Baron of Kingston, wth the unanimous approbation of the Brethern then attending his Lordship at the Grand Lodge.

"KINGSTON, G. M."

"ST. JOHN'S DAY, June 24th, 1732.—A Grand Lodge was held on said day at Brothr. Phairs, when said Lodge was adjourn'd to the 25th of July next, and it is unanimously agreed yt all such members as are duly served and wont attend, yt they shall pay ye fine of five shillings and five pennce, or to be admonished or expold for sd. misdemeanor.

"ADAM NEWMAN, D. G. M.
Wm. GALWEY, Mastr. of ye Lodge."

"June 23, 1733.—At a consultation held for adjourning the Grand Lodge, St. John's Day happning on Sunday, the Grand Lodge was accordinly adjourn'd to Monday, the 25th inst.

"ADm. NEWMAN, D. G. M."

The Grand Lodge was again adjourned to July 26th, and further adjourned to October 3, the order being signed as before. There are no further minutes of this Grand Lodge, but the following Regulations are given, though of anterior date by over three years:

"GENERAL REGULATIONS MADE AT A GRAND LODGE HELD IN CORKE ON ST. JOHN Yᴇ EVANGELIST'S DAY, 1728.

"THE HONble. JAMES O'BRYEN, ESQr., GRAND MASTr.:

"In due Honour, Respect and obedience to ye Right Worshipfull the Grand Master, that his Worship may be properly attended for the more Solemn and proper holding our Grand Lodge on St. John the Baptist's day, annually, for ever, and for ye propagating, exerting, and exercising Brotherly Love and affection as becometh true Masons, and that our ancient Regularity, Unanimity, and Universality may in Lawdable and usual manner be preserv'd according to immemorial usage of our most ancient and Rt Worshipful Society, the following Regulations are agreed to.

1. "That every Brother who shall be Mastr. or Warden of a Lodge, shall appear and attend, and shall allso prevail with and oblige as many of ye Brethren of his Lodge as can, to attend ye Grand Lodge.

2. "Every constituted Lodge, if the Master and Wardens thereof cannot attend, shall send at least five of ye Brethren to attend the Grand Lodge.

3. "That every Master of a Lodge shall give timely Notice in writing to yᵉ Master of the Lodge where yᵉ Grand Lodge is to be held, eight days before yᵉ Grand Lodge, what number of Brethern will appear from his Lodge at the Grand Lodge.

4. "That if it shou'd happ'n that yᵉ Master and Wardens or Five of yᵉ Brethern of any Lodge shou'd not be able to attend at yᵉ Grand Lodge, then such Lodge so failing shall send yᵉ sum of twenty and three shill : to be paid to the Grand Mastʳ. or his Deputy.

5. "That all & singular yᵉ Brethern of such Lodges where the Grand Lodge shall be held, shall attend such Grand Lodge, or the person absenting to pay a British Crown.

6. "That these Regulations be duly entered in yᵉ Books of each Lodge, and sign'd by the Master, Wardens, and all yᵉ Brethern of such Lodge, and that at yᵉ making of any new Brother, care be taken that he sign such Regulations.

7. "That an exact Duplicate of these Regulations sign'd by the Master and Wardens and all the Brethern be delivered with convenient speed to the Rᵗ. Worshipful Grand Master, of each Lodge.

8. "That every new Brother who has not sign'd such Duplicate before it be deliver'd to the Grand Master, shall be oblig'd to attend at the next Grand Lodge which shall be held after his admission, there to sign such Duplicate.

9. "That no person pretending to be a Mason shall be considered as such within yᵉ precincts of our Grand Lodge, or deem'd duly matriculated into yᵉ Society of Freemasons until he hath subscribed in some Lodge to thes regulatns., and oblig'd himself to sign yᵉ before mention'd Duplicate, at wch time he sall be furnish'd with proper means to convince yᵉ authentick Brethern yᵗ he has duly complyed.

10. "That the Master and Wardens of each Lodge take care that their Lodge be furnish'd with the Constitution, printed in London in yᵉ year of Masonry 5723, Anno Dom. 1723, Intitled the Constitution of Free Masons, containing the History, Charges, Regulations, &c., of THAT MOST ANCIENT AND RT. WORSHIPFULL FRATERNITY.

"To due and full observance of the foregoing Regulations we, the subscribers, do Solemnly, Strictly, & Religiously, on our obligations as Masons, hereby oblige ourselves this Twenty-seventh day of December, in the year of Masonry 5728, and Anno Dm. 1728.

"The foregoing Regulations and form of obligation were read and approved by ye Grand Master and Grand Lodge afore mentioned, & ord'd to be observ'd as yᵉ original Warrant under yᵉ Grand Master's hand, and attested by all the Brethern then present, which Warrant is deposited with yᵉ other records of this Lodge of Cork.

"THOˢ. WALLIS, G. W.   FRANˢ. HEALY, Mastʳ.
THOMAS GORDON,   JAMES CROOKE, ⎫
HIGNETT KEELING,   ⎬ Wardens."
THOS. RIGGS,   ⎭

(And ten other Brethren.)

MINUTES OF THE LODGE.

" December yᵉ 8th, 1726.

"In a meeting of this Lodge this day at Mr. Herbert Phaires, it was unanimously agreed that Mr. Thoˢ. Holldˢ., a poor Brother, be every Lodge night a constant attendᵗ of this Lodge, and that every night he so attends a brittish crown be allow'd him for yᵉ relief of his distress'd Family. " Mastʳ. Springett Penn."

"Wardens, ⎧ The above named Thomas Holland missbehaveing himself at the Grand
Thomas Gordon. ⎨ Lodge held on St. John's Day, the 27ᵗʰ of Decembr, 1726, Order'd the
Thomas Riggs. ⎩ above order continue no longer in force.
" D. G. Master, Springer Penn."

Passing the entry of February, we come to that of
" Novembr 20th, 1727.

" By an ordʳ in writing from the Honble. James O'Bryan, Esq., our present Grand Mastʳ., to us, directed for the convening a Lodge to choose Mastr. and Wardens for the Worshipfull Lodge of Freemasons in Corke, wee having accordingly conven'd a sufficient Lodge at the House of Brother Herbert Pair on this day, proceeded to the election, and then and there Wm. Lane, Esq., was duly chosn Mastʳ. of sᵈ. Lodge, and the Honble. Sr John Dickson Hamman, Knt. Barnt., and Mr. Thos. Wallis were duly chosn Wardens.
" Thos. Gordon.   Frans Fook."

"At the same time Mʳ. James Crooke, Junʳ., was chosen Treasurʳ and Secretary to said Lodge.

" W. Lane, Master, ⎫
Jaˢ. Dickson Haman, ⎬ Wardens."
Thoˢ. Wallis, ⎭

The following is signed by thirty-three brethren :
" We who have hereunto subscribed do resolve & oblige ourselves as Masons to meet on the first Monday of every month at the House of Broʳ Phaire (or such convenient place as shall be appointed) for the holding of a Lodge in a Brotherly or Friendly manner. Each member of the Lodge being absent to pay thirteen pence.
" Dated 22nd August, 1728."

" December the Second, 1728.

" The yeare of the Master & Wardens being expired the twentieth of last month, it was this day agreed to in a proper Lodge of the Worshipfull ffraternity of ffreemasons in the City of Corke assembled at the house of Brother Herbert Phaire, that ffrancis Healy, of the said City, Merchant, be elected to serve as Master, and James Crooke, Junr., and Joseph Collins, Merchants, be Wardens of the said ffraternity for the ensuing yeare, in the Room and place of the late Master and Wardens, which was consented & agreed to Nemine Contradicente.

" Fras. Healy, Mastr.   Wm. Lane, late Mr.
Jo Collins, ⎫   Thos. Wallis, G.W.
James Crooke, Junr. ⎬ Wardens.
                   ⎭   John Flower."

Passing the minutes of March 13, 1728, and January, 1729, the following are the next in order:

"CORK, Monday the first Day of March, 173⅔.

"At a Lodge held by adjournment this day for the election of Master and Wardens for the Lodge of Cork, by unaminous Consent W^m. Gallway, Esq, was chosen Master, M^r. Abraham Dickson and M^r. Sept^s. Peacock, Wardens, for the year ensuing.

"W^m. GALWEY, Master.   TH^{os}. WALLIS, late Mr.
ABRA^m DICKSON, } Wardens.   TH^{os}. RIGGS, D. G. M.
                               JOHN GAMBLE, G. W."

"CORK, 12th Augt. 1731.

"Att a Lodge held at Bro. Phairs, W^m. Newerham, Esq., appeared and acted as Mast^r., ye Mast^r. being absent, and only one Warden, at which time Thomas Evans, Rowland Bateman, William Armstrong, and George Bateman, Esq^{rs}., were admitted Enter'd Prentices."

The only other entry which is preserved, begins on the reverse of the leaf containing the first part of the Regulations of 1728, and concludes on the next page after the Grand Lodge record of June 24, 1728, and is to the following effect:

"CORK, June the 21, 1749.

"At a Lodge held at brother Hignett Keelings on the day above written, the Master and Wardens being present, Mr. Willm. Bridges was Rec^d Enter prentice, and did then and there perform the Requisite Due.

"FRAN^s COOKE, Mastr.
HERBERT PHAIRE, } Wardens.
HIG^t. KEELING, }
THOS. RELY.
S^r. GEORGE VAN LAWEN.
JOHN HART, M. D."

IN BRIEF:

In 1726 Col. James O'Brien was elected Grand Master, and Springett Penn Deputy Grand Master.

In 1728 O'Brien was still Grand Master, and Robert Longfield Deputy Grand Master. General Regulations made at a Grand Lodge at Cork this year.

1729. Col. William Maynard was Grand Master, and Thomas Riggs Deputy Grand Master. In this year the Grand Lodge of Ireland laid the cornerstone of the Parliament House, Dublin.

In 1731 the Right Hon. James King, Lord Kingston, was elected and installed Grand Master of Ireland, having been Grand Master of England the preceding year.

In 1733 Lord Kingston was re-elected Grand Master, and Lord Viscount Nitterville Deputy Grand Master.

1738. The Grand Lodge established a Committee of Charity.

"The General Regulations of the Free and Accepted Masons in the Kingdom of Ireland, pursuant to the English Constitutions," were approved of and agreed upon by the Grand Lodge in Dublin, on the 24th June, 1741. Tullamore, Grand Master.

1751. In this year the Book of the Irish Constitutions was published by Edward Pratt.

In 1838 there was a notable Masonic celebration in Dublin by the brethren of St. Patrick's Lodge, No. 50. The principal object of this *fête* was to honor the Countess of Mulgrave, and it was graced by over a thousand guests, comprising many of the most fashionable and distinguished members of Dublin society. The entertainment was given at the Rotunda. Soon after the arrival of the Viceroy and the Countess of Mulgrave and suite, a procession was formed to conduct the distinguished guests to the rooms where refreshments awaited them, the rooms being beautifully decorated with Masonic banners, etc., and brilliantly illuminated.

All accounts represent this as being the most magnificent as well as one of the most agreeable entertainments that ever occurred in Dublin.*

NOTES FROM AUTHORITIES.

1. In Shropshire there is a hill bearing evidence of ancient fortifications, and where tradition says that a great battle took place.

2. That the corporation of builders were established in Britain as early as 52 B.C. is shown by the inscription on a tubular stone found at Chichester in 1725, on which was chronicled the fact that a temple to Minerva and another to Neptune had been erected at that place.

Another notice of the presence of the Roman Colleges in Britain at an early period is a votive tablet on which those Craftsmen allude to the safety of Claudius Cæsar's family, also to the dedication of a temple to Neptune and Minerva. A learned antiquary has decided that this

* Mitchell, vol. i., pp. 336–342.

stone is the oldest memorial of the Romans in Britain hitherto discovered. See Gould, vol. i., p. 38.

3. No sooner was the Roman conquest of Britain begun, and a modicum of territory obtained, than we find a collegium in our own civitates Regnorum ; a collegium faborum. And this was while Claudius was still Emperor. The colleges of course multiplied and spread throughout our islands, remaining during the whole of the imperial rule, and surviving, with our provincial ancestors, the various barbarian conquests. Gould, vol. i., p. 37.

4. H. C. Coote, in Romans of Britain, p. 440, says that the Romans of Britain survived all the barbarian conquests, and that they retained their own law, with its own procedure and police ; their own lands, with the tenures and obligations appertaining to them ; their own cities and municipal government, their Christianity and private colleges.

5. And in another place, comparing the internal working of the colleges, cutlorum dei, with the Guilds established in London, Cambridge, and Exeter, composed of gentlemen, he concludes thus : "These coincidences, which cannot be attributed to imitation or mere copying, demonstrates the absolute identity of the guild of England with the collegium of Rome and of Roman Britain." Gould, vol. i., p. 43.

6. Lappenberg, speaking of the Roman corporations, says : "This form of social unions, as well as the hereditary obligations under which the trades were conducted, was propagated in Britain, and was the original germ of those guilds which became so influential in Europe some centuries after the cessation of the Roman dominion." History of England Under the Anglo-Saxon Kings, by B. Thorpe, vol. i, p. 36 ; also Gould, vol. i., p. 37.

7. When the Anglo-Saxons arrived in Britain they found the colleges in full play, and they left the Romans at liberty to continue them. The name guild, by which they were afterward known, was due to the contributions upon which the colleges had from time to time subsisted. See History of Freemasonry, by Gould, p. 38.

8. From early in this century the Roman Empire was agitated by rivals for the throne ; and in several such cases Britain not only afforded the pretenders an asylum but the means of advocating their claims. Among these claimants was Carrausius.

9. St. Alban, the first Martyr of Britain, was born at Verulam, in the third century, and after long living as a heathen, was converted to Christianity, but put to death at the commencement of Diocletian's persecution of the Christians. His anniversary is celebrated on June 22d. The town of St. Albans, which bears his name, is believed to stand on the site of his birthplace or the scene of his martyrdom. Chambers's Encyclopædia, vol. i., p. 165, Student's Ed.

10. Caledonians, the name given by the Romans to the people of North Britain. They were afterward known as Picts, and were joined by the Scoti, or Scots, from the north of Ireland.

11. No two of the MSS. were exactly alike, though there is a substantial agreement between them all, and evidently they had a common origin, just as they were designed to serve a common purpose. It is probable that each lodge, prior to the last century, had one of these "Old Charges" among its effects, which was read to an apprentice on his introduction to the craft. Gould, vol. i., p. 59.

12. During the eleventh and twelfth centuries, the Society of Constructors, or Free Masons, had become established on a solid basis, and began to exercise a wide-spread and salutary influence upon the architecture of Europe.

At this epoch the Free Masons formed a numerous and powerful corporation, and architecture, together with many other arts, at this time passed from the monasteries into the possession of lay architects, organized into fraternities of Masons. Fort, Early History and Antiquities of Free Masonry, pp. 73, 74.

13. It is worthy of remark, and perhaps here is the most proper place to make it, that Masonry conforms to the practice of the Egyptians, in prohibiting to slaves a participation of its mystic rites. It excludes all, also, who possess any bodily defect.

The Levites, among the Jews, were subjected to the same rigid discipline; no one who had the least bodily blemish could be admitted into the sacerdotal order.

This circumstance alone is a strong proof of the ancient origin of the Masonic order. Mysteries, p. 137.

14. The author of The Master Key to the Door of Freemasonry has judiciously remarked, "That the word 'free' was added to masonry by the society, because none but the freeborn was admitted into it;" and for a very obvious reason, for there could be no safety in confiding secrets to slaves which might at any time be extorted from them by their masters. Besides, this was in conformity with the rule established in the Egyptian Mysteries. Mysteries, p. 258.

15. In his survey of the cities of London and Westminster, Seymour gives the date of the incorporation of the Masons company at about 1410, and adds: "They having been called Free Masons, a Fraternity of great account, who having been honored by several Kings; and very many of the nobility and gentry being of their Society." Gould, vol. iii., p. 154.

16. In 1421, at Catterick Church, a "luge" of four rooms is specified as having to be made for the Masons. In 1426 the Masons engaged to build Walberswick steeple, were to be provided with "hows" to eat, drink, work, and sleep in, and to "make mete in," *i.e.*, fitting or convenient. As I have shown, these lodges were formerly thatched, but one properly "tiled" was to be provided at the expense of some parishes in Suffolk. In 1432, a "luge" was erected in the cemetery at Durham. And 1541, Thomas Phillips, *Freemason*, and John Petit, covenanted "To set up and fully finish" Coventry Cross, and at their own Charge "to prepare, find and make a house or lodge for Masons to work in during the time of making the

same cross." Various customs of trade are mentioned in the manuscript constitutions of the latter date. Gould, vol. ii., p. 304.

17. In a work entitled The Display of Heraldry, by John Guillim, it is stated that the company of Masons, being otherwise termed *freemasons*, of ancient standing and good reckoning, by means of affable and kind meetings, divers times did frequent this mutual assembly in the time of King Henry VI., in the twelfth year of his reign, 1434. Mysteries, p. 253.

18. "The conclusion forces itself irresistibly upon the mind of every candid and intelligent person that there existed in London, in 1709, and for a **long time** before, a society known as Freemasons, having certain distinct modes of recognition, and as the proof of it is to be found, not in the assertion of Masonic writers and historians, but in a standard work unaccompanied by explanation, because it needed none then, as it needs none now, and is one of these sure and infallible guide marks whence the materials for truthful history are taken, and by which its veracity is tested." J. L. Lewis, Masonic Eclectic, vol. i.

19. In his Early History of Free Masonry, Halliwell, quoting Aubrey, says: "This May the 18th being Monday 1692, after Rogation Sunday, is a great convention at St. Paul's Church of the Fraternity of the *adopted* Masons, where Sir Christopher Wren is to be adopted a brother and Sir Henry Goodric of the Tower and divers others."

The Postboy, March 2 to March 5, 1723, has the following: "London, March 5, this evening the corpse of that worthy Free Mason, Sir Christopher Wren, Knight, is to be interred under the Dome of St. Paul's Cathedral." A similar announcement appeared in the British Journal, March 9th, viz., "Sir Christopher Wren, that worthy Free Mason, was splendidly interred in St. Paul's Church on Tuesday night last."

20. As it is by the term Speculative that Free Masonry is distinguished from ancient Operative Masonry, light concerning the word will be of interest in this connection. In Webster's definition of the word we find the following: "Involving or formed by speculation; ideal; theoretical; inquisitive." And its masonic import will appear from the following quotations from Lord Bacon and others. Bacon, speaking of philosophy, says: "These be the two parts of natural philosophy, the inquisition of causes, and the production of effects; speculative and operative."

Worsop, speaking of a learned Craftsman, says: "He understandeth Arithmetike Geometrie, and Prospective, both speculatively and practically, singularly well." In the Lexicon Technicorum it is stated that "Geometry is usually divided into speculative and practicle."

21. "Although, for convenience sake, the year 1717 is made to marke the epoch of authentic, *i.e.*, officially credited Masonic history, the existence in England of a widely diffused system of freemasonry in the first half of the seventeenth century is demonstrable, whence we shall be justified in concluding that for its period of origin in South Britain, a **far higher antiquity** may be claimed and conceded." Gould, vol. iii., p. 2.

NOTES FROM AUTHORITIES—ENGLAND.

22. "Speculative Masonry has perpetuated intact for centuries that which has come down from the very twilight of time. In passing through the various nationalities which have successively fallen to decay, this brotherhood has survived, and through the long line of ages continued to guard the relics of a remote antiquity." Fort, Early History and Antiquities, p. 184.

23. During his second term of office as Grand Master, Payne *compiled* the *General Regulations*, which were afterward finally arranged and published by Dr. Anderson, in 1723. He continued an active member of the Grand Lodge until 1754, on April 27th of which year he was appointed a member of the committee to revise the "Constitution" (afterward brought out by Entick in 1756). According to the Minutes of the Grand Lodge he was present there for the last time in the following November.

It is certain that upon Anderson, rather than either Payne or Desaguliers, devolved the leading rôle in the consolidation of the Grand Lodge of England. Gould, vol. iv., pp. 348–356.

24. The earliest book of "Constitutions" was published by Dr. James Anderson, conformably with the directions of the Grand Lodge, to which body it was submitted in print on Jan. 17, 1723, and finally approved. It was the joint production of Anderson, Desaguliers, and the antiquary, George Payne, the two last named of whom had filled the office of Grand Master. Payne compiled the "Regulations" which constitute the chief feature of the work; Desaguliers wrote the preface, and Anderson digested the subject matter. Gould, vol. iii., p. 7.

25. It is called the Quarterly Communication, because it should meet quarterly according to ancient usage. When the Grand Master is present it is a lodge in Ample Form: otherwise in Due Form, yet having the same authority with Ample Form.

26. Then followed the more important changes in the Constitutions, known as those of 1738; those emanated from a representation made to the Grand Lodge by Dr. Anderson, on February 24, 1735. The subject went to a committee, was reported, and resulted in a new edition of the Constitutions published in 1738, and which have been regarded as the basis of Masonic History, whether in or out of the Craft. Thus became firmly established the first Grand Governing Power of the Masonic Fraternity.

27. "There was a great Lodge or ancient Society of the Free Masons held last week at the Horn Tavern, in Palace Yard; at which were present the Earl of Dalkeith, their Grand Master, the Deputy Grand Master, the Duke of Richmond, and several other persons of quality, at which time the Lord Carmichael, Colonel Carpenter, Sir Thomas Pendergast, Colonel Paget, and Colonel Saunderson, were accepted Free Masons, and went Home in their leather Aprons and Gloves." Gould, vol. iv., p. 342.

The Schism, 1747–52.

28. It appears to me that the summary erasures of lodges for non-attendance at the Quarterly Communications, and for not "Paying in their Charity," was one of the leading causes of the schism, which, as before expressed, I think must have taken place during the presidency

of Lord Byron. In the ten years, speaking roundly, commencing June 24, 1742, and ending November 30, 1752, no less than forty-five lodges, or about a third of the total of those meeting in the metropolis, were struck out of the list. Gould, iv., p. 398.

29. Of Laurence Dermott, the first Grand Secretary of the Seceders, it may be said, without erring on the side of panegyric, that he was the most remarkable Mason that ever existed.

As Grand Secretary, and later as Deputy Grand Master, he was simply the life and soul of the body with which he was so closely associated. He was also its historian, and to the influence of his writings must be attributed, in a great measure, the marvellous success of the schism.

The epithets of "Ancient and Modern" applied by Dermott to the usages of his own and of the older society respectively, produced a really wonderful result. Gould, iv., p. 435.

30. Dermott, referring to the Moderns, said : " As they differ in matters of Masonry, so they did in matters of calumny ; for while some were charging me with forgery, others said that I was so illiterate as not to know how to write my name. But what may appear more strange is, that some insisted that I had neither father nor mother, but that I grew up spontaneously in the corner of a potato garden in Ireland." Gould, vol. iv., p. 437.

CHAPTER IX.

ANCIENT YORK, ENGLAND.—EPITOME OF ITS MASONIC HISTORY.

This was the Chief Town of one of the Native Tribes when the Romans Landed in Britain.—Remodelled by the Colleges of Builders.—Several Roman Emperors Resided here when Visiting the Island.—The First English Parliament was Held in this City.—King Edwin, Athelstan and Edmund.—Tragic Fate of the Latter.—The City was the Scene of the First General Assembly of Masons ever Convened, and it has Held a Conspicuous Place in Masonic History since the Tenth Century.

This ancient city is situated at the junction of the rivers Ouse and Foss, in the north of England, and has a population of 45,000.

At the time of the Roman invasion, 55 B.C., it was one of the chief towns of the Brigantes, the most numerous and powerful of the British tribes. In A.D. 79, Agricola established a Roman station here, and named it Eboracum. During the Roman occupation of Britain, York was a city of the first importance. Hadrian lived here, and Constantine Chlorus, the father of Constantine the Great, died here. When the Roman emperors visited the province, York was the place of their residence. King Edwin resided at Audley, five miles from York. Subsequently it became the capital of Northumbria. Here also the first English Parliament was held by Henry II., in 1160.

The Masonic interest in this ancient city lies in the tradition that a General Assembly of the craft was held here under the patronage of King Athelstan, A.D. 926, and a document was adopted and promulgated known as the Charter of York.*

As considerable confusion exists concerning King Athelstan and Prince Edwin—the latter having been made to take a prominent part in the calling

---

* Notes 4, 5, 7, 8, and 9, pp. 393, 394; Woodford, Old Charges, British Freemasons, p. xiv; Mackey, p. 95.

of this noted assembly—a brief sketch of the lives of each will assist in rendering the subject intelligible.

Edwin was born in 586, and after passing through various vicissitudes he ascended the throne in 617. He was pre-eminent among contemporary Anglo-Saxon kings for military genius, statesmanship, and for his promotion of the builder's art. He employed the craft in building a church, and on other works in York. So inflexible was his administration of justice, that in his reign a woman or child might carry anywhere a purse of gold without danger of robbery—high commendation in those days of almost unbridled rapine.

In the eleventh year of his reign Edwin and his nobles embraced Christianity, and were baptized, and thereafter he became the most powerful prince in England. He subdued a part of Wales, and his power extended north to the Lothians. He fell in battle at Hatfield Chase in 634.*

Athelstan, the grandson of Alfred the Great, was born A.D. 895, and was the first Saxon monarch who took the title of King of England. He was crowned at Kingston-upon-Thames in 925, and seems to have possessed great ambition and great talents. It is supposed that his design was to unite under his sway the entire island of Britain. His resources, however, were not equal to the undertaking, and he had to content himself with the acquisition of portions of Cornwall and Wales. On the death of Sigtric, King of Northumbria, who married one of his daughters, Athelstan took possession of his dominions. This excited the alarm and animosity of the neighboring states, and a league, composed of Welch, Scotch, and Irish, was formed against the English king for the purpose of placing Aulaff, the son of Sigtric, on his father's throne. A fierce and decisive battle was fought at Brunenburg, in which the allies were utterly defeated, and which became famous in Saxon song. After this, the reputation of Athelstan spread to the Continent. His sisters married into the Royal families of France and Germany, and he himself enjoyed the greatest influence and consideration.

Athelstan was liberal in his ideas, like his grandfather, Alfred the Great; he was a promoter of civilization: patronized learning, built many churches and monasteries, and encouraged the translation of the Scriptures. He also

---

* Notes 1, 2, and 3, p. 393; Hume, vol. i., pp. 34–37; Chambers, vol. iv., pp. 737-739; Mackey, p. 241; Hughan, pp. 113-168.

gave charters to several Masonic Guilds, and otherwise encouraged them. In his reign the "Frithgildan," free guild or sodalities, were incorporated by law.

Athelstan died A.D. 941, and was succeeded by Edmund, who after reigning five years, came to a singular and tragic death. While solemnizing a festival in Gloucester he was astonished to see Leolf, a noted robber whom he had banished, coolly enter the hall where he himself had dined and take a seat at the table with his attendants. Enraged at such presumption, he sprang upon him and seized him by the hair, when the robber gave him a thrust with his dagger that killed him.*

Therefore, as Athelstan was succeeded by Edmund, and there being no respectable authority who will stand sponsor for Prince Edwin as son of Athelstan, the Edwin of Masonic history will have to be relegated to the domain of myths; and for Edwin, substitute Edmund.

The only *real* Edwin who, as Prince or King, figured in early English history, was *Edwin*, King of Northumbria, whose reign was in the first part of the seventh century, as previously stated; and the tradition of his being a promoter of the arts and an encourager of the craft, did in some way reach the assembly of A.D. 926, and became mixed up with that event; or Edwin has been, by the magic of the old Masonic pen, made like Naymus Grecus, to jump centuries in order to accommodate the dealers in fables.

THE CHARTER OF YORK,

A.D. 926.

The Articles which pertain to Speculative Masonry.

ARTICLE I.—Your first duty is, that you reverence God with sincerity and submit to the laws of the Noachides, because they are divine laws. For this reason you should also avoid false doctrine and offending against God.

ARTICLE II.—You should be faithful to your King, without treason, and obedient to constituted authority, without deception, wherever you may find yourself, to the end that high treason should be unknown to you; but if you should be apprised of it, you must immediately inform the King.

* Hume, vol. i., pp. 85–88; Chambers, vol. iv., p. 893.

ARTICLE III.—You should be serviceable to all men, and a faithful friend to the extent of your ability, without disquieting yourself as to what religion or opinion they shall hold or belong to.

ARTICLE IV.—You should be, above all, faithful among yourselves, instructing each other and aiding each other, not calumniating one another, but doing to each other as you would have done to yourself; so that, according as a brother shall have failed in his engagement with his fellow, you ought to help him to repair his fault, in order that he may reform.

ARTICLE V.—You should assist assiduously at the discussions and labors of your brethren in the Lodge, and keep the secret of the signs from all who are not brethren.

ARTICLE VI.—Each should guard against infidelity, seeing that without fidelity and probity the fraternity cannot exist, and a good reputation is a valuable property. Also constantly hold to the interests of the master whom you may serve, and honestly finish your labor.

ARTICLE VII.—You should always pay honorably that which you owe, and in general, do nothing that will injure the good reputation of the Fraternity.

ARTICLE XI.—Furthermore, no Master or Fellow-craftsman should accept indemnity for admitting any person as a Mason, if he be not free-born, of good reputation, of good capacity, and sound of limbs.

ARTICLE XV.—Furthermore, all Masons should receive their fellows coming from abroad, and who will give the signs; but they ought to be careful, and as they have been taught. They also ought to come to the relief of brethren who may need assistance, as soon as they shall learn, in manner as they have been taught, that such assistance is necessary, and the distance be within half a league.

These are the duties which he well and truly ought to observe. Those which shall yet be found good and useful in the future ought always to be written and published by the chiefs of the lodges, for all the brothers to learn the same, and to be sworn to their performance.

This Charter was based upon the ancient documents, laws and privileges of

ANCIENT YORK, LODGE MEETINGS.

the Roman College of Builders, and it is claimed by some to be the basis of the English Masonic Constitutions.*

The General Assemblies and Lodges continued to meet at York and in its vicinity, and in 1705, under Sir George Tempest, Bart., then Grand Master, there were several Lodges in that city, and many worthy men were initiated in them. Sir George was succeeded by the Right Hon. Robert Benson, Mayor of York, and a number of meetings of the Fraternity were held there at different times.

Among the York Records and Minutes of the transactions of the Fraternity still extant are the following:

"March the 19th, 1712.—At a private Lodge, held at the house of John Boreham, situated in Stonegate, in the city of York, Mr. Thomas Shipton, Mr. Caleb Greenbury, Mr. John Norrisson, Mr. John Russell, John Whitehead and Francis Norrisson, were all of them severally sworn and admitted into the honorable Society and Fraternity of Free Masons.

"1714.—At a General Lodge held on the 24th of June at Mr. James Boreham's, situated in Stonegate, in York, John Taylor of Langton in the Woulds, was admitted and sworn into the honorable Society and Company of Free Masons in the City of York, before the Worshipful Charles Fairfax, Esq.†

"At St. John's Lodge in Christmas, 1716, at the house of Mr. James Boreham, situated at Stonegate, in York, being a General Lodge, held then by the Honorable Society and Company of Free Masons, in the City of York, John Turner, Esq., was sworn and admitted into the said Honorable Society and Fraternity of Free Masons."

"CHARLES FAIRFAX, ESQ., *Dep. Prest.*
"JOHN TURNER."

"On January 10th, 1722–3; at the same time the following persons were acknowledged as Brethren of this ancient Society." (Names given.) "And on February 4th, 1722–3, at the same time and place, the two persons, whose names are underwritten, were, upon their examination, received as Masons, and as such were accordingly introduced and admitted into this Lodge.‡

"GEO. REYNOLDSON,
"BARNABY BAWTRY."

* Rebold, p. 350.   † Gould, vol. iv., pp. 271, 272.   ‡ Hughan, p. 56.

Old Rules.

The following was copied from a Sheet of Parchment, endorsed, "*Old Rules of the Grand Lodge at York, 1725, No. 8 :*"*

Articles agreed to be kept and observed by the Ancient Society of Free Masons in the City of York, and to be subscribed by every member thereof at their Admittance into the said Society.

1. Imprimis. That every first Wednesday in the month a Lodge shall be held at the house of a Brother, according as their turn shall fall out.
2. All Subscribers to these articles, not appearing at the monthly Lodge, shall forfeit Sixpence each time.
3. If any brother appear at a Lodge that is not a Subscriber to these articles, he shall pay over and above his club the sum of one shilling.
4. The bowl shall be filled at the monthly Lodges with Punch once, Ale, Bread, Cheese and Tobacco in common; but if anything more shall be called for by any Brother, either for eating or drinking, that Brother so calling shall pay for it himself besides his club.
5. The Master or Deputy shall be obliged to call for a Bill exactly at ten o'clock, if they meet in the evening, and discharge it.
6. None to be admitted to the making of a Brother but such as have subscribed to these articles.
7. Timely notice shall be given to all the Subscribers when a Brother or Brothers are to be made.
8. Any Brother or Brothers presuming to call a Lodge with a design to make a Mason or Masons, without the Master or Deputy, or one of them deputed, for every such offence shall forfeit the sum of Five Pounds.
9. Any Brother that shall interrupt the Examination of a Brother shall forfeit one shilling.
10. Clerk's Salary for keeping the Books and Accounts shall be one Shilling, to be paid him by each Brother and his admittance; and at each of the two Grand days he shall receive such gratuity as the Company shall think proper.

*See Gould vol. iv., p. 407; Hughan, p. 61.

11. A Steward to be chosen for keeping the Stocks at the Grand Lodge, at Christmas, and the Accounts to be passed three days after each Lodge.

12. If any dispute arise, the Master shall silence them by a knock of the Mallet; any Brother that shall presume to disobey shall immediately be obliged to leave the company or forfeit Five Shillings.

13. An hour shall be set apart to talk Masonry.

14. No person shall be admitted into the Lodge but after having been strictly examined.

15. No more persons shall be admitted as Brothers of this Society, that shall keep a public house.

16. That these articles shall at Lodge be laid upon the table to be perused by the members, and also when any new Brothers are made, the Clerk shall publicly read them.

Concerning the question of priority between the Grand Lodge at York and the Grand Lodge at London, the following letter appears in evidence:

"Sir: In compliance with your request to be satisfied of the existence of a Grand Lodge at York, previous to the establishment of that at London in 1717, I have inspected an Original Minute Book of this Grand Lodge, beginning at 1705, and ending in 1734, from which I have extracted the names of the Grand Masters during that period as follows:

"1705, Sir George Tempest, Baronet;

"1707, The Right Honourable Robert Lord Mayor of York;

"1708, Sir Walter Robinson, Bar.;

"1713, Sir George Tempest, Bar.;

"1714, Charles Fairfax, Esq.;

"1720, Sir Walter Hawkeworth, Bar.;

"1725, Edward Bell, Esq.;

"1726, Charles Bathurst, Esq.;

"1729, Edward Thompson, Esq., M.P.;

"1733, John Johnson, Esq., M.D.;

"1734, John Marsden, Esq.

"In short, the superior antiquity of the Grand Lodge of York, to all other

ANCIENT YORK, MASONIC RELICS.

Lodges in the Kingdom, will not admit a Doubt. All the books which treat on the subject agree that it was founded so early as the year 926, and that in the reign of Queen Elizabeth it was so numerous that mistaking the purport of their Meetings, she was at the trouble of sending an armed Force to dislodge the Brethren. It appears, by the Lodge books since that Time that this Lodge has been regularly continued and particularly by the Book above. I am, with true regard, your most faithful Brother and Obedient Servant,

"JACOB BUSSEY, G. S.

"To MR. BENJAMIN BRADLEY,
"No. 4 Clements Lane, Lombard Street, London.
"York, 29th Aug. 1778." †

Furthermore, it is clear that, so far as England is concerned, the distinction of having preserved the earliest evidences of its transactions belongs to York, as will be seen by the following schedule of implements, records, etc., belonging to the Grand Lodge of all England, taken the 15th of September, 1779:

An oak wainscoat repository with three locks and keys in the upper part, and an iron bolt and staple inside.

* An old brass plate for the Summonses;
* A new one for the like;
* A new one for the Certificates;
* A Seal and Counter Seal, the first bearing the arms of Prince Edwin, and the other the arms of Masonry;
* An old Seal of Prince Edwin's arms;
* An iron Screw Press;
* A wooden Square, Level and Plumb;
* A white Staff for the G. M.;
* A blue cloth Coat with a red Collar for the Tyler;
* Records and Papers in a paper Box:

No. 1. A parchment Roll in three slips, containing the Constitutions of Masonry, and by an Endorsement appears to have been in Pontefract Castle at the demolition, and given to the Grand Lodge by Bro. Drake.

* No. 2. Another like Roll in three slips, Endorsed "Constitutions for Masonry."

† Gould, vol. iv., pp. 408, 409.

No. 3. A parchment Roll of Charges on Masonry, 1630.

* No. 4. A paper Roll of Charges on Masonry, 1693. Given to the Grand Lodge by Bro. Walker, 1777.

* No. 5. Part of another paper Roll of Charges on Masonry.

No. 6. A parchment Roll of Charges, whereof the bottom part is wanting.

Holy Bible bound in crimson velvet, gilt.

* A large Painting of the Ancient Grand Lodge with Masonic Emblems.

Two brass Branches. A large mahogany Pedestal upon Castors.

* A Cushion with a crimson Velvet Cover, gold Fringe round the edge, the gift of Bro. Sir Thos. Gascoigne, Baronet.

* Three Candlesticks of the Doric, Ionic, and Corinthian Orders, with silver Sockets;

Two painted Floor Cloths; A broad basket-hilted Sword;

A Hanger, green Handle, Silver-mounted; One ditto, ditto;

* A pair of gold Compasses, enriched with a Ruby and steel points;

* A silver Square; * Level; * Plumb;

* Cross Keys;

* A Bible and Jewel for the Grand Chaplain, the gift of Bro. Kitson;

* A large Square; * A small square; A pair of brass Compasses; Two small Pedestals;

* A Lewis let into Masonry; * A silver Extinguisher; * A wood Box lined with green baize;

* A mahogany Balloting Box with two Drawers in; An Apron for the G. M.;

* Four Aprons lined with pink silk;

* Three Ebony Mallets; Three brass letters, J. B. C., and small green Bags;

* A large silk Banner with the Society's Arms painted on each side, silk Fringed;

* Two lesser Banners; Five Aprons; A still earlier mahogany flat rule or gauge, with the following names and year incised:

William ✠ Baron, of Yorke, 1663, John Drake, John ✠ Baron.†

† Hughan, p. 33; Gould, vol. iv., p. 401.

The * denotes that the article or articles are still preserved at York, and were, in August, 1870, in the Archives of York Lodge, No. 236, in that city, as certified by Bro. William Cowling, P. M. and Treasurer P. Prov. S. G. W., N. and E. Yorkshire.

The Ecclesiastics of York Minster have long held that the Free Masons of the Middle Ages were convened for secret meetings in the crypt of that historic old edifice; and recent research has brought to light an ancient Lodge Minute Book, in which is noted a meeting of a Lodge there. This Lodge is described as being a secret recess in the Cathedral crypt. The present York Lodge preserves with zealous care an old painting of this subterranean hall, showing that the walls were beautifully decorated and made instructive by Masonic symbols.*

We also know from other sources, that during the last of the period that the Masonic Fraternities operated under and with the ecclesiastics, they met in church crypts and in other secure apartments of church establishments.

EXTRACTS FROM A SPEECH MADE BEFORE THE GRAND LODGE IN THE CITY OF YORK ON ST. JOHN'S DAY, DECEMBER 27, 1726, IN WHICH SOME IMPORTANT POINTS IN MASONIC HISTORY APPEAR.†

"In Egypt we still see their Pyramids, which answer to the description that have been made of them; and I question not, but a stranger might find out some Remains of the labyrinth that covered a whole province, and had a hundred temples disposed among its several quarters and divisions.

"The Wall of China is one of these Eastern pieces of magnificence, which makes a figure even in the map of the world, although an account of it would have been thought fabulous, were not the wall itself extant.

"We are obliged to Devotion for the noblest buildings that have adorned the several countries of the World. It is this which has set Men at Work on Temples, and Public Places of Worship; not only that they might by the Magnificence of the Building invite the Deity to reside there, but that such

* See Fort, pp. 197, 198. † Hughan, p. 111.

stupendous Works might at the same Time open the Mind to vast Conceptions, and fit it to converse with the Divinity of the Place.

"To the Romans, indeed, our Ancestors owe the Origin of useful Learning amongst them, which made a very good exchange for the Loss of their Freedom; for Cæsar in his Commentary tells us, that the Britons had no walled Towns nor Houses, but only fortified their Dwellings with Woods and Marshes: But when after that, our first Saxon Kings, having thrown off the barbarous Ignorance of the Usefulness of Arts and Sciences, this of course answering the necessary End of Self-Preservation, as well as Grandeur and Devotion, must be allowed to be first sought after; and tho' 'Old Verulam,' since call'd St. Albans, may justly claim Precedency as the first built Town in Britain, yet you know we can boast that the first Grand Lodge ever held in England was held in this City (York) where Edwin the first Christian King of the Northumbers, about the Six Hundredth Year after Christ, and who laid the Foundation of our Cathedral, sat as Grand Master. This is sufficient to make us dispute the Superiority with the Lodges at London: But as nought of that Kind ought to be amongst so amicable a Fraternity, we are content that they enjoy the Title of Grand Master of England; but the Totius Angliæ we claim as our undoubted Right.

"A Word of Advice, or two, and I have done. To you, my Brethren, the Working Masons, I recommend carefully to peruse our Constitutions: There are in them excellent Rules laid down for your Conduct, and I need not insist upon them here.

"To you, that are of other trades and occupations, and have the honor to be admitted into this Society, I speak thus: First mind the business of your calling. Let not Masonry so far get the ascendant, as to make you neglect the Support of yourselves and families. You cannot be so absurd as to think that a taylor, when admitted a Free Mason, is able to build a church; and for that reason your own vocation ought to be your most important study. False Brethren, 'tis true, may build castles in the air; but a good Mason works upon no such fickle foundation. So square your actions as to live within compass. Be obedient to the officers chosen to govern the Lodge; consider they are of your own appointing and are trusted with an unlimited power by you. As well henceforwards, as on this solemn day, let each salute his

Brethren with a cheerful countenance; that as long as our feet shall stand upon this earthly foundation, we may join heart and hand, and, as it were, with one voice issuing from the same throat, declare our principles of Brotherly Love, Relief and Truth, to one another."*

MS. Constitutions, No. 4, York, 1693.

This is written on a large roll of paper, slightly mutilated, and endorsed, "Brother Geo. Walker of Wetherby, to the Grand Lodge of York, 1777, No. 4, 1693," and the date is further certified by "These be the Constitucions of the noble and famous history called Masonry, made and now in practice by the best Masters and Fellows for directing and guideing all that use the said craft, scripted "p. me vicesimo tertio die Octobris, anno Regni regis et Regina Gulielmy et Marie quinto anno que Domini 1693 Mark Kypling.†

. . . Jht of the Father of Heaven, ye wisdom. . . sed Son through the goodness of the. . . Ghost be with us at our begining & give us grace soe to governe our lives that we may come to Eternal Joyes. Good Brethren & Fellowes oure purpose is to tell you how and in what manner the Craft of Masonry was first begun, and afterwards how it was knowne by Mighty Kings and worthy princes & many other worshipfull men, and to them that be here, we declare the charge that belongs to every true Mason to Keepe for in good faith, if you take heed thereto, it is well worthy to be Kept for a worshipful Craft and for a Curious Science, for there be several & seaven liberall sciences of the which it be one, as follows. The first is grammar that teacheth to pronounce and speak truly, the second Lodieck that teacheth to deserne the truth from fallsehood; the third Rhetorick that learns to speak in substill tearmes; the fourth is Musick, that teacheth the art of Song and Voice of Harp and Organ; the fifth is Arithmetick, yt teacheth to number; the sixth is Geometry, that teacheth to measure the Earth and other things of which is Masonry; the seaventh is Astronomy, that teacheth the course of Sun, and moone & other ornaments of the Heavens. The seaven liberall sciences which all one science, viz.:—Geometry it teacheth mett and Measure ponderation and weights of all manner of things in the world, and there is noe man that worketh by any Craft but he worketh by some measure, & all this

* Hughan, p. 106.   † Gould, vol. i., p. 68; Hughan, p. 91.

is Geometry.* . . . And it befell in dayes the Lords and States of ye Land (Egypt) had so many sons that they had gotten some by their wives and some by other Ladies of the Realme, for the land was holden and Replenished by generation, wherefore they were sore trobled in mind in what sort to provide for them, and the King maid proclamation through the Realme if there were any man that could inform them, that he should come unto him, and that he should be well rewarded for his travell, and that him selfe should be well pleased. After this crye and proclamation was made came the worthy Clark, Euclid, and said to the King and his Lords, if you will give me your Children to govern and teach as gentlemen should, under condition that you will grant me and them a commission that I have to Rule honestly as that science ought to be used and Ruled. And the King granted anon, and sealled their commission, & then the worthy doctor tooke the Lord's sons, and taught the science of Geometry in practise to work in stone all manner of worthy worke that belonged to Castels, Courts, Tempels, and Churches and other buildings, and he gave them a charge in manner following, viz., first that they should be true to the King, and to the Lords whome they served, & that they should love well together, and be true one to another, and that they should call each other fellow, and not servant, nor his Knave, nor any foull name, & that they should ordain the wisest among them to master of the Lord's worke, and neither for love of great Riches nor hirrings to let any that had little understanding to be master of the Lord's worke, whereby the Lord should be evill served and they disgraced, and that they should call the governor of the work Mr whilst they wrought with him, and many other charges which were tedious to Relate; and to all other charges he made them sweare a great oath used at that time, and ordained for them Reasonable pay that they might live honestly by it. And that they should come and assemble themselves, and have counsell in the Art of Geometry governed there, and that worthy Mr gave it the name and it was called Masonry in this land, since long after the children of Issrael were come into the Land of Behest, it is now called amongst us the Land of Jerusalem. King David began the Temple of Jerusalem which is called with them devine templu, and the same King

---

* Where this MS. is nearly identical with the Lansdowne, it is omitted here. See Lansdowne MS., p. 325.

David loved Masons well and Cherished them, and gave them good pay, and he gave them the Charges and manners as he had it out of *Egypt* . . . and the same Sollamon Conformed the Charges and manners his father had given Masons. And this was the worthy Craft of Masonry in the land of Israell and Citty of Jerusalem, and in many other Kingdoms, glorious workmen walked abroad, some because learning more Craft, & others to teach theire Craft.

. . . .

England was now all this while void of Masons until the time of St. Albons. In his time the King of England was a Pagan and builded the town called Albons. After that in Albons tome, was a worthy Knt. Chief-Steward to the King & had governmt of the Realme and the Erecting of the towne walles, & he loved Masons well and Cherrished them, and their wages was Right standing as the Realme did require, for he gave them every weeke 3s. 6d. to their double patment or wages; before that time through all the land a Mason took but a penny a day, and afterwards St. Albons amended it much, and gott them a Charter from the King and his Counsell, and gave it the name of assembly, and there at himselfe was made Mason and gave them Charges as you shall hear afterwards. Right soon after the death of St. Albons came great warrs into England by divers nations, soe that the good Rule of Masonry was destroyed untill the time of Athelstone who was a worthy King of England, brought the land into great peace and builded many famoss buildings as Abbeys & Castles, etc., and he loved Masons well, and he had a son whose name was Hedwin, and he loved Masons much more than his father, for he was full of practise in Geometry wherefore he drew himselfe much to commune with Masons to learn their Craft, and after for the love he had to Masons, and the Craft he was made a Mason himselfe & gott of the King, his father, a Charter and a commission hold every year an assembly, where he would. within the Realme & to correct within themselves Enormities and tresspasses that was done within the Craft. And he made himselfe an assembly at Yorke, and there he made Masons, and gave them Charges and taught them the manners of Masons, and did command that Rule to be kept ever after; and to them he gave a Charter and Commission to keep and make ordinances that it should be Ruled from King to King. When this assembly was gathered, he made a Cry that all Masons that had aney writeings, or understanding the Craft that was made in this land, or in aney other Land, that they should shew them forth, and there was some in French, some in Greeke, and Lattine, & some in English and other Languages, and the Intent thereof was found, and he commanded a booke thereof to bee made how the Craft was first found, and commanded that it should be Read and tould where aney Masons was to be made, and to give them their Charges, and from that time Masons had kept in this form and order as well as men might govern it. Furthermore, at divers assemblyes there have bene added to it divers charges more and more by the best Maisters, and follows advices. Now you have heard in pticular how this nouble and famous Craft of Masonry was first Invented and how Maraculusly it was preserved, And since how it hath beene Loved and Cherrished both by Kings and potentates from the first beginning to this very day and how it should & ought still to be loved and kept in high repute and Estimation by all manner of persons whatsoever.

The one of the Elders taking the Booke and that he . . . that is to be made a Mason, shall lay their hands thereon and the charge shall be given.

CHARGES.

Every man that is a Mason take heed to his Charge, if you find yourselves gilty in anye of these crimes, strive to amend & especially you that is to be Charged, take heed that you keepe the Charge for it is a great perill and danger to the soulle for a man to forsweare himselfe on a booke. The first articelle of your Charge is that you shall be true to God and the holy Church, And you see noe hersie no error to youer understanding, alsoe you shall be true Liege Men to the King without Treason, but you shall mend it if you may, also warne the King or his counsell thereof. Thirdly you shall be true one to another, viz. To every Mr and fellow of the Craft of Masonry that be masons allowed, that you doe to them as you would they should to you.

And also that every Mason shall keep true Chamber and Lodg & all other counsell that ought to be kept by way of Masonry. Fourthly that you shall be true to, the Mr and the lord you serve, and truly seek his profitt and advantage. Fifthly that you shall call all Masons fellowes or else Brethern, and noe other foull name, neither shall you take your fellowes wife in villany, nor desire his daughter unlawfully nor his servant. Sixthly you shall pay truly for table & for meate and drinke where you goe to board. These be the Charges in generall that every Mason should hold, both Masters and Fellowes. Now will I Rehears the Charges in Generall that belong to every true Mr and fellow.

That no Mr or fellowe shall take aney allowance to be made Mason without the consent of his fellow at least in number 5 or 6 & if he that is to be made shall be free borne, and of a good kindred and noe bondman, and that he has his Right Limbs as a man ought to have.

Alsoe that noe fellowe shall slander another behind his backe to make him loose his good name or his worldly goods alsoe that noe fellow within the Lodg or without, may answer his fellow unrespectively without a Reasonable cause, & every Mason shall prefer his Elder and put him to worshipe, alsoe that noe fellowe go into the towne in the night time without some fellow with him to beare testamony he was in honest place.

. . . .

The Apprentice Charge.

That he shall be true to God and the holy Church, the prince, his Mr and dame who he shall serve, And that he shall not steal nor pike away his Mr or dames goods or absent himself from their service, nor go from them about his own pleasure by day or by night without their Licence, And that he do not commit adultry or fornication in his Masters house with his wife, daughter or servant or any other, and that he shall keepe councell in all things spoken in Lodg or Chamber by any Masons, fellowes or freemasons. And that he shall not hold any disbedient argument against any freemason nor disclose any secret whereby any difference may arise amongst any Masons or fellowes or apprentises, but Reverently to behave himself to all freemasons being sworne brethern, to his Mr and not to use any carding, diceing or any other unlawfull games, nor haunt Tavernes or alehouses there to waste any mans goods without Licence of his said Mr or, some other freemason, and that he shall not commit adultry in any mans house where he shall work or be tabled. And that he shall not purloyn nor steale the goods of any pson nor willing suffer harme or shame or consent thereto during his said apprentisshyp either to his Mr or dame, or any other freemason. But to withstand the same to the utmost of his power, And thereof to informe his said Mr or some other freemason, with all convenient speed that may bee.

These be the Constitutions of the noble and famous history called Masonry, made and now in practice by the best masters and fellowes for directing and guideing all that use the said craft, scripted p me nicesimo terito die octobris, Anno Regni Regis et Regina Gulielmg et Marie Quinto Annoque Domini 1693.

MARK KYPLING,
WILLIAM SIMPSON,   CHRISTOPHER THOMPSON,
ANTHONY HORSMAN,   CHRISTOPHER GILL,
Mr ISAAC BRENT, Lodg Ward.

We, the undersigned, have compared this with the original Document in the possession of the "York Lodge" No. 236 and formerly belonging to "The Antient Grand Lodge of all England," held in the City of York, and thereby certify that it is a true and correct copy.

WILLIAM COWLING, P. M. and Treasurer, 236.
RALPH L. DAVISON, P. M.. 236.

York, May 13, 1870.

The original document is a roll of paper slightly mutilated, endorsed:

No. 4.
1693.

BROTHER GEO. WALKER, of Wetherby,
To
the Grand Lodge of 177..

There are altogether six of the Old York MSS., but this being one of the best, comprising the important points of the others, it was selected for use here.

Concerning the *antiquity* of York Masonry, Hughan in his Reprints, p. 169, says:

"WILLIAM PRESTON saw this so clearly that his history on early Free Masonry in England is but the history of operative companies brought from Rome, first by Abanus, then Augustine, then by the famous builders, Benedict Biscop, St. Swithin, Paulinus, who baptized Edwin at York and built the Yorkshire Minsters with Roman Masons, then Archbishop Wilfred, and others, especially Dunstan, and latterly Gundolph, Bishop of Rochester, after the Norman Conquest.

"All these men were the great builders of those times; and in the early chronicles we read how in almost every case they brought artificers, or masons, "cementarii," from Rome, who would thus perpetuate the old Roman sodality under Christian auspices and control.

"This is the theory of Mr. Hope in his well-known essay on architecture, and I confess has always seemed to me to contain the only true history of our fraternity in those early days. I am, therefore, by no means indisposed to accept the very ancient tradition that the Masons met together under Edwin (A.D. 600), and were actually incorporated under Athelstan (926), though for the proof of such statement we must probably rely on our own traditions, which so clearly connect us with York and these early patrons of Free Masonry. I am aware that in saying this I run counter to a great deal that has lately been advanced both in England and Germany on this subject, but I am writing as I really believe, and am only advancing an opinion which my own studies for many years now have tended entirely to confirm."

The same, at p. 129, quoting Godfrey Higgins:

1. "From a Masonic document now in my possession, I can prove that no very long time ago the Chaldees of York were Free Masons, that they constituted the Grand Lodge of England, and that they held their meetings in the Crypt under the Grand Cathedral of that city. Vol. i., page 718. . . . After I had been led to suspect from various causes that the Culdees noticed in the Notitia Monastica, c, in the last chapter, and there stated to have been found in the Cathedral at York, were Masons, I searched the Masonic records in London, and I found a document which upon the face of it seemed to show that the Lodge, which was the Grand Lodge of all England, had been held under the Cathedral in the Crypt at York. In consequence of this I went to York and applied to the only survivor of the Lodge, who showed me from the documents which he possessed, that the Druidical Lodge, or Chapter of Royal Arch Masons, or Templar Encampment, all of which it calls itself, was held for the last time in the Crypt, on Sunday, May 27th, 1778." . . . . . .

Again, from Hughan, at p. 133:

"In page 41, 'History of Free Masonry in York,' we alluded to the doubtful connection of Craft Masonry with the Royal Arch degree under the York Rite. The Minute Book of the Grand Lodge, however, which we shall now refer to, is more confirmatory of Bro. John Yarker's opinion, then of our own, as to recognition. According to all the known records when we wrote that work, none exhibited any authorization by the Grand Lodge of all England, of Royal Arch and Knight Templar Masonry, *but we find now* that some of the then missing documents *decidedly support* the statement made by Bro. John Yarker in 'Notes on the Orders of the Temple and St. John,' *respecting* the *opening* of a *Grand Chapter* and *Encampment* under the authority of the Grand Lodge."

In conclusion, notwithstanding that much of what has been published concerning early York Masonry, including the charter of 926, is traditional and apocryphal, yet, from the foregoing, it will be seen that there is abundance of well-attested history and other evidence to establish the fact, that the first important step from Guild Masonry toward the free Masonry of 1717 was taken here by an assembly of the craft in the early part of the tenth century, probably about 926; and that the result of their deliberations was a Code of Regulation which was preserved by tradition or otherwise, and subsequently served as the basis of the Constitutions of 1717.

NOTES FROM AUTHORITIES.

1. Edwin, the Northumbrian king, who reigned from A.D. 620 to 634, resided at Audley, near York, and built the first Metropolitan Church ever built in England. A church of wood was hastily run up at York for the new Converts, which were numerous. Shortly after Edwin laid the foundation of a Church of Free Stone, but it was finished by Oswald, his successor. Rapin, p. 246; Bede, L. 2, C. 13.

2. In the famous speech delivered by Drake, the antiquary and historian before the Grand Lodge at York December 27, 1726, he said, " Yet you know we can boast that the first Grand Lodge ever held in England was held in that City, where Edwin the first Christian King, of Northumbers, about the six hundredth year after Christ, and who laid the foundation of our Cathedral, sat as Grand Master." Gould, vol. iii., p. 247; Hughan, p. 168; Mackey, p. 905.

3. According to Drake, the Edwin mentioned in the legend was *not* the brother of Athelstan, but Edwin, King of Northumbria (born 587, ascended the throne 617, and died 633), who laid the foundation-stone of York Cathedral about 626. Royal Masonic Cyclopedia, p. 774.

4. The Rev. Mr. Woodford, in an essay on the connection of York with the history of Free Masonry in England, critically discussed this subject, and thus endorses the Antiquary Drake: "I see no reason, therefore, to reject so old a tradition, that under Athelstan the Operative Masons obtained his patronage and met in General Assembly." To that verdict I subscribe. Woodford, Old Charges of the British Freemasons, p. xiv; Hughan, p. 168; Mackey, p. 905.

5. In England, we have already seen that the stonemasons, under the distinctive appellation of Free Masons, held a general assembly at the city of York, in the year 926, and there adopted those constitutions which have always been looked upon as the fundamental law of English Masonry. Of course, the very calling of this assembly proves that the Free Masons were previously in activity in the kingdom, which is in fact otherwise proved by the records

of the building at an earlier date by them of cathedrals, abbeys, and castles. But we date the York assembly as the first known and acknowledged organization of the Craft in England into a national body, or Grand Lodge. Their history differs but little from that which has already been detailed. Stonemasons, in fact, but in the possession of many professional secrets originally derived from their monkish teachers, as well as from the Roman Colleges, with which, like the Masons of France, they had an intimate communication through the legions which had been encamped for so many years in England. Mackey, pp. 749, 750.

6. Hargrave states that "In searching the Archives of Masonry, we find that the first lodge was instituted in this city (York) at a very early period; indeed, even prior to any other recorded in England."

7. "That it was an honorable, as well as an ancient Society, is abundantly proved by reference to those of its valuable records which are happily still preserved and zealously guarded by their careful custodians, the members of the York Lodge." Gould, vol. iv., p. 114.

8. "We have, indeed, in the fabric rolls of York Minster, published by the Surtees Society, the fact established beyond all doubt of the existence of the Free Masons as working under the chapter in 1370.

"We have rules laid down for their government; we obtain glimpses, though only few and far between, of their habits and customs, and we are told of 'Le Loge,' of the 'Magister,' of the 'Guardiani' (Wardens), of the 'Marjores,' of the 'Felowes,' and of the apprentices." Hughan's Reprints, p. 169.

9. "There is the strongest internal evidence that all the manuscripts, from the Halliwell to the Papworth, had a common *original*, from which they were copied with more or less accuracy, or on which they were framed with more or less modification. And this *original* I suppose to be the Constitution which must have been adopted at the General Assembly at York." Mackey, p. 905.

CHAPTER X.

SCOTLAND.—ITS EARLY FREE MASONRY.

Free Masonry makes its Appearance in this Country in the Fourteenth Century.—Quaint and Highly Interesting Records of the Old Lodges at Perth, Scone, and Aberdeen.—Old Documents, in which the Novel Ideas of the Ancient Scotch Craftsmen are Expressed in the Rich Dialect of that Period.—A Singular Ancient Masonic Seal.—Robert Burns Master of a Lodge.—A Masonic Relic left by Him.

Soon after the Roman occupation of Britain they were harassed by a people from north of the Frith of Forth, whom they called Picts, and later Caledonians. Subsequently, this people were joined by the Scoti or Scots, from whom Scotland derived its name.

The Scoti were from Ireland, and their first settlement in North Britain was in Argyle, from whence they spread along the west coast from the Frith of Clyde to the modern Ross. The first king of the British Scots was Fergus, who crossed over to Britain in 503.*

Passing from this to A.D. 787, we find that a treaty was entered into between the King of France and the King of the Scots, which was observed down to the union of the crowns of England and Scotland.

Next in this connection we come to Macbeth, King of Scotland, and patron of the Culdees. From his father Finlegh, the son of Ruadhri, he inherited the rule of the province of Moray; and became allied with the royal line, by his marriage with Gruoch MacBoedhe, the grand-daughter of King Kenneth Macduff. He made grants to the *Culdees* † of Loch Leven, and in the year 1050 he went on a pilgrimage to Rome.

---

* See Chambers, vol. x., p. 787
† Ibid., vol. vii., p. 726, and vol. iv., p. 83.

THE CULDEES.

The Culdees (Colidie) were first heard of on the Continent in the sixth century, and next in Scotland in the ninth century. A leaf of the Register of St. Andrew's relates that Brude, the last King of the Picts (who ceased to reign in 843), gave an island in Loch Leven to *God*, St. Servan, and the Culdee hermits serving God there. They were governed by an Abbot, and about the year 1093 gave up their island to the Bishop of St. Andrew's.

In 926 they were the officiating clergy in the Cathedral Church of St. Peter's at *York*, the duties of their office being both *religious* and *charitable*.

During the march of King Athelstan against the Scotch in 926, he halted at York, and besought the clergy of St. Peter's (the Culdees) to invoke the aid of God in his behalf, promising them if he was victorious he would confer certain favors upon them. Being successful in his campaign, he returned to the church and publicly returned thanks to God for his success; and then granted to the Culdees and their successors, for the promotion of their charitable purposes, a thrave of corn from every plough-land in the diocese of York.

Subsequently, the Culdees founded a hospital in the same city for their poor. In his inquiry into the origin of all languages, nations, and religions, the author of "Anacalypsis" states as his belief, that the Essenes and Culdees were Free Masons, in progressive stages of development. Another writer of note (Higgins) says: "I request my reader to think upon the Culidei or Culdies in the crypt of the Cathedral of York, and at Ripon, and in Scotland and Ireland—that these Culdies or *Chaldeans* were Masons and Mathematici —builders of the Temple of Solomon."*

According to Lenning and Gadicke, the Culdees comprised in their system both *religion* and *architecture*—that in fact, they were similar to the Roman Colleges of Builders, differing only in the matter of religion. They are credited with having built many sacred edifices in Scotland.

Gadicke also claims that the York Constitutions were derived from the Culdees.

* See Chambers, vol. iv., p. 82; and Gould, vol. i., pp. 50–55.

KILWINNING LODGE—ITS ORIGIN.

The Abbey of Kilwinning was founded in the year 1140 by Hugh Morville, and dedicated to St. Winning. It was situated in the Bailwick of Cunningham, about three miles north of the burg of Irving, near the Irish Sea. This large and beautiful edifice was built by the " Travelling Free Masons."* And although the earlier records of Kilwinning Lodge are not now in existence, yet, as some of the fraternity usually remained and settled at or near the scene of their labors, they would continue their social and business relations —their Lodges, and receive into their brotherhood men of the locality who had assisted in the work, and by them be succeeded in their Lodge. In no other way can the great antiquity assigned by tradition to Kilwinning Lodge be accounted for.†

In the reign of James II., 1437–1460, the Barons of Roslin, patrons of Scotch Masonry, held their annual meetings at Kilwinning.

MELROSE ABBEY.

This Abbey was founded by David I. in 1136. It was destroyed during the wars of the Succession, but was rebuilt in 1326. It was in the Second Pointed Style, and was the most beautiful edifice that Scotland possessed in the Middle Ages.‡

One of the first reliable accounts of Masons in Scotland is found engraved, in nearly obliterated character, on the walls of this Abbey.

The earliest minutes of Melrose Lodge is to the effect that " be the voyce of the ludge," no master shall take an apprentice under seven years, the latter to pay eight pounds (Scotts) for " meit and drink," and 40s. (Scotts) for the " use

---

* See Mackey, p. 395.

† From the Edinburgh Encyclopædia : "The earliest appearance of Free Masonry in modern times was under the form of a travelling association of Italian, Greek, German, and French artists, who were denominated Free Masons, and went about erecting churches and cathedrals. The members lived in a camp of huts. They were under a surveyor, who directed the establishment, and every tenth man was called a warden, and overlooked those under his charge. By means of this 'travelling association' the mysteries of Masonry seem to have been introduced into Kilwinning, and York, in England, at a very early day."

‡ Chambers, vol. vii., p. 986.

of the box, by and allow y^m sufficient gloves." It was also " condescendet on y^t w^never a prentice is mad frier mason, he must pay four pund Scotts."

An agreement made January 29, 1675, " betwixt the Maisones of the Lodge of Melrose," is signed by no less than eighty of its members; several of whom append their designations, as "maltman," weaver, vinter and hostler, thereby proving that at the period mentioned (1675) many of the brethren were not operative Masons, though connected with the Lodge as Free Masons.

"27. Dec. 1690 f is votted that a verie meason that takes the place in the kirk befor his elder broy^rs is a great ase." *

In December, 1835, the Lodge at Melrose renewed its ancient custom of forming a torchlight procession and marching round the ruins of "St. David's holy pile,"

AISLE, MELROSE ABBEY.

preceded by solemn music. Dr. Oliver gives the following description of one of these processions:

" Nothing could be more singular or impressive than the spectacle which presented itself. The red glaring light of the flambeaux, as it flashed upon the pillars and projections of the ancient abbey, discovering the grotesque faces and figures of grinning monks sculptured on the corbels and capitals of many a moldering arch, contrasted slightingly with the deep, mysterious gloom of the

* Gould, vol. ii., pp. 448–452; Fort, pp. 75–113.

retiring aisles and cloisters, whose darkness, indeed, was ever and anon partially illuminated as the singular procession passed along. Every step which the brethren trod, as they slowly advanced up the interior of the edifice, was upon hallowed dust. In the language of him whose name is linked with that of the place,

> 'Beneath the lettered stone were laid
> The ashes of their fathers dead;
> From many a garnished niche around
> Stern saints and tortured martyrs frowned.'" *

Extracts from the Records of the Lodge of Aberdeen.

The records of this ancient Lodge commence in 1319, and with the exception of a hiatus between 1414 and 1433, they are complete.

The first volume contains an account of an early contract between the " Comownys of Abden " on the one part, and two " Masonys " on the other part, which was agreed to on the feast of St. Michael the Archangel. The work contracted for was to hew xii dures, and xii wyndowys, in fre tailly," and the work was to be delivered in good order at any quay in Aberdeen.†

It was recorded that on June 27, 1483, the "master of the kirkwark," appointed, decreed, and ordained that the " Masownys of the luge," consisting of six members, whose names are duly recorded, were to pay 20s. and 40s. to the Parish Church (Saint Nicholace Wark) for the first and second offences respectively, in the event of either of them raising any debate or controversy, for it appears that previously there had been disputes in consequence of their so doing. It was also provided that "gif thai fautit the thrid (third) tym," they were " to be excludit out of the luge as a common forfactour."

Two of the members were particularly specified as offenders, and were cautioned that, should either of them break the rule they had agreed to, " he beis fundyn in the faute thai of salbe expellit the luge fra that tyme furtht."

A " statute annent the government of the maister mason of the college kirk of St. Giles, 1491," as extracted from the burgh records of Aberdeen:

The master and his servants were to begin work in the summer at 5 A.M., and continue until 8, then to be allowed half an hour, resuming labor from

---

* Mitchell, pp. 351, 352. † Gould, vol. i. p. 422.

8.30 A.M. to 11, when two hours were given, one o'clock witnessing the resumption of work, until 4 P.M.; and then "to gett a recreation in the *commoun luge* be the space of half an hour," the remainder of the time from 4.30 P.M. to 7 being devoted to labor continually. In winter the work was to commence with the welcome appearance of daylight, the hours else to be kept as before, provided the men having "bot thair none shanks allanerly afternone, and labour until *daylicht begane*."*

The master mason who was employed on church work by the Town Council of Aberdeen received £24 16s. 8d. Scots quarterly (*i.e.*, a little over £2 sterling), and his journeymen 20 marks per annum (£1 6s. 8d.). In 1500, the masons engaged on the steeple of the "old Tolbooth" were paid weekly, each journeyman 9s. Scots and £10 Scots for his apprentice, per annum; and at Lundie, Fife, in 1661, the master had per day 10d., and his journeymen 9d., "*and all the diet in the house*."

The tradition concerning the first Cathedral Church of Aberdeen is, that a mason named Scott, with several assistants from Kelso, was employed by Matthew Kininmonth, Bishop of Aberdeen, in building St. Machar's Cathedral, about 1165, and that by Scott and his associates the Aberdeen Lodge was founded. That the Lodge of Aberdeen existed at a very early date, can be verified without recourse to the traditions of the craft.†

On May 6, 1541, the Seal of Cause of the masons and wrights was confirmed under the common seal of the burgh, and then included coopers, carvers, and painters. From this confirmation the Fraternity in Aberdeen date the institution of the Lodge.

Among the laws and statutes of the Lodge of Aberdeen, A.D. 1670, are:

"FIRST STATUTE—FOR THE MAISTER.—The Master Masons and 'Entered Apprentices' who are subscribers to the book, vow and agrees to own the Lodge on all occasions, unless prevented by sickness or absence, as they did at their entry, and on receiving the 'Mason Word.'

"SECOND STATUTE—MAISTER CONTINUED.—The Master to act as judge in all disputes, to inflict fines, pardon faults, 'always taking the voice of the honorable company;' and he may instruct his officer to impound the working

---

* Gould, voi. ii., p. 403.   † Ibid., vol. ii., pp. 424, 425.

SCOTLAND.—ITS EARLY FREE MASONRY.

tools of malcontents, who, if they are further rebellious, shall be expelled from the Lodge.

"THIRD STATUTE—WARDENS.—By the oath at entry, the warden is acknowledged as the next in power to the Maister, and in the absence of the latter he is to possess similar authority and to continue in office according to the will of the company. The Master is to be annually elected on St. John's Day, also the box master and clerk, no salary being allowed the latter, it being only a piece of preferment. The officer to be continued till another be entered in the Lodge. No Lodge was to be held within an *inhabited dwelling-house*, save in '*ill weather*,' then only in such a building where '*no person shall heir or see us.*' Otherwise the meetings were to take place in the *open fields*." *

NAMES OF THE MEMBERS OF ABERDEEN LODGE IN 1670.

THE: NAMES OF: US: ALL: WHO: ARE: THE: AUTHOIRES: OF: AND: SUBSCRYUERS: OF: THIS: BOOK: IN: ORDER: AS: FOLLOWETH.

1. Harrie Elphinston: *Tutor* of Airth: *Collector of the Kinges Customes* of Aberdein: Measson: and: *Master* of our Honorable: Lodge of Aberdein.
2. Alexander: Charles: *Wrighte* and: Measson: and Master of our Lodge.
3. William: Kempte: Measson.
4. James: Crombie: Measson.
5. William Mackleud: Measson and Warden: of: our Lodge.
6. Patrick: Steuison: Measson.
7. John Roland: Measson: and Warden: of: our: Lodge. And ye first Warden of our Lodge.
8. Dauid Murray: Measson. *Key Master*, 1686–1687.
9. John Caddell: Measson.
10. William: George: *Smith:* and Measson: and Maister: of: our: Lodge.
11. James: Anderson: *Glassier* and Measson: and *Wreatter* of this Book, 1670. (And Master of our Lodge in y year of God 1688 and 1694.)

* Gould, vol. ii., p. 428.

12. John : Montgomrie : Measson : and Warden : of : our : Lodge.
13. The : Earle : of : Findlator : Measson.
14. The : Lord : Pitsligo : Measson.
15. George : Cattaneuch : *Piriuige : Macker :* and : Measson.
16. John : Barnett : Measson.
17. Mr. William : Frasser : *Minister : of : Slaines :* and Measson.
18. Mr. Georg : Alexander : *Aduocat :* in : Edinburgh : and : Measson.
19. Alexander : Patterson : *Armourer :* and : Measson. (And m of our Lodge in the year of God 1690–1692–1698.)
20. Alexander : Charles. Yonger, *Glassier :* and : Measson.
21. James : King : *Wrighte :* and : Measson : and : Theassurer of our Lodge.
22. Maister : George : Liddell, Professor of *Mathematickes.*
23. Mr Alex Iruing : Measson.
24. Walter : Simpson : *Piriuige : Macker :* and : Measson.
25. William : Rickard : *Merchand* & Measson : and Treasurer : of : our : Lodge.
26. Thomas : Walker : *Wright* and : Measson.
27. John : Skeen : *Merchand :* and : Measson.
28. John : Craurie : *Merchand :* and : Measson.
29. William : Youngson : *Chyrurgeon* and : Measson.
30. John : Thompson : *Chryrurgeon :* and Measson.
31. Earle : of : Dunfermline, Measson. (1679.)
32. Earle : of : Errolle : Measson.
33. John : Gray : Younger : of Chrichi : and Measson.
34. Mr George : Seatton : *Minister of Fyvie :* and Measson.
35. George : Rait : of : Midepla ; Measson. (1679.)
36. John Forbes : *Merchand :* and : Measson.
37. George Gray. *Wright,* and Measson.
38. John Duggade : *Sklaiter :* and Measson. (1677.)
39. Robert : Gordon : *Carde : Macker :* and Measson.
40. Patrick : Norrie : *Merchand :* and Measson.
41. James : Lumesden : *Merchand :* and : Measson.
42. John : Cowie : *Merchand* and Theassurer of our Lodge.

43. Allexander : Moore : *Hook : Macker :* and : Measson.
44. David : Achterlounie : *Merchand :* and : Measson.
45. Mr. George : Iruing : Measson : and : *Preacher.*
46. Patrick : Matthewson : *Sklaiter :* and Measson. [Patrick Mathewson.]
47. John : Burnet : Meason. [John Burnet.]
48. William : Donaldson : *Merchand :* and Meason.
49. Alexander : Forbes, *Sklaiter :* and Meason.

"In the opinion of Mr. Jamieson, eight only of the forty-nine members described as "authors" and "subscribers" were *operative* Masons. . . . . . The Master for the year 1670, was a tutor and Collector of the Customs, and enjoyed the distinction of presiding (in the Lodge) over four noblemen, three ministers, an advocate, a professor of mathematics, nine merchants, two surgeons, two glaziers, a smith, three slaters, two peruke-makers, an armorer, four carpenters, and several gentlemen, besides eight or more masons, and a few other tradesmen."

"If what we have been considering does not amount to 'speculative' Free Masonry, I, for one, should despair of ever satisfying those by whom the proofs I have adduced are deemed insufficient to sustain my contention." . . . .

"It may be safely assumed that, as the Lodge of Aberdeen was doubtless in its inception a purely operative body, many years must have elapsed prior to 1670 before such a predominance of the speculative element would have been possible."

"The existing records of the Lodge of Aberdeen afford conclusive evidence, not only of 'speculative' customs, but actually of speculative ascendency, in the year 1670. The power of the Master was then even more absolute than it is now, and the duties of the warden correspond very closely with those peculiar to that position in modern times. The 'officers' received a gratuity in those days from initiates, such as many Tylers do now, and no more precautions are taken under the modern system to secure privacy than in the days of yore. The charitable nature of the Fraternity is embodied in the rules for the 'Poor-box.'" . . . . *

* Gould, vol. ii., pp. 430, 436, 437.

Scoon and Perth Lodge.

This is one of the oldest Lodges in Scotland, having a well-kept record extending back over two hundred years.

The following extracts are from its unique documents—conclusion of its old Charter: "And Lastlie, wee, and all of ws off ane mynd, consent, and assent, doe bind and obleidge ws, and our successoris, to mantayne and yphold the haill liberties and previledges of the said Lodge of Scoon, as ane frie Lodge, for entering and passing within ourselves, as the bodie thereof, residing within the burgh of Perth as sd is; And that soe long as the Sun ryseth in the East and setteth in the West, as we wold wish the blessing of God to attend ws in all our wayes and actiones.*

" 1. No frieman to contradict another unlawfully.

" 2. Nor goe to no other Lodge nor mak ane Lodge among themselves, seeing this Lodge is the prinle within the Shrye.

" 3. If any frieman leave the Lodge for another, he can only return on payment of three times the sum exigible on his joining either, *and shall 'be put cleane from the company of the Lodge he was last in.'*

" 4. The master and warden before named to see these rules carried out.

" 5. No master to take another's work unless so entitled.

" 8. All fellow-crafts passed in this Lodge shall pay £16 (Scots), besides the gloves and dues, with £3 (Scots) at their first incoming, efter they are passed.

" 9. If these sums are not paid at once, 'cautioners' must be obtained outside the Lodge."

Concerning the Milneses.

" According to the ' Knowledge of our predecessoris ther cam one from the North countrie named Johne Mylne, ane measone or man weille experted in his calling, who entered himselff both frieman and burges of this burgh.'

" His son, John Milne, succeeded him in both offices, in the reign of his Majestie King James the Sixt, of blessed memory, who, by the said seconde Johne Mylne, was (be the King's own desire) entered Freeman, measone, and

* Gould, vol. ii., p. 411.

fellow-craft." This royal initiation naturally caused special remark, hence we read. " During all his lyfetime he mantayned the same as ane member of the Lodge of Scoon, so that this Lodge is the most famous Lodge (iff weill ordered) within the kingdom."

From the Records of Lodge No. 1, Edinburgh.*

May 20, 1640, James Hamiltone being Deacon, and Johne Meyenis, Warden, " and the rest off Mrs. off meson off edenbr. conuened," was admitted the Right Hon. " Alexander Hamiltone, general of the artelerie of thes kindom, to be felow and Mr. off the forsed craft."

Other entries show the admission of William Maxwell, " doctor off Fisek," July 27, 1647; and on March 2, 1653, of James Neilson, " master skliatter to his majestie," who had been " *entered* and *past* in the Lodge of Linlithgow."

General Hamiltone was present with the Scottish army at Newcastle, May 20, 1641, on which day, together with certain masters and others of the Lodge of Edinburgh, he took part in the admission of " Mr. Robert Moray (Murray), General Quarter Mr. to the armie off Scotlan." The proceedings of this emergent meeting were duly accepted by the authorities, though taking place beyond the boundaries of the Scottish Kingdom. The Minute states that " the same being approven be the hell mester off the mesone of the Log. off Edenbroth," and the entry is ratified by the signatures and marks of four brethren, including the two Generals.

Hume of Polwarth was admitted as "fellow of craft and Master;" on June 24, 1670, the Right Hon. " Mr. William Morray, His Mai'ties Justice Depute, Mr. Walter Pringle, Advocate," and the Right Hon. Sir John Harper of Cambusnethen, as brothers, and fellow-crafts.†

Prior to October, 1736, William St. Clair, of Roslin, was said to be the hereditary,‡ and ostensible head of all the Lodges of the craft in Scotland. At that time, however, four Lodges in Edinburgh congregated for the purpose

* Gould, vol. ii., pp. 407, 411, 412.
† The terms Master Mason, Fellow Craft, Entered Apprentice, and Cowan, appear, from documentary evidence, to have been in common use in Scotland, from the year 1598 down to our own times. Gould, vol. iv., p. 319.
‡ Gould, vol. v., pp. 48–52.

of "framing proposals, to be laid before the several Lodges, in order to the choosing of a Grand Master for Scotland. These were Mary's Chapel, Canongate Kilwinning, Kilwinning Scots Arms, and Leith Kilwinning. The result of the meeting was, that on the 30th of November, of the same year, thirty-three Lodges met in Mary's Chapel, Edinburgh, and organized the Grand Lodge of Scotland. Learning of this determination of the Lodges, St. Clair decided to resign his office of Grand Master, and at the meeting of the thirty-three Lodges he presented his resignation as follows:

"I, WILLIAM ST. CLAIR OF ROSSLINE, ESQUIRE,

Taking into my consideration that the Massons in Scotland did, by several deeds, constitute and appoint William and Sir William St. Clairs of Rossline, my ancestors, and their heirs, to be their patrons, protectors, judges, or masters; and that my holding or claiming any such jurisdiction, right or privilege, might be prejudiciall to the Craft and vocation of Massonrie, whereof I am a member, and I, being desireous to advance and promote the good and utility of the said Craft of Massonrie to the utmost of my power, doe therefore hereby, for me and my heirs, renounce, quit, claim, overgive, and discharge, all right, claim, or pretence that I, or my heirs, had, have, or any ways may have, pretend to, or claim, to be patron, protector, judge or master of the Massons in Scotland, in virtue of any deed or deeds made and granted by the said Massons, or of any grant or charter made by any of the Kings of Scotland, to and in favours of the said William and Sir William St. Clairs of Rossline, or any others of my predecessors, or any other manner of way whatsomever, for now and ever; And I bind and oblige me, and my heirs, to warrand this present renounciation and discharge at all hands; and I consent to the registration hereof in the Books of Councill and Session, or any other judge's books competent, therein to remain for preservation; and thereto I constitute my procurators, &c.

In witness whereof I have subscribed these presents (written by David Maul, Writer to the Signet), at Edinburgh, the twenty-fourth day of November one thousand seven hundred and thirty-six years, before these witnesses, George Fraser, Deputy Auditor of the Excise in Scotland, Master of the

Cannongate Lodge; and William Montgomerie, Merchant in Leith, Master of the Leith Lodge.

"Sic Subscribitur, WM. ST. CLAIR.
"GEO. FRASER, Canongate Kilwinning, witness.
"WM. MONTGOMERI, Leith Kilwinning, witness."

"Several, at least, and possible a majority of the representatives present, had been instructed to vote for the Earl of Home, while none of the Lodges, with the exception of Canongate Kilwinning—of which St. Clair was a member—up to the period of election, appear to have been aware upon what grounds the latter's claims were to be urged. Nevertheless, the brethren were so fascinated with the apparent magnanimity, disinterestedness, and zeal displayed in his 'Resignation,' that the Deed was accepted with a unanimity that must have been very gratifying to the Lodge at whose instance it had been drawn, and the abdication of an *obsolete* office in Operative Masonry was made the ground of St. Clair being chosen to fill the post of first Grand Master in the Scottish Grand Lodge of *Speculative* Masons." *

St. Clair was initiated in Canongate Kilwinning, May 18, 1736, within eight months after the "choosing of a Grand Master" had been first discussed in that Lodge, and was "advanced to the degree of Fellow Craft" in the following month, "paying into the box as usual." John Douglas, an influential member of the Lodge of Kirkcaldy, next appears on the scene. He was—August 4, 1736—in consideration "of proofs done and to be done," affiliated by Canongate Kilwinning, and at the same time appointed "Secretary for the time, with power to appoint his own deputy, in order to his making out the scheme for electing St. Clair Grand Master for Scotland." Eight days prior to the election, St. Clair was advanced to "the degree of Master Mason," and two days later he signed the document that was to facilitate the election of a Grand Master, which was written and attested by three leading members of *his Mother-Lodge.*

The magnanimity of this act overcame the determination to elect another G. M., and Lord St. Clair was elected the first Grand Master of Scotland under the speculative system.

* Gould, vol. v., pp. 49, 50.

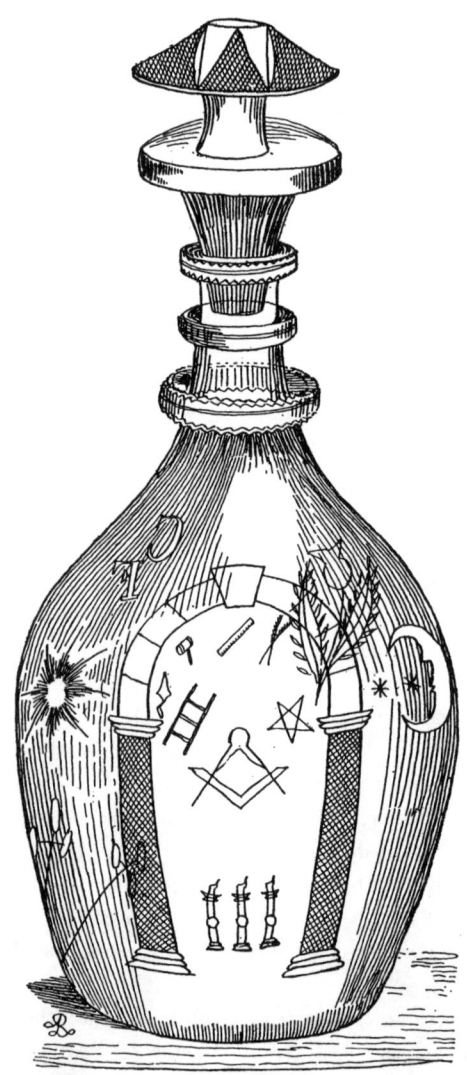

DECANTER BELONGING TO ROBERT BURNS'S FAMILY.

The Lodge Mary's Chapel, exhibiting an act in due form, which carried its origin to the year 1598, was placed at the head of the list of Lodges, and took the rank of No. 1. The Lodge Canongate Kilwinning claimed the first place, stating that their origin reached back to the year 1128—a claim that was admitted; but this Lodge, having lost its papers during the inactivity of a century and a half, could not now produce them, and was denied the preference. This caused Kilwinning Lodge to refuse connection with the new Grand Lodge, and to set itself up as an independent constituent power at Edinburgh in 1744 — at first under the name of the "Mother Lodge of Kilwinning," and subsequently as the "Royal Grand Lodge and Chapter of the Order of Herodium of Kilwinning."

"In the year 1807, however, this Lodge placed itself under the jurisdiction of the Grand Lodge as 'Canongate Kilwinning, No. 2.'

"November 30th, 1737, St. Clair was succeeded as Grand

SCOTLAND.—ITS EARLY FREE MASONRY.

Master by George, the third and last Earl of Cromarty, who in turn was succeeded in 1738 by John, third Earl of Kintore. Elections in the Grand Lodge of Scotland, by resolution, are held on the 30th of November, the birthday of St. Andrew, the tutelar Saint of Scotland."*

BURNS.

Among the noted names that figure in the annals of Free Masonry in Scotland is that of Robert Burns, the poet. He was born at Kirk Alloway, near Ayr, on the 25th of January, 1759. He was made a Mason at Irvine, in 1781. Subsequently he was elected Master of a Lodge at Mauchline.

The following is from his farewell to the brethren of Tarbolton Lodge:

"Adieu! A heart warm, fond adieu!
Dear brothers of the mystic tie!"†

The illustration opposite, is from an accurate sketch made from a decanter long in use in the Burns family.

THE SCHAW MSS., 1598.

At Halyrude House Edinburgh the XXVIIJ day of December, the zeir of God Im Vc four scoir awchtene zeiris, the Statutis and Ordinanceis to be obseruit be all the Maister-Maissounis within this realme sett doun be Williame Schaw Maister of Wark to his Maiestie and generall Wardene of the said Craft with the consent of the Maisteris efter specifeit.

ITEM. First that thay obserue and keip all the gude Ordinanceis sett doun of befoir concernying the priviligeis of thair predecessoris of gude memorie, and specially That thay be trew ane to ane vther and leve cheritablie togidder as becomis sworne brether and companzeounis of Craft.

ITEM. That thay be obedient to their Wardeneis Dekynnis and Maisteris in all thingis concernying thair Craft.

ITEM. That thay be honest faithfull and diligent in thair calling and deill uprichtlie wt the maisteris or awnaris of the warkis that thay sall tak vpoun hand be it in task meit & fie or owlklie wage.

ITEM. That nane tak vpoun hand ony wark gritt or small quhilk he is

* McClenachan, vol. i., p. 49.   † Mackey, p. 135.

nocht abill to performe qualifeitlie vnder the paine of fourtie pundis money or ellis the fourt part of the worth and valour of the said wark and that by and attour ane condigne amendis and satisfaccione to be maid to the awnaris of the wark at the sycht and discretione of the generall Wardene or in his abscence at the sycht of the Wárdeneis Dekynnis and Maisteris of the Sheriffdome quhair the said wark is interprisit and wrocht.

ITEM. That na Maister sall tak ane vther Maisteris wark over his heid efter that the first Maister has aggreit wt the awnar of the wark ather be contract arles or verball conditione vnder the paine of fourtie pundis.

ITEM. That na Maister sall tak the wirking of ony wark that vther Maisteris wrocht at of befoir vnto that the tyme that the first wirkaris be satisfeit for the wark quhilk thay haif wrocht vnder the paine foirsaid.

ITEM. That thair be ane Wardene chosin and electit ilk zeir to haif the charge over everie Ludge as thay are devidit particularlie and that be the voitis of the Maisteris of the saids Ludgeis and consent of thair Wardene generall gif he happenis to be present and vtherwayis that he be aduerteist that sic ane Wardene is chosin for sic ane zeir to the effect that the Wardene generall may send sic directions to that Wardene electit as effeiris.

ITEM. That na Maister sall tak ony ma Prenteissis nor thre during his lyfetyme wtout ane speciall consent of the haill Wardeneis Dekynnis and Maisteris of the Sheriffdome quhair the said Prenteiss that is to be ressavit dwellis and remanis.

ITEM. That na Maister ressave ony Prenteiss bund for fewar zeiris nor sevin at the leist and siclyke it sall nocht be lesum to mak the said Prenteiss Brother and Fallow-in-Craft vnto the tyme that he haif seruit the space of vther sevin zeiris efter the ische of his said Prenteisship wtout ane speciall licence granttit be the Wardeneis Dekynnis and Maisteris assemblit for that caus and that sufficient tryall be tane of the worthynes qualificationis and skill of the persone that desyris to be made Fallow-in-Craft and that vnder the paine of fourtie pundis to be upliftit as ane pecuniall penaltie fra the persone that is maid Fallow-in-Craft aganis this ordour besyde the penalteis to be sett doun aganis his persone accordying to the ordour of the Ludge quhair he remanis.

ITEM. It sall nocht be lesum to na Maister to sell his Prenteiss to ony vther Maister nor zit to dispens wt the zeiris of his Prenteisship be selling yrof to the Prenteissis self vnder the paine of fourtie pundis.

ITEM. That na Maister ressave ony Prenteiss wtout he signifie the samyn to the Wardene of the Ludge quhair he dwellis to the effect that the said Prenteissis name and the day of his ressavying may be orderlie buikit.

ITEM. That na Maister or Fallow-of-Craft be ressavit nor admittit wtout the numer of six Maisteris and tua enterit Prenteissis the Wardene of that Ludge being ane of the said six and that the day of the ressavyng of the said Fallow-of-Craft or Maister be orderlie buikit and his name and mark insert in the said buik wt the names of his six admittors and enterit Prenteissis and the names of the intendaris that sal be chosin in eurie persone to be alsua insert in the buik. Providing alway is that na man be admittit wtout ane assay and sufficient tryall of his skill and worthynes in his vocatioun and craft.

ITEM. That na Maister wirk ony Maissoun wark vnder charge or command of any vthr craftsman that takis vpoun hand or vpoun him the wirking of ony Maissoun wark.

ITEM. That na Maister or Fallow-of-Craft ressave ony cowanis to wirk in his societie or cumpanye nor send nane of his servands to wirk wt cowanis vnder the paine of twentie pundis so often as ony persone offends heirintill.

ITEM. It sall nocht be lesum to na enterit Prenteiss to tak ony vther gritter task or wark vpoun hand fra a awnar nor will extend to the summe of ten pundis vnder the paine foirsaid to wit xx lib and that task being done thay sall interpryiss na mair wtout licence of the Maisteris or Wardenes quhair thay dwelle.

ITEM. Gif ony questionis stryfe or variance sall fall out among ony of the Maisteris Servands or entert Prenteissis that the parteis that fallis in questioun or debat sall signifie the causis of thair querrell to the perticular Wardenis or Dekynnis of thair Ludge wtin the space of xxiiij hours vnder the paine of ten pundis to the effect that thay may be reconcilit and agreit and thair variance removit be thair saids Wardenis, Dekynnis and Maisteris and gif ony of the saids parteis sal happin to remane wilfull or obstinat that thay sal be depravit of the privilege of thair Ludge and nocht permittit to wirk y^{r}at vnto the tyme tha thay submitt thame selffis to ressoun at the sycht of thair Wardenis Dekynnis and Maisters as said is.

ITEM. That all Maisteris interpriseris of wark is be verray carefull to se thair skaffoldis and futegangis surelie sett and placit to the effect that throw thair negilgence and sloth na hurt or skaith cum vnto ony personis that wirkis at the said wark vnder the paine of dischargeing of thaim yrefter to wirk as Maisteris havand charge of ane wark bot sall ever be subiect all the rest of thair dayis to wirk vnder or wt ane other principall Maister havand charge of the wark.

ITEM. That na Maister ressave or resett ane vther Maisteris Prenteiss or Servand that sal happin to ryn awa fra his Maisteris seruice nor intertayne him in his cumpanye efter he has gottin knowledge y^r of vnder the paine of fourtie pundis.

ITEM. That all personis of the Maissounis Craft conuene in tyme and place being lawchfullie warnit vnder the paine of ten pundis.

ITEM. That all the Maisteris that sal happin to be sent for to ony assemblie or meitting sall be sworne be thair grit that thay sall hyde nor conceille na fawltis nor wrangis done to ane vther nor zit the faultis or wrangis that ony man hes done to the awnaris of the warkis that thay haif had in hand sa far as thay knaw and that vnder the paine of ten pundis to be takin vp fra the conceillars of the saidis faultis.

ITEM. It is ordanit that all thir foirsaids penalteis sal be liftit and tane vp fra the offendaris and breakaris of thir ordinanceis be the Wardeneis Dekynnis and Maisteris of the Ludges quhair the offendaris dwellis and to be distributit ad pios usus accordyng to gude conscience be the advys of the foirsaids. And for fulfilling and obseruing of thir ordinanceis sett doun as said is the haill Maisteris conuenit the foirsaid day bindis and oblisses thaim heirto faithfullie and thairfore hes requeistit thair said Wardene generall to subscrive thir presentis wt his awin hand to the effect that ane autentik copy heirof may be sent to euerie particular Ludge wtin this realme." *

WILLIAM SCHAW,
Maister of Wark.

* Hughan, p. 213.

"THE EGLINTON MS.," A.D. 1599.

(From an Exact Copy made by D. Murray Lyon, of Ayr, Scotland, for Bro. W. James Hughan, of Truro, England.)

xxviii December, 1599.

First. It is ordanit that the wardene within the boundis of Kilwynning and vtheris places subject to thair ludge, sal be chosen and electit zeirlie be mony of the maisteris voites of the said ludge, vpon the twentie day of December, and that within the kirk at Kilwynning, as the heid and secund ludge of Scotland, and therefter that the generall warden be advertysit zeirlie quha is chosin warden of the ludge, immediatelie efter his electioun.

Item. It is thocht neidful and expedient by my lord warden generall, that every ludge within Scotland sall have in tyme cuming the auld and antient liberties thereof vsit and wont of befoir; and in speciall, that the ludge of Kilwynning, secund lodge of Scotland, sall haif thair warden present at the election of the wardenis within the boundis of the Nether Waird of Cliddisdaill, Glasgow, Air, and boundis of Carrik; with power to the said warden and dekyn of Kilwynning to convene the remanent wardenis and dekynis within the boundis foir said quhan thay haif ony neid of importance ado, and thay to be judgit be the warden and dekyn of Kilwynning quhen it sall pleis thame to convene for the tyme, aither in Kilwynning, or within any vther part of the west of Scotland and boundis foirsaid.

Item. It is thocht neidfull and expedient be my lord warden generall, that Edinburgh sal be in all tyme cuming, as of befoir, the first and principal lodge in Scotland; and that Kilwynning be the secund ludge, as of befoir is not ourlie manifest in our awld antient writtis; and that Stirueling sal be the thrid ludge, conforme to the auld privileges thairof.

Item. It is thocht expedient that the wardenis of everie ilk ludge salbe answerable to the presbyteryes within their schirefdomes for the maissounis subject to the lugeis anent all offensis ony of them sall committ; and the third part of the vnlawis sal be employit to the godlie vsis of the ludge quhair ony offens sal happin to be committit.

Item. That ther be tryall takin zeirlie be the wardenis and maist antient maisteris of the ludge, extending to sex personis, quha sall tak tryall of the offensis, that punishment may be execut conforme to equitie and iustice and guid conscience and the antient ordour.

Item. It is ordanit be my lord warden generall, that the warden of Kilwynning, as secund in Scotland, elect and chuis sex of the maist perfyte and worthiest of memorie within (thair boundis) to tak tryall of the qualificatioun of the haill masonis within the boundis foirsaid, of thair art, craft, scyance, and antient memorie; to the effect the warden deakin may be answer-

HOLYROOD ABBEY.

able heiraftir for sic personis as is committit to him, and within his boundis and jurisdictioun.

Item. Commissioun is gewin and deakon of Kilwynning, as second ludge, to secluid and away put furth of their societie and cumpanie all personis disobedient to fulfil and obey the hail actis and antient statutis sett doun of befoir of guid memorie; and all personis disobedient ather to kirk, craft, counsall, and otheris statutis and acts to be maid heiraftir for ane guid ordour.

Item. It is ordainit to be the warden generall, that the warden and deacon to be present of (with?) his quarter maisteris, elect cheis and constitut ane famour notar, as ordinar clark and scryb; and that the said notar to be chosinge sall occupye the office, and that all indentouris discharges and vtheris wrytis quhatsumever, perteining to the craft, sal be onlie wrytin be the clark; and that na maner of wryt, neyther tityll nor other evident, to be admit be the said warden and deacon befoir thame, except it be maid be the said clark, and subscryuit with his hand.

Item. It is ordainit be my lord generall, that the hale auld antient actis and statutis maid of befoir be the predecessouris of the masounis of Kilwynning, be observit faithfullie and kepit be the crafts in all tymes cuminge; and that na prenteis nor craftis man, in ony tymes heiraftir, be admittit nor enterit bot onlie within the kirk of Kilwynning, as his paroche and secund ludge; and that all bankattis for entrie of prenteis or fallow of craftis to be maid within the said ludge of Kilwynning.

Item. It is ordainit that all fallows of craft at his entrie pay to the commoun bokis of the ludge the soume of ten pundis mone, with x s. worthe of gluffis, or euir he be admittit, and that for the bankatt; and that he be not admittit without ane sufficient essay and pruife of memorie and art of craft, be the warden, deacon, and quarter maisteris of the ludge, conforme to the foirmer; and quhairthrow thai may be the mair answerable to the generall warden.

Item. That all prenteissis to be admittit be not admittit quhill thai first pay to the commoun bankat foiresaid, the soume of sex pundis money; utherwyes to the bankat for the haill members of craft within the said ludge and prenteissis thairof.

Item. It is ordainit that the warden and deaconis of the secund ludge of Scotland, present of Kilwynning, sall tak the aythe, fidelitie and trewthe of all maisteris and fallowis of craft within the haill boundis commit to thair chairge, zeirlie, that thay sall not accumpanie with cowanis, nor work with thame, nor any of their servandis or prenteisses, undir the pain of the penaltie contenit in the foirmer acts, ane peying thairof.

Item. It is ordainit be the generall warden, that the luge of Kilwynning, being the secund luge in Scotland, tak tryall of the art of memorie and science theirof, of everie fallow of craft and everie prenteiss, according to ather of their vocationis; and in cais that thai have lost onie point thairof, eurie of thame to pay the penaltie as followis, for their slewthfulness, viz., ilk fallow of craft xx s. ilk prenteiss xi s. and that to be payit to the box for the commoun weill zeirlie; and that conforme to the commoun vse and pratik of the commoun lugis of this realm.

And for the fulfilling, observinge and keeping of thir statutis, and all thair actis and statutis maid of befoir, and to be maid be the warden, deaconis, and quarter maisteris of the lugis foirsaidis, for guid ordour keeping, conforme to equitie, justice, and antient ordour; to the making and setting doun quhairof, the generall warden hes gevin his power and commission to the said warden and others abvnevritten, to set doun and mak actis conforme as accordis to the office and law. And in signe and taking thairof, I, the generall warden of Scotland, hes sett doun and causit pen their actis and statutis, and hes subscryuit the samynis with my hand efter the testimoniale.

Be it kend to the warden, dekyn, and to the maisteris of the ludge of Kilwynning, the Archibald Barclay, being directit commissioner fra the said ludge, comperit in Edinburgh, the twentie seven and twenty awcht of December instant, quhair the said Archibald, in presens of the warden generall, and the maisteris of the ludge of Edinburgh, producit his commissioun and behaifit himself verie honestlie and cairfullie for the discharge of sik thingis as was committit into him; bot be ressone of the abscence of his Maiestie out of the toun, and that thair was na maisteris but the ludge of Edinburgh convenit of this tyme, we culd nocht get sik ane satlat ordour (as the privileges of the craft requyris) tane at this time; bot heirefter, quhan occasion sall be offerit we sall get his Maiesties warrand, baith for the authorizing of the ludgeis privileges, and ane penaltie sett downe for the dissobedient personis and perturberis of all guid ordour: Thus far I thocht guid to signifie vnto the haill brether of the ludge, vnto the neist commoditie: In witness heirof, I have subscriut thir presents with my hand, at Halyrudhous, the twentie awcht day of December, the zeir of God I^m Vc fourscoir nynetene zeirs.*

WILLIAM SHAW,
Maistir of Wark, Warden of the Maisonis.

* Hughan, p. 218.

THE ST. CLAIR CHARTERS.

No. I.

Be it kend till all men be thir present lris. Ws deacones maisteris and frie men of the Maissones w'tin the realme of Scotland with expres consent & assent of W'm Schaw Maister of Wark to our sou'ane lord ffor sa mekle as from aige to aige it hes bene observit amangs ws that the Lairds of rosling hes ever bene patrones and protectors of ws and our privileges lyckas our predecessors hes obeyit and acknawledgeit thame as patrones and Ptectoris Quhill that w'in thir few yiers throwch negligence and slewthfulness the samyn hes past furth of vse Quhairby nocht onlie hes the Laird of Rosling lyne owt of his just vrycht bot also our haill craft hes bene destitute of ane patrone protectour and oversear q'lk hes genderit manyfauld corruptiones and imperfectiones baith amangis ourselfis and in our craft and hes gevin occasioun to many persones to consave evill opinioun of ws and our craft and to lieve off great inerpryses of pollecie Be ressone of our great misbehavior w'out correction Quhairby not onelie the committairs of the faultis bot also the honest men ar disapoyntit of thair eraft and Pffeit. As lyckwayes quhen dyvers and sindrie contraverses fallis out amangis ourselfis thair follows great & manyfald inconveniencis throw want of ane (patrone and protector) we nocht being abill to await vpoun the ordiner judges & judgment of this realme throw the occasioun of our powertie and langsumnes of process ffor remeid of q'r' of and for keping of guid ordour amangis ws in all tymes cummying and for advancement our craft and vocatioun within this realme and furtherens of policie w't' in the samin. We for our selffis & in name of our haill bretherene and craftismen w't consent foirsaid aggreis and consentis that W'm Sinclair now of roslin for himself & his airis purches and obteine at ye hands of our Sou'ane Lord libertie friedome and jurisdictioun vpone ws and our successoures in all times cummying as patrones & judges to us and the haill Pfessoris of our craft w't' in this realme quhom of we have power and commissioun Swa that heirafter we may acknawledge him and his airis as our patrone and judge vnfer our Sou'ane Lord w't' out ony kynd of appellatioun or declyng from his judgment with power to the said Williame and his airis to depute judges ane or mæ vnder him and to vse sick ampill and lairge jurisdictione vpoun ws & our successors als weill as burghe as land as it sall pleis our souerane lord to grant to him and his airis.*

WILLIAM SHAW.

That *Schaw* was a man of note, both in the Masonic Fraternity and socially, appears from the following : †

First, at an early period of his life, he was connected with the royal household, and his signature was attached to the original parchment deed of the National Covenant, which was signed by King James VI. and his household at the Palace of Holyrood, January 28, 1580–81.

Second, in 1584, Schaw became successor to Sir Robert Drummond, of Carnock, as Master of Works. This high official appointment placed under his superintendence all the royal buildings and palaces in Scotland; and in the Treasurer's accounts of a subsequent period various sums are entered as having been paid to him in connection with these buildings for improvements, repairs, and additions. Thus, in September, 1585, the sum of £315 was paid "to *William Schaw, his Majestie's Maister of Wark*, for the reparation and mending of the Castell of Striueling," and in May, 1590, £400, by his Majesty's precept, was "delyverit to William Schaw, the Maister of Wark, for reparation of the hous of Dumfermling, befoir the Queen's Majestie passing thairto."

Third, Sir James Melville, being appointed to receive the three Danish Ambassadors who came to Scotland in 1585 (with overtures for an alliance with one of the daughters of Frederick II.), he requested the king that two other persons might be joined with him, and for this purpose he named *Schaw* and James Meldrum, of Seggie, one of the Lords of Session. It further appears that Schaw had been employed in various missions to France. He accompanied James VI. to Denmark in the winter of 1589, previous to the king's marriage with the Princess Anna of Denmark, which was celebrated at Upslo, in Norway, on November 23d. The king and his attendants remained during the winter season in Denmark, but Schaw returned to Scotland on March 16, 1589–90, for the purpose of making the necessary

* Hughan, p. 220.   † See Mackey, p. 691.

arrangements for the reception of the wedding-party. He brought with him a paper subscribed by the king, containing the "Ordour set down be his Majestie to be effectuate be his Heines Secreit Counsall, and preparit agane his Majestie's returne in Scotland," dated in February, 1589-90.

The king and his royal bride arrived in Leith on May 1st, and remained there six days, in a building called "The King's Work," until the Palace of Holyrood was prepared for their reception. Extensive alterations had been made at Holyrood, as a warrant was issued by the Provost and Council of Edinburgh to deliver to William Schaw, Maister of Wark, the sum of £1,000, "restand of the last taxation of £20,000" granted by the Royal Buroughs in Scotland, the sum to be expended "in biggin and repairing of his Hienes Palice of Halyrud-house," March 14, 1589-90. Subsequent payments to Schaw occur in the Treasurer's accounts for broad scarlet cloth and other stuff for "burde claythes and coverings to forms and windows bayth in the Kirk and Palace of Halyrudhouse." On this occasion various sums were also paid by a precept from the king for dresses, etc., to the ministers and others connected with the royal household. At another time he received £133 6s. 8d.

The queen was crowned on May 17th, and two days following she made her first public entrance into Edinburgh.

The inscription on Schaw's monument states that he was, in addition to his office of Master of the Works, "Sacris ceremoniis præpositus" and "Reginæ Quæstor," which Monteith translated "Sacrist and Queen's Chamberlain." This appointment of Chamberlain evinces the high regard in which the queen held him; but there can be no doubt that the former words relate to his holding the office of General Warden of the ceremonies of the Masonic Craft, an office analogous to that of Substitute Grand Master in the Grand Lodge of Scotland.

William Schaw died April 18, 1602, and was buried in the Abbey Church of Dunfermline, where a monument was erected to his memory by his grateful mistress, the Queen. On this monument is his name and monogram cut in a marble slab, which, tradition says, was executed by his own hand, and containing his Mason's mark, and an inscription in Latin, in which he is described as one imbued with every liberal art and science, most *skilful in architecture*, and in labors and business not only unwearied and indefatigable, but ever assiduous and energetic. No man appears, from the records, to have lived with more of the commendation, or died with more of the regret of others, than this old Scottish Mason.

SEAL OF THE ABBEY OF ARBROATH.

The Seal of the Ancient Abbey of Arbroath, Scotland.

Concerning this Seal, the Rev. Charles Cordinet, in his "Description of the Ruins of North Britain," says:

"The figures sculptured on the seal marked **initiation**, evidently represent some formidable ceremony in a sacred place where a pontiff presides in state; one hand on his breast expressive of seriousness, the other stretched out at a right angle, holding a rod and a cross, the badge of high office, while he makes some awful appeal respecting a suppliant, who, in a loose robe, blindfolded, with seeming terror kneels before the steps of an altar, while several attendants with drawn swords, brandish them over his head;" bringing to remembrance a description that *Plutarch*, in his famous essay, "De Osiris" gives of the engraving of a seal which the Priests of Isis used in their solemnities, namely, that of a man kneeling with his hands bound, a knife at his throat, etc. "And (says he) it is not a little remarkable, in how many particulars the mysterious fate of Osiris, as recorded by the above celebrated author, corresponds with the account of Hiram; 'The rod and cross, the badge of high office,' held by the pontiff, is precisely a copy of the measure of the Nile, which was originally put into the hands of a figure of Anubis, to indicate the rise of the inundation upon which mainly depended the subsistence, or temporal salvation of Egypt."

This rod afterward obtained, says Pluche, the name of Caduceus, or Mercury's wand, and was borne as a sceptre or staff of honor, indicating a sacred person. The figure (10), a cabalistic number, shows its original to have been a measure.*

* See Mysteries, pp. 241, 242.

CHAPTER XI.

THE EASTERN HEMISPHERE.

RAPID SPREAD OF FREE MASONRY THROUGHOUT THIS HALF OF THE GLOBE

Its Introduction into Europe, Asia, and Africa.—Free Masonry in Egypt, Greece, Turkey, including Jerusalem and Damascus.—In Persia, Bombay, Calcutta, China, Australasia, etc.

THE history of Free Masonry having been traced to Britain, and its reorganization at London in 1717 described, its introduction into all the principal countries of the world will next follow.

EUROPE.

Belgium.—The first foreign Lodge in accordance with reorganized Free Masonry, was warranted at Mons, June 4, 1721,* by Grand Master Lord Montagu, under the title of Perfect Union. Lodges then increased so rapidly that in 1736 the Catholic priests became jealous of their influence and prevailed upon Charles VI. to issue an edict for their suppression throughout the Netherlands. Notwithstanding this, as the Lodges comprised men of note and determination, they continued to meet, but not as openly as before. This state of things went on until 1740, when the influence of Francis of Lorraine (Imperial Consort of Maria Theresa) secured toleration of Free Masonry until 1764, when its tireless enemies, the Catholics, again succeeded

---

* The first Lodge was instituted at Mons, June 4, 1721, under the title of "Perfect Union" by the Duke of Montagu, then Grand Master of the Grand Lodge of London. Rebold, History of Free Masonry in Europe, p. 118.

The Duke of Montagu, on June 4, 1721, authorized the establishment of a Lodge at Mons, Belgium ; and in 1730 another Lodge was established at Ghent, by authority from Austria. McClenachan, History of Free Masonry in New York, p. 60. See, also, Annales Maçonniques des Pays-Bas.

in having the institution suppressed. But, as before, the Craft soon rallied and rendered the edict inoperative. The influence of the Church of Rome however, has been so strong against them, that as late as 1901 there were only nineteen Lodges in Belgium.*

Holland.—In 1731 a Lodge was opened at The Hague, under a warrant from Montagu, G. M. of the Grand Lodge of England. It was, however, only a Lodge of emergency, having been called to initiate the Duke of Tuscany, afterward Francis I., Emperor of Germany.

The ceremony was performed by Dr. Desaguliers and the Earl of Chesterfield. The first was deputed by the Grand Master of England, and the second was ambassador at the Hague. The first regular Lodge of which there is any record, was established at the same place in 1734, which, ten years after, took the name of the Union Mother Lodge.

Another Lodge was founded at The Hague, in the same year, composed of eminent men, but upon the announcement in the newspapers of a Masonic assembly, which would be presided over by the new Provincial Grand Master Rademacher, the magistracy of the Hague issued an ordinance interdicting all such assemblies.†

But as this Lodge numbered among its members the most prominent men in the city, it disregarded the prohibition, and continued its labors. Upon learning of this, the Catholic clergy proceeded to stir up the ignorant class against it, and caused its place of meeting to be invaded by a mob of fanatics, who burned the property of the Lodge, and otherwise exhibited a disposition to proceed to the most violent measures. Therefore the general Government, with the object of preventing a recurrence of such action, intervened, and prohibited Masonic assemblies. One Lodge, however, in defiance of this prohibition, continued to meet in secret, but their secrecy was not proof against a Church that could locate a heretic by intuition, and persecute him to the extent of its powers. Therefore, Papal spies soon discovered that this Lodge still met regularly; and after making sure that a meeting was in session—that their prey was bagged—they broke into the Lodge and made

---

* Rebold, p. 118 ; Gould, vol. v., p. 210.
† Mackey, p. 527 ; Rebold, pp. 123, 124 ; Gould, vol. v., p. 202.

prisoners of its members. On the following day they were brought before the tribunal of the city, and although the prisoners knew that Papal injustice would be administered without stint, they did not ask their prosecutors to prove their allegations, but boldly declared that they were Masons, and were assembled in the Lodge as such. Not only this, but the officers defended and upheld their institution, and challenged the Court to select any honorable man whom they could initiate, and according to his report they were willing to be dealt with. But as the Court was convened to convict and sentence, the challenge was at first declined. The firmness of the men, and the justice of their proposal, however, was so obvious to the judge and the spectators, that it was finally acceded to, and the Town Secretary * was selected; whereupon the members were paroled, convened a Lodge, and duly initiated the candidate. The initiate was so well pleased with what he learned, that he endorsed the institution zealously, and not only secured the prisoners' discharge, but induced the magistrate and other high officials to apply for initiation.

Another, but more ludicrous, case of persecution was that of two young officers of good families, who applied to the priest of the parish in which they resided to examine them on certain points of religion, agreeable to the requirements of the Church, and then grant them a certificate to entitle them to receive the Holy Sacrament. After the examination had ended, and the priest satisfied in regard to their qualifications, he asked them if they were Free Masons. Being answered in the affirmative, he refused to grant them certificates, which in that country was equivalent to expulsion from the Communion. This transaction raised such an uproar, that at last the Grand Assembly of the States General took it into consideration, and ordered that for the future no clergyman should ask either that or any other question regarding Free Masonry, in the execution of his ecclesiastical duty, and ordered the priest, before whom the officers had been examined, to immediately grant their certificates.

In 1756 there were fourteen Lodges in Holland and vicinity. These met on the 25th of December of that year and constituted a Grand Lodge, known as the Grand Lodge of the Netherlands, and elected Baron Aerssen Beyeren as Grand Master, and Baron Von Boetzelaar, Deputy Grand Master.

* Mitchell, vol. i., p. 327.

Amsterdam—Montalban's Tower.

FREE MASONRY IN EUROPE.

This jurisdiction now comprises 93 Lodges, of which 53, with 3,307 members, are in Europe; 23 at, and in the vicinity of the Cape of Good Hope, and 17 in the other Dutch colonies. Total, 4,938 members.

GERMANY.—A Lodge was established at HAMBURG in 1733—Karl Sarry, Master. On the 30th of October, 1740, this Lodge was merged into Absalom Lodge, which Lodge was raised by the Grand Lodge of England to the rank of Provincial Grand Lodge of Hamburg and Lower Saxony—Lutman, Grand Master. It was by a deputation of this Lodge that Prince Frederick of Prussia, subsequently Frederick the Great, was initiated at Brunswick.* In 1901, there were 36 Lodges under this jurisdiction, with 3,322 members. From Hamburg, Free Masonry passed in 1738 to Dresden; in 1740 to Berlin; in 1741 to Leipsic; in 1744 to Brunswick, and in 1746 to Hanover.

THE GRAND LODGE "SUN," AT BAYREUTH.

On the 21st of January, 1741, the Margrave, Frederick of Brandenburg-Kulmbach, opened, in his castle at Bayreuth, the capital of his dominions, a Lodge which he named the "Sun," of which he assumed control and remained Master until his death in 1763. December 5, 1741, this Castle Lodge, the "Sun," instituted in Bayreuth a *City* "Sun" with great pomp, the Margrave himself taking a conspicuous part in the procession. The *Castle* "Sun" soon added to itself a directory of Scots Masters, which partially discharged the functions of a non-representative Grand Lodge.

December 13, 1811, the Provincial Grand Lodge, the Sun, declared itself an independent Grand Lodge.

In 1872 Bluntschli was Grand Master, and in 1878, Feustel. The present Grand Master is Dr. Lowe. In January, 1901, this Grand Lodge had thirty-four Lodges under its rule, chiefly in Bavaria and Baden, one each in Hamburg, Bremen, and Norway, and two in Wurtemberg, where Masonry was forbidden in 1784, but has asserted itself since 1835. The membership of these thirty-four Lodges was 2,842, an average of 88 per Lodge. Later a second Norwegian Lodge has been erected.

* See Gould, vol. v., p. 225; Rebold, p. 128; McClenachan, vol. i., p. 60.

Grand Lodge "Zur Eintracht" (Concord), at Darmstadt.

February 27, 1846, three Lodges met, proclaimed the Grand Lodge "Concord," and elected J. H. Lotheissen, President of the Court of Appeal, as their first Grand Master.

In 1851, the Grand Lodge Concord—consisting of three Lodges in all—elected Betz as Grand Master.

In January, 1901, there were 8 Lodges and 803 members, an average of 100 per Lodge. The Grand Master was then Philip Brand, and the Protector of the Brotherhood was the Grand Duke, Louis IV., who succeeded his uncle, Louis III., in 1877, and, like the latter, has not been enrolled as a member of the Fraternity.

Three Globes—Lodge and Grand Lodge.

In 1738 the King of Prussia manifested considerable hostility to Free Masonry, but Count Albert Wolfgang of Lippe-Buckeburg took its part so successfully as to awake in the Crown Prince Frederick a desire to join the Craft. Under the circumstances, great secrecy was necessary in carrying out such a project. The arrangements were undertaken by Count Albert, and as the King had announced his intention of visiting Brunswick during the annual fair, it was resolved that the ceremony of initiation should be performed in that city. To Von Oberg, Master of the Lodge in Hamburg, was confided the management of the affair, and he, with the Secretary, Bielfeld, and a Baron von Lowen, travelled to Brunswick, where they met, by arrangement, the Count of Kielmansegge, F. C. Albedyll, from Hanover, and Count Albert. Count Wartensleben joined the Prince as a *second candidate.* Late in the evening of August 14–15, 1738, the Prince and his friend came to the hotel where the Hamburg brethren were staying, and after midnight the two candidates were received and initiated in due form, no difference being made as regarded the Prince, in compliance with his own special request. The brethren then separated and returned home as quickly as possible, because, as Bielfeld wrote, "there is here one crowned head too many, who, if he discovered that we had initiated the Prince, his son, might in his ill-humor fail in the respect due to the *Most Worshipful Masters!*"

FREE MASONRY IN EUROPE.

Subsequently Von Oberg erected and presided over a Lodge in the Prince's castle of Rheinsberg, and when he left for Hamburg, in 1739, Frederick himself assumed the chair. Soon after his father's death, in 1740, Frederick openly acknowledged himself a Mason, and June 20th, same year, he presided over a Lodge in the Royal Palace of Charlottenburg, with Bielfeld and Jordan as his Wardens. On that occasion the following candidates were initiated by the King in person: his two brothers, August Wilhelm, and Heinrich Wilhelm; his brother-in-law, Karl, Margrave of Brandenburg-Onolzbach; and the Duke of Holstein-Beck. Afterward he initiated the Margrave of Brandenburg-Bayreuth.

Soon after his accession Frederick empowered Jordan, the Secretary of his Lodge, to open a Lodge in Berlin for the numerous Masons there resident. Its first meeting was held September 13, 1740, and it took the name of "The *Three Globes.*" Later, by the order of Frederick, it became a Grand Lodge of the same name, founded simply on the King's authority, who from the first assumed all the privileges of a Grand Master in his dominions.

In October a deputation from the Lodge initiated Karl Frederick, Duke of Saxe-Meiningen, and "The Three Globes" issued its first warrant of constitution to a Lodge, "The Three Compasses," in that prince's chief city.

On November 9, 1740, the first code of by-laws was drawn up and accepted.

Prior to 1744 six warrants of constitution were granted, some of which were for localities beyond the confines of Prussia. On June 24, 1744, the Lodge assumed the title of "Grand Royal Mother-Lodge OF THE THREE Globes." It did not cease, however, on that account to continue working as a private Lodge. Frederick the Great was nominally Grand Master, and in September, 1747, the Duke of Holstein-Beck, Governor of Berlin, was elected Deputy Grand Master. These offices, however, were rather ornamental than useful, as the real power in the Lodge was still vested in the Master. Von Printzen was initiated March 18, 1748, elected Master of the Lodge May 5, 1749, held the post until June 5, 1752, and was one of the foremost figures in its early history.

On the 9th of December, 1754, a second Lodge was constituted at Berlin, under the name of La Petite Concorde, but with very limited powers.

Feeling the humility and inconvenience of this arrangement, this Lodge took advantage of irregularities in the election of the officers of the Mother-Lodge, May, 28, 1755, to protest and declare itself independent. Lord James Keith, who was then Governor of Berlin, professing to be Deputy G. M. of all English Lodges in North Germany, interfered to prevent the "Concord" being closed by force, and promised it an English constitution. In May, 1757, Von Printzen was once more called to the direction of affairs. His first efforts to restore peace between the Three Globes and the Concord were, however, only partially successful. In 1758 the Concord also erected for itself a Scots Lodge, under the name of "Harmony."

February 24, 1759, the Mother-Lodge constituted the Berlin Lodge of the "Flaming Star," of which C. A. Marschall von Bieberstein was Worshipful Master. This Lodge, with the Three Globes and the Concord, now formed one body under the *Scots* Lodge. This culminated in such confusion that in 1787 steps had to be taken to remedy the difficulty.

On the 16th of November, 1770, the Crown Prince, afterward Frederick William II., wrote to the Lodge of the Three Globes assuring it of his protection.

June 26, 1780, the first step toward a representative system was made by a resolution conferring honorary membership of Grand Lodge on all acting Masters of subordinate Lodges.

In 1782 the meeting of the Wilhelmsbad Convent, and with it the practical subversion of the Strict Observance, took place. This furnished an opportunity for the Three Globes to avow its position and principles. In a circular of November 11, 1783, it declared its independence of all superior authority, but was willing to honor Duke Ferdinand, as before, in the capacity of Grand Master; it refused, however, to conform to the rectified Templar system, but offered to recognize as legitimate all Masons of every system as far as concerned the first three degrees (excepting the Illuminati), and counselled all Grand Lodges to follow its example.

In 1783 three Lodges were warranted, and in 1784 Theden became W. M. of the Three Globes.

In 1787 one new Lodge was warranted, and in 1788 the first list was published, showing 16 subordinate Lodges, with 763 members. In 1790, the

The Three Crowns Tavern, Ryegate.

mutual interdiction between the Lodges under the "Three Globes" and the *National* G. L. was terminated, and was succeeded by a pact of tolerance and amity. In 1791, the continual absence from Berlin of the G. M., Prince Frederick Augustus, necessitated the presence of a Deputy, — Zollner was elected to fill that position.

October 20, 1798, a royal edict appeared suppressing all secret societies. The three Grand Lodges in Berlin, however, and Lodges holding under them, were expressly exempted from its provisions; but Lodges erected in Prussia by *other* Grand Lodges were declared illegitimate. The names of all such members were to be handed to the police authorities yearly. The Grand Masters and the Deputy Grand Masters were asked whether their names should be also cited, and whether they would accept the accompanying responsibility. They declined, and resigned their posts in February, 1799.

Between 1788–98 six Lodges were warranted, and the number of active Lodges had increased to twenty, with a total membership of nine hundred and forty-one.

It was determined, March 7, 1799, not to elect any special National Grand Master, but to consider the W. M. of the *Three Globes* as such pro tem. Zollner, therefore, thenceforth took the title of Grand Master. June 24th, new statutes were agreed to; but these must not be confounded with the constitutions, as German Grand Lodges make a distinction between the two, although it is at times difficult to discover the difference. February 10, 1801, the special constitutions of the Inner Orient received final approbation; and November 1, 1804, the Constitutions were revised; the Grand Lodge to consist of eleven Grand Officers and thirty-six active members.

On the 12th of September, 1804, Grand Master Zollner died, and was succeeded by Guionneau, a past Grand Master. Prince Frederick Augustus, Duke of Brunswick, died November 8, 1805.

On the entry of the French troops into Berlin, in October, 1806, the Lodges there under the Three Globes system were ordered to *suspend work*. The committees of the Grand Lodge continued, however, to meet and transact all necessary business.

December 16, 1808, the Berlin Lodges resumed work. During the *preceding* ten years forty Lodges had been added to the roll, but owing to a few dropping out, the total of active Lodges had only risen from twenty to fifty-five, with a membership of 3,694, or an average of sixty-seven per Lodge.

During the next ten years thirty-nine Lodges had been added to the roll, and after allowing for those that had become extinct the total had only risen to seventy-four in 1818, with 6,545 members, an average of eighty-eight per Lodge.

In 1821, an edict was issued by the Czar closing the Polish Lodges. This caused a loss of several Lodges to Berlin; and the revision of the Statutes in 1825, once more enforced the regulation that a Jew could neither be initiated, affiliated, nor received as a visitor. In 1821, O'Etzel, the subsequent Grand Master, joined Lodge Concord, and in 1822 he was elected a member of the Grand Lodge.

Between 1818 and 1828 fifteen Lodges had been constituted, bringing the total number of active Lodges up to eighty-seven, with a membership of 6,842, an average of seventy-eight per Lodge.

September 13, 1840, the Grand Lodge held its centenary festival, on which occasion it was presented by the Master of the Lodge " *Horus* " with the sword used at the initiation of Frederick the Great at Brunswick in 1738; whereupon it was resolved, that the W. M. of Lodge Horus, although under another jurisdiction, be ex-officio an honorary member of the Grand Lodge of the Three Globes.

February 20, 1868, it was resolved to present every initiate with a copy of O'Etzel's " History of the Three Globes."

On August 14, 1838, this Grand Lodge celebrated the 150th anniversary of the initiation of Frederick the Great. In 1900 it had 134 St. John Lodges, 69 Scottish Lodges, with a total membership of 14,272, and 997 honorary members. It also had 64 St. Andrew's Chapters, and 400 benevolent institutions.

Royal York.

On the 5th of May, 1760, the Lodge of the Three Globes received from the French Masons of Berlin, a petition for a warrant to enable them to meet as a Lodge—" Joy and Peace "—to initiate Frenchmen only, offering to pay all their income into the funds of the Mother-Lodge. Practically, it was to be merely a French branch of the Three Globes. The petition was granted, and in the same year, August 10th, Von Printzen constituted the Lodge under the name of the "Three Doves." In March, 1761, the Mother-Lodge took into consideration a request to enlarge the powers of the Three Doves, as it was found impossible to recruit the Lodge solely from Frenchmen, and to carry it on without funds. The petition was acceded to, and a new warrant granted April 12th, whereby the Lodge became an independent sister-Lodge of the Three Globes, and its title was altered to "Friendship of the Three Doves." In the same year this Lodge joined with the "Three Globes" and "Concord" in forming a Masonic Tribunal—electing Von Printzen Grand Master.

On the 27th of July, 1765, H. R. H. Edward Augustus, Duke of York, brother of George III., and his companion, Colonel Henry St. John, were initiated. And on August 2d the Prince authorized the Lodge to assume the name of "Royal York of Friendship"

In 1798, a Royal Edict appeared wherein the Royal York was named as one of the three authorized Grand Lodges of Prussia.

In 1798, December the 20th, the Berlin Lodge, "VICTORIOUS TRUTH," initiated and admitted to active membership H. R. H. Augustus Frederick, Duke of Sussex, son of George III., and nephew to the Duke of York, who was initiated in 1765.

In 1901 the Grand Lodge "ROYAL YORK" comprised 67 Lodges, with 6,507 members, an average of 97 members per Lodge. Of these Lodges 4 are outside of Prussia—3 in Alsace-Lorraine, and 1 in Bremen. It has, also, 1 Provincial Grand Lodge, Silesia, and 12 Inner Orients.

GRAND LODGE OF SAXONY—DRESDEN.

The first Lodge in this jurisdiction was the "Three Eagles," opened at Dresden in 1738. The next Lodge was the "Three Golden Swords," opened in 1739. In January, 1901, the number of Lodges on the roll was 23, with a membership of 4,296, an average of 183 per Lodge. The honorary members number 454. The two Lodges at Meiningen and Greitz are not in the Kingdom of Saxony. On the other hand, two Lodges at Leipsic do not belong to the Union, but are independent. The ritual in this Jurisdiction is Schroeder's, with the exception of the Bautzen Lodge, which still retains that of the Three Globes, and the Freiberg Lodge, which adheres to Fessler's. The present Grand Master is Dr. Bernhard A. Erdmann. The benevolent institutions number 112.

The Grand Lodge of Free Masons.—National Grand Lodge.

This G. L. was established in Berlin in 1770. It was originated by Zinzendorf, and is a very pretentious body.

On the 5th of November, 1853, the initiation of Prince Frederick William of Prussia took place. The ceremony was performed in the palace, and his father presided in person, in the presence of the Grand Officers of the three Prussian Grand Lodges, and in the name of the National Grand Lodge, of which he became a member. The Master's gavel used on that occasion was the one formerly belonging to Frederick the Great.

The eighth and last of the Berlin Lodges under this system was constituted two years afterwards—November 5, 1855, and named in his honor "Frederick William of the Dawn."

April 26, 1860, Selasinsky died, and Prince Frederick William of Prussia accepted the office of Master of the Order on June 24th following.

On June 24, 1870, the Grand Lodge celebrated its centenary, with the Prince in the chair.

Two years later, A. Von Ziegler had been appointed Grand Master, and he was succeeded by F. R. A. Neuland, the present Grand Master.

In 1901, the National Grand Lodge had 114 Lodges, with 11,941 members, and 592 honorary members. There are also 23 St. Andrew's Chapters, with 2,542 members.

This Grand Lodge had at this time 148 benevolent institutions.

Grand Lodge "Eclectic Union"—Frankfort-on-the-Main.

The first permanent Lodge in this jurisdiction was established in 1742. Others followed, so that the statistics of this Grand Lodge for 1901, showed 20 subordinate Lodges, with 2,832 members and 55 benevolent institutions.

There are also in Germany five independent Lodges, all with English charters, and although not under any Grand Lodge jurisdiction, yet they are recognized as regular by the German Grand Lodge bodies. In 1890, these independent Lodges had 1,400 members.

THE GRAND LODGE LEAGUE OF GERMANY now comprises the following Grand Lodges, and in the order here given:
1. Three Globes at Berlin.
2. Grand Lodge of Free Masons of Germany (National) at Berlin.
3. G. L Royal York—Berlin.
4. G. L. of Hamburg—Hamburg.
5. G. L. of Saxony—Dresden.
6. G. M. L. Eclectic Union—Frankfort.
7. G. L. Sun—Bayreuth.
8. G. L. Zur Eintracht (Concord), Darmstadt.

Number of Lodges in the G. L. League in 1901, 505. Number of members, 47,015. In addition to this there are, as above stated, 5 independent Lodges with 1,400 members.

THE LAST DAYS OF THE EMPEROR FREDERICK IIL—HIS DEATH AND THE LODGE OF SORROW.*

At the convention of the Grand Lodge League held in Berlin, May 20, 1888, it was resolved to send a telegram to the Emperor Frederick III., with the sincerest wishes for his welfare, and for his recovery from severe illness, to which the following telegram was received:

"By order of His Majesty, the Emperor and King, I transmit to the Grand Lodge League the heartfelt and fraternal thanks of His Majesty for the greetings and wishes. The Emperor hopes that the Supreme Architect of the Universe will grant His blessing to the work and endeavor of the Grand Lodge League."

After the death of the Emperor a Lodge of Sorrow was held in his

* See Report on Correspondence in Proceedings of the Grand Lodge of New York for 1889, pp. 98–105.

memory, and the following Grand Lodges participated in this solemn and imposing ceremony:

The Grand Lodge of the "Three Globes," Berlin. Grand Lodge of Prussia, "Royal York." Grand Lodge of Hamburg. Grand Lodge of Saxony. Grand Mother Lodge of the Eclectic Union at Frankfort-on-the-Main. Grand Lodge "Zur Sonne," at Bayreuth. "Zur Intracht," at Darmstadt. Grand Lodge of Free Masons of Germany at Berlin, of which the Grand Master presided.

The four isolated, but regularly recognized, St. John Lodges in Germany, by their delegate, Brother Carus.

The presiding Grand Master, Brother Neuland, opened the Lodge session with prayer and an impressive address.

The orator of the day, Grand Master Brand, reviewed the Masonic career of the deceased Emperor, and mentioned especially the words addressed to him by his father, Emperor Wilhelm I., on the occasion of his initiation and of his raising to the Master's Degree. In conclusion G. M. Brand made allusions to utterances of the ancestors of the deceased; first, of Frederick II., called the Great, viz.:

"In my country everyone shall get to Heaven in his own way."

Then the words of Emperor Wilhelm I., spoken a short time before his death to his daughter,

"I have no time to get tired;" and quoted the words of the deceased addressed to his son,

"Learn to suffer without complaining."

On this occasion the Grand Lodges of England and of the Netherlands expressed, through their representatives, their sympathy; and the following telegram was received from the Grand Orient of Italy, dated Rome, June 15, 1888:

"WORSHIPFUL AND DEAR BRETHREN: In the name and on behalf of the Grand Orient and of all Free Masons of Italy, please accept for the Imperial Family, and for all Subordinate Lodges, and for all Masons in Germany, the feelings of the sincerest and deepest condolence at the death of the valiant Brother, His Majesty Emperor Frederick III. Alas, his too early parting from life is an immense misfortune to the whole Fraternity, whose principles he adopted with such great enthusiasm, and which he propagated and defended with such great endurance and fidelity.

"The firmness and hero-like devotion with which he suffered during the long and severe torments of his malady, show to the world the vigor and tenacity with which he would have persevered in the fight for all human and civil progress, and his endeavor to bless mankind with true freedom, fraternity, and peace. Glory to his sublime virtues.

(Signed) "The Grand Master,
"ADRIANO LEMMI."

Hanover.—Free Masonry was established in this kingdom in 1746; and in a Provincial Grand Lodge, in 1826, under the Grand Mastership of the reigning king, it declared its independence as a Masonic authority.

In November, 1813, Ernest Augustus, Duke of Cumberland, son of George III., visited the Lodge "Frederick of the WHITE HORSE," and at the ensuing banquet applied for admission, and the application was granted. In 1815, Hanover was raised to the rank of a kingdom, and its boundaries were enlarged. In the same year the Provincial Grand Lodge constituted a Lodge at Nienburg, and affiliated the one warranted in Celle, by Hamburg, in the previous year. It also received the adhesion of several Lodges that belonged to the Grand Lodge of Westphalia.

In 1837, William IV. died; Hanover became an independent kingdom, and the Duke of Cumberland, the then Grand Master, succeeded to the throne. He died in 1851, and was succeeded by his son, George V. Although not a Mason, King George assumed the patronage of the craft, and in 1857 was initiated in the "Black Bear."

On the 30th of September, 1867, the Minister of Justice, by virtue of the old edict (1798), closed the Grand Lodge of Hanover; consequently the subordinate Lodges had to choose new superiors. Velzen, Goslar, and Osnabruck joined the "Three Globes;" Buckeburg joined the Grand Lodge of Hamburg; Walsrode dissolved; "Cedar," in Hanover, joined the National Grand Lodge; the other seventeen Lodges affiliated with the Grand Lodge Royal York, and were of material weight in carrying the more liberal Constitutions of that Grand Lodge in 1872.

FREE MASONRY IN EUROPE.

Denmark. — Free Masonry was introduced into this country at Copenhagen in 1743, under a charter from the Lodge "Three Globes" at Berlin. H. R. H. the Crown Prince Frederick was Grand Master. There were 10 Lodges in Denmark, including the Lodges of Instruction, with 4,243 members in 1901.

The Grand Lodge meets in a superb hall, richly ornamented, built for that purpose in 1761. There are also several Lodges in the Danish West India possessions, under the Constitution of the Grand Lodge of Copenhagen.

The Fraternity is recognized by the State, and the reigning kings have always been the Grand Masters.

Sweden. — Masonry was introduced into Sweden at Stockholm, in 1735; but the interdictions pronounced against it by the Catholic Church in nearly every European State also affected it here, and the Masonic meetings were prohibited in 1738. Nevertheless, new Lodges were subsequently established, and in the year 1759. the Grand Lodge of Sweden was organized at Stockholm. One of the first acts of the Fraternity of this country was the establishment of an orphan asylum, which is to-day the glory of Swedish Masonry.

The Grand Lodge meets in Stockholm. H. M. the King of Sweden and Norway is Grand Master. Number of Lodges, 33; members, 10,985.

Switzerland. — In 1736 a Lodge was established in the city of Geneva, a naturalized Scotchman, George Hamilton, being Master. On March 5th, of the same year, he was forbidden by the Republic to initiate native citizens (a decree which was, however, systematically violated), and in 1737 he was appointed by the Grand Lodge of England, Provincial Grand Master of all Lodges in the State. The present Grand Lodge, Alpina, has thirty-two subordinate Lodges, with 3,424 members.

Russia. — In 1731, under the reign of the Empress Anna Ivanowa, the Grand Lodge of London established a Lodge at Moscow; and for the purpose of constituting others in that country, appointed John Phillips Provincial Grand Master. Free Masonry made so little progress, however, in Russia, that it was not until the year 1771 that the first Lodge was organized at St. Petersburg. In 1772, the Grand Lodge of London delivered to John

FREE MASONRY IN EUROPE.

Yelaguine, Senator and Privy Councillor, a patent constituting him Provincial Grand Master of Russia. After his death he was succeeded by the Count Roman Woronsow.*

Austria.—Free Masonry was introduced into this country in 1742; but owing to the hostility of the Catholic Church but little progress has been made. †

Hungary.—This jurisdiction comprises 46 Lodges, with 3,324 members.

Roumania.—The First Lodge was opened here in 1859. Number of Lodges in 1883, 27; Chapters, 12.

Servia has two Lodges at Belgrade.

FRANCE.—*Introduction of Free Masonry into that Country, and Leading Events in its History.*—The first Lodge in France, in accordance with the new dispensation, was established at Dunkirk, in 1721. The next was founded in Paris, on June 12, 1726, under the title of "St. Thomas." Its members held their Lodge at the house of Hurre, in the street of the St. Germain Market. The second Lodge in Paris was established on May 7, 1729, under the name of Louis d'Argent. December 11th of the same year, a third Lodge was constituted, under the title of "Arts Sainte Marguerite." Its meetings were held at the house of Gaustand. On November 29, 1732, a fourth Lodge was constituted, under the name of "Buci," and after having initiated the Duke of Aumont, it took the name of "Lodge of Aumont." ‡

It has been claimed that the above-named Lodges in Paris were founded by "Lord Derwentwater" and two other Englishmen, then stopping in that city. But as there is neither evidence nor probability that Derwentwater was a Mason, his connection with the Fraternity, further than to intrigue for their assistance politically, is very doubtful; § consequently, while these Lodges were doubtless organized in accordance with the formula of Speculative Masonry as acquired in London, yet they were, like their old operative predecessors, self-constituted bodies.

* Gould, vol. v., p. 214. † Ibid., vol. vi, p. 286. § Ibid., vol. v., p. 139.
‡ Rebold, p. 80.

The first Lodge established in France under the then only constituting authority, the Grand Lodge of England, was numbered and named on its list of 1730-1732 as No. 90, the King's Head, Paris.

The second Lodge, under the same authority, was constituted at Valenciennes—No. 127. The third was established at the Castle of Aubigny in 1735. In 1738 the Duc d'Antin, a peer of France, was elected Grand Master ad vitam of Free Masons.

In 1743 d'Antin died, and on December 11, 1743, sixteen Masters of Paris Lodges elected as his successor Prince Louis de Bourbon, Comte de Clermont.*

In 1740, degrees termed *Scottish* or *Scots* degrees, appeared, and soon became numerous. From these arose the Scots Mother Lodges, and finally the A. and A. Scottish Rite.

In 1761, the Grand Lodge was, on account of quarrels, divided into two factions, each asserting the authority of a Grand Lodge. In this year the faction or Grand Lodge, headed by Lacorne and Jonville, held a joint meeting with the Emperors of the East and West, and among its acts was the grant to Morin of his famous patent.†

1771. Death of Grand Master Clermont, and reorganization of the Grand Lodge. The Duke of Chartres elected Grand Master.

1772. August 9th, union of the Supreme Council of the Emperors of the East and the Grand Lodge—new title of "Sovereign and Respectable Grand Lodge of France."

June 26, 1773, the National Grand Lodge of France was established. December 27th, it changed its name to Grand Orient.‡

August 12, 1774, the Grand Orient, having completed its new premises in the Rue Pot-de-Fer, took possession of them.

In 1775 a compact was formulated between the Scots Directories of the 2d, and 3d, and 5th Provinces, and the Grand Orient.

By this compact the Templar Lodges were to use their own ritual and obey their own superiors, but must be chartered by the Grand Orient, and pay fees to that body.

In February, 1778, the Grand Orient published a list of 258 Lodges.

* Gould, vol. v., p. 140. † Ibid., vol. v., p. 145. ‡ Ibid., vol. v., p. 153.

For the next three years there is nothing very remarkable to be recorded.

November 5, 1781, a compact was formed between the Grand Orient and the Scots Philosophic Rite.

In 1784, nine of the Paris Lodges dependent upon the Grand Orient, possessed a Rose-Croix Chapter.

February 17, 1786. The Grand Orient resolved to amalgamate with the Grand Chapter.

1787.—Union of the Grand Orient and Grand Chapter.

Article 6 provided that the chapter shall in future be called Chapitre Metropolitain, receiving a patent from the Grand Orient.

Article 11. The four grades worked by the Chapter were to be continued until otherwise decreed. As the Ritual remained nearly the same, this accounts for the four extra degrees of the French Grand Orient, denominated the Modern or French Rite. The first order comprised the Kadosch Degrees, renamed the Secret Elect; the second, the Scots Degrees, called the Order of Scottish Knights; the third, the Crusading Degrees, under the style of Knights of the East and West; and the fourth, the Rose-Croix Degrees, under the appellation, Knights of the Eagle and Pelican.*

In 1804 Hacquet and De Grasse Tilly arrived in Paris from New York and South Carolina, respectively; the first with his revived Rite of Perfection 25°, and Tilly with the A. and A. S. R. 33°. Around Tilly rallied the dissatisfied Scots Masons; and during the next eight months he dispensed the 32° and 33°, right and left, and erected his Supreme Council 33°.

October 21, 1805, Joseph Bonaparte was proclaimed Grand Master in the Grand Orient. In December the Grand Orient celebrated the *solstitial* fête of the Order.†

October 27, 1813, the Supreme Council of America sought amalgamation with the Grand Orient, then sole authority in Masonic matters, the other rites being merely supplementary.

In 1880, from the chaos of French rites, a symbolic Grand Lodge was evolved. It acknowledged the jurisdiction of the Supreme Council, in all matters concerning the high degrees, over such of its members as passed

* Gould, vol. v., p. 161. † Ibid., vol. v., pp. 164–167.

beyond the third degree. The first declaration of principles read, " Free Masonry rests on the solidarité humaine."

The Grand Lodge was composed of deputies from each Lodge, who need not be members of Provincial Lodges, but must be of the Paris Lodges, and also residents of the metropolis. The members of the Grand Lodges were elected as the Executive Commission; they could not accept or hold grand office. A President was substituted for the Grand Master, who directed the meetings of the Grand Lodge, but had no executive power.*

In 1885, the Grand Orient had 294 Lodges, of which 32 had a Chapter or other body attached to them.

At the same time the Supreme Council of the A. and A. Scottish Rite had 80 Lodges, 19 Chapters, and 5 Areopagi; and the Mother Lodge, " the Rainbow," of the Rite of Misraim, claimed 5 subordinate Lodges.

SPAIN.—The first Lodge in Spain was founded by the Duke of Wharton, in his apartments at Madrid, February 15, 1728, under a deputation granted by Lord Coleraine, Grand Master of England.†

But as the Romish Church has always, where it was in power, arrogated to itself the sole privilege of holding secret meetings and tribunals, it has relentlessly persecuted Free Masons wherever it could reach them by treachery or force, or both. Therefore, the introduction of Free Masonry into Spain, the hot-bed of Popery and congenial soil of its Inquisition, was considered so presumptuous that it must be summarily dealt with. Accordingly the bloodhounds of the Inquisition were let loose, and they soon discovered a Lodge, and seized eight of its members. These were, after a form of examination, condemned to the galleys—a slow torture.

Yet the Fraternity persisted in meeting, and the Lodges increased for a short time; but only for a short time, for, on July 2, 1751, Torrubia, a member of the Inquisition, obtained from Ferdinand VI. a decree condemning Masons to death without the benefit of a trial of any kind. To facilitate his operations, Torrubia treacherously caused himself to be initiated. He then betrayed every member's name to the Inquisitors, and to alarm the Inquisition and spur it to greater exertions, he reported ninety-seven Lodges in Spain.

* Gould, vol. v., p. 193. † Ibid., vol. vi., p. 312.

PRISON OF THE INQUISITION.

This resulted in an extensive persecution of the craft. Nevertheless meetings continued to be held, even in Madrid.

According to Don Rafael Sunye, Spanish Free Masonry declared itself independent of England in 1767, and the Free Masons' "Calendar" of 1776 alludes to an independent Lodge in Spain. In the former year the Count d'Aranda, the Prime Minister of Charles III., and Grand Master of Masons, had succeeded in procuring the banishment of the Jesuits. Subsequently this Grand Lodge became permeated with French ideas, and took the name of Grand Orient. In 1795 Count d'Aranda having lost his liberty, his nominee, the Count de Montijo, was elected Grand Master. In 1806 the Royal Order of Scotland at Rouen was enabled to found a Spanish Grand Lodge of the Order at Xeres. This appears to have been followed by the erection of a real *Scottish* Lodge in 1807, the "Desired Reunion," numbering 276 on the roll of the Grand Lodge of Scotland; and in the same year, James Gordon was appointed Prov. Grand Master "over all the Lodges under that jurisdiction," east of Balbos in Andalusia."

Again, however, the war between fanaticism and Free Masonry was to be renewed. For on the return to power of Ferdinand VII., he commenced a fresh persecution of the craft. On May 4, 1814, he re-established the Inquisition, and declared Free Masonry treason. This petty despot began his work in September, by the arrest and imprisonment of twenty-five members of the craft in Madrid, among whom was General Alava, Wellington's aide-de-camp. The plan he followed was to hand the suspected persons over to the bloody Inquisition. But instead of being intimidated by this Popish tool, it consolidated its position, and at its head was found the liberal leaders of the day.* In 1818, Riego Arguelles, the brothers San Miguel, and others assisted in the deliberations in Madrid, which resulted in a union of the two Supreme Councils of which Riego became Grand Master. This was followed by the uprising in 1820, headed by Riego, which brought his Catholic majesty to terms, and on the 9th of July he regranted the Liberal Constitution, abolished the Inquisition, and expelled the Jesuits. But in 1823, Ferdinand, with the assistance of French troops, suppressed the Brotherhood. He then had Riego shot; and on the 1st of August, 1824, he issued an edict by which all Free

* Gould, vol. vi., p. 315.

FREE MASONRY IN EUROPE.

Masons who failed to deliver up their papers and renounce the Society in thirty days, were to be executed without trial. Therefore, September 9, 1825, a Lodge at Granada having been surprised, seven of its members were murdered, and the candidate for admission was given eight years of forced labor.

Lieutenant-Colonel Galvez was hanged in Barcelona, and two other members of the craft were condemned to the galleys for life. Notwithstanding this persecution, the craft continued to consolidate, although compelled to exercise great secrecy in its proceedings.

There were, in 1885, 60 Lodges under the Grand National Orient; under the Grand Orient of Perez, in 1881, 60 Lodges; under the Grand Lodge, in 1885, there were 100 Lodges. G. L. of Seville, 25; under the G. O. of Portugal, 41 Lodges. Under French Bodies, 6; G. O. of Italy, 1. Besides these, there is the Grand Spanish, Independent Symbolic Lodge, established at Seville on February 7, 1881, with jurisdiction over the first three degrees.*

PORTUGAL.—The Masonic Institution was established in this country in 1736, when a Lodge was established at Lisbon, under a deputation to George Gordon from Lord Weymouth, Grand Master of England. In 1743 an attempt was made by John Coustos to establish a second Lodge, but he and his companions were arrested by the Inquisition, and the Lodge suppressed, yet Free Masonry continued to exist, although secretly practised. In 1776 other arrests were made by the Inquisition, and for over half a century the history of Masonry in Portugal was blackened by a relentless persecution carried on by the Church. In 1805, however, the Fraternity had become sufficiently numerous to establish a Grand Lodge at Lisbon, of which Egaz-Moritz was elected Grand Master.† During his exile, John VI. issued from Santa Cruz a decree which declared that every Mason who should be arrested should suffer death, and his property be confiscated to the State; and this law was extended to foreigners residing in Portugal as well as to natives. On his restoration to the throne, in 1823, this bigot promulgated another decree against the Order, and Free Masonry fell into abeyance; but in 1834 the Institution again revived. In addition to the persecutions dissensions in reference to

---
* Gould, vol. vi., p. 318.   † Mackey, p. 594.

Masonic authority arose among the Fraternity of Portugal, which increased the confusion in the history of the Order in that country.

Previous to 1846, there were no less than four bodies claiming Masonic jurisdiction, namely, a Grande Oriente Lusitano, which had existed for over a quarter of a century, and which, in 1846, received Letters-Patent from the Supreme Council of Brazil for the establishment of a Supreme Council; a Provincial Grand Lodge under the jurisdiction of the Grand Lodge of Ireland, with a Chapter of Rose-Croix, under the authority of the Grand Council of Rites of Ireland; and two Grand Orients working under contending Grand Masters. To add to the difficulty, another body calling itself the Orient of the Masonic Confederation appeared in the field in 1862. But all embarrassments were removed in 1871 by the union of the different bodies, so that the Masonic interests of Portugal are now prosperously conducted by one governing power—the " Grande Oriente Lusitano Unido. Supremo Conselho de Maconaria Portugueza." Lodges in 1885, 70. Members, 2,800.

ITALY.—Returning to Italy, the cradle of the Colleges of Builders, a few of her renowned craftsmen will first be noticed. John de Medicis, of the house of Medici,* and after him his son, Cosmo I., were educated at Florence, and each became Master or Superior of the Masons, and the Society or Lodge was called the Revivers, because they were instrumental in reviving the Augustan style of architecture.

Following these, in 1465, came the celebrated Bramante. He studied Masonry at Milan, examined the remains of architecture throughout Italy, and became so proficient in the art as to be employed by two successive Popes in building public edifices. Finally, under Pope Julian II., he was ordered to draw the design for St. Peter's at Rome, and at the head of a large assembly of cardinals, clergymen, and craftsmen, he levelled the cornerstone, A.D. 1507. But Bramante only lived to superintend the work seven years. He died in 1514, and by order of Pope Leo X. was buried in the church.

Raphael, who had studied Masonry under Bramante, succeeded him as superintendent of St. Peter's until he died, A.D. 1520. He was followed by

* Mitchell, vol. i., p. 142.

Jocunde and Anthony San Gallo, who superintended this vast work until they died, 1535, when Pope Paul III. appointed Michael Angelo. Angelo was then the most celebrated draughtsman, and subsequently the most distinguished architect, of that, or perhaps any other, age. Not liking the draughts of his predecessors, he made a new model, by which that lofty and magnificent temple was carried on to completion. He died at the age of ninety years, but he did not cease to be the recipient of honors even after his death, for the Grand Duke of Tuscany stole the corpse and followed it, at the head of a long procession of Masons, to St. Croce, at Florence, where it was interred with Masonic honors.

Cosmo the Second was created Grand Duke of Tuscany; and he soon became so eminent for his knowledge of architecture and his devotion to Masonry that Pope Pius V. and the Emperor Ferdinand styled him the Great Duke of Tuscany. He was general Supervisor of all the Masons of Italy; and he it was who established the famous College at Pisa for the education and improvement of apprentices. He died A.D. 1574.

Passing from names that have rendered Operative Masonry famous, we come to *Speculative* Masonry in Italy; and in no country has the Institution been subjected to greater vicissitudes of fortune than here.

The first traces of Free Masonry in Italy are found at Florence, a Lodge having been established there in 1733 by the Duke of Dorset.*

In 1750 there was a Lodge opened by a Greek at Naples, and soon after this Masonry became wide-spread through the cities of Italy.

In 1764 a National Grand Lodge was erected with four Lodges at Naples, and an equal number distributed throughout the other cities of the kingdom.

Free Masonry was introduced into Rome at an early date, and on August 16, 1735, a regular Lodge was opened there under J. Colton.† August the 17th, 1737, the Inquisition seized its members, and on the 20th it was closed. In 1738 the bull of Clement XII. was published, and was confirmed by a further edict in 1739, forbidding Free Masonry throughout the Papal States under pain of death and confiscation of property. Notwithstanding this, another Lodge was established at Rome in 1787, but was surprised by the Inquisition,

* Mackey, p. 371. † Gould, vol. vi., p. 299.

FREE MASONRY IN EUROPE. 451

December 27, 1789. A convenient secret passage facilitated the escape of the brethren, but the property and archives were seized.

Passing from this to 1872, we find that in that year, the new Constitutions were accepted, and in 1873 the Supreme Council at Palermo amalgamated with the Grand Orient, which has ever since been the governing Masonic body in Italy, and under which Free Masonry has flourished. In 1901 there were 109 Lodges and 13,500 members. The seat of the Grand Orient is now at Rome, and Popery can contemplate its presence with impotent rage.

The other Grand Bodies are the Supreme Council at Palermo (A. and A. S. R.), 39 Lodges, and the Grand Council at Milan (Craft), 7-8 Lodges.*

Greece.—The first Lodges opened in this country were established at Corfu by the Grand Orient of France; the first in 1809 and the second in 1810.

In 1835 the third Lodge, Pythagoras, was opened at the same place. Later a Royal Arch Chapter was attached to this Lodge. In 1840 a Grand Lodge was organized at Corfu, Calichiopulo Grand Master.

Between 1860 and 1866 eight additional Lodges were established at Athens, Syra, Piræus, Chalkis, Corfu, Patras, Lamia, and Argos. These were under the Grand Orient of Italy. In 1867 these Lodges, with the consent of the Grand Orient of Italy, formed an independent Grand Lodge of Greece. In 1872 Prince Rhodocanakis, of Scio, was elected Grand Master. This G. M. held the office until 1881, when he was succeeded by Nicholas Damaschino. There is also a Supreme Council, 33 degrees, established here. All the different bodies are in a flourishing condition. There were 12 Lodges in 1901.

Malta.—Free Masonry was established here, in 1735. In 1740 the Bull of Clement XII., forbidding the meetings of Masons, was published at Malta. But the institution has survived papal anathemas, and there are now 8 Lodges on the island.

* Gould, vol. vi., pp. 299-305.

ASIA.

Turkey.*—It is claimed that there was a Masonic meeting in Constantinople in 1748, at which some Turks were initiated, but that the government prohibited the meetings. Organized Masonry was not introduced into Turkey until 1838, when Lodges were chartered by the Grand Lodge of England. They were likewise soon discontinued, in consequence of the opposition of the Mohammedan hierarchy.

The late war with Russia, and the threatening attitude of that and other great powers toward Turkey, has had the effect, however, of securing from that country an enforced tolerance of the institutions of civilization, especially Free Masonry. So that there are now twelve Lodges in the Mohammedan capital, two at Beyrout, one at Ephesus; and even in ancient Damascus, that hot-bed of Mohammedanism, there is a Lodge in successful operation. And last but not least, there is a Lodge at Jerusalem. In fact, there have been two Lodges established here, one of which was opened in a vault under the very site of King Solomon's Temple. But from the difficulty in reaching this singular Lodge-room, the meetings did not long continue.

Not only Lodges, but Chapters, Rose-Croix Chapters, and Councils are becoming numerous, both in Constantinople and Smyrna.

Number of Lodges in Turkey, 31.†

Persia has one Lodge. It is located at the capital, and comprises the members of the Court.

Bombay.—First Lodge established in 1758. Number of Lodges in 1903, 29.

Bengal.—A deputation was granted by the Grand Lodge of England to George Pomfret, in 1728, authorizing him "to open a Lodge in Bengal." He was succeeded by Captain Ralph Farwinter. In 1730 another Lodge was duly established, which is described as No. 72, at Bengal, in the East Indies.

Farwinter was followed by James Dawson and Zech Gee, who held the office in 1740; after whom came Roger Drake, who was appointed April 10,

---

* Placed in Asia because a large part of its present territory is in that division of the globe.
† Gould, vol. vi., pp. 320, 321.

RELIC OF AN OLD INSTITUTION.

1755. Drake was Governor of Calcutta at the time of the attack made by Surajah Dowlah, in 1756. He escaped the horrors of the Black Hole by flying to the shipping, but had the satisfaction of being present at the retaking of Calcutta by the forces under Clive and Watson, in January, 1757.

William Mackett was the next Provincial Grand Master, 1760, Culling Smith in 1762, and Samuel Middleton in 1767.

The number of Lodges under the Grand Lodge of Bengal, previous to 1903, was 51; under the Grand Lodge of Scotland, 11.

There were also Lodges at Chandernagore, Patna, Burdwan, Dacca, and Moorshedabad. The Provincial Grand Lodge under England worked in perfect harmony with a similar body under Holland. The officers and members of the two societies exchanged visits and walked together in processions.

On the 14th of January, 1789, a grand ball and supper was given by the Prov. Grand Lodge, to which invitations were sent to residents in Calcutta, to Titsingh, Governor of Chinsurah, and other Masons of that colony; to Bretel and the other Masons of Chandernagore; also to the Masons of Serampore and other colonies, according to custom on such occasions in India.

Madras.—The first Lodge in Southern India was established at Madras in 1752. Three others were formed at the same station in 1765. Later, about 1766, Captain Edmond Pascal was appointed Provincial Grand Master for Madras and its dependencies; and in the following year a fifth Lodge was erected at St. George. For a brief period this Presidency predominated over the other English settlements in India; and from 1750 to 1800 the continuous wars with the French, and afterward with Hyder Ali and his son, caused the Carnatic to figure largely in Indian history.

A Lodge was established by the Athol Grand Lodge of England at *Fort St. George*, in 1768; and in 1773 a Lodge was opened by the Grand Lodge of Holland at Negapatam.

The next important event was the initiation, in 1776, of Umdat-ul-Umara, eldest son of the Nabob of Arcot, at Trichinopoly. In his reply to the congratulations of the Grand Lodge of England, he stated that "he considered the title of an English Mason as one of the most honorable he possessed." There were 27 Lodges in 1903.

China.—The first Lodge opened in this country was at Canton in 1767. The number of Lodges in 1903 was 18.

Japan.—The first Lodge here was established in 1866. The number of Lodges in 1903 was 6.

Ceylon.—The first Lodge was opened at Colombo, this island, by the Grand Lodge of Holland in 1771; and another by the same authority at Point de Galle, 1773. In 1795 the English took possession of the Dutch settlements on the island, and annexed them to the Presidency of Madras; and in 1801, Ceylon was formed into a separate Crown colony. The number of Lodges in 1886 was six.

Sumatra.—A Lodge was established at Bencoolen in 1765, and two others at Fort Marlborough in 1772 and 1796, respectively.

In 1886 there were two Lodges on the island, one, Mata Hari, at Padang; the other, Prince Frederick, at Kotta Raja—both constituted by the Grand Lodge of Holland.

AFRICA.

Egypt.—It is claimed that Free Masonry was introduced into this country by Napoleon and his officers, in 1798. In 1802, a Lodge was established at Alexandria, and another at the same place in 1806. Others followed, at Cairo, Mansourah, Ismaila, Port Said, and Suez.

The governing body is styled the " National Grand Lodge." Grand Master, in 1890, the Khedive. Number of Lodges at the same time, 20; members, 600. Egypt has also a Grand Orient.

Tunis.—The first Lodge was established here, in 1860. In 1886, there were 6 French Lodges, two English, and one under the Grand Orient of Italy. Of the French Lodges, two hail from the Grand Orient. One of them bearing the name, New Carthage.

From the leading journal of this country it appears that there is in existence an extensive system of " Moslem Political Free Masonry." It has five subdivisions, one of which—the powerful confraternity of Sidi Abdel Kader el Chiliani—has a college at Kairwan.

Algeria.—The first Lodge founded in this country was by the French in 1832. There were in 1886 ten Lodges under the Grand Orient, and five under the S. C. 33 degrees of France. Throughout Northern Africa, the people who take the most intelligent interest in Free Masonry are the *Arabs* of Algeria, of whom the late heroic Abdel Kader was a prominent example.

Ciprian Kuerevoski, an eminent Mason, thus describes in an Egyptian newspaper his visit to an Arabian Lodge: "The Temple is richly ornamented in oriental style; the chair in the East is higher and five steps guide to it. The rear of the chair is painted blue, and adorned with stars; also the moon in silver, and the sun in gold are seen. Over the seat of the Master is a canopy of velvet with gilt fringes. In the midst of the Temple is the Altar with the Constitution. In the west, right and left, are the seats of the Wardens. The apron is white, with a green triangle. The Master and officers wear a green sash across the breast. There were fifty members belonging to this Lodge." *

Morocco.—In 1867, a Lodge was formed at Tangier under the S. C. of France. There is another, under the Grand Orient of Spain, at Ceuta.

The first Lodge established in the western portion of the dark Continent, was at **Bulam**, in 1792. This was followed by Torridzonian Lodge, at Cape Coast Castle, in 1810.

Two other English Lodges were established in this district—one, at **Cape Coast Castle,** 1859; and another at **West Coast,** in 1867—both of which are active.

At **Senegal**—French Senegambia, there are two Lodges; one was opened in 1874 under the Grand Orient of France, and the other is under the Grand Orient of Italy.

Liberia.—This little Republic was founded in 1821 by the American Colonization Society, for a home for the freed slaves from the United States.

* See Report of Correspondence in Proceedings of Grand Lodge of New York, 1890, p. 153.

It has since been recruited by emigrants of the same class and by the cargoes of captured slave vessels. It was recognized as an independent Republic by Europe in 1848. The date of the advent of Free Masonry here is uncertain, but in 1867 a Grand Lodge was organized.

Cape of Good Hope—South Africa.—Two Dutch Lodges were opened at Cape Town, the first in 1772, and the second in 1802. Other Lodges followed, not only at Cape Town, but in the Orange Free State, Transvaal, and the Boer Republics. So that in 1886 there were altogether 91 Lodges.

Mozambique.—This island lies near the southeast coast of Africa, and, with the town, forms the capital of the Portuguese possessions here. It has two Lodges, both of which are under the United Grand Lusitanian Orient.

Mauritius—Isle of France.—Prior to 1790, four Lodges, under the G. O. of France, were established at Port Louis—the first in 1778; the second in 1785; the third in 1786; and the fourth in 1790.

The Azores.—These islands, which form a province of Portugal, have one Lodge—under the United Grand Lusitanian Orient. In MADEIRA there are three Lodges, and in the CANARIES nine, holding warrants from the same Grand Orient.

St. Helena.—A Lodge was opened on this island in 1764, and another, under the Grand Lodge of England, in 1798. Both Lodges were extinct in 1832; but, in 1843, another Lodge was established here, and a second in 1862, both of which meet at James Town

AUSTRALASIA.

New Zealand, Tasmania, and Australia were originally under the government of New South Wales, but they subsequently became independent colonies.

New South Wales.—The first Lodge heard of here, was that of Social and Military Virtues, attached to the Forty-sixth Foot; and was at work at Sydney in 1816.

FREE MASONRY IN AUSTRALASIA.

This was followed by the establishment of stationary Lodges at Sydney, the capital, in 1820, 1824, and 1828.

The next Lodges were established at Paramatta in 1838. During the last decade Free Masonry has increased rapidly in this colony—their reports showing, in 1901, 187 Lodges, with a membership of 8,186.

Victoria.—A Lodge was opened at Melbourne by the Grand Lodge of England in 1841, and two others in 1846.

The number of Lodges in 1900 was 186. This includes one at Levuka, Fiji.

South Australia.—The first Lodge was constituted in 1834. Two others were established at Adelaide in 1844.

In 1901, the number of Lodges established in South Australia was 43.

West Australia.—The first Lodge formed in this colony was St. John, at Perth, in 1842. Number of Lodges, 49.

Tasmania.—Lodges under the Grand Lodge of Ireland were established at Hobart Town as early as 1823. In 1846 English Masonry obtained a footing on the island, and Tasmanian Union was formed at Hobart Town. A second English Lodge was opened in 1852. Number of Lodges in 1901, 20.

New Zealand.—The first Lodge established in this colony was at Akaroa, in 1843; the second was opened at Auckland in 1844; and the third in 1845. Later, Lodges were established at Lyttelton, Christ Church, New Plymouth, Auckland, Wanganui, Nelson, Kaiapoi, Napier, and Dunedin.

There were in 1901 117 Lodges, with a membership of 5,385.

North Island.—Auckland District.—In this colony there were in 1886 eighteen Lodges under the G. L. of England, and six each, under those of Scotland and Ireland.

In the **Wellington District** there were thirty Lodges at the same date.

Middle, or South Island.—Canterbury District.—The District Grand Masters in 1886 were Henry Thomson and the Rev. James Hill, who ruled over nineteen, and nine Lodges respectively.

Otago and Southland District has two District Grand Lodges with fourteen Lodges each.

Westland District has nine Lodges.

Marlborough and Nelson District have six Lodges.

Fiji Islands.— The first Lodge formed in these once cannibal islands, was at Levuka, in 1872, and by consent of King Thakombau. In 1874 the islands were annexed to England, and on February 1, 1875, a Scottish charter was granted to a Lodge here. A second English Lodge was established in the archipelago by the Grand Lodge of England in 1881. Three Lodges in 1903.

For other small countries, see table of statistics, page 557.

CHAPTER XII.

THE WESTERN HEMISPHERE.

INTRODUCTION OF FREE MASONRY INTO NORTH AND SOUTH AMERICA, AND ADJACENT ISLANDS.

The United States.—The First Lodges, and Grand Lodges in all the different States and Territories.—Primitive Proceedings in Early Lodges. —Remarkable Masonic and Social Career of a Prominent Mason.— He builds a Castle and Marries a Beautiful Indian Girl.—Destruction of his Castle by the Indians.—Establishment of a Lodge at Crown Point in the Stirring Days of the Revolution.—A Mason bound to the Stake by the Indians to be Burnt, but is Saved by Making the Sign of Distress.—Original and Highly Interesting Records of various Old Lodges. —Washington's Headquarters at Morristown, N. J., in the Winters of 1777 and 1779.—A Lodge Opened there, in which General Lafayette was Initiated.—Free Masonry in the Dominion of Canada, and in the Countries of South America and the West India Islands.—Statistics of Free Masonry throughout the World in 1890-91.

IN considering the time and place of the opening of the first lodge in this hemisphere the question arises as to what constituted the introduction of the institution into a country, after its reorganization in 1717. Whether a deputation or warrant from the Mother Grand Lodge in London, empowering a certain person to act as Master, or Grand Master, was necessary, or whether the action of a number of reputable members of the Fraternity, in meeting, constituting themselves a Lodge of Free Masons, and working as such, was all that was required. That Masonic Lodges met and did work very nearly the same as is done in the Lodges of the present day, practised Free Masonry long before the transformation in London in 1717, long before the era of Grand Lodges as now constituted, is a fact well known in Masonic history.*

It is also well understood that for at least a decade of years after the establishment of the Grand Lodge in London, its functions and prerogatives were poorly defined and worse understood. Therefore it is not strange that during this period members in a distant country should meet, establish Lodges, and do the work of Free Masonry without warrant.

That this was the case is shown by the Masonic records of several of the American colonies, notably Massachusetts, Pennsylvania, and New York.

Among the early settlers of this country were members of the Masonic Fraternity, men who had been made Masons in Europe, principally in England, and early in the eighteenth century had commenced in several places to hold Lodge meetings. In 1730 they were deemed to be sufficiently numerous by the Grand Lodge of England to entitle them to a Grand Master. Accordingly Daniel Coxe was appointed for New York, New Jersey, and Pennsylvania; and soon after this, Henry Price was appointed for Massachusetts.

It is claimed by some, however, that during the incumbency of Coxe he did not do an official act; while others assert that Price's commission was not genuine; still the fact stands as previously stated, that the Grand Lodge of England considered the Fraternity sufficiently strong in the above-named Colonies, in 1730–1733, to require the presence of Grand Masters. But at what particular place, or at what time, the *first meeting* of Free Masons took place in North America, there is no certain data for determining.

THE UNITED STATES.

New York.—That Free Masonry was practised in New York as early as in any part of this country will appear from the following: The Grand Lodges of Pennsylvania and Massachusetts both claim priority as to the establishment of the institution in the American Colonies, and while both granted warrants for Lodges in the Provinces, States, and Territories, and even in four foreign countries, they never warranted a Lodge for New York.

In 1730, Daniel Coxe received a deputation from the Grand Lodge of

* Notes 3, 6, 8, and 9, pp. 560–561.

England constituting him Provincial Grand Master of New York, Pennsylvania, and New Jersey. But, as above stated, Lodges had met in this country, doubtless in New York City, previous to this date.

From the Text of the Deputation to Coxe.

"Norfolk, Grand Master.

"To all and every our Right Worshipful and loving brethren now residing, or who may hereafter reside, in the Province of New York, New Jersey, and Pennsylvania, His Grace Thomas, Duke of Norfolk, Grand Master of Free and Accepted Masons of England,

"SENDETH GREETING:

" *Whereas*, application has been made unto us by our Right Worshipful and well-beloved Brother, Daniel Coxe, of New Jersey, and by *several other* brethren, Free and Accepted Masons, residing and about to reside in the said province of New York, New Jersey, and Pennsylvania, that we should be pleased to nominate and appoint a Provincial Grand Master of the said Provinces: Now know ye that we have nominated, ordained, constituted and appointed, and do by these Presents nominate, ordain, constitute and appoint, our Right Worshipful and well-beloved Brother, the said Daniel Coxe, Provincial Grand Master of the said Provinces of New York, New Jersey, and Pennsylvania, with full power and authority to nominate and appoint his Deputy Grand Master and Grand Wardens, for the space of two years, from the feast of St. John the Baptist, now next ensuing, after which time it is our will and pleasure, and we do hereby ordain, that the brethren who do not reside in all or any of the said Provinces, shall and they are hereby empowered every other year, on the feast of St. John the Baptist, to elect a Provincial Grand Master, who shall have the power of nominating and appointing his Deputy Grand Master and Grand Wardens. And we do hereby empower our said Provincial Grand Master, and the Grand Master, Deputy Grand Master and Grand Wardens for the time being, for us and in our place and stead, to constitute the said brethren (Free and Accepted Masons) now residing, or who shall hereafter reside, in these parts, into one or more regular

Lodge or Lodges, as he shall think fit, and as often as occasion shall require.

" Given under hand and seal of Office, at London, this fifth day of June, 1730, and of Masonry 5730." *

Colonel Coxe was born in London, in August, 1673. He was the son of a London physician, and in 1703 he received his appointment as Colonel of all the military forces in West Jersey. In 1705 he was made a member of the Provincial Council, and so continued until 1713.

The Coxe family mansion at Trenton, New Jersey, was burned by the British troops in 1777, and with it were destroyed many of the family records and papers.†

The second Provincial Grand Master of New York was *Richard Riggs*, under a deputation granted by the Earl of Darnley, November 15, 1737.

The third deputation for the Grand Mastership was granted by Lord Byron to *Francis Goelet*, in 1751.

Further than that the anniversaries were celebrated during Goelet's incumbency, the records do not inform us.

The fourth deputation was granted by R. W. John Proby, Baron of Carysfort, June 9, 1753, to *George Harrison;* but he was not installed until December 27th, the ceremony then took place in Trinity Church.

His energetic administration gave the Masonic institution a powerful impetus not only in New York, but in neighboring States.

The fifth Grand Master, under a deputation from the Grand Lodge of England, was Sir John Johnson, son of Sir William Johnson.

From the records of St. Patrick's Lodge, it appears that he was commissioned by Lord Blaney in 1767, but he was not installed as Grand Master until 1771.

As newspapers always afford good current history of passing events and serve to verify regular history, quotations from the press of the day will be made.

* Note 16, p. 562. † Note 17, p. 562.

From the New York Gazette,* November 28, 1737.

"There being a new and unusual sect or Society of Persons of late appeared in our native Country, and from thence spread into some other Kingdoms & Common Wealths, and at least has extended to these parts of America, their Principle, Practices and Designs not being known, nor by them published to the World, has been the reason that in Holland, France, Italy, and in other places they have been suppressed.

"All other societies that have appeared in the World have published their Principles and Practices; and when they meet set open their meeting-house doors for all that will come in and see and hear them, but this society called FREE MASONS, meet with their doors shut, and a Guard at the outside to prevent any to approach near to hear or see what they are doing. And as they do not publish their Principles or Practices, so they oblige all their Proselytes to keep them secret, as may appear by the severe oath they are obliged to take at their first admittance."

Here follows an oath similar to the obligation now used.

The *Gazette* of May 21, 1738, announces the arrival of Captain Riggs, from London, in seven weeks from Land's End; and that Lord De La War continues as Governor of New York.

New York Mercury, December 31, 1753.

"On Thursday last, at a Grand Lodge of the Ancient and Worshipful Fraternity of Free and Accepted Masons, a Commission from the Honorable John Proby, Baron of Carysfort, appointing George Harrison, Esquire, to be Provincial Grand Master, was solemnly published, we hear, to the universal satisfaction of all the brethren present; after which, it being the festival of St. John the Evangelist, the members attended service at Trinity Church.

"The order in which they proceeded was as follows:

"First walked the Sword Bearer, carrying a drawn sword; then four Stewards with white maces, followed by the Treasurer and Secretary, who bore each a crimson damask cushion, on which lay a gilt Bible, and the book of

---

* The New York *Gazette* was the first newspaper published in the Province; its publication commenced in 1725, and was edited by Wm. Bradford.

Constitution; after these came the Grand Warden and Wardens; then came the Grand Master himself, bearing a trunchion and other badges of his office, followed by the rest of the Brotherhood, according to their respective ranks —Masters, Fellow Crafts, and Prentices, to about the number of fifty, all clothed with their jewels, aprons, white gloves, and stockings. The whole ceremony was concluded with the utmost decorum, under a discharge of guns from some vessels in the harbor, and made a genteel appearance. We hear they afterwards conferred a generous donation of fifteen pounds from the public stock of the Society to be expended in clothing for the poor children belonging to our charity school; and they made a handsome private contribution for the relief of indigent prisoners."

Mercury, July 2, 1753.

"Sunday the 24th ult., being the Anniversary of the Festival of St. John the Baptist, the Ancient and Right Worshipful Society of Free and Accepted Masons of this City, assembled at Spring Garden the next day, and being properly clothed made a regular procession in due form to the King's Arms Tavern, in Broad Street, near the Long Bridge, where an elegant entertainment was provided; and after drinking His Majesty's and several loyal toasts, the day was concluded in the most social manner, and to the entire satisfaction of all the company."

Mercury, November 19, 1753.

"The Members of the Provincial Lodge of Free and Accepted Masons, in New York, are desired to meet at the King's Arms Tavern on Wednesday, the 19th day of December, on business of importance.

"By order of the Grand Master,

"H. GAINE, *Secretary.*"

Mercury, December 25, 1758.

"The members of Temple Lodge of Free and Accepted Masons, in the city of New York, and also all strange brethren who can conveniently, are desired to attend at the Fountain Tavern, on Wednesday, the 27th inst., in order to celebrate the Festival of St. John. Tickets (without which none will be admitted) for that purpose may be had at the printing office, Hanover Square, until 10 o'clock on Wednesday.

" By order of the Master,
" JOHN ARMSTRONG, *Secretary.*"

Mercury, June 22, 1767.

" The members of the Ancient and Honorable Society of Free and Accepted Masons who are disposed to celebrate the anniversary of St. John, on Wednesday the 24th inst., in conjunction with the members of Trinity Lodge, at their Lodge Hall, are desired to give timely notice to Mr. John Marshall, at the Masons' Arms, at the upper end of Queen Street."

Mercury, December 28, 1767.

" The brethren composing the St. John's Trinity Union and King Solomon's Lodges of Free and Accepted Masons of this city, propose to celebrate the Festival of St. John the Evangelist at the house of Mr. John Jones, Vintner, at the sign of the Masons' Arms, in the fields. Sojourners in the city, members of the Fraternity, are invited to join upon the occasion."

THE ANCIENTS AND THE ATHOL WARRANT.

Following the Grand Mastership of Sir John Johnson, came that of Rev. William Walter.

On January 23, 1781, the Masters and Past Masters of No. 212, English Registry, 441, Registry of Ireland, Zion's Lodge, U. D., and the field Lodges, Nos. 169, 133, 210, convened for the purpose of improving their Grand Lodge, and electing officers. Accordingly, after the Grand Lodge had been opened in due form, the following brethren were nominated and unanimously elected : The Rev. William Walter, Grand Master ; John Stedholme Browning, Sen., Grand Warden ; and John Beardsley, Jun., Grand Warden. Soon after this, a petition was forwarded to the Grand Lodge of England—Ancients, for a Provincial Grand Lodge.*

The request of the petitioners was, on September 5th, granted in what is

---

* Early History and Proceedings of the Grand Lodge of New York, vol. i., p. xiii.

known as the "Athol Charter," of which the following is a copy. (Omitting the long list of titles pertaining to the Duke of Athol.)

No. 219.

(Seal)

ATHOL, Grand Master,
WILLIAM DICKEY, D. G. M.,
JAMES JONES, S. G. W.,
JAMES READ, J. G. W.,

To all whom it may concern :

We, the Grand Lodge of the Most Ancient and Honourable Fraternity of Free and Accepted Masons (according to the old Constitution granted by His Royal Highness, Prince Edwin, at York, Anno Domini, Nine Hundred Twenty and Six, and in the year of Masonry, Four Thousand Nine Hundred Twenty and Six), in ample form assembled, viz. : The Right Worshipful and Most Noble Prince, John the Third, Duke, Marquis, and Earl of Athol, Grand Master of Masons ; do, by these Presents, authorize and empower our Trusty and Well-beloved Brethren, Free and Accepted Ancient Masons, who at the time of this present Writing are or hereafter shall become inhabitants of the Province of New York, in North America, to congregate, form and hold a Provincial Grand Lodge in the City of New York, aforesaid, independent of any former Dispensation, Warrant or Constitution, ordered given or granted by us or any of our Predecessors, Grand Masters of England, to any Mason or Masons residing within the Masonical Jurisdiction, aforesaid ; such Provincial Grand Lodge, when duly constituted, to be held annually, Half-yearly, Quarterly, Monthly, or at any seasonable Time or Times as occasion shall require. And We do hereby nominate, constitute and appoint Our Right Trusty and Well-beloved Brother, William Walter, Master of Arts, to be our Provincial Grand Master ; John Stedholme Browning, Esq., to be our Provincial Senior Grand Warden ; and our Right Trusty and Well-beloved Brother the Reverend John Beardsley, Master of Arts, to be our Provincial Junior Grand Warden, with the Masonical Jurisdiction aforesaid ; who together with the aforesaid Provincial Grand Master and his Deputy, when appointed and installed, and Provincial Grand Wardens, shall be addressed by the Stile and Title of the Right Worshipful Provincial Grand Master, Grand

Wardens, &c. And We do hereby further authorize and empower our said Right Worshipful Provincial Grand Master, William Walter, his deputy, and Grand Wardens, John Stedholme Browning, Esq., and John Beardsley, with the approbation and advice of their Grand Lodge, to grant dispensations, warrants and Constitutions, for the congregating and making Free and Accepted Masons, forming and holding of Lodges within the Jurisdiction aforesaid, according to the most Ancient and Honorable custom of the Royal Craft, in all Ages and Nations throughout the known World. And We do, by these Presents, further authorize and empower our said Trusty and Right Worshipful Brethren, the Provincial Grand Master, Grand Wardens and their legal successors, when in regular Grand Lodge formed, to hear, adjust, and impartially determine all and singular matters of complaint, dispute, debate or controversy, relative to the Craft, within the Jurisdiction aforesaid; strictly requiring all and every of our worthy and loving brethren within the Jurisdiction aforesaid, to be conformable to all and every of the good rules, orders, issues and decrees, which shall from time to time be ordered, issued or decreed by the said Right Worshipful Provincial Grand Lodge; herein reserving to ourselves our ancient prerogative of hearing Appeals, and Administration of such things as shall (bona fide) appear absolutely necessary for the honor and benefit of the Craft in general. And lastly, we do hereby authorize and empower our said Trusty and Right Worshipful Grand Master and Grand Wardens, together with their lawful associates being the installed Masters, Wardens, and Past Masters, of the regular Lodges within the Jurisdiction aforesaid, in Grand Lodge assembled, to nominate, choose and install their successors to whom they shall deliver this warrant, and invest them with their particular jewels and Masonical powers and dignities as Provincial Grand Officers, etc., etc., etc.

And such successors shall in like manner nominate, choose, and install their successors, such installation to be upon or near every Saint John's Day, the twenty-fourth of June, during the continuance of the Provincial Grand Lodge forever. Providing the said Right Worshipful Wiiliam Walter, John Stedholme Browning, Esq, John Beardsley and all the successors, Grand Officers of the said Provincial Grand Lodge, do continually pay due respect to the Right Worshipful Grand Lodge of the most Ancient and Honorable

Fraternity of Free and Accepted Masons, by whom this warrant is granted, otherwise this warrant and Constitution to be of no Force nor Virtue.

Given under our hands and seal of the Grand Lodge in London, the fifth day of September, in the year of our Lord, One Thousand Seven Hundred Eighty and One, in the year of Masonry, Five Thousand Seven hundred Eighty and one, and in the Seventh year of the Grand Mastership of His Grace the Duke ATHOL, &c., &c., &c.*

CHARLES BEARBLOCK, *Grand Secretary*.

Although the Athol warrant was granted in September, 1781, yet the Grand Lodge was not organized under it until December 5, 1782, when William Walter was continued Grand Master by virtue of his appointment in that warrant.

At the first meeting of this G. L., nine Lodges were represented, three belonging to the city, and six " Regimental Lodges " connected with the British army.

At the evacuation of the city, in the fall of 1783, the Regimental Lodges left the country, and with them the Grand Master and other Grand Lodge Officers.

A few days previous to the departure of the British, a Grand Lodge of Emergency was opened, in which the Rev. William Walter resigned his office of Grand Master and nominated as his successor William Cock, who was elected. The Grand Lodge then proceeded to fill the other vacant offices.†

On February 4, 1784, William Cock was succeeded by Robert R. Livingston, whose installation followed on February 18th. Livingston was continued in office until 1800.

March 7, 1787, the Grand Lodge resolved that a Committee be appointed to consider the propriety of continuing the Grand Lodge under the *Athol Warrant*. On June 6th following, the Committee reported in favor of holding under the Athol authority. The following is the report:

"That the Grand Lodge of this State is established, according to the ancient and universal usages of Masonry, upon a Constitution formed by the

---

* See Early History and Proceedings of the Grand Lodge of New York, vol. i., pp. xii.–xvi. ; Mitchel, p. 503. † McClenachan, History of Free Masonry in New York, p. 142.

representatives of the regular Lodges, convened under a legal warrant from the Grand Lodge of England, dated the 5th day of September, in the year of Masonry, five thousand seven hundred and eighty-one, the Most Noble Prince, John the Third, Duke Athol, being the then Grand Master. And your Committee further beg leave to report that, in their opinion, nothing is necessary or essential in the future proceeding of the Grand Lodge upon the subject matter referred to them; but that a Committee be appointed to prepare a draft of the style of warrant to be hereafter granted by the Grand Lodge, co   to the said Constitution. All of which is, nevertheless, most respectfully submitted to the wisdom of the Most Worshipful Grand Lodge.

"Witness our hands this sixth day of June, 5787.
            (Signed)   " W. COCK,
                                     " PETER MCDOUGALL,
                                     " WHITE MATLACK,
                                     " ROBERT COCK." *

The report of the Committee was accepted and confirmed, thus *ratifying* the *Athol Warrant*.

The seal of the Grand Lodge was not, however, changed until August 27, 1788, when " Grand Lodge of the State of New York " was substituted for the previous title.

The next question to be disposed of was that of the rank of Lodges, concerning which the Grand Lodge adopted this recommendation : " That as soon as the Committee appointed to establish the precedency of rank of the Lodges of this city do report, that then all the Lodges in the State be required to take out new warrants and deliver up the old ones, the dues to the Grand Lodge being previously paid."

The report and determination of this subject was finally made June 3, 1789.

* McClenachan, History of Free Masonry in New York, pp. 115, 116.

472 FREE MASONRY IN THE UNITED STATES.

EARLY LODGES IN THE CITY OF NEW YORK, WITH THE DATE OF THEIR ORIGINAL WARRANT AND PLACE OF MEETING.

Title.	Rank.	Date of Warrant.	Place of Meeting.
St. John's Lodge,	No. 1,	1757,	Ann Street, City Hotel, and Green Bay-Tree Tavern.
Ind'p'd't Royal Arch Lodge,	" 2,	1760,	Nassau St., No. 9-87.
St. Andrew's Lodge,	" 3,	1771,	No. 66 Liberty St.
Zion's Lodge,		1773,	
St. John's Lodge,	" 6,	1783,	No. 3 South St.
Hiram,	" 7,	1779,	
Holland,	" 8,	1787,	City Hotel.
Howard,	" 9,	1795,	City Hotel.
Trinity,	" 10,	1795,	St. John's Hall.
Phœnix,	" 11,	1795,	No. 3 South St.
L'Union, Française,	" 14,	1798,	
Abrams,	" 15,	1800,	St. John's Hall.
Washington,	" 16,	1800,	
Warren,	" 17,	1800,	
Adelphi,	" 18,	1802,	St. John's Hall.

Lodge 210, English Registry—Ancients, Warranted February 20, 1779, was located in the city of New York, and was one of the principal Lodges at the organization of the Grand Lodge in 1781-82. On the retirement of the British, the warrant was retained by order of the G. L., and in 1789, the G. L. granted its members a new warrant, as Temple's Lodge, No. 4. In 1794, this name was changed to Jerusalem Lodge. Later, owing to a split in the Lodge, the warrant was revoked, the Lodge divided, and new warrants granted to the members, as Trinity, No. 10, and Phœnix, No. 11.

Solomon's Lodge, No. 212, English Registry—Ancients, was warranted in 1780, and located in the city of New York. This Lodge took part in the formation of the Grand Lodge. In 1788, the name was changed to St. Patrick's, and in 1789 it ranked as No. 5.

Zion's Lodge, U. D.—an Army Lodge, was warranted in 1780. Located in the City of New York, and was represented at the formation of the Grand Lodge.

NOTED LODGES AND MASONIC HALLS.

ST. JOHN'S LODGE, No. 1.

The warrant for this Lodge was granted by George Harrison, Provincial Grand Master, December 7, 1757. It stood No. 2 Provincial Register and 272 English Register. March 3, 1784, St. John's Lodge surrendered its old charter to the Grand Lodge of New York, then in session; and on March 27, 1785, a Grand Steward's Lodge of emergency adopted this resolution:

"*Resolved*, 1st, that St. John's Lodge No. 2, having surrendered its warrant to the Grand Lodge on the 3d of March inst., and agreed to conform to its regulations, be entitled to all the rights and privileges of members of said Grand Lodge, and take rank of all Lodges that may be constituted by the Grand Lodge, after said surrender."

At a session of the Grand Lodge, June 3, 1789, the committee appointed to ascertain the ranks of the several Lodges, from the dates of their respective warrants: "Reported that said St. John's Lodge, No. 2, be considered the oldest Lodge in this city, and take rank as *first*, which was confirmed by the Grand Lodge." This rank the Lodge has retained to the present date.

The following is from a letter written by M. W. John L. Lewis, Jr., G. M., in reply to an invitation to participate with the Lodge at its Centennial Anniversary, December 7, 1857:

"St. John's, No. 1, has not only been the Alma Mater of Lodges, but of Grand Lodges, as well as 'the mother of men;' and on the registry of the Craft in this State has ever maintained the precedency accorded to its numerical position. Ever foremost and earnest in every good work, true and faithful to the Brotherhood, and respectful and loyal to its Masonic superiors, even while zealously maintaining its own chartered rights, it has set a brilliant example for other Lodges to follow; and I can truly rejoice with you that its prosperity has been commensurate with its just deserts as a bright star in our firmament. Long may it so continue; and may the events of your

Anniversary kindle anew such a spirit as will make it indeed 'a light, a landmark, on the cliff of fame.'"

Its Lodge-room was at first in Ann Street; the building was burnt in March, 1770, and rebuilt, and the Lodge opened in it the following November. This Lodge is in possession of the Washington Bible, the one upon which, on April 30, 1789, the oath of office was administered to George Washington, on the occasion of his inauguration as President of the United States. On the cover of this historic Bible is the following: "God shall establish."

St. John's Lodge constituted 5757; burnt down March 8, 5770; rebuilt and opened November 28, 5770; officers then present, Jonathan Hampton, Master; William Butler, Senior Warden; Isaac Heron, Junior Warden."

From the records of this Lodge we learn that the notorious Captain Shays, who headed "Shays' Rebellion," recommended a candidate for initiation, the following being the recommendation:

"Bros: Our friend, Joseph Burnham, has for a considerable time manifested a desire of being initiated in the (friendly or charitable) Society of Free and Accepted Masons at Fishkill. We do therefore recommend him, from personal acquaintance, to be such a person as, when admitted, will do honor to the Craft, and for that purpose beg your assistance and influence.

(Signed) "DANIEL SHAYS, *Captain.*
"OLIVER OWEN, *Lieutenant.*
"IVORY HOLLAND, *Lieutenant.*

"SOLDIERS FORTUNE, April 26th, 1778."

In 1779 the Lodge-room was in the Green Bay-Tree Tavern, in Fair Street. In that year Burnham was taken prisoner by the British, then in possession of New York.

At a later date we get the following from the Lodge Minutes:

"It so happened that Joseph Burnham, a prisoner of war, who was brought to New York, and of course confined in prison, made his escape; but not knowing where to fly, fortunately found his way to the Green Bay-Tree Tavern, in Fair Street, where St. John's Lodge was held, and, indeed, the only one held in this city at the time, where he was kindly received, and a brotherly protection afforded him by Brother Hopkins, the keeper of the house. Brother Hopkins soon prepared a habitation of safety from the pursuers of the afflicted prisoner by securing him in his garret. One evening, after the Lodge had convened, the prisoner, to pass the night, laid himself down to rest on some planks that formed the ceiling of a closet, that opened directly to the centre of the Lodge-room. The boards being unnailed, naturally slipped from their places, and the whole gave way; the door, too, being only fastened by a wooden button, flew open, and gave the Lodge an unexpected visitor, for the poor prisoner stood aghast in the middle of the room. The Brethren, chiefly British officers, enveloped in surprise, called in Brother Hopkins, who explained all, and acknowledged what he had done. They gave him credit for his charitable behaviour to a Brother, and made a generous contribution, with their advice, which was, that Brother Hopkins should transport him as secretly and as expeditiously as possible to the Jersey shore."

Holland Lodge.

This was another Lodge that figured conspicuously in the early history of the order in this city. This Lodge was established in 1787, but the location of its first Lodge-room is uncertain. In 1788, it was in Beekman's house in Cortlandt Street, and later in the old Tontine Tavern, subsequently known as the City Hotel, Broadway and Thames Street (Rector).

Among the first Masters of Holland Lodge were DeWitt Clinton, Elias Hicks, and John Jacob Astor. With these were associated a long list of names prominent in the early history of the city and State. Under date of February 5, 1790, the name of General Jackson appears on the records as a visitor.

Old Masonic Buildings and Halls.

St. John's Hall was at the head of Frankfort Street, on ground afterward covered by French's Hotel. This famous building comprised a hotel, a hall used for political purposes, and a large Lodge-room, which was used by several Lodges of the day.

The City Hotel—the old Tontine—was also a favorite place for Lodge meetings, as St. John's and St. Andrew's Lodges met there for some time;

and it was from this hotel that the Bible was taken on which General Washington took the oath of office as President of the United States.

Masonic Hall was another edifice of note in 1830. It was erected by the Masonic Fraternity in 1826, and stood on the east side of Broadway, between

St. John's Hall.

Duane and Pearl Streets. On the second floor was a saloon 90 feet long by 47 feet wide and 25 feet high, finished in the best style of Gothic architecture. The ceiling was divided into eight arches, from which were pendent numerous ornaments in imitation of the Chapel of Henry the Eighth. This room was used for public meetings, concerts, and balls, and was considered at that time the most splendid apartment of the kind in this country. The third floor was handsomely furnished for the meetings of the Fraternity.

FREE MASONRY IN THE UNITED STATES. 477

This building remained up to a recent date, when it was taken down, and the site is now occupied by Nos. 314 and 316 Broadway.

Morton Commandery and General Lafayette.—Recollections of an Old Mason.

"The coming dedication of a statue to the memory of Marquis de Lafayette having given rise to the question of when and where the Marquis was created a Knight Templar, we, the subscribers, now the only surviving witnesses to the fact, do say as follows:

"I, Adolphus Andreas, now residing in Eighty-sixth Street, in New York City, certify as follows: I was born in the city of New York; was initiated, passed, and raised in German Union Lodge, No. 63, October 14, 1819; was made a Royal Arch Mason in Rising Sun Chapter, No. 16, in 1824, and was Knighted in Morton Encampment, No. 4, in the year 1824. That at the *same time and place* were Knighted the Marquis de Lafayette and his son, George Washington Lafayette; that I received my orders with him at St. John's Hall, then situated in Frankfort Street. That Sir Knight Dr. William H. Piatt was E. C.; Sir Knight Richard Pennell was Generalissimo; that Sir Knight Jared L. Moore was Captain General; and Sir Knight Lebbeus Chapman was Recorder at the time; that I fully recollect the occasion, it being at that time an event to indelibly fix itself upon the memory.

The City Hotel—Old Tontine.

"This conclave, being of the character described, the members of other encampments were invited to be present, and were so; and I have no doubt that this fact has given rise to the impression of the orders of Knighthood having been conferred in another than Morton Commandery.

"I distinctly remember the names of the following Sir Knights who were present at the time.

"Jared L. Moore, William E. Ross, Samuel Maverick, Henry Reill, of Columbian, No. 1, John W. Timson, John Gairen, Lebbeus Chapman (Recorder at the time), and Robert P. Morris, who was the composer of the ode sung at the banquet given by the Grand Lodge to the Marquis and his son, at Washington Hall, then on the corner of Broadway and Reade Street.

MASONIC HALL, BROADWAY AND DUANE STREET, NEW YORK.

"I also remember that on the evening of conferring the order of Knighthood on the Marquis de Lafayette, the order of the Red Cross was conferred.

"I was afterwards Recorder of Morton Commandery, No. 4, and distinctly remember having many times seen the signatures of the Marquis and his son to the by-laws of the encampment.

"A. ANDREAS.

"New York, January, 1889."

"I, John W. Timson, a Sir Knight of Manhattan Commandery, do certify that at that time I was a member of Morton Commandery, No. 4, and was present on the occasion mentioned above, and that the statement of Sir Knight Andreas is true in every respect.

"JOHN TIMSON, SR."

(Timson was a Past Commander of Manhattan at the time of Lafayette's visit.)

"We may add to the foregoing that the Sir Peter Brewer, who acted as one of the officers on that occasion, and Past Master William E. Lathrop, still living, have frequently made statements in our presence to the same effect as the foregoing.

"J. W. SIMONS."

"I do certify that Wesley B. Church was Recorder of Morton Commandery, No. 4, and was also a Notary August 14, 1876, and that Sir Knight Adolphus Andreas and Sir Knight John W. Timson did appear before him on that date and affirm to the facts above. Sir Knight Adolphus Andreas is still living and visits his Lodge and Commandery.

"JOHN W. KEELER,
"Ex-Commander Morton Commandery, No. 4, K. T.

"January 26, 1889."

"Sir Knight Adolphus Andreas and Sir Knight John W. Timson did affirm to the fact above before me.

"WESLEY B. CHURCH, *Notary.*
"August 14, 1876."

"Sir Knight Adolphus Andreas is still living and visits his Lodge and Commandery quite often.

"JOHN W. KEELER,
"Ex-Commander Morton Commandery, No. 4, K. T.

"January 26, 1889."

"The first information I had of a meeting of Masons in this city was June, 1799, at the City Hotel, corner Broadway and Thomas Street; the next was in old Tammany Hall, corner Spruce and Nassau, opposite the Tribune building, southeast corner, also old St. John's Hall, at No. 8 Frankfort Street, also at Oliver and Henry Streets in 1823. Age between 89 and 90 years, will be

90 in June, 1889. I was at the funeral procession of George Washington, carried in my mother's arms.

"In June, 1889, I will be in Masonry (70) seventy years, and now feel that I have as much interest in Free Masonry as I ever had.

"Adolphus Andreas.

"January 28, 1889."

Solomon's Lodge, No. 1, Afterward No. 5, Poughkeepsie.

This city was settled by the Dutch in 1690, and was the State Capital during the Revolution, and it was also here that the Convention to ratify the Constitution of the United States met in 1788.

Solomon's Lodge received its Warrant from Provincial Grand Master George Harrison, in 1771.

The following are extracts from its records:

"At a meeting of the Brethren of the Ancient and Honorable Society of Free Masons at the house of Lewis Duboise at Poughkeepsie in Dutchess County.

"Present:

"Robert R. Livingston, Master of Union Lodge in New York,
James Livingston,   Anthony Hoffman,
Jonathan Lewis,   Philip J. Livingston,
John Childs,   Malcolm Morrison,
Andrew Bostwick,   Michael Hopkins.

"Robert R. Livingston read the Deputy Grand Master's Warrant for Constituting this Lodge by the name of Solomon's Lodge, No. 1, of Poughkeepsie. Following the reading of the warrant,

"Robert R. Livingston gave a brotherly Charge to the Members present, and having opened the Lodge in Due Form, installed the following officers:

"James Livingston, Master,

"Jonathan Lewis, Senior Warden,

"John Child, Junior Warden.

"The Lodge then proceeded to make the following rules and orders for their future Government:

"That all Candidates on being made entered Apprentices shall pay fee of Five Pounds, York money, into the Treasury.

'That all Master Masons on being admitted Members of this Lodge shall pay forty shillings in like manner.

"That all Fellow Craft on the like admission shall pay fifty shillings in like manner.

"That all Entered Apprentices on the like admission shall pay Three Pounds in like manner.

"That all Members (not Master Masons) shall receive their degrees without other fees than above mentioned.

"That the Members of this Lodge shall pay into the Treasury thereof eight shillings each Quarterly.

"That on ballotting for a Candidate or Member one black bean shall exclude without any further Question.

"That all Candidates on being proposed to the Lodge shall be ballotted for on the Regular Lodge night following their being proposed; and if found worthy to remain on the books till the next Lodge night, then to be admitted.

"The Master and Junior Warden then proposed to the Lodge Lewis Duboise as a Candidate.

"On being ballotted for and found worthy, ordered that he be admitted next Lodge night.

"Michael Hopkins proposed Reuben Hopkins as a Candidate, and being balloted for and found worthy, ordered as above.

"The Lodge Closed in due form to be opened again on Wednesday in June term next, being the 12th of the Month.

"The Lodge met according to adjournment on Wednesday, the 12th of June, 1771, at the house of Lewis Duboise, in Poughkeepsie. Present:

" James Livingston, in the chair,	" Michael Hopkins,
" Jonathan Lewis, Senior Warden,	" Richard Warner,
" John Child, Junior Warden.	" Andrew Bostwick.

" Visiting Brethren:

" Robert R. Livingston, Junr.,

" Peter Hepburn,

At a full assemblage of the Lodge on May 16, 1781, Andrew Billings Master in the East; Brothers Everett and Myer, Wardens, pro tem. . . .

"Ordered, that the name of Benedict Arnold be considered as obliterated from the minutes of this Lodge."

The name is thoroughly crossed and recrossed, and the letter N placed before, and B after his name, thus: " N. *Benedict Arnold* B."

A committee reported on April 12, 1785, in favor of moving to Brother Vemout's, where they could have candles and fire-wood for twelve pounds a year. The report was accepted and recommendation adopted.

. . . .

Brother Brooks was fined on October 3d, to the extent of one shilling, for not attending Lodge and keeping the keys of the refreshment closet. Thereupon on next Lodge night Brother Brooks resigned as Steward.

On June 23, 1787, John Thomas was elected Master. After the dinner, however, the Lodge having resumed business, the following was placed upon its minutes: "It's the sence of this Lodge that John McBride be expeld with infamy for defrauding the Lodge of its dues." And again on June 23, 1788, that "It's the sence of this Lodge that Brother Reyley be expel'd this Lodge for his unmasonick and fraudulent conduct, and that circular letters be sent to the several Lodges within our acquaintance."

One of the Old By-Laws of Solomon's Lodge.

"Article 1.—In open Lodge without order or decence a dissolution must be the consequence.

"Therefore, at the third stroke of the Master's hammer, a profound silence shall be observed; and if any brother curses, swears, or says anything irreligious, obscene or ludicrous, holds private committees, disputes about Religion or Politics, offers to lay any Wagers, interrupts another brother who is speaking to the Master, or hisses at what he is, or has been speaking, is not on his legs when he has anything to say to the Master, sits down unclothed or with his hat on, or smokes tobacco in open Lodge, or is disguised in Liquor during Lodge hours, such offending Brother shall for the first offence be gently reproved and admonished by the Master; for the second offence shall be fined one shilling; for the third offence be fined two shillings, and for the fourth offence to be immediately expelled from the Lodge and never be admitted again as a visitor or a member unless he be ballotted for and received in like manner with a strange brother, paying all fines due as per these bye Laws and Eight Shillings as a new admission fee if he chooses to be reinstated as a Member."

St. Patrick's Lodge, No. 4.

Among the Lodges that were closely connected with the early history, not only of Free Masonry but of the country, was St. Patrick's Lodge at Johnstown. This Lodge was organized May 23, 1766, under a warrant from George Harrison. Sir William Johnson was the founder and first Master; Guy Johnson was Senior Warden, and Daniel Claus, Junior Warden. The Lodge was organized with fifteen members, and the place of meeting was an upper hall in Sir William's castle known as Johnson Hall.* Sir William continued as Master until December 6, 1770, when he resigned, and Colonel Guy Johnson was elected Master, Daniel Claus, Senior Warden, and Michael Byrne, Junior Warden.

In July, 1771, the Lodge was convened to assist in laying the capstone of the church at Johnstown.

Daniel Claus succeeded Guy Johnson as Master.

Sir William Johnson presented the Lodge with a set of silver jewels that he procured from England.

During the Revolution the jewels and charter were carried to Canada by Colonel Guy Johnson, but were returned after the restoration of peace, and with them a ring belonging to Sir William, which bore the date of 1739. These relics, with his portrait, are carefully preserved in the archives of the Lodge.

The only thing that now marks his grave is a mound which is seen from a window of the Lodge-room.

---

* During the French and Indian Wars Sir William gained a great victory over the French and their allies, under Baron Dieskau, for which the King of England granted him such territory in the Valley of the Mohawk as enabled him to build the castle and live like a feudal baron of mediæval times.

The castle was flanked by strong forts, and armed with cannon to hold the surrounding tribes in subjection and awe.

St. Patrick's Lodge was the pioneer of Free Masonry in the then wilderness of New York west of the Hudson; and its old records bear many names well known in the history of the country.

As Sir William Johnson was a conspicuous figure in the early history of Free Masonry in Central New York, a brief sketch of his life will be given in this connection: He was a native of Ireland, and was born in 1714. He was a nephew of Sir Peter Warren, the naval commander who distinguished himself at the siege of Louisburg, in 1745. Previous to this, Sir Peter had married a sister of Chief-Justice De Lancey, of New York, and had further identified himself with American interests by the purchase of a large tract of country on the Mohawk River; and in 1735 he sent for his nephew, the subject of this sketch, to come over and take charge of his land estate.

In response to this proposal, young Johnson, though only about twenty years of age, came to America and settled on his uncle's lands at Caughnawaga on the Mohawk River. The Mohawk Valley at that time was but sparsely settled by white men, and for many years his principal neighbors and associates were the Indians of the Six Nations, known as the Confederacy of the Iroquois. He learned their language, and often joined with them in hunting, fishing, and other recreations, and by his adroitness and tact obtained an almost unbounded influence over them. He became skilled in their diplomacy, in their traditionary legends, and in their religious ceremonies; and to promote his interests he adapted himself to many of their customs. Soon after his arrival the English Government appointed him its Superintendent of Indian Affairs in the Colony of New York. His official position and his intimacy with the various tribes around him gave him great advantages for traffic, and he made large gains by exchanging European goods for the rich furs of the Indian hunters.

Being genial as well as crafty, many amusing incidents of his intercourse with his Indian neighbors have come down to us.

On one occasion, Hendrick, the chief of the Mohawks, was charmed with the sight of a fine gold-laced coat which Johnson had just procured for himself from England. The cupidity of the chief was excited, and he went to its owner the next day, saying he had dreamed.

"Well, what did you dream?" said Johnson.

"I dreamed," said the chief, "that you gave me the fine coat."

The hint was too strong to be mistaken or unheeded, and the proud chief went away wearing the coat, well pleased with his pretended dream. Soon afterward, meeting the chief, Johnson said to him that he also had dreamed.

"Well, what did you dream?" said Hendrick.

"I dreamed that you gave me a tract of land," said Johnson, describing it.

The chief paused a moment at the enormity of the quantity, but soon said: "You may have the land, but me no dream again; you dream too hard for me."

The tract of land thus gained is said to have been about twelve miles square, and the title was subsequently confirmed to Johnson, by the King of England.

Sir William was twice married. His first wife was a young German girl who had been sold on her arrival in America for her passage-money as a redemptioner, to a Mr. Philips, in the Mohawk Valley. She was so beautiful as to attract the attention of Sir William, and on a friend's advising him to get the pretty girl for a housekeeper, he did so, and subsequently married her.

She was the mother of his son, Sir John Johnson, and of two daughters, who afterward became the wives of Guy Johnson and Colonel Claus.

His second marriage was highly romantic, his wife being a sister of the celebrated *Brant*, an Indian *protégé* of Sir William. She was a Mohawk girl of rare beauty and agility, and being present one day at a military review, she playfully asked an officer to allow her to ride upon his horse with him.

He gave his consent, without thinking she would dare to attempt it; but to his astonishment she sprang with the swiftness of a gazelle upon the horse behind him, and, with her arm around his waist and her dark hair streaming in the wind, she rode about the parade-ground to the amusement and admiration of all present, except the young officer who became so unexpectedly the gallant of the forest fairy. Sir William, who witnessed the spectacle, became enamored with the wild beauty before him, and soon after took her to his house as his wife, in accordance with Indian customs. He treated her with kindness and affection, and she is said to have made him a devoted and faithful wife, and to have borne him several children, which he legitimatized by marrying her according to the ceremonies of the Episcopal Church, a short time before his death. Many of the descendants of Sir William and Molly Brant, it is said, are still living.

He died in 1774, and his death was regarded by our Government as a public loss; for it is believed that, had he lived, he would have used his powerful influence with the Indians to prevent their taking up arms in behalf of the English in the then impending war.

At his death he left a large sum of money to be expended in providing mourning dresses for his Indian friends, and all were provided with some badge to wear with which to show their sorrow for his loss. His authority over the Mohawks had been almost kingly; and no white man ever attained a greater influence with the American Indians than Sir William Johnson.*

Sir John Johnson, son of Sir William, succeeded to his father's position and estates; but instead of exercising his authority and influence over the Indians on the side of his adopted country, he proved to be one of the most vindictive and contemptible Tories that figured in the Revolutionary War. He incited the Indians to murder and plunder even to the destruction of his own settlement. This last act he did not do, however, until he and his Indian allies were defeated by General Sullivan, when finding his cause hopeless, he permitted, if he did not direct, Brant and his dusky warriors to destroy the American settlement on the Mohawk; and whether Johnson intended that his establishment should be included or not, the Indians ransacked his castle. This historic old building is still standing, and in such a state of preservation as to indicate its old time grandeur. On the stair-railings are seen marks made by Indian tomahawks when Brant plundered the house.

Crown Point Lodge.

Crown Point, noted in American history, is on the west shore of Lake Champlain, and seventy five miles north of Albany. In 1758 that section was embraced in Canada, and was under the domination of the French. In 1759 the British took it from the French, and subsequently, by the war of the

* The foregoing account has been drawn largely from Washington and His Masonic Compeers, by Hayden.

Revolution and under the succeeding treaty, the United States gained possession of it. Finally the adjoining territory became a part of New York. In 1758, Jeremy Gridley, of Massachusetts, Provincial Grand Master, authorized Abraham Savage to congregate all Free and Accepted Masons engaged in the expedition intended against Canada into one or more Lodges, as he should think fit, and appoint thereunto proper officers.

On the 4th of August Crown Point surrendered. A Lodge, called Crown Point Lodge, was opened, and twelve officers of the First Infantry were made Masons, Abraham Savage being Master.

An incident transpired here that showed that signs given by a Mason in distress are often talismans sufficiently potent to ward off the shafts of death.

General Isaac Putnam was the subject of the incident that barely stopped short of tragedy. He was born in Massachusetts, was a farmer in early life in Connecticut, and finally a general in the French War. He was captured by the Indians at Crown Point in 1758, and would have been burned alive but for the Mystic Tie. After being bound to a tree, preparatory to burning him, he as a last resort made the sign of distress before the French officer in charge, who happening to be a Mason, he caused the savages to release their intended victim, and thus saved his life. The legend is still related to tourists visiting this historic spot that the intercession by the French officer, in behalf of General Putnam, was in consequence of his recognizing him as a Masonic Brother.

The tree to which he was bound stood a short distance from a creek, on Indian Ridge, and has always been known as "Put's Oak." It was blown down a few years ago, but the stump, eight feet in height, remains as Put's monument.*

From the By-laws of Union Lodge, Albany.

ARTICLE I.—That from and after this 29th day of April, 1773, this Lodge shall assemble on Thursday every Fortnight at the hour to which the same is adjourned, which shall be deemed general or public Lodge Nights, but the Worshipful Master may convene an extra or private Lodge whenever he shall deem it expedient.

* History of Free Masonry in New York, p. 204.

ARTICLE II.—That a member neglecting to attend a public Lodge shall pay a Fine of two Shillings, and a private Lodge one Shilling if duly summoned to such private Lodge, unless he makes Excuse satisfactory to the Body; and a Member coming to Lodge after the appointed Time, shall pay a fine of six Pence, for which Purpose the Secretary shall every Lodge Evening call the Roll and make Report of those who are finable.

ARTICLE V.—That every member of this Lodge shall pay to the Treasurer the annual sum of ten Shillings by quarterly payments, commencing from the Feast of St. John Ye Baptist, and if anyone shall refuse or neglect to pay the same in three months from every such quarter day, having had notice thereof from the Secretary, he shall be expelled and excluded from visiting this Lodge, unless good Cause be shown to the Master and Brethren to induce a Forbearance.

ARTICLE X.—That a visitor shall pay two Shillings for every Visit, except ye first.

ARTICLE XVI.—That when a person is proposed to be made a Mason or become a Member and is rejected, no Member or visitor discover who the members were that opposed his admission, or he shall be expelled if a Member, and if a Visitor never more be admitted to visit.

ARTICLE XX.—That every member refusing to pay his fines shall be forever expelled this Lodge, but the Master with Consent of the Body may remit any Fines.

The above Laws are made and enacted at a public Lodge held on thursday, the xxixth day of april, AL 5773. AD 1773.

THE MORGAN INCIDENT.

In 1826 a Masonic renegade suddenly disappeared from his home in Western New York, and this circumstance was seized upon by political demagogues of the day, who (by the fraudulent claim that the Masonic Fraternity were in league with the opposite political party) succeeded in creating such a feeling against the Order that work was suspended in many Lodges, and the weaker ones gave in to the popular clamor, and surrendered their Charters to their Grand Lodges. But as the structure of Masonry rests on principles

FREE MASONRY IN THE UNITED STATES. 489

that commend themselves to all thinking men, the prejudice against the Institution soon died out, and, phœnix-like, it rose and resumed its operations with such renewed vitality that in the short space of time intervening between the Morgan episode and the present year of grace (1903), it has achieved a membership of over one million, comprising a large proportion of the incumbents of offices, political and commercial, in this country.

GRAND LODGE OFFICERS, FROM 1730 TO 1783.

When Appointed.

1730. Daniel Coxe, Grand Master, by appointment from the Grand Lodge of England.
1737. Richard Riggs, by appointment from the Grand Lodge of England.
1751. Francis Goelet, by appointment from the Grand Lodge of England.
1753. George Harrison, by appointment from the Grand Lodge of England.
1767. Sir John Johnson, by appointment from the Grand Lodge of England.
1781. William Walter, elected from the Grand Lodge of England.
1782. William Walter, by appointment; William Cock, Grand Secretary.
1783, September 19. Walter resigned, and William Cock elected Grand Master; James Clark, Grand Secretary.

TERMINATION OF THE PROVINCIAL GRAND LODGE, AND PRACTICAL COMMENCEMENT OF THE GRAND LODGE OF THE STATE OF NEW YORK.

	Grand Masters.	*Grand Secretaries.*
1783 to February 4, 1784,	William Cock.	James Clark.
1784, February 4,	Robert R. Livingston.	John Lawrence & James Giles.
1785.	Robert R. Livingston.	John Lawrence & James Giles.
1786.	Robert R. Livingston.	James Scott.
1787.	Robert R. Livingston.	James Scott.
1788.	Robert R. Livingston.	Jacob Morton.
1789.	Robert R. Livingston.	Jacob Morton.
1790.	Robert R. Livingston.	Jacob Morton.
1791.	Robert R. Livingston.	Jacob Morton.
1792.	Robert R. Livingston.	John Abrams.
1793.	Robert R. Livingston	John Abrams.

	Grand Masters.	Grand Secretaries.
1794.	Robert R. Livingston.	John Abrams.
1795.	Robert R. Livingston.	John Abrams.
1796.	Robert R. Livingston.	John Abrams.
1797.	Robert R. Livingston.	John Abrams.
1798.	Robert R. Livingston.	John Abrams.
1799.	Robert R. Livingston.	John Abrams.
1800.	Robert R. Livingston.	Rin: Jan Vandenbroeck.
1801.	Jacob Morton.	Daniel D. Tompkins.
1802.	Jacob Morton.	Daniel D. Tompkins.
1803.	Jacob Morton.	Daniel D. Tompkins.
1804.	Jacob Morton.	Daniel D. Tompkins.
1805.	Jacob Morton.	John Wells.
1806.	DeWitt Clinton.	John Wells.
1807.	DeWitt Clinton.	John Wells.
1808.	DeWitt Clinton.	John Wells.
1809.	DeWitt Clinton.	John Wells.
1810.	DeWitt Clinton.	John Wells.
1811.	DeWitt Clinton.	John Wells.
1812.	DeWitt Clinton.	John Wells.
1813.	DeWitt Clinton.	John Wells.
1814.	DeWitt Clinton.	John Wells.
1815.	DeWitt Clinton.	John Wells.
1816.	DeWitt Clinton.	John Wells.
1817.	DeWitt Clinton.	Elias Hicks.
1818.	DeWitt Clinton.	Elias Hicks.
1819.	DeWitt Clinton.	Elias Hicks.
1820.	Daniel D. Tompkins.	Elias Hicks.
1821.	Daniel D. Tompkins.	Elias Hicks.
1822.	Joseph Enos.	Elias Hicks.
1823.	{ Martin Hoffman. { Joseph Enos.	Elias Hicks. Charles G. Haines.
1824.	{ Martin Hoffman. { Joseph Enos.	Elias Hicks. John W. Oakley.

	Grand Masters.	Grand Secretaries.
1825.	Martin Hoffman. Steph. Van Rensselaer.	Elias Hicks. Ebenezer Wadsworth.
1826.	Elisha W. King. Steph. Van Rensselaer.	Elias Hicks. Ebenezer Wadsworth.

Pennsylvania.—The first Lodge or meeting of Free Masons in this Jurisdiction, must have been opened prior to 1730; for, as previously stated, Daniel Coxe received a deputation at that time constituting him Grand Master of New York, Pennsylvania, and New Jersey; therefore the Fraternity were sufficiently numerous to have formed at least one Lodge in each of those Provinces, or there would have been no occasion for a Grand Master.*

From an old Lodge Ledger recently discovered, it appears that there was a Lodge established in Philadelphia as early as the latter part of 1730, or the first part of 1731. It commenced with thirteen members, and met on the first Monday of each month.

This Ledger was entitled "Libre B." It was the Secretary's Ledger, embracing the time from June 24, 1731, to June 24, 1738, and comprises the names of fifty members. "Libre B" indicates that there was, or had been, a Libre A, a still older Ledger, used in an older Lodge.†

In Libre B, Benjamin Franklin figures conspicuously, for in it he is charged (June 24, 1731), "To remainder of your £3. Entrance is £2.0s." He had apparently paid the sum of £1, five months before or some time during that period, as he was also charged with five months' previous dues, indicating that he was made a Mason in February, 1731. The last entries in these records were made by Franklin, and a report drawn up June 5, 1732, by a committee of the members, was in his handwriting.

The following are among the resolutions agreed to by Franklin and the other members of the committee:

"1. That since the excellent Science of *Geometry* and *Architecture* is so much recommended in our Ancient Constitutions, Masonry being first instituted with this design, among others, to distinguish the true skilful Architect from

---

* In 1715, John Moore, Collector for the port of Philadelphia, in a letter to a friend, mentions having spent some evenings with his Masonic Brethren. See Proceedings of the Grand Lodge of Pennsylvania, 1882, p. 152.   † Notes 4, 5, 7, 10, 11, 12, and 13, pp. 560, 561.

unskilful Pretenders; *total ignorance of this art* is very *unbecoming* a Man who bears the worthy Name and Character of *Mason*.

"We therefore conclude, that it is the Duty of every Member to make himself, in some Measure, acquainted therewith, as he should honour the Society he belongs to, and conform to the Constitutions.

"2. That every Member may have an Opportunity of so doing, the present Cash to be laid out in the best Books of Architecture, suitable Mathematical Instruments, etc." *

At the expiration of the Grand Mastership of Daniel Coxe, in 1732, the brethren proceeded to elect a Grand Master to succeed him. This event was thus chronicled in the *Pennsylvania Gazette*:

"Philadelphia, June 26, 1732.

"Saturday last being St. John's Day, a Grand Lodge of the Ancient and Honourable Society of Free and Accepted Masons was held at the Sun † Tavern, in Water Street, when, after a handsome entertainment, the Worshipful W. Allen, Esq., was unanimously chosen Grand Master of the Province for the year ensuing, who was pleased to appoint Mr. William Pringle, Deputy Master. Wardens chosen for the ensuing year were Thomas Boude and Benjamin Franklin."

On June 27, 1734, Franklin was elected Grand Master.‡ After his election, he appointed John Crap, Deputy, and James Hamilton and Thomas Hopkinson, Wardens. Among the members present were the Governor and other notables.

From the Gazette, June 27, 1734.

"Monday last a Grand Lodge of the Ancient and Honourable Society of Free and Accepted Masons in this Province, was held at the Sun Tavern, in Water Street, when Benjamin Franklin, being elected Grand Master for the ensuing year, appointed Mr. John Crap to be his Deputy; and James Hamilton, Esq., and Thomas Hopkinson, Gent., were chosen Wardens. After which a very elegant entertainment was provided, and the Proprietor (Thomas Penn), the Governor, and several other persons of distinction honored the Society with their presence."

* Gould, vol. vi., p. 430.　　†Note 15, p. 562.　　‡ Note 14, p. 562.

Franklin served a second term, which was inaugurated at the "Royal Standard," on Market Street near Second, where he appointed Dr. Thomas Boude, D. G. M., Joseph Shippen, S. G. W., and Philip Syng, J. G. W.

Subsequently, during his diplomatic career, and while a resident in France, Franklin joined the Lodge of the Nine Muses, of which Lalande and other literary celebrities were members. He took a prominent part in the initiation of Voltaire, and on the death of that philosopher acted as S. W. of the Lodge of Sorrow held to celebrate his memory.

In 1735 the Grand Lodge changed its quarters from the Sun Tavern to the Indian King, at the corner of Biddle's Alley, in Market Street, below Third.

June 7, 1758, a Lodge, the present No. 2, was warranted for Philadelphia by the Grand Lodge of the Ancients, and three years later a second Lodge was warranted by the same body.

In 1764 the Ancients warranted a Provincial Grand Lodge for Pennsylvania, and appointed William Ball Grand Master. Soon after the arrivals of warrants from the Ancients, the Grand Lodge and subordinates working under the Grand Lodge of England began to decline in this Jurisdiction, and finally ceased to act under that body.

On September 25, 1786, Lodges Nos. 2, 3, 5, 9, 12, 14, 18, 33, 44, and 45 met and dissolved the Provincial Grand Lodge. These Lodges met with Lodge No. 25 in a little Lodge room in Vidall's Alley, near Second and Chestnut Streets, Philadelphia, and formed the Independent "Grand Lodge of Pennsylvania," and Masonic Jurisdiction thereunto belonging to be held in Philadelphia. William Adock was elected Grand Master. Recognition was then sought from the Grand Lodge of England, and on September 5, 1792, the interchange of friendship and amity became reciprocal.

This Grand Lodge had, in 1891, 387 subordinates, and nearly 41,000 members. In 1799 it set aside one-third of its receipts for a charity fund, which now amounts to $80,000. It has also a Stephen Girard Fund, with an invested capital of over $63,000. The Ahiman Rezon of 1738 exacted of every member one shilling quarterly, and of every initiate five shillings for the Charity Fund.

These two funds furnish an annual income of over $6,000 for charitable

494   FREE MASONRY IN THE UNITED STATES.

purposes. On March 27, 1884, an act of incorporation granted to twenty-six brethren, authority to establish a "Home for the .Free and Accepted Masons of Pennsylvania." These brethren organized June 24th of that year, as the representatives of forty-five bodies, and secured a handsome property on Broad Street, size 200 by 160 feet, the seat of the Home—a commodious structure, upon which there is no incumbrance.

The Grand Lodge Library had its origin in 1787, when it was "ordered that the Treasurer buy every book for the use of this Lodge which may appear interesting on Masonry." In 1816 a committee was appointed to devise the best means of establishing a Masonic Library, which has resulted in a collection of the most valuable character, the catalogue of which, in 1880, covered sixty-six pages.

The present Masonic Temple is on Broad Street, Philadelphia. It covers an area 150 by 250 feet in size, and is one of the finest edifices of the kind in the world.

PROVINCIAL GRAND MASTERS OF PENNSYLVANIA, UNDER THE GRAND LODGE OF ENGLAND—MODERNS.

1730.	Daniel Coxe—for New York, New Jersey, and Pennsylvania.	1736.	Thomas Hopkinson.
		1737.	William Plumstead.
1732.	William Allen.	1738.	Joseph Shippen.
1733.	Humphrey Murray.	1741.	Philip Syng.
1734.	Benjamin Franklin.	1749.	Benjamin Franklin.
1735.	James Hamilton.	1750.	William Allen.

GRAND MASTERS UNDER THE ANCIENTS.

1764–1781. William Ball (First Grand Master).
1782–1786. William Adcock.

In the last-named year William Adcock was elected the first Grand Master under the independent Grand Lodge of Pennsylvania, as it is now constituted.*

* History of Free Masonry in New York, vol. i., p. 74.

THE MASONIC TEMPLE AT PHILADELPHIA.

FREE MASONRY IN THE UNITED STATES.

Massachusetts.—In the *spring* of 1733 Henry Price arrived in Boston from London, bringing a deputation from the Grand Lodge of England, appointing him Grand Master of New England and Dominions and Territories thereto belonging. On the 30th of *July following*, Price selected *ten members of the Fraternity*, opened a Provincial Grand Lodge, and initiated eight applicants. On the 31st of August, Grand Master Price and the eighteen members constituted a regular Lodge, which was known as St. John's Lodge, and it met at the Bunch of Grapes Tavern.

From the fact that Price *selected ten* members with which to constitute his Grand Lodge, it would appear that previous to his arrival there was in Boston and vicinity a considerable number of Free Masons who met in Lodge and worked as such; but on the arrival of Price they availed themselves of his authority from the Grand Lodge of England, and petitioned to be organized in accordance therewith, hence the meeting above described. Either this, or Price on his arrival, might have seen fit to ignore the existence of the Lodge or Lodges then established, and organize a Lodge under his dispensation. There is a tradition that there was a Lodge established in Boston in 1720.*

In 1704, Governor Belcher, of Massachusetts, while stopping in London, was admitted into the Fraternity there.

From the Deputation to Henry Price.

Montague (L. S.) Grand Master.

To all and every Our Right Worshipful and Loving Brethren, *now* Residing, or who may hereafter Reside in New England,

Sendeth Greeting:

The Right Honorable and Right Worshipful Antony, Lord Viscount Montague, Grand Master of the Free and Accepted Masons of England:

Whereas, Application has been made unto us by Our Right Worshipful and well-Beloved Brother, Mr. Henry Price, in behalf of himself and several other brethren, *now* residing in New England, aforesaid Free and Accepted

---

* See Proceedings of the Grand Lodge of Massachusetts, 1883, p. 155.

Masons, that we would be pleased to nominate and appoint a Provincial Grand Master of Free and Accepted Masons in New England, aforesaid.

Now Know Ye That we have Nominated, Ordained, Constituted and Appointed, and by these presents Nominate, Ordain, Constitute and Appoint Our said Worshipful and well-Beloved Brother, Mr. Henry Price, Provincial Grand Master of New England aforesaid and Dominions and Territories thereunto belonging, with full power and authority to Nominate and Appoint his Deputy Grand Master and Grand Wardens.

And we do also hereby empower the said Mr. Henry Price, for us in our Place and Stead, to constitute the Brethren (Free and Accepted Masons) now residing or who shall hereafter reside in those parts, into one or more regular Lodge or Lodges, as he shall think fit, and as often as occasion shall require.

He, the said Mr. Henry Price, taking special care that all and every Member of any Lodge or Lodges so to be Constituted have been or shall be made regular Masons.

And lastly, we will and require that our said Provincial Grand Master of New England, do Annually cause the brethren to keep the feast of St. John the Evangelist, and dine together on that Day, or (in case any accident should happen to prevent their dining together on that Day) on any other day near that time, as he shall judge most fit, as is done here, and that at all quarterly communications he recommend a General Charity, to be established for the relief of poor brethren in these parts.

Given under our hand and seal of office at London the thirtieth day of April, 1733, and of Masonry, 5733.

By the Grand Master's Command,

THOS. BATSON, D. G. M.
G. ROOKS, S. G. W.
J. SMYTHE, J. G. W.

In 1737 Robert Tomlinson was appointed Provincial Grand Master by John, Earl of Loudon, Grand Master of the Grand Lodge of England, and was duly installed April 20th of that year.

February 15, 1749, St. John's Lodge, No. 2, was established by warrant from the Grand Lodge of England. This being the second Lodge warranted for Massachusetts. It met at the British Coffee House in King Street, Boston.

On September 23, 1743, Thomas Oxnard was appointed Provincial Grand Master of North America by John, Lord Ward, Baron of Birmingham, Grand Master of the Grand Lodge of England.

Attorney-General Gridley, an initiate of St. John's Lodge, was installed as Provincial Grand Master by Henry Price, October 1, 1755, with great pomp and ceremony; the two brethren, clothed with their jewels and badges, walking together in the procession to Trinity Church, after the close of the Masonic meeting.

A number of Masons in this city, who were highly impressed with the name of "Ancient Masonry," petitioned the Grand Lodge of Scotland for a warrant to form a Lodge of Ancient Masons. The Grand Lodge of Scotland granted their request, by issuing a deputation, dated November 30, 1752, signed by Lord Aberdour, Grand Master of Scotland. This warrant constituted the petitioners into a Lodge, under the name of Saint Andrew's.

Joseph Warren was initiated in St. Andrew's Lodge in 1761. Subsequently this Lodge, with the assistance of the three travelling Lodges in the British Army, organized the Grand Lodge of Ancients of Massachusetts, and elected General Warren Grand Master.

December 27, 1769, St. Andrew's Grand Lodge celebrated the festival of St. John the Evangelist; and at this meeting a commission from the Right Honorable George, Earl of Dalhousie, Grand Master of Scotland, was read, dated May 30, 1769, appointing Joseph Warren to be Grand Master of Masons in Boston, and within one hundred miles of the same, whereupon he was duly proclaimed and installed.

By a further Scottish patent, signed by the Earl of Dumfries, March 3, 1772, Joseph Warren was appointed Grand Master for the Continent of America.

On April 18, 1775, the day before the battle of Lexington, General Warren, hearing of the intended advance of the British under General Gage, on Concord and Lexington, despatched Paul Revere to the latter town, via Charlestown, to announce the British expedition. On June 17th of the same year General Warren fell while gallantly defending the works on Bunker

Hill, and was buried on the spot where he fell. Subsequently the Masons of Boston disinterred the body, and conveyed it to the State House, from which place it was followed by a large concourse of people to the Stone Chapel, where an appropriate eulogium was delivered by Perez Morton, after which the burial took place with Masonic honors, according to the ancient usages of the Order.

Paul Revere was an active member of St. Andrew's Lodge, and after filling both Wardens' chairs and twice holding the office of Deputy Grand Master of the Grand Lodge of Massachusetts, he served as Grand Master of the (United) Grand Lodge of that State, 1795–97. He was one of the Boston "tea party" and hero of that night ride to Lexington, celebrated in picture, song and story, which fired the people when Gage marched on Boston.

Notwithstanding the conflict of authority between the Ancients and Moderns, but little hostility was manifested; and on January 29, 1773, a resolution was passed by the original Grand Lodge (Moderns), John Rowe, "Grand Master," that the members of St. Andrew's and other Lodges under the Massachusetts Grand Lodge (Ancients), should be admitted as visiting brethren in the Lodges under the jurisdiction of the Moderns; and on December 16, 1772, one of the Lodges at Falmouth took the following action:

"In order to establish harmony amongst the Free Masons in this town, it is voted that (for the future) the Lodge be opened one evening in the Modern form and the next evening in the Ancient form, which is to be continued till the Lodge vote to the contrary."

In 1783, Massachusetts contained an equal number of Lodges holding warrants from the two Grand Lodges in England; but on June 19, 1792, these bodies united and formed the "Grand Lodge of the Most Ancient and Honorable Society of Free and Accepted Masons for the Commonwealth of Massachusetts," John Cutler, Grand Master.

On that occasion, the only allusion to the different rites was the simple proviso that "All distinctions between Ancient and Modern Masons shall be abolished as far as practicable."

Concerning the first Grand Master, Henry Price, we find that he was born about 1697, and came to New England in 1723. Subsequently he returned to London, but came again to Boston in 1733, and in the same year

Governor Jonathan Belcher appointed him cornet in his troop of guards, with the rank of Major, and from that time he was known as Major Price.

In 1736 he entered into partnership with Francis Beteille, who was a shopkeeper, while Price himself carried on the tailoring department. In 1741, Price became the sole partner, and as a merchant or shopkeeper carried on the business alone until 1750, when he retired. In May, 1780, while using an axe in splitting rails, it glanced and struck him in the abdomen, inflicting a fatal wound. He lingered until May 20th, when he died at his homestead in Townsend, aged eighty-three years. He left an estate of considerable value.

The procession, in connection with the feast of St. John the Evangelist, at Boston, in 1747, challenged great curiosity, and moved a native poet to perpetrate the following:

"Entertainment for a winter's evening, being a full and true account of a very strange and wonderful sight seen in Boston, December 27, 1747, at noon-day, the truth of which can be attested by a great number of people who actually saw the same with their own eyes."

"See Buck, before the aproned throng,
Marches with sword and book along.
The stately Ram with courage bold
So stalks before the fleecy fold.
And so the Gander, on the brink
Of river, leads his Geese to drink."

The landlord of the Royal Exchange Tavern got the following:

"Where's honest Luke, that cook from London?
For without Luke, the Lodge is undone;
'Twas he who oft dispelled their sadness,
And filled the brethren's heart with gladness.
Luke in return is made a brother,
As good and true as any other,
And still, though broke with age and wine,
Preserves the token and the sign."

Lodges Warranted by the Provincial Grand Lodge at Boston.

Philadelphia, Pennsylvania, 1734.
Portsmouth, New Hampshire, 1735.
Charleston, South Carolina, 1735.
Boston, Master's Lodge, 1738.
Antigua, West Indies, 1738.
Annapolis, Nova Scotia, 1738.
Newfoundland, 1746.
Newport, Rhode Island, 1749.
Boston, Second Lodge of, 1750.
Boston, Third Lodge, 1750.
Annapolis, Maryland, 1750.
Halifax, Nova Scotia, 1750.
New Haven, Connecticut, 1750.
Philadelphia, Pennsylvania, 1752.
New London, Connecticut, 1753.
Middletown, Connecticut, 1754.
Lake George, Canada, 1757.
Louisburg, 28th Foot, Military, 1758.
Crown Point, Canada, 1758.
Providence, Rhode Island, 1757.
Newport (Master's Lodge), 1759.

Marblehead, Massachusetts, 1760.
Surinam (Dutch Guiana), 1761.
Hartford, Connecticut, 1762.
Falmouth, Massachusetts, 1762.
Elizabethtown, New Jersey, 1762.
Quebec, 1764.
Crown Point (Province Troops), 1764.
Waterbury, Connecticut, 1765.
Prince Town, New Jersey, 1765.
Norwich, Connecticut, 1766.
Virginia, 1766.
Salem, 1766.
St. Christopher, West Indies, 1766.
Barbadoes, 1766.
Pitt County, North Carolina, 1766.
Newbury, Massachusetts, 1766.
Newfoundland, Second Lodge of, 1766.
Wallingford, Connecticut, 1769.
Sherburne, Massachusetts, 1771.
Guilford, Connecticut, 1771.
Boston, 4th Lodge (Rising Sun), 1772.*

Connecticut.—In a voyage to Boston in 1750, Captain David Wooster, who had been an officer in the Regular Army during the Indian war, and then commanding a trading vessel, applied to the Provincial Grand Lodge of Massachusetts for a Charter, to establish a Lodge of Ancient Free and Accepted Masons in the town of New Haven, Connecticut. This petition was received favorably, and the Charter granted August 12, 1750.

This Lodge was first named New Haven Lodge, but was afterward called Hiram, No. 1. It held its first communication December 27, 1750, at the house of Jehiel Tuttle, at which twelve members were present, and from

* Gould, vol. vi., p. 448.

MASONIC TEMPLE, BOSTON.

the records it appears that "Each brother paid thirty shillings." Benedict Westcut paid one hundred shillings advance money; Lodge received of Brother Lyman two dozen gloves, at £10 12s. 6d. = £21 5s. Received of Brother B. Westcut in full for admittance £9.

General Wooster was mortally wounded in leading an attack against General Tryon, at Ridgefield, April 27, 1777, a musket-ball having entered his spine. He expired May 2d. A fitting monument marks his grave, the corner-stone of which was laid by the Grand Master of Connecticut, April 27, 1854.

Thomas, the son of General Wooster, was initiated in Hiram Lodge, April 14, 1777, a few days previous to his father's death.

The second Lodge in Connecticut was opened under a dispensation granted January 12, 1753, upon a petition from brethren residing at New London. The third Lodge was opened at Middletown, under a warrant granted February 4, 1754, by Provincial Grand Master Thomas Oxnard, of Boston.

St. John is a favorite name in this jurisdiction, as it has five Lodges designated "St. John's," as follows:

St. John's Lodge, No. 1, was established at Fairfield, chartered by Provincial Grand Master Harrison, of New York, in 1762. This Lodge is now No. 3, at Bridgeport.

St. John's Lodge, No. 2, was warranted by Provincial Grand Master Oxnard, of Massachusetts, at Middletown, 1754.

St. John's Lodge, No. 3 (present number), by Provincial Grand Master Gridley, at Hartford, 1763.

St. John's Lodge, No. 4, by Provincial Grand Master Harrison, at Norwalk, 1765. (Now No. 6.)

St. John's Lodge, No. 5, by Grand Master Harrison, at Stratford, 1766. (Now No. 8.)

A warrant for a Lodge was obtained from the Grand Lodge of Massachusetts (Ancients) by the brethren of Colchester, dated January 12, 1781, the name of which was Wooster, in honor of the General; and as another mark of honor and affection for the original patron of Masonry in Connecticut, a second Lodge named Wooster was chartered at a recent date for New Haven.

In response to the recommendation of a committee of thirteen Lodges a convention of delegates from twelve Lodges met at New Haven, April 29, 1783, and formed what was practically a Grand Lodge; though in place of Grand Lodge officers they elected a Moderator and Clerk.

Comfort Sages was elected to the former office, and Pierpont Edwards to the latter. The object was to consider and determine "the sums to be paid for the admitting, passing, and raising Brethren; the ceremonies to be observed at the admission of visiting Brethren, who have none to vouch for them; the time that persons shall stand proposed before admission, and such other matters of general concern as in their opinion may, without trenching upon the By-laws of particular Lodges, be objects of general regulation." These matters were all duly considered and adjusted.

This arrangement appeared to work satisfactorily until May 14, 1789, when "a Convention of Delegates from the several Lodges in the State was convened at Hartford to consider the state of the Lodges, and advise upon the question of establishing a Grand Lodge."

Of this convention William Judd was President, and Ephraim Kirby, Secretary. The result was the appointment of a committee of four—Pierpont Edwards, William Judd, Asher Miller, and Ephraim Kirby—"to prepare a systematic plan for forming a Grand Lodge in this State." The convention then adjourned to July 8, 1789.

At the above date, the Lodges assembled in New Haven and adopted a Constitution, regulations, and ordinances for the government of the Grand Lodge, and proceeded to the election of Grand Lodge officers for the year ensuing. Pierpont Edwards was elected Grand Master, with William Judd as his Deputy; Ralph Pomeroy, Senior Grand Warden; Samuel Wyllys, Junior Grand Warden; Elias Shipman, Grand Secretary.

At a meeting in October, 1791, it was "Resolved that the Grand Communications in future be holden on Wednesday next following the second Thursday in May at Hartford; and on Wednesday next following the second Thursday in October at New Haven."

New Hampshire.—On February 5, 1736, a petition to hold a Lodge was addressed by the brethren at Portsmouth, N. H., to Henry Price. In the petition they style Price Grand Master of the Society of Free and Accepted

Masons held in Boston, and describe themselves as of the holy and exquisite Lodge of St. John. They asked for power to hold a Lodge according to order as is, and has been, granted to faithful brothers in all parts of the world, and declare that they had their Constitutions both in print and manuscript as good and as *ancient* as any that England can afford. This was asked, because they had heard that there was a superior Lodge held in Boston.

As Portsmouth was settled over one hundred years previous to this, and principally by the English, it is probable that there had been one or more Lodges at work in New Hampshire several years prior to 1736. Concerning this matter, Gould, in his History of Free Masonry, vol. vi., p. 444, thus comments:

"Be it noted this was early in 1736, when no Lodge had been warranted in Portsmouth; and as the brethren stated they possessed 'Constitutions' in manuscript—which it is hardly possible could have been anything else than a copy of the 'Old Charges'—as well as in print, the evidence is consistent with the supposition that, while at the date named, the Lodge must have been some years in existence, its origin may have reached back even to the seventeenth century.

"I am anxious not to lay too much stress on the precise meaning attached by me to the mention of manuscript Constitutions; nevertheless, I think the petition may be taken as fair evidence that in 1736 there were brethren in New Hampshire, meeting as Masons in a Lodge, who possessed a copy (or reprint) of the English Constitutions published in *1723*, as well as a version of an *older* set of laws in MS., thus pointing to the possible existence of the Grand Lodge era of 1716–17."

And in reference to the above, McClenachan, in his History of Free Masonry in New York, p. 90, says:

"It will be observed from the deduction made by Brother Gould, that in like manner as Grand Master Henry Price issued authority to warrant a Lodge to the eighteen Masons in Boston who petitioned in behalf of themselves and 'other brethren,' therefore the brethren had been meeting as a Lodge anterior thereto and discharging Masonic duties; convening and meeting as Masons without other authority than that of ancient immemorial right which the craft had many decades before exercised, of meeting when and where circumstances permitted or required, and choosing their own temporary Master; it is probable that thus many of the old Masons in America had been admitted to the Mystic Rites.*

The Grand Lodge of New Hampshire was organized July 8, 1789, and General John Sullivan, Governor of the State, was elected Grand Master. There were then five Lodges in the State.

Rhode Island.—In the spring of 1658 Mordecai Campannell, and others, in all fifteen families, arrived at Newport from Holland. They brought with them the first three degrees of Masonry and worked them in the house of Campannell, and continued to do so, they and their successors, to the year 1742.†

The first warranted Lodge established in Rhode Island was St. John's, at Newport, December 27, 1749, by St. John's Provincial Grand Lodge of Massachusetts, Oxnard, Grand Master.

The second Lodge in this State was established at Providence, January 18, 1757, also by warrant from the Massachusetts Grand Lodge.

Governor Jabez Bowen was the Junior Warden of the last-mentioned Lodge in 1762, and again from 1765 to 1769.

In 1769 the meetings ceased and the Lodge was closed, principally for the want of funds. The Lodge remained closed until July 15, 1778, when Bowen, under commission from John Rowe, Provincial Grand Master of Massachusetts, reopened the Lodge and took charge of the same as Master. On St. John's Day a public celebration was held, seventy-one of the members being present, including brethren from the army. Bowen remained Master until 1790.

In 1791, the Grand Lodge of Rhode Island was organized under the title, "The Grand Lodge of the Most Worshipful and Honorable Society of Free and Accepted Masons for the State of Rhode Island and Providence Plantations," when Bowen was elected Deputy Grand Master, and Grand Master in 1794, which office he retained till the close of 1798.

*Notes 1 and 2, p. 560.
† See Guide to the Chapter, Gould, and Paterson's History of Rhode Island.

FREE MASONRY IN THE UNITED STATES. 509

The Grand Chapter was organized in March, 1798, and the Grand Council in October, 1860. The Grand Commandery forms a part of a common body known as the Grand Commandery of Massachusetts and Rhode Island. It was formed in 1805, and the celebrated Thomas Smith Webb was its first presiding officer.

New Jersey.—Daniel Coxe, the first Provincial Grand Master appointed by the Grand Lodge of England for any American Province, was a resident of Burlington, N. J., and represented Gloucester County in the Assembly of 1716.

In May, 1761, a constitutional number of Master Masons in and near the town of Newark petitioned for, and received from George Harrison, Provincial Grand Master of New York, a Dispensation, empowering William Tukey as Master, and others as officers, to meet and operate as a Lodge. The first meeting was held at the Rising Sun Tavern. The Lodge was called St. John's Lodge, No. 1, and still preserves its original minutes. Two other Lodges were opened in this Province, under charters from Boston, in 1762–63.*

On December 18, 1786, a convention of Master Masons was held for the consideration of the formation of a Grand Lodge for the State. This resulted in the adoption of a Constitution, April 2, 1787. The Hon. David Brearly, Chief Justice of the State, was chosen the first Grand Master.

It was in 1777, the darkest period of the Revolution, while Washington held his winter quarters at Morristown, that Pennsylvania, aside from her troops of the line, raised a regiment of artillery under the command of Colonel Thomas Proctor, to join the army. At the same time the Grand Lodge of Pennsylvania issued a travelling Lodge warrant to Colonel Proctor to hold Lodges in his regiment wherever he might be stationed.

The organization of this regiment and its accompanying Lodge, by Colonel Proctor, seem to have been contemporaneous, for Lodges were held in Morristown during that winter at Washington's headquarters, in the old *Freeman's Tavern*, on the north side of the Green.

* Anderson, in his History of Masonry, states that a warrant was issued by the Grand Lodge of England in 1729, for a Provincial Grand Lodge in New Jersey, America. History of Free Masonry in New York, p. 104 ; Mitchell, p. 587 ; Gould, vol. vi., p. 456.

510 FREE MASONRY IN THE UNITED STATES.

The furniture used in this military Lodge belonged to St. John's Lodge, of Newark, whose labors had been suspended on account of the war; and it was generously loaned to Colonel Proctor's Lodge, and removed to Morristown, two of the members of St. John's Lodge being responsible for its safe return.

In the New Jersey Historical Society's Archives is this record:

" An account of sundry articles taken out of the Lodge-chest of Newark.

" St. John's Lodge No. 1, by consent of Bro. John Robinson, Bro. Lewis Ogden, Bro. Moses Ogden, and lent unto Bro. Kinney and Bro. Jesse Bruen to carry as far as Morristown.

" Said Bros. Kinney and Bruen promise with word of Brothers to return the same articles as per inventory below with our Bro. John Robinson, Secretary, when called for. (24 aprons, 2 ebony Truncheons, 3 candlesticks, etc., etc.)

Signed : " THOMAS KINNEY.
" JESSE BRUEN."

THE OLD FREEMAN'S TAVERN, AND ITS HISTORIC ASSOCIATIONS.

It was in a room over the office of this Tavern, that General Lafayette was made a Mason, and it is said that General Washington himself presided on the occasion.* General Lafayette was then but twenty years of age, and, as a curious coincidence, that was the age of Washington when he was made a Mason.†

This historic old building (the Freeman's Tavern) now contains a large collection of relics of the Revolution, and among them twenty different pieces of furniture which General Washington and his wife are known to have actually used when here in the winter of 1779 ‡ and 1780 ; and these, with the old Watts Psalm-book, which the former used when attending service in the church which preceded the present one on the Green, commands particular notice and attention. So also does the Commission appointing Washington

---

* Quarterly Review of Free Masonry, vol. ii., p. 574.

† According to the late C. W. Moore, all the American generals of the Revolution, with the exception of Benedict Arnold, were Free Masons. The Marquis de Lafayette was among the number. Gould, vol. vi., p. 419.

‡ Washington's head-quarters were at Morristown both in the winters of 1777 and 1779. See Lossing's History of the United States, pp. 269 and 306.

Commander-in-Chief, which latter is dated Philadelphia, June 19, 1775, and signed "*John Hancock, President of the Fourteen United Colonies.*"

The room at the southwest corner contains, among other interesting articles, the veritable writing-desk or secretary upon which the General wrote his letters.

In the parlor where hangs the Commission, Mrs. Martha Washington held her New Year's reception in that memorable winter of 1780. While her guests came dressed in silks and ruffles, " they were surprised," says the historian Lossing, " to find their hostess habited in a very plain gown made of home-made stuff, a white 'kerchief covered her neck and bosom, a neat cap, and no ornament but a plain gold wedding-ring. While with her right hand she gave each a kindly greeting, in her left hand she held a half-knit stocking, the ball of yarn laying in an outside pocket hanging at her side." When seated, she plied her needles incessantly, knitting socks for not only her husband, but the poor soldiers camped amid the snows of an almost Arctic winter, talking much also as she worked of the great sufferings of the patriot army, thus affording, in mien and occupation, a wise rebuke to her idle, handsomely attired visitors."

Among the most noted military Lodges that were organized in the American Army, was the " American Union," and a festival was held by this Lodge at Morristown, in December, 1779, at which General Washington was present.

From the minutes of the American Union Lodge the following appears :

"MORRISTOWN, December 27, 1779.

" An entered Apprentices' Lodge was held this day, for the celebration of the Festival of St. John the Evangelist.

" Officers present : Brothers Jonathan Hart, Worshipful Master; Richard Sill, S. W.; Robert Warner, J. W.; William Richards, Treasurer; John R. Watrous, Secretary; Thomas Grosvenor, S. D.; Brother Little, J. D.; Lorian and Binns, Tylers.

" Visitors present : Brothers Washington, Gibbs, Kinney, Van Rensselaer, etc.

" The Lodge was opened, and after the usual ceremonies had been performed, the Brethren formed a procession in the following order :

"1. Brother Binns, to clear the way.
"2. The Band of Music.
"3. Brother Lorian.
"4. The Deacons with their Rods.
"5. The Brethren, by Juniority.
"6. The Past Masters.
"7. The Secretary and Treasurer.
"8. The Wardens with their Wands.
"9. The Worshipful Master.

"The Brethren then proceeded to the Meeting-house, where a very polite discourse, adapted to the occasion, was delivered by the Rev. Dr. Baldwin, of the Connecticut line.*

In September, 1824, while General Lafayette was in Newark, he received an invitation to visit Morristown, and in his acceptance he expressed "his wish and intention to visit a place endeared to him by so many recollections of the Revolution."

On the day appointed the General was escorted to Morristown from Hoboken by a joint committee from Paterson and Morristown, accompanied by Governor Williamson.

Georgia.—According to Hayden, in Washington and His Masonic Compeers, p. 342, the first Lodge was established at Savannah in this State in 1735,† and was known as King Solomon's Lodge.

Whitfield, in his diary at Savannah, June 24, 1738, has the following: "Was enabled to read prayer and preach with power before the Free Masons, with whom I afterward dined."

And tradition says that this Lodge commenced work under an old oak-tree. Union Lodge, No. 2, at Savannah, was warranted in 1774, and Grenadier's Lodge in 1775.

South Carolina.—The first Lodge established in this State was under a warrant granted in 1735 by Lord Weymouth, of the Grand Lodge of

---

* On December 27, 1779, the head-quarters of the army being then at Morristown, N. J., the American Union Lodge met to celebrate the festival of St. John. Gould, vol. vi., p. 419.
† Savannah settled in 1732. Lossing's History of the United States, p. 171.

The Old Fireman's Tavern, Morristown.

England, for the establishment of a Lodge in the city of Charleston. It was organized August 28, 1736, by the name of Solomon's Lodge.

The first Provincial *Grand* Lodge here was established by authority from the Earl of Loudoun, in the same year. The next Lodge was warranted in 1738, by St. John's Grand Lodge of Boston, Mass., for a Lodge also at Charleston. This was followed in 1743, 1755, and 1756, by warrants from the Grand Lodge of England establishing Prince George's Lodge at Winyaw, Union Lodge and Master's Lodge at Charleston, and a Lodge at Beaufort.

In 1760 the Grand Lodge of Scotland warranted Union Lodge, No. 98, and St. Mark's Lodge was warranted by the Grand Lodge of England in 1763.

In 1754 a *second* Provincial Grand Lodge was established by a deputation from the Marquis of Carnarvon to Chief Justice Leigh. In 1777 this Grand Lodge assumed independence, and became the "Grand Lodge of Free and Accepted Masons," Barnard Elliott being the first Grand Master.

In 1783 the Athol or Ancient Masons invaded this jurisdiction, and in 1787 they held a Convention and organized the "Grand Lodge of Ancient York Masons." This caused much strife until 1817, when a union was permanently established, the two Grand Lodges merging into one, under the name of the "Grand Lodge of Ancient Free Masons."

Virginia.—The first Lodge in Virginia was St. John's Lodge, established at Norfolk in 1741, under a warrant from the Grand Lodge of Scotland.

The next Lodge in Virginia was the one in which **George Washington** was made a **Mason.**

This is the Lodge that was opened at Fredericksburg in 1751, under a dispensation from the G. L. of Massachusetts. It was not chartered, however, until July 21, 1758.

Swan Tavern Lodge at Yorktown was warranted August 1, 1755, by the Grand Lodge of England, as was Botetourt Lodge, November 6, 1773; and Williamsburg Lodge at Williamsburg in the same year.

In 1788, Lodge No. 39, at Alexandria, which had hitherto been working under the Grand Lodge of Pennsylvania, transferred its allegiance to Virginia and elected George Washington, Master.

The following is from its records: "On May 29, 1788, the Lodge proceeded to the appointment of Master and Deputy Master to be recommended to the Grand Lodge of Virginia, when George Washington, Esq., was unanimously chosen Master; Robert McCrea, Deputy Master; William Hunter, Jr., Senior Warden; John Allison, Junior Warden."

The Warrant (under which the Lodge is still working) was granted to Washington as Master. The appointing clause is in the following words:

"Know ye that we, Edmund Randolph, Esquire, Governor of the Commonwealth aforesaid, and Grand Master of the most Ancient and Honorable Society of Free Masons within the same, by and with the consent of the Grand Lodge of Virginia, do hereby constitute and appoint our illustrious and well-beloved Brother, George Washington, Esquire, late General and Commander-in-Chief of the forces of the United States of America, and our worthy Brethren Robert McCrea, William Hunter, Jr., and John Allison, Esqs., together with all such other brethren as may be admitted to associate with them, to be a just, true, and regular Lodge of Free Masons, by the name, title, and designation of the Alexandria Lodge, No 22." *

The formation of the Grand Lodge will be given from its old records.†

"At a convention of delegates from the Lodges below mentioned, we met in the city of Williamsburg, on Tuesday, May 6, 1777, in consequence of a petition of the Williamsburg Lodge, recommending that the Worshipful Master and Wardens of the different Lodges, or their Deputies, should meet in Williamsburg, for the purpose of choosing a Grand Master for the State of Virginia:

"Matthew Phripp, Esq., Deputy from the Norfolk Lodge.

"James Kemp, from the Kilwinning, Port Royal Cross Lodge.

"Duncan Rose, from the Blandford Lodge.

"William Waddill and John Rowsay, from the Williamsburg Lodge.

"William Simmons and John Crawford, from the Cabin Point Royal Arch Lodge.

"Matthew Phripp, Esq., being elected President, and James Kemp, Clerk.

"Brother Waddill laid the following letters before the convention, which were directed to the Williamsburg Lodge, viz.: A letter from the

* Mackey, pp 870, 871.   † Mitchell, History of Free Masonry, p. 580.

Fredericksburg Lodge, enclosing an order of that Lodge (a letter from the Botetourt Lodge, also a letter from James Taylor, as Master of the Norfolk Lodge), which were severally read, and referred to the Williamsburg Lodge for proper answers.

"A motion being made, and it being the unanimous opinion of this Convention, that a Grand Master ought to be chosen to preside over the Craft in this Commonweath :

"*Resolved:* That a Committee be appointed for drawing up reasons why a Grand Master should be chosen, consisting of Duncan Rose, William Waddill, James Kemp, and John Crawford, and that their proceedings be laid before the Convention, on Tuesday, May 13th, at six o'clock P.M.

"Tuesday, May 13, 1777. The Convention met agreeably to adjournment.

"Brother Phripp being absent upon business, Brother Rose was elected President.

"Brother Waddill reported that the Committee, having met, had drawn up their reasons why they thought a Grand Master should be chosen, which he delivered to the Chair; and being read it was agreed that the same should be recorded—and are as follows :

"To the Right Worshipful Master, Worshipful Wardens, and Worthy Brethren of the ———— Lodge :

"1. We find that the Lodges in this State hold their charters under five distinct and separate authorities, viz.: The Grand Master of England, Scotland, Ireland, Pennsylvania, and America (the last at second-hand).

"2. We cannot discover, upon inquiry, that Masonry has ever derived any benefit from the foreign appointment of a Grand Master in this country, they being little known and as little acknowledged.

"We, the Deputies aforesaid, for ourselves and our respective Lodges, humbly beseech and desire that you will be pleased to take the foregoing reasons into consideration, and that you will favor us with your attendance, by Deputation, in this Lodge, for the purpose of electing a Grand Master for this State, on June 23d next, at ten o'clock A.M., for the first time, and ever after, at such time and place as the Grand Lodge shall determine." As there was not a majority of the Lodges present, the next Convention failed to elect; but a Convention of the Craft assembled at Williamsburg, October 13, 1778, and elected John Blair Grand Master. Following Blair, in 1784 James Mercer was elected Grand Master, with Edmund Randolph as Deputy Grand Master, and in 1786 Edmund Randolph was elected Grand Master.*

GEORGE WASHINGTON.

In the records of the old Lodge at Fredericksburg, Va., is the following entry: "November 4th, 1752. This evening Mr. George Washington was initiated as an E. P." The fee of two pounds and three shillings is also acknowledged.

March 3d, in the following year, the records show that "Mr. George Washington was passed to the degree of Fellowcraft, and that on the 4th of the following August he was raised to the sublime degree of Master Mason.†
In 1778 he was elected Master of Alexandria Lodge as previously shown. Subsequently he showed his interest in the institution by taking at least one of the higher degrees in a military Lodge attached to the Forty-sixth Regiment while it was stationed at or near Halifax during the French war.‡
April 30, 1789, he took his oath of office as President of the United States, in New York City, being sworn in by Chancellor Livingston, Grand Master of New York, on the Bible belonging to St. John's Lodge.

We next come to a memorable event in the history of the United States, the laying of the corner-stone of the Capitol of what is destined to be the greatest Nation of the world. These important ceremonies were to be conducted by members of the most ancient existing Order known to history, under its chief Officer, and fit Representative of the American Nation.

At ten o'clock on Wednesday, September the 21st, 1793, under a large military escort, including artillery, the President, George Washington, crossed the Potomac and was received in Maryland by the officers and members of No. 22, Virginia (Washington's Lodge), and No. 9, Maryland, whom the President then headed. They were preceded by a band of music; and the Alexandria artillery brought up the rear. In this order they proceeded to President's Square, in the city of Washington, where they were met and

---

* Mitchell's History of Free Masonry, pp. 581, 582.
† Hayden, Washington and His Masonic Compeers, p. 23. ‡ Gould, vol. vi., p. 421.

saluted by Lodge No. 15 of that city, headed by Joseph Clarke, Rt. W. G. M., P. T., and conducted to a large Lodge prepared for their reception. After a brief time spent here, the procession was formed to proceed to Capitol Hill, and in the following order:

   The Surveying Department of the City of Washington.
    Mayor and Corporation of Georgetown.
     Virginia Artillery.
 Commissioners of the City of Washington and their Attendants.
    Stone-cutters, and other Mechanics.
      The Sword-bearer.
     Masons of the first degree.
     Bible, etc., on Grand Cushions.
     Deacons, with staffs of office.
     Masons of the second degree.
      Stewards, with wands.
     Masons of the third degree.
     Wardens, with truncheons.
    Secretaries, with implements of office.
     Past Masters, with their regalia.
     Treasurers, with their jewels.
       Band of music.
 Lodge No. 22, of Virginia, disposed in their own order.
      Corn, Wine, and Oil.
The Grand Master pro tem., Worshipful Master of No. 22 of Virginia, and
       George Washington.
       Grand Sword-bearer.

On arrival at the proposed site of the Capitol, and the preliminary ceremonies concluded, "the artillery discharged a volley. The Grand Marshal then delivered to the commissioners a large silver plate with an inscription thereon, which the commissioners ordered to be read, and was as follows:

"This southeast corner-stone of the Capitol of the United States of America, in the City of Washington, was laid on the 18th day of September, 1793, in the thirteenth year of American Independence, in the first year of the second term of the presidency of George Washington, whose virtues in the civil administratien of his country have been as conspicuous and beneficial, as his military valor and prudence have been useful in establishing her liberties, and in the year of Masonry, 5793, by the President of the United States, in concert with the Grand Lodge of Maryland, several Lodges under its jurisdiction, and Lodge No. 22 from Alexandria, Virginia.

"Thomas Johnson, David Steuart, and Daniel Carroll, Commissioners; Joseph Clarke, R. W. G. M. P. T.; James Hoban and Stephen Hallate, Architects; Collin Williamson, M. Mason.

" The artillery discharged a volley, the plate was delivered to the President, who, attended by the Grand Master P. T., and three Most Worshipful Masters, descended to the cavazion trench and placed it on the *corner-stone of the Capitol of the United States of America*, on which was deposed Corn, Wine, and Oil, when the whole congregation joined in prayer, which was succeeded by Masonic chanting honors, and a volley from the artillery.

" The President of the United States and his attendant brethren ascended from the cavazion to the east of the corner-stone; and there the Grand Master P. T., elevated on a triple rostrum, delivered an oration fitting the great occasion. . . . At intervals, during the delivery of the oration, volleys were discharged by the artillery. The ceremony ended in prayer, Masonic chanting honors, and 15 volleys from the artillery.

"The whole was witnessed by a vast concourse of people, among whom the strictest order prevailed throughout the ceremonies." *

THE SABLE CURTAIN FALLS.

After a career that enrolled his name among the greatest characters known to history, General Washington died at his residence, Mount Vernon, on December 14, 1799.

" The funeral ceremonies were arranged by a committee of Lodge No. 22, at Alexandria, consisting of Dr. Elisha Cullen Dick, its Master; Colonel George Deneale, its Senior Warden; and Colonels Charles Little and Charles Simms, members. On Monday, the 16th, an emergent meeting of this Lodge was called, at which Dr. Dick presided. Forty-one of its members were

* See Hayden in Washington and His Masonic Compeers, pp. 149–159.

present, and two visiting brethren, one from Fredericksburg, where Washington was made a Mason, and the other from Philadelphia.

A committee from No. 22, consisting of Brothers Joseph Neale and Thomas Petrekin, was appointed to confer with Lodge No. 47 ; and the joint committee of both Lodges agreed upon the ceremonies as arranged by the former committee of Lodge No. 22. There were also two other Lodges at that time in the Federal District. These were Potomac No. 9, at Georgetown, and Federal Lodge No. 15, at Washington. A messenger was appointed by No. 22 to wait on these Lodges on Tuesday, and invite them to join the funeral procession at Mount Vernon on Wednesday, at twelve o'clock. The deacons of the Lodge were directed to have the Orders cleaned and prepared, and to furnish spermaceti candles for them. The secretary was also directed to have the case in which the charter was kept repaired and gilded for the occasion. It was also arranged that the military companies of Alexandria should join in the procession as an escort and guard of honor. They were at that time under command of Colonel Deneale, the Senior Warden of Washington's Lodge.

On Wednesday, December 18th, the citizens about Mount Vernon commenced assembling at eleven o'clock, and the encoffined body of the illustrious dead was placed in the piazza of the old mansion where, while living, he had been accustomed to walk and muse, or converse with visitors. On an ornament at the head of the coffin was inscribed, Surge ad Judicitum, and beneath it Gloria Deo ; and upon a silver plate on the middle of the lid was inscribed,

GENERAL
GEORGE WASHINGTON.
Departed this Life on the 14th December,
1799, æt. 68.

The sun had passed its meridian before the Masonic and military escort arrived from Alexandria. A Masonic apron and two crossed swords were then placed upon the coffin, a few mystic words were spoken, and the brethren one by one filed by the noble form, majestic even in death, and took a last sad look of one they had loved so well.

The Procession.

Cavalry.
Infantry and Guard, with arms reversed.
Band of Music, with muffled drums.
Four clergymen, three of whom were Masons.
Washington's war horse, carrying the saddle, holsters,
and pistols, and led by two grooms, dressed in black.
The body on a bier, with a dark pall.
Six pall-bearers, all Masons, and wearing on their
left arms badges of black crape.
Relatives and family friends.
Officers and members of Washington's Lodge.
Officers of the Corporation of Alexandria.
Overseers of the Mount Vernon estate, and domestics.
Citizens at large.

Arrived at the family vault, the military escort halted and formed their lines. "The body, the clergy, the mourning relatives, and the Masonic brethren then passed between them and approached the door of the tomb. There the encoffined Washington rested on his bier before them. Dr. Dick, the Master of the Lodge, and the Rev. Thomas Davis, rector of Christ Church, stood at its head, the mourning relatives at its foot, and the Fraternity in a circle around the tomb."

The Rev. Mr. Davis broke the silence by repeating from the sacred writings, "I am the resurrection and the life; he that believeth in Me, though he were dead, yet shall he live."

Prayer, a short address, a pause; and then the Master of the Lodge performed the mystic funeral rites of Masonry, as the last service at the burial of Washington. The apron and the swords were removed from the coffin, for their place was no longer there—it was ready for entombment. The brethren one by one cast upon it an evergreen sprig.

The silence was so profound throughout the gathered multitude of citizens, that they might almost have heard the echoes of the acacia as it fell

FREE MASONRY IN THE UNITED STATES. 523

with trembling lightness upon the coffin-lid. The pall-bearers placed the body in the tomb's cold embrace, earth was cast on the threshold, and the words were spoken: "Earth to earth—ashes to ashes—dust to dust," and the entombment of Washington was finished. The mystic public burial honors of Masonry were next given by each brother with lifted hands, saying in his heart, "Alas, my Brother." The mystic chain was reunited in the circle there, the cannon on the vessel and on the banks above fired their burial salute, and Mount Vernon's tomb was left in possession of its noblest sleeper. The sun was setting, and the pall of night mantled the pathway of the Masonic brethren as they sadly returned to their homes.*

Other Illustrious Names
in the
HISTORY OF FREE MASONRY
and of the United States.

PEYTON RANDOLPH,
First President of the Continental Congress, and last
Provincial Grand Master of Virginia.

EDMUND RANDOLPH,
Governor of Virginia, and Grand Master of Masons
in that Commonwealth.

BENJAMIN FRANKLIN,
Master of the First Warranted Lodge in Pennsylvania,
and Provincial Grand Master of that Province.

PIERPONT EDWARDS,
The First Grand Master of Connecticut.

JABEZ BOWEN, LL.D.,
Lieutenant-Governor of Rhode Island, and Grand Master
of Masons in that State.

JOHN SULLIVAN, LL.D.,
A Major-General of the Revolution; first Grand Master of the Grand Lodge of New
Hampshire, and Governor of that State.

GENERAL JOSEPH WARREN,
The hero of Bunker Hill and Grand Master of Masons in Massachusetts.

* See Hayden in Washington and His Masonic Compeers, pp. 195-203.

PAUL REVERE,
One of the most earnest of the patriots of the Revolution, and Grand Master of the Grand Lodge of Massachusetts.

GENERAL RUFUS PUTNAM,
First Grand Master of Ohio.

Delaware.—The first Lodge in this jurisdiction was established under warrant from the Grand Lodge of Scotland in 1751.

The succeeding five Lodges were warranted by the Grand Lodge of Pennsylvania between 1765 and 1802.

The Grand Lodge was organized June 6, 1806.

Maryland.—The first Lodge in this State was established at Annapolis in 1750, under a warrant from Thomas Oxnard, Provincial Grand Master of the Grand Lodge of Massachusetts, granted August 12th.

The Grand Lodge of Maryland was organized July 31, 1787, by a Convention of five Lodges, there being eight in the State at the time.

Lord Baltimore, who was proprietary Governor, resided in the Province from 1732 to 1734. He was made a Mason in England in 1730, and assisted in forming the Lodge at which Frederick, Prince of Wales, was initiated.

Florida.—The first Lodge opened in this jurisdiction was a Military Lodge, warranted by the Ancients at St. Augustine in 1759.

The next Lodge organized was St. Fernando, by authority of the Grand Lodge of Georgia. This Lodge was also at St. Augustine. In the year 1811, it was suppressed by the Spanish Government. In 1820, the Grand Lodge of South Carolina granted a Charter to Floridian Virtue Lodge, No. 28, but, in consequence of the hostility of the Catholics, it did not long exist. In 1824, the Grand Lodge of South Carolina granted another Charter, for Esperanza Lodge, at St. Augustine, which body, however, became extinct after a year by the removal of most of its members to Havana. In 1826, the Grand Lodges of Tennessee and Georgia granted warrants for the establishment, respectively, of Jackson Lodge at Tallahassee, Washington Lodge at Quincy, and Harmony Lodge at Mariana. On July 5, 1830, delegates from these three Lodges met at Tallahassee, and organized the Grand Lodge of Florida.

Missouri.—In 1763, Pierre Liguste Laclede received from the Director General the exclusive privilege to trade with the Indians of Missouri, and on February 15, 1764, Laclede and his party landed at the spot now occupied by the city of St. Louis, where he proceeded to clear the land and draw the lines of a town. This town he afterward named St. Louis, in honor of Louis XV., of France, and it subsequently became the capital of Upper Louisiana, and is now one of the great cities of the West.

At this time Western merchants procured their goods from Philadelphia, to which city they resorted once a year. Here several of them took the degrees. This was done in the old French Lodge, No. 73. As soon as the Masons were sufficiently numerous in the territory, they resolved to form a Lodge, and, upon application, a warrant was granted them by the Grand Lodge of Pennsylvania—in 1807–8. Other Lodges were erected here by the Grand Lodge of Tennessee in 1816–1819, and by that of Indiana in 1820.

On February 22, 1821, in response to an invitation sent by the Missouri Lodge, No. 12, of St. Louis, to the several Lodges in that State, their representatives assembled in the hall of Missouri Lodge; and having resolved to organize a Grand Lodge, they appointed a committee consisting of William Bates, Nathaniel Simons, and Edward Bates, to draft a Constitution and Code of By-laws for the government of the Grand Lodge. They then adjourned to meet at the same place on the 23d day of April following, to organize a Grand Lodge—which they did.

Louisiana.—The first Lodge in this jurisdiction, La Consolante Maconne, was established at New Orleans by the Lodge Anglaise de Bordeaux, in 1764. Subsequently, refugees, chiefly from the island of Guadeloupe, established the Lodges Perfect Union and Polar Star, the first working the "York" and the second the French or Modern Rite, and holding warrants from the Grand Lodge of South Carolina, and "La Parfaite" of Marseilles, respectively.

In 1804 more fugitives arrived from San Domingo, including the members of "La Réunion Désirée," of Port au Prince, who obtained a duplicate Charter from the Grand Orient of France in 1806, but changed it in 1808 for a warrant from the Grand Lodge of Pennsylvania.

The first Lodge that worked in the English language was "Louisiana," established by the Grand Lodge of New York in 1807. A Grand Lodge was established in 1820, and a second in 1848. In 1850 the two Grand Lodges united and formed the Grand Lodge of Louisiana.*

Vermont.—The first Lodge intended for this State was warranted for a Lodge at Cornish ; but which, upon the establishment of the line between Vermont and New Hampshire, proved to be in the latter, whereupon the Lodge was moved to Windsor on the Vermont side of the Connecticut River, on June 24, 1785, and took the name of Vermont Lodge, No. 1. Later a Lodge was opened in the town of Manchester. Both this and the first Lodge were warranted by the Grand Lodge of Massachusetts.

The third Lodge was authorized by Sir John Johnson, Provincial Grand Master of Lower Canada (formerly of New York), in 1791, by a warrant granted to Governor Thomas Chittenden and others.

The fourth and fifth Lodges opened in this jurisdiction were warranted in 1793–94 by the Grand Lodge of Connecticut.

The representatives of these five Lodges met in Convention at Rutland, October 10, 1794, organized a Grand Lodge October 14th, and that body held a meeting October 15th.

The anti-Masonic party exercised so much influence in this State that the Grand Lodge was compelled to suspend its labors in 1833.

The G. L., however, did not dissolve, but maintained its legal existence by regular, although private, communications of the officers, and by adjournments, until 1846, when it resumed vigor. Nathan B. Haswell, who was the Grand Master at the time of the suspension, took the chair at the resumed communication in January, 1846.

The Grand Chapter in this State was organized December 20, 1804, Jonathan Wells being first Grand High Priest.

The Grand Council of R. and S. Masters was organized August 19, 1854, by a convention of four Councils held at Vergennes ; Nathan B. Haswell being elected Grand Master.

Kentucky.—Free Masonry was introduced into this State (then a territory), by the Grand Lodge of Virginia, which in 1788 granted a charter for

* Gould, vol. vi., p. 461.

Lexington Lodge, No. 25, at Lexington. This was the first Lodge instituted west of the Alleghany Mountains. Three other Lodges were subsequently chartered by Virginia—at Paris, Georgetown, and Frankford, and a dispensation granted for a fifth at Shelbyville. These five Lodges met in convention at Lexington on September 8, 1800, and having resolved that it was expedient to organize a Grand Lodge, they prepared an address to the Grand Lodge of Virginia, and the convention adjourned to October 16th. On that day it reassembled, and organized the Grand Lodge of Kentucky, William Murray being elected Grand Master.

Chapters of Royal Arch Masons were first established in Kentucky by Thomas Smith Webb in 1816, and the Grand Chapter was formed December 4, 1817.

Ohio.—On April 23, 1783, "American Union" met for the last time as an Army Lodge; it was then ordered to stand closed until the W. Master should call them together. In 1790 a colony from New England, including members of American Union Lodge, having become established northwest of the Ohio, the old Lodge was reopened at Marietta by Jonathan Heart, Master, with Benjamin Tupper and Rufus Putnam officiating as Wardens.

The Grand Lodge of Ohio was organized at Chillicothe, January 8th, by the following Delegates:

Robert Oliver and Ichabod Nye, Delegates from Union Lodge, No. 13.

William Skinner, Thomas Henderson, and Francis Mennessier, Delegates from Cincinnati Lodge, No. 13.

Thomas Gibson and Elias Langham, Delegates from Scioto Lodge, No. 2.

John W. Seely and George Todd, Delegates from Erie Lodge, No. 41.

Isaac Vanhorn, Delegate from Amity Lodge, No. 105.[*]

That distinguished patriot, General Rufus Putnam, of Marietta, was elected Grand Master, but being unable from age and infirmity to journey to Chillicothe and discharge the labors of his appointment, he sent his letter of declination. Therefore, under the Constitution, Samuel Huntington became the first Grand Master; Lewis Cass, first D. G. M.; William Skinner, S. G. W.; William Rayen, J. D. W.; Henry Massie, G. T.; Henry Brush, S.;

[*] Gould, vol. vi., p. 460, and Mitchell, p. 605.

528   FREE MASONRY IN THE UNITED STATES.

Philemon Beecher, S. D.; Thomas Kirker, J. D.; John Woodbridge, G. M.; Peter Spurch, G. S. and Tyler.

Michigan.—Zion Lodge, No. 1, of Detroit, was instituted under a warrant from the Grand Lodge of England in 1793. This Lodge affiliated with the Provincial Grand Lodge of Lower Canada in 1794, and with the Grand Lodge of New York in 1806, remaining on the roll of the latter until the formation of the Grand Lodge of Michigan in 1826, when Detroit, Oakland, and Menominee Lodges were organized.

The Grand Lodge of Michigan was originally organized at Detroit June 26, 1826, by Henry J. Hunt, John L. Whiting, Austin E. Wing, Levi Cook, John Garrison, Charles Jackson, Andrew G. Whitney, Marshall Chapin, Orville Cook, and John Anderson.

In consequence of the Morgan excitement the Grand Lodge became dormant in 1829, but was revived in 1841. This step being deemed irregular by the other American jurisdictions, a majority of the Lodges again met in Convention, and organized the present Grand Lodge in 1844.

Indiana—The first Lodge was opened in this State in 1807—Vincennes Lodge, No. 15, at Vincennes—under a warrant granted by the Grand Lodge of Kentucky. Five other Lodges were subsequently chartered by the same authority. On December 3, 1817, a convention assembled at Corydon, at which were present the representatives of six chartered Lodges, and two under dispensation from Kentucky, and one under dispensation from Ohio. The convention, having taken the preliminary steps, adjourned to meet at Madison on January 12, 1818, on which day the Grand Lodge was organized.

The Grand Chapter was established in 1845, the Grand Commandery on May 16, 1854, and the Grand Council of Royal and Select Masters on December 11, 1855.

Mississippi.—The first Lodge in this State was organized in 1801, under warrant from the Grand Lodge of Kentucky. Two other Lodges were also warranted by Kentucky, and two by Tennessee. The representatives of three of these Lodges met July 27, 1818, and organized the Grand Lodge of Mississippi.

Masonic Temple, Cincinnati, O.

District of Columbia.—In 1793, Lodge No. 15, of Washington, took part in laying the corner-stone of the Capitol, and on the 11th of December, 1810, a Convention was held at Washington, and took the preliminary steps to form a Grand Lodge. Pursuant to the action of the Convention, the Grand Lodge of the District of Columbia was organized January 8, 1811.

Tennessee.—The first Lodges in this State were warranted by the Grand Lodge of North Carolina. The Grand Lodge was established in 1813. This was done by the Delegates of eight Lodges. Thomas Claiborne was the first Grand Master.

Maine.—This State was formerly a part of Massachusetts, but became an independent State in 1820, and a Grand Lodge was organized in it by twenty-four Lodges on June 1st of that year. The Grand Lodge of Massachusetts very gracefully consented to an equitable division of the charity and other funds, when asked to do so by the new Grand Lodge.

Alabama.—The first Lodge in this jurisdiction was opened in 1819, under warrant from the Grand Lodge of South Carolina. The Grand Lodge of this State was organized June 14, 1821, by seven Lodges.

Texas.—The first Lodge in this State, then a part of Mexico, was Holland Lodge, and the following graphic piece of history is from one of the organizers of that Lodge:

"In the winter of 1834–35, five Master Masons, who had made themselves known to each other, consulted among themselves, and, after various interviews and much deliberation, resolved to take measures to establish a Lodge of their Order in Texas. This resolution was not formed without a full appreciation of its consequences to the individuals concerned. Every movement in Texas was watched at that time with jealousy and distrust by the Mexican Government, and already had its spies and emissaries denounced some of our best citizens as factionists and disaffected persons; already were the future intended victims of a despotic power being selected. It was well known that Free Masonry was particularly odious to the Catholic priesthood, whose influence in the country at that time was all-powerful. The dangers, therefore, attendant upon an organization of Masons at this time, which was 'trying men's souls,' were neither few nor unimportant. But zeal for a beloved institution predominated; all fears of personal consequences were thrown aside, and the resolution to establish a Lodge was adopted. The five brethren were John H. Wharton, Asa Brigham, James A. E. Phelps, Alexander Russell, and Anson Jones, and tney appointed a time and place of meeting to concert measures to carry their resolution into effect. In the meantime another Master Mason came into their plans—Brother J. P. Caldwell. The place of meeting was back of the town Brazoria, near the place known as General John Austin's, in a little grove of wild laurel, and which had been selected as a family burying-ground by that distinguished soldier and citizen. The spot was secluded, and out of the way of 'cowans and eaves-droppers,' and they felt they were alone. Here, and under such circumstances, at ten o'clock in the morning of a day in March, 1835, was held the first formal Masonic meeting in Texas. The six brethren I have mentioned were all present; and it was concluded to apply to the Grand Lodge of Louisiana for a dispensation to form and open a Lodge, to be called Holland Lodge, in honor to the then M. W. G. Master of that body, J. H. Holland. The funds were raised by a contribution to defray the expenses, to which each contributed. A petition was in due time drawn up and signed by them, which was forwarded to New Orleans, having been previously signed by another Master Mason, Brother W. D. C. Hall. The officers named in the petition were: For W. M., Anson Jones; S. W., Asa Brigham; J. W., J. P. Caldwell, who filled those offices, respectively, until the close of 1837. The Dispensation was granted, after some delay, to these Brethren, and Holland Lodge, No. 36, U. D., was instituted and opened at Brazoria, on December 27, 1835. Brother Phelps was chosen Treasurer, and M. C. Patton, Secretary. The Lodge held its meetings at Brazoria, in the second story of the old Court-house, which room was afterward occupied by St. John's Lodge, No. 5. About this time the difficulties with Mexico broke out into open hostilities, and our work was very much retarded by that circumstance, and by the members having to be absent in the service of the country. Still, there were a few others from time to time, introduced into the Order, either by receiving the degrees or by affiliation. The Lodge struggled on until

February, 1836, when I presided over its last meeting at Brazoria. I well recollect the night, and the fact that Brother Fannin, who one month later became so celebrated for his misfortunes and those of his unfortunate party at Goliad, acted as Senior Deacon. It seemed, indeed, that the gloom which prevailed in the Lodge that night was a foreshadowing of its and their unhappy fate, which was so soon to overtake both.

"In March, Brazoria was abandoned. Urea soon after took possession of the place at the head of a detachment of the Mexican army, and the records, books, jewels, and everything belonging to the Lodge were utterly destroyed by them, and our members were scattered in every direction. Brothers Wharton, Phelps, and myself joined the Texan troops on the Colorado, about the 18th of March. In the meantime, the Grand Lodge of Louisiana had issued a Charter for Holland Lodge, No. 36, and it was brought over to Texas by Brother John M. Allen. This, together with some letters from the Grand Secretary, was handed to me by Brother Allen, on the prairie between Groce's and San Jacinto, while we were on the march, and carried by me in my saddle-bags to the encampment of the army on Buffalo Bayou, at Lynchburg. Had we been beaten here, Santa Anna would have captured the Charter of Holland Lodge, at San Jacinto, as Urea had the Dispensation for it at Brazoria. Such an event, however, was impossible. The Charter and papers were taken safely to Brazoria; but, as the members had been lessened in numbers by death, or scattered in the army and elsewhere in the service of the country, no attempt was ever made to revive the work of the Lodge at *that* place.

"In October, 1837, however, it was reopened by myself and others, at the City of Houston, having then been in existence about two years."

In the meantime two other Lodges, with charters from the Grand Lodge of Louisiana, were established in Texas—Milam, at Nacogdoches, and Temple Lodge, No. 4, at Houston. MacFarlane Lodge, No. 3, at San Augustin, and St. John's Lodge, at Brazoria, originated from the Grand Lodge of Mississippi.

In May, 1838, a convention of Delegates from the above-named Lodges met at Houston, the then capital of the *Republic* of Texas, and organized a Grand Lodge.*

---

* See Reprint of Proceedings of the Grand Lodge of Texas, published by A. S. Ruthven, Grand Secretary. Also World's Masonic Register, pp. 404-406.

Arkansas.—According to some authorities, Masonry was introduced into Arkansas by the Spanish more than a century ago. The present Grand Lodge was formed in 1838 by four Lodges, two holding warrants from Louisiana, and one each from Alabama and Tennessee.

Wisconsin.—The history of organized Free Masonry in Wisconsin commenced in 1843 by the establishment of Mineral Point Lodge at Mineral Point, Melody Lodge at Platteville, and Milwaukee Lodge at Milwaukee, all under the authority of the Grand Lodge of Missouri. On the 18th of the following December, delegates from these three Lodges assembled in convention at Madison, and organized the Grand Lodge of Wisconsin, Rev. B. T. Kavanaugh, the Master of Melody Lodge, being elected Grand Master.

The Grand Chapter was established February 13, 1850, and Dwight F. Lawton elected Grand High Priest.

Iowa.—The advent of Free Masonry into Iowa was on November 20, 1840, at Burlington, where a Lodge was opened under a Warrant from the Grand Lodge of Missouri. Theodore S. Parvin, since Grand Master and later G. Sec., was one of the founders of this Lodge, and James R. Hartsock, another Past Grand Master, was the first initiate. A second Lodge was formed at Bloomington (now Muscatine) February 4, 1841; a third at Dubuque, October 20, 1841; and a fourth at Iowa City, October 10, 1842. On January 2, 1844, a convention was held and a Grand Lodge organized; Oliver Cock being elected M. W. Grand Master, and Theodore S. Parvin, G. S.

The Grand Chapter was organized June 8, 1854; the Grand Council in 1857, and the Grand Commandery June 6, 1854. The A. & A. 33° has also been introduced into the State, and there is a Grand Consistory and several subordinate bodies.

Illinois.—The first Lodge opened in Illinois was warranted by Pennsylvania, June 2, 1806, for Western Star Lodge, at the ancient town of Kaskaskia. On the 28th of August, 1815, the G. L. of Kentucky warranted a Lodge for Shawneetown. On October 6, 1819, the G. L. of Tennessee warranted a Lodge at Edwardsville.

In 1822, the G. L. of Missouri granted warrants for the following Lodges:

Olive Branch—Vandalia, at Vandalia—Sangamon, at Springfield—Union, at Jonesboro, and Edon Lodge. These were all warranted between October 3d and 22d, of that year. And in the same year Indiana granted a dispensation for Albion Lodge.

The Grand Lodge was established in 1823, became extinct in 1828, and was reorganized in 1840, by six Lodges; there being twelve Lodges in the State at that time.

California.—The first Lodge in this jurisdiction was California Lodge, established at San Francisco under a warrant from the Grand Lodge of the District of Columbia, bearing date November 9, 1848, Levi Stowell, W. M., William Van Voorhis, S. W. The second Lodge was Connecticut, No. 75, chartered January 31, 1849, by the Grand Lodge of Connecticut. This Lodge was opened at Sacramento, Caleb Fenner, W. M., and L. J. Wilder, S. W. The third Lodge was chartered by the Grand Lodge of Missouri, May 10, 1848, and was organized at Benton City October 30, 1849; Sachel Woods, W. M., L. E. Stewart, S. W. The fourth Lodge was opened at Sacramento City, December 4, 1849, under dispensation from the Grand Lodge of New Jersey, W. N. Dougherty, W. M., and Barryman Jennings, S. W. April 19, 1850, the Grand Lodge of California was organized at Sacramento by the first three above-named Lodges, Jonathan D. Stevenson being Grand Master, and John H. Gihon, Grand Secretary.

Oregon.—The Grand Lodge of Oregon was established in 1855. The officers were John Elliott, G. M.; J. C. Ainsworth, D. G. M.; A. M. Belt, S. G. W.; A. W. Ferguson, J. G. W.; Robert Thompson, G. Treasurer; Benjamin Stark, G. Secretary.

Nebraska.—Unique commencement of its Masonic career.—The first Lodge organized in Nebraska, Bellevue, met in the second story of the Trading Post of General Sarpy, near the Steamboat landing at Bellevue, in 1855. Concerning the early days of this Frontier Lodge, A. R. Gilmore, one of the members, gives the following:

"This venerable specimen of primitive architecture still graces the spot where it then stood, and around and within its rude walls are clustered many highly valued associations. Within its rough walls the sound of the gavel first hailed the Craft and called them to their first 'labor.' In this humble room the pioneer band of the 'Brotherhood' first assembled around their altar, and received their first charge from the lips of their first Master (L. B. Kinney), who set the Craft to work under 'due instructions' in this then extreme limit of civilization. The official regalia, or rather the jewels, of the Lodge,

The Old Trading Post, and First Lodge in Nebraska.

were skilfully made of tin by a craftsman, who afterward established the manufacture of tinware in this city.*

"During the fall of 1855 General Peter A. Sarpy handed in his petition for initiation. The report of the committee to whom it was referred was favorable to his admission, and a ballot was proposed, seconded, and carried. The preparation for this duty developed the fact that we were destitute of both box and ballot, and to relieve ourselves from this awkward dilemma we were forced to substitute an empty gallon pickle-jar for a ballot-box, and a box

* From A. R. Gilmore, Masonic Register, pp. 255, 256.

of small gravel-stones, which I had gathered as specimens, and which I still had in my possession, were selected to serve the friendly office, while a cup of 'leaden bullets' were to perform the 'darker colored' service. The jar, the stones, and bullets were then placed upon our primitive altar (two trunks covered with a blue blanket), when we gravely proceeded with our ballot. This done, our W. M. ordered the 'contents of the bottle' analyzed and the result proclaimed, a task that was speedily and scientifically performed by the J. and S. W., who gave their unanimous opinion that the presence of 'lead' was not discovered or detected, and that the ballot was clear in favor of the candidate. A few evenings thereafter, as many of our members as could leave accompanied the 'candidate' to Council Bluffs, it being the evening of the regular meeting of the Council Bluff Lodge. They closed their Lodge in the early part of the evening, and kindly tendered Bellevue Lodge the use of their room, furniture, tools, and aid. Whereupon our Lodge was opened in due form, General L. L. Bowen presiding, and the Entered Apprentice Degree duly conferred upon General Peter A. Sarpy, the hardy pioneer and Indian trader of thirty-six years' standing."

This was the first degree conferred by Bellevue Lodge—the first in Nebraska. The Grand Lodge of Nebraska was duly organized in 1857, and in 1902 the number of Lodges in this jurisdiction was 236 and the number of members 13,115.

Minnesota.—Lodges were first established in Minnesota in 1850. In 1853 three Lodges united and formed the Grand Lodge of Minnesota. Four years later there were nineteen Lodges in this jurisdiction, and in 1902 there were 228 Lodges, and 17,528 members.

Kansas.—The first Lodges in the then Territory of Kansas were opened in 1854. And in the year 1855, there were three Lodges in Kansas holding warrants from the Grand Lodge of Missouri. On November 14, 1855, two of these Lodges met in convention at Leavenworth, but in consequence of the absence of the third Lodge, the convention adjourned until December 27, 1855. At that date the two Lodges of Smithton and Leavenworth met (Wyandot Lodge being again absent), and organized the Grand Lodge of Kansas, and elected Richard R. Reece Grand Master.

Washington.—Free Masonry was introduced into this jurisdiction in 1857. The first Lodges were Olympia, Steilacoom, Grand Mound, and Washington.

On December 6 to 9, 1858, delegates from these four Lodges met in convention at the city of Olympia, and organized the Grand Lodge of Free and Accepted Masons of the Territory of Washington. T. F. McElroy was elected Grand Master, and T. M. Reed, Grand Secretary.

The high degrees of the American Rite have not yet been established in Washington Territory; but in 1872 the Ancient and Accepted Scottish Rite was introduced by Brother Edwin A. Sherman, the agent of the Supreme Council of the Southern Jurisdiction, and several bodies of that Rite were organized.

Colorado.—The first Lodge in this jurisdiction was opened in 1860, under a charter from the Grand Lodge of Kansas. In 1861 Rocky Mountain and Summit Lodges were chartered, and in the same year the Grand Lodge was organized.

Nevada.—This was originally a part of California, and when it separated from that State, in 1865, it had eight Lodges. These met in that year at Virginia City, and organized the Grand Lodge of Nevada.

West Virginia.—Originally a part of Virginia, the Lodges here were under the Grand Lodge of that State. But the new State of West Virginia having been formed in 1863, nine Lodges sent delegates to a convention held at Fairmount, April 12, 1865, which, after some discussion, adjourned to meet again on May 10th of the same year, when the Grand Lodge of West Virginia was organized, and W. J. Bates elected Grand Master.

The Grand Chapter of Royal Arch Masons of West Virginia was organized, November 16, 1871, by a convention of five Chapters.

Idaho.—The first four Lodges in this jurisdiction were chartered by the Grand Lodge of Oregon and the Grand Lodge of Washington (one by the latter). In 1867 these Lodges met in convention and organized the Grand Lodge of Idaho.

MASONIC TEMPLE, DENVER, COL.

Utah.—The first Lodge in this jurisdiction was Wasatch, chartered October 7, 1867, by the Grand Lodge of Montana.

Mount Moriah Lodge, No. 70, was chartered October 21, 1868, by the Grand Lodge of Kansas, and Argenta Lodge, No. 21, by the Grand Lodge of Colorado, September 26, 1871. All of these Lodges are situated in Salt Lake City. On January 16 to 20, 1872, the representatives of the three Lodges met at Salt Lake City and organized the Grand Lodge of Utah, O. F. Strickland being elected Grand Master.

Montana.—This Grand Lodge was organized in 1866.

New Mexico.—The Grand Lodge for this jurisdiction was organized in 1877.

Indian Territory.—The Grand Lodge in this Territory was organized in 1874.

Wyoming.—The Grand Lodge for this jurisdiction was organized in 1883.

Colored Masons.—In 1775, Prince Hall and fourteen colored men of Boston were initiated in a Military Lodge attached to General Gage's army, and in 1784 they applied to the Grand Lodge of England for a Charter. Their request was granted September 29th of that year, but the warrant did not arrive in Boston until 1787. It bore the number 459, and the title "Africa Lodge." Prince Hall, who was the first Master, established a Lodge by his own authority in Philadelphia in 1797, and a second at Providence, R. I., shortly afterward. The three Lodges formed a Grand Lodge in 1808. In 1847 there were three colored Grand Lodges in the United States—one at Boston and two in Pennsylvania. These met in convention and organized a National Grand Lodge, which has met triennially.* There were in 1901 thirty-one Grand Lodges in the different States of the Union and one in Canada, with a membership of 39,253.

* Gould, vol. vi., p. 464.

DOMINION OF CANADA.

Nova Scotia.—By the conditions of the treaty of Utrecht, in 1712, France resigned to England what subsequently became the Provinces of Canada, Nova Scotia, Prince Edward Island, and the Hudson Bay Territory, and by the Treaty of Paris, in 1763, she resigned to the same power Cape Breton, together with all her remaining North American possessions east of the Mississippi.

Shortly after its cession, in 1712, the British troops took possession of, and commenced a settlement at, that part of Nova Scotia known as Annapolis Royal, and the next settlement was made at Halifax in 1750.

In 1738, under authority from Henry Price, of Boston, Mass., a military Lodge was established at Annapolis by Erasmus James Philips, and in 1750 another was established at Halifax, but whether it was a military or permanent Lodge is uncertain. In 1757 Philips was appointed Provincial Grand Master by the Ancients, and two Lodges were warranted by the same body at that time. Three others sprang up under the same authority; the first two in 1768, and the third in 1781. By St. Andrew's and St. John's Lodges, four dispensations were granted. At this time, however, three of the Lodges warranted by the Ancients were extinct.[*]

In 1784 a Provincial Grand Lodge was organized at Halifax, under a warrant from the Ancients, its subordinates numbering nineteen, in 1789.

"The seal of this Grand Lodge is of the largest size, circular, and heraldic, presenting a quartered shield, bearing on its compartments respectively the figures of a lion, an ox, a man, and an eagle; and enclosed on either side by a palm branch, with supporters in the form of full-length figures of the cherubim and seraphim, so called, hieroglyphically composed of the superior parts of the man and posterior parts of the ox.

The crest is the ark of alliance, supported by cherubim and seraphim kneeling, with wings extended toward each other and meeting above the ark. The motto or legend on a scroll at the base of the shield is " Kodes al Adonai," being the value in Roman letters of the Hebrew characters on the frontlet of

[*] See Gould, vol. vi., p. 467.

a High Priest's mitre, and the circumscription Provincial Grand Lodge of Nova Scotia, with the date 1784 at the base below the scroll."*

The first Lodge organized by the Provincial Grand Lodge outside of Halifax was that at Guysborough (then called Chedabucto), bearing the name of Temple Lodge. The Grand Master Pyke retained the office but one year, when an election took place. The Grand Lodge officers elected were described in print as follows :

"His Excellency, John Parr, Captain General and Governor in Chief in and over his Majesty's Province of Nova Scotia, the Islands of St. John and Cape Breton and their Dependencies, Vice Admiral of the same, &c., &c., &c., Right Worshipful Grand Master of Ancient Masons.

" The Right Worshipful Mr. William Campbell, Deputy Grand Master.

" The Honorable and Right Worshipful Richard Bulkeley, Senior Grand Warden.

"The Right Worshipful Mr. George Deblois, Junior, Junior Grand Warden.

" The Right Worshipful Mr. Joseph Peters, Grand Secretary.

" The Right Worshipful Mr. John Fillis, Junior, Grand Treasurer.

" The Rev. Joshua Wingate Weeks, Grand Chaplain.

" Mr. John Cannell, Deputy Grand Secretary.

" Mr. John Lewis, Grand Pursuivant.

" Mr. William Stewart, Grand Tyler."

In 1837 Scotland began to warrant Lodges here, and in 1866, established a Grand Lodge, with a constituency of ten Lodges. On June 24, 1869, a union between this Grand Lodge and the Provincial Grand Lodge under England took place, and the Grand Lodge of Nova Scotia was established.†

Relics.

In 1827 Dr. Charles T. Jackson and Francis Alger, of Boston, made a mineralogical survey of Nova Scotia, and while prosecuting their examination on Goat Island in Annapolis Basin, they discovered on the shore a flat stone slab, of such appearance as to challenge their curiosity. And upon removing the sand which partially covered it, they were surprised to find the square and compass cut in, near the upper edge of the face of the slab, and

* Rebold, p. 384.   † Gould, vol. vi., p. 467.

below this the date, 1606. Both the square and compass and the date were plainly drawn and deep cut. At about that time a small band of French emigrants located on Goat Island, near where this slab was found. And to commemorate the date of their settlement, or of their first cultivation of the soil here, they set up this stone, the inscriptions on which evidenced the presence of one or more of the Masonic craft.

In 1872, J. Fletcher Brennan, compiler of Rebold's History of Free Masonry, saw in the chest of the Lodge at Annapolis a copy of Anderson's Book of Constitutions, of 1723. This was a copy of the reprint by Benjamin Franklin in 1734. On the fly-leaf was written: "Presented to the Old Lodge by *Grand Master E. J. Phillips.*"

On the 5th of June, 1800, Edward, Duke of Kent * (at that time in command of H. M. troops in British North America), laid the corner-stone of Free Masons' Hall, Halifax. In 1876 this building was taken down and the present Hall, erected on its site. When erecting the new Hall the old corner-stone was carefully guarded and given a conspicuous place, where it is now seen. It bears the following inscription:

In the name of
God,
In the Reign of George III.,
His Royal Highness,
Prince Edward, Duke of Kent,
Commander-in-Chief of British N. America,
G. M. of Lower Canada,
In behalf R^D Bulkley,
Member of His Majesty's Council.
G. M. of N. Scotia,
Laid this Foundation-Stone of
Free Masons' Hall,
5th June, Anno Domini 1800,
And of Masonry 5800.

Hon. W. Ross, *Grand Secretary.*

* Father of Queen Victoria.

FREE MASONRY IN CANADA.

New Brunswick.—A warrant was granted to Ephraim Betts and others, in 1792, to form and hold Solomon's Lodge at St. Ann's—now Fredericton—and this Lodge is still active.

The Grand Lodge of New Brunswick was organized October 10, 1867, by sixteen Lodges—twelve English, three Irish, and one Scottish—there being at the time twenty-six Lodges in this Jurisdiction, viz., twenty English, three Irish, and three Scottish.

Canada.—The Merchant's Lodge of Quebec was established in 1761, under a warrant from New England. This was the first authorized Lodge in Canada. This was soon followed by other Lodges, one at Montreal, and five at Quebec; one of which was a Sea and Field Lodge in H. M. S. Canceux, and the Fifty-second Foot. Between 1787 and 1793 further Lodges were warranted by the Grand Lodge of England—some for Montreal, and four for Upper Canada.

Canada was divided in 1791 into what was called Upper and Lower Canada—it was next designated Canada East and Canada West, but is now known as Ontario and Quebec. In 1799 the number of Lodges under the authority of the Ancients was fourteen in Upper, and sixteen in Lower, Canada. Previous to 1857 forty-one additional Lodges were warranted from England. Ireland comes next, having warranted sixteen Lodges, the first in 1821, and the last in 1855. A Scottish Lodge was opened in Quebec in 1851.

SEVERANCE FROM THE GRAND LODGE OF ENGLAND.

Finding that they were neglected, the Fraternity determined to establish an independent Grand Lodge. At this time (1855) there were eighty-three Lodges in Canada, forty-one of which were represented in the Convention that established the Grand Lodge of Canada.

The English Provincial Grand Lodge of Canada West discountenanced this movement, and on September 9, 1857, declared its independence, assuming the title of "Ancient Grand Lodge of Canada." But this state of things was short-lived, for on July 14, 1858, articles of union were agreed to, the junior body dissolved, and its officers and Lodges accorded their relative rank in the

G. L. of Canada. The G. L. was formally recognized by the G. L. of England in the following December. March 23, 1859, the Earl of Zetland, in a letter to Grand Master Wilson, acknowledged the jurisdiction of the G. L. of Canada, excepting the Lodges still adhering to their original allegiance, in Quebec and Montreal, retaining for them the full privileges as individual Lodges, together with the rights and privileges of their Provincial G. Lodges, which stipulation was agreed to by the Grand Master of Canada.

In 1867 Canada East, Canada West (Ontario), Nova Scotia, and New Brunswick, united and formed the "Dominion of Canada."* To these were added, in 1869, the territory of the Hudson's Bay Company, now the Province of Manitoba, British Columbia in 1871, and Prince Edward Island in 1873.

In 1869 Quebec organized its Grand Lodge, upon the principle of exclusive jurisdiction, which was contested by the Grand Lodge of Canada. The present G. M. of Quebec is Isaac H. Stearns, and the number of Lodges 57. The G. M. of Canada is R. T. Walkem, and the number of Lodges on the roll is 362.

There are three English Lodges in Montreal, under a Deputy Grand Master, appointed by the G. L. of England. These have hitherto declined to affiliate with the Grand Lodge; and the Grand Lodge of England, while interposing no obstacle to a transfer of their allegiance, wisely holds that the point is one which those Lodges are entitled to settle according to their own judgment, without pressure of any kind.

Prince Edward Island.—Two Military Lodges were formed here under warrants from Nova Scotia; the first in 1781 and the second in 1797. The latter became a stationary Lodge. A Scottish Charter was issued in 1858, and the Lodge so formed, with seven on the registry of England, organized the Grand Lodge June 23, 1875.

Newfoundland.—The first two Lodges on this island were established under warrants from Boston. Other Lodges were erected by the Grand Lodge of England in 1784–85, and five by the ancients prior to 1778. In 1867 there were two jurisdictions on the island; and each had its District Grand Master with in one case six, and in the other two, Lodges to supervise.

* Gould, vol. vi., pp. 466–468.

FREE MASONRY IN MEXICO.

Manitoba.—The first Lodge in this province was established by the Grand Lodge of Canada in 1870. Two others were warranted soon after. These united and formed the Grand Lodge of Manitoba, May 12, 1875. There was a schism in 1877, during which year, and a part of the next, there were two Grand Lodges in the province; but a union was effected in 1879.

British Columbia.—Between 1859 and 1867 there were four Lodges established in this territory and Vancouver's Island, under warrants from England,

THE GREAT CATHEDRAL, MEXICO.

and five were opened under warrants from Scotland in 1862–69. Eight of these organized the Grand Lodge September 21, 1871.

Mexico.—The first Lodge in this country was established in 1816, at Vera Cruz, and the second at Campeachy in 1817.

Soon after the introduction of Free Masonry into Mexico it was seized upon by the political parties as a means of promoting their interests. So that between the complications of politics, and the warfare against it by the Catholic Church, it has been subject to many vicissitudes of fortune—now prosperous and vigorous with a numerous following, next paralyzed by

TYPES, MEXICO.

the Church, or by the defeat of the political party to which it was principally attached.

In 1883, there were 7 Grand Lodges and 42 Lodges. In the same year, 12 Lodges met at the Capital and established the Grand Lodge of the City of Mexico.

THE WEST INDIES AND CENTRAL AMERICA.

Cuba.—First Lodge in 1804. Number of Lodges, 28. The Spanish Catholics, true to their national instincts and the dogmas of a Pagan religion, have relentlessly persecuted the Fraternity here. As a sample, a Spanish officer ordered the arrest and imprisonment of a large number of Masons in Santiago de Cuba, of whom he had eighteen shot in cold blood. The name of this representative of Spain was Gonzales Bret, and the date, not in the Dark Ages, but in 1889.

Hispaniola.—The first Lodge on this island was established in 1749. After passing through numberless vicissitudes, and surviving many black dynasties, Republicanism and Free Masonry still flourish, there being now two Republics, 66 Lodges, and 2,000 Masons.

For the other West India Islands, see *statistics*, p. 558.

Costa Rica.—The first Lodge was opened at San Jose, in 1867, by warrant from New Granada. A G. O. and S. P. C. 33° for Central America was established at the same place in 1870.

The Sov. G. Com. in 1890 was Manuel B. Boilla, and there were 24 Lodges under the G. O.

Guatemala.—The first Lodge opened in this Republic was by warrant from the G. O. of Colombia, at Carthagenia. In 1890 the number of members was 250.

San Salvador.—Its first Lodge was established at the Capital, in 1882, by authority of the G. O. of Central America. Soon after this a Lodge was established at Tecla.

SOUTH AMERICA.

Venezuela.—Free Masonry was introduced into this country early in the nineteenth century, by the Grand Orient of Spain. In 1827, Bolivar prohibited all secret societies. After passing through many vicissitudes, it appeared in 1884 under a Grand Orient, the same being divided into a Grand Lodge, Grand Chapter, Grand Consistory, and a Supreme Council, each body being entirely independent of the others. In 1901 there were 35 Lodges under the Grand Lodge.

Venezuela has recently erected a Masonic Temple at the capital, Caracas, out of the funds of the State, and at its dedication, the President of the Republic officiated as G. M.

Colombia.—The first Lodge was established in this country in 1833. Number of Lodges, 7.

Bolivia.—The first Lodge was chartered in 1875 by authority from Lima. There are four Lodges in Bolivia under the G. L. of Peru.

British Guiana.—There were two Lodges in existence at Georgetown or Demerara, in the last century. The first, St. Jean de la Re-Union, was established by the Grand Lodge of Holland in 1771; and the second, by the Grand Lodge of Ireland, in 1796.

Dutch Guiana.—The Lodge La Vertueuse was established in 1769, and La Fidèle Sincérité, in 1771, at Batavia; these were followed by Concordia in 1762, La Zélée in 1767, and Le Croissant des Trois Clefs in 1768, at Surinam.

French Guiana—Cayenne.—The first Lodge, L'Anglaise, was established here in 1755 by the Mother-Lodge of the same name at Bordeaux; the second, La Parfaite Union, in 1829, by the Grand Orient of France; and the third, La France Equinoxiale, in 1844, by the Supreme Council 33° of the same country. There is but one lodge at work now, a penal colony not being congenial to Free Masonry.

Brazil.—In 1815 a Lodge was established at Rio Janeiro, under a French warrant. This is believed to have been the first lodge in Brazil. In 1821 this Lodge was divided into three parts, and these by their deputies formed the first Grand Orient of Brazil.

In the same year Dom Pedro, Regent, and afterward Emperor of Brazil, was initiated in one of these Lodges. Subsequently, however, finding that the Masonic associations were being used for political purposes, he ordered their meetings to be discontinued.

After the abdication of Dom Pedro, a "Grand Brazilian Orient" was established, which led to the revival of the *original* "Grand Orient of Brazil." Political machinations soon made their presence felt—the old Grand Orient was despotic, and the new one Democratic, and therefore hostile to each other.

In 1860 there were 130 Lodges in Brazil, with the original G. O. in possession of the field. In 1863 there was strife, and the Grand Orient split into two parts, each of which became known by the name of the street in which it assembled. One body, the G. O. of Lavradio Valley, chose as its G. M. Baron Cayru, who was succeeded by Dr. Joachim Marcellino do Brito in 1865, and by the Visconde do Rio Branco in 1870. The other G. O., Benedictine Valley, elected Joachim Saldanha Marinho, G. M.

Following this, the Church again endeavored to get in some of its work. The Bishop of the Diocese of Pernambuco, at the bidding of the Jesuits, attempted to enforce a Papal bull against the Free Masons, and had counted on the support of the people; but his high-handed measures turned the tide of popular feeling, and he was mobbed in his own palace, his life only being saved by the military. Subsequently the Government interfered, and the Bishop was sentenced to four years' imprisonment.

In January, 1883, a union between the two Grand Orients was perfected, and Francisco Jose Cardoso proclaimed G. M. and Sov. G. Com. of the then only Grand Orient of Brazil.

Three rites are recognized by this body—the A. and A., S. R. 33°, the modern French (7), and the Adonhiramite rites. There were at this time 139 Lodges, 48 of which meet in the city of Rio Janeiro. In 1886 the total number of Lodges under the G. O. was 210. There were also three European Lodges at work in Brazil at that time.

Buenos Ayres.—After forming for some years a distinct State, it re-entered in 1860, the Confederacy of the Argentine Republic, of which it constitutes the head. The first Lodge was chartered at the city of Buenos Ayres by the Grand Lodge of Pennsylvania, September 5, 1825. In 1861 the Grand Lodge of England commenced chartering Lodges here. Number of Lodges, 68.

In 1858 the Roman Catholic Bishop fulminated a bull against all Masons within his bishopric. In this bull he declared the marriage contract dissolved in all cases where the husband refused to renounce Masonry.

An appeal was taken from his decree to His Holiness Pius IX., at Rome. Not receiving any reply, an inquiry was instituted as to the cause of the delay, when it was found that, during a sojourn at Montevideo in 1816, the Pontiff himself, then a young man, received the degrees of Masonry. This, however, is not considered good history.

Uruguay.—This country has a large, well-built, and pleasant capital, Montevideo, of which one-third of the residents are foreigners. According to Dr. Mackey, Free Masonry was introduced into this Republic in 1827, by the Grand Orient of France, which in that year chartered a Lodge called the "Children of the New World." But as the Republic was not fully established until 1828, there is some doubt as to the above date. A Lodge was regularly chartered in Montevideo by the Grand Lodge of Pennsylvania, February 6, 1832. In 1841, a Lodge, Chapter, Areopagus, and Consistory, were established by the Grand Orient of France. Further Lodges were erected under warrants from Brazil. In 1855, authority was obtained from one of the then existing Grand Orients at Rio Janeiro to establish a governing Masonic body, and the Supreme Council and Grand Orient of Uruguay were formally constituted at Montevideo. In 1886, the Sov. G. Com. and G. M. was Dr. Carlos de Castro. The number of subordinate Lodges was then 34.

Paraguay.—At the time this country declared its independence of Spain, the reins of government were seized by Dr. Francia, who, among his measures for advancing the material interests of the State, sealed it up from all communication with the outer world, so that Paraguay was for a long period as effectually closed as ever Japan had been. Nearly the same exclusive policy was pursued by his successors—Don Carlos Antonio Lopez, and his son, Don Francisco Solano Lopez. During the reign of the latter, a small band of Masons—mostly foreign residents, English, Americans, and Germans—occasionally met secretly and carried on the work of Masonry. For this they were arrested, repeatedly tortured, and finally ten of them were shot. But retribution was close at hand, as Lopez had involved the country in a war with

FREE MASONRY IN SOUTH AMERICA.

Brazil, Uruguay, and the Argentine Republic, the result of which to Paraguay was a loss of half of its male population and nearly one-half of its territory.

Peru.—Free Masonry was introduced into this country in 1825, after the independence of the Republic was achieved.

In that year, General Valero, a member of the Grand Orient of Columbia, visited Lima, and as a representative of that G. O., proceeded first to legitimate the Lodges in the new Republic, and afterward to organize others. At this time there were four Lodges at the capital, and nine others were soon after erected in the provincial towns.

In March, 1882, five Lodges met in convention at Lima and organized the "Grand Lodge of Peru." There are now 33 Lodges.

Chili.—The first Lodge in this Republic was L'Étoile du Pacifique, established at Valparaiso by the Grand Orient of France, September 12, 1851. The next was Pacific Lodge, formed shortly afterward under a dispensation from the G. M. of California. After this came L'Union Fraternelle, under the G. O. of France, also at Valparaiso, chartered in 1854. Number of Lodges in 1901, 10; members, 500.

Sandwich or Hawaiian Islands.—The first Lodge opened in this part of the world was warranted by the Supreme Council of France in 1850. In 1852, Hawaiian and Wailukee Lodges were authorized by the Grand Lodge of California. The last is at Maui; the others meet at Honolulu, where they occupy a hall in common. These three Lodges are composed of Americans, Englishmen, Germans, and natives. King Kalakaua was an active member of Le Progrès de l'Océanie, and his brother, William Pitt Leleihoku, is a member of the Hawaiian. The former visited many foreign countries and evinced the same interest in Masonry while on his travels as at home. On January 7, 1874, he was entertained by the Lodge, Columbian, of Boston, and on May 22, 1881, by the National Grand Lodge of Egypt. By the latter body the King was elected an Honorary Grand Master, and afterward delivered an oration, in which he expressed his belief that Egypt was the cradle, both of Operative and Speculative Masonry.*

* Gould, vol. vi., p. 395.

As the Sandwich Islands and their history are unique, a sketch of the latter will be of interest here. They were discovered by Captain James Cook in 1778. In *Owhyhee* or *Hawaii*, one of these islands, he fell a victim to the sudden resentment of the natives, February 14, 1779. The king and queen visited London in 1824, and died there in July. These people have made great progress in civilization, and embraced Christianity before any missionaries were settled among them. Population in 1884, 80,578. Numbers of native population said to be stationary. King Kaméhaméha IV. married Miss Emma Rooker, 1856. She came to England in 1865, landing at Southampton, July 13th, and visited the queen September 9th. The king died November, 1863. The Duke of Edinburgh warmly received at Honolulu, July 21, 1869. Kaméhaméha V. died, unmarried, December 11, 1872. Wm. C. Lunalilo crowned January 8, 1873; died February 3, 1874. Reciprocity treaty concluded between Hawaii and the United States, 1875. David Kalakaua (born November 16, 1836), elected king in opposition to Queen Emma, February 12th; visits the President at Washington, December 12, 1876; visits Europe; at Rome, July 1st; received by the queen of England at Windsor, July 12, 1881; crowned February 12, 1883. Queen Kapiolani arrives at Liverpool to be present at the royal jubilee service, June 2d; arrives in London June 8, 1887. See Hayden's Dictionary of Dates, p. 793.

Queen Liliuokalani was deposed in 1894. In 1898 Hawaii was annexed to the United States.

STATISTICS OF FREE MASONRY THROUGHOUT THE WORLD.

THE EASTERN HEMISPHERE.

EUROPE.

	First Lodge.	Grand Lodge.	Number of Lodges.		Members.
England,	1703,	1717,	2,465	(at home and abroad),	475,000.
Ireland,	1726,	1726,	426.		
Scotland,	1727,	1736,	663.		
Belgium,	1721,	1818,	19.		
Holland,	1734,	1756,	93,		4,938.
Germany,	1733,	1740,	505,		47,015.
Norway,		1891,	9,		1,791.
Denmark,	1743,	1743,	12,		4,243.
Sweden,	1735,	1759,	33,		10,985.
Russia,	1739,	1772.			
Austria,	1742,	1784.			
Hungary,		1870,	46,		3,324.
Roumania,	1859,	1880,	23.		
Switzerland,	1736,		32,		3,424.
France,	1721,	1738,	374	(80 being under the A. & A. Rite).	
Spain,	1729,	1767,	95.		
Portugal,	1735,	1869,	70,		2,800.
Italy,	1750,	1764,	109,		13,500.
Greece,	1837,	1867,	12,		2,000.
Turkey,	1748,		31.		
Malta,	1735,		6.		

Lodges, 5,023. Members given, 679,020.
Members estimated, 161,489.*

---

* On the basis of the average membership of Lodges in the countries of Europe where the number of members *is* given, the membership of the remaining countries is estimated.

Asia.

First Lodge.		Number of Lodges.	Members.
Bombay,	1758,	29.	
Bengal,	1728,	51.	
Madras,	1752,	33.	
Ceylon,	1771,	6.	
Sumatra,	1765,	2.	
Java,	1769,	8.	
Penang,	1809,	1.	
Singapore,	1845,	2.	
China,	1767,	18.	
Japan,	1866,	5.	
Borneo,	1885,	1.	
Philippines,	1800,	4.	
		160	Members estimated at **40** per Lodge, 6,400.

Africa and Islands.

First Lodge.		Number of Lodges.	Members.
Egypt,	1802,	20.	750.
Tunis,	1860,	14.	
Algiers,	1832,	15.	
Morocco,	1867,	2.	
Cape Coast,	1736,	1.	
Lagos,	1867,	1.	
Senegal,	1874,	2.	
Liberia,	1867,	6.	125.
Cape Town & Orange Free States, etc.,	1772,	91.	
Mozambique,		2.	
St. Helena,	1764,	2.	
Madeira,		3.	
Canaries,		9.	
Bourbon,	1775,	1.	125.
Mauritius,	1778,	2.	
		171	Members given, 1,000.

Remaining countries estimated at 35 per Lodge.............. 5,040.

STATISTICS OF FREE MASONRY.

Australasia.

First Lodge.		First Grand Lodge.	Number of Lodges.	Members.
N. S. Wales,	1820,	1839,	187.	8,186.
Victoria,	1841,	1883,	186.	
South Australia,	1884,		43.	2,594.
West Australia,	1842,		49.	2,584.
Tasmania,	1846,	1875,	20.	
New Zealand,	1843,		117.	5,385.
			602.	Given, 18,749.

Estimated on an average of 47 per Lodge .... 9,752.

Oceanica.

First Lodge.		Number of Lodges.	Members.
New Caledonia,	1868,	2.	
Society Islands,	1834.	1.	
			Estimated, 102.

Totals in the Eastern Hemisphere:

Lodges...	5,959.
Members given...................................	698,769.
" estimated.............................	182,783.
Non-affiliates *.................................	240,000.
Total...	1,121,552.

THE WESTERN HEMISPHERE.
THE UNITED STATES.

Grand Lodges....................................	50.
Lodges...	12,008.
Members...	890,886.
Non-affiliated Members *.........................	375,000.
Grand total in United States, Members...........	1,265,886.

British America.

Lodges...	635.
Members...	43,269.

Mexico.

Lodges...	53.
Members...	15,000.

Totals in North America:

Grand Lodges....................................	57.
Lodges...	12,696.
Members...	1,324,155.

* This includes the aged and infirm.

STATISTICS OF FREE MASONRY.

West India Islands.

First Lodge.		First Grand Lodge.	Number of Lodges.	Number of Members.
Cuba,	1804,	1859,	28.	1,308.
Hayti,	1749,		40.	
Jamaica,	1739,		11.	
Porto Rico,	1800,		15.	396.
Santa Cruz,	1760,		1.	
St. Thomas,	1792,		3.	
Caribbean Islands,	1739,		23.	
Antigua,	1739,		2.	
Barbadoes,	1740,		2.	
Curaçoa,	1757,		2.	
Dominica,	1773,		26.	
Guadeloupe,	1784,		3.	
Martinique,	1738,		1.	
Bahamas,	1752,		4.	
Bermudas,	1761,		7.	

Lodges, 168.   Given, 1,704.
Estimated on an average of 40 per Lodge.................. 5,080.

Central America and South America.

First Lodge.		First Grand Lodge.	Number of Lodges.	Number of Members.
Nicaragua,	1763,		1.	
Costa Rica,	1867,		23.	
Guatemala,	1881,		4.	200
San Salvador,	1882,		2.	
Colombia,	1833,	1863,	7.	
Venezuela,	1824,	1838,	35.	
The Guianas,	1771,		7.	
Brazil,	1815,	1821,	214.	
Argentine Republic,	1825,	1858,	23.	
Uruguay,	1827,	1855,	34.	
Ecuador,	1857.		4.	
Bolivia,	1875,			541
Peru,	1825,	1831,	33.	550.
Chili,	1840,	1862,	10.	500.
Sandwich Islands,	1870.		3.	
Paraguay,	1896,		8.	

Lodges in Central and South America .... 408.   Given, 1,791.
Estimated on an average of 50 per Lodge.................. 18,050.

Totals in South America and West India Islands:

Lodges.. 576.
Members... 26,625.

STATISTICS OF FREE MASONRY.

SUMMARY.

Eastern Hemisphere.—Lodges .... 5,959.
" " Members .... 1,121,552.
Western Hemisphere.—Lodges .... 13,272.
" " Members .... 1,350,780.
Grand Totals.—Lodges .... 19,231.
Members .... 2,472,332.

Notwithstanding that innumerable orders have been established and are now in operation, and that the old institution has been and is now being assailed by fanatics and cranks, it is everywhere in a flourishing condition. In consequence of its antiquity, numerical strength, and of the fact that it comprises the best men in every community, it is regarded as an aristocratic institution; and inversely, the influence of its humane and noble principles have done much toward making good and true men—fit material of which to make Free Masons.

In North America the institution has more than kept pace with the growth of the country, and throughout its whole extent it is increasing rapidly.

In Europe Grand Lodges are among the prominent and permanent institutions of all of its different countries, and Lodges are to be found in every locality of any importance from England to the Bosphorus.

In Asia Lodges are numerous, and on the increase in all its principal countries.

In fact, the institution is thoroughly established and flourishing in the four quarters of the globe; proving that the "Universality of Free Masonry" is not a meaningless expression, but a wonderful fact in history.

After encountering and overcoming bigotry and fanaticism for many centuries, the institution stands forth throughout the world in its might and majesty, as the great conserver and exponent of morality, and promoter of the true fellowship of man.

NOTES FROM AUTHORITIES.

1. In the History of Rhode Island and Newport, in the Past, by the Rev. Edward Peterson, we find the following : "In the spring of 1658, Mordecai Campannell, Moses Peckeckoe Levi, and others, in all fifteen families, arrived at Newport, from Holland. They brought with them the first three degrees of Masonry, and worked them in the house of Campannell, and continued to do so, they and their successors, to the year 1742.

2. When and by whom these and other old Lodges were constituted, cannot now be decided, but that they or similar combinations of Free Masons existed centuries before the Grand Lodge cannot be doubted. See McClenachan, in History of Free Masonry in the State of New York, vol. i., pp. 33–94.

3. It is evident that Brethren who had left the Old World, and brought to their new homes a knowledge of the Craft, were as much within their rights in holding Lodges in Philadelphia, Portsmouth (New Hampshire), and elsewhere in America, as those who assembled in like manner in England and Scotland. . . . Gould, vol. vi., p. 436.

4. Clifford P. MacCalla of Philadelphia, discovered in 1884, an original Masonic record, dating from 1731. This book is bound in vellum, and bears on the front cover the words, "*Philadelphia City, St. John's Lodge, Libre B.*" The *second* record of that Lodge.

5. "The documentary evidence showing the existence of a Lodge reaches back to 1731, and as we there only commenced with 'Libre B,' the actual date at which the Brethren who are named in it (or those they may have succeeded) associated together as a body, must remain a pure matter of conjecture. 'Libre A,' if produced, might, indeed, bring us within measurable distance of this period; but on the other hand, it is equally possible, not to say probable, that it would point to an uninterrupted succession of Philadelphia Masons meeting at St. John's Lodge . . . "from time immemorial." Gould, vol. vi , pp. 429, 435.

6. But without going back any further than the year 1731, we shall do well to reflect that the sovereignty of Grand Lodges was then only on its trial. Such bodies had been formed, it is true, at London, York, and Dublin. . . . But in Scotland, the most ancient home of Masonic precedent, there was as yet no chartered Lodges ; and assemblies of Brethren, formed in Philadelphia, were the only Masonic associations existing in that country. Brethren united to form Lodges in neighborhoods where there were fair chances of their continuance. . . .

7. The Fraternity there (Philadelphia) must be held to have been as much and as legally a Grand Lodge as that of "All England at York." Their meetings, for all we know to the contrary, may have been held before the era of Grand Lodges, and they certainly were before the influence of the earliest of these bodies had made itself felt across the seas. Gould, vol. vi., p. 436.

8. It must not be forgotten that but few records were ever made of the making of Masons, prior to the organization of the Grand Lodge of England, in 1717. Free Masons assembled when and where they chose ; opened a Lodge and made Masons, without being responsible or amenable to any higher authority : and hence it is not very remarkable that we have no records of their meetings." Mitchell : Masonic History, pp. 578, 579.

9. And even before *regular* Lodges were constituted, it cannot be doubted that informal receptions into our Fraternity took place whenever a few Masons met together. Wherever the earliest Lodges existed, there we find traces of previous meetings, and in no other way can the presence in the first stated Lodges, of undoubted Masons initiated elsewhere, be accounted for. Gould, vol. v., p. 78.

10. There appeared in the *Pennsylvania Gazette*, No. 108, December 3–8, 1730, the following article on the first page: "As there are several lodges of Free Masons erected in this Province, and people have been much amused with conjectures concerning them, we think the following account of Free Masonry from London will be acceptable to our readers : " By the death of a gentleman who was one of the Brotherhood of Free Masons, there has lately happened a discovery of abundance of their secret signs and wonders, with the mysterious manner of their admission into that Fraternity, contained in a manuscript found among his papers." McClenachan, vol. i., p. 73.

11. Letters from Henry Bell, of Lancaster, Pa., to Dr. Thomas Cadwallader, of Philadelphia. " As you well know, I was one of the originators of the first Masonic Lodges in Philadelphia. A party used to meet at the Tun Tavern, in Water Street, and sometimes open a Lodge there. Once in the fall of 1730, we formed the design of obtaining a charter for a regular Lodge, and made application to the Grand Lodge of England for one, but before receiving it, we heard that Daniel Coxe, of New Jersey, had been appointed by that Grand Lodge as Provincial Grand Master of New York, New Jersey, and Philadelphia. We therefore made application to him and our request was granted."

12. In reference to this letter, the Library Committee of the Grand Lodge of Pennsylvania stated that : " The letter was exhibited in the Grand Secretary's office (Philadelphia) in 1872. It bore all the marks of being genuine, and we have no doubt of its being correct."

From the Pennsylvania Gazette, June 26, 1732.

13. "Saturday last being St. John's day, a Grand Lodge of the Ancient and Honorable Society of Free and Accepted Masons was held at the Sun Tavern, in Water Street, when, after a handsome entertainment, the Worshipful W. Allen, Esq., was unanimously chosen Grand Master of this Province for the year ensuing, who was pleased to appoint Mr. William Pringle, Deputy Master. Wardens chosen for the year ensuing were, Thomas Boude, and Benjamin Franklin."

Pennsylvania Gazette, Philadelphia, June 27, 1734.

14. "Monday last a Grand Lodge of the Ancient and Honorable Society of Free and Accepted Masons in this Province was held at the Tun Tavern, in Water Street, when Benjamin Franklin being elected Grand Master for the year ensuing, appointed Mr. John Crap to be his Deputy ; and James Hamilton, Esq., and Thomas Hopkins, Gent., were chosen Wardens, after which a very elegant entertainment was provided and the proprietor, Thomas Penn, the Governor, and several other persons of distinction, honored the Society with their presence." Also see Gould, vol. vi., pp. 430, 431.

15. "There was a Sun as well as a 'Tun' Tavern in Water Street, Philadelphia. According to Franklin's Gazette the 'Grand Lodge' in 1732 met at the former, and the two following years at the latter. All three designations, Sun, Tun, or Hoop, are believed by McCalla to apply to one public-house at different dates not far apart." Gould, vol. vi., p. 442.

16. That Daniel Coxe was a Mason several years previous to this will be seen from the records of a meeting at Devil's Tavern ? within Temple Bar, London, April 25, 1722, where these names appear : Claude Crespigny (Master), Edw. Ravennell (S. W.), John Houghton, and Daniel Coxe.

The first minute book of that body (the Grand Lodge of England) relates the proceedings of the Grand Lodge, from June 24, 1723, to March 17, 1731. In the same volume are contained several lists of Lodges, with the names of their members, and copies of various deputations granted to Brethren in foreign parts, and among them the exact text of the patent issued to Daniel Cox. Gould, vol. vi., p. 443.

17. Daniel Cox was the son of Dr. Daniel Cox, of London, who from the year 1687 to 1690, was the largest landed proprietor and also Governor of the Province of West Jersey. He was appointed associate Justice of New Jersey in 1734, an office held by him until his death, which is thus announced in the *Pennsylvania Gazette* of April 26, 1739 :

"Yesterday morning died at Trenton, the Honorable Daniel Cox, Esq., one of the Justices of the Supreme Court of the Province of New Jersey."

CHAPTER XIII.

THE MARKS OF THE ANCIENT BUILDERS.

Marks used at the Building of King Solomon's Temple.—Marks found at Tyre and Sidon.—Marks found in the Crypts of Old Churches and Cathedrals in various Places in Europe.—Singular Old Masonic Medals.

IN connection with the symbols, the marks of the ancient builders may be considered, as many of them are nearly identical, and others are similar to the symbols of Free Masonry. These marks were found on the foundation walls enclosing K. S. T. at Jerusalem, in other parts of Palestine, and in the crypts of churches and cathedrals throughout Europe. Most of the marks found on the walls of K. S. T. were made with some red mineral substance so durable that those on the lower courses, which had been covered with earth, were as bright as when put on, nearly three thousand years ago.*

At the building of King Solomon's Temple certain competent craftsmen were appointed, called *mark*-men, whose duties were to place a private *mark* on the stones as they were finished by the Masons, both to show the quality and value of each man's work and to show the place of such work in the Temple. These marks consisted of certain mathematical figures, the square, the cross, the level, the perpendicular, etc.

Masonic signs and marks constituted an elementary portion of the Lodge Ritual during the period of the Guilds. They were also a testimonial of honor; and each entered apprentice was given a mark on his admission to the degree of a Fellow. An ancient rule made it necessary that each Mason should select his mark, based upon a geometrical figure, and Masonic tribunals had jurisdiction in all matters pertaining to proprietary marks. This system of ownership of marks was recognized at a very early date in England.

*Gould, vol. ii., pp. 460–465; Fort, pp. 326–337.

THE MARKS OF THE ANCIENT BUILDERS.

Upon the termination of apprenticeship, and receiving the degree of Fellow, the Craftsman was entitled to possess a separate mark, which he must thenceforth cut upon his work. The presentation of the mark was accompanied with a ceremony and feast. After the presentation, the mark was enrolled upon the Master's tablet or Book of Tokens. A record of this kind, dating back to a remote period, is still preserved at Basle. The use of such tablets is of the highest antiquity.

FIGURE 1.—This ancient mark was found on a fragment of stone in the rubbish just outside the wall, near the Damascus gate, north side of Jerusalem.

FIGURE 2.—Was found at Samaria, Carlisle Abbey, England, in the crypts of an ancient cathedral in Glasgow, and at other places.

FIGURE 3.—This mark was found at Hebron, seventeen miles from Jerusalem, at Geneva, and with figure 2 in the crypt of the Cathedral in Glasgow.

FIGURE 4.—A primitive square and compass interlaced—found at Sidon, Tyre, Samaria, in Fountain's Abbey, and at Glasgow—a common mark among the ancient Craftsmen.

FIGURE 5.—Triple triangle. This mark was found at Samaria, and it is seen also in the interior of St. Pierre, at Poitiers, and in a fine state of preservation.

FIGURE 6.—In St. Radigonde Chapel there is a double intertwined triangle resembling a six-pointed star.

FIGURE 7.—Found over one of the doors in Melrose Abbey, Scotland.

FIGURE 8.—This figure is cut in an embossed escutcheon springing from one of the columns in the Cologne Cathedral.

FIGURE 9.—The equilateral triangle, with a dot in the centre, is found in several of the great cathedrals of Europe. One of this style is carved in the Cologne Minster, and is surmounted by a figure 4.

FIGURE 10.—There is visible, upon the pilasters flanking the entrance to St. Mark's Cathedral at Venice, a double triangle. It is mounted by a straight line, with intersecting lines at the top, which give it the appearance of the feathered end of an arrow. This character was used by the Byzantine Craftsmen, and is wide-spread and numerous.

FIGURES 11 and 12 are in Saint Ninian's Lodge at Brechin.

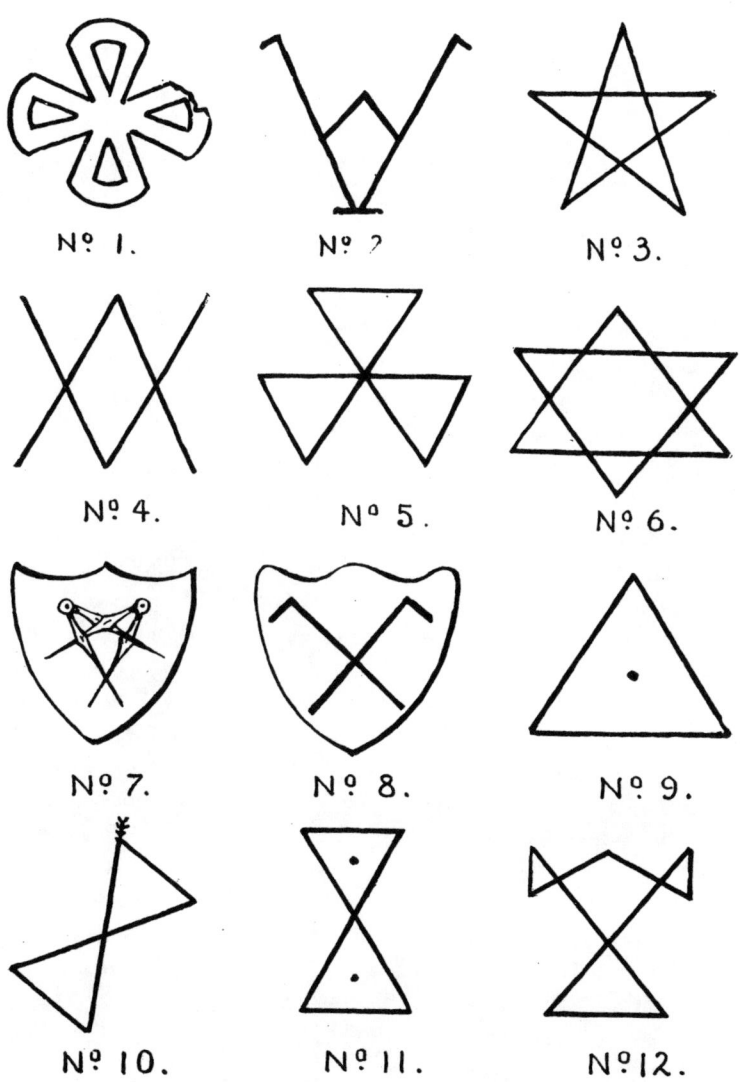

MARKS OF THE ANCIENT CRAFTSMEN.

THE MARKS OF THE ANCIENT BUILDERS. 567

On the ruined walls of St. Mary's Abbey at York, is a pentalpha, also two interlaced squares. On the façade of Santa Croce, Florence, two blazing stars are seen. The most singular representation, however, in the cathedral appears on the main portal, being the figure of Christ holding in his hand a perfect square. In York Minster, several double triangles conjoined at the outer edges are visible on the stone pavements leading to the crypt.

On one of the supporting columns at the principal entrance of the Freiburg Church, a life-sized statue of King Solomon stands, his head covered with a mitred crown, and a mace in one hand.

In St. Margaret's Church, at York, there are figures embossed in a concave circle in the arched doorways. One of these images stands before an altar with upraised arms. A learned antiquary believes that this figure represents King Solomon. His head-dress contains a triad, which was interpreted to signify the three attributes of that monarch—wisdom, strength, and beauty. The portico in which this is found is much older than the main building, having been erected in the eleventh century.

In the turrets surmounting the side entrance to the Duomo of Florence are three beautiful canopied niches, in each of which a martyred saint appears, and in a position of significance to the initiated eye.

Fallou and Stieglitz, two German writers of note, have furnished engravings of two symbolic columns of remote antiquity, copied from originals in the Wurzburg Cathedral, which was founded in the eleventh century. That these columns once belonged to a much older edifice, Stieglitz has clearly demonstrated. A square entablature surmounts these columns, and on the outer edge of one is visible, in nearly obliterated letters, the word Jachin; on the inner edge of the other is the name Boaz.

ABRAXAS

Signifies the adorable, blessed name—the unutterable word. In this last it corresponds with the unspeakable Omnific, and ineffable Tetragammaton, the Jehovah of the Jews. When written in the form of a triangle and suspended about the neck it had the virtues of an amulet. As such it was used by the Syrians for the purpose of invocation. This word was usually engraved upon abraxas stones, and with it the name of Jehovah, Jaw, or Jao.

The faculty of abrax is the system known to us as the cabala, the philosophical theology of many of the distinguished English Protestants of a still later date, being widely accepted as the current biblical interpretation of Jewish scholars.

It is in the speculations of the cabala, that many of the traditions of previous ages have reached us, and under forms which Masons, especially in the Chapter Degrees, are accustomed to receive them.

The word abrak is also to be found in the Bible as a salutation to Joseph by the Egyptians upon his accession to royal power.

As late as the thirteenth century, cabalistic rites were openly practised in France by the Jews. After the destruction of the first temple, many of the Jews emigrated to Egypt, and there, Judaic culture found a congenial soil, and the active phantasis of the Hebrews readily merged portions of the Egyptian, Persian, and Greek elements into the Holy Scriptures.*

The vitality exhibited by this strange truth constitutes a curious fact in history. That a name so sacredly guarded, so potent in its influence, should be preserved by mystic societies through the many ages and finally be enshrined in Free Masonry, is significant. For it is only in Free Masonry that the "Divine Word" is held in due reverence.

An Abraxas Stone.

The head represents the image of the Creator, under the name of Jupiter Ammon. The sun and moon upon the reverse are the Osiris and Isis of the Egyptians, hieroglyphically representing the omnipotence, omniscience, and eternity of God. The star denotes prudence. The scorpion represents malice, and the serpent represents wicked subtlety.

---

* An account of the word Abrak was given in a pamphlet written by Henry VI. of England, about the middle of the fifteenth century, containing a record of an official investigation into the principles of Free Masonry, in which it is claimed that the Venetians brought Free Masonry from the East.

It is only in the Masonic Order that the divine word is a living reality and a subject of interest to the thought of our modern world. Rev. J. F. Garrison, Fort, pp. 417–444.

An Abraxas Stone

CHAPTER XIV.

ROYAL ARCH MASONRY.—ITS ORIGIN, ETC.

Origin of the Royal Arch Degrees.—The Captivity.—The Vaults Discovered under the Site of King Solomon's Temple.—Remains of the Citadel and Tomb of Cyrus, King of Persia.—The Astronomical Royal Arch.—Establishment of the First Royal Arch Chapters in the United States.—Statistics of that Body.

WITH the exception of the third, there is no other degree in Free Masonry that is as important in its historical and symbolical import, nor one that has been so extensively patronized, as the Royal Arch. Its sublime significance has challenged for it the prefix of "The Holy Royal Arch." Dr. Oliver says that it is "indescribably more august, sublime, and important than any which preceded it, and is, in fact, the summit and perfection of ancient Masonry."

But as it is uncertain whether the Royal Arch was at first a degree, or only the completion of one, its origin is difficult to determine, and it can only be approximated by considering the facts and circumstances bearing on the question. Therefore the condition of Free Masonry in 1717–50, in those countries that took part in its origin and formation, will be noticed. One of the first two Lodges opened on the Continent under the banner of Speculative Masonry, was established in France, and the institution so commended itself to the French, that they have ever been its zealous promoters. Scotland, since the Middle Ages, has been a congenial field for the Masonic Craftsmen; and it is among the earliest, if not the earliest country in which the spirit of *Free Masonry* was manifested. To England also, as Chapter VIII. has shown, is Free Masonry indebted for much of its early development. In fact the history of Free Masonry, during the first half of the eighteenth century, in the above-named countries, was characterized by such zeal of its votaries as would indicate that they would, instead of burying the talent entrusted to them, endeavor to improve it. That they did this will be seen further on.

In prosecuting his researches into the history of Free Masonry, Dr. Oliver discovered a Master Mason's tracing-board, bearing the date of 1725. This board displays near its top an arch scroll containing an inscription in which the true Word is conspicuous. On the right side are an arch and key-stone, and a sun darting its rays obliquely. In the centre are two interlaced triangles, with a sun in the centre, all surrounded by a circle. On one side of this is a seven-branched candlestick.

Soon after the date of this tracing-board, the Chevalier Ramsay, a Scotchman, appears in Masonic history, being credited by some authorities with the invention of new degrees, one of which, the Royal Arch of Enoch,* comprised the essentials of the Royal Arch. Others claim that he never invented a degree.† However this may have been, in 1738, being a resident in France and Orator of the Grand Lodge in Paris, he delivered an address before that body in which higher degrees were suggested.‡

At this time, and even earlier, there were resident in France a large number of Ramsay's countrymen, men of note, Free Masons. These naturally entered into the spirit of progress then manifest in French Masonic circles. Therefore it is not strange that new degrees began to make their appearance, termed Scots, or Scottish degrees. Many have supposed that these degrees were carried from Scotland, but this is not the case.§ All that their originators carried from their native land of this nature, was their Scottish zeal for Free Masonry. From these Scots degrees it is claimed that the Royal Arch originated.||

From the foregoing, the circumstances which led up to the establishment of the Royal Arch degree will be apparent; and from which the following conclusions are obvious: As early as 1725—probably earlier—the idea of the Royal Arch had been conceived in England, and in that year it was expressed on the tracing-board, as previously described. The conception of this degree was primarily based upon the legends and traditions of the discovery of a

---

* Mackey, p. 629. † Gould, vol. v., p. 86. ‡ Ibid., vol. v., p. 83.
§ Ibid., vol. v., pp. 78–92. || Ibid., vol. iv., p. 457.

ROYAL ARCH MASONRY. 573

vault (containing the lost Word) under King Solomon's Temple, and later the grand arch of heaven was considered in this connection. Upon this cornerstone the structure of Royal Arch Masonry was erected. Ramsay, and his countrymen in France, furnished the plan of the edifice, and the plan was appropriated by the Seceders *—Ancients, in England, and from which, under their enterprising leader, Dermott, they reared the Royal Arch.

It was at first *used* as a component part—the concluding portion of the Master's degree; † but between 1740 and 1746 it was dissevered from this connection and given its proper and independent position.

Laurence Dermott ‡ was at this time pushing "Ancient" Masonry in England, and was ambitious of making such additions to it as would bring it into prominence, and render it superior to his rival the G. L. of England. Therefore it is believed that he either acted on Ramsay's suggestions and formulated a part of this degree, or received it from France. Subsequently Thomas Dunckerley, a Mason of brilliant intellect, greatly improved it.

Ramsay, commonly known as the Chevalier Ramsay, was born at Ayr, in Scotland, June 9, 1668. His father being a possessor of considerable property, was enabled to give his son a liberal education. He was accordingly sent to school in his native burgh, and afterward to the University of Edinburgh, where he was distinguished for his abilities and diligence. Subsequently he went to Holland, residing for some time at Leyden. There he became acquainted with Pierre Poiret, one of the most celebrated teachers of the *mystic* theology which then prevailed on the continent. From him Ramsay learned the principal tenets of that system; and was thus indoctrinated with a love of mystical speculations.

Ramsay was also, by nature and association, an aristocrat; hence, in proposing his theory of the origin of Free Masonry, he placed its birth-place in Palestine, among those kings and knights who had gone forth to battle as Crusaders for the conquest of Jerusalem. Therefore it was in accordance with his views to suggest higher degrees.

---
* Gould in Guide to the Chapter, p. 16.
† See History of Free Masonry and Concordant Orders, p. 556.
‡ Dermott was at first Grand Secretary, and then Deputy Grand Master of the Ancients.

From Dermott's Ahiman Rezon.

" Rules and regulations for the introduction to, and government of, the Holy Royal Arch Chapters, under the protection of, and supported by, the Ancient Grand Lodge of England, made at several times. Revised and corrected at a General Grand Chapter, held at the Crown Anchor Tavern, in the Strand, London.

"That the said Chapters of the Royal arch (Holy) may be held and conducted with the regularity, discipline, and solemnity becoming the sublime intention with which they have, from time immemorial, been held as an essential component part of ancient Masonry.

" I.—That no Chapter of Holy Royal Arch shall be held or convened within the kingdom of England, or Masonic jurisdiction thereunto belonging, but under the authority and sanction of a regular subsisting warrant, granted by the Grand Lodge, according to the old institutions.

" II.—That no Chapter of Holy Royal Arch shall be convened and held, for the purpose of exalting to the degree of Holy Royal Arch Mason, unless six regular registered Royal Arch Masons be present.

" III.—That no brother shall be admitted into the Holy Royal Arch, but he who has regularly and faithfully passed through the three progressive degrees, and has performed the duties in his Lodge, to the satisfaction of the brethren.

" VIII.—That all registered Royal Arch brothers shall be entitled to a Grand Royal Arch certificate, either on paper or parchment, on the payment of three shillings for the same."

In 1834, changes were made in the ceremonies of exaltation, but the general outline of the system was preserved. The degree is the fourth in the Masonic Series, and a Master Mason who has been so for twelve months is eligible for exaltation. The principal officers of an English Chapter are: three principals, Zerubbabel, Haggai, and Joshua; three Sojourners, and two Scribes, Ezra and Nehemiah; a Treasurer, and a Janitor.

Finally, this degree came to the United States through warrants issued by the Grand Lodge of the Ancients, the Athol Grand Lodge. And the first

Chapter held in this country was in 1758, in Philadelphia. This was doubtless the oldest distinct organization of Royal Arch Masons ever held on this continent.

Following this, was St. Andrew's Royal Arch Lodge, organized in Boston, in 1769.

Previous to the organization of a Grand Chapter there were in the city of New York two Chapters, one known as the Old Chapter, and the other called Washington Chapter. Washington Chapter issued charters to subordinate Chapters, in which it styled itself "The Mother Chapter."

The first Chapter in Rhode Island was chartered in 1793 by Washington Chapter. The first Chapter in Connecticut, Hiram Chapter, No. 1, at Newtown, was also chartered by Washington Chapter. Its charter bearing date April 29, A. L. 5791, was signed by Josiah O. Hoffman, H. P. W. C. R. A. M., George Anthon, K-g W. C. R. A. M. and Martin Hoffman, S-e, W. C. R. A. M.*

The first convention of the Chapters in Connecticut was held on the first Wednesday of July, 1796, at Hartford, in which all the Chapters above named were represented by delegates, except Franklin, at New Haven. A regular organization was perfected, and articles of agreement were entered into for the government of the several Chapters in the State.

The organization was at first called, "A Convention of Committees of the Chapters of R. A. M. in Connecticut," and was, so far as can be learned, the first governing body in Royal Arch Masonry organized in the United States. The Grand Chapter of Pennsylvania was also established in 1796.

The first meeting of delegates at Boston, out of which arose the *General* Grand Chapter, occurred October 24, 1797 ; and the first meeting of the General R. A. Chapter took place at Middletown, Ct., in September, 1798. It was then styled the Grand R. A. Chapter of the Northern States of America. In 1816 the title was changed to the General Grand Chapter of R. A. Masons for the U. S. A.

* The Masonic Mirror and Keystone, vol. iii., p. 15, January 1854 ; also History of Free Masonry, by Mitchell, vol. i., p. 670 ; Guide to the Chapter, pp. 37, 39 and 40.

The Triple Tau

Constitutes the jewel of the Royal Arch as practised in England, where it is called the "emblem of all emblems," the grand emblem of Royal Arch Masonry.

The tau is the Greek letter "T," which by the ancients was held to be a symbol of life, a sacred mark; and was placed upon the foreheads of those who escaped from any great peril, in token of their deliverance from death. See Ezekiel ix. 4-6. The triple tau is the tau three times repeated.

The Lost Word—Grand Omnific Word.

Among the Jews the pronunciation of the true name was supposed to be followed by such tremendous effects that a substitute was enjoined. Accordingly, we find in the Old Testament that, wherever the name of God occurs, the substitute "Adonai," or Lord, is used. From the long-continued use of a substitute, the real word was believed to be lost; and from this originated the many superstitions and legends in relation to the "grand omnific word." Dr. Mackey, in Encyclopædia of Free Masonry, page 477, says: "no matter what was the word, no matter how it was lost," . . . this word was nothing but the pass-word, that which went with the sign by which the initiated could make themselves known to one another."

The Royal Arch degree is founded on the captivity of the children of Israel, the legends attending the rebuilding of the Temple of Solomon, the finding of the Book of the Law, and the Discovery of the Lost Word.

The preliminary degrees are: Mark, Past, and Most Excellent Master; and the principal officers are: High Priest, King, Scribe, and Captain of the Host, Principal Sojourner, Royal Arch Captain, and three Masters of the Veils.

The Captivity.

The house of David being divided into the Kingdoms of Israel and Judah, and consequently weakened, they were both subjected to dire disasters.

Nebuchadnezzar, King of Babylon, with no other cause than conquest, marched against Jerusalem, and after a siege of eighteen months the city was taken, the temple pillaged and destroyed, the city reduced to ruins, and the

AN ÆSTHETIC VALUE UNDER THE ELECTRIC LIGHT.

The Tomb of Cyrus.

ROYAL ARCH MASONRY. 581

king, nobles, priests, and all the better sort of people were carried captive to Babylon. This took place in 508 B.C.

Subsequently Babylon itself was taken by Cyrus, King of Persia, of whom it was foretold by the Prophet Isaiah, that he should liberate the captives.

The captivity is computed to have lasted seventy years, but this is not strictly correct; it lasted seventy years, if reckoned from the appearance of Nebuchadnezzar in Anterior Asia (606), and fifty-two counting from the destruction of Jerusalem. When Cyrus had overthrown the Babylonian kingdom (538 B.C.) the condition of the Hebrews began to improve. Daniel rose higher and higher in dignity and power, and finally became "supreme head of the Pashes to whom the provinces of the Persian empire were committed." Through his influence, Cyrus was prevailed upon to issue an edict permitting the exiles to return home.*

THE PROCLAMATION.

"The Lord God of heaven hath given me all the kingdom of the earth, and he has charged me to build him a house at Jerusalem, which is in Judah. Who is there among you of all his people? his God be with him, and let him go up to Jerusalem, and build the house of the Lord God of Israel" (Ezra i. 2, 3).

In response to this, upward of forty thousand persons, including four of the twenty-four courses of priests, set out under the leadership of Zerubbabel, a descendant of their old kings.†

Those who had valuable possessions in Babylonia, and preferred to remain, committed valuable gifts to the hands of their more zealous brethren.

Cyrus also caused the sacred vessels of gold and silver which Nebuchadnezzar had taken from the temple to be restored. A minute account of the circumstances attending this joyous event is given in the Books of Ezra and Nehemiah.

LEGENDS OF THE VAULTS.

When preparing for the rebuilding of the Temple, 535 B.C., the ruins of the Temple of Solomon were cleared away, and while doing this, the workmen unearthed, first a keystone, which led to the discovery of a subterranean

---

* See Chambers, vol. vii., p. 149.   † See Kitto, vol. i., p. 92.

vault, which from its situation had escaped the conflagration at the time of the destruction of the Temple. This vault was supported by seven pairs of pillars, and was built by King Solomon for a secure depository of certain invaluable matters, in case of disaster to the city and Temple. From this vault a secret passage led to his palace.* When the débris was being cleared away, preparatory to building the mosque now standing on the site of the Temple, a passage was discovered which led down into a remarkable vault or subterranean chamber, the roof of which is supported by beautiful columns, and the whole is still in a good state of preservation.

Philostorgius, and after him Nicephorus, relate that, at the clearing of the foundations (when Julian, the Apostate, set himself to rebuild the Temple), a stone was taken up that covered the mouth of a deep cave, cut out of the rock in a cubical form, into which one of the laborers was lowered by a rope fastened around his middle. At the bottom he found water a foot deep, and in the centre an altar reaching above the surface of the water, on which lay the roll of a book wrapped in fine linen cloth. Being drawn up, the linen was observed to be fresh and undecayed; and the roll being unfolded was found, to the amazement of both Jews and Gentiles, to contain the first words of the Gospel of St. John, written in capital letters—" IN THE BEGINNING WAS THE WORD, AND THE WORD WAS WITH GOD, AND THE WORD WAS GOD."†

Another legend says that Enoch built a subterranean temple consisting of nine vaults, situated perpendicularly over each other. To a triangular stone of agate, a plate of gold, each side of which was a cubit long and enriched with precious stones, was attached. On this plate was engraved the word—true name of God; and this was placed on a cubical stone in the ninth or lowest arch and the arch sealed up. ‡

In consequence of the deluge all knowledge of this secret temple, together with the sacred and ineffable name, was lost for ages. The word was however subsequently found in this long-forgotten subterranean temple by David, when excavating for the temple of Solomon his son.

* Note 1, p. 15.
† Traditions of Free Masonry, pp. 368–372 ; Prime, Tent Life in the Holy Land ; Barclay, City of the Great King ; and Bartlett, Walks About Jerusalem.   ‡ Mackey, p. 256.

Remains of Ecbatana, the Ancient Persian Capitol.

In confirmation of these legends is the testimony of Talmudic writers, and the following fact: In 637, the Caliph Omar erected a mosque on the site of the ancient Temple, covering the Dome of the Rock—the highest point of Mount Moriah and as previously stated, a passage leading down into a large vault was discovered.

The Mohammedans believing that Mahomet ascended to Heaven from this rock, hold the whole of the ancient Temple enclosure as sacred ground, and in 687 repaired and added to the mosque, so that even at this day it is not only in a good state of preservation, but is a beautiful and unique structure—known as El-Kubet-es-Sukhra, or Dome of the Rock.

These legends agree in the main particulars, that the "word" was deposited—secreted deep under-ground, in the lowest arch; that it was there lost, "buried in darkness" for many years, and then found and brought to light.

From Plutarch we learn that, "when the sun was in Scorpio, in the month of Athyr, the Egyptians inclosed the body of their god Osiris in an ark or chest, and during this ceremony a great annual festival was celebrated. Three days after the priests had inclosed Osiris in the ark, they pretended to have found him again. In brief the Jewish ark, like the Egyptian ark, contained something symbolically representing the true God.*

Palace and Castle of Darius.

In the time of Cyrus and Darius, there were two capital cities in Persia, one being known as Ecbatana and the other Ecbatane. Ecbatana was the capital of Northern Media and was located in latitude 36° 28', and longitude 47° 9'. This city was founded 728 B.C., and was situated upon a conical hill which was surmounted by a temple of the Sun. It was enclosed by seven concentric walls, the two innermost of which were gilded and the others, in their order outward, were painted *orange, blue, scarlet, black,* and *white,* respectively.†

As they rose one above the other toward the centre or highest point in the city, they presented a view both unique and beautiful. One of the principal

* Note 1, p. 591.   † Chambers, vol. iv., p. 694.

structures was its citadel, where the archives were kept in which Darius found the edict of Cyrus the Great concerning the building of the Temple in Jerusalem.

The conical hill, one hundred and fifty feet high, which is the site of this singular ancient city, is covered from base to top with massive ruins. Its ramparts were constructed of large blocks of squared stone, and can easily be traced their entire circuit. On one side of the hill and near the top is a remarkable pool of clear, cool water. This city continued to be an important place down to A.D. 1200, when it began to decline. It is now known as Hamadan, and has a population of thirty thousand.

A large number of Jews reside here, and their rabbins claim that this ancient city was the residence of Ahasuerus, and show within its precincts the Tomb of Esther and Mordecai. The ruins of the castle and palace of Darius are still quite conspicuous.

The Astronomical Royal Arch.

The Royal Arch is primarily the great zodiacal arch, reaching from the vernal to the autumnal equinox. It is supported by three of the cardinal points of the zodiac: being the equinoctial points at each base, and the solstitial point at the summit.*

At the time of the building of King Solomon's Temple the celestial equator cut the ecliptic at about 10 of the constellation Aries. Therefore at that period the constellation Leo was near the solstitial point, and the summit of the zodiacal arch. Now, as the summit or key of an arch is its strongest point, and the sun, when it reaches that point has also the greatest power, it being the summer solstice and when the day is the longest—that point is emblematic of strength. The vernal equinox marks the opening of spring, the season of beauty; therefore it signifies beauty. The autumnal equinox being the season of maturity, denotes wisdom.

To observe the constellations as they were at the summer solstice, 1012 B.C.—the time of the building of King Solomon's Temple—the heavens should be viewed on or about the 5th of February, at which time the same stars are visible at midnight.

* Notes 2, 3, and 4, p. 591.

THE ROYAL ARCH OF HEAVEN

LIBRA ♎ VIRGO ♍ LEO ♌ SUMMER SOLSTICE ☉ GEMINI ♊ TAURUS ♉ ARIES ♈

AUTUMNAL EQUINOX

VERNAL EQUINOX

Therefore, if the intelligent Craftsman will on a clear night, at low twelve, about the 5th of February, take a position facing south and raise his eyes to the vast arch of heaven, he will be rewarded by a magnificent spectacle eloquent with the fundamental truths of his institution. For far up in the azure vault, within less than 30° of the summit, or key-stone, of the arch, will be seen the constellation Leo; on one side of which will be seen Aries, and on the other, Libra, constellations which anciently marked the equinoctial points, and upon which bases the whole of the majestic arch appears to rest.

Libra is typical of Wisdom, the wisdom which, in the scales of Reason, duly weighs all things; Aries, marking the ancient place of the vernal equinox, —spring, is typical of beauty, and also indicates that the sun, which lies dead in the cold embrace of winter, will rise again clothed with new life and power. The sign Aries is therefore also a symbol of immortality, teaching that the soul of man will rise in glory from the darkness of the grave.

Next to Libra, in the east, is the constellation Virgo, the Virgin. In her left hand shines the bright star Spica; and at a short distance north is brilliant Arcturus. In the west Taurus, with the Pleiades, is conspicuous. Sublime in his majesty Orion is seen. Lower down, and near the horizon, is the beautiful sun-star Sirius. While higher up the sky, Procyon shines almost with equal glory. Lastly Gemini, Castor and Pollux, Cassiopeia in her golden chair, the great bear, Cephas, and Andromeda bound to the rock with chains, the polar star, and around the pole the scaly dragon, all come in to add beauty and grandeur to the view.

This illustration shows the relative positions of the various constellations and signs of the first great arch. The summer solstice, with the astronomical sign of the sun inscribed upon it, represents the key-stone of the arch, and signifies the exaltation of the sun to the summit of the arch.

The Key-stone.

The key-stone alludes to the summer solstice, or key of the zodiacal arch, in close proximity to which it is now seen, and where anciently was located the constellation Leo, also typical of strength.

The circle inscribed in the masonic key-stone is the Egyptian astronomical sign of the sun. In the key-stone it denotes the sun in the summer solstice, exalted to the summit of the zodiacal arch and completing it.

The six signs of the zodiac, that constitute the Celestial Royal Arch, are represented with geometrical precision by the points of the *triple tau*. The vernal and autumnal equinox represent the base, and the summer solstice the summit. The triple tau is therefore a correct symbol of the Royal Arch; while the quadruple tau, being composed entirely of "right angles, horizontals, and perpendiculars," embraces all the secret signs of Free Masonry.

The Number Seven.

As the sun makes his apparent revolution in twenty-four hours, that created the division of time into days. The next division was suggested by the revolution of the moon about the earth. The latter division was called "moons," by the Ancients; hence the word "month." The Egyptian hieroglyphic sign for month was the crescent of the moon. In each lunar month the moon passes through four distinct phases in regular periods of seven days each, the new moon, first quarter, full moon, and last quarter. The last division was called a week.

Strength of R. A. Masonry, in the United States and Canada.

General Chapters.	Members.	General Chapters.	Members.	General Chapters.	Members.
Alabama	856	Maine	6,715	Oklahoma	603
Arizona	320	Maryland	2,051	Oregon	1,509
Arkansas	1,975	Massachusetts	16,557	Pennsylvania	21,240
California	6,232	Michigan	13,983	Quebec	590
Canada	6,215	Minnesota	5,396	Rhode Island	2,728
Colorado	2,739	Mississippi	2,083	South Carolina	710
Connecticut	6,049	Missouri	7,518	South Dakota	1,637
Delaware	737	Montana	866	Tennessee	2,721
District of Columbia	2,451	Nebraska	2,951	Texas	8,416
Florida	781	Nevada	304	Utah	401
Georgia	3,450	New Brunswick	463	Vermont	3,087
Idaho	397	New Hampshire	3,669	Virginia	2,935
Illinois	18,123	New Jersey	3,559	Washington	1,400
Indiana	7,519	New Mexico	462	West Virginia	2,024
Indian Territory	1,133	New York	23,289	Wisconsin	6,328
Iowa	8,238	North Carolina	797	Wyoming	454
Kansas	5,343	North Dakota	1,025		
Kentucky	3,844	Nova Scotia	698		244,002
Louisiana	1,244	Ohio	17,187		

NOTES FROM AUTHORITIES.

1. There is nothing more commonly found in the monuments of Egypt, than a small chest, a van, a serpent, a human head. Many ancient monuments testify to the use of these articles. Mysteries, p. 167.

2. It is believed the Royal Arch degree owes its title, partly, to the imaginary arch made in the heavens by the course of King Osiris, the sun from the vernal to the autumnal equinox.

3. The Royal arch, like the greater mysteries, contains a scenical representation of a journey from this world to the next. In the way are four guarded passes, called veils, emblematical of the equinoxes and solstices, allegorically denominated gates of heaven, through which lies the sun's course. The high priest is dressed in a white robe, with a breast-plate of brilliants consisting of 12 pieces (to represent the 12 signs of the zodiac), an apron, and a mitre. Mysteries of Free Masonry, pp. 297, 298, and 300.

4. "Ye Priests!" says Volney, alluding to Catholic priests, "you wear his (the sun's) emblems all over your bodies; your tonsure is the disk of the sun, your stole is his zodiac, your rosaries are symbols of the stars and planets. Ye Pontiffs and Prelates! your mitre, your crosiers, your mantles, are those of Osiris." Mysteries, pp. 35-46, 167-315.

CHAPTER XV.

THE A. AND A. SCOTTISH RITE, 33°.

Origin of this Rite.—Its Development and Rapid Spread in the East and West.—Its Advent in the West Indies and the United States.—Formation of the Different Bodies Representing the A. and A. Rite in this Country. —The Southern Jurisdiction.—Northern Jurisdiction.

SOON after the establishment of Free Masonry in France, that country became very prolific of rites and degrees. Prominent and vigorous among the new ones were those termed Scottish or Scots degrees;* these soon became so numerous, that they were able to usurp the privileges and prerogatives of a Grand Lodge, and issue warrants of constitution. Thus arose the Scots Mother Lodges—bodies that developed systems of degrees of their own, which were worked in chapters; but independent of each other.

As early as 1740, not only new degrees, but new rites were multiplying both in France and in Germany; and many of the new rites took the name, Scottish, to designate their systems.

In 1743 the Masons of Lyons invented the Kadosch degree, representing the vengeance of the Templars, and thus laid the foundation of Templar Rites. It was at first called Junior Elect; but developed into Elect of 9, or of Perignan, Elect of 15, Illustrious Master, Knight of Aurora, Grand Inquisitor, Grand Elect, Commander of the Temple, etc.

The Chapter of Clermont was established in 1754, and was a Templar continuation of the Scots degrees. From this the Emperors of the East and West were developed; and these subsequently grew into the Ancient and Accepted Scottish Rite, 33°.†

In 1756 the Knights of the East, Princes and Sovereigns of Masonry was established—it consisted principally of the middle class of people—a rival of the Chapter of Clermont. Its divisions were termed *colleges*.

---

* Notes 1 and 2, p. 610. † Gould, vol. v., pp. 92-98, and 141-144; Folger, p. 50.

THE A. AND A. SCOTTISH RITE.

In 1758, the Chapter of Clermont developed into the Council of the Emperors of the East and West, Sovereign Prince Masons. This body organized "The Rite of Perfection," consisting of twenty-five degrees, the highest of which was styled "Sovereign Prince of the Royal Secret."

The 25 degrees were divided into 7 classes, the first class of which comprised Free Masonry. These constitutions are the groundwork of the system known as the Ancient and Accepted Scottish Rite, 33°.*

This Rite flourished and extended throughout Europe; and on the 27th of August, 1761, Stephen Morin was commissioned Inspector-General for North America by this Council and the Grand Lodge; his patent being signed by the officers of both bodies.†

Immediately after this he sailed for Port au Prince, St. Domingo, and after remaining there a short time, he went to Kingston, Jamaica, all the while zealously propagating the Rite of Perfection. Soon after his arrival at Kingston he established a Council of Princes of the Royal Secret. Additional Councils were established at Jamaica and Santo Domingo, which developed into a G. C. of Princes of the Royal Secret, and Sovereign Council and Sublime Orient at Kingston in 1798.‡

In 1762, nine Commissioners from Paris and Bordeaux, appointed *ad hoc* by the Sovereign Grand Council of the Princes of the Royal Secret, met at Bordeaux and drew up constitutions and regulations, comprising thirty-five articles, for the government of the Order. These Constitutions were *transmitted* to Morin; and in Article XXVII., concerning petitions, is the following:

"The propper *Grand Inspectors*, may each . . . *create, constitute*, . . . revoke and exclude, according as their judgement may direct. They may for greater dispatch, appoint Deputies, etc."

By this and other articles of this document, and by Morin's patent, it will be seen that he and his legitimate successors had sufficient authority for establishing Supreme Councils.§

---

* Notes 3 and 4, p. 616; Gould, vol. v., p. 97; Mackey, p. 697.
† Gould, vol. v., pp. 126,127; Folger, p. 281; Notes 5 and 6, pp. 616, 617.
‡ Historical Inquiry, by Albert Pike, pp. 177-199; also Masonic Chronicle, vol. xiii., pp. 201-203.
§ See Document 29, Article 27, p. 304, Masonic History, by Folger; also Constitutions of 1762, issued by the Grand Consistory of Louisiana, and quotation at top of p. 594.

594   THE A. AND A. SCOTTISH RITE.

In the Circular issued by the Supreme Council at Charleston in 1802, is the following:

"On the 25th of October, 1762, the Grand Masonic Constitutions were ratified in Berlin, and proclaimed for the government of all the Lodges of Sublime and Perfect Masons, Chapters, Councils. . . . over the surface of the two hemispheres. In the same year the Constitutions were transmitted to our illustrious Brother, Stephen Morin, who had been appointed *Inspector-General over all Lodges*, etc., in the New World. On May 1, 1786, the Grand Constitutions of the Thirty-third Degree, called the Supreme Council of Sovereign Grand Inspectors-General, was finally ratified by His Majesty, the King of Prussia, who possessed the Sovereign Masonic power over all the Craft. . . This high power was conferred on a Supreme Council of *nine* brethren in *each* nation, who possess *all* the Masonic prerogatives in their own district, that His Majesty individually possessed, and are Sovereigns of Masonry.*

In 1762, Morin appointed Henry A. Francken Deputy Inspector-General.

Francken, continuing the transmission of the degrees and authority from Morin, conferred them on M. Hays, in 1765, and Hays conferred on Berand Spitzer, of Charleston, June 25, 1781.

These inspectors met at Philadelphia and conferred on Moses Cohen, of Jamaica, and he on Isaac Long, who at Charleston *created* Delahogue, De Grasse, Croze Magnan, St. Paul, Robin, Petit, and Marie. This was attested by J. L. Long, D. G. I. G., at Charleston, May 3, 1797, and countersigned by Delahogue, D. G. I., Prince Mason, Sov. Grand Commander.†

CHARLESTON,—THE SOUTHERN JURISDICTION.

In 1783, Deputy Inspector-General Isaac Da Costa (appointed by Hays) established a Sublime Grand Lodge of Perfection at Charleston; and on February 20, 1788, a Grand Council of Princes of Jerusalem was opened there by Myers, Spitzer, and A. Forst, Deputy Inspectors-General for South Carolina, Georgia, and Virginia, respectively. January 12, 1797, a Sublime Council of Princes of the Royal Secret was also established at Charleston by authority of the Sov. Grand Consistory at Kingston.‡

August 2, 1795, Spitzer conferred the degrees on John Mitchell, Mitchell

---

* See Document No. 7, pp. 43, 44, of Documents in Masonic History, by Folger.

† Reprint Proceedings, Northern Jurisdiction, 1781 to 1851, vol. i., Part 1, p. 4; Folger, p. 37; J. J. Gorman's Address, 1889, pp. 29-31; Notes 6½ and 7, p. 617, and Note 13, p. 618.

‡ Folger, p. 38; Historical Inquiry by Albert Pike, pp. 177-190; History of Free Masonry and Concordant Orders, p. 799.

conferred them on Dalcho, and the last two conferred them on Isaac Auld and Emanuel De La Motta. As the conferring of degrees indiscriminately by individual Deputy Grand Inspectors-General without organization led to confusion, an attempt was made to correct the evil in 1801, by organizing a supreme governing body at Charleston.* This Council was opened by John Mitchell and Frederick Dalcho, and on the basis of the Constitutions drawn up at Bordeaux in 1762. This organization was not, however, at first successful, and it soon ceased action and remained nearly dormant until 1822. It then revived and continued its functions until 1830, when it was acknowledged by the Grand Orient of France, and appeared in the published Annuary of that body. Between 1830 and 1844 but little of note transpired. In the latter year Dr. Albert G. Mackey became Secretary General. Continuing its course down to 1852, it chartered a Consistory in the city of New Orleans, for the State of Louisiana. The New Orleans Consistory continued through various vicissitudes until the year 1855, at which time it formed a union with the old Consistory of Cerneau, that was established in 1813 in that city, and was reinforced from the Cerneau body in New York in 1839.† Immediately after this union, the "united body" entered into a concordat with the Supreme Council at Charleston, and became its dependent for the State of Louisiana.

In 1859 Albert Pike became S. G. C., and filled that position to the time of his death—April, 1891. Immediately after the accession of Pike, the Constitutions were made to conform to those alleged to have been authorized by Frederick the Great in 1789. By the terms of this document, Frederick's power in the matter was to be vested in a Council of *nine* in each nation—*ad vitam* Officers. These Constitutions were first published in 1832, in French, and in 1834 another version was published in Latin. While agreeing in the main, the two versions differ in some of their details. The Southern jurisdiction recognizes the Latin version, and the Northern jurisdiction the French.

Concerning the Constitutions of 1789, Pike says:

"I first saw the *Latin* version of the Constitutions at New Orleans in 1857, in one of the copies published at Paris, in 1834, by the Supreme Council of France. These Constitutions had been adopted two years before by the Hicks-St. Laurent United Hemisphere Council at

---

* Folger, pp. 281–311, 312 and 313.
† American edition of Gould's History of Free Masonry, vol. iv., pp. 698, 699.

its origin, and were no doubt sent to New York by the Supreme Council of France, by the hands of St. Laurent."

"The French copy, which, as it has been published by us, . . . was adopted as the law of the rite, the organic law of its being, on the 31st of May, 1801, by the Supreme Council of the United States, then established at Charleston." " We accepted first the *French*, and then the Latin Constitutions."

"Thus, then, the first Supreme Council in the world had the right to make for itself, or to adopt ready-made, an organic law for the Rite which it owned, and to call that law Grand Constitutions. It did either make or adopt the French version, purporting to have been first adopted in 1786, . . . and the Rite was governed by them for fifty-eight years—until 1859 ; and then, in the exercise of the same plenary power, it adopted the Latin version, and it and the Rite have been governed by this in the Southern jurisdiction for over a quarter of a century." Official Bulletin of the Supreme Council for the Southern Jurisdiction for 1885, pp. 21-27.

In reference to the eight degrees above the twenty-fifth it is claimed that they were composed by the Charleston body in 1801. But this was not the case, as those degrees were simply modifications of existing French degrees, as will be seen by the following :

The 26th degree was taken from the system known as Saint Martinism, composed by Paschalis Martinez,—introduced into some provincial Lodges in France in 1743 ; subsequently Paschalis went to St. Domingo, and died there.*

The 27th, Pyron, in his Abridgement of the History of the Scottish Rite, admits to have been practised in France from time out of mind.

The 28th was composed about 1770 by Dom Pometti, a Benedictine monk, who died at an advanced age in 1800.

The 29th was taken from the system of the Baron de Tchoudy, author of the Flaming Star, published at Frankfort in 1766.

The 30th, Kadosch, was composed by Paschalis at Lyons in 1743.

The 31st was originally the seventh and last in the philosophic Rite, instituted by De Boileau in 1776.

32°—Sublime Prince of the Royal Secret. 33°—Inspector-General.†

This Rite has been known as the " Ineffable," the " Sublime," the " Exalted or High degrees," the " Philosophical," the " Scottish System," the " Rite of Perfection," the " Right of Heredom, of Kilwinning," and lastly as the " Ancient and Accepted Scottish Rite 33°." ‡

* Folger, pp. 48–53 ; Mackey, p. 488.   † Notes 8, 9 and 10, pp. 617, 618.
‡ Folger, pp. 15, 51-58.

Classification of the Degrees of the A. and A. Rite.

First Series. *Symbolic Degrees.*
1. Entered Apprentice. 2. Fellow Craft. 3. Master Mason.

II. *Perfection Lodge—The Ineffable Degrees.*
4. Secret Master.
5. Perfect Master.
6. Intimate Secretary.
7. Provost and Judge.
8. Intendant of the Buildings.
9. Elect of Nine.
10. Knight Elect of Fifteen.
11. Sublime Knight Elected.
12. Grand Master Architect.
13. Royal Arch of Enoch.
14. Grand Elect, Perfect. And Sublime Master Mason.

III. *Council of Princes—Historical Degree.*
15. Knight of the East or Sword. 16. Prince of Jerusalem.

IV. *Rose-Croix Chapter—Philosophical Degrees.*
17. Knight of the East and West. 18. Knight of the Rose-Croix de H. R. D. M.

V. *Areopagus—Historical and Philosophical Degrees.*
19. Grand Pontiff.
20. Grand Master of *all Symbolic Lodges.*
21. Noachite, or Prussian Knight.
22. Knight of the Royal Axe.
23. Chief of the Tabernacle.
24. Prince of the Tabernacle.
25. Knight of the Brazen Serpent.
26. Prince of Mercy.
27. Commander of the Temple.
28. Knight of the Sun.
29. Knight of St. Andrew, or Patriarch of the Crusades.

VI. *Consistory—Chivalric Degrees.*
30. Knight of Kadosch.
31. Grand Inspector, Inquisitor, Commander.
32. Sublime Prince of the Royal Secret.

VII. *Supreme Council—Official and Executive.*
33. Inspector-General—33d Degree and last Grade.*

* Book of the A. and A. Rite, by McClennachan, pp. 9 and 10.

The De La Motta—Gourgas—Raymond—Northern Jurisdiction.

On February 21, 1802, De Grasse Tilley received a patent from the Supreme Council at Charleston, creating him a Sovereign Grand Inspector-General, and giving him authority over the French West India Islands. On the following September De Grasse created Antoine Bideaud a Sovereign Grand Inspector-General. In 1804, Abraham Jacobs arrived in New York and commenced conferring degrees. He had been residing in Jamaica, where he received his authority from Moses Cohen.* In 1806, Bideaud also appeared in New York, and on August 4th commenced business by conferring the degrees up to the thirty-second on J. J. J. Gourgas, John B. Des Doity, John G. Tardy, Louis de Soulles, and Pierre A. Du Peyrot, and August 6th they opened a Consistory. On November 8, 1808, according to Gourgas, Daniel D. Tompkins, Richard Riker, and Sampson Simpson received the degrees up to the thirty second in this Consistory. And on November 12th, 16th, and 18th he (Gourgas) Piexotto, and Des Doity were made Deputy Inspectors-General. In 1813, Emanuel de la Motta, an officer third in rank, in the Supreme Council at Charleston visited them, declared their proceedings regular, and gave them a certificate to that effect. August 5th, the same year, De la Motta conferred the thirty-third degree on Simpson and Gourgas. These three then opened a provisional Supreme Council, and conferred the degree on Daniel D. Tompkins, Riker, Peixotto, and Tardy. De la Motta then proceeded to organize the **Second** Supreme Council for the United States. Tompkins was appointed Grand Commander, and Simpson Lieutenant Grand Commander. De la Motta's proceedings were ratified by the Supreme Council at Charleston, in the following December. †

In 1822, Giles Fonda Yates, having found the warrant of the Lodge at Albany, granted by Francken, patents issued by him and a copy of the Constitutions left by him at Albany, he by the assistance of the surviving members, succeeded in reviving the old Lodge. The necessary steps were then taken to place the same, under the superintendence of a Grand Council of Princes of Jerusalem, and such Council was subsequently opened in that city.

---

* Folger, pp. 130, 131 ; History of Free Masonry and Concordant Orders, pp. 802, 803.

† Ibid., pp. 803–806; Folger, pp. 158, 159; American edition of Gould's History of Free Masonry, vol. iv., pp 654, 655.

In 1824, a Consistory was organized at Albany, and bodies of the rite were established at Boston under authority of the Supreme Council at Charleston. In 1825, the thirty-third degree was conferred on Yates by Joseph McCosh, Grand Secretary-General, and Special Deputy * of the same body.

In the year 1844 Gourgas assumed, as of right in seniority, the position of Grand Commander of the dormant De La Motta Council, Yates becoming Lieut. Grand Commander.† Soon after this, Gourgas entered into a contract with others, whom he had inducted into the mysteries, whereby it was agreed to institute a new Supreme Council, but retaining the previous title "The Supreme Council of the *Northern* Jurisdiction," antedating its organization to August 5, 1813; ‡ and in 1848 he issued an edict containing the following names as members of this Council: J. J. J. Gourgas, Giles Fonda Yates, Edward A. Raymond, Killian H. Van Rensselaer, John Christe, Charles W. Moore, and Archibald Bull. This Council established its East in the city of New York, and claimed Masonic Jurisdiction over all the northern part of the United States of America.

In 1851 the seat of this Supreme Council was removed to Boston, and Gourgas resigned the position of Sovereign Grand Commander in favor of Giles Fonda Yates, who immediately resigned in favor of Edward A. Raymond. The Council proceeded harmoniously until August, 1860, when a split occurred, one branch remaining under Raymond, while the other subsequently elected Killian Van Rensselaer S. G. C.

Raymond proceeded to fill the offices made vacant by the schism, and in the published proceedings of the session of May 21, 1861, the following names appeared as the first two officers:

        Edward A. Raymond........................ S. G. C.
        Simon W. Robinson........................ Lieut. G. C. and G. Treas.

On February 7, 1863, a Treaty of Union was entered into, between the Gourgas-Raymond Council, commanded by Ed. A. Raymond, and the Cerneau-Hays Council, and a new Council evolved under the name of the Supreme Council of the Ancient and Accepted Scottish Rite for the United States of America, its Territories and Dependencies, Hays becoming the

---

* Deputized to confer on Yates. History of Free Masonry and Concordant Orders, pp. 806, 807.
† Ibid., pp. 807, 808, 822.
‡ Condensed History of A. & A. Rite, 1887, p. 12 ; Folger, p. 246.

Grand Commander, and Ed. A. Raymond Deputy Grand Commander. Thus the bodies known as the Cerneau Supreme Council and the Raymond Supreme Council were merged into the new organization.

In 1864 Edward A. Raymond died. December 14, 1865, Edmund B. Hays resigned his office, and Simon W. Robinson succeeded as Sovereign Grand Commander in his place.

The Union had hardly continued two years, before members of the United Council, who were formerly members of the *Raymond* body, began to agitate the question of re-establishing the body known as the Supreme Council of the Northern Jurisdiction, and at a meeting of this S. C., held September 11, 1865, a committee was appointed for the purpose of taking into consideration the propriety of "resuming" the old name "Supreme Council for the Northern Jurisdiction," * etc. Subsequently the Committee reported favorably, the report was adopted, and the Raymond Council resuscitated.

On November 27, 1866, Simon W. Robinson issued a summons for a meeting of the Council. Time, December 13th.

At the beginning of this meeting, Robinson announced that, consequent upon the death of Bro. E. A. Raymond, late Sovereign Grand Commander, he had succeeded to the Grand Commandership of the old Raymond Council. A board of officers was selected. The S. G. Commander then caused it to be proclaimed that the Supreme Council, 33°, for the Northern Jurisdiction United States of America, was fully organized, and proceeded to install the officers.† Thus the *Northern* Jurisdiction, as now known, became an established fact. They next altered their constitution, raising the number of active members of their S. C. to 33, and then elected the following Brethren to active membership, viz.,

Daniel Sickles,	John Innes,	Thomas J. Corson,
Henry C. Banks,	Geo. M. Randall,	J. Clarke Hagey,
Geo. W. Bently,	Henry L. Palmer,	John F. Currier.
Hopkins Thompson,	Aaron King,	

Bro. Daniel Sickles was chosen G. Sec. Gen. H. E.

---

* Pp. 201, 202 printed proceedings Northern Jurisdiction; Condensed History of A. & A. S. Rite, pp. 12 to 22; Gorman's Address, before the Supreme Council, U. S. A., 1889, p. 38.

† Ibid., p. 41; Folger, pp. 81 to 86, Supplement; also p. 21, Condensed History of the A. & A. Rite.

In 1867 Robinson resigned, and Josiah Drummond became Sov. G. Commander. He held the office until 1879, when he resigned, and was succeeded by H. L. Palmer.

POWER OR PATENT OF STEPHEN MORIN.*

T∴ T∴ G∴ O∴ T∴ G∴ A∴ O∴ T∴ U∴

And in accordance with the will and pleasure of his Most Sovereign Highness Illustrious Brother Louis of Bourbon, Count of Clermont, Prince of the Blood, Grand Master and Protector of all the Lodges.

At the East, in a place well lighted, and where dwell *Peace, Silence, Concord*, Anno Lucis, 5761, and according to the Christian Era, August 27, 1761.

Lux ex tenebris, veritas, concordia fratrum.

We, the undersigned, Substitutes General of the Royal Art, Grand Wardens and Officers of the Grand and Sovereign Lodge of St. John, established at the Grand East of Paris. And we, Sovereign Grand Master of the Grand Council of the Lodges of France, under the protection of the Sovereign Grand Lodge, under the sacred and mysterious numbers, do hereby declare, certify, and ordain to all Brethren, Knights, and Princes, spread throughout both hemispheres, that having assembled by order of the Deputy General, President of the Grand Council, a request to us, communicated, was read at our sitting.

That our Dear Brother Stephen Morin, Grand, Elect, Perfect, formerly Sublime Master, Prince Mason, Knight and Sublime Prince of all the Orders of the Masonry of Perfection, Member of the Trinity Royal Lodge, etc., being about to leave for America, and wishing to be enabled to work regularly, to the advantage and improvement of the Royal Art in all its perfection, may it please the Sovereign Grand Council and the Grand Lodge to grant him Letters Patent for Constitution.

A report having been made to us, and being acquainted with the eminent qualities of Brother Stephen Morin, we have, without hesitation, granted this satisfaction for the services which he has always rendered to the order, and the continuation of which is to us guaranteed by his zeal.

* Folger, Document No. 4, p. 29, Supplement of Masonic History.

'Wherefore, and for other good reasons, after approving and confirming dear Brother Morin in his designs, and wishing to give him testimonies of our gratitude, we have unanimously constituted and instituted him, and by these presents do constitute and institute him, and we do give full power and authority to said Brother Stephen Morin, the signature of whom stands in the margin of these presents, to form and establish a Lodge for the purpose of receiving and multiplying the Royal Order of Free Masons in all the perfect and sublime degrees, to take due care that the general and particular statutes and regulations of the Grand and Sovereign Lodge be kept and observed, and to admit therein none but true and legitimate brethren of Sublime Masonry.

To regulate and govern all the members which may compose his said Lodge, which he is authorized to establish in the four parts of the world whither he may arrive or where he may dwell, under the title of *Lodge of St. John*, and by surname *The Perfect Harmony*.

Power is hereby to him granted to select such officers as he may think proper to help him in the government of his Lodge, and to whom we command and enjoin to obey and respect him.

We do command and ordain to all Masters of regular Lodges spread all over the earth, and of whatsoever dignity they might be, we request and enjoin them in the name of the Royal order, and in the presence of our Most Illustrious Grand Master, to recognize, as we do ourselves hereby recognize, our dear Brother Stephen Morin as Worshipful Master of the Perfect Harmony Lodge; and we commission him as our *Grand Inspector** in every part of the new world, to rectify the observance of our laws in general, etc., and by these presents we do institute our dearest brother Stephen Morin, our Grand Master Inspector, authorizing him and giving him full power to establish Perfect and Sublime Masonry in every part of the world, etc.

We therefore request the brethren in general to grant to said Stephen Morin such aid and assistance as may be in their power, and we do require him to act in a similar manner toward all the brethren members of the Lodge,

---

* This was a title and not a degree. This title was, and is still at this day, bestowed on brethren commissioned to examine the work of the Lodges, in order to report upon the regularity of their proceedings and their work. Leblanc de Marconnay, p. 28.

or such as he might have admitted or constituted, or whom he might hereafter admit and constitute in the Sublime Degree of Perfection which we grant him, with full power and authority to make Inspectors wherever the Sublime degrees have not been established, as we are well satisfied with his great information and capacity.

In testimony whereof, we have delivered him these presents, signed by the Deputy General of the Order, Grand Commander of the White and Black Eagle, Sublime Prince of the Royal Secret, and by us, Grand Inspectors, Sublime Officers of the Grand Council and of the Grand Lodge established in this capital, and we have hereunto affixed the Grand Seal of our Illustrious Grand Master, His Royal Highness, Louis of Bourbon, Count of Clermont, Prince of the blood, etc., and that of our Grand Lodge and Sovereign Grand Council.

At the Grand East of Paris, A. L. 5761, or of the Christian Era, August 29, 1761.

(Signed) *Manu propria,*

CHAILLON DE JOINVILLE, Deputy General of the Order, Worshipful Master of the First Lodge in France, called Br∴ F∴ Thomas, Chief of the Eminent degrees, Commander and Sublime Prince of the Royal Secret.

PRINCE DE ROHAN, Master of the Grand Lodge " *The Intelligence,*" Sovereign Prince of Masonry.

LACORNE, Deputy Grand Master, Master of Trinity Lodge, Grand, Elect, Perfect, Knight, and Prince Mason.

SALVALETTE DE BUCKOLAY, Grand Keeper of the Seals, Grand, Elect, Grand Knight, and Prince Mason.

TAUPIN, Prince Mason.

BREST DE LA CHAUSSÉE, Grand, Elect, Prince Mason.

COUNT DE CHOISEUL, Prince Mason.

CHEVALIER DE LENONCOURT, Prince Mason.

By order of the Grand Lodge, (Signed)

D'AUBERTIN, Grand, Elect, Perfect, Master, and Sovereign Prince Mason, Master of the St. Alphonso Lodge, and of the Sublime Council of Perfect Masons of France.

FRANCKEN.

After receiving his patent from Moren, Francken remained several years in the West Indies. He then came to the United States, and in 1767, instituted a Lodge of Perfection at Albany.

In this patent Francken declares himself authorized to confer personally from the 4th to the 29th degrees, inclusive.†

From Francken's Patent to the Albany Body.

Lux Ex Tenebris.

Unitas, Concordia, Fratrum.

By virtue of a full power and authority committed to me by the Most Illustrious, Most Respectable, and Most Sublime Brother *Stephen Moren*, Grand Inspector of all Lodges relative to the Superior degrees of Masonry, from Secret Master to the 29th degree, *and confirmed* by the Grand Council of Princes of Masons, in the island of *Jamaica*, &c., &c., We, Hen.·. And'w Francken, Dep'y Ins'r Gen'l of all the Superior degrees of Masons in the West Indies and North America, have duly examined and found worthy our dear Brethren William Gamble, Francis Joseph Von Pfister, Thomas Swords, Thomas Lynott, and Richard Cartwright, and find them well qualified in the mysteries of Masonry, to the 14th degree, known by us to be the highest degree of ancient Masonry by the name of Perfection of Masonry. Know ye that in consequence of such power *we have constituted*, and by these presents *we do constitute*, our said worthy Brethren William Gamble, Francis Joseph Von Pfister, Thomas Swords, Thomas Lynott, and Richard Cartwright into a Regular Lodge of Perfection, by the name of *Ineffable;* to be held at the City of Albany, in the Province of New York.

Done near the B. B. at New York, the Day and Year above written.

Hen'y and W. Francken,
Sov'n Prince of Masons, Dep'y Gr'd Insp'r Gen'l.

---

* See Gorman's Address, 1889, pp. 73, 74.
† Proceedings of Northern Jurisdiction for 1869, p. 8; Folger, p. 276.

THE A. AND A. SCOTTISH RITE.

LEADING EVENTS IN THE HISTORY OF THE A. AND A. RITE.

1754. Chapter of Clermont established.

1758. Council of the Emperors of the East and West organized.

1761. Morin's Patent granted by the G. L. of France and the Council of the Emperors.

In the same year Morin goes to St. Domingo, and soon after to Jamaica, where he confers the degrees and authority on Francken.* Francken confers on Hays in 1763, and Hays confers on others.

1762. The noted Constitutions of 1762 drawn up by nine Commissioners at Bordeaux.

1766. Morin's Patent annulled.

1767. Francken at Albany, N. Y., and organizes a Lodge of Perfection there.

1770. G. C. of S. P. of the R. S.† established at Kingston, Jamaica.

1781. A Lodge of Perfection opened in Philadelphia.

1783. Lodge of Perfection opened at Charleston by Deputy Inspector Hays.

1788. A G. C. of P. of J. organized at Charleston.

1797. Sublime Council of Princes of the Royal Secret est. at Charleston, developed into a Supreme Council which conferred the degrees upon Dalcho, May 25, 1801.

1798. The Council at Charleston recognized by the Council at Kingston.

1801. Supreme Council opened at Charleston by Mitchell and Dalcho, May 31.

1802. De Grasse Tilley had the 33° conferred on him by the Supreme Council at Charleston.

1804. De Grasse Tilley organizes a Supreme Council for France in Paris.

1824. Jeremy L. Cross receives a Patent from the Southern Jurisdiction, constituting him a S. G. I. G.

---

* Folger, pp. 37–79 ; American edition of Gould's History, vol. iv., p. 635 ; Reprint of Proceedings of Northern Jurisdiction, vol. i., part I., p. 4, 1781, 1851 ; Picton in Masonic Chronicle, vol. xii., p. 69 ; Gorman's Address for 1889, pp. 29–31.

† Abbreviations will be used for preposterously long titles.

1824. Giles F. Yates receives a Patent from the same body, authorizing the establishment of a Consistory at Albany.

1825. Yates made a S. G. I. G., by McCosh, an officer of the Southern Jurisdiction.

1846. The Southern Supreme Council established a Consistory of P. of the R. S., 32°, at Natchez, Miss.

1852. The same body established a Consistory at New Orleans.

1859-91. Albert Pike, S. G. C.

1891-1900. Thos. H. Caswell, S. G. C.

The Northern Jurisdiction.

1806. A Consistory of P. R. S. organized in New York by Antoine Bideaud. Among the members present were: Tardy and Gourgas.

1808. A G. C. of P. of J., and a Lodge of P., were organized in New York, by Abraham Jacobs.

1813. Bideaud's Consistory of 1806, was reorganized by De La Motta as a Supreme Council.

1845. The Northern Supreme Council reorganized by J. J. J. Gourgas.

1846. England.—A Supreme Council of the 33° established in that country by authority of a Patent granted by the Supreme Council of the Northern Jurisdiction, to Robert T. Cucefix, of London.

1851. G. F. Yates, S. G. C. He transfers the office to E. A. Raymond, and in the same year the Council moves to Boston.

1860. Split—Raymond S. G. C. of one wing, and Van Rensselaer of the other.

1863. Union of the Gourgas Raymond Council, and the Cerneau-Hays Council.

1864. Raymond dies.

1865. Hays resigns and Robinson becomes S. G. C.

1866. The Union Council dissolved, and the Northern Supreme Council revived.

1867. The Robinson and Van Rensselaer Councils unite and take the title, *Northern* Jurisdiction. Josiah Drummond, S. G. C.

1879.—H. L. Palmer, S. G. C.

CERNEAU.*

1787. He goes to St. Domingo.

1806. Receives his patent from Dupotet at Baracoa.†
In the same year he proceeds to New York.

1807. He establishes a Sov. G. Consistory in New York and was Sovereign Grand Commander.

1809. The Consistory reorganized—became the Sovereign Chapter of Rose Croix—title, "Triple Amity."

1812. He est. Supr. Council of the 33° in New York.

1813. The Supreme Council warrants a Consistory of Sub. P. of the R. S., at Newport, R. I.

1814. A Grand Encampment of Knights Templars was opened by the Cerneau S. G. Consistory.

In the same year a Sub. C. of P. of the R. S., was authorized by Cerneau, at Charleston.

1821-23. J. W. Mulligan, S. G. C. ‡

1823-25. De Witt Clinton, S. G. C.

1825. General De Lafayette, S. G. C.§

1826-28. De Witt Clinton, S. G. C.

1828-44. Elias Hicks, Sov. G. Commander.

1832. Union of the Supreme Council of the U. S. of America, etc. (Cerneau), with the Sup. Council of Mexico, Terra Firma, South America, etc.— the Hicks Laurent Council.

1846. The union between these two bodies was dissolved. ||

1845-51. H. C. Atwood, S. G. C.

1851. Jeremy L. Cross, S. G. C.

1852-60. H. C. Atwood, S. G. C.

1860-65. E. B. Hays, S. G. C.

1862. A Consistory (Cerneau) opened at Trenton, N. J.

1863. A Consistory opened by the same at Boston.

---

* Cerneau bodies are regarded as illicit by other organizations. Note 17, p. 612.

† Picton in Masonic Chronicle, vol. xii.. pp. 45, 46 ; also Acta Lattamorum, vol. i., p. 236.

‡ J. J. Gorman's Address before the S. C. (Cerneau), 1888. pp. 30, 31. § Note 16, p. 612.

|| Gorman's Address, 1889. pp. 33, 34.

THE PRESENT CERNEAU BODIES.

Cerneau-Gorgas.

This Council claims succession to Cerneau through H. G. Seymour and E. B. Hays.

1872, 1880. Harry J. Seymore, S. G. C.
1880–87. William H. Peckham, S. G. C.
1887–90. F. J. S. Gorgas, S. G. C.
1890–92. P. F. D. Hibbs, S. G. C.

Cerneau-Gorman.

1881. The adherents of the Cerneau-Hays Council decide to revive it. Hopkins Thompson, first S. G. C.

1883. E. W. Atwood, S. G. C.
1885. John B. Harris, S. G. C.
1886. John Haigh, S. G. C.
1887–92. John J. Gorman, S. G. C.

Claims of the A. and A. Rite, under its Nova Instituta Secreta, over the Degrees of Free Masonry.

"Therefore, and from motives of important interest, we have gathered and united into **one** body of **Free Masonry,** all the rites of the Scottish System, the doctrines of which are universally acknowledged as agreeing with the Ancient Institutions, tending to the same end, forming the principal branches of **one** and the same tree."

. . . "Taking therefore as the basis of our Conservatory reformation, the **First** of those rites, and the number of **Hierarchical** degrees of the **Last,** we declare that thus united and agglomerated, those degrees constituted one *single* Order, which professes the dogmas and pure doctrine of Ancient Free Masonry, and embraces all the systems of Scotch Masonry, united under the name of Ancient and Accepted Scotch Rite."

Therefore, the doctrine shall be imparted to *Masons* in **Thirty-three** degrees, divided into seven Temples or classes, which each of them shall be bound successively to pass through before being initiated to the most sublime and last, and to wait for each degree the delays, and undergo the trials, which the *Secret Institutes,* and ancient and modern rescripts of the Order of Perfection, require.

THE A. AND A. SCOTTISH RITE.

The First degree shall be subject to the second, this one to the third, and so on, up to the most sublime, or thirty-third, which shall watch over all the others and reprehend them, and command them, the assemblage, or re-union of all those who are there to be initiated, forming for that purpose the Grand Supreme Dogmatic Council, Conservator of the order, which it shall govern and administer in conformity with the present institutes, under the Constitutions soon to be established.*

De La Motta, in his Replication, says:

"Although Sublime Masons have not, in this country, initiated into the Blue or Symbolic degrees, yet their councils possess the indefeasible right of granting warrants for that purpose. It is common on the continent of Europe, and may be the case here, should circumstances render the exercise of that power necessary." †

Drummond, in Proceedings of Supreme Council Northern Jurisdiction, 1869, p. 27, said:

"The conclusion which I have reached, after considerable thought, is, that if the power of punishment with all its necessary consequences is withheld from the subordinates in any case or class of cases, the power to try should also be withheld.

"Any one of three methods might be adopted to effect this.

"1. To require charges in all cases to be filed and tried in the body of the highest grade of which the accused is a member.

"2. To provide for the appointment of a commission of the peers of the accused."

In "Transactions," 1857 to 1866, p. 357, Pike states:

"Undoubtedly we have ample power to commission a Deputy Inspector-General to confer the Blue degrees and to create Symbolic Lodges in any unoccupied country."

NOTES FROM AUTHORITIES.

1. As these degrees did not emanate from the G. L. of Scotland, nor were in any way connected with that body, the term Scottish doubtless originated from the fact that those new degrees were instituted by Scotch Masons residing in France. See Gould, vol. v., pp. 78, 92.

2. It cannot be too strongly insisted upon, that all so-called Scottish Masonry has nothing whatever to do with the Grand Lodge of Scotland, nor, with one possible exception—that of the Royal Order of Scotland—did it ever originate in that country. If we add to this rite that of the Ancient and Accepted Scottish Rite of 33° we may even maintain that none of the Scots degrees were at any time practised in Scotland. Gould, vol. v., p. 92.

In France, however, some of the Scots Lodges would appear to have clearly manufactured

---

* Folger, pp. 78, 79. † Ibid., p. 159.

new degrees, connecting these very distinguished Scots Masons with the Knights Templars, and thus given rise to the subsequent flood of Knight Templarism. The earliest of all are supposed to have been the Masons of Lyons, who invented the Kadosch degree, representing the vengeance of the Templars, in 1741.

From that time new rites multiplied in France and Germany, but all those of French origin contain knightly, and almost all, Templar grades.

The Scots Lodge ultimately usurped the prerogatives of a Grand Lodge, and issued warrants of constitution. In this way rose the so-called Scots Mother-Lodges.

Many of these Mother-Lodges developed systems of degrees of their own, which were worked in Chapters, independent of each other. Gould, vol. v., p. 93.

3. In 1758, the Chapter of Clermont added further degrees, and developed into the Council of the Emperors of the East and West, Sovereign Prince Masons, Substitutes General of the Royal Art, Grand Surveillants and officers of the Grand Lodge of St. John of Jerusalem. Their system also took the title of "Heredom of Perfection." Gould, vol. v., p. 97.

4. The Sovereign Council of Paris united in 1762 with their own offspring, the Sovereign Council of Princes of the Royal Secret, to formulate the grand Constitution of the system or Rite of Perfection, or Heredom, or of Emperors of the East and West, for all these names refer to the same association. According to these Statutes the rite was built up of 25 degrees, in seven classes : the first class comprised Free Masonry ; the second, 5 additional degrees ; in the fourth class, 13°, we find Knights of the Royal Arch ; in the fifth class, 15°, Knights of the East ; 17°, Knights of the East and West ; 18°, Sovereign Prince Rose-Croix ; and the 25° and last of the seventh class was the Sovereign Prince of the Royal Secret. The other degrees may be here omitted. These constitutions are still acknowledged by the Ancient and Accepted Scottish Rite 33° as the groundwork of their present system. Gould, vol. v., p. 97.

5. The original source for transmission of authority derived from France, the cradle of Scottish Rite Masonry is universally admitted to be the patent of Stephen Morin, from whence are descended all the Inspectors to be found on this soil. We know that prior to 1767 he appointed as his deputy, Andrew Francken, whose patent was endorsed by a Grand Council of Prince Masons at Kingston, Jamaica, which became recognized as the Metropolitan, or head of the order in America. See Gorman's Address in 1889, before the S. P. C. for the U. S , etc., pp. 29–31.

In 1801 there was in St. Domingo a Grand Consistory established by the Kingston authority, of which Cerneau and Hacquet were members. In consequence of the negro insurrection this Consistory was transferred to Baracoa, Cuba. Page 46, Masonic Chronicle, 1890.

6. Morin was an Inspector and a Prince Mason. The Inspectorship was an office created *ad hoc*, not a degree. He was empowered to nominate other Inspectors, but the high functionaries who signed his patent do not call themselves Inspectors. When the Rite returned to Europe in 1804, the Prince Masons had been promoted to the 32d degree, and a 33d and

THE A. AND A. SCOTTISH RITE. 611

last degree, consisting of Sovereign Inspectors General, had been created. The purely administrative office. had, in other words, been converted into a degree, and the office-holders had usurped authority; an analogy may be found in the position of an English Past Master.

6½. The second document in the golden book summarizes the genealogy of De Grasse Tilley's Inspectorship. Morin conferred it on Francken, of Jamaica, and the latter on Dr. Moses Hayes, at that time G. Commander at Boston, while Hayes in turn conferred it on Dr. Spitzer, of Charleston. All the Inspectors met at Philadelphia, and gave it to Moses Cohen, of Jamaica, and he in his turn passed it on to Isaac Long, who at Charleston created Delahogue, De Grasse, Croze Magnan, St. Paul, Robin, Petit, and Marie. Attested by J. Long, D. G. I. G. at Charleston, May 3, 1797, and countersigned by Delahogue, D. G. I., Prince Mason, Sov. G. Commander. Gould, vol. v., p. 128.

7. The Register of Delahogue, which was made out in 1798 and 1799, now deposited in the archives of the Supreme Council at Charleston, contains as its first entry, the filiation of the powers of Morin as Inspector-General. It states that he conferred his degrees and authority on Francken at Jamaica, he on M. M. Hays, and he on Spitzer, at Charleston, S. C. Folger, p. 37, also Registers of Aveilhe, 1797.

8. It is apparent that toward the very close of the last century the rite of Perfection was extended by the grouping of other degrees from time to time into its system; and unquestionably concurred in by Secret Articles agreed upon between the various Deputy Inspectors, deriving their powers as Sovereign Princes of the Royal Secret from Morin directly; or by communication from those he had invested. The powers of all these were coequal and coextensive. Indeed, owing to the closing of all the Masonic bodies, especially those of the Scottish Rite in France in 1789, caused by the Revolution, the Grand Deputy Inspectors in America, whether on the continent or in the islands, became independent; and as Principals, and by virtue of their own sovereign authority, remodelled and extended the Rite of Perfection by cumulating what had been previously controlled as honorary or side degrees; thus creating, when perfected, what is now known as the Ancient and Accepted Scottish Rite, adding to the series the controlling degree of Sovereign Grand Inspector-General. Constitutions and History of the A. & A. Rite, p. 16.

9. From Kaufman's History of Free Masonry, it appears "that the Scottish Rite in 33 degrees was established at Namur, a Province of Belgium, in 1770."

And from Chemin, Dupont's Encyclopédie Maçonnique, vol. iii., page 390, edition of 1823, the following: "We have seen, handled, and copied precisely a patent of the thirty-third degree delivered by a Consistory in Geneva, in 1791, to worshipful Brother Viele, an active officer of the Grand Orient of France." See Address of J. J. Gorman, before the Supreme Council A. and A. Rite for the U. S. A., 1889, p. 30, also Acta Latomorum, vol. i., pp. 318, 320.

10. Vassal contends that the Grand Lodge of France possessed the Scottish Rite before it was known in the New World, and that the Scottish Rite brought into France by the Count De Grasse, remodelled, is the same as that which the Grand Lodge had possessed for forty years.

11. Joseph Cerneau's Patent from Dupotet is given in full in the American edition of Gould's History, vol. iv., pp. 556, 557.

12. Cerneau had his Patent from Dupotet. History of Free Masonry and Concordant Orders, p. 813.

13. About 1765 there was established at Kingston, Jamaica, a Supreme Grand Council of Prince Masons, which countersigned the patent issued to Henry A. Francken, the first deputy appointed by Morin. Picton.

14. The Masonic Calendar of St. Domingo for 1802, testifies to the existence of a Supreme Council upon that island, of which Cerneau and Germain Hacquet were members.

15. 1807, the Grand Consistory at Baracoa constitutes a Consistory of Princes of the Royal Secret at New York, United States of America. It is promulgated October 28, 1808. Acta Latomorum, vol. i., p. 236.

16. In 1824 General De Lafayette was made a Sovereign Grand Inspector-General, 33° and last degree of Free Masonry, in Supreme Council in New York, by his Excellency Ill. De Witt Clinton, then Grand Commander. Address of J. J. Gorman, S. G. C., before the Supr. Council, A. & A. S. Rite, November 20, 1888, p. 30 ; also see Folger, p. 179.

17. The Grand Lodge of Iowa, by a vote of 781 against 429 at its session for 1893, decided to sustain the law opposed to the Cerneau bodies, thus in effect reaffirming that those bodies are illicit and clandestine.

CHAPTER XVI.

THE KNIGHTS TEMPLARS.

Origin of this Ancient Order.—The Knights of Chivalry.—Origin of the Crusades.—Peter the Hermit and his Hosts set out for Jerusalem, but are nearly Annihilated by the Turks in Asia Minor.—Subsequent Crusades.—The Knights Templars and Knights Hospitalers, their Desperate Valor, and Wonderful Career of over Two Hundred Years.— They defeat the Mohammedans in many Bloody Battles, but were finally Overwhelmed by Numbers and afterward Robbed and Suppressed by the Pope and King of France.—De Molai and Two Hundred Knights put to Death.—Suppressed, but still Undaunted, they Maintain their Organization in Different Countries.—They ultimately Unite with the Free Masons and Hospitalers, and thus give Rise to Modern Knight Templary. Establishment of the First Encampment in North America.— Grandeur of the Organization.—Statistics.

NATIONS, like individuals, become corrupt, diseased; and like individuals, perish if the disease is not arrested. Thus it was with Europe in the last part of the tenth century. Court circles and high life were corrupt to the core, and at the same time armies of soldiers that had been discharged at the close of the civil wars, were, for the want of occupation and bread, banded together and roamed over the land as robbers and tramps. Therefore Europe, like a diseased individual, must have relief or perish, and the relief came with Peter the Hermit and his crusade, which purged the country of its corrupt and vicious elements.

PALESTINE.

This small and mountainous country, that has occupied such a space in the world's history, as the theatre of its most momentous events, is a strip of territory 130 miles in length, with an average width of 40 miles; an area not as large as the State of New York. The " Great Sea " (Mediterranean) on the west, and the Jordan valley on the east, enclose the Holy Land on the east and west sides. The deserts of Arabia on the south, through which the forty years' migration of the Israelites occurred, make a defence equally formidable upon that end.

After the advent of Christianity, the next event of importance in this connection was occasioned by the spread of the Mohammedan religion. The Moslems, having pushed their doctrines by fire and sword, rapidly subdued Palestine and Egypt. The victorious Omar, having overrun the surrounding country, sat down before Jerusalem A.D. 637, and after a siege of four months, took it by capitulation; and notwithstanding the antagonism of the two creeds, Mohammedan and Christian, the conquerors generously respected the religious views of the Pilgrims to the Holy Sepulchre, and permitted them to come and go at their will. This leniency continued until the conquest of Syria by the Fatimides of Egypt (A.D. 980), when the position of the Christians became dangerous; but the culmination of their troubles did not come until the subjugation of the country by the Seljuk Turks. These, although they were good Mohammedans at home, yet when abroad were as regardless of the Koran as of the Bible; they therefore followed the instincts of their brutal natures, and perpetrated atrocities on all alike, Mohammedan and Christian; this rendered the situation intolerable for the Pilgrims, and led to the crusades.

This was also a period of unrest for Europe. It was believed that the end of the world was near, and prophets found plenty of credulous and excited hearers. The country was overrun with discharged soldiers, now helpless and driven to plunder, and their ranks were augmented by adventurers and vagabonds. Therefore bands of robbers were roving everywhere at will. Suddenly the situation took a turn and found vent in the crusades. One only thought pervaded the country. Great and little, poor and rich, male and female, parents and children, priests and people, all were turning their faces toward the Holy Land, as though they had a great duty to discharge there. All wished to sell their property, with no one to purchase, except what was portable.

This was the condition of Europe when Peter the Hermit, mounted on a white mule, commenced riding from village to village, from province to province, his lank body enveloped in a pilgrim's mantle of the commonest stuff; his feet naked, his cowl thrown back, leaving his head bare. His singular raiment, austerity of demeanor, fiery zeal, and vehemence of speech and gesture, had such effect upon the people, that they followed him in rapidly increasing crowds.

Such was the man who inaugurated the crusades, who applied the torch to combustible Europe.

Peter was a native of Amiens, France. A zealous religionist by nature and teaching.

This impelled him to make a pilgrimage to the Holy Sepulchre, which he did in company with others. Arrived in Jerusalem, he soon witnessed scenes that filled him with terror and indignation. After having followed his brethren to Calvary and the tomb of Christ, he repaired to the Patriarch of Jerusalem, and they consulted together over the sufferings of the Christians.

The result of this interview was that Peter returned to Europe, charged with letters asking for assistance. He crossed the sea, landed in Italy, and hastened to the feet of the Pope.

The chair of St. Peter was then occupied (A.D. 1088) by Urban II., who embraced with ardor a project which had been entertained by his predecessors; he received Peter as a prophet, applauded his design, and bade him go forth and announce the approaching deliverance of Jerusalem. The preacher of the Holy War was everywhere received as a messenger from God, and the people esteemed it a great favor to even touch his vestments.

While Peter was preaching the crusade, the Pope called a council of the western nations, which he addressed with such effect that, when he had ceased to speak, loud acclamations burst from the multitude. Pity, indignation, and despair at the same time agitated and rendered tumultuous this assembly of the faithful. According to their temperaments, some shed tears over Jerusalem and the fate of the Christians; while others swore to exterminate the Infidels.

Thus the agitation went on till the spring, A.D. 1096, when it had become impossible to longer restrain the impatience of the people. Penitence and piety, the most sincere and fervent, were now to associate with impurity—virtue and vice making common cause against the Infidel.

From the Mediterranean to the Northern Ocean, from Portugal to the Danube, men, women, and children were hurrying to the crusade. Those who were to remain were in tears, while those marching toward Asia showed smiles of hope and joy. They declared themselves the volunteers of heaven, and would not hear of any mixture of what was human. At every village it was asked "Is that Jerusalem?" Happy in their ignorance, not a word of reason came from old or young, clerk or layman. To all classes of people the crusade became the great object of life—all things else were insignificant in comparison.

Even the clergy dare not miss this new plan of salvation, so fell into line with the rest. With the good and pure came also the blasphemers, cursers, pickpockets, and robbers—large parties of the most audacious ruffians, and the most shameless Delilahs and Jezebels, and the like, who joined the crowd for profit and a glorious old time, as they said.

From this mass of wild humanity the military leaders first endeavored to rid themselves of the riff-raff, but with poor success.

Next, all the mobs of different nationalities were gotten together in *three* divisions, with the zealous Peter as fit leader of the *first*. He believing that a red-hot will was sufficient to insure obedience, even from an undisciplined host, figured at the head of that burlesque on an army, everywhere distinguished by his unique costume and his mount, the same white mule which had carried him over Europe. This division comprised 100,000 men. Following in the rear was a long train of primitive vehicles containing the sick, decrepit, women, and children, who would not be turned back.*

At length, after passing through many vicissitudes, Peter reached Semlin, where he found sixteen not dead men, but the garments and arms of so many of his vanguard, stuck up by way of caution to deter his army from following the example of those plunderers. At sight of this Peter waxed hot, and gave the signal for war, the blast of a trumpet; when his desperate legions rushed

---

* At this point there is a conflict of testimony as to the number of men assembled, the number of divisions in which they proceed, etc. But as Addison gave this subject a careful investigation, both in Europe and the Holy Land, his statements are accepted as reliable on all important questions in the history of the Templars. See Addison's Knights Templars (Macoy), p. 92.

Preaching the First Crusade.

THE KNIGHTS TEMPLARS. 619

to the attack and slew 40,000 of the peaceable inhabitants. Upon learning of this atrocious massacre, the King of Hungary, with a large army, hastened after Peter.

But before the King's arrival, Peter and his army had run away and escaped across the River Save. There they found the country abandoned. Everyone had sought refuge in the hills and woods from the threatened danger.

The next place of importance reached by the now famishing crowd, was the fortified town of Nyssa. Here they could not enter, but were given a little food beneath its walls, on their promise of forthwith proceeding without perpetrating any misdemeanor. Yet a party of them recklessly fired some wind-mills in the vicinity, upon which the citizens, armed, charged the rear and put many to death, and took a large number of prisoners, including mothers and infants, many of whom were found living there in bondage years afterward. The remnant hastened forward, reduced in numbers and in a miserable condition.

Following Peter was the *second* division, and worse than the first; they were from the north of the Rhine and led by a priest of the name of Gotschalk. These warriors varied the tedium of the march by such diversion as pillage, rapes, quarrels, robbery, and murder. What Peter had told them concerning Christ and the Holy Sepulchre they had soon forgotten, or disregarded it for the congenial pursuits now within their reach. Strife between parties and individuals for the same plunder, constantly led to sanguinary arguments; so that this noble band would soon have worn itself out, if it had not fallen a victim to better disciplined barbarians.

As bad as were these two divisions of the followers of the Hermit, yet there was a *third*, that, for every form of vice and crime, completely overshadowed them.

The idea that freemen who had been born and reared in hovels and in the open air, should yield to military or ecclesiastical rule, or submit to any restraint whatever, was to them a huge joke; that they were crusaders, soldiers of Christ, was sufficient for them to know. That freed them from all responsibility, moral and otherwise. Therefore they could commit the most diabolical crimes with impunity, considering that for the wonderful service they were rendering the state, all the riches on earth were insufficient to recompense them. Consequently all that should fall into their hands was their own, and even that was but a small part of what was due them. As to the proprietors of the land they were traversing, they should thank them if they left them with their hides on. They frequently took a goat, and made it march at their head, and assured astonished beholders that it was equal to any priest or bishop.

The greatest sufferers on their line of march were the Jews, whom they blamed for the Crucifixion of Christ, and for which, they robbed and murdered them with the most abominable tortures.

They were as vain of the destruction of these defenceless people as though they had vanquished the Saracens. Retribution, however, was close at hand, as the Hungarians, becoming exasperated at this assemblage of brutes, exercised their keen-edged swords on them so mercilessly that only a small portion of it survived to join the Hermit at Constantinople.

With these stragglers and the remnants of the other divisions, reinforced by Venetians and Normans, Peter got together another army of a hundred thousand men, quite as reckless, undisciplined, and wicked as his first. As Constantinople was suffering from the neighborhood of the crusaders, the emperor gladly furnished vessels to transport them out of his way into Asia. After disembarking his army, Peter advanced to the neighborhood of Nice with the same ignorance and disregard of military tactics and caution as he had exhibited from the start, consequently a Turkish army came upon him and routed and slaughtered his army almost to a man. His Lieutenant, Sansavior, was literally cut to pieces, and the Hermit barely escaped with his life. Thus in a single day that whole vast collection of men disappeared, and left only their remains in the valley (near Nice) that was the scene of the slaughter.

Christendom was horror struck at learning of this disaster, for of the four hundred thousand crusaders she had sent out nearly all had now perished. But thus purged of this deadly incubus, the knightly prowess of Europe asserted itself. The leaders of the real crusade, with Godfrey de Bouillon at their head, gathered nearly all the most illustrious military men of the time, and horses and equipments were in such demand that the funds of a great estate hardly sufficed to arm and mount a single knight. But when equipped and en route

THE FOUR LEADERS OF THE FIRST REAL CRUSADE.

they presented an imposing appearance, and thus in a measure re-established the honor of the crusaders in the countries they passed through. Reaching Constantinople, they entered it with the honors and demonstrations of a public welcome. Finally, the Emperor generously furnished them transportation across the Bosphorus, and they advanced toward Nice, but had proceeded but a few leagues when they met a few survivors of Peter's army, and further on they came to the battle-field, covered with human bones, telling of that terrible slaughter. Wolves and vultures had consumed their flesh, and the bleached bones was all that remained of the Hermit's ill-fated hosts. This spectacle determined the crusaders to avenge the slaughter of their countrymen. Therefore they made a fierce attack on Nice, and took it, June 20, 1097, and a few days later gained the bloody but glorious victory at Dorylæum. Upon entering the Turkish camp at the latter place they were surprised to see camels, animals till then unknown in Europe.

On July 6th the crusaders renewed their march toward Jerusalem, and met with no further resistance throughout Asia Minor, until they reached Antioch, as the affair at Dorylæum showed the Turks that they had now a foe worthy of their steel; but upon reaching Antioch (October 18th) the crusaders found it thoroughly prepared for a siege. This city was then four miles in circumference and contained a population of over two hundred thousand. It was surrounded by a deep and wide ditch, and had massive walls of defence. Its garrison of 30,000 was commanded by Baghasian, a brave general, who made such a stubborn resistance that nearly seven months intervened before the city was taken. The capture was effected May 3, A.D. 1098.

The crusaders then prepared for rest, but were soon astonished at finding themselves assailed by a host of Mohammedans from every quarter of the surrounding country. Twenty-eight Emirs led as many divisions of their forces, to rescue this important city and stronghold from the Christians. Their army, of over 300,000, was led by Kerboga, Prince of Mosul, Lieutenant of the Sultan of Persia. The attack by such numbers drove the crusaders within the walls, where they in turn were compelled to suffer a siege. A series of desperate battles followed; and at last, after a prodigious display of valor by the crusaders, the Moslems were so badly defeated that they retreated to the east of the Euphrates.

The beautiful capital of Syria, with its massive fortifications, was at last in quiet possession of the Latins, but consequent on such a sacrifice of life that of all who left Europe, only about 50,000 were now left.

The remaining distance to Jerusalem, of nearly three hundred miles, was over a country one of the worst for military aggression in the world ; a path so hemmed in between the Lebanon Mountains and the sea that there is rarely room for the narrowest column to deploy ; where flanking parties can destroy the mightiest forces in detail. Such was the route from Antioch to Jerusalem.

In view of the natural obstacles, and the terrible depletion of their ranks, a year was spent in recuperation and recruiting the army, so that it was March, 1099, before the crusaders were prepared to resume their march to the Holy City. Prince Bohemond remained in charge at Antioch. By a forced arrangement the cities down the coast, Tripoli, Beyrout, Sidon, Tyre, Acre, Cæsarea, and Joppa were to supply them with provisions as they passed.

Bountiful harvests had just been gathered, so there was no lack of supplies. The crusaders' fleet sailed along the coast, most of the time in full view, until the army reached Joppa. The successive and overwhelming defeats the Moslems had experienced filled them with such wholesome fear of the invaders, that not even the narrowest defiles on the route were seriously defended. They traversed the rich territory of Beyrout, Sidon, and Tyre—rested in the gardens of those ancient cities, and refreshed themselves with their cool waters; the Moslems remaining unwilling spectators within their walls, but sending provisions to the passing pilgrims and conjuring them not to damage their orchards or flowers.

Early in June they reached, and took, Lydia and Ramleh, eighteen miles from Jerusalem. Proceeding again, they were met at Emmaus by a deputation of Christians from Bethlehem, who solicited a guard to protect the venerable church of the Nativity. In compliance, Tancred was sent forward at midnight with a choice detachment of soldiers, and took possession of that place. During the same night, June 9th, an eclipse of the moon occurred which has been of great service to historians and chronologers ever since, as it served to fix not only the date of the capture of Jerusalem by the crusaders, but of subsequent events.

At dawn of day, June 10th, the army reached the top of the mountains northwest of Jerusalem, and beheld for the first time the Holy City. The effect was magical. Jerusalem! Jerusalem! was shouted by the enraptured hosts. Some knelt and prayed; and some cast themselves down and kissed the earth. But their joy was of brief duration; for a hazardous task confronted them—the capture of the city. Iftikhar Eddaulah, in command of Jerusalem, was a brave and energetic ruler, and he had ravaged the suburbs of the city, destroyed the fruit-trees, broken the tanks and cisterns, and poisoned the springs. He had also caused provisions for a long siege to be collected, and had compelled his prisoners and large numbers of his people to repair the walls and bulwarks, deepen the ditches, and construct machines of war. The garrison was estimated at 80,000, while the assailants now counted less than 50,000. Besides, Jerusalem against the then mode of warfare, was nearly impregnable, as it had deep rough ravines upon three sides, and immense walls all around it.

On June 15, 1099, the fifth day after their arrival, the chiefs of the crusade, having divided among themselves the work of assault, made the first attack upon Jerusalem.

By the plan of attack, the space between the Joppa gate and the Damascus gate was assigned to Godfrey De Bouillon and Baldwin de Bourg.* The tent of Godfrey was pitched where the Russian Convent now stands, and was distinguished by a silver cross on its summit. Robert, Duke of Normandy, Robert, Count of Flanders, and Tancred were assigned the northeast corner of the city. After having stationed a garrison at Bethlehem, five miles south, Tancred rode around by way of Mount Olivet to take part in the assault.

The space between this last division and that of Godfrey was entrusted to Duke Alain Fergent, commanding the Bretons. The western wall was given to Raymond, Count of Toulouse.

Everything being in readiness, a terrible assault took place, and was wellnigh successful—yet fell short of victory, and the crusaders had to haul off for rest and repairs; this also gave the Saracens time to repair their walls. After great preparation on both sides the assault was renewed with desperate determination. The enthusiasm was so great that even the old, sick, and

* Near the Damascus gate, Captain Warren found in August, 1867, a stone with a Templar Cross engraved upon it.

feeble lent what aid they could, while the women hurried through the ranks, bringing water to assuage the thirst of the assailants.

Still, the Saracens made such a stout defence, that when more than half the day was spent the crusaders were repulsed at all quarters. At this critical juncture a soldier suddenly appeared on Mount Olivet, waving on the crusaders. Where he came from does not appear, or whether he was not the mere creature of imagination. But this apparition so raised the hopes of the Christians, that almost supernatural efforts were now made. The tower of Godfrey de Bouillon was rolled up until it touched the wall, upon which Letoldus of Tournay, his brother Engelbert, and Godfrey himself, sprang. They were followed by a stream of fierce warriors, and soon the ensign of the Cross announced to the anxious eyes of the army, that Christians stood upon the battlements of Jerusalem. Nearly simultaneous with this, the crusaders burst into the city from other points, and in an inconceivable short space of time Jerusalem had changed hands. The Moslems retreated into their Mosques, fighting as they went; a large number of them huddled in the Mosque of Omar upon Mount Moriah, where, without further struggle, they submitted their necks to the inevitable slaughter. Thus was Jerusalem taken by the first crusaders. As for Peter the Hermit, the great agitator, if not the originator of this crusade, his grotesque war record had brought him into such disrepute among military men, that after remaining a short time in Palestine, he returned to France and spent the remainder of his life in a monastery. He died in 1115.

The Knights Templars.

Although the Infidels had been driven out of Jerusalem, they had not by any means been driven from Palestine. The mountains on the sea-coast still continued to be infested by warlike bands of Mussulmen, the worst now being the fugitive soldiers from Jerusalem, who maintained themselves in castles and strongholds, from whence they came forth upon the roads, and robbed and maltreated all travellers, of both sexes, taking life when any resistance was offered; thus gratifying their love of plunder and revenging themselves for the destruction of their habitations and property by the crusaders. The Bedouin horsemen from east of the Jordan also hovered around the routes of the pilgrims, so that whether they approached Jerusalem by sea, by way of Joppa, or by any other route, they were alike exposed to robbery and death. To remedy this state of things, and guard the honor of saintly women, Hugh de Payens, and eight brave crusaders who had greatly distinguished themselves at the siege and capture of Jerusalem, entered into a solemn compact to aid one another in guarding the highways, and in protecting the pilgrims on their way to and from Jerusalem. Animated by the sacredness of the cause to which they had devoted their swords, they called themselves the " Poor Soldiers of Jesus."

In the Holy Church of the Resurrection, in the year 1113, in the presence of Arnulph, Patriarch of Jerusalem, they embraced vows of perpetual chastity, obedience, and poverty. When duly organized, they selected as their first Master Hugh de Payens.

The Christian Church of the Virgin, erected about A. D. 540 by the Emperor Justinian, on the southern end of the Temple enclosure, was on the conquest of Jerusalem by the Moslems, A. D. 637, converted into the Mosque-el aksa ; and as Hugh de Payens and his rapidly increasing band had no church and no particular place of abode, this Mosque and adjacent buildings were appropriated to them. And later, the court extending between that building and the Dome of the Rock, a distance of about five hundred feet, was also conceded to them. King Baldwin, the barons of the Latin kingdom, and the patriarchs and prelates of Jerusalem, assigned them various gifts and revenues for their maintenance and support. With their revenues and a permanent place of abode, the Knights soon began to gain in numbers, entertain more extended views, and seek a larger theatre for the exercise of their profession.

Each Knight was allowed a squire or serving brother-at-arms, and three horses, but all gilded and superfluous ornaments were forbidden, and their dress was prescribed to be white, as a mark of their profession to which they were bound by vows of poverty, and they lived on the coarsest food.

When not engaged in combating the enemies of Christ they remained secluded in the house assigned to them, furbishing their armor and mending their clothes. They were forbidden to play at chess, draughts, or dice ; and as their number increased they formed a hardy and determined band of warriors, devoted to the cause of their institution.

The reception of a Knight into the Order was an impressive ceremonial. When a candidate presented himself for admission the Chapter assembled, and the gates of the Temple were scrupulously closed, while every officer occupied his proper place in the assembly, which usually met by torchlight, at the dead of night, in the church. The candidate attended outside, and the presiding officer three several times deputed two brethren to ask him whether he was firmly determined to enter the Order. On his reply in the affirmative, he was admitted, and then thrice, humbly kneeling on his knees, solicited bread and water, and his admission to the Order. He was then addressed in the following terms by the Preceptor or other President: "You are about to subscribe to heavy engagements. You will be exposed to many difficulties and dangers; you will have to watch when you would desire to sleep, to suffer the pangs of hunger when you would desire to eat and drink, and depart into one country when you would desire to be in another." He was then asked whether he was in good health; whether married or betrothed; whether he belonged to any other Order; and finally, whether he had any debts to pay. When the candidate had satisfactorily replied to these questions, he pronounced the three vows of chastity, poverty, and obedience. "I swear," said the novice, "to consecrate my thoughts, my energy, and my life to the defence of the unity of God and the mysteries of the faith, etc. I promise to be submissive and obedient to the Grand Master, whensoever necessity shall arise. I agree to pass over the seas to the battle-field. I will give my aid in fighting infidel kings and princes; and in the presence of three opponents, I will not turn and fly, but will encounter them if they be Infidels." He then received the mantle of the Order, and the Knights present gave him the kiss of fraternity.

The dress of the Templar consisted of a long white tunic nearly resembling that of the priests in shape, with a red cross on the front and back, and under this was his linen shirt clasped by a girdle. Over all was the white mantle with the red cross pattee. The head was covered with a cap or hood attached to the mantle. The arms were a sword, lance, mace, and shield.

Those entering the Order abandoned their property of every kind to it. Hence, although they were individually poor, as a body they rapidly became enormously rich, and their power increased in proportion. The principal officer was the Grand Master, who ranked as a prince at the courts of Europe, and under him were Preceptors or Grand Priors, Visitors, and Commanders. At first the Grand Master resided at Jerusalem; subsequently, when that city was lost to the Christians, he resided at Acre, and finally at Cyprus; but as his duties required him to be in the Holy Land, he never resided in Europe.

The Grand Master was elected for life from among the Knights, and when an election was completed it was duly announced to the assembled brethren. The Prior then thus addressed the elect: " In the name of God the Father, the Son, and the Holy Ghost, we have chosen, and do choose thee, Brother D, to be our Master ;" then turning to the Brethren, he said: " Beloved Sirs and Brethren, give thanks unto God; behold here our Master."

Following the Grand Master in the Order of their rank, were, 1st, the Seneschal, who was his representative and lieutenant; 2d, the Marshal, who was the General of the Order ; 3d, the Treasurer, who was also the Admiral; 4th, the Draper, who had charge of the clothing, a kind of Commissary General; 5th, the Turcopolier, Commander of the light-horse. Next came a class of officers called Visitors, whose duties, as their name imports, was to visit the different provinces, and correct abuses. Lastly, there were some subordinate offices appropriated to the Serving Brethren, such as Sub-Marshal, Standard Bearer, Farrier, etc.

The foregoing officers, with the Grand Preceptors of the Provinces and distinguished Knights who could attend, constituted the General Chapter, where all laws and regulations were made and great officers elected. This assembly was seldom convened, and in the intervals its powers were exercised by the Chapter at Jerusalem.

As the Order increased in prosperity and augmented its possessions in the East and in Europe, it was divided into Provinces, each of which was governed by a Grand Preceptor, or Grand Prior, for the titles were indiscriminately used. That, however, of Preceptor, was peculiar to the Templars, while that of Prior was common both to the Templars and the Knights Hospitalers. The Provinces were fifteen in number, viz., Jerusalem, Tripoli, Antioch, Cyprus, Portugal, Castile and Leon, Aragon, France and Auvergne, Normandy, Acquitaine, Provence, England, including Scotland and Ireland, Germany, Upper and Central Italy, Apulia and Sicily.

In each Province there were numerous Templar houses called Preceptories, presided over by a Preceptor; and in each of the large Preceptories there was a Chapter, in which local regulations were made and members received into the Order. The number three, was peculiarly sacred among the Templars. They observed three great fasts; they communicated thrice a year; alms were given, in all the houses of the Order, thrice in every week.

Among the accessions to their ranks were many of the best architects of the day, and thus they became a warlike and mechanical Order. The ruins of the fortified towns and castles built by them attest their skill and energy.

In 1124, Hugh de Payens and five of his brethren proceeded to Rome and were received with great honor and distinction by the Pope. Subsequently, a great ecclesiastical council was assembled at Troyes, in France, to which De Payens and his brethren were invited to attend, and were there again shown great honor.

In fact, the aim and scope of their noble work had become so well known, that an astonishing enthusiasm was excited throughout Christendom in their behalf; princes and nobles, sovereigns and their subjects, vied with each other in heaping benefits and gifts upon them.

Scarce a will of importance was made without an article in it in their favor. Many illustrious persons on their deathbed took the vows, so that they might be buried in the habit of the Order. Sovereigns and princes quitted the government of their kingdoms, enrolled themselves among this Fraternity, and bequeathed even their dominions to the Master and the Brethren of the Temple.

The Beauséant, assumed by the Templars as a standard, was formed of black and white cloth, and for nearly two hundred years its presence carried dismay into the ranks of the Infidels.

The Knights Hospitalers.

As the Knights Hospitalers and Knights Templars both originated in Jerusalem, and were in many respects similar, their history has been very much mixed up; therefore a few words concerning the Hospitalers will render the subject more intelligible.

THE KNIGHTS TEMPLARS.

In 1047, some wealthy merchants of Amalfi, a city of Naples, while trading in Egypt, obtained from the Caliph Monstaser Billah permission to establish hospitals in the city of Jerusalem for the use of the poor and sick pilgrims. The site assigned to them was near the Holy Sepulchre, and there they erected a chapel and two hospitals, one for each sex, for the reception of pilgrims. Later, each of the hospitals had a separate chapel annexed to it, that for the men being dedicated to St. John the Almoner, and the other, for the women, to St. Mary Magdalen. Many of the pilgrims who had experienced the kindness so liberally bestowed upon wayfarers, abandoned the idea of returning to Europe, and formed themselves into a band of charitable assistants; and, without assuming any regular religious profession, devoted themselves to the service of the hospitals and the care of their sick inmates. The chief cities of the south of Europe subscribed liberally for the support of this institution. The merchants of Amalfi, who were its original founders, acted as the stewards of their bounty.*

This society first assumed the name Hospitalers of Jerusalem; afterward, taking up arms for the protection of the holy places against the Moslems, they styled themselves Knights Hospitalers of St. John; later Knights of Rhodes, and finally Knights of Malta. They were reorganized on a military basis in 1100, but their first military exploit of note was in 1168,† when Almeric was King of Jerusalem, and Gilbert de Assalit was Guardian of the Hospital. The latter being ambitious and reckless, in defiance of existing treaties, united with the King in an invasion of Egypt, the King promising the Hospitalers, as their share of the conquest, the wealthy city of Belbeis (Ancient Pelusium), in perpetual sovereignty. Not looking for an attack from people with whom they were at peace, the Egyptians were taken by surprise, Belbeis was carried by assault, and its inhabitants barbarously massacred. This treachery was speedily avenged, as the Egyptians rallied, gave the Christians battle, and defeated them with great slaughter, so that only a fragment of their army, with the king, escaped to Jerusalem. The history of the Knights Hospitalers from this time is but a chronicle of continued

---

* When the crusaders took Jerusalem (July 15, 1099), a large number of their wounded soldiers were received and cared for by the Hospitalers. Mackey, p. 351; Addison's Knights Templars, p. 167.
† Ibid., pp. 168, 169.

warfare, but mostly in connection with the Knights Templars, against the Moslems. When Jerusalem was captured by Saladin, in 1187, the Hospitalers retired to Margat, a town and fortress of Palestine. In 1191 they made Acre, which they had helped to capture, their principal place of residence. Finally, when Syria was abandoned by the Latin race, the Hospitalers found refuge in the island of Cyprus, where they established their convent. But in time, their residence in Cyprus became so unpleasant, by reason of the heavy taxes and other exactions imposed by the king, that they determined to secure some other residence. As the neighborhood of Rhodes had long been the refuge of Turkish corsairs, Fulk de Villaret, the Grand Master of the Hospital, with the assistance of several European States, made a descent upon the island, and after months of hard fighting, he, on the 15th of August, 1310, planted the standard of the Order on the walls of that famous city.

Hence they were often called the "Knights of Rhodes."

After holding Rhodes over 200 years—until 1522, the Hospitalers were overpowered and compelled to surrender the island to Solyman. They next secured the cession of the islands of Malta and Gozzo, which they retained as their headquarters for 268 years.

The degree of Malta is conferred in the United States, as an appendant order in a Commandery of Knights Templars.

There is a ritual attached to the degree, but usually communicated after the candidate has been created a Knight Templar.

As the history of this Order is henceforth intimately mixed up with that of the Knights Templars, mention of them hereafter will only be made in connection with that Order.

The Latin Kingdom.

At what time the crusaders conceived the idea of establishing a kingdom in Palestine is uncertain; but within one month after they entered Jerusalem, an assembly of princes and priests was held, and Godfrey de Bouillon was chosen king, and thus was the Latin Kingdom of Palestine established. Godfrey had not enjoyed his new honors a month before intelligence was received that Al Aphdal, a noted Moslem leader, had entered the Holy Land at the head of a host of Turks and Egyptians, and was marching on Jerusalem. To

Malta.

meet this emergency, Godfrey hastily got together a force of 20,000 men and met the invaders at Ascalon. Here a bloody battle was fought, in which the Moslems were routed, and left nearly 30,000 dead on the field.

The Latin Kingdom* now had a period of comparative rest until 1136; but at this time the religious fanaticism of the Moslems was again directed against the Christians, by Zinghis and his son Noureddin, warlike chieftains of the East, and, from a lack of organization and preparation, the Templars were defeated in several engagements. This so alarmed the Oriental Clergy, that they sent urgent letters to the Pope, and the Templars in Europe, for assistance.

Upon receipt of this important intelligence from the Holy Land, a General Chapter of the Templars was convened in Paris, at which were present Louis VII., King of France, Pope Eugenius III., and many princes and nobles from all parts of Europe.

The result of the deliberations of this assembly was the second crusade, 1146. This expedition advanced into Asia Minor, the first division of which was led by Conrad, Emperor of Germany, who had not advanced far into the enemies' country, before he was met by the Moslems and defeated; his army being so badly cut up that only Conrad and a small portion of his forces escaped from the scene of their disaster. They afterward united at Constantinople, where they found passage on some merchant vessels to Joppa, and thence proceeded by land to Jerusalem. Here they were joined by King Louis, with the second division of the crusaders. Soon after the arrival of Louis, he, Conrad, and the Templars decided to proceed against Damascus; they accordingly marched across the mountains to the beautiful valley in which this remarkable ancient city is situated. But again this crusade was doomed to disaster; for Noureddin was in command, and not only defended the city, but compelled the invaders to retreat with immense loss—such loss as left but little further life in the second crusade. Subsequently the Saracens crossed the Jordan and advanced to the Mount of Olives, opposite Jerusalem; but too much confidence brought them to grief, as the Templars surprised them in the night and routed them with terrible slaughter.

* From the election of Godfrey de Bouillon in 1099, to 1205, the Holy Land was known as the Latin Kingdom of Palestine.

To offset this success, the Templars were afterward drawn into an ambuscade near Tiberias, and badly cut up.

Notwithstanding that the Templars strenuously opposed the invasion of Egypt by King Almeric, yet, in retaliation for the perfidy of the King, they were now to be confronted with a far more dangerous enemy than they had hitherto met. This was the famous Saladin, who, though he was at first unsuccessful, ultimately contributed largely to the destruction of the Templars in Palestine. Acting under instructions from the Fatimite Caliph, Saladin first stirred up the Moslems to take vengeance upon the Christians for their invasion of Egypt. He then got together an army of 40,000 men, crossed the Desert, and besieged the fortified City of Gaza, which belonged to the Knights, and was the key of Palestine toward Egypt. Luxuriant gardens, the palm and olive groves of this city of the wilderness, were destroyed by the wild cavalry of the Desert, and the tents of the Arab host were thickly clustered on the neighboring sand-hills.

The Templars and warlike monks first invoked the aid of the God of battles, and then made a desperate defence, and in a sally upon the enemy's camp they performed such prodigies of valor that Saladin, despairing of taking the place, abandoned the siege and returned to Egypt.

On the death of Noureddin, Sultan of Damascus, in 1175, Saladin managed to secure the sovereignty both of Egypt and Syria. He then levied a second great army, crossed the Desert, and again invaded Palestine. His forces were composed of over 60,000 men, comprising 8,000 cavalry. But in a battle fought near Ascalon, November 1st, Odo de St. Amand, Grand Master of the Temple, at the head of his Knights, broke through the Mameluke Guard, slew their commander, and penetrated to the imperial tent, from which Saladin escaped nearly naked, and with great difficulty, upon a fleet dromedary.

The following year the Templars, in order to protect the road leading from Damascus to Jerusalem, commenced the erection of a strong fortress near Jacob's Ford, on the River Jordan. To oppose the progress of this work, Saladin advanced at the head of his forces, while Baldwin IV., King of Jerusalem, and all the chivalry of the Latin Kingdom, gathered together in the plain to protect the Templars and workmen. After a few days of skirmishing between the cavalry a general engagement took place, in which most of the Templars and Hospitalers were killed or taken prisoners. With a few followers, the Count of Tripoli at last cut his way through the Infidels and fled to Tyre, twenty-five miles distant. The Grand Master of the Hospitalers swam across the Jordan, and fled, covered with wounds, to the Castle of Beaufort. Saladin then laid siege to the newly erected fortress, and after a gallant defence on the part of the garrison, set it on fire and then stormed it.

Causes which Led to Disaster.

At this period, Palestine was covered with castles and fortified towns, which were occupied and commanded by petty barons, Knights Hospitalers, and Knights Templars; but all subject to the King at Jerusalem. Yet the commanders of these fortresses declared war and made peace nearly at their own will and pleasure, not only against the common enemy, but against one another; and what rendered this state of things more surprising is, that the Christian occupants of Palestine were nearly surrounded by warlike and watchful enemies, ready to improve the first opportunity for their destruction. Yet at this time, under the leadership of a man of even ordinary ability, order might have been restored and the Christian rule perpetuated in the Holy Land. But this opportunity for consolidating their power was soon lost; for in 1186 the throne was, by the aid of the Grand Master of the Temple, usurped by Guy of Lusignan, who had many enemies, and at least one powerful rival. Among the petty rulers at this time were Count Raymond of Tripoli, and Raynald of Chatillon, who had associated with them a large number of Knights Templars.

So great was the indignation of the Count of Tripoli and the barons when they learned that Lusignan was in possession of the throne, that they raised the standard of revolt and proclaimed the Princess Isabelle, the younger sister of Sybilla (who had been married to Humphrey de Thoran), Queen of Jerusalem.

Upon hearing of these proceedings Humphrey de Thoran, with his wife the princess, hurried to Jerusalem aad tendered their allegiance to Lusignan. This turn of affairs struck dismay into the hearts of the conspirators, most of whom now proceeded to Jerusalem to do homage; while the Count of Tripoli retired to the strong citadel of Tiberias, of which place he was the feudal lord, and there prepared to defend himself.

At first the King sought the co-operation of the Templars against his vassal, but they refused. He then gave orders for the concentration of an army at Nazareth, upon which it is claimed the Count called upon the Sultan for assistance, and entered into an alliance with him. The friends of the King foreseeing that Saladin would not fail to take advantage of a civil war, besought his Majesty to offer terms of reconciliation to the Count. To this the King agreed, and the Grand Master of the Templars, De Riderfort, and of the Hospitalers, De Moulin, with others, were appointed to proceed to Tiberias, and endeavor to bring back the Count to his allegiance. This party set out from Jerusalem, and slept the first night at Nablous, thirty miles north, and the next day proceeded toward Nazareth, forty miles farther. As the Grand Master of the Templars was eating his supper in the "Castle of La Feue," intelligence was brought him that a strong force of Mussulman cavalry, under Male-al-Afadal, one of Saladin's sons, had crossed the Jordan and was marching through the territories of the Count of Tripoli.

As soon as the Grand Master received this startling intelligence, he sent messengers to a castle of the Templars, "the Convent of Casco," and mustered all the forces within reach, about 600 men all told. This small band set out in quest of the enemy and had proceeded about seven miles in the direction of the Jordan, when they came suddenly upon a column of Mussulman cavalry, amounting to several thousand, who were watering their horses at the brook Kishon.

Without stopping to consider their great inferiority in numbers, the Templars raised their war-cry and dashed into the midst of the enemy; but after a sharp and bloody contest they were routed and nearly exterminated; the killed included the Grand Master of the Hospital and all his Knights, and all the Templars, except the Grand Master De Riderfort and two of his Knights, who broke through the dense ranks of the Moslems and made their escape to Nazareth. The barbarians cut off the heads of the Templars, and attaching them to the points of their lances, proceeded in the direction of Tiberias. This battle took place May 1, 1187.

Thoroughly alarmed by the disaster to the Templars, the Count of Tripoli consented to become reconciled to the King, and for this purpose immediately set out from Tiberias for Jerusalem. The reconciliation took place at Jacob's Well, near Nablous, in the presence of the Templars and Hospitalers, and the bishops and barons. The King and Count then returned together to Nablous, to take measures for the defence of the country. While these dissensions were weakening the Christians, their powerful enemy was pushing his preparations for the reconquest of Jerusalem, the long-cherished enterprise of the Moslems.

In his call to all the Faithful to join him, Saladin promised them plunder, luxury, and sensual delights.

This drew crowds of Mohammedans from all parts of Asia to his standard; and the Caliph of Bagdad and all the Imaums put up daily prayers for the success of his arms. After protecting the return of the spring caravan from Mecca, Saladin marched to Ashtara, near Damascus, where he met his son Al Malek-al-Afdal, and other chiefs, and reviewed the vast forces under their command.

He next received intelligence of the reconciliation of the Count of Tripoli with the King of Jerusalem, which determined him to immediately attack Tiberias.

Therefore he advanced first upon Al Soheira, a village situated at the northern end of the Lake of Tiberias, where he encamped for the night. Early in the morning of the next day he marched around to the west of the lake toward Tiberias, and on the 21st, took the town by storm, put all who resisted to the sword, and made slaves of the survivors. All except the citadel was then set on fire and burned to the ground. The wife of the Count of Tripoli, with the remnant of the garrison, took refuge in the citadel, and despatched a messenger to her husband and the King of Jerusalem, earnestly imploring instant succor.

Upon receipt of the intelligence that the Moslems had invaded Palestine, all the Christian forces of the Latin Kingdom were summoned to join the King. The call was promptly responded to, and a camp was formed at the fountain of Sepphoris, five miles north of Nazareth on the road to Acre. Here the Templars and Hospitalers collected together the forces from their different castles and fortresses. During all the time since the battle of the brook of Kishon, Saladin's cavalry had ravaged and laid waste the country from Tiberias to Bethoron, and from the mountains of Gilboa to Nazareth. From all directions nothing was to be seen except the smoking ruins of villages and scattered dwellings of the Christian population. The camp was filled with fugitives who had fled with terror before the merciless Moslems. To render the situation more hopeless, the King was so irresolute as to destroy the confidence of his officers, and the Count of Tripoli was either weak or treacherous: this came out unmistakably at the council of war held on the arrival of messengers from Tiberias.

At this critical time the Count, although his capital was in flames and his wife in great peril, advised the King to remain inactive where he was. Upon hearing this advice the Grand Master of the Temple rose before the assembly and stigmatized the Count as a traitor, and urged the King to march immediately to the relief of Tiberias. It was determined, however, that the army should remain at Sepphoris.

Notwithstanding this, the Grand Master, in a secret interview with the King that night, so wrought upon his pride and feelings that he consented to march to the relief of Tiberias, and the rescue of the wife of the Count.

In vain did Raymond and the weaker barons oppose this movement. The King and the Templars remained resolute; and early on the morning of July 3d, the hosts of the Cross in full array were marching on Tiberias. The Christian forces numbered nearly 50,000, and the Saracens over 70,000.

As soon as the scouts of Saladin brought in word of the advance of the Christian army, he turned the siege of the citadel of Tiberias into a blockade,* called in his cavalry, and hastened to occupy the passes and defiles of the mountains leading to Tiberias. He then encamped on the hills west of that place, with his left wing upon the lake, and his cavalry stationed in the valleys six miles distant. As soon as the Latin forces had arrived within nine miles of Tiberias, they were engaged by the hosts of Saladin, and that afternoon the battle raged furiously with varying success; but when evening came the Latins found that they had merely been able to hold their ground, and, worst

* After the battle of Hattin, the citadel surrendered, and the wife of the Count of Tripoli was set at liberty.

of all, they were compelled to spend the night without water, the enemy being between them and the lake.

When the Saracens saw where the Christians had pitched their tents, they regarded them as their prey, and came and encamped so close to them that the soldiers of the two armies could converse together.

The night was hot and sultry, and both men and horses, after the hardships of the day, threw themselves on the parched ground, sighing for water. But not a drop of that precious element touched their lips, and the soldiers rose exhausted and unprepared for the fierce conflict of the next day.

Impelled by their terrible condition, the Templars and Hospitalers formed in battle array in the van of the Christian army, determined to open a passage to the lake.

But the ground was so broken and the defiles so narrow, that the Knights could not place their lances in rest, nor bring their chargers to the career, while from the heights above, the enemy rained down upon them clouds of death-dealing missiles.

At one time the Templars reached within a short distance of the lake, so near that its placid blue waters were seen winding gracefully among the hills; but every inch of the route was so fiercely contested that the Christians could not reach it, and instead of quenching their terrible thirst at the lake, the soil was drenched with their blood. Finally, after almost superhuman exertions, the Templars and Hospitalers made a stand, and sent to the King for succor.

But at this critical juncture, Raymond of Tripoli, whose conduct from first had been suspicious, dashed with a few followers through a force of Mussulmen who opened their ranks to let him pass, and retreated to Tyre.

The defection of this nobleman gave rise to a sudden panic, and the troops that were advancing to the support of the Templars were driven in a confused mass upon the main body.

The infantry being composed principally of the native population, crowded together in confusion around the bishops and the holy cross, and refused to longer obey their leaders. Many of the Knights and lesser barons however collected their followers together, rushed over the rocks, down the mountain sides, pierced through the enemy's squadrons, and leaving the infantry to their fate, made their escape to the sea-coast. The Arab cavalry dashed on, and surrounding with terrific cries the trembling and unresisting foot-soldiers, they mowed them down until they were nearly exterminated.

The King, Gerard de Riderfort, the Grand Master of the Templars, the Marquis of Montferrat, Reginald de Chatillon, the immediate author of the disaster, and many other nobles and Knights, were taken prisoners. When the darkness of night had put an end to the slaughter, a crowd of fugitives who still survived the frightful carnage gained the summit of Mount Hattin, a mile northward, in the vain hope of escaping from the field of blood under cover of the night. But they were so carefully watched, that when morning came they were found huddled together on the summit of the mountain, but in a position so strong that they at first successfully resisted the attacks of the Moslems.

The latter then set fire to the dry grass, which soon enveloped the fugitives in smoke and flames, and compelled them to surrender. This eventful battle was commenced on the afternoon of Thursday, the 3d of July, 1187, and terminated on the morning of Saturday, the 5th.

As soon as the battle was over, Saladin gave orders to have his illustrious prisoners, Guy, King of Jerusalem, De Riderfort, the Grand Master of the Temple, and Reginald de Chatillon, brought into his tent.

Reginald had incurred the bitter enmity of the Moslems, especially of Saladin, by leading several piratical expeditions against the caravans of pilgrims to Mecca.

On the arrival of the prisoners, Saladin ordered a bowl of sherbet (the sacred pledge among the Arabs of hospitality and security) to be presented to the King and to the Grand Master of the Temple. But when Reginald would have drunk thereof, Saladin prevented him, and after reproaching him for his perfidy and impiety, he commanded him to instantly acknowledge the Prophet or meet the death he had so often deserved. On his refusal, Saladin struck him with his scimitar, which was a signal for the guards, who immediately despatched him.

On the following Sunday, barbarian fanaticism was further gratified by the cold-blooded murder of other eminent prisoners. At sunset of that day the monks of the Temple and the Hospital were brought out on a hill overlooking the Lake of Tiberias, and there decapitated.

Knowing the effect of this terrible defeat at Hattin, physically and morally, upon the Latin Kingdom, Saladin proceeded to take advantage of it and subjugated much of the country in the vicinity of Jerusalem.

He then moved forward toward that city, and on the 2d day of October, 1187, a few of his horsemen were seen on the hills to the westward of the city—just as the bells of the churches were tolling to vespers. These were immediately followed by the vast hosts of Saladin, like a dark, rushing cloud sweeping over the hills, shouting " El Khuds! El Khuds!" (the Holy City) and their singular banners were to be seen upon the hills in every direction, gleaming brightly in the last rays of the setting sun.

The beleaguered inhabitants were not kept long in suspense, for that very night, when the Mussulmens had finished their prayers, and ere darkness had covered the land, amid the loud blasts of trumpets, Saladin summoned the Christians to surrender. But they answered that the city should not be surrendered; the attack did not begin, however, that night, but at sunrise the next morning the inhabitants were awakened by the loud clash of arms, and the fierce cries of the savage enemy. Terrified women and children rushed into the churches and prostrated themselves before the altars, weeping, and lifting up their hands in supplication to heaven, while the men rushed to the battlements; and although the Knights had lost heavily in recent battles, yet the few who remained, by their experience and undaunted valor, enabled the people to successfully resist the onslaught of the enemy for fifteen days.

The barbarous warfare carried on by Saladin in Palestine, had filled Jerusalem with so many fugitives that the houses could not contain them, and the streets were crowded with women and children, who slept night after night upon the cold pavements.

Finding his attacks continually repulsed, Saladin retired from the walls, and constructed additional and powerful military engines, and made other preparations. He then renewed the assault, directing his efforts against the northern wall of the city, between St. Stephen's gate and Joppa gate—the same part of the wall against which the successful assaults had been made by the crusaders in 1099, eighty-eight years before.

To cover the forces operating the battering rams, Saladin constructed machines' for throwing stones and flaming combustibles upon the ramparts and over into the city. The foundations of the towers were also sapped, and in the night of October the 16th, the angle of the wall at the northwest, where it touches the valley of Hinnon, was thrown down with a tremendous crash. This appalling disaster filled the besieged with consternation, as they saw that all was lost.

Early the next morning, a deputation proceeded to Saladin to implore his mercy, but ere they reached his tent the assault had commenced, and Moslem banners waved in triumph over the breach; therefore the Sultan treated the messengers with contempt, declaring that he would take Jerusalem from the Franks as they had taken it from the Moslems, sword in hand.

But the garrison, led by the Templars and Hospitalers, manned the breach, and in a last desperate struggle the Moslems were driven out with great slaughter and their standards torn down. The messengers were again sent to Saladin, and boldly declared that if he refused to treat for the surrender of Jerusalem the Christians would set fire to the Mohammedan temple (Mosque of Omar), destroy all the treasures in the city, and massacre their prisoners. The announcement of this desperate determination being accompanied with the offer of a ransom, induced Saladin to listen to terms, and a treaty was entered into by which the city was to be surrendered to Saladin, and the liberty and security of the inhabitants were to be purchased by paying to him ten golden bezants ($750) as a ransom for each man; for every woman, five; and every child under seven years, one bezant.

On the announcement of these terms in the city, nothing could exceed the grief and despair of the poorer classes of people, as they had no money wherewith to pay this enormous ransom, and would be delivered up to perpetual bondage. But to the everlasting praise, however, of the few Templars and Hospitalers then in Jerusalem, they spent all the money they possessed in ransoming the poor, and then escorted them in safety to Tripoli, two hundred miles northward. Those who were unable to pay the ransom were sold in the common slave markets, and distributed through the Mussulman countries of Asia. The women often becoming the concubines and hand-maids of their masters.

Thus, in 1187, 88 years after its conquest by Godfrey de Bouillon and the crusaders, Jerusalem again passed under Mohammedan rule.

THE KNIGHTS TEMPLARS. 645

After rehabilitating the Temple in accordance with the Moslem religion, restoring the fortifications of the city, founding schools, etc., Saladin renewed his military operations in the field.

Notwithstanding the loss of the Holy City and their other misfortunes, the Templars still maintained themselves in some of the strongest castles of Palestine, and the city of Tyre continued to resist all the attacks of the Moslems. From the Feast of St. Martin, up to the time of the Circumcision, Saladin had besieged Tyre. But on the vigils of St. Sylvester, Conrad, the Marquis of Montferrat, with the assistance of the Brethren of the Temple, engaged the galleys of Saladin in the harbor, captured eleven of them, and took prisoners the Admiral of Alexandria and eight other admirals, a large number of the Infidels being slain. The rest of the Mussulman galleys being in danger of capture, were run aground by Saladin's command and burnt.

Saladin was so overwhelmed with rage and grief at this repulse, that he cut off the ears and tail of his horse, and then rode the mutilated animal through his army in the sight of all. He continued the siege, however, until the winter set in, and then despairing of taking the city, he burnt his catapults and battering rams, and retired to Damascus.

After a short season of rest Saladin again took the field, and after taking several strongholds belonging to the Christians, he appeared before the rich city of Antioch.

This city was then occupied by a strong force of Templars under the command of the Grand Master De Riderfort, and by a numerous and well-organized force under Prince Bohemond, all fully prepared for a desperate struggle in defence of the city. Therefore, upon learning of the great strength of the place, Saladin contented himself by plundering and destroying the surrounding country, and finally concluded a treaty with Bohemond, whereby a suspension of arms was agreed upon for the term of eight months, in which it was stipulated that all the Moslem prisoners detained in Antioch should be liberated.

The news of the disaster at Hattin and of the fall of Jerusalem had in the meantime reached Europe. But instead of being disheartened by the intelligence, the people were everywhere inspired with rage against the Moslems and a determination to recapture the Holy City.

Therefore, crowds of armed men again quitted the shores of Europe for Palestine; and in response to the calls of their brethren in the East, a large number of Templars from the different preceptories of England, Scotland, and Ireland hastened to their assistance, taking with them arms, horses, clothing, and munitions of war, with a vast amount of treasure that had been collected at the churches.

The Grand Master De Riderfort, and De Lusignan, King of Jerusalem, placed themselves at the head of the newly-arrived battalions, and established their headquarters at Ras el Ain, a small village on the mainland, two miles southeast of Tyre.

Their accessions had been such, that at the commencement of the summer of 1189, they took the field at the head of a large force, marched down the coast, and laid siege to the city of Acre.

Upon learning of this, Saladin sent messengers to all the governors of the Moslem provinces, requiring them to join him at Sepphoris without delay. From thence he advanced to a hill near Acre, and after a reconnoissance of the position of the Christian army he encamped, and disposed of his forces in such a manner that the besiegers themselves became the besieged. He then surprised a weak part of the Christian camp, broke through the lines, penetrated to one of the city gates, and threw into it a reinforcement of 5,000 men laden with arms, provisions, and clothing. He then effected his retreat to his camp. Soon after this the recruits from Europe, eager to exhibit their prowess against the Moslems, marched out of their entrenchments and attacked Saladin's camp, broke through the right wing of his army, and produced a temporary panic in his ranks. Then thinking that the day was their own, they rushed heedlessly on after the Infidels, and reaching the tent of Saladin, abandoned themselves to plunder. De Riderfort, foreseeing the result, collected the forces of the Order around him, and none too soon, as the enemy rallied, led by Saladin in person, and the Christian army would have been annihilated but for the Templars. But they, firm and immovable, presented for over an hour an unbroken front to the advancing Moslems, and thus gained time for the foolish crusaders to recover from their terror and confusion.

In this affair the Grand Master Gerard de Riderfort and the Seneschal of the Order were slain, and over half of the Templars present were killed.

De Riderfort was succeeded by Walter as Grand Master. For over two years the siege was fiercely prosecuted, and during that time nine pitched battles were fought, in which 300,000 Saracens and nearly as many Christians are computed to have perished.

The tents of the dead were constantly replenished by the living—the recruits from Europe.

The vessels of Saladin often succored the city, and the Christian ships continually landed supplies and men for the besiegers, until the contest seemed interminable.

In July, 1191, however, the combined fleets of France and England completely shut off all supplies by sea, and the garrison, reduced to great straits, were perishing from hunger. This brought Saladin to terms, and on July 13th the city was surrendered, the kings of France and England being present.

The terms of the surrender were, that the inhabitants of Acre pay a ransom of 200,000 pieces of gold for their lives and liberties, 2,500 Christian captives be set at liberty, and the True Cross, which had been taken at the battle of Tiberias, was to be restored.

The capture of this stronghold cost the Christian powers nearly 300,000 men, including six archbishops, twelve bishops, forty earls, and many barons.

On August 21st, the Templars, with the forces of King Richard, left Acre for Jerusalem; after halting for three days on the banks of the River Belus, to collect their troops, they resumed their march down the coast. At the same time the fleet, loaded with supplies, moved along the shore in sight of the army. Well knowing that Jerusalem was at stake, after the loss of Acre, Saladin got together an immense force and so harassed the Christian army, that the march to Joppa was but little less than a continuous battle. Masses of Arab cavalry hovered upon their flanks, cut off the stragglers, and put every prisoner they took to death. The next night after leaving the Belus, both the Templars and the Crusaders encamped around wells in the plain between Acre and Caifa. On August 26th, they forded the brook Kishon, fought their way to Caifa, and there halted one day. On the 28th, they forced the passes of Mount Carmel, although the heights were covered with dense masses of Moslems who disputed the ground inch by inch.

On September 7th, the Christian army found Saladin occupying a strong position at Arsoof, determined to stop their progress; accordingly an engagement took place, fiercely contested on both sides, but resulting in the defeat of the Moslems, with heavy loss.

After a brief period of rest, the march toward Jerusalem was again resumed, the Templars leading, and the Hospitaler cavalry protecting the rear of the army.

But the rainy season had now set in, and storms of rain, hail, thunder and lightning, succeeded one another without cessation; the tents were torn to pieces by furious tempests, and the provisions were destroyed by the wet. Horses, camels, and beasts of burden perished from inclemency of the weather, until finally shelter was sought in Joppa, fifteen miles west. Here they remained until the 18th of January, when King Richard and the Templars advanced along the coast twenty-eight miles, and encamped amid the ruins of Ascalon. During the march they again suffered great hardships from terrific showers of hail and sleet; and on their arrival they were appalled at hearing of the shipwreck of their vessels freighted with provisions. They, however, pitched their tents and remained for five months encamped amid the desolate ruins of the once proud Ascalon, and during this time they employed themselves in intercepting the caravans which were crossing the neighboring desert from Egypt to Palestine. In the caravans were many Christian captives whom they liberated. The tents were at last struck and they resumed their march, with the intention of laying siege to Jerusalem. They proceeded by easy marches across the plain of Ramleh, and on the 11th of June, five days after leaving Ascalon, they reached Beitnubah. Here they halted for a space of an entire month, professedly waiting for Henry, the King of Jerusalem, and the forces marching under his command from Tyre and Acre. But the real cause of the delay was the rugged mountains between Beitnubah and Jerusalem, the defiles of which could be easily defended by the Moslem hosts.

Being worn out with incessant warfare, Saladin fixed his headquarters in Jerusalem, leaving the main body of his army encamped among the mountains. His Mamelukes had also become impatient, if not disheartened, by the long continuance of the war and the determination and fortitude of the Christian soldiers. This, and the ill-health of King Richard and Saladin, created a desire for a cessation of hostilities, if not of the war. Therefore a treaty of peace was entered into whereby it was stipulated that Christian pilgrims should enjoy the privilege of visiting the Holy City and the Holy Sepulchre without tribute or molestation ; that Tyre, Acre, and Joppa, with the sea-coast between them, should belong to the Latins, but that the fortifications of Ascalon should be demolished.

The Templars were now to be relieved of one of their dangerous foes, as Saladin died on the 13th of March, A.D. 1193, aged fifty-seven years. Soon after this event the vast empire he had consolidated and ruled for nineteen years began to fall to pieces. The titles to the thrones of Syria and Egypt were disputed between the brothers and sons of the deceased Sultan. These dissensions suggested to the Pope a favorable opportunity for the recovery of the Holy City, he therefore ignored the treaty and caused a crusade to be preached—the fourth. The result was that two expeditions were organized in Germany and proceeded to Palestine. On their arrival at Acre, they insisted on the immediate commencement of hostilities, but the Templars and Hospitalers remonstrated against the violation of the truce, not only because it would be a breach of faith, but bad policy. Remonstrance, however, was in vain, the headstrong Germans sallied out of Acre, and committed such frightful ravages and atrocities in the Moslem territories that the Mohammedans immediately ceased their dissensions, united against their common enemy, and rushed to arms.

From Egypt, Arabia, and the remote confines of Syria, the followers of Mohammed rallied again around the banner of Islam. Saphadin took command of the Moslem forces and speedily proved himself a worthy successor to his brother Saladin. He soon collected a vast army, and by rapid movements compelled the Germans to quit the open country, and shut themselves up in the city of Joppa. By a well-executed manœuvre, on the Feast of St. Martin, he induced them to make a rash sortie from the town, then suddenly charged upon the main body of their forces, and defeated them with terrific slaughter.

He followed the fugitives pell-mell into the city and nearly annihilated the entire German force. The small garrison of the Templars was also massacred, and the fortifications razed to the ground.

Fuller, in his "Holy War," says : "At this time the spring-time of their mirth so drowned their souls, that the Turks, coming in upon them, cut every one of their throats to the number of 20,000. The camp was their shambles, the Turks their butchers, and themselves the beeves, from which the beastly drunkards differed but little."

Three weeks after the terrible affair at Joppa, the second division of the Crusaders, under the command of the Dukes of Saxony and Brabant, arrived, and with the Templars took the field. Their first engagement took place between Tyre and Sidon, where they defeated a large force of Moslem cavalry with great slaughter; and then engaged and defeated the entire Moslem army. In this battle Saphadin was badly wounded, but effected a retreat to Damascus. Beyrout was next taken, then Gebal, Laodicea, and all the maritime towns between Tripoli and Jaffa.

Soon after this, intelligence reached Palestine of the death of the Emperor Henry VI., whereupon all the German chieftains abandoned their brethren in the East and hurried home, intent on schemes of private ambition.

This brings us to the year 1201, with Philippe Duplessis Grand Master of the Temple; shortly after his accession to power, he became engaged in hostilities with Leon I., King of Armenia, who had taken possession of the castle of Gaston which belonged to the Templars.

The Templars defeated Leon, compelled him to give up the castle and sue for peace. At this period the Templars had recovered possession of most of their castles and strongholds throughout Palestine, and were looking forward to a period of peace and rest, when they were again disturbed by hearing that some European vessels had been plundered by pirates. For this the Templars made reprisals on the Moslems, extending their ravages eastward to the banks of the Jordan, and collecting together a vast booty.

Following this exploit, the Sultan of Damascus assembled a large force at Sephoris, and marched against the hill fort Doc, which belonged to the Templars. This place being only three miles distant from Acre, the population of that town was thrown into the utmost consternation. But the Templars assembled their forces from all quarters, repulsed the invaders, and restored peace to the Latin kingdom.

At the expiration of the truce with the Infidels, 1205, Duplessis, the Grand Master, refused to renew it. Consequently hostilities were commenced in earnest, and Pope Innocent III., emulating the example of Urban

II., called together a general council of the Church to prevail upon Europe to arm again for the recovery of the Holy City.

This resulted in the *fifth* crusade. The first to set out on this enterprise were the King of Hungary and the Dukes of Austria and Bavaria.

At the head of an army made up of many nationalities, they landed at Acre at the commencement of the year 1217, and after a few days spent in the city they marched out and pitched their tents upon the bank of the brook Kishon. On the day following, the monks from the Templars and Hospitalers marched with great pomp and solemnity into the camp, bearing with them a piece of the true Cross—a piece that had been miraculously preserved for the occasion. The kings and princes went out barefooted and uncovered to receive the holy relic, which they placed at the head of their army, and under the guidance of the Templars they immediately commenced their march toward the Jordan.

They followed the course of the brook Kishon through the valley of Jezreel, and traversed the paths through the mountains of Gilboa, descended into the valley of the Jordan, and pitched their tents on the bank of that river. They next proceeded up the Jordan to Lake Tiberias, skirted its beautiful shores, and thence across the country to Acre, without meeting an enemy.

The Templars and crusaders next besieged the strong fortress of Mount Tabor. But finally, the height and steepness of the mountain and other obstacles, among which were the enemy, afforded excuses for the abandonment of the siege. The usual consequences of a retreat then followed. Bodies of Arab cavalry harassed the flanks and rear of the retiring crusaders, and the retreat would have been disastrous but for the gallant conduct of the Templars and Hospitalers. As it was, the army suffered great loss in men and horses, and when they regained their quarters at Acre, they were a worn-out and disgusted body of men.

The Grand Master, Duplessis, died a few days after the return of the army. He was succeeded by William de Chartres, who shortly after his election took command of a large fleet, fitted out by the Templars against the Egyptians. He sailed from Acre in May, 1217, anchored at the mouth of the Nile, and proceeded to lay siege to the wealthy city of Damietta. On their arrival, the Templars pitched their tents on the left bank of the river, opposite the town, and surrounded their position with a ditch and wall.

With their galleys, and rafts furnished with military engines, they first attacked a castle on an island in the river, called the Castle of Taphnis, but the towers erected upon rafts to protect their operations were constantly destroyed by the terrible Greek fire, which was blown out of long copper tubes, and could be extinguished with nothing but vinegar and sand.

At length, however, a great tower was erected on a raft, and so high that it overlooked the castle.

This tower was divided into stages filled with archers, the sides were pierced with numerous loopholes, and the whole structure was thickly covered with raw-hides to preserve it from the dreaded Greek fire. Everything being in readiness on August 24th, this vast floating tower was towed to the point of attack, and while the enemy in the castle were preparing to discharge the Greek fire and pour boiling oil upon the assailants, the Templars stationed in the lowest platform of their tower threw out grappling irons, and made a lodgement upon the causeway in front of the castle. They then battered in the door of the fortress and threw their lighted combustibles into it, which instantly enveloped the place in smoke and flames, and compelled the garrison to surrender at discretion. The great chain that had been stretched between the castle and the river was then cut, and the vessels of the crusaders ascended the Nile and took up a position in front of the town; but before it could be taken a strong north wind arose and impeded the descent of the waters to the Mediterranean. The Christian camp was flooded, the Templars losing their provisions, arms, and baggage, and when the waters receded live fish and reptiles were found in their tents. An epidemic fever followed the inundation and carried off the Grand Master and many of the brethren. The Grand Master was succeeded by the veteran Templar, Peter de Montaign.

In the summer of 1223, urged by the Pope, the Emperor Frederick II., to fulfil the vow that he had made eight years before, sailed for Acre with a powerful army to succor the Holy Land. But he was at sea only three days when he became sea-sick, and returned to land on a plea of ill-health. This enraged the Pope, and his Holiness excommunicated the Emperor in the church of Anagni. Without noticing the Holy See, he again embarked and arrived in

THE KNIGHTS TEMPLARS. 653

the harbor of Acre, September the 8th. The Pope then commanded the Templars not to join his standard, and they accordingly refused to take the field. Therefore, as the forces of the Emperor only amounted to 10,000 men, he remained inactive during the winter.

But notwithstanding this small showing of numbers and energy, the Emperor managed to open negotiations with the Moslems which resulted in a treaty, whereby Jerusalem was nominally surrendered to him.

By the terms of this singular treaty the Christian and Mohammedan religions were to meet with equal toleration in the Holy City; the followers of Mohammed were to retain the Mosque of Omar, and the Christians the Church of the Resurrection. The Moslems were to be governed by their own laws, and the Court of Judicature, in the forum of Al Rostak, was to be under the direction of a Moslem governor.

In consummation of this treaty, the Emperor proceeded to Jerusalem with a few attendants, and went through the farce of crowning himself in the Church of the Resurrection. Then, after a stay of a few days he hurried back to Acre, and soon departed for Europe. No Christian garrison was established in the city, nor did the Templars and Hospitalers venture to take any advantage of this visionary conquest.

In 1233, the Grand Master, Peter de Montaign, died at Acre, at an advanced age, and was succeeded by Herman de Perigord. Shortly after his accession to power the truce with the Sultan expired, and William de Montferrat besieged a fortress of the Infidels, but was surrounded and his forces nearly destroyed. The standard-bearer of the Templars on this occasion performed prodigies of valor. Although covered with wounds, yet he unflinchingly bore the Beauséant aloft with his bleeding arms, through the thickest of the fight, until he at last fell dead upon a heap of his slaughtered comrades.

The *sixth* crusade against the Infidels was now preached. Although not manifesting the fiery zeal of his predecessors, yet Pope Gregory IX. earnestly urged Europe to make this war.

Therefore the Templars, expecting speedy assistance and being desirous of taking advantage of the dissensions among the Saracens, had recommenced hostilities with the Sultans of Egypt and Damascus; and soon after this Thibaut I., King of Navarre, the Duke of Burgundy, and the Counts of Brittany and Bar, arrived in Palestine with a considerable force, which uniting with the Templars, marched to attack the Sultan of Egypt, while the Grand Master, De Perigord, prepared to invade the territory of the Sultan of Damascus. The invasion of Egypt ended in disaster, for in a bloody battle fought with the Mamelukes, near Gaza, the Count de Bar, many Knights, and nearly all the foot-soldiers were slain, the Count de Montfort taken prisoner, and the equipage and baggage of the army was lost. The King of Navarre and the survivors then retreated to Joppa, and sailed for Acre. On their arrival, they joined De Perigord, who was encamped at the Palm Grove of Caifa. From this place they marched toward Tiberias; but on their arrival at Sephoris they met messengers who were on their way from the Sultan of Damascus to the Grand Master of the Temple, with overtures of peace and offers to surrender Jerusalem, which were accepted. The terms proposed were: that the Moslem and Christian prisoners of war were to be immediately liberated; and Palestine, between the coast and the Jordan, excepting the cities of St. Abraham, Nablous, and Bethshean, was to be surrendered to the Christians.

The latter were then to assist the Sultan of Damascus in a war between him and the Sultan of Egypt, and were to occupy Joppa and Ascalon, to prevent the latter from marching through Palestine, to attack the Sultan of Damascus. Lastly, no truce was to be entered into with the Sultan of Egypt by the Christians, unless the Sultan of Damascus was included therein.

The fortifications of Jerusalem having been dismantled by Malek Kamel, at the period of the siege of Damietta, in 1238, when alarmed at the success of the Franks, the Sultan was now willing to purchase the safety of the rest of the country by the cession of that defenceless city. Consequently the Templars entered Jerusalem without resistance, the Mussulman population abandoning their dwellings on the approach of their old enemies.

The Templars hastened in martial array, with sound of trumpets, through the deserted streets to take possession of their ancient quarters on Mount Moriah, vacant for over one hundred years.

Again the Crescent came down from the lofty pinnacle of the Mosque of Omar, and the glittering Cross took its place. The Mosque el Aksa was purified, and its halls and spacious areas were once more graced with the white habit of the Knights of the Temple.

THE KNIGHTS TEMPLARS.

As the Sultan of Egypt had not been a party to the surrender of Jerusalem, he determined to drive out the Templars before they had time to repair the fortifications. Upon learning of this, the Templars assembled their forces and advanced to meet the Egyptians, and having possession of the passes through the hill country leading to Jerusalem, they gained a great victory over them, driving the survivors into the desert. The Sultan now finding himself unable to resist the alliance of the Templars with Saleh Ismal, Sultan of Damascus, called to his assistance the fierce tribes of the Kharizmians. These, although a warlike people, had been driven from their abodes in the neighborhood of the Caspian, by the Mogul Tartars. They then rushed headlong upon the weak and effeminate nations of the south, and had thus far devastated Armenia and Northwestern Persia, cutting off by the sword, or dragging away into captivity, all who opposed their progress.

At this time, 1244, the Kharizmians were encamped on the east bank of the Euphrates, and were considering what people to assail next, when their chief, Barbeh Khan, received a deputation from the Sultan of Egypt, inviting their co-operation in the reduction of Palestine. Their cupidity was aroused by a glowing account of the fertility and wealth of the country, and they were offered a settlement in Palestine, if they would help to rescue it from the hands of the Franks. The messengers presented to the Kharizmian chief rich shawls and magnificent presents, and returned to the Sultan at Cairo with promises of speedy co-operation. Barbeh Khan assembled his hosts, and crossed the Euphrates in their leathern boats, and as soon as they were well across, they proceeded to ravage the territories of the Sultan of Aleppo, and then marched up the plain of the Orontes to Homs, wasting all the country around with fire and sword.

Intelligence of these events reached the Grand Master, De Perigord, when he was engaged in rebuilding the fortifications around Jerusalem. He immediately called a council of war, and as the city was untenable, it was decided to abandon it. Barbeh Khan, having advanced into the plain of Ramleh, by way of Baalbec, Tiberias, and Nablous, directed his march toward Jerusalem, which his hordes entered sword in hand, massacred the remaining Christians that were crowded into the Church of the Holy Sepulchre, then plundered the city, and rifled the tombs of the Kings for treasure.

Having completed their work in Jerusalem, they marched upon Gaza, stormed that city, and put the garrison to the sword, after which they sent messengers to the Sultan of Egypt to announce their successes. Highly gratified at the intelligence, Ayoub immediately sent a robe of honor and sumptuous gifts to the chief of the savages, and despatched his army from Cairo, to join them before Gaza.

In the meantime the Templars hurriedly collected their forces together, and formed a junction with the troops of the Sultan of Damascus. They then rapidly advanced upon Gaza, attacked the Egyptians and Kharizmians, but after a bloody battle of two days' continuance, were nearly exterminated. In this engagement De Perigord and the flower of his chivalry perished, and the Grand Master of the Hospital was taken prisoner.

Notwithstanding the temporary success of the wild Kharizmians, their annihilation soon followed; for the Sultan of Egypt, having no further use for their services, left them to take care of themselves in the lands they had devastated. They were first attacked by the Sultans of Aleppo and Homs, and were pursued with equal fury by Moslems and Christians. Large bodies of them were cut up in detail by the Templars and Hospitalers, until they were exterminated.

In 1249, notwithstanding the fate of their countrymen, another horde of Tartars made their way into Palestine; first into Armenia, then into the Principality of Antioch. Here they ravaged both banks of the Orontes, gathering up everything of value, then under a guard they sent the better class of people back into Tartary, captives. To meet these barbarians a considerable force was assembled, and in a long and bloody engagement fought near the iron bridge over the Orontes, the Tartars were routed with great slaughter, and the small remnant of them that survived fled from the country with all possible speed.

Again, in 1257, another army of Tartars invaded Palestine, this time under the command of the famous Holagou; and in revenge for previous disasters, they made a clean sweep wherever they went, destroying human life like a deadly pestilence.

The Templars, entirely underestimating the strength of the invaders, hastened to meet them, and were cut to pieces in a sanguinary battle. This so demoralized the Christians that the Tartars were enabled to besiege and capture the rich and populous cities of Aleppo, Hamah, Homs, Damascus, Tiberias, and Nablous; and finally they reached the climax of their operations by entering in triumph the city of Jerusalem. But Egypt was destined to send forth a scourge not only against the Tartars but the Christians. This scourge was the Mamelukes, who under the command of the notorious Bendocdar, came upon the Tartars near Tiberias and defeated them with terrible slaughter. So complete was the rout, that the remnant of them scarcely halted till they reached and crossed the Euphrates. Bendocdar then returned to Egypt, clothed with such popularity that he aspired to the possession of the throne which he had so successfully defended, and finally slew with his own hands his sovereign, Kothuz, the third Mameluke Sultan of Egypt. The Mamelukes then hailed Bendocdar with acclamations as their sovereign.

The Sultan first proceeded to exact the submission and homage of the rulers and people of Aleppo; he then made a hostile demonstration against the wealthy city of Antioch; but finding the place strong and well defended, he retired with his army to Egypt. The next year he crossed the desert at the head of 30,000 cavalry, and overran Palestine up to the very gates of Acre. He burned the churches of Nazareth and Mount Tabor, and sought to waken the zeal and enthusiasm of his soldiers in behalf of Islam, by performing a pilgrimage to Jerusalem and to the Mosque of Omar.

He then returned to Egypt, and the Templars and Hospitalers in turn became the aggressors. They surprised and took the castle of Lillion, razed the walls and fortifications to the ground, and brought off many prisoners of both sexes, together with much booty. They next marched to the neighborhood of Ascalon, where they surprised and slew a band of Mamelukes. Then turning toward the Jordan, they destroyed Bethshean, and laid waste all of the Jordan valley as far as Lake Tiberias.

In the following winter Bendocdar again collected his forces together, and advanced by rapid marches toward Cæsarea. He disguised his plans, made a long march during the night, and at morning dawn suddenly attacked the city. His troops descended into the ditch by means of ropes and ladders, and climbed the walls with the aid of iron hooks and spikes, then burst open the gates, massacred the sentinels, and planted the standard of the Prophet on the ramparts, ere the inhabitants had hardly time to rouse themselves from their morning slumbers.

1265. Caifa, Arsoof, and Safed shared the fate of Cæsarea; after gaining possession of the latter place, he treacherously massacred 1,500 of the surviving Templars. Following this, he concentrated his forces at Aleppo, and marched against the Province of Armenia, where all the castles of the Templars were assaulted and taken, and the garrisons massacred. The people were plundered of everything of value, and the young and fair were tied together with cords and driven to Aleppo. There, with much music and many dancing girls, the brutal Bendocdar celebrated his exploits.

He next marched against Acre, and by using the banners of the Templars as a ruse, he attempted to gain an entrance through the east gate of the city; but the Templars were on the alert and foiled the barbarians in their attempt. In revenge for this they slaughtered over five hundred unarmed people outside the walls, and put a part of their heads in sacks, and mounted the others on stakes. They then destroyed the windmills, dwellings, and fruit-trees, and poisoned the wells.

On March 7, Bendocdar stormed Joppa, put the garrison to the sword, and set fire to the town. He then divided his army into three corps, which he sent by different routes against Antioch.

The first division approached the city from the north. The second secured the mouth of the Orontes, so as to prevent assistance from the sea, and the third division, led by Bendocdar in person, approached Antioch from the south, and when the different divisions had arrived and were assigned their positions, the works of defence were furiously assaulted; this was continued incessantly for three days, with varying success; but on the fourth day the Moslems scaled the walls where they touched the sides of the mountain, and rushing across the ramparts, sword in hand, into the city, they soon put nearly ten thousand Christians to the sword. The survivors of the Templars and populace fled from the scene of carnage to the citadel, and there defended themselves with the energy of despair. Finally, Bendocdar granted them their lives, and they surrendered. They were then bound with cords, and the long string of prisoners passed in review before the Sultan, who caused his notaries to take down the names of each person.

The next thing in order was the plunder. This being a rich city, the spoils were immense, requiring several days to collect it from the homes and shops of the inhabitants. When it had been brought together, it was taken to the plain near the city and divided among the Moslems. There was so much gold and silver that it was distributed by measure, and merchandise and property of all kinds, piled up in heaps, was drawn for by lot. The women and girls were distributed among the soldiery, and they were so numerous that even the male slaves of the conquerors were permitted to have captives at their disposal.

The Sultan halted here for several weeks, and permitted his soldiers to hold a market for the sale of their booty. This market was attended by Jews and adventurers from all parts of the East, who greedily bought up the rich property and costly valuables of the unfortunate citizens of Antioch. Yet the loss of property was a small matter compared with the fate of the captives. When the mother saw her daughter handed over to a brutal soldier, when she herself was sold into irredeemable bondage, the bitter cries that resounded through the plain touched even the hearts of the Moslems. "It was," says a Mohammedan writer, "a fearful and heartrending sight. Even the hard stones were softened with grief."

Not only was all the personal property pillaged, but the ornaments and decorations of the churches, and the lead from the roofs of the buildings, were carried away. The city was then fired in different places, amid the exultant shouts of the brutal Mohammedans, and with the exception of the churches, was soon destroyed. The great churches of St. Paul and St. Peter, burnt with terrific fury for several days; at last, however, nothing remained of wealthy, happy Antioch but a vast black field of ruins.

Thus was the history of this grand city closed in 1268, one hundred and seventy years after its recovery from the Infidels by the Crusaders. For nearly six centuries the blighting genius of Mohammedanism has rested over the site of this ancient metropolis of the East, therefore it is, at this date, nothing more than a miserable Arab village; the Arabs doubtless being descendants of the conquerors and destroyers of the city. The renowned Church of Antioch which, in the fourth century, numbered 100,000 people, now consists of a few Greek families, who still cling to the Christian faith amid the insults and persecutions of the Infidels.

Upon the capture of the city, Bendocdar caused the following letter to be written to the Prince of Antioch, who was at Tripoli: "Since not a soul has escaped to tell you what has happened, we will undertake the pleasing task of informing you. We have slain all whom you appointed to defend Antioch. We have crushed your knights beneath the feet of our horses, and have given up your provinces to pillage. Your gold and silver have been divided among us by the quintal, and four of your women have been bought and sold for a crown. There is not a single Christian in the province that does not now march bound before us, nor a single young girl that is not in our possession. Your churches have been made level with the dust, and our chariot wheels have passed over the sites of your dwellings."

The doughty Bendocdar's victorious career was checked, however, by the arrival of Prince Edward of England, who joined Thomas Berard, Grand Master of the Temple, at the head of a reinforcement of knights and foot-soldiers. Various successes were then obtained over the Infidels, and on April 23, A.D. 1272, a truce was agreed upon for a space of ten years and ten months, but it only comprised the town and plain of Acre, and the road to Nazareth.

Soon after this Prince Edward was stabbed with a poisoned dagger by an assassin. Though dangerously wounded, he struck his assailant to the ground, and caused him to be immediately despatched by the guards. The Prince then made his will, Thomas Berard, the Grand Master, signing as a witness. The life of the Prince, however, was preserved, the effects of the poison being neutralized by an antidote; and on September 14th, the same year, he returned to Europe, and thus terminated the last expedition undertaken for the relief of the Holy Land.

Of all the places of note in sacred and profane history in Palestine, the last was soon again to pass under the domination of the Infidels. Tripoli was taken in January, 1287, and with it a great amount of plunder, as over four thousand bales of silk, together with many rich ornaments, and much coin, was divided among the soldiers. Next Gebal, Beyrout, and the other towns and cities between Sidon and Laodicea fell into their hands, and Sultan Kelaoun was preparing to attack the important and populous city of Acre, when death terminated his victorious career.

THE KNIGHTS TEMPLARS. 661

Kelaoun was succeeded by his son, Aschraf Khalil, who hastened to execute the projects of his father. Khalil marched against Acre, at the head of 60,000 horse and 140,000 foot.

Acre, next to Jerusalem, was now the most important city in Palestine, for after the loss of Jerusalem, in A.D. 1187, this city had become the metropolis of the Christians, and it was adorned with a great cathedral, numerous stately churches, and other elegant buildings, with aqueducts, and an artificial port.

The fortifications were vast and massive, consisting of a double wall strengthened at intervals with lofty towers, and defended by a castle called the King's Tower, and by the fortress of the Temple. Between the ramparts extended a large space of ground covered with beautiful residences, occupied by the nobility of Palestine. To man these extensive works there was only a small garrison of 12,000 men, under the command of the Grand Master of the Temple. The siege lasted from April 1, 1291, to May 20th, during the whole of which period the fighting was incessant. Great stones and pots of burning naphtha were incessantly poured into the city. The walls were battered, and the foundations were sapped by miners who were continually advancing their works. More than six hundred catapults and other instruments of destruction were directed against the fortifications, and the movable towers of the Moslems overtopped the walls of the city.

Finally, on May 4th, after thirty-three days of constant fighting and battering with their engines, the great tower, the key of the fortifications, and called by the Moslems "The Cursed Tower," was thrown down.

From this time till the 16th, the breach was carried and recovered several times, the knights at last closing up the passage shoulder to shoulder, presented a wall of steel to the advance of the enemy.

The Grand Masters of the Temple and the Hospitalers fought side by side at the head of their knights, and for a time successfully resisted all the efforts of the enemy. But as knight after knight fell beneath the scimitars of the Moslems, there was none left to take his place, and at last the Grand Master of the Templars was also stricken down.

Upon hearing of this, thousands of the people became panic stricken and rushed to the harbor, where they sought with frantic violence to gain possession of the ships and boats in the port; but a terrible thunder-storm was raging over the dark waters of the sea and many of the boats and vessels were swamped by the surging waves, so that the bitter cries of the perishing fugitives ascended alike from sea and the doomed city.

A small band of Templars, the sole survivors of the Order in Acre, kept together and successfully withstood the victorious Mamelukes. In a compact column they fought their way, followed by hundreds of Christian fugitives, to the convent of the Temple and secured the gates.

They then assembled in solemn chapter, and appointed the Knight Templar Gaudini, Grand Master. The Temple was a place of great extent and strength, so strong, that on the following morning favorable terms were offered the Templars by the Sultan, and they agreed to evacuate the Temple, on condition that a vessel should be placed at their disposal, and they be allowed to retire in safety with the fugitives under their protection, and retain as much of their effects as each person could carry.

The Sultan pledged himself to the fulfilment of these conditions, and sent a guard of three hundred soldiers charged to see that the articles of capitulation were properly carried into effect, but the soldiers, attracted by the beauty of some of the women, broke through all restraint and outraged them. Upon this the enraged Templars closed and barricaded the gates, and then set upon the treacherous Infidels and put every one of them to death. Before this massacre was terminated the Moslem trumpets sounded to the assault; but the Templars defended themselves until the next day, when the Marshal of the Order and several of the brethren were deputed by Gaudini, with a flag of truce, to the Sultan, to explain the cause of the massacre of his guard. The enraged monarch, however, had no sooner got them in his power than he ordered them to be beheaded, and then fiercely pressed the siege.

In the night Grand Master Gaudini, with a chosen band of his companions, collected the treasure of the Order and the ornaments of the church, and making their way through a secret passage leading to the harbor, they got on board a small vessel, and escaped to the Island of Cyprus.

The remainder of the Templars retired into a large tower of the Temple, which they defended with desperate energy. The Mamelukes were repeatedly driven back, and the little fortress was everywhere surrounded with heaps of their slain. But the Sultan at last ordered it to be undermined, and the huge tower fell with a tremendous crash, and buried the brave Templars in its ruins. The Sultan next set fire to the town, and thus was the last stronghold of the Christian power in Palestine reduced to black ruins.

In 1291, after this disaster, the Templars established their headquarters at Limisso, in the Island of Cyprus, and sent urgent letters to Europe for succor. In the meantime the armies of Sultan Kelaoun assaulted and captured Tyre, Sidon, Tortosa, Caiphas, and the castle at Athlit. The last three places belonged to the Templars, and were stoutly defended; but being attacked by the Egyptian fleet by sea, and by large armies of Moslems by land, they were at last taken and destroyed.

1295. The Grand Master Gaudini died, and was succeeded by James de Molay (Jaques de Molai), a member of a noble family in Burgundy, who was the twenty-second and last Grand Master of the Templars. He was first appointed Visitor-General, then Grand Preceptor of England, where he then resided. He afterward became the head of the entire Fraternity.

Soon after his election he sailed for Cyprus, carrying out with him a large body of English and French knights, and a considerable amount of treasure. Immediately after his arrival he was invited by the famous Casan Cham, Emperor of the Mogul Tartars, and a descendant of Ghenghis Khan, to join him in an expedition against the Sultan of Egypt. Casan Cham married the daughter of Leon, King of Armenia, a Christian princess of great beauty, to whom he was strongly attached, and who was permitted the full exercise of the Christian worship.

Therefore the Tartar Emperor became favorably disposed toward the Christians, and sought an alliance as above indicated.

De Molay acceded to his proposal, and in April, 1299, he, with his force of Templars, landed at Suadia, and formed a junction with the Tartar army which was encamped amid the ruins of Antioch. A force of thirty thousand men was then placed by the Emperor under the command of De Molay, and the combined forces moved up the valley of the Orontes toward Damascus, and in a great battle fought at Homs, the armies of the Sultans of Damascus and Egypt were routed and pursued with great slaughter until nightfall. Aleppo, Homs, Damascus, and all the principal cities, surrendered to the victorious Moguls and Templars, and the latter again entered Jerusalem in triumph. The Emperor then sent ambassadors to Europe to the Pope, and to the sovereigns, announcing the success of the allies and soliciting their alliance, for which he offered them in return the possession of Palestine. But the so-called Christian nations were too much engrossed with their selfish ends to meet the call.

1299. De Molay next advanced to Gaza, and drove the Saracens into the desert of Egypt; but a Saracen chief who had been appointed by the Tartars to be governor of Damascus, treacherously instigated the Mussulman population of Syria to revolt, and the Grand Master was obliged to hastily retreat to Jerusalem. He was there joined by the Tartar General, Cotulosse, who had been sent by Casan across the Euphrates to support him.

The combined armies were once more preparing to march upon Damascus, when the sudden illness of Casan disconcerted their arrangements, and deprived the Grand Master of his Tartar allies. The Templars were therefore compelled to retreat to the sea-coast and embark their forces on board their vessels. The Grand Master then sailed to Limisso, stationing a strong detachment of his soldiers on the island of Aradus, which they fortified. But that position was soon after attacked by a fleet of twenty vessels and an army of ten thousand men, and after a gallant defence the garrison were all killed or taken prisoners. This terminated the dominion and career of the Templars in Palestine, and for a long time closed the long and sanguinary struggle between the Crescent and the Cross. The few remaining Templars and Christians in the Holy Land were pursued from the ruins of one place to the ruins of another, until they were all exterminated.

Everything along the coast that could afford a shelter or foothold for crusaders was carefully destroyed. The houses were all burned, the olive-groves and other trees were cut down and burnt, and the land everywhere made a blackened waste.

List of the Eight Crusades.

The First Crusade was started by Peter the Hermit, A.D. 1096, and was promoted by Pope Urban II. The civilized and successful portion of this crusade was commanded by Godfrey de Bouillon, and resulted in the capture of Jerusalem, July 15, 1099.

The Second Crusade, commenced A.D. 1142, preached by Bernard, and led by the Emperor Conrad II., of Germany, and Louis VII., of France. Both armies were nearly destroyed while passing through Asia Minor; terminated in 1148.

The Third Crusade, A.D. 1188, led by King Richard, of England, Philip II. and the Emperor Frederick I., of France and Germany, resulted in the capture of Acre, 1191.

The Fourth Crusade, A.D. 1195, was led by Henry VI., of Germany. Some victories were gained, but the crusade was ruined by internal dissensions. Terminated 1198.

The Fifth Crusade, A.D. 1198, led by Baldwin, Count of Flanders, was changed to the conquest of Constantinople, 1202, and so terminated.

The Sixth Crusade, A.D. 1238, was led by the Emperor Frederick II., of Germany, who entered Jerusalem. This was accompanied by that preposterous episode, "The Children's Crusade."

The Seventh Crusade, commenced A.D. 1256, was led by King Louis IX., of France (called St. Louis), who was defeated and captured at Mansourah, Africa.

The Eighth Crusade, A.D. 1270, led by the same Louis, who died at Carthage, Africa. Although the Popes had had enough of crusades, yet Pope Clement IV. could not prevent this one.

In 1291 the Turks took Acre, and by the year 1300 the last of the remaining Templars in the Holy Land had been driven out or exterminated, and De Molay, the last Grand Master, had returned to France.

An immediate consequence of the overthrow of the Templars in Palestine was the loss of prestige and respect at home. Hitherto they had occupied the highest position in the state, both civil and military; but they were now like Sampson shorn of his hair, helpless.

The great wealth and influence of the organization had rendered them objects of envy and hatred, both to the Romish Church and the Catholic despots of Europe; consequently they soon became victims of their rapacity and bigotry.

The Pope as prime mover, Philip, King of France, and Edward II., of England, united in a scheme of persecution and plunder against the Templars, which resulted in the murder of a large number of them, and the division of their property among these robbers, and the Hospitalers. Thousands of the Templars were seized simultaneously in France, Italy, and England, and thrust into dungeons, from whence, after undergoing a farce of a trial, they were dragged forth to the stake, the favorite form of murder by Popery. When the mock trials commenced, the prisons were full of knights, and all who did not voluntarily confess to crimes that would compromise them, were subjected to the most barbarous tortures in use. The cries and groans of those who were torn with hot pincers, and had their limbs torn asunder in the torture, were heard throughout the land; some to escape the awful agony, confessed whatever was required of them, but most of the knights, in the midst of the most fearful tortures, maintained their principles with invincible fortitude.

His *Holiness* the Pope, becoming impatient of the delay of even a form of a trial, declared that if the Templars could not otherwise be condemned, the *plenitude* of the *Pontifical power* would supply everything; and that he would condemn them by way of expedient.

One of the first scenes in the bloody drama was the burning of fifty-four Templars. The place selected for this tragedy was in the open country, at Porte St. Antoine des Champs. Here fifty-four stakes were set in the ground in the form of a crescent, and around these stakes were piled fagots and charcoal. To this spot the doomed men were conducted, and marched by the semi-circle in single file, one being left at each stake as they passed, where they were taken charge of by the executioners and chained to the stakes. The fires were then lighted, but the fuel was so arranged as to burn slowly, and thus prolong their sufferings, and give the victims time to realize their awful situation. As soon as the fire began to reach their bodies the inquisitors, thinking that they would then yield, approached, and once more offered them pardon if they would make the confession that was required; but the fortitude of the Templars was equal to the fiery ordeal before them, and they replied that they would not; that they considered death, even the horrid death they were doomed to die, far preferable to perjury and dishonor. They were then left to the jeers of the Catholic mob till their bodies were consumed, thus affording a spectacle so cruel and inhuman as has rarely ever been witnessed in any civilized or even barbarous nation, and showing that, of all the animal kingdom, none are so cruel and vindictive to their kind as man, when impelled by religious fanaticism or the lust for gain.

After a vast number of the knights had been condemned and burned, the crowning act in this bloody drama came in the martyrdom of the Grand Master De Molay, and his illustrious companion Guy, the Preceptor.

As De Molay had rendered the Church and State such important services as to render him popular with the people, it was deemed expedient to proceed with caution in his case; therefore, instead of bringing him to the stake with the others, he was kept confined in prison and frequently subjected to cruel tortures to force a confession, also with a view to terminating his life in that way; but his strong constitution had so far survived all the barbarities inflicted on him.

On the 18th of March, 1313, De Molay and his companion were led forth to a scaffold that had been erected on an island in the Seine, opposite the king's gardens.

Upon the appearance of the knights, chained like wild animals, and haggard from long suffering, a murmur of astonishment ran through the crowd of spectators. This, however, was suppressed by the guards, and as soon as silence was secured the Bishop of Alba proceeded to read aloud the eighty-eight articles of accusation, followed by what purported to be their confessions. At the conclusion of the reading, the papal legate turned to the doomed men and requested them to avow their guilt. This they refused to do, and never for a moment did either of these noble martyrs flinch, nor by word or gesture indicative of fear or death did they gratify their fiendish persecutors. But by their wonderful fortitude and heroic death they added another bright page to the closing history of their Order.

When the fires were lighted and De Molay was nearly stifled with smoke, he, in a loud voice, summoned the Pope to appear before the tribunal of God in forty days, and Philip within a year. In less than thirteen months both of these worthies died miserable deaths. All the people shed tears at the tragical spectacle of this execution. Convinced of their innocence, many persons gathered the ashes of these noble victims and preserved them as precious relics. During the five years in which the bitterest of this persecution was carried on, the Pope and Catholic sovereigns of Europe confiscated and appropriated to their own use the vast wealth of the Templars, including their ornaments, jewelry, and the treasures of their churches.

List of Grand Masters of Knights Templars, from the Organization of the Order, until the Death of De Molay in 1313.*

	Installed.		Installed.
1. Hugh de Payens	1113	12. Gilbert Horal	1194
2. Robert of Burgundy	1136	13. Philip Duplessis	1201
3. Everard de Barri	1146	14. William de Chartres	1217
4. Bernard de Tremellay	1151	15. Peter Montaign	1218
5. Bertrand de Blanquefort	1154	16. Herman de Perigord	1233
6. Philip of Nablous	1167	17. William de Sonnac	1247
7. Odo de St. Amand	1170	18. Reginald de Vichier	1251
8. Arnold de Troye	1180	19. Thomas Berard	1257
9. Gerard de Riderfort	1185	20. William de Beaujen	1273
10. Walter	1189	21. Theobald de Gaudini	1291
11. Robert de Sable	1191	22. Jaques de Molai	1295

Successors to De Molay, according to the French System.†

	Installed.		Installed.
1. John Mark Larmenius	1313	14. Gaspard de Galtiaco Tavanensis	1544
2. Francis Thomas Theobald	1324	15. Henry de Montmorency	1574
3. Arnold de Braque	1340	16. Charles de Valois	1615
4. John de Claremont	1349	17. James Ruxellius de Granceio	1651
5. Bertrand du Guesclin	1357	18. James Henry, Duc de Duras	1681
6. John Arminiacus	1381	19. Philip, Duke of Orleans	1705
7. Bernard Arminiacus	1392	20. Louis Augustus Bourbon	1724
8. John Arminiacus	1419	21. Louis Henry, Bourbon Comde	1737
9. John de Croy	1451	22. Louis Francis, Bourbon Conty	1741
10. Bernard Imbault	1472	23. Louis Hercules Timoleon	1776
11. Robert Lenoncourt	1478	24. Claude M. R. Chevillon	1792
12. Galeatius Salazar	1497	25. Bernard Raymund Fabre Palaprat	1804
13. Philip Chabot	1516	26. Sir William Sydney Smith	1838

* Addison's Knights Templars, p. 136; Mackey, p. 427.   † Ibid., p. 541.

THE KNIGHTS TEMPLARS. 669

Many have supposed that the schemes of robbery and murder carried on against the Templars resulted in the destruction of their organization. But this was not the case, as they were suppressed, not exterminated, for we soon hear of them again in Scotland, Portugal, and even in France and England.

Inspired by the grand history and noble principles of the old Order, their successors have developed an organization, military and masonic, that is both numerous and powerful in Europe and North America, and as a public pageant, they constitute the crowning glory of Free Masonry.

Soon after the overthrow of the Templars in Europe, Dennis I., King of Portugal, obtained from Pope John XXII. permission to re-establish the Order in his dominions, but under the title of the Order of Christ. To this the Pope consented, approved the statutes which were submitted to him, and subsequently, under certain restrictions, confirmed the institution.

During the persecution of the Templars many of them fled to Scotland and joined their more fortunate brethren there. For, although the ban against them throughout Europe affected them here to the extent, that much of their property was transferred to the Hospitalers, and their sphere of action contracted, yet they continued to reside in the preceptories left to them.

A part of the Scottish Knights Templars even united with the Knights Hospitalers and lived with them amicably in the same houses, until the Reformation, when many of them united with the Free Masons* and established the Ancient Lodge at Sterling, where they conferred the degrees of Knight of Malta and Knight Templar.

In 1808 the Order received accessions of men of eminence which gave it a new impulse, and in 1828 it numbered forty encampments in the British Dominions.

Soon after the establishment of the Scots or Scottish degrees in France, the Scots Lodges instituted degrees having reference to the history and chivalry of the Knights Templars; being incited thereto undoubtedly by members of Templar bodies that had been secretly maintained in Paris, and by the celebrated oration of the Chevalier Ramsey.

Among the earliest of these degrees was the Kadosch, which represented

---

* See Addison's Knights Templars, pp. 543–551; Laurie's History of Free Masonry and Grand Lodge of Scotland; Mackey, p. 428.

the vengeance of the Templars; subsequently nearly all of the new rites of French origin contained Templar grades.

The English Masonic Templars were derived from the "Baldwin Body," or from one of the four co-ordinate Bodies of London, Bath, York, and Salisbury, which were formed by the members of the preceptories which had long existed at Bristol, and who, on the dissolution of their Order, are supposed to have united with the Masonic Fraternity.

The Successors to the Ancient Templars.—Modern Templarism.

From the foregoing we get the different lines of descent from the Knight Templars of Chivalry to the Knight Templars of the present time, viz.: From the Scottish Templars in Scotland, from Scottish and French Templarism in France, and from their old establishments in England.*

When it was desirable to form an Encampment, the Knights, in the absence of any central authority, acted by virtue of their inherent rights and proceeded to organize an encampment, and do the work thereof; thus were the first encampments established in the United States.

At first it was not necessary to be a Mason to become a Templar in this country; yet Blue Lodges sometimes conferred the Templar degrees.

The first appearance of Knight Templarism in this country was in 1769, when St. Andrew's Lodge, of Boston, conferred the "Order of Knight Templar." The first encampments of Knights Templars, established in this country, were located, respectively, at Charleston, in New York City, at Stillwater, N. Y., in Philadelphia, and at Newburyport, Mass. All established prior to 1797.†

In 1802 Boston Encampment was formed by ten Knights of the Red Cross, and St. John's Encampment was formed at Providence. In 1805 Darius Council, of Portland, was organized; and prior to 1813 Rising Sun, Jerusalem, and Columbian Encampments were formed in the City of New York.

In 1811, Joseph Cerneau appeared in the history of Knighthood, and

---

* Mackey, pp. 428, 429; History of Free Masonry and Concordant Orders, pp. 766–769; Addison's Knights Templars, pp. 565–575; Dr. J. Burnes's Sketch of the History of the Knights Templars.

† Gould's History of Free Masonry, American edition, vol. iv., pp. 542–661; Folger, pp. 122–125; History of Free Masonry and Concordant Orders, pp. 711–713.

commenced conferring its degrees, including Knight Templar, Knight of the Red Cross, and Knights of Malta.

In 1807 he established the Sovereign Grand Consistory of the Ancient and Accepted Rite for the United States of America, etc.; and in 1812, a system was organized by this Sovereign Grand Consistory in which they made the "Knights of the Red Cross" the first; the "Knights Templars" the second; the "Knights of Malta" or "St. John of Jerusalem" the third; the "Knights of the Christian Mark" the fourth; and the "Knights of the Holy Sepulchre" the fifth and last.*

These degrees were conferred at that time according to the ritual of the Ancient and Accepted Scottish Rite. The Lecturers, however, soon remodelled them and formulated a system of lectures which, in the year 1816, was adopted by the General Grand Encampment then formed.

The Sovereign Grand Consistory, at its session on January 22, 1814, decreed, by a unanimous vote, the establishment of a Grand Encampment of Knights Templars and Appendant Orders for the State of New York, and immediately proceeded to its formation by choosing the Grand Officers thereof, as follows: DeWitt Clinton, Grand Master; Martin Hoffman, Grand Generalissimo; John W. Mulligan, Senior Grand Warden; James B. Durrand, Junior Grand Warden; Elias Hicks, Grand Orator.

On June 18th following, this encampment again met, the object of the meeting being that of hearing the report of the committee appointed for the purpose of drafting a constitution. After the encampment was duly opened, the Grand Orator of the day took occasion to deliver a short discourse, in which he gave a historical sketch of the foundation of the Order of Knights Templars, and also the following account of the formation of the Grand Encampment on January 14th, *previous*.†

"The numerous encampments of Knights Templars," said he, "now existing within this State, being self-created bodies, are consequently governed by their own private and individual laws, acknowledging no superior authority, because in fact none heretofore existed.

---

* Folger, pp. 124, 125.

† Proceedings of the Grand Encampment of the State of New York for 1844-1851; also reprint of Proceedings for 1860; History of Free Masonry and Concordant Orders, pp. 718-721.

"A longer continuance of this state of things could but be productive of ill consequences, inasmuch as it was to be apprehended that this sort of unconstituted associations, so rapidly increasing in number, would sooner or later have lessened, if not entirely destroyed, that commanding respect due to so dignified a degree as that of Knight Templar.

"The want of superior authority, which alone can regulate and preserve order in the proceedings of subordinate encampments, not only might have induced such isolated corps to encroach upon prerogatives not their own, but must have ended in producing some serious misunderstanding among themselves, thereby producing a schism equally injurious to the prosperity and glory of exalted Masonry."

"Accordingly, the Sov. Grand Consistory of Chiefs of Exalted Masonry, fully impressed with the necessity and importance of this subject, has at its session of the 22d day of January, A.D. 1814, as aforesaid, decreed, by an unanimous vote, the establishment of a Grand Encampment of Sir Knights Templars and Appendant Orders for the State of New York, and immediately proceeded to its formation by choosing the Grand Officers thereof; taking (for this time only) from among its own members; and the majority of the votes proved in favor of

DeWitt Clinton, Thrice Illustrious Grand Master; Martin Hoffman, Grand Generalissimo; John W. Mulligan, Grand Captain-General; James B. Durrand, Senior Grand Warden; Jacob Schieffelin, Junior Grand Warden; Elias Hicks, Grand Orator; Anthony Reinetaux, Grand Recorder; Joseph Gouin, Grand Treasurer.

"They were accordingly installed into their respective offices, and the establishment of the Grand Encampment of Sir Knights Templars and Appendant Orders for the State of New York was proclaimed in ample form."

In 1814 Rising Sun Encampment stood as No. 1, and Columbian as No. 5.

At the meeting of the Grand Encampment in May, 1815, Columbian applied for and received a charter from the Grand Body, in which it retained its previous name and number.

At the same meeting of the Grand Encampment it was decided that Nos. 1, 2, 3, and 4 should remain open for the encampments established, should they apply for a renewal of their Charters under the *Grand Encampment.*

Soon after this, Temple Encampment was acknowledged as No. 2. An Encampment at New Orleans, and one at Utica, N. Y., were chartered and numbered respectively 6 and 7. Subsequently Columbian was given the place of No. 1. Morton Encampment was chartered August 16, 1823, and designated No. 4. In December, 1824, General Lafayette and his son Washington were knighted by this Encampment, at St. John's Hall, in Frankfort Street.

Palestine Encampment was constituted in 1851, its number being 18.

On June 21, 1816, the General Grand Encampment for the United States was formed in the city of New York. DeWitt Clinton was elected General Grand Master, and Thomas Smith Webb, Deputy General Grand Master.

In 1857 the title "Encampment" was changed to "Commandery," and "Grand Master" was changed to "Grand Commander."

That the Order is now in a flourishing condition, not only in the United States, but throughout the world, will be seen from the following statistics.

	Members.		Members.
Alabama	463	Montana	460
Arizona	194	Nebraska	1,735
Arkansas	571	New Hampshire	2,333
California	3,779	New Jersey	1,678
Colorado	1,699	New Mexico	325
Connecticut	2,747	New York	13,578
District of Columbia	1,576	North Carolina	438
Florida	374	North Dakota	618
Georgia	946	Ohio	9,918
Illinois	9,842	Oklahoma	344
Indiana	4,003	Oregon	504
Indian Territory	223	Pennsylvania	13,950
Iowa	4,844	South Dakota	838
Kansas	3,532	Tennessee	984
Kentucky	2,631	Texas	2,383
Louisiana	376	Vermont	1,861
Maine	3,829	Virginia	1,713
Maryland	1,286	Washington	710
Massachusetts and Rhode Island	13,692	West Virginia	1,540
Michigan	6,107	Wisconsin	3,268
Minnesota	2,889	Wyoming	397
Mississippi	778	Grand Encampment	1,330
Missouri	4,770		
Total in the United States			132,356

OTHER COUNTRIES.

	Members.
Canada	2,104
England and Wales	3,026
Ireland	1,080
Scotland	525
Victoria, Australia	93
	6,828
Total in the world	139,184

CHAPTER XVII.

THE MYSTIC SHRINE.

Reported Origin and History of the New Organization.—Institution of Mecca Temple in New York.—Establishment of Other Temples.—Growth of the Order in America.—List of Temples

THE Ancient Arabian Order of the Nobles of the Mystic Shrine is an organization composed exclusively of Knights Templar and of Thirty-second degree Masons, and purports to be an ornamental branch of Free Masonry.

The story of the origin of the Order of Nobles of the Mystic Shrine is interesting and romantic, but might be out of place in this History. The account given of the introduction of the Shrine to America is to the effect that William J. Florence, 32°, the famed actor, was initiated in the mysteries of the Shrine, in August, 1870, in Marseilles, France; that a copy of the ritual was given to him on the day of his departure from that city for Algiers; that nearly every member of the several diplomatic corps, many influential bankers, merchants, and learned and powerful Mohammedans of that port, met each evening in the Shrine there; that Mr. Florence then, and at other times, received manuscripts which related the history, and described and explained the monitorial and other work of the Order; and that the Shrines in America were founded by authority given, and work under instructions conveyed by these manuscripts.

A number of Knights Templar and Thirty-second degree Masons met in Masonic Hall, at No. 114 East Thirteenth street, New York City, on the 16th of June, 1871, and Sherwood C. Campbell, James S. Chappell, Edward Eddy, Charles T. McClenachan, Oswald Merle d'Aubigné, George W. Millar, John A. Moore, Albert P. Moriarity, William S. Paterson, Daniel Sickels and John W. Simons were received into the Order by Mr. Florence and Dr. Walter Fleming.

676   FREE MASONRY IN THE UNITED STATES.

A session was called in the same hall on September 26th, 1872, and Mecca Temple was then instituted, the thirteen brethren above named being its charter members. The first officers of Mecca Temple were Walter Fleming, Potentate; Charles T. McClenachan, Chief Rabban; John A. Moore, Assistant Rabban; William S. Paterson, Recorder; Edward Eddy, High Priest; James S. Chappell, Treasurer; George W. Millar, Oriental Guide; Oswald M. d'Aubigné, Captain of Guard.

George F. Loder and seven associates were received into the Order on the 4th of January, 1875, and in the same year instituted Damascus Temple of Rochester, N. Y. The work of that Temple created wider interest in the new order, and during that year a number of influential Masons were empowered to establish subordinate Temples.

Twenty-five neophytes took the obligations of the Shrine on June 16th, 1876, in Masonic Hall, in New York City. At the same time and place the Imperial Council of the Ancient Arabian Order of the Nobles of the Mystic Shrine for the United States of America, was duly organized, with the following list of officers: Walter M. Fleming, Imperial Potentate; George F. Loder, Rochester, N. Y., Deputy Potentate; Philip F. Lenhart, Brooklyn, N. Y., Chief Rabban; Edward M. Ehlers, New York City, Assistant Rabban; William H. Whiting, Rochester, High Priest; Samuel R. Carter, Rochester, Oriental Guide; Aaron L. Northrup, New York City, Treasurer; William S. Paterson, New York City, Recorder; Albert P Moriarity, New York City, Financial Secretary; John L. Stettinus, Cincinnati, Ohio, First Ceremonial Master; Benson Sherwood, New York City, Second Ceremonial Master; Samuel Harper, Pittsburg, Pa., Marshal; Frank H. Bascom, Montpelier, Vt., Captain of Guard; George Scott, Paterson, N. J., Outer Guard.

The first of the resolutions adopted by the newly instituted Imperial Council, declared that "The Grand Orient of this Imperial Council shall be at the City of New York, N. Y." It was also resolved, that the prerequisites for reception into the Order of the Shrine in America shall be, that the applicant must be either a Knight Templar, according to the requirements of the Grand Encampment of Knights Templar for the United States of America, or a Mason of the Thirty-second degree of the Ancient Accepted Scottish Rite.

At a session of Mecca Temple, held in the New Masonic Hall in New York

City, January 16th, 1877, the Imperial Potentate announced that Temples, deputies, representatives and members of the Shrine were then to be found in every part of the jurisdiction, from its Extreme East to the far West, from its North to its South, and that the Order was destined to become a most powerful one in America.

Two years later it was said that there were then thirty active members in the Council, and thirteen Temples, which had a membership of four hundred and thirty-eight Nobles, showing an increase of thirteen over the number reported for the next preceding year. It was officially declared, at the end of the year 1903, that the membership of the several Temples in America included nearly seventy five thousand Nobles. The list of Temples at that time was as follows:

Zamora,	Birmingham,	Ala.	Tangier,	Omaha,	Neb.
Sahara,	Pine Bluff,	Ark.	Ballut Abyad,	Albuquerque,	N. Mex.
Al Malaikah,	Los Angeles,	Cal.	Cyprus,	Albany,	N. Y.
Islam,	San Francisco,	Cal.	Kismet,	Brooklyn,	N. Y.
Rameses,	Toronto,	Can.	Ismailia,	Buffalo,	N. Y.
El Jebel,	Denver,	Col.	Mecca,	New York,	N. Y.
Pyramid,	Bridgeport,	Conn.	Damascus,	Rochester,	N. Y.
Almas,	Washington,	D. C.	Oriental,	Troy,	N. Y.
Morocco,	Jacksonville,	Fla.	Ziyara,	Utica,	N. Y.
Yaarab,	Atlanta,	Ga.	Media,	Watertown,	N. Y.
Medinah,	Chicago,	Ill.	El Zagal,	Fargo,	N. D.
Tabala,	Rockford,	Ill.	Syrian,	Cincinnati,	O.
Mohammed,	Peoria,	Ill.	Al Koran,	Cleveland,	O.
El Kahir,	Cedar Rapids,	Ia.	Aladdin,	Columbus,	O.
Kaaba,	Davenport,	Ia.	India,	Oklahoma,	O. T.
Murat,	Indianapolis,	Ind.	Al Kader,	Portland,	Ore.
Abdallah,	Leavenworth,	Kan.	Zem Zem,	Erie,	Pa.
Isis,	Salina,	Kan.	Lu Lu,	Philadelphia,	Pa.
Kosair,	Louisville,	Ky.	Syria,	Pittsburg,	Pa.
Jerusalem,	New Orleans,	La.	Rajah,	Reading,	Pa.
Kora,	Lewiston,	Me.	Palestine,	Providence,	R. I.
Boumi,	Baltimore,	Md.	Naja,	Deadwood,	S. D.

Aleppo,	Boston,	Mass.	El Riad,	Sioux Falls,	S. D.
Moslem,	Detroit,	Mich.	Alhambra.	Chattanooga,	Tenn.
Saladin,	Grand Rapids,	Mich.	Al Chymia,	Memphis,	Tenn.
Ahmed,	Marquette,	Mich.	Ben Hur,	Austin,	Tex.
Zuhrah,	Minneapolis,	Minn.	Hella,	Dallas,	Tex.
Osman,	St. Paul,	Minn.	El Kalah,	Salt Lake City,	Utah.
Hamasa,	Meridian,	Miss.	Mount Sinai,	Montpelier,	Vt.
Ararat,	Kansas City,	Mo.	Acca,	Richmond,	Va.
Moila,	St. Joseph,	Mo.	El Katif,	Spokane,	Wash.
Moolah,	St. Louis,	Mo.	Afifi,	Tacoma,	Wash.
Algeria,	Helena,	Mont.	Osiris,	Wheeling,	W. Va.
Sesostris,	Lincoln,	Neb.	Tripoli,	Milwaukee,	Wisconsin.
El Zaribah,	Phœnix,	Arizona.	Oasis,	Charlotte,	N. C.
Sphinx,	Hartford,	Conn.	Antioch,	Dayton,	Ohio.
Alee,	Savannah,	Georgia.	Irem,	Wilkes-Barre,	Penna.
El Korah,	Boise City,	Idaho.	Beni Kedem,	Charleston,	W. Va.
Melha,	Springfield,	Mass.	Korein,	Rawlins,	Wyoming.
Za-Ga-Zig,	Des Moines,	Iowa,	Aloha,	Honolulu,	Hawaiian Islands.
Kalurah,	Binghampton,	N. Y.,	Zenobia,	Toledo,	Ohio.
Karnak,	Montreal,	Canada,	El Mina,	Galveston,	Texas.

CHAPTER XVIII.

MISCELLANY.—INCIDENTAL TO THE HISTORY OF FREE MASONRY.

Unique Old Documents.—The Grand Mystery of the Free Masons as Revealed by an Outsider in 1725.—Examination of Craftsmen in the Olden Time.—Dr. Plotts' Account of the Free Masons.—The Four Crowned Martyrs.—Tomb of Adoniram at Saguntum.—Concerning King Canute, the Dane.—A Law of Edward VI., which Regulated Everybody's Business but his Own.—The Punishment of Cowans in the Fifteenth Century.—Kit Cotti's House, Its Symbolic Signification.—Bagdad, a Singular Old City Built by the Masonic Craftsmen.—Allahabad.—Masonic Marks on its Ancient Walls.—Satirical Lecture Given to a Young Craftsman in 1350.—Egyptian Origin of Free Masonry.—Relics of King Solomon's Temple.—Ancient Mexico, Its Mysteries.—Masonic Symbols Found in the Ruins of its Old Temples.—Ancient Peru, Its Hieroglyphics.—Free Masonry among the Aborigines of North America.

A MASON'S EXAMINATION IN 1723.*

WHEN a Free Mason is enter'd, after having given all present of the Fraternity a Pair of men and Woman's gloves and a Leathern Apron, he is to hear the. . . . belonging to the Society read to him by the Master of the Lodge. Then a Warden leads him to the Master and Fellows; to each of them he is to say,

> I fain would a Fellow-Mason be,
> As all your worships may plainly see.

After this, he swears to reveal no Secrets of the Worshipful Fraternity, on pain of having his Thr. ct, and having a double Porrion (portion) of Hl and Dmntn hereafter. Then he is blind-folded, and the ceremony of . . . is

---

* Gould, vol. vi., p. 487.

performed. After which he is to behold a Thousand different Postures and Grimaces, all of which he must exactly imitate, or undergo the Discipline till he does.

After this the word Mgh'bn is whispered by the youngest Mason to the next, and so on, till it comes to the Master, who whispers it to the entered Mason, who must have his face in due order to receive it. Then the Neophyte says what follows:

> An enter'd Mason I have been,
> Boaz and Jachin I have seen;
> A Fellow I was sworn most rare,
> And know the Astler, Diamond, and Square:
> I know the Master's Part full well,
> As honest Mgh'bn will you tell.

Then the Master says:

> If a Master-Mason you would be,
> Observe you well the rule of three;
> And what you want in Masonry,
> Thy mark and Mgh'bn makes thee free.

In 1827, Humber Lodge, No. 73, at Kingston-upon-Hull, laid the cornerstone of a new Masonic Hall. and the following were the questions and answers in the ceremony.

" I hereby, in the presence of these Worshipful Masters, Wardens, and Deacons, and in the presence of these Master Masons, worthy and diligent workmen of our secret Craft, do ask of you and of your company, if you know yourself at this time to have done anything contrary to the laws of Masonry which has not been told to the provincial authorities, and whereby you should be suspended from your work?

" W. M.—We are good Masons at this very time.

" D. P. G. M.—Have you among your company any brother guilty of brawlings, strife, and disobedience in open Lodge?

" W. M.—We have none, Right Worshipful Master.

" D. P. G. M.—Have you among your company any brother who in open Lodge is guilty of drunkenness, common swearing, or profane words?

MISCELLANY.

"W. M.—We have none, Right Worshipful Master.

"D. P. G. M.—Have you authority to do this day's work?

"W. M.—We have, Right Worshipful Master, and, with your permission, will here read it."

The authority was then read, the procession formed, and the corner-stone laid in ample form.

Signs to Know a True Mason.

1. To put off the hat with two fingers and a thumb.
2. To strike with the right hand on the inside of the little finger of the left three times, as if hewing.
3. By making a square, viz., by setting your heels together and the toes of both feet straight, at a distance, or by any other way of triangle.
4. To take hand in hand, with left and right thumbs close, and touch each wrist three times with the forefinger.
5. You must whisper, saying thus, The Masters and Fellows of the Worshipful Company from whence I came greet you all well.

The other will answer, God greet well the Masters and Fellows of the Worshipful Company from whence you came.

6. Stroke two of your forefingers over your eyelids three times.
7. Turn a glass, or any other thing that is hollow, downward after you have drunk out of it.
8. Ask how you do; and your Brothers drink to each other.
9. Ask what Lodge they were made Free Masons at.

The Grand Mystery of Free Masons.

The following was discovered in 1725, by a busy body, who hastened to announce it to the world.

"This piece having been found in the custody of a Free Mason, who died suddenly, it was thought proper to publish it in the very words of the copy, that the Public may, at last, have something Genuine concerning the Grand Mystery of Free Masons." Proceeding, we shall first present our readers with

The Free Masons' Signs,*

A, Guttural >   A, Pedestal Z   A, Manual <   A, Pectoral ×

Examination upon Entrance into the Lodge.

Peace be here.
Answer. I hope there is.
Q. What a-clock is it?
A. It's going to six, or going to twelve.
Q. Are you very busy?
A. No.
Q. Will you give, or take?
A. Both; or which you please.
Q How go squares?
A. Straight.
Q. Are you rich, or poor?
A. Neither.
Q. In the name of, etc., are you a Mason? What is a Mason?
A. A man born of a woman, brother to a King.
Q. What is a fellow?
A. A companion of a Prince.
Q. How shall I know you are a Free Mason?
A. By signs, tokens, and points of my entry.
Q Which is the point of your entry?
A. I hear and conceal, under the penalty of having my throat cut, or my tongue pulled out of my head.
Q. Where was you made a Free Mason?
A. In a just and perfect Lodge.
Q. How many make a Lodge?
A. God and the Square, with five or seven right and perfect Masons, on the highest mountains or the lowest valleys in the world.
Q. Why do odds make a Lodge?
A. Because all odds are men's advantage.
Q. What Lodge are you of?
A. The Lodge of St. John.
Q. How does it stand?
A. Perfect East and West, as all Temples do.

* Gould, vol. vi., p. 476.

Q. Where is the Mason's Point?
A. At the East window, waiting at the Rising of the Sun, to set his Men at Work.
Q. Where is the Warden's Point?
A. At the West window, waiting the Setting of the Sun, to dismiss the Entered Apprentices.
Q. Who rules and governs the Lodge, and is Master of it?
A. Irah, or the Right Pillar, Iachin.
Q. How is it governed?
A. Of Square and Rule.
Q. Have you the Key of the Lodge?
A. Yes, I have.
Q. What is its Virtue?
A. To open and shut, and shut and open.
Q. Where do you keep it?
A. In an Ivory Box, between my tongue and my teeth, or within my Heart, where all my Secrets are kept.
Q. Have you the Chain to the Key?
A. Yes, I have.
Q. How long is it?
A. As long as from my Tongue to my Heart.
Q. How many precious Jewels?
A. Three: a square Asher, a Diamond, and a Square.
Q. How many lights?
A. Three, a Right East, South, and West.
Q. What do they represent?
A. The Three Persons, Father, Son, and Holy Ghost.
Q. How many Pillars?
A. Two: Iachin and Boaz.
Q. What do they represent?
A. A Strength and Stability of the Church in all Ages.
Q. How many Angles in St. John's Lodge?
A. Four, bordering on Squares?
Q. How is the Meridian found out?
A. When the Sun leaves the South, and breaks in at the West end of the Lodge.
Q. In what part of the Temple was the Lodge kept?
A. In Solomon's Porch, at the West end of the Temple, where the two Pillars were set up.
Q. How many steps belong to a right Mason?
A. Three.

Q. Give me the Solution?
A. I will—The Right Worshipful, Worshipful Masters, and Worshipful Fellows, of the Right Worshipful Lodge from whence I came, greet you well.
Response. That Great God to us greeting, be at this our meeting, and with the Right Worshipful Lodge from whence you came, and you are.
Q. Give me the Jerusalem Word?
A. Giblin.
Q. Give me the Universal Word?
A. Boaz.
Q. Right Brother of ours, your Name?
A. N. or M.
Response. Welcome, Brother M. or N., to our Society.
Q. How many particular Points pertain to a Free Mason?
A. Three: Fraternity, Fidelity, and Taciturnity.
Q. What do they represent?
A. Brotherly Love, Relief and Truth among all Right Masons; for which all Masons were ordained at the Building of the Tower of Babel, and at the Temple of Jerusalem.
Q. How many proper points?
A. Five: Ft to foot, Kn to knee, Han to Hand, hrt to heart, and E to Ear.
Q. Whence is an Arch Deriv'd?
A. From Architecture.
Q. How many orders in Architecture?
A. Five: the Tuscan, Doric, Ionic, Corinthian, and Composite.
Q. What do they answer?
A. They answer to the Base, Perpendicular, Diameter, Circumference, and Square.
Q. What is the right word or right Point of a Mason?
A. Adieu.

The Free Mason's Oath.

You must serve God according to the best of your knowledge and Institution, and be a true Liege Man to the King, and help and assist any Brother as far as your Ability will allow. By the Contents of the Sacred Writ you will perform this Oath. So help you God.*

They cause him who is about to be received to swear that he will not reveal to father nor mother, wife nor children, priest nor clerk, not even in confession, that which he is about to do and witness; and for this purpose they choose a tavern, which they call "The Mother," because there it is that they usually assemble, as if at their common mother's, in which they choose two rooms conveniently placed for going from one into another, one serving for their ceremonies, and the other for the banquet. They close the doors carefully and the windows

* Gould, vol. vi., pp. 476–487.

in order not to be seen or surprised by any means. Secondly, they cause the candidate to elect sponsors (*un parrain et une marraine*); give him a new name, such as they may decide on ; baptize him and perform other ceremonies peculiar to the craft, according te their traditions.

Concerning King Canute.

In 1080, this doughty warrior made a pilgrimage to Rome. On the road he visited the most celebrated churches, leaving everywhere proofs of his devotion and liberality. On his return, he proceeded to Denmark, but dispatched the Abbot of Tavistock to England with a letter describing the object and issue of his journey. In this letter he says, " It is long since I bound myself by my vow to make this pilgrimage; but I had been hitherto prevented by affairs of state, and other impediments."

He concludes his letter as follows: " Lastly, I entreat all my bishops, and all the sheriffs, by the fidelity which they owe to me and to God, that the church dues, according to the ancient laws, may be paid before my return; namely, the *plow-arms*, the *tithes of cattle* of the present year, the *Peter-pence*, the *tithes of fruit* in the middle of August, and the *kirk-shot* at the feast of St. Martin, to the parish church. Should this be omitted, at my return, I will punish the offender by exacting the whole fine appointed by law. Fare ye well."

2 and 3 Edward VI., Chapter XV., a.d. 1548.

An Acte Towchinge Victuallers and Handycraftes Men.

Forasmuche as of late days diverse sellers of vittayles, not contented withe moderate and reasonable gayne but myndinge to have and to take for their vittayles so muche as lyste them, have conspyred and covented together to sell their vittells at unreasonable price ; and lykewise **Artificers** handycraftsmen and labourers have made confederacyes and pmyses (promises), and have sworn mutual othes, not onlye that they shoulde not meddle one withe anothers worke, and pforme (perform) and fynishe that another hathe begone, but also to constitute and appoynt howe muche worke they shoulde doe in a daye, and what howers and tymes they shall worke, contrarie to the Lawes and Statutes of this Realme, to the greate hurte and ympoverishment of the Kinges Majesties Subjectes.

1. For Reformacion thereof it is ordeyned and enacted by the Kinge, our Soveraigne Lorde, the Lords & Comons in this present Parliament assembled, and by the authoritie of the same, that yf any Bochers, Bruers, Bakers, Poulters, Cooks, Costerdmongers, or Frewterers, shall at any

tyme from and after the first day of Marche next comynge, conspire covennte promyse or make any othes that they shall not sell their vittelles but at certen prices; or yf any **Artificers** Workemen or Laborers doe conspire covennte or promyse together or make any othes that they shall not make or doe their workes but at a certeyne price and rate, or shall not enterprice or take upon them to fynishe that another hathe begone, or shall doe but a certen worke in a daye, or shall not worke but at certain howers and tymes, that then everie person so conspiring covenntinge swearinge or offendinge beinge laufullye convicte thereof by witnes confession or otherwise, shall forfeit for the first offence tenne pounds to the King's Highness, and yf he have sufficient to paye the same and doe also paye the same within sixe dayes next after his conviction, or ells shall suffer for the firste offence twentie dayes ymprisonment, and shall onely have bread and water for his sustenance; and for the seconde offence shall forfeyte twentie poundes to the Kinge, yf he have sufficient to paye the same and doe pay the same within sixe dayes next after his conviccion, or ells shall suffer of the seconde offence punyshement of the pillorye. (Statutes relating to the Free Masons, pp. 373, 374.)

The Cowan.

From the lectures in use in the fifteenth century, it appears that the following curious punishment was inflicted on a detected cowan: "To be placed under the eaves of the house in rainy weather, till the water runs in at his shoulders and out at his shoes."

The Four Martyrs, a.d. 284.

In the reign of the Emperor Diocletian, he ordered a temple to be erected to the Sun god Apollo, and went to the province of Pannonia and superintended the procuring and forwarding of metals to be used in the construction and adornment of the temple. Among the artisans whom he collected for the construction of this edifice were four skilled masons by the names of Claudius, Castorius, Symphorianus and Nicostratus. They had renounced Paganism and embraced Christianity. In the company with the four workmen, there worked another mason, by name Simplicius, who was a heathen. While working with the others he wondered to see how much they surpassed all the other artisans in skill and amount of work done. So finally, he went to Claudius and said: "Strengthen, I beseech thee, my tools, that they may no longer break." Upon which Claudius took them in his hands and said: "In the name of the Lord Jesus Christ, be these tools henceforth strong and faithful to their work." From this time Simplicius succeeded in all he attempted to do. Amazed at the change, Simplicius asked: "Was not this done by the god Zeus?" Claudius replied: "Repent, O my brother, of what thou hast said, for thou hast blasphemed God our Creator whom alone we worship. That which our hands have made, we do not recognize as a god." By such arguments Simplicius became converted and refused to sacrifice to the heathen gods.

Soon after the conversion of Simplicius, Diocletian issued an order that a statue of Apollo should be constructed out of marble. Therefore the philosophers and workmen began to consult upon the subject, particularly as to the kind of stone to be used, but at length decided upon a huge block of stone that had been brought from the Isle of Thasos. It appears however that the five Christian workmen objected not to the stone, but declined to work upon the idol. Then began the philosophers to rail against them, saying: "Why do ye not hearken to the commands of our devout Emperor Diocletian and obey his will?" To this, Claudius answered: "Because we cannot offend our Creator and commit a sin whereof we should be found guilty in his sight." Then said the philosophers: "From this it appears that you are Christians." And Claudius replied: "Truly we are Christians." Whereupon the philosophers selected other artisans and directed them to carve the statue. Then said the Emperor to the philosophers: "If your accusations be true, let them suffer the punishment of sacrilege." He then sent for the Tribune Lampadius and said to him, "If they refuse to offer sacrifice to the Sun god Apollo, let them be scourged with scorpions." For five days thereafter, Lampadius sat in his place before the Sun god and called on them by proclamation of the herald, and showed them many dreadful things and all sorts of instruments for the punishment of martyrs, and then said to them: "Hearken to me and avoid the doom of martyrdom, and be obedient to the mighty prince and offer sacrifice to the Sun god." But Claudius replied with great boldness, saying: "This let the Emperor Diocletian know: that we truly are Christians and never can depart from the worship of our God." Thereupon Lampadius, becoming enraged, caused them to be stripped and scourged with scorpions. While the barbarous punishment was being inflicted, a herald proclaimed that this was done because they had disobeyed the commands of the Emperor. Within the same hour Lampadius died on his seat of judgment. As soon as the Emperor heard of the death of Lampadius, he ordered leaden coffins to be made for the Christians and had them secured therein alive and thrown into the river. This order was obeyed and thus these faithful Masons suffered a terrible death for their principles.

Reference to these martyrs has been found not only in Roman art, but in the old sculpture and stained glass of Germany; their effigies are easily distinguished by the fact that they stand in a row bearing palms, with crowns upon their heads and with masonic implements at their feet.

Frederick II., King of Prussia, wrote in defence of Free Masonry, and upheld it against Roman Catholic Europe with all the influence and power of his position as a sovereign, and chief of the order. He considered the dissemination of Masonic principles to be of the utmost importance in securing the permanence of his empire. He required his nobles, and all persons occupying places of trust in his government, to become Free Masons.

Secrecy.

Origen, a noted ancient chronicler, born A.D. 135, in replying to Celsus, who charged that the Christians had a secret doctrine, said: "Inasmuch as the essential and important doctrines of Christianity are openly taught, it is foolish to object that there are other things that are recondite; for this is common to Christian discipline with that of those philosophers in whose teachings some things were exoteric and some esoteric; and it is enough to say that it was so with the disciples of Pythagoras."

Persecution in the Nineteenth Century.

In 1814, the spirit of Popery was again manifested by the appearance of an edict issued by Pope Pius. In this edict, His Holiness pronounces dire penalties, even to death, against all who are alleged to be Free Masons. As these persecutions were inspired as much by a desire for plunder as from bigotry, the Pope did not omit the usual clause—"confiscation of the victims' property." Simultaneously with the issuance of this edict, and almost identical with it, interdicts were proclaimed by the different rulers under Papal domination in Europe. The result of this onslaught against Free Masonry was the seizure and imprisonment of large numbers of Masons, and many of them were

Fortress and City of Allahabad.

subjected to tortures to compel confession and renunciation of the Masonic obligations; and not a few of those who remained true to their principles were put to death and their property confiscated. Yet, as the majority of the members were men of the better class, they were not only not intimidated by persecution, but in many places continued their meetings in a spirit of defiance against their persecutors, and ultimately overcame all opposition; so that at present there is hardly a civilized country remaining in which Free Masonry is not openly practised—even in Rome and within gunshot of the Vatican, lodges meet regularly.

Relics.

A celebrated piece of antiquity was recently standing near Maidstone, called Kit's Cotti House. This was a dark chamber of probation; for Kit is no other than Ked, or Ceridwen, the British Ceres; and Cotti or Cetti meant an ark or chest; hence the compound word referred to the Ark of the Diluvian God Noah, whose mysterious rites were celebrated in Britain; and Ceridwen was either the consort of Noah, or the Ark itself; symbolically the great mother of mankind. Mysteries, p. 235.

In rebuilding an ancient bridge, near Limerick, Ireland, there was found, under one of the stones, a brass square much corroded, having on its sides the following: " I. will. strive. to. Live. with. Love. & Care.—Upon. The. Leul. By. The. Square.—" expressing the Masonic idea of living on the level and by the square. The date was 1517. Mackey, p. 735.

Bagdad.

This singular old city was founded by the Calif Almansur, 762 A.D., on the site of ancient Ctesiphon. Almansur employed the Craftsmen of all nations that were convenient, and the work was pushed rapidly, especially on the mosques and other public edifices. The streets, and the exterior of the private buildings, do not present an inviting appearance, but many of the interiors demonstrate the great skill of the Masons of that period.

Allahabad (the Holy City).—Masons' Marks.

This ancient city is situated in the northwestern part of India. It contains several singular old monuments, elaborate and costly. What their original purpose was is uncertain, but they are fine examples of the work of the Craftsmen of the period. This city also had an ancient castle of great extent, which had lofty towers, and was a work of great strength when it fell into the hands of the English. In reconstructing a part of the works, Masonic marks and symbols were found on the blocks of red granite in the lower courses of the walls.

Tomb of Adoniram.

In Margoliouth's History of the Jews, we find the following legend: That early in the fifteenth century there was discovered at Saguntum, in Spain, a singular ancient tomb bearing the inscription: " This is the grave of Adoniram, the servant of King Solomon, who came to collect the duty."

The same historian says that subsequently, Villipandus being desirous of ascertaining if the account concerning the tomb was true, directed the students who resided at Murviedro, a small village on the ruins of Saguntum, to make strict search for the tomb. After a long and careful search the students discovered a mound, having in its side a stone bearing a Hebrew inscription nearly obliterated by time. This stone the natives held in great reverence, as they claimed that it was " The stone of Solomon's collector." But this being unsatisfactory, they continued the search, and by the aid of an old priest, discovered in the Cathedral a manuscript written in ancient Spanish, containing the following: " At Saguntum, in the citadel, in the year of our Lord 1480, was discovered a sepulchre of surprising antiquity, which contained an embalmed corpse—a mummy of a man of unusual stature. On the front of the sepulchre are two lines in ancient Hebrew signifying: 'The sepulchre of Adoniram, the servant of King Solomon, who came hither to collect tribute.' "

Sofism.

The Sofs are a secret sect that comprises many of the most erudite and influential men of the Orient. Their principal writers are familiar with the doctrines of Plato and Aristotle, and their works abound with quotations from those renowned philosophers. Sir John Malcom compares the school of Sofism to that of Pythagoras. The principal features of their ceremony of initiation are very similar to those of Free Masons. Their rites comprise four degrees.

Skoustusm.

In the first there is little besides an obligation of secrecy and religious instruction. In the second the candidate is received within the pale of Sofism. The third degree signifies wisdom, and he who receives it is supposed to have attained superior natural knowledge. The fourth is designated truth. In each degree there are secrets that are held to be sacred and inviolable.

As the origin of this order is placed as far back as the second century of Mohammedanism, the close coincidences of its rites and doctrines with those of Free Masonry, suggest the inquiry as to whether Sofism is not a branch of ancient Masonry.

The Chinese claim that they have occupied the same country from the creation of the world; and were it not for the modern improvements and discoveries in astronomy, we should be driven to the Bible alone to correct their chronological calendar. The celebrated Cassini, however, observing their account of a remarkable conjunction of the sun, moon, and other planets, which took place, according to *their* showing, immediately after the creation, or about six thousand years ago, calculated back, and proved that such a conjunction was visible in China 1812 B.C.—*in the time of Abraham.*

This people possessed a knowledge of architecture in an eminent degree, before they built the Great Wall; and have a very ancient order similar to the *ancient Masons.*

The Smith's Lecture.

SATIRICAL LECTURE GIVEN A YOUNG SMITH AT THE CONCLUSION OF THE CEREMONIES CELEBRATING THE TERMINATION OF HIS APPRENTICESHIP.

My son, I am to tell you much about craft usages, and even though you have forgotten more than I can tell, yet will I tell you what I know. I will tell you it is pleasant to wander, between Easter and Whitsuntide, when it is nice and warm, when the purse is well filled and the hose well darned, and the hair sticks up through the crown of the hat, then is it pleasant to wander. My son, if to-day or to-morrow you wish to wander, take a fine farewell of your master on Sunday afternoon, after meals and prayer, and not of a week day, for it is not craft usages to cease work during the week. And if you have served your time with him, speak thus: "I give you thanks for having helped me to an honorable craft; it stands to be repaid at the disposal of any of yours." Say not your disposal; for who has once been master is not accustomed willingly to resume his wanderings. But if you have only served him for weekly pay, then say: "Master, I thank you that you have been pleased to employ me so long; it stands to be repaid to any of yours to-day or to-morrow." Then go to your mistress and say: "Mistress, I thank you that you have kept me in washing so long; it stands to be repaid at the disposal of any of yours to-day or to-morrow." If you do not wish to carry your bundle to the tavern (house of call), but desire to leave it at your master's house, then speak to the master, and say thus: "Master, I wish to beg you to harbour my bundle for one night more."

My son, if to-day or to-morrow you wish to travel, go not alone out of the gates, but acquire a good name with the fellows; first stand a can of beer or wine; you may also ask the pipers and several fellows to accompany you beyond the gates to give you good convoy; and being come out before the gates, take three feathers in your right hand and blow them from you; one will fly to the right, the other to the left, the third straight ahead. Which one will you follow? If you follow the one to the right, it will perhaps fly over the wall back into the town, because you have a sweetheart there? But some Masons are bad fellows, they do not fasten the stones well, you might perchance fall down, and perhaps break your neck, and thus you would lose your young life—we our godson, and your father and mother their son—that would be bad for all three of us. No, my son! do not so. The other feather on the left will fly over a large sheet of water; if you follow it you may find probably a Bohemian cheese, or, as we say in German, a millstone; roll that into the water; if it swims across you can also follow, but if it falls to the bottom stay you behind, for it is perchance deep, and you might fall in and be drowned; and thus you lose your young life. Therefore, my son, do not this also. The third feather will fly straight ahead, so fine and crisp, follow you that (a lesson in prudence and perseverance). Thus you will arrive at a pond, and sitting around it you will see a crowd of green men, who will cry, "Croak, croak, croak." But you will say, "Why should I croak? I have not had much to croak over in my apprentice years;" therefore bother yourself not about it, but proceed straight on (courage and perseverance).

You will come to a mill, it will repeat always "turn again, turn again." But you will reflect, "Shall I turn again? Why, I have only just set out!" Do that not, but go right into the mill-wife. Speak thus to her: "Good day, dame mother, how goes your cow, has the calf fodder? How is your dog, and is the cat still well? How go your hens, do they still lay fine eggs? How are your daughters, have they still many swains?" Then the mill-wife will consider. "That is a polite son; he asks after all my small cattle; what will he not do for the great?" Then she will come quickly and fetch a ladder and mount to the pantry shelf, and reach you down a sausage. But let her not mount herself, but you mount for her and hand her down a string of them. But be not so rude as to seize the largest and cram it into your pocket, but wait till she give it to you. Having received one, thank her kindly and proceed bravely on your way. A mill-axe might be lying about, and you might be tempted to examine it and think if only I could also make such an axe; but the miller might be led to think you wished to steal it; therefore, do it not, and look not long about thee, for some millers are loose cards, and have, perhaps, behind the door an earwig, that is, a balance beam, and might lay it about your back. Therefore, be careful and go straight forward (a lesson in politeness and to avoid impertinent curiosity).

You will then come to a field, and the shepherd will watch the sheep, and the young ones will spring round about the old ones. "Ah," you will think, "if I were with my mother I would also spring about;" but ponder not thereon, only keep straight ahead, and you will come to a high hill, and you will think: "Almighty Lord, how shall I get my bundle up to the top of so high a hill?" But be not afraid, and help yourself. You will probably have a string or piece of whip-cord about you; the smiths have ever been fond of carrying a piece of whip-cord—take it and tie it to your bundle, and drag it behind you to the top. But let it not be too long, for in such high mountains there may be robbers who might perhaps cut the bundle off, and you would thus lose your goods. Having come to the top, you will not know how to get down the other side. "Dear Lord," you will say, "up it is; if it were only down again;" and you may, perhaps, take your bundle and roll it down the hill. But do that not, for there might be someone there to take the bundle, and you would lose your things. Better keep it between your shoulders, and then no one can take it up or down the hill. Having got to the bottom of the hill, you will be thirsty, and you will come to a spring and wish to drink; lay your bundle down and keep it not on your back, for the bundle might take a swing and carry you with it, and you would fall in and be drowned, and thus you would lose your young life. That do not, but put bundle down before you drink, yet place it not too far off, lest someone come and take it, and you thus lose your bundle (prudence, forethought). Having drunk your fill behave honourably; post no sentinel in the neighborhood, lest some honest man come to the same place and wish to drink; he would say what a common fellow has been here and left his true sign (Wahrzeichen) everywhere. Do it not (decency of behaviour).

Having drunk go straight on, and you will come to a green wood where the birds sing, young and old, and your young heart will be pleased, and you will also commence to sing. And probably a rich merchant in a scarlet velvet cloak will come riding past and say, "Good luck to ye! why so jolly, youngster?" Then say, "And why should I not be jolly? I have all my father's goods with me." He will then think you have a few thousand ducats on you, and propose an exchange, his red fox fur against your tattered coat. But exchange not at once, hesitate a little, and he will once more offer you the exchange. But do it not yet; but if he offer it a third time, exchange with him, but not too fast, nor give him your coat first, but let him give you his fox skin. For if you give him yours first he might up and away, for he has four legs and you only two, so you could not follow him. But if he gives you his red fox skin, throw him your tattered coat, and make yourself scarce with the fox fur, nor look about you too much, for when he shall have searched the torn coat and found no ducats, he might come back, take back his furs, and cut your neck in two (a lesson in worldly prudence, at the expense of strict morality). Having proceeded some distance further you will see a gallows-tree.

Will you be pleased or sorry at the sight? My son, you shall not be pleased thereat, neither shall you mourn as though you were fated to be hung on it, but you shall rejoice, inasmuch as you are then in the neighborhood of a town. For if you go further you will see it, and hear the hammers clang and the smiths sing, and your heart will rejoice that you are able to earn your bread. And it is customary that before some cities sentinels are placed, and when you are come unto the town and the sentry cries, "Whence come you?" do not give him the name of a place forty or fifty miles off, but the next town or the village where you passed the night. And they will ask you what craft you are of, and you may answer that you are a smith. They will then say, that you ought to bring a sign to the master in the town; and if you wish to enter the town, say, "Sirs, I pray you, keep my bundle for me, whilst I fetch a token from a master in the city." And you will be obliged to leave your bundle in the gate; give it to a sub-officer. And when you go into the city, go into the first smith's shop that you see, and pass no master by, and say, "Good-day, and good luck; God honour the craft, master and fellows;" and they will thank you and say, "Welcome, smith." And sometimes it is an old fellow who stands by the bellows and a young master by the hearth. Go to him who stands by the bellows, and say, "By your leave, let me ask, is that the master who stands by the hearth?" and he will put you right. After that speak to the master, "Master, I would beg you to give me a token, that I may pass my bundle through the gates." And the father (*i.e.*, master) will give you a token—a hammer, or a horseshoe, or a ring. Take the token and go to the gates, and show it and say, "Will that do?" and they will say, "Give it here;" but give it not, as they might plague you to give them a drink. But speak thus, "I would willingly stand you something, but have nothing myself." So take your bundle and go straight back to the master, and you may perhaps meet a small white animal, with a fine bushy tail—I call it a dog; and you will think, "What a fine feather that would make for my hat!" and you might take the token and throw it at the dog; but do not, for in these large towns are many deep wells and cellars; the token might fall into one, and the master say, "Who shall lend you a token if you bring it not back?" Therefore, go to the house and say, "By leave, that I may enter; good day and good luck; God honour the craft, master and fellows. Master, I would speak to you in the name of the craft, if you would let me lay my bundle down here, that I may go further with honour and God;" that is, if you do not wish to spend the night there. But if you desire to rest the night, then say, "Master, I would speak to you in the name of the craft, if you would harbour me and my bundle, that I may go further with God and honour;" and he will say, "Put it down." And you will already have the bundle hanging on one shoulder only; but carry it not into the room and hang it on the wall where the peasants hang their baskets, or the other lads may think you have many pence therein; and they may chaff you and say, "Smith, you must have lots of bread and bacon in your bundle, that you are afraid to put it down on the ground." But place it readily under the bellows or the hammer bench (humility and confidence); if the father loses not his hammer, you will not lose your bundle. And when they go to sup, be you ready to seat yourself at the door of the room. And if the father say, "Smith, come hither and partake," go not at once. But if he say again,

"Smith, come hither and partake," then go in and eat with them; but take not your seat directly at the top of the board, but seat yourself beside the stroke master, and when they begin, cut yourself a lump of bread, so that they can hardly see you behind it; and having eaten that, cut small pieces at a time, so that you may have finished at the same time as the others; for if the others were satisfied, and you had still a large piece of bread before you, the master would say, "Where have you learnt that—with the boors?" But if you are satisfied, put not up your knife before the others have finished, or they might say, "What a small-eating smith; he evidently wishes to shame us by eating so little." And if the father drink to you, you may also drink. If there is much in the cup you may drink deeply, but if there be only little you must drink very little. But if you have much coin you may drink it all up and say, "Can one have a messenger? I wish to pay for a can of beer."

Having eaten, they will go to rest; but say not to the dame mother or maid sister, "Where shall I sleep?" But wait, and she will surely conduct you to your chamber. Then untie one shoe-string, and re-tie the other; and if she go not then from you, take a wisp of straw and point to the door; and if she will not even then, why, take her to thee, embrace her, and kiss her twenty-four fold. And when morning breaks and the other fellows rise, do not you rise first, nor even with them, for they might think you wished to put them to shame, but remain in bed for another half-hour; but not too long, for if the master come intending to give thee work, and you were yet asleep, he might say, "That must be a lazy smith, he likes to sleep late. I can do that myself, and need no smith to help me." And being risen, go not at once to the kitchen and chat with the cook, but go first to the workshop and wash yourself, and take up a hammer and work bravely with the others. But if no hammer be there, take an axe; and if no axe, seize the crowbar and work away, and the master will think, "That is surely a trusty smith, him will I give work." And it will then be breakfast-time, and they will take you with them. Therefore, go in and partake; and having eaten, go to the master and return thanks, and say, "Master, I thank you that you have harboured me and my bundle, and for your food, and drink, and good will; it remains owing to be repaid to any of yours to-day or to-morrow." Say not, "to you," for who has once been master does not willingly resume his wanderings. Afterwards go to the lads and say, "By leave, my lads, I thank you for your donation and pledge; if to-day or to-morrow one or other comes to me where I am at work, I will pledge him in a can of beer or wine, as may be within my means, according to craft custom and usage." Then resume your journey. If the sentinel ask you, "Whither away?" answer him, "Who knows where the wind may carry me when I get outside?" Therefore, peg ahead and run a hole into the world, so large that a haystack would not fill it.

From Dr. Plot's Account of Free Masons.

"Into which Society, when any are admitted, they call a meeting, or Lodge, as they term it in some places, which must consist at least of five or six of the Ancients of the Order, whom the candidates present with gloves. This ended, they proceed to the admission of them, which chiefly consists in the communication of certain secret signs, whereby they are known to one another all over the nation, by which means they have maintenance whither ever they travel ; for if any man appear, though altogether unknown, that can shew any of these seignes to a Fellow of the Society whom they otherwise call an Accepted Mason, he is obliged presently to come to him, from what company or place soever he be in, nay, tho' from the top of a steeple (what hazard or inconvenience soever he run), to know his pleasure, and assist him ; viz., if he want work he is bound to find him some ; or if he cannot do that, to give him money, or otherwise support him till work can be had ; which is one of their articles. Gould, vol. iii., p. 164.

THE EGYPTIAN ORIGIN OF MASONRY.—THE MYSTERIES.

Translated from the French of M. Rhigellini.

Certain authors have supposed that the rites of Masonry are derived from the ceremonies and ancient Mysteries, which passed directly from Egypt and Phœnicia into Europe; others assert that Masonry took its birth in the schools of Pythagoras and Plato.

Whatever doubts may have been suggested by some writers regarding the antiquity of Free Masonry, we do not the less persist in believing that it had its cradle in the Egyptian Mysteries. This opinion is justified by the first three degrees called Blue Masonry; the ceremonies, the instructions, and the results are the same; everything is alike, notwithstanding the difference of the machines which were at the disposal of the initiating priests of antiquity, of the period of time which they employed in the preparation of the neophyte, and of that which was necessary for the study of those sciences to whose nomenclature alone the masonic initiation is limited.

All historians, ancient and modern, are of the opinion that Egypt was once the cradle of the arts and sciences, and, as the learned Dupuis has demonstrated, that contemporary nations thence derived their religious and political opinions. As a tree old as the world itself, Egypt has raised her majestic head from out of the chaos of eternity, and enriched all parts of the earth with her fruit; she has extended her roots to posterity, under different forms, apparently changed and heterogeneous, but ever constant in essence, *and sent down, even to our own days*, her religion, her morals, and her sciences.

The Magi of Persia, the Greek philosophers, the Jewish priests, or the twelve patriarchs who preceded Moses, during the captivity in Egypt, all learned from the Egyptian priests their doctrines, their Mysteries, and their science, with the art of governing the people in accordance with their moral dispositions, their civilization, and the nature of their climate.

These Mysteries and these sciences were carefully guarded and taught by the priests, who were exclusively intrusted with their control; and, to prevent men without character, firmness of purpose, or intelligence from being admitted to them, they established a law that all initiates should be subjected to the trials of the four elements—trials so severe that the fact of their existence would be incredible to us, did we not find detailed descriptions of them in many ancient and modern writers. *These trials were intended to secure an assurance of the courage, morality, and intelligence of the neophyte, and to repel slaves and the dregs of the people.*

We preserve in the Masonic trials of initiation at the present day the ancient names of the voyages to which the candidate was subjected at his initiation in the Mysteries; and we also preserve the Egyptian inscription, which is read on the sarcophagus of Hiram, in the vault at the admission into the sublime degree of Knight of Kadosch: " Whoever has made these voyages alone, and without fear, will be purified by fire, by water, and by air, and having overcome the dread of death, and having his soul prepared to receive the light, will be permitted to issue from the bosom of the earth, and be admitted to the revelation of the great Mysteries.

The initiate was naked, and wore only an apron in front. He was naked, to teach him that he should, in perfect frankness, permit his most secret thoughts to be unveiled. He was deprived of all profane ornaments, as well as of every metal, to remind him, by this deprivation, that his new condition demanded of him the practice of virtue, and that gold and other precious things were almost always the instruments of human corruption, as iron was of human revenge. We will not here descend to any minute details of the Masonic initiation, as every brother will readily recognize their type in these ceremonies. But let us hope that after these considerations, it will become evident that the object of our meetings is something more than the enjoyment of sumptuous banquets, and that they are intended to promote an elevated and useful moral and theosophic purpose.

The neophyte, after having surmounted the first obstacles—after having descended into the mysterious well, and passed through the sacred vault—was still permitted, if he chose, to retrace his steps; but this was no longer the case after he had passed the gate defended by the three guards. These guards were armed priests, wearing helmets, which represented the heads of animals, symbolic of the mysteries which they were then celebrating. The helmet was in the form of the head of a cock or a serpent, if the Mysteries were those of Osiris or the sun; of an ox, if the Mysteries were those of Apis; and of a dog, if they were those of Anubis.

The neophyte, having passed this gate, could no longer return. If firmness now failed him in the trials which he was to undergo, he spent the remainder of his life in apartments attached to the temple, where, however, he could yet, by zealous efforts, arrive at the rank of a subaltern officer.

In the Masonic initiation, which is a faithful imitation of the Egyptian, there is a period of time when the alternate is offered to the candidate of withdrawing or of going forward.

Every man could present himself for the Egyptian initiation, but all were not admitted without distinction; a regulation which was subsequently adopted by the Greeks, the primitive Christians, and the Masons.

We learn that Nero, in his voyage to Greece, visited the temple of Eleusis, and expressed a desire to participate in the Mysteries; but the voice of the herald forbade him to enter; he respected the command, and retired. This same Nero, afterward passing by Delphos, wished to interrogate the oracle. The pythoness loaded him with reproaches, and classed him as a matricide with Alcmæon and Orestes. Nero was so enraged at this, that having determined to put an end to the oracle, he caused several men to be slain, and their blood shed at the mouth of the cave, after which he ordered it to be closed.

The hierophant in the Egyptian Mysteries represented the Creator; he wore across his breast a plate, on which these words were engraved—Truth, Wisdom, Science; his vest was of embroidered purple; a diadem of brilliant stones, which formed characters explaining the power of God, adorned his forehead, and in the performance of the ceremonies he was clothed in a garment of white linen, fastened by a girdle of various colors.

When an initiate was admitted to the greater Mysteries, he became a priest, and then all deceptions ceased. The instructions consisted in teaching him the weakness of humanity, the abstruse operations of nature, the course of the stars, and the order of the universe. The knowledge of these things necessarily brought the candidate to a recognition of the Grand Architect of the Universe. The illusions of mysterious ceremonies were now at an end; the acolyte was henceforth subjected only to an explanation of certain truths, undoubted and general in their nature, and which were founded on the purest philosophy.

In all the rites of Masonry, and especially in Ecossaism and the degrees which are derived from it, the formalities of the Egyptian ceremonial trials have been preserved; the instruction is the same, the result to which they lead is the same, with this difference, that the ancient priests of initiation constituted a part of the government, were, indeed, its very life and soul, and owned large possessions annexed to their temples, where the common people had no right to enter. The priests, by their power and their physical knowledge, could control the character of their candidates, for initiation was the basis of the ancient religions, as it is of that of Masonry.

The kings of Egypt often exercised the functions of the priesthood; and they were initiated into the sacred science as soon as they attained the throne. So at Athens, the first magistrate, or archon-king, superintended the Mysteries. This was an image of the union that existed between the priesthood and royalty, in those early times when legislators and kings sought, in religion, a potent political instrument.

Cicero says that the initiates not only received lessons which made life more agreeable, but drew from the ceremonies happy hopes for the moment of death. Socrates says that those who were so fortunate as to be admitted to the Mysteries, possessed, when dying, the most glorious hopes of eternity. Aristides says that "they not only procure the initiates consolations in the present life, and means of deliverance from the great weight of their evils, but also the precious advantage of passing after death to a happier state.

Seneca, comparing philosophy to initiation, says that the most sacred ceremonies could be known to the adepts alone; but that many of their precepts were known even to the profane. Such was the case with the doctrine of a future life, and a state of rewards and punishments beyond the grave. The ancient legislators clothed this doctrine in the pomp of a mysterious ceremony, in mystic words and magical representations, to impress upon the mind the truths they taught, by the strong influence of such scenic displays upon the senses and imagination.

Entrance to the temples was forbidden to all who had committed homicide, even if it were involuntary. So it is stated by both Isocrates and Theon, that Magicians, who pretended to be possessed by evil spirits, were excluded from the sanctuaries. Even impious person and criminal was rejected; and Lampridius states that before the celebration of the Mysteries public notice was given, that none need apply to enter but those against whom their conscience uttered no reproach, and who were certain of their own innocence.

Orpheus, author of the Grecian Mysteries, which he carried from Egypt to Greece, consecrated the symbol (the mystic egg); and taught that matter, uncreated and informous, existed from all eternity, unorganized as chaos; containing in itself the principles of all existences confused and intermingled— light with darkness, the dry with the humid, heat with cold; from which it, after long ages, taking the shape of an immense egg, issued the purest matter, or first substance, and the residue was divided into the four elements, from which proceeded heaven and earth, and all things else. This grand cosmogonic idea he taught in the Mysteries; and thus the hierophant explained the meaning of the mystic egg seen by the initiates in the sanctuary.

Says Creuzer: "In the Orphic and Bacchic sects, in the Eleusinian and Samothracian Mysteries, was treasured up the secret doctrine of the old theological and philosophical myths, which had once constituted the primitive legendary stock of Greece in the hands of the original priesthood and in the ages anterior to Homer. The Mysteries of Greece were thus traced up to the earliest ages, and represented as the only faithful depositories of that purer theology and physics which had been originally communicated, though under the unavoidable inconvenience of a symbolical expression, by an enlightened priesthood.

"To form symbols and to interpret symbols were the main occupation of the ancient priesthood."*

* American Masonic Quarterly Review, vol. ii., pp. 81–455.

RAMESES II.

RAMESES III. 1300 B.C.

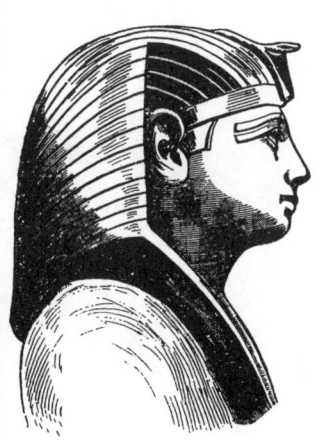
THOTMES III. 1500 B.C.

SHESHONK I.—(SHISHAK). 960 B.C.

HEADS OF EGYPTIAN KINGS.

MISCELLANY.

THE RELICS AND REMAINS OF THE TEMPLE.—THE OLD QUARRIES.

FROM "TENT LIFE IN THE HOLY LAND," BY WILLIAM C. PRIME.

"Most visitors of Jerusalem have mentioned the vast caverns under the northeastern part of the city, but few have found their way into them, and the statement is, by many, regarded as apocryphal.

"Moses, servant in the house of Antonio, had, at some time, visited them, and volunteered as a guide. We formed a party one afternoon, and sallied out of the Damascus gate, near which on the east is the entrance to these subterranean halls, which in extent, height, and depth surpass all that has been hinted at concerning them.

"Turning short to the right as we left the gate, and following the city wall to the point where it crosses a high precipitous bluff of rock, we found a small dark hole under this bluff itself.

"Lying on my face and entering, feet first, the narrow hole, just large enough to admit my body, I pushed myself in some six feet, and then found my feet unsupported, so that advancing slowly, I at length bent my legs downward, and with due discretion dropped into the arms of Moses, who stood ready to receive me. Having helped in the other gentlemen and Rev. Dr. Bonar, of Scotland, who had joined us at the Damascus gate, we advanced a few steps, when we found ourselves on the edge of the earth, described as filling up the mouth of the cavern. It now fell off at such an angle that we slid rather than walked down the sharp descent of thirty or forty feet, and found ourselves in a mighty cavern, with a magnificent roof far over us, and vast pillars of unhewn rock supporting it.

"Nearly, or quite all, that part of Jerusalem which lies north of the Via Dolorosa and east of the Damascus gate, leading therefrom to the old bath at the corner of the Via Dolorosa, stands on arches or pillars of rock in this subterraneous cavern. The floor is irregular, often having deep pits, out of which blocks of stone had been taken. The total descent in the deepest part must be, at least, a hundred and fifty feet.

"There was one deep excavation, in the white stone, the deepest in the whole cavern, at the bottom of which we found the bones of a skeleton, the remains of a man who was missing for many years from his home in the city, and who was at length found here, where he had evidently fallen from the lofty side which hung a hundred feet above the pit.

"In one place, nearly under the line of the street of the Damascus gate, we found water, clear, limpid, and bright, trickling, drop by drop, from the wall into a sort of rock basin. But I have seldom tasted a more vile stuff than it was. Although filtered as clear as crystal, it was the wash of the street, if not a worse drain from above, and in no sense a living spring. That the whole was a *quarry* was amply evident. The unfinished stone, the marks of places whence many had been taken, the galleries, in the ends of which were marked out the blocks to be cut, and the vast masses cut but never removed, all showed sufficiently the effect of the cutting.

But date or inscription we looked in vain for, and conjecture is left free here. I wandered hour after hour, through the vast halls, seeking some evidence of their origin.

"One thing, to me, is very manifest. There has been solid stone taken from the excavation sufficient to build the walls of Jerusalem and the Temple of Solomon. The size of many of the stones taken from here appears to be very great. I know of no place to which the stone can have been carried but to these works, and I know no other quarries in the neighborhood from which the great stone of the walls would seem to have come. These two connected ideas impelled me strongly toward the belief that this was the ancient quarry whence the city and Temple were built.

Specimens of the Work.

"In the wall that bounds the temple enclosure on the east, and which overhangs the valley of Jehoshaphat, there are built many *pieces* of *columns*, laid on the wall, with the *round ends projecting* like cannon, and built in as the wall was laid up. Three of these are side by side not far from the tower and projection known as the Golden gate, and from their character and location there is no reason to doubt that *they formed a portion of the walls of the Temple.* The commonly received opinion is, that they were columns of the gate which was called Beautiful. Travellers have hammered at these until the ends are mere projecting globes, and without hammer or chisel it is impossible now to procure pieces.

Stones from the Temple.

"Before it was quite dark we visited another part of the western wall of the area of the mosk and ancient temple, which is now very properly known by the name of its discoverer— as Robinson's Arch—and with which the name of that distinguished scholar will be forever connected as a monument of his learning and research.

"The huge stones which form this broken relic of a great arch were often noticed, as, doubtless, portions of the ancient temple walls, but no one, till Dr. Robinson's visit in 1842, imagined them to be, what he immediately named them, the remains of the great bridge which Josephus describes as connecting Zion and the temple.

"One of the stones is crumbling to pieces; and a broken piece of this, which I added to my collection of relics, I think myself safe in believing, without doubt, a part of the identical walls of the ancient temple—possibly, of the Temple of Solomon.

"In closing this chapter, I may add, by way of answer to the repeated queries that all men make about Jerusalem, that there are many portions of the wall, that inclosed the temple courts, still standing; and there is no reasonable doubt whatever that they have never been moved since they were originally laid.

"On the eastern side of the enclosure, the wall that overhangs the valley of Jehoshaphat is largely composed of immense blocks of stone, some of which I found to measure twenty-three feet by five and a half, and their thickness that of the wall, from five to seven feet. These stones are evidently of ancient times and in ancient positions. Of the relics of those times, within the sacred enclosure, I shall speak in another chapter. When I come to speak of the topography of ancient Jerusalem, I shall remark on the common error that supposes that Jerusalem was overthrown and demolished by Titus. For the present it is enough to say that the prophecy of Christ, which is often referred to, of the total demolition of the stone structures of the temple, if at all literal, had reference only to the buildings themselves, which are now gone ; **but** parts of the ***enclosing walls,*** and ***the crypts*** that formed the foundations of the **southern** parts of the temple, ***remain to this day.***

THE ROCK OF THE TEMPLE.—DOME OF THE ROCK.

"There has been no age of the world, since the time of David, when there have not been hearts yearning toward the rock of the temple. No period when, somewhere on its broad surface, there have not been men dying with faces turned thitherward, and dim eyes gazing through tears or through the films of death, to catch, with the first power of supernatural vision, the longed-for view of the threshing-floor of the Jebusite, the holy of holies of Solomon. Blessed were our eyes that, in the flesh, beheld the spot where the daily incense was wont to be offered, where the ark of God for so many generations rested, where the cherubim overhung the altar, and the visible glory of Jehovah was wont to be seen by the eyes of sinful men.

"Jews and Mohammedans alike believe in the sacredness of this rock, and the former have faith that the ark is within its bosom now. It is a faith that needs not much argument to sustain. I know not why we should believe that the rod of Aaron and the pot of manna, that were so long preserved, should have been suffered to go to dust at last ; nor can I assign any date to such a change in the miraculous intentions of God. It is pleasant to believe that somewhere, on or in the earth, these relics of his terrible judgments as well as of his merciful dealings, are preserved ; and I am not disposed to dispute the Jew, who believes them to be in the rocky heart of Es-Sukhrah."

ANOTHER ACCOUNT OF THE GREAT QUARRY

is furnished by Dr. Barclay, an American missionary at Jerusalem, in his work entitled "The City of the Great King." (See the American *Quarterly Review,* vol. i., pp. 514, 515.)

While a resident of the Holy City, having heard vague accounts of an immense cavern beneath the city, he was constantly on the alert to gain any information that might lead to the precise locality of this interesting place. On walking around the northern wall, immediately opposite the cave of Jeremiah (as long the jealous eye of the Turk would allow, in the immediate vicinity of the Damascus gate, which is kept under constant guard), his attention was attracted by his dog, apparently on the scent for game or food, for which he forthwith commenced active mining operations with his forepaws, and soon effected an entrance. No time was lost in crawling in, feet foremost, through a narrow hole, barely large enough to admit the body. A complete exploration of this gigantic artificial quarry occupied the entire night. The plot shows it to be more than a thousand feet in circumference, with immense labyrinthine halls, having their roofs supported by pillars, apparently left for that purpose, and galleries and crypts, in the end of which were visible the marked blocks to be cut, as well as several large masses, prepared but never removed. Above a beautiful pellucid little pool of brackish and bitter water, may be seen petrified stalactites, that sparkle like chandeliers in a brilliantly-lighted ball-room, when exposed to the light of the flambeaux. Small pieces of crockery were also observed, beautifully encrusted in sparry deposits. In the southern end of the quarry was found a most singular skull, now in the Academy of Natural Sciences in this city. Imagination is left free in assigning to this person a locality, or unravelling the mystery of his death. Who can say but that the bleached hand of this adventurous explorer, three thousand years ago,

"Held, by Solomon's own invitation,
A torch at the great temple's dedication."

On comparing some of the chippings of the blocks in the cave with the huge stones in the temple wall, the origin of these immense stones, and the means by which Hiram, the great Phœnician architect, placed them in this position in the temple, by rolling them down the inclined plane, is at once made apparent. Is not this fact also explanatory of what Ezra mentions in relation of some of the large rocks in the temple, repaired by Zerubbabel, which he calls the stones of rolling?

The Famous Columns in Arabia.

According to Diodorus, there were two columns erected near Nysa, in Arabia, where, it was said, were two of the tombs of Osiris and Isis. On one was this inscription: " I am Isis, Queen of this country. I was instructed by Mercury. No one can destroy the laws which I have established. I am the eldest daughter of Saturn, most ancient of the gods. I am the wife and sister of Osiris the King. I first made known to mortals the use of wheat. I am the mother of Orus, the King. In my honor was the city of Bubaste built. Rejoice, O Egypt, rejoice, land that gave me birth! . . ." And on the other was this: " I am Osiris the King, who led my armies into all parts of the world, to the most thickly inhabited countries of India, the North, the Danube, and the Ocean. I am the eldest son of Saturn; I was born of the brilliant and magnificent egg, and my substance is of the same nature as that which composes light. There is no place in the universe where I have not appeared, to bestow my benefits and make known my discoveries." The rest was illegible.

ANCIENT MEXICO.

As Masonic emblems have been found engraved on stones among the ruins of temples in Mexico, it is believed that the ancient Americans practised rites and ceremonies similar to those of ancient Masons. Therefore a brief sketch of the early history of Mexico and its temples will be of interest here.

The history of Mexico commenced with the arrival of the Toltecs in Anahuac, between the fifth and sixth century. For nearly four hundred years the Toltecs lived in peace and prosperity. But misfortunes came: famine, wars, and disasters drove them from their homes, and they migrated southward to Yucatan, where they communicated many of the arts they had elaborated in Anahuac.

It is generally admitted that the Toltecs were descended from the Esquimaux, and that the Aztecs were allied to the Red Indians.

The conquerors, or at least the successors, of the Toltecs in Mexico were the Aztecs, whose greatest period of prosperity was immediately before the Spanish conquest.

In Yucatan there is a different race, but whether they were originally Caribs cannot be ascertained. In Peru there is a strongly developed Polynesian element.

The account of the domestic animals and other important details given by Hoei Shin when he returned to China, in 499, points to Vancouver's Island or the coast in that vicinity as the place described by him. From this and other evidences, there is no doubt but that Northern America was in communication with Northern Asia as early at least as the fifth century.

Advancing eastward from the Valley of the Euphrates, the forms of art are found to be more and more like those of Central America. At Suku, in Java, there is a teocalli (temple) which is almost identical with that of Tehuantepec. In Cambodia there are teocallis at Bakong and Bakeng.

The principal monuments in the Valley of Mexico are the teocallis, built in *terraces* and surmounted by a temple.

The largest and the oldest of the teocallis is that of Cholulu. Its dimensions are nearly 1,440 feet square by 177 feet in height. It has four stories or stages, which are surmounted by a temple.

The Egyptian and Assyrian pyramids were likewise built in stages or terraces, and the upper platform was crowned by a chamber, or temple.

Notwithstanding this, however, there are a few monuments in Mexico, like that at Mitla, which are entirely original.

YUCATAN.

In Central America also, remarkable ruins have been discovered, notably at Kabah, Uxmal, Palenque, and Chichen Itza.

These ruins belonged to a people whose architecture was in many respects similar to that of the East.

At Palenque there is a pyramid which is nearly 280 feet square, and 60 feet in height. It is surmounted by a temple, 76 feet wide in front and 25

RUINS AT CHICHEN ITZA.

feet deep, ornamented in stucco with basso-relievo. In it were large hieroglyphical tablets, whose decipherment would doubtless reveal the history of these buildings and afford a clue to the history of their builders.

At the time of the conquest of Peru by the Spanish, the twelfth descendant of Manco Capac was on the throne, but his father having married a

REMAINS OF THE HOUSE OF MANCO CAPAC, CUZCO.

woman of the Indian race, the purity of the Inca blood was considered tarnished, and civil war ensued, which greatly aided the Spanish conquest.

CHRONOLOGY.

	Dates. A.D.
Toltecs arrived in Anahuac	648.
Toltecs abandoned the country	1051.
Chichemecas arrived	1170.
Acolhuans arrived about	1200.
Aztecs reached Tula	1196.
City of Mexico founded	1125.
Almitzolt conquered Guatemala beginning of the 16th century.	
Spaniards arrived	1519.

THE MASONIC MYSTERIES OF THE INDIANS.

FROM HISTORY OF FREE MASONRY IN NEW YORK.

It is a fact well known in the history of the American Indians that they held their secret societies in great reverence. These societies were of a nature to show that they originated in an old and high state of civilization, that must have come from the Eastern hemisphere. They were bound by mystic ties and possessed an esoteric knowledge, which they carefully concealed from all but the initiated. A native minister who had been initiated, stated that the number of members was limited to fifteen, of whom six were to be of the Seneca tribe, five of the Oneidas, two of the Cayugas, and two of the St. Regis. They all claim that their institution has existed from time immemorial. The place and time of their meetings were kept secret, and their proceedings were shrouded in mystery.

Brinton, in "The Myths of the New World," informs us that among the red race of America the priests formed societies of different grades of illumination, only to be entered by those willing to undergo trying ordeals, whose secrets were not to be revealed under the severest penalties.

"The Algonkins had three such grades—the *waubeno*, the *meda*, and the *jossakeed*, the last being the highest. To this no white man was ever admitted. All tribes appear to have been controlled by these secret societies. Alexander von Humboldt mentions one, called that of the Botuto, among the Indians of the Orinoco, whose members were compelled to vow celibacy, and submit to severe scourgings and fasts. The Collahuayas of Peru were a guild of itinerant magicians, who never remained permanently in one spot.

The traditions and legends of the American Indians reach back to a remote antiquity, and the traditions most revered are those concerning their secret society—a society whose internal workings are very similar to those of Free Masonry. George Copway, one of the chiefs of the Ojibways, was very intelligent, highly educated, and well versed in Indian history and traditions. He was also a member of the Masonic Fraternity. His lectures in 1851, on the history, religion, and mysteries of the Indians, were so interesting, and so eloquently delivered, that he drew crowded and select audiences who listened with profound attention, especially the more learned of the Masonic Fraternity. He stated that the medicine men of the tribes excelled, not merely in knowledge of medicine, but they were the *religious* teachers and *prophets* of the nation; that they were members of a fraternity who were under the strictest obligations of secrecy, and passed through four degrees in their advancement. He further asserted that the secret elements of the Masonic institution had long been known among the Indians of America. From his account it appeared that the *medicine* men were the *Grand Masters* of their secret societies, and that the advanced members had a symbolic badge which was worn nearest the skin on the left breast. This served as a diploma—a talisman and mystic voucher of his character and standing in the order whereever he went. An emblem like this was worn among all of the most intelligent of the Indian tribes.

That these aboriginal Masons had some conception of the Masonic sign of distress is shown by several singular incidents in the early history of this country. Francis Lewis, chaplain in a military expedition to Port Royal, S. C., and father of General Morgan Lewis, Grand Master of Masons of New York from 1830–1843, was taken captive in the French war by some Tuscarora Indians and condemned to death. These Indians, from their dialect, appeared to be of *Welsh* descent; and upon being given the sign of distress, and addressed in the *native Welsh* language, a sachem recognized the secret appeal and saved his life.

Among the practices of these societies, similar to those of Free Masonry, is that of circumambulation round the council or Lodge-room, which are always of an oblong square form. The procession moved in Indian file, following the course of the sun, and stopped at the east end of the room, where the three oldest chiefs were seated, dressed in the most *ancient* costume of the nation. Of these chiefs questions were asked and answers returned each time round. The procession consisted of nine, two of whom were the bearers of a sacrifice to the Great Spirit, whom they recognize as their Creator, Governor, and Benefactor.

Eli S. Parker was grandson of the renowned Red Jacket, and highly educated. At a banquet in a Western city, he said: "I am almost the sole remnant of what was once a noble race, which is as rapidly disappearing as the dew before the morning sun. I found my race wasting away, and I asked myself, 'Where shall I find home and sympathy, when our last council-fire is extinguished?' I said, 'I will knock at the door of Masonry, and see if the white race will recognize me, as they did my ancestors, when we were strong and the white man weak.' I knocked at the door of the Blue Lodge, and found brotherhood around its altar; I went before the great light in the

Chapter, and found companionship beneath the Royal Arch. I entered the Encampment, and found there valiant Sir Knights willing to shield me without regard to race or nation."

After a brief pause he continued: "I have in my possession a memento which I highly prize. I wear it near my heart. It came from my ancestors to me as their successor in office. It was a present from Washington to my grandfather, Red Jacket, when our nation was in its infancy. You will be glad to see and handle it." He then drew from his bosom a large oval medal, about seven inches by five, and it was eagerly sought for, and passed from hand to hand along the tables. On one side of this medal were engraved the figures of two chiefs, Red Jacket, in costume, presenting the pipe of peace, and Washington, with right hand extended, in the act of receiving it. On the other side the *Masonic emblems* with the date 1792.

INDEX.

A

	PAGE
Astronomy	79
Architecture	89
Assyria	101
Arch	103
Architecture, Grecian	103
Architecture, Roman	109
Architecture, Byzantine	114
Architecture, Gothic	126
Alaric, the Goth	209
Attila, the Hun	209
Anglo-Saxons	279
Ashmole, Elias	296
Athelstan	376
Aberdeen, Lodge of	399
Arbroath Seal	421
Asia—Free Masonry	452
Africa—Free Masonry	456
Algeria	457
Australasia	458
America	461
Ancients, Athol Warrant	467
Alabama, its First Lodge	531
Abraxas	567
Astronomical Royal Arch	584
A. & A. Scottish Rite	592
A. & A. Scottish Summary	611
Antioch	629, 651, 664
Acre	653, 667
Allahabad	695
Adoniram	696

B

Boadicea	263
Burns, Robert	409
Belgium	422
Bombay	452
Bengal	452
Brazil	550
Buenos Ayres	551
Battle of Dorylæum	629
Battle of Hattin	647
Bendocdar	663
Bagdad	695

C

Cabiri of Samothracia	33
Cathedrals	134
Cedars of Lebanon	158
Colleges of Builders	182
Constitutions, Strasburg	215
Charter of Cologne	230
Compagnons, France	254
Cæsar in England	262
Caractacus	263
Carrausius	267
Constantinus	268
Canterbury Cathedral	283
Chichester Cathedral	293
Charges, etc., in 14th Century	333
Charges, etc., in 1723	340
General Regulations, 1723	346
Culdees	396
China	456
Ceylon	456
Cape of Good Hope	458
Connecticut, its first Lodges	502
California	535
Colorado	538
Colored Masons	541
Canada, Severance from the Grand Lodge of England	545, 546
Chili	553
Captivity, the	576
Clermont, Chapter of	592
Cerneau—his Patent	604-608
Crusades	620
Crusaders take Antioch	629
Crusaders take Jerusalem	632
Crusades, a List of	668
Cyprus	670
Cassan Cham	669

D

Degrees in the Mysteries	25, 30
Dionysian Mysteries and Architects	33
Dome	103
Dedication of K. S. Temple	164
Dome of the Rock-Mosque	169
Druids of England	275
Denmark	440
Delaware	524
Dominion of Canada	542
Dermott	573
Darius, his Castle	583
De La Motta	595, 598
Degrees, eight additional	596
Degrees, Classification of	597
Damietta	657
De Molai	669
De Molai, his Martyrdom	673

E

Egyptian Mysteries	19
Eleusinian Mysteries	26
Essenes	37
England	262
Edwin, King of England	376
Edinburgh Lodge, No. 1	405
Emperors of the East and West	592

F

First Temples of Egypt	41
France	242
Free Mason, Origin of the Term	295

INDEX.

Free Masonry, its Spread over the Eastern Hemisphere 422
Frederick III., Last Days of 437
France, Free Masonry in. 441
Franklin, Benjamin...... 491
Freeman's Tavern, Washington's Headquarters, and Masonic Lodge Room................ 509
Florida................ 524
Four Martyrs, the....... 688

G

Gnostics 33
Grecian Architecture 103
Guilds................. 197
Germany 199–240
Guilds in Britain........ 287
Grand Lodge, 1717...... 303
Grand Masters—England. 315
Germany—Free Masonry. 427
Greece—Free Masonry .. 451
Georgia 512
Gourgas 598
Gaudini 669

H

Houses, Egyptian....... 99
Hiram, Abif............ 169
Hiram's Tomb.......... 175
Halliwell MSS.......... 323
Harleian MSS 331
Holyrood Abbey 414
Holland 423
Humber Lodge......... 682

I

Interiors of Cathedrals... 131
Ireland, Free Masonry in. 362
Italy, Free Masonry in... 449
Indiana................ 528
Illinois 534
Iowa 534
Idaho 538
Indian Territory 541
Indians, American, and Ancient Masonry...... 717

J

Judgment of the Dead... 52
Jacques, Maître......... 257
Japan 456
Jerusalem taken by the Crusaders............ 632
Jerusalem taken by Saladin.................. 650
Jerusalem taken by the Templars 660

K

Karnak................ 95
Kentucky 526
Kansas 537
Knights Templars...619, 632
Knights Hospitalers..... 636
Kharizmians........... 661
King Canute 687

L

Lombardy 211
Lansdowne MSS 325
List of old MSS......... 338
Landmarks, Ancient..... 361
Liberia 457
Lafayette 605
Louisiana.............. 625
Latin Kingdom......... 638

M

Mysteries, Egyptian and Greek 24–26
Mithraism 34
Meydoun Monument 90
Martel, Charles 244
Macbeth............... 395
Melrose Abbey 397
Malta 451
Madras................ 455
Morocco............... 457
Massachusetts, its First Lodges 497
Maryland 524
Missouri, its First Lodges 525
Michigan 528
Mississippi............. 528
Maine 531
Minnesota 537
Montana............... 541
Manitoba.............. 547

Mexico............547–715
Marks of the Builders.... 563
Morin 593
Morin, his Patent....... 601
Martyrdom of the Templars 672
Masters of the Templars from 1113 to 1838..... 674
Masons' Examination in 1723 681
Mystery of Free Masons.. 683
Mystic Shrine........... 675

N

Notes, Chapter I........ 53
Notes, Chapter II 86
Notes, Chapter III...... 146
Notes, Chapter IV...... 180
Notes, Chapter V...... 195
Notes, Chapter VI...... 260
Notes, Chapter VIII..... 369
Notes, Chapter IX 393
Notes, Chapter XII..... 560
Notes, Chapter XV..... 616
Norega, Battle of........ 199
New Zealand........... 459
New York, its First Lodges.............. 463
New York, its Noted Masonic Halls.......... 475
New Hampshire, its first Lodges.............. 506
New Jersey, its First Lodges and Museum of Masonic Relics....... 509
Noted Masons.......... 523
Nebraska 535
Nevada 538
New Mexico............ 541
Nova Scotia 542
Newfoundland 546
Nobles of the Mystic Shrine............... 675

O

Origin of Free Masonry.. 704
Old Documents, German. 219–235
Old Documents, French..249–254
Old Documents, England. 323
Old Documents, York.... 386
Old Documents, Scotland. 409
Officers, G. L. New York, 1730–1827 489

INDEX.

	PAGE
Ohio, First Lodges	527
Oregon	535
Omnific Word	576

P

	PAGE
Pythagoras	39
Pyramids, The	91
Principles of Free Masonry	339
Portugal	448
Persia	452
Pennsylvania	491
Philadelphia	493
Prince Edward Island	546
Paraguay	552
Peru	553
Pike, Albert	595
Palestine	619
Peter the Hermit	621
Peter's Hosts Destroyed	626
Persecution of Masons	690
Peru—Relics	717

Q

Quarry, Jerusalem	152

R

Religion, Egypt	50
Races	193
Romans in Germany	199
Romans in Gaul	242
Romans in Britain	262
Roman Walls in Britain	267
Roman Relics in Britain	271–
" " "	275
Russia	440
Royal Arch Masonry	571
Royal Arch, First Chapters	575
Royal Arch, Statistics of	588
Raymond, E. A	599
Robinson, S. W	599

	PAGE
Relics and Remains of Solomon's Temple	711

S

Stones from the Temple	712
Symbols	61
Saccarah, Pyramid	92
St. Sophia	119
St. Mark's Cathedral	120
Strasburg	215
Soubise, M	258
Severus Septimus	267
Speculative Masonry	302
Schisms	313
St. Paul's Cathedral	321
Scotland	395
Scoon and Perth Lodges	404
St. Clair of Rossline	406
Schaw MSS	409
Sweden	440
Switzerland	440
Spain	444
Senegal	457
Solomon's Lodge, N. Y.	480
St. Patrick's Lodge, N. Y.	483
South America	549
Sandwich Islands	553
Statistics of Free Masonry throughout the World	555–559
Sickles, Daniel	600
Seymour-Gorgas	607

T

Temple of Solomon	151
Temples of Jerusalem	175
Tyre	176
Torgau Ordinances	227
Travelling Craftsmen	237
Transition State	284
Tower of London, The	289
Three Globes, Berlin	431
Texas—Graphic History	531
Templars, Knights	632

	PAGE
Tartars	661
Templarism, Modern	675, 676
The Smith's Lecture, Sarcastic	699

U

United States	462
Union Lodge, Albany	487
Utah	541
Uruguay	552

V

Varus Defeated	205
Virginia, its First Lodges	515
Vermont, its First Lodges	526
Virginia, West	538
Vaults, Legends of	579

W

Wren, Sir Christopher	318
Western Hemisphere	461
Washington's Masonic Career in Virginia—at Morristown, N. J.—Laying the Corner-stone of the Capitol at Washington	510, 518-520
Wisconsin	534
Washington, on the Pacific	538
Wyoming	541
West Indies	549

Y

York, England	375
York, Charter of	377
York, Old Rules	381
York, Relics	382
York—A Masonic Speech	384
Yates, G. F	598
Yucatan	716